from
Betsy Flavell
7 Springhill Lane
Marristown, N.J.
07960

THE BEST OF
FOOD&WINE
1991 COLLECTION

THE BEST OF
FOOD&WINE
1991 COLLECTION

American Express
Publishing Corporation
New York

TABLE OF CONTENTS

FOREWORD	7
VINTAGE RATINGS	8
MATCHING WINE AND FOOD	10
BEVERAGES	18
APPETIZERS & FIRST COURSES	24
SOUPS	42
FISH & SHELLFISH	50
POULTRY	62
MEAT	86
PASTA, RICE & GRAINS	106
VEGETABLES	120
SALADS	134
SANDWICHES & BREADSTUFFS	152
PIES, CAKES & COOKIES	166
DESSERTS	198
LOW-CALORIE COOKING	218
SAUCES, CONDIMENTS & PRESERVES	254
INDEX	260
CONTRIBUTORS	271

THE BEST OF FOOD & WINE/1991 COLLECTION
Editor/Designer: Kate Slate
Art Director: Elizabeth G. Woodson
Illustrators: Hong Chow, David Gordon

Published by American Express Publishing Corporation
1120 Avenue of the Americas, New York, New York 10036

Manufactured in the United States of America

ISBN 0-916103-13-7

♈

FOREWORD

I am delighted to present *The Best of Food & Wine*, the sixth annual collection of recipes from the magazine. Here you will find the way to prepare dishes for every occasion, season and mood. Some of these recipes are for the normal days of our lives, the ones that demand good, nutritious meals that can be prepared in little time. Others are for those times when no effort is too great—holiday meals or special dinner parties or weekends when you feel like taking on a challenging menu. What is consistent throughout is the quality of the finished dish. The exhaustive process of testing recipes at *Food & Wine* goes way beyond the practical matters of method and technique; what Diana Sturgis, the director of our test kitchen, often refers to as "the payoff" is as important as anything else.

We are also attentive to the second part of the magazine's name: wine, which is so connected to fine dining. Month after month, our coverage extends from our wine columns, which feature particular labels or particular winegrowing regions, to specific wine recommendations for featured dishes, to ways of building a menu around a bottle. This edition of *The Best of Food & Wine* is greatly enhanced by a wonderful chapter on matching wine with food by Elin McCoy and John Frederick Walker, who have written a column for the magazine for 10 years. You will find it charming to read and full of intelligent, useful information.

So, you have at hand a guidebook to the pleasures of the table, one of the marks of civilized life, no matter how simple. We are, after all, the only animals who cook our food, and it seems unarguable that winemaking is one of our great achievements. I hope this cookbook becomes one of your favorites.

Carole Lalli

Carole Lalli
Editor-in-Chief

FOOD & WINE'S VINTAGE RATINGS
1979-1989

COMPILED BY ELIN McCOY & JOHN FREDERICK WALKER

	1979	1980	1981	1982	1983
Red Bordeaux	8½ Fruity & well-balanced. Start drinking.	5 Small-scale, lightweight, pleasant. Drink up.	7½ Full, attractive wines. Start drinking.	9½ Rich, massive. Start sampling now.	7½ Firm, powerful. Start drinking.
Sauternes	6 Light but has character. Drink up.	7 Attractive, small-scale. Start drinking.	7½ Well-balanced wines. Start drinking.	7 Variable. Best are big, powerful wines. Start drinking.	9 Rich, classic wines. Start drinking.
Red Burgundy	6 Soft, supple, fading. Drink up.	6 Mostly light wines. Drink up.	5½ Variable vintage. Thin. Drink up.	7 Big, soft wines. Drink now.	8 Variable. Some very good. Start drinking.
White Burgundy	7 Attractive, fruity wines. Drink up.	5 Variable; the best are attractive. Drink up.	8 Attractive wines. Drink up.	8 Big, rich wines. Drink now.	8 Good, rich wines. Drink up.
Napa/Sonoma Cabernet Sauvignon	7 Uneven quality; some very good. Drink now.	8 Powerful, tannic. Start drinking.	8 Variable. Many attractive. Drink now.	7 Lighter style; some attractive. Drink now.	7 Good, but not great. Start drinking.
Napa/Sonoma Chardonnay	8 Rich, intense, fading. Drink up.	8½ Balanced but fading. Drink up.	7 Soft, ripe wines. Fading. Drink up.	7½ Variable, light, fading. Drink up.	7 Good moderate year. Drink up.
Barolo & Barbaresco	8 Elegant, well-balanced wines. Start drinking.	6 Uneven. Best are well-balanced, attractive. Drink now.	6½ Firm, solid wines. Start drinking.	8½ Big, powerful wines; very promising. Wait 1-4 years.	7 Lighter vintage. Start sampling.
Chianti	7 Attractive, ripe wines. Drink up.	6 Uneven; best are small-scale. Drink up.	7 Good, firm wines. Drink up.	7½ Attractive but early maturing. Drink now.	7 Attractive, early maturing. Drink now.
Germany	7 Good quality & balance. Drink up.	5 Light & lean. Drink up.	7 Well-balanced, attractive. Drink up.	7 Soft, fruity. Drink up.	9 Excellent year. Marvelous late-harvest wines. Drink now.
Vintage Porto	No vintage declared.	7 Light but good. Start sampling.	No vintage declared.	7 Soft, well-balanced. Sample in 3-6 years.	8 Firm, solid wines. Sample in 3-7 years.

8

The following ratings and comments reflect a variety of opinions, including our own, on the quality and character of various categories of wines from recent vintages. The ratings—0 for the worst, 10 for the best—are averages, and better or worse wine than indicated can be found in each vintage. Assessments of the most current vintages are more predictive and hence less exact than those of older vintages.

Scores are based on a wine's quality at maturity. A lower-rated but mature wine will often be superior to a higher-rated but immature wine. When-to-drink advice is based on how such wines seemed to be developing in mid-1990, and presumes good storage. The earliest date suggested for consumption applies to the lesser wines of the vintage, which will mature faster than the finest examples of the year.

1984	1985	1986	1987	1988	1989
6 Small-scale, firm. Start drinking.	8½ Soft, delicious, elegant. Start sampling.	9 Mixed vintage. Some classic tannic wines. Try in 5 years.	7 Flavorsome but lightweight. Start drinking.	7½ Good, somewhat tannic wines. Wait.	9 Variable. Some big fleshy wines.
5½ Mixed quality. Few good. Drink now.	7½ Soft, full, good. Sample now.	8½ Luscious & rich. Sample now.	6 Light, lean; few good wines.	9 Superlative, rich, concentrated. Start sampling.	9 Very promising. Rich & powerful.
5½ Variable, thin wines. Drink up.	9½ Glorious, rich & round. Start drinking.	7 Variable; mostly light wines. Sample now.	7½ Stylish wines. Sample now.	9 Concentrated, fruity, classic. Start sampling.	8½ Promising. Big fruity wines.
7 Crisp wines. Some fine. Drink up.	8 Big but soft. Start drinking.	9 Crisp, balanced, classic. Start drinking.	7 Light, round, soft. For early drinking.	7½ Good; some very fine.	8½ Attractive, fruity. Start sampling.
8 Big, rich, powerful. Start drinking.	9½ Brilliant, deep & elegant. Wait 3 years.	8 Deep, full & powerful. Wait 2 years.	8½ Dark, firm, promising. Wait 2 years.	7½ Mixed vintage; some concentrated. Wait.	7½ Difficult vintage; variable quality.
7 Good full wines. Drink up.	8 Lovely, balanced. Drink now.	9 Crisp, leaner style. Drink now.	8 Elegant & crisp. Drink now.	8 Good, fruity wines. Start drinking.	7 Uneven quality. Some good.
5½ Light, variable. For early drinking.	9 Splendid, rich. Wait 3 years.	8 Well-balanced & fruity. Wait 3 years.	7½ Round, fruity. Wait 3 years.	8½ Rich, full wines. Wait.	9 Big, powerful, promising wines.
5 Spotty. Drink up.	9½ Superb balance & flavor. Start drinking.	7½ Good quality. Start drinking.	7 Average quality. Start drinking.	8 Ripe, fruity, balanced. Sample now.	7 Fruity, pleasant wines.
6½ Lean & tart. Drink now.	8½ Excellent. Start drinking.	6 Light, crisp wines. Start drinking.	7 Mostly lean, some fine. Start sampling.	9 Outstanding, full-flavored, fruity. Start sampling.	9 Promising. Rich & fruity.
No vintage declared.	9 Marvelous, deep & fruity. Wait 10 years.	—	—	—	—

MATCHING WINE AND FOOD

By Elin McCoy & John Frederick Walker, authors of Wines & Spirits

Good wine is a natural accompaniment to good food. It adds a civilized grace note to the simplest meal, transforming it into something special. As you sip and savor the wine, the pace of a meal becomes more relaxed, more pleasurable: mere eating becomes real dining.

The appreciation of wine in America has kept pace with the national passion for fine food and its preparation, but selecting an appropriate wine for a meal or menu is still regarded by many as an esoteric art—which it isn't. Choosing the right wine is a matter of understanding how the tastes of different wines interact with food, balancing those tastes in a menu, and taking the setting and occasion into consideration when making a final selection. The whole point of serving one wine rather than another is simply to make the meal taste better.

Our approach is down-to-earth and practical. In this section you'll find the rationale behind the wine suggestions made throughout *The Best of Food & Wine* as well as all the information you need to choose an ideal wine for virtually any dish, menu or occasion from pea soup to poundcake, picnic to formal dinner.

MYTHS AND MISCONCEPTIONS

Before getting down to some of the basic principles and details of matching wine with food, let's get rid of a few common misconceptions. The first is that trying to match food and wine is silly and pretentious. It's true that many people find the idea of rules on the subject ridiculous. All over the world, they point out, people happily wash down their meals with whatever wine is at hand and never give it a second thought. Fussing over what is the per-

fect wine to go with a particular dish, they feel, is thus just a lot of nonsense. Behind this is a second misconception: that it really doesn't make any difference what wine you serve with a dish, anyway.

Admittedly, if you lived in a small European wine town—say, a village in Burgundy—you could adopt that attitude and never be the worse for it, because the local cuisine and the local wines have developed in tandem over the centuries and go together perfectly. Outside such an isolated gastronomic island, however, there's a jungle of conflicting tastes.

Today the dishes Americans prepare at home—or find in restaurants—run the gamut from simple to sophisticated, home-grown standard to exotic new wave. To drink what you like drinking with whatever you happen to be eating sounds laudably simple, but

those who enjoy both red Bordeaux and Mexican cuisine would rightly hesitate to pick *grand cru* St-Emilion to go with enchiladas—the taste of each would hardly enhance the other. In addition, the bewildering spectrum of flavors derived from dozens of newly popular cuisines and foodstuffs now available from every corner of the world constitute an exciting but uncharted territory for wine matching where old rules of thumb—white with fish, red with meat—aren't much help. And now there's also an amazing variety of wines available to choose from: any well-stocked wine store or wine list of a good restaurant may offer literally hundreds of choices of every wine type from the world's wine regions.

Nevertheless, although no list of memorized rules can cover most of today's situa-

tions, that doesn't mean the art of matching wine and food has become so complex you need a computer to do it. What you do need is a grasp of how the tastes of wine and food interact. Armed with such information you can readily find attractive combinations and with experience refine them to suit your own tastes and that of your guests. To make successful matches you don't need to know the flavors of thousands of individual wines and dishes, but you do need to be aware of the basic taste categories—the broad strokes, as it were—of the dishes and wines you plan to pair.

The key is to remember that since wine is primarily consumed at meals, you need to think of it as a special kind of food, one with a variety of flavors that can enliven the tastes of other dishes. That way deciding what wine is likely to taste good with certain foods is no greater challenge than deciding which side dishes go well with the roast. It's the same sort of thinking process—a matter of pondering possible taste combinations to come up with an ensemble that's likely to work on the table. In matching wine and food you're looking for synergy, a third taste that results when the flavors of the food and wine interact and create something more marvelous than either of them alone. If you care enough about food to find attractive combinations to cook, serve, and eat, there's every reason to select wines to enhance particular meals.

Which brings us to a third misconception: the idea that the best wine to serve at a meal is the best wine you can afford. It isn't. *The best wine to serve is the one that goes best with the meal.* The most palate-pleasing choice may be a modest wine, which, while not thrilling by itself, may provide just the right accent to the dish you are serving. With a rich cassoulet, for example, it's pointless to serve an expensive bottle of *grand cru* red Burgundy whose subtleties would be wiped out by the welter of flavors when a much less costly bottle of hearty Australian Shiraz would doubtless make a far more satisfying match.

HOW WINE INTERACTS WITH FOOD

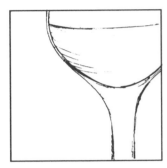

When it comes to interacting with food, a wine does one of four things: It *complements* the food in a pleasant way, *contrasts* with it in a different but equally pleasant way, *clashes* with it in an unpleasant way, or does none of those things—in which case, it's *neutral*.

• If a wine *complements* a dish, it appears to have a similarity with it. It may harmonize with or echo some aspect of the dish—the flavor, texture, intensity or spice. A rich, round, buttery Chardonnay from California, for example, echoes the flavor and texture of lobster with drawn butter. A peppery red Rhône harmonizes with steak au poivre.

• If a wine *contrasts* a dish, it provides an alternative but pleasing countertaste or texture. On the simplest level a wine can offer a contrast simply by being a different temperature than the food—for example, a cold white Zinfandel sipped between bites of hot, spicy Buffalo chicken wings. A contrasting wine may provide tartness to accent a mild dish or offer a completely different taste, the way the rich sweetness of a ruby port contrasts with the tangy saltiness of Stilton cheese.

• If a wine *clashes* with a dish, it creates an unpleasant flavor. When you taste a young, tannic Cabernet Sauvignon with cold sardines, for example, the wine seems to have a metallic tang.

• If a wine is *neutral*, it has little effect on the food's flavors. A bland jug white, for example, will just taste wet alongside chiles rellenos.

The most basic principle in matching wine and food successfully is to pair wines and foods that have an affinity or an attractive contrast.

There are obviously levels of interaction too, from merely pleasant to downright dramatic. A really wonderful match usually operates on several levels at once, both complementing the taste (as Cabernet Sauvignon does lamb) while providing a contrast (the wine's tannin cuts the fatty richness of the meat).

To know whether the flavors of a wine will complement or contrast with a particular dish, you need to know the main taste elements in wine and how they interact with food. The taste of any wine has three easily perceived components: *sweetness*, *acidity* and *bitterness*. All three shape the specific flavor the wine has and your impression of its body. These taste elements interact with food in various ways.

• *Sweetness* in wine—or the lack of it—can actually be measured. (In fact, you may see the amount of "residual sugar" listed on a back label. That's what remains of the natural grape sugar after fermentation.) A dry wine has no residual sugar, or at least no perceptible sweetness. To most people, a wine tastes dry when it contains less than .5% residual sugar. Wines with a slight hint of sweetness are often called "off-dry" because they taste more fruity than sweet. Truly sweet wines, such as Sauternes, are unmistakably honey-sweet.

The level of sweetness in a wine is an important factor to consider when matching it with food. Dry wines allow most food flavors to come forward. But sweet ones can overpower the flavors of many foods, and completely mask delicate tastes. That's why very sweet wines are usually served with a sweet dessert—or alone. But slightly sweet wines contrast and thus balance very spicy, smoky and salty foods and they harmonize attractively with many mild and fruity flavors.

• *Acidity* in wine gives it tartness or crispness. These natural fruit acids add liveliness to the flavor and give the wine a refreshing edge or bite. Acidity is more noticeable in whites, but is an essential part of the taste of all wines, red and white. Lower-acid wines taste soft; wines with too little acidity taste flabby and dull. Acidity is basically a contrasting element; it points up flavors and provides an accent for mild flavored foods.

• *Bitterness* is an element found primarily in red wines.

11

It is derived from the tannin extracted from the grape skins during fermentation. Tannins are also imparted to any wine aged in oak, which includes some whites, primarily fine Chardonnays and white Burgundies. They give a wine an astringent or mouth-puckering quality.

An excessive amount of tanins is perceived as bitterness, but a slightly tannic wine has a pleasing assertiveness, which, like acidity, checks richness in foods. In fact, foods too rich to contrast with merely acidic wines can be contrasted by a tannic wine. Tannic wines have a distinct dryness in the mouth, which cuts fat and oily or unctuous flavors and seems to have the effect of cleansing the palate.

Beside these elements there are specific flavors found in wines that derive primarily from the particular grape variety used to make the wine. These are the tastes that often harmonize with similar flavors in foods and spices. Pinot Noir, for example, reminds many people of cherries. Cabernet Sauvignon often has a taste of olives or currants. Sauvignon Blanc's flavor is distinctly reminiscent of herbs. Some red Burgundies are earthy, like mushrooms. Chenin Blanc can have a peachlike fruitiness. Oak aging contributes a vanillalike nuance to wine. (Interestingly, flavor is conveyed primarily by smell although we think of it as an aspect of taste. What your nose tells you is aug-

mented by the actual taste in the mouth.)

Another element of wines that affects the way they interact with food is body, or the tactile impression of a wine's weight and texture. Alcohol accounts for much of the impression of thickness or viscosity in a wine. A German Mosel of 9-percent alcohol inevitably strikes you as light and delicate in comparison with a 14-percent-alcohol Italian Barolo, which seems big and weighty. An intense wine—one that seems packed with flavor— also seems weightier than one with weaker flavors. Big wines (and sweet ones) often have a creamy round texture or feel in the mouth; a tannic one has a certain roughness.

While a contrast in textures can be attractive, in matching wine and food it's important for the weight and intensity of the wine to match that of the food. Light, delicate food flavors and textures will be lost if you serve a weighty, intense wine. And if you drink a light, delicate wine with a rich stew, you won't be able to taste any of the wine's fleeting flavors at all.

Of course, when you taste a wine, you get an overall impression just as you do when you taste a dish. Some wines appear very balanced, with no one characteristic that stands out. Others will strike you immediately as primarily acidic, fruity, rich and so on. Both sorts of wines have their uses on the table.

MATCHING THE MENU: FROM APPETIZER TO DESSERT

There are two principles to remember when you pick wines for a particular menu. First, you want to choose wines that complement or contrast the tastes of a dish. For the simplest meals, all that's required is a single wine matched to the main course. Since side dishes are often chosen to complement the main dish, they'll probably co-

exist happily with any wine you'd pair with the principal food. Rice, noodles, steamed vegetables and the like have a supporting role and aren't likely to override those dominant flavors. Sharp or fruity side dishes served for contrast—such as cranberry relish with roast turkey—may be less than ideal with the chosen wine, but will rarely undermine the basic wine-and-food combination.

But in a more formal, multi-course meal, you also need to consider the role and place of each wine in the menu as a whole. An aperitif wine, for example, needs to taste good with the appetizer, but it also needs to pave the way for the wines and food that follow. It shouldn't be too heavy or rich;

it should be appetizing and refreshing. A dessert wine ought to match the sweetness of the dessert as well as end the meal with a flourish. If you've served a strong-flavored, rich rabbit stew with a thick-textured Brunello di Montalcino, you probably want to end with a light dessert—and a lighter, more acidic dessert wine.

APERITIFS

These wines are usually served before a meal in the placed of mixed drinks and may or may not be accompanied by some kind of appetizer. The simplest choice is a glass of whatever you'll be drinking with the meal, but a crisp, light white best refresh-

es the palate and because of its tartness, stimulates the appetite. Typical choices include Pinot Blanc and Macon from France, Soave and Pinot Grigio from Italy, Sauvignon Blanc from California or Sémillon from Washington State, all of which pair well with a wide variety of fish and vegetable appetizers.

White wines don't have to be bone-dry to be light, refreshing and appetizing. A Riesling from the Mosel region in Germany or a Chenin Blanc from California, both of which have a fruity ripeness balanced by a lively fresh acidity, are easier to drink without food than drier wines are. Thus they are an excellent choice if you're not serving an appetizer at all. But they also go particularly well with spicy tidbits such as curried shrimp—the touch of sweetness in the wine assuages the palate.

Champagne and other sparkling wines and dry sherry are two classic aperitif wines that can also be drunk on their own. The effervescence and crispness of dry sparkling wines and *brut* Champagne seem to whet the appetite, especially alongside nutty, salty and smoky-flavored foods such as smoked almonds, bits of crumbly Parmesan, cheese twists or smoked fish. And if you want to add a celebratory note to a dinner, Champagne is the aperitif to pick. (Interestingly, it's the bubbles in Champagne that make it easy to match to a wide variety of foods. They provide both a cleansing effect on the palate and an interesting contrast, which is probably why many people think that you can serve Champagne throughout a meal. But there is almost always a better wine choice for every course.) Besides the classic Champagnes of France you can choose from a number of excellent sparkling wines from California and good value *cavas* from Spain.

Sherry is a neglected aperitif wine in the United States, doubtless because it is thought of solely as a sweet drink. But in Spain, the homeland of sherry, virtually all the sherry consumed is *Fino*, a pale straw-colored, bone-dry, savory type of sherry that is served icy cold as an accompaniment to *tapas*, the spicy Spanish appetizers. Dry sherry's strong, savory character

---

HARD-TO-MATCH FOODS

It's important to realize that not all foods are friendly. Spiciness can be a problem: a bite of red-hot chili or vindaloo curry will make any wine sampled afterwards taste bitter and stripped of flavor.

Asian and Indian dishes, if reasonably mild, can be attractive with wine. But sweet and sour flavors, the use of citrus, and spices such as ginger and curry powder undermine the subtler flavors of wine. A modest off-dry fruity white is likely to fare best next to unfamiliar dishes with Asian ingredients and flavors.

Tomatoes, eggs, artichokes, asparagus, raw greens and vinegar are often cited as foods that can alter the taste of wine for the worse. However if not overly strong or if balanced by other foods these ingredients rarely cause insurmountable trouble. But if the wine and food combination is untried, it makes more sense to go down the wine scale to a simple white or red that will happily play the role of supporting refreshment.

The flavor of coffee is too bitter to match successfully with wine—which is also why coffee itself should never be served with or before any wine. And chocolate is usually too palate-coating, sweet and/or bitter for wines to pair with. That makes it a poor flavor choice when you want to serve wine with dessert. But there are exceptions—a not-too-sweet chocolate génoise with a not-too-tart raspberry sauce, for example, can be paired with a fruity, sweet red ruby port, which will play off the texture of the cake and the fruit in the sauce.

---

can match olives, smoked ham, sardines or spicy sausages in intensity.

SOUPS

In traditional formal dinners, dry sherry or Champagne was served with the soup. The rationale for the match was to provide some textural contrast—such as higher alcohol or bubbles—between two liquids. This idea is still valid, but the predominant flavor and the heaviness of the soup are really the most important factors when choosing a wine match. A light mussel soup, for example, would be complemented by a savory, dry

white wine, such as Muscadet or Sauvignon Blanc, which would underscore the soup's briny flavor. A ham and pea soup, on the other hand, could be contrasted with an off-dry Riesling whose fruitiness would balance the saltiness of the meat.

Heartier main-course soups naturally call for heartier wines. For a rich seafood chowder, a deep-flavored Chardonnay would be a good accompaniment. For a thick leek and potato soup, a light red such as Pinot Noir would contrast the soup's mild taste with a piquant, fruity flavor. A flavorful minestrone, however, suggests a medium-bod-

ied flavorful red such as Chianti or Rioja. Hearty main-course soups and souplike stews are often dominated by the flavor of the main ingredient—fish, chicken, ham, veal, beef—which in turn influences the choice of wine.

FISH

The main principle to remember in choosing a wine match for fish is to react to the dish, not the category. This means considering the kind of fish and how it is prepared. Is the fish mild in flavor, like sole or tilefish? Or is it full-flavored and oily, like mackerel or bluefish? Is it baked, poached, grilled or smoked? Is it served plain with a wedge of lemon or covered with a rich caper sauce?

White wine, traditionally recommended for all fish dishes, is still the best match for many. Fish with delicate flavors (sole, perch, snapper, flounder, trout, etc.) that are simply prepared (poached, broiled or sautéed in butter, or lightly sauced) show best with light delicate white wines (Italian Chardonnay, white Rioja, Alsace or German Riesling) that harmonize. A heavier, more strongly flavored wine would mask the flavors of the fish—unless it's served with a rich cream sauce.

Lobster and crab are richer and sweeter in texture and flavor, and the best match is often a round, elegant but not overly powerful Chardonnay that echoes their succulence and sweetness.

Shellfish such as oysters, mussels and clams are briny

13

and succulent but less meaty than lobster and crab. Crisp, acidic whites are usually—and correctly—recommended with these shellfish because the tartness of the wine acts as a needed accent, much as a squeeze of lemon does. The classic combination of oysters and Chablis (from France) is attractive precisely because the acidity of the wine cuts the fatty gelatinous character of the oyster while the wine's lean, savory, mineral flavors carry through the saline taste of the oysters. But again, the sauce and preparation count a great deal. A creamy oyster stew needs a wine with a thicker texture—a not-too-heavy Chardonnay.

The flavors of some fish such as bluefish and mackerel overwhelm many white wines. That's why they require assertive whites with plenty of character and bite such as Sauvignon Blanc, Pinot Gris, white Graves and whites from Sicily.

Rich fleshy fish such as tuna, swordfish and salmon work well with correspondingly rich, fleshy Chardonnays or white Burgundies.

Yet despite the affinity of fish for white wines, they aren't always the best choice. Some types of fish and sauces add up to rich dishes that are better matched to a red wine. Raw oysters are one thing, breaded oysters another—the crusty breading tunes the flavors toward a light red such as Beaujolais. Another example is grilled tuna steaks with a tomato-y provençal sauce, which are wonderful with a sturdy red Côtes-du-Rhône. It's the strong garlic, tomato

---

CLASSIC AFFINITIES

There is something to be said for so-called classic matches, because if a particular combination of food and wine has been a traditional favorite for generations there is doubtless something about it that works. There are those who find these combinations obvious and boring, but far more find them timeless and gratifying.

Take the combination of roast lamb and red Bordeaux or other wines based on Cabernet Sauvignon and related grapes. These wines are normally tannic in character. The richness of the meat mutes this astringency; at the same time the wine's acerbity checks the fattiness of the meat. In addition, the nutty flavor of lamb has an affinity for the flavor of Caberent Sauvignon, which is often olivelike and herba-

ceous, echoing spices such as thyme, garlic, rosemary and pepper—spices often used to season roast lamb. The result is a synergy of tastes that's a step up from the basic, simple attraction of red wine and red meat.

There are dozens of classic combinations. A few examples: red Burgundy and roast beef; vintage port and Stilton cheese; Sauternes and Roquefort cheese; oysters and French Chablis. All are worth experiencing.

But the important thing to remember is that there is nothing mandatory about classic matches. Roast lamb, for example, is splendid with a number of reds, such as Côte Rôtie or Brunello di Montalcino. And Bordeaux is equally delicious with duck, pot roast, squab and a host of other dishes.

---

and olive flavors that direct the match toward red wine. Grilling salmon or swordfish also adds a meaty character that marries well with a red. Such fleshy fish are particularly good with red wine sauces, whose flavors naturally call for a red wine accompaniment.

The key in picking a red wine to go with fish is to choose light or medium-bodied reds that are not too fruity or tannic and that have high acid. Lighter St-Emilions, Chinons, Long Island Merlots and Pacific Northwest Cabernet Sauvignons are all good choices. The low tannin is important: the tannins in many reds can taste unpleasantly

metallic alongside various fish flavors, and not just strong ones like sardines but even mild ones such as lobster.

CHICKEN, VEAL & PORK

More than for most foods, the recipe is what counts when trying to match a wine to poultry and lighter meats, such as veal or pork. That's because their mild, light flavors are versatile by themselves and easily dominated by the flavors of the preparation and sauce, so much so that both red and white wines might be equally suitable, depending on the dish.

The mildness of plain roast chicken can be comple-

mented—in different ways, of course—by a light white such as dry Chenin Blanc or by a light, fruity red such as Gamay. But a richer preparation—say, chicken breasts with mushrooms and cream—needs a richer, rounder wine with earthy overtones to echo the mushrooms. A not-too-buttery California Chardonnay would be a good choice. The smoky, spicy flavors of barbecued chicken, on the other hand, point to a medium-bodied red—Beaujolais, Chianti and the like.

A similar rationale (and wine choices) applies to veal and pork, although the fattiness of pork can be attractively balanced by tannic reds that would overpower chicken or veal, such as Rhône wines, or by big whites that have a hint of astringency such as Alsace Gewürztraminer. Barbecued ribs, not surprisingly, call for full-throttle reds—Shiraz, Zinfandel and Barolo.

RED MEAT & GAME

There's a reason why red meat, particularly beef and lamb, are almost always paired with red wines. The fat and depth of flavor of the meat need the counterbalance of strong tannins and full flavors found in red wines like Bordeaux, Cabernet Sauvignons and Merlots. Most white wines—whose structure is based on acidity—lack sufficient weight, bite and depth to stand up to that fat and flavor. (One exception is the combination of a powerful California Chardonnay with rare baby lamb chops.) The herbs often used with lamb—rosemary and thyme—also have an affinity with the flavors found in wines based on Cabernet Sauvignon.

But preparation and seasoning also matter when choosing a wine match for a red meat dish. Grilled, highly seasoned and tomato-accented meats (pepper steaks, grilled butterflied leg of lamb, braised beef) need young reds that are even more assertive (Zinfandel or Barbaresco, for example). On the other hand, the succulent, almost sweet flavors of prime rib of beef won't mask the subtleties of a good red Burgundy, whose silky texture and complex, earthy flavors stand out next to the direct juicy character of the beef.

Game is not necessarily any stronger in taste than lamb. When simply roasted, the sweet flavors of quail and pheasant match well with the fruitiness of Pinot Noir and red Burgundy; with rich stuffings and side dishes, a complex old Bordeaux would be an ideal accompaniment.

Venison, like lamb, is better matched in flavor by Cabernet Sauvignon and Bordeaux. But again, a richer or heavier dish such as venison stew needs a deep, thick-textured, weighty wine with obvious flavors, like Cornas, Hermitage or California Petite Sirah.

Pâtés, sausages and cold meats go with a wide variety of red wines including both hearty and light fruity red wines. But the tartness of an off-dry white, especially Riesling, will also cut across the richness of these meats.

HAM

The saltiness of ham and the sweet glazes often used in its preparation are the primary factors affecting your choice of wine. These diminish the flavor of most red and dry white wines. An off-dry rosé (such as California rosé of Cabernet Sauvignon) and a fruity-tart Riesling provide a refreshing contrast to the salty flavors. Tart acidity in the wines prevents the sweetness in the dish from being cloying.

VEGETARIAN ENTREES & VEGETABLES

With the increase of vegetables and grains in today's diets, vegetarian main courses are becoming familiar. In choosing an accompanying wine, the most important things to consider are first, whether vegetables, tomatoes, eggs, cream or cheese dominate the flavor, and second, how rich and heavy the dish is.

Dishes that feature green vegetables and sweet peppers tend to be lighter and have an affinity with wines that have a somewhat vegetal flavor: Sauvignon Blanc or Sancerre. Their tart herbaceousness complements meatless pasta dishes like pasta primavera and main-dish summer salads. Dishes dominated by root vegetables and beans, such as a vegetable stew, need a white with less obvious acidity, such as Chardonnay or a light fruity red such as Dolcetto to add a piquant contrast. Dishes where tomatoes (and often eggplant) dominate need a flavorful red that's not too fruity such as Chianti, Rioja or Dão.

Most dishes with the flavors of eggs, cream or cheese are on the richer side and need a wine with more body and texture. A pleasant white with some body and flavor but not too much assertiveness such as Orvieto Secco will harmonize with creamy pasta sauces while richer dishes like spinach lasagna need a medium-bodied red that has some tannin to provide a flavor and texture contrast. A Merlot would be a good choice.

Many vegetable side dishes will be served alongside meat, fish or poultry entrées. But because few vegetables other than plain artichokes will noticeably affect the taste of the wine, let the flavor of the main dish guide your choice.

CHEESE

The basic fact to remember when choosing a wine to accompany cheese is that despite its reputation, cheese is often not a flattering companion to wine—especially an older wine with complex flavors. Strongly flavored cheeses such as Pont l'Evêque and Camembert are simply far too pungent and intense for subtle wines and easily overwhelm their flavors. That's why young assertive reds—say, a Châteauneuf-du-Pape—are the best choice for most cheeses. With mild cheeses such as Monterey Jack, a fruity white wine such as Sylvaner provides a pleasing contrast. The tartness and herbaceous flavor of Sauvignon Blanc or Sancerre echoes the acidic flavors of goat cheese and contrasts nicely with its creamy texture.

DESSERT

The key to successful matching of wine to desserts is to be sure that the dessert is *less*

PICKING YOUR OWN HOUSE WINE

In restaurants a house wine is what you get when you order just a glass of red or white wine. In a good restaurant, it's an attractive wine that will go well with most things on the menu. It's rarely an exciting wine, but it should be reliable.

At home, even if you have a wine cellar, it makes sense to have your own house wines on hand—an everyday red and white that can be enjoyed with a great variety of foods.

For a red, Beaujolais or California Gamay is a top choice. The combination of high acidity, low tannin and maximum fruitness pairs happily with foods as different as sausages and salmon.

For a white, the crisp herbaceousness of California Sauvignon Blanc (also called Fumé Blanc)—and its French cousins Sancerre and crisp Bordeaux Blancs—give it great versatility as an accompaniment to seafood, pastas and salads. Another useful white is Alsace Sylvaner or Riesling—dry, light, aromatic and savory, they pair with a number of light entrées and makes a first-rate aperitif.

sweet than the dessert wine. Very sugary desserts, particularly those based on cream or those with buttercream as a filling or icing, will strip the flavor from a fine dessert wine. Not-too-sweet, simply prepared fruit-based tarts, pies or cobblers and plain poundcakes and nut cakes are the best types of desserts to pair with wines such as rich Sauternes, Muscat de Beaumes-de-Venise, late-harvest Rieslings and Italian Moscatos. The most wine-compatible fruits to use in desserts are strawberries, raspberries, pears, peaches and cooked apples. Citrus fruits—except as a flavoring—have too much acidity to pair well with wine.

Hint: If you're unsure about the relative sweetness of the dessert and the wine, serve the wine before the dessert so it can be appreciated on its own first.

A SENSE OF OCCASION

Another principle to keep in mind is to suit the wine to the occasion.

You won't pick the same kinds of wines for a picnic that you would for a grand anniversary dinner—even if both feature steak as the main course. The type of occasion is a more important element to keep in mind when matching food and wine than most people realize. If you're not fussing with the food, it isn't necessary to fuss with the wine. A precise match isn't of critical importance on a picnic, but it can be fun to work on the ideal combination for a sophisticated dinner party.

Before choosing a wine, consider: Will the occasion be casual or formal? Will it take place indoors or out? On a hot summer afternoon or a snowy winter evening? With a boisterous crowd or a few wine-loving friends?

Here are some guidelines.

SEASON

Choose heavy, rich wines for cold weather and light, chillable ones for warm weather. A glass of rich red port may be just the thing to sip by the fireside on a raw winter's day, but it would seem far too powerful in a summer garden, when a glass of chilled fruity Vouvray would be much more appealing and refreshing. Not surprisingly, substantial winter dishes like stews and roasts are best with hearty, satisfying reds and big, flavorful whites, while spring and summer menus are best matched with lighter reds and—especially in hot weather—well-chilled rosés and whites.

CASUAL AFFAIRS

At most casual parties, whether indoors or out, it's difficult for guests to focus on the subtleties of a wine. And when a variety of foods is served at the same time, as often happens at large parties, buffets or picnics, offering a precise wine match for each dish just isn't possible. Hence what's needed are wines with direct clear flavors that bridge a broad range of food tastes. For a red, pick a wine with a modest amount of tannin and a lively, fruity flavor—Beaujolais, Gamay or a lighter Côtes-du-Rhône. For whites, look for crisp, clean-flavored wines—a refreshing lively quality is more important than depth or complexity. Pinot Blanc from Alsace, Galestro from Tuscany and Vinho Verde from Portugal are good bets. Since guests will be making their own choices from the selection of food, it makes sense to offer them a choice of red and white wines as well.

LUNCH & DINNER PARTIES

It's possible to offer a different wine match for different dishes when they're served in a series of courses at a lunch or dinner. For a five-course dinner you could match each course with a separate wine—sparkling wine to start, followed by a white with a fish course, then a red with a meat course, another red with the cheese and a sweet wine with dessert. For a formal dinner party, a special celebration or an anniversary, serving a different wine with each course makes the meal very grand.

But however many courses and wines you plan to serve, the standard advice for serving a sequence of wines is the same: white before red, young before old, dry before sweet. Though these rules can be bent successfully with certain menus, the underlying concept—that a series of wines should appear to build in intensity and enhance each other as well as the food—is a valid one. Most whites taste insubstantial if served after a red because reds normally have greater depth of flavor (but bear in mind that a huge fleshy Chardonnay served before a delicate Pinot Noir would certainly diminish the red; the power in this case belongs to the white). And it's usually more appropriate to serve a sweet wine at the end of the meal with dessert because dry wines stimulate the appetite while very sweet ones satiate it. One of the few exceptions to this—and a classic—is pairing an unctuously sweet Sauternes with rich foie gras as a first course.

The "young before old" dictum, however, doesn't always apply. If you serve a powerful young Cabernet Sauvignon before an old, subtle Bordeaux, the older wine will seem thin and weak by comparison. With two such wines, it would make more sense to serve the older wine first with the main course, and bring out the bigger red with the cheese.

BEVERAGES

BEVERAGES

RICE-ALMOND COOLER

In Mexico a cold, milky drink called *orchata* is sold by street vendors. Made of ground rice and almonds or melon seeds, it's a boon to anyone who can't drink cow's milk but craves something milky. This version is more highly flavored than the typical Mexican one. You can use an aromatic basmati-style rice, but Carolina rice works fine too (just avoid using processed rice).

————— *4 Servings* —————
⅓ cup whole blanched almonds
    (2 ounces)
3 to 4 cups boiling water
½ cup white rice
2 tablespoons sugar or honey
¼ teaspoon vanilla extract
1 drop of almond extract

1. In a small bowl, cover the almonds with 1 cup of the boiling water and let soak for 4 hours.

2. Meanwhile, in a strainer, rinse the rice until the water runs clear. Drain the rice and place it in a small bowl. Cover it with another cup of boiling water and set aside to soak for 4 hours.

3. In a blender, combine the soaked almonds and rice and their soaking liquids. (If all the liquid has been absorbed during soaking, add 1 cup of boiling water to the blender to get it started.) Blend for 3 minutes to pulverize the solids as fine as possible.

4. Add the sugar, vanilla, almond extract and enough boiling water to bring the volume to 4½ cups. Blend for 1 minute. Strain the liquid through several layers of dampened cheesecloth. Refrigerate until cold and serve over ice.

—*Deborah Madison*

• • •

RASPBERRY OR ORANGE ICE CUBES

Place one cube in the bottom of each Champagne flute and pour Champagne over to serve.

————— *Makes 16 Cubes* —————
1 box (10 ounces) frozen raspberries in light syrup, completely thawed
1 can (6 ounces) orange juice concentrate

1. For raspberry ice cubes, push the raspberries and their syrup through a fine-mesh sieve to remove the seeds. Transfer the raspberry puree to a 1-cup measure and add enough water to make 1 cup.

2. For orange ice cubes, in a medium bowl, dilute the orange juice concentrate with ⅓ cup water. Mix well to blend.

3. Pour the raspberry or the orange mixture into an ice cube tray, filling it ¾ full. Be careful not to make the cubes too large; they should fit into a Champagne flute. Freeze for at least 4 hours, or preferably overnight.

—*Paul Grimes*

• • •

THE REVITALIZER

This spicy tomato-based drink can be served hot or cold.

————— *6 Servings* —————
1 can (48 ounces) tomato juice cocktail, such as V-8
2 cups assorted sliced vegetables (such as mushrooms, tomatoes, onions, green bell pepper, red bell pepper or snow peas)
2 celery ribs, chopped
1 large carrot, chopped
1 bunch of parsley
2 bay leaves
1 to 2 teaspoons hot pepper flakes
2 teaspoons fresh rosemary or 1 teaspoon dried

½ teaspoon fennel seeds
2 tablespoons chopped fresh basil

1. In a large nonreactive saucepan, combine the tomato juice cocktail, sliced vegetables, celery, carrot, parsley, bay leaves, hot pepper, rosemary, fennel seeds, basil and 1½ cups of water. Bring to a boil over moderate heat. Reduce the heat to low and simmer for 40 minutes.

2. Transfer to a strainer set over a bowl and press with a wooden spoon to extract all the juices (or process in a food mill); discard the pulp.

—*Michel Stroot, Cal-a-Vie, Vista, California*

• • •

MANGO RASPBERRY COOLER

————— *4 Large Servings* —————
1 ripe mango—peeled, pitted and cut into chunks
1 cup fresh or frozen unsweetened raspberries
2½ cups fresh orange juice
1 cup crushed or shaved ice
1 cup seltzer or club soda
Orange wedges, for garnish

In a blender, combine the mango, raspberries, orange juice and ice. Puree at high speed until smooth, about 1 minute. Pour into 4 tall glasses. Top off with seltzer and stir. Garnish each glass with an orange wedge.

—*Michel Stroot, Cal-a-Vie, Vista, California*

• • •

MULLED CIDER

——— 2 Servings ———
2½ cups unfiltered, unpasteurized
    apple cider
1 teaspoon finely grated lemon zest
1 cardamom pod, slightly crushed,
    or a pinch of ground cardamom
1 large cinnamon stick, broken
    in half
3 whole cloves, slightly crushed
2 whole allspice berries, slightly
    crushed
1 slice of orange, halved, or coarsely
    grated orange zest, for garnish
Cinnamon, for sprinkling

In a small saucepan, combine the cider, lemon zest, cardamom, cinnamon stick, cloves and allspice. Bring to a boil over high heat. Reduce the heat to very low and simmer for 10 minutes. Strain the cider into two mugs. Float half an orange slice sprinkled with cinnamon in each, or stir in the grated zest and sprinkle cinnamon on top. Serve hot.
——Linda Merinoff

• • •

BARLEY TEA

Barley tea, a popular beverage in Japan and Korea, has a subtle, smoky flavor and no sugar, caffeine, calories or other worrisome elements. It is made with roasted barley and water and can be served hot or cold. Other flavorings, such as orange or lemon zest, a pinch of cardamom, nutmeg, cinnamon or clove, or orange or rose water, can be added to steep along with the barley. Although roasted barley is available at Japanese markets, it is very simple to roast your own.

——— Makes About 5½ Cups ———
3 tablespoons pearl barley
Honey and lemon slices, for serving
    (optional)

1. In a small, dry, cast-iron skillet, cook the barley over moderate heat, shaking the pan from time to time, until the grains have a toasty aroma and begin to brown, 5 to 7 minutes.
2. Transfer the barley to a medium saucepan. Add 6 cups of water and bring to a boil over moderate heat. Reduce the heat and simmer for 7 minutes. Strain and drink hot or let cool, refrigerate and serve over ice. If you like, serve the tea with honey and a slice of lemon.
——Deborah Madison

• • •

LA MAISON DU CHOCOLAT'S HOT CHOCOLATE

This recipe hails from the world-renowned chocolatier Robert Linxe and his Parisian shop La Maison du Chocolat. If desired, serve this luscious, rich, hot beverage with a dollop of whipped cream, and—as they do in Paris—a glass of water on the side.

——— 6 Servings ———
7 ounces imported bittersweet
    chocolate, preferably Valrhona
    Bittersweet Couverture, chopped
3 cups milk

1. In a medium saucepan, combine the chocolate, milk and 1 cup of water. Bring to a boil over moderately high heat, whisking constantly to prevent scorching, 15 to 18 minutes.
2. Reduce the heat to moderate and simmer, stirring occasionally with a wooden spoon, for 3 minutes.
3. Remove from the heat and let cool slightly, about 3 minutes. Whisk briskly to create a froth. Pour into 6 cups and serve at once.
——Robert Linxe, La Maison
    du Chocolat, Paris

• • •

CAFE BRULOT DIABOLIQUE

Restaurant Antoine's is famous for its tableside preparation of this after-dinner hot toddy.

——— 6 Servings ———
8 whole cloves
1 cinnamon stick
Zest of 1 lemon, cut in strips
1½ tablespoons sugar
3 ounces Cognac or other brandy
3 cups hot strong black coffee

In a medium saucepan, combine the cloves, cinnamon, lemon zest, sugar and Cognac. Cook over moderate heat until hot but not boiling, about 3 minutes. Remove from the heat and, using a long kitchen match, ignite the brandy and let it burn for 1 minute. Stir in the hot coffee to extinguish the flames. Ladle the coffee into demitasse cups and serve at once.
——Antoine's, New Orleans

• • •

COFFEE-HAZELNUT NIGHTCAPS

For this toddy use tall, narrow mugs with big handles; they'll help keep your drink and your hands warm.

——— 6 Servings ———
3 tablespoons sugar
1½ tablespoons unsweetened cocoa
    powder
1 cup light cream or milk
3 cups freshly brewed coffee
¾ cup Frangelico (hazelnut liqueur)
Lightly sweetened whipped cream
    and cinnamon, for garnish

1. In a medium saucepan, whisk together the sugar and cocoa. Stir in 1 cup of water and bring to a boil over moderate heat. Boil, stirring, for 1 minute; then stir in the cream and coffee. Bring almost to a boil, stirring occasionally. Remove the saucepan from the heat.

2. Pour 2 tablespoons of the Frangelico into each of 6 coffee mugs, then add enough coffee to reach within ¾ inch of the rim. Top each serving with a dollop of whipped cream and a pinch of cinnamon. Serve at once.

—*Ken Haedrich*

• • •

MILK PUNCH

At Commander's Palace, each drink is made separately in a hand shaker and chilled. We've adapted this recipe so that you can make six soothing cocktails at once in a blender.

—————— **6 Servings** ——————
1 cup milk
¾ cup plus 2 tablespoons bourbon
* or brandy*
¾ cup half-and-half or light cream
2 tablespoons superfine sugar
1 tablespoon vanilla extract
1 cup small ice cubes
Freshly grated nutmeg

In a blender, combine the milk, bourbon, half-and-half, sugar, vanilla and the ice. Blend until foamy, about 1 minute. Pour into glasses and top each serving with a pinch of nutmeg.

—*Commander's Palace, New Orleans*

• • •

U.N. PLAZA EGGNOG

For many of us, eggnog is the quintessential holiday season beverage. This rich, coffee-almond flavored cup from the United Nations Plaza Hotel in New York can easily be multiplied to fill your holiday punch bowl.

—————— **1 Serving** ——————
3 ounces eggnog, chilled
1 ounce Amaretto
½ ounce Kahlúa
Dark bitter chocolate, shaved, for
* garnish*

Pour into an old-fashioned glass and gently stir. Garnish with shaved dark bitter chocolate.

—*Warren Picower*

• • •

FRAGOLINO

Danny Meyer, the owner of the Union Square Cafe in New York City, describes the popular house cocktail as "having an Italian basis with a French twist, because that's also the restaurant's personality."

—————— **1 Serving** ——————
½ ounce Fraise de Bourgogne
4 ounces Prosecco brut or other
* Italian sparkling white wine,*
* chilled*
Fresh raspberry or strawberry

Pour both ingredients into a Champagne glass. Garnish with either a raspberry or strawberry.

—*Warren Picower*

• • •

POIRE ROYALE

From Windows in Rosslyn, Virginia, this mix of fine Champagne and intense fruit flavors seems to make the view across the Potomac of Washington, D.C., just a bit more majestic.

—————— **1 Serving** ——————
½ ounce pear brandy, such as Pear
* William (Poire Williams)*
½ ounce framboise
4½ ounces brut Champagne, chilled

Pour all the ingredients into a chilled Champagne glass.

—*Warren Picower*

• • •

FRENCH 75

This, the ultimate brandy and soda, was created by World War I doughboys who named it after the French army's 75 mm howitzer (known for its devastating firepower). We've only added the luxury of ice cubes. For years this splendid drink was all but lost in the obscurity of bar guides, which corrupted the original straightforward formula with the addition of quantities of lemon juice and sugar, and even replaced Cognac with gin. A writer we know likes to serve these to Sunday afternoon guests before they sit down to a sandwich lunch and pro football on TV. Though essentially a purist, he does allow a dash of bitters and a twist of lemon peel if requested. Many brut Champagnes are currently made with enough of a touch of sweetening dosage to be used instead of the sec.

—————— **1 Serving** ——————
3 ounces Cognac
Extra-sec or sec Champagne, chilled
Dash Angostura bitters (optional)
Twist of lemon rind, for garnish
* (optional)*

Fill a large (12 ounces or more) snifter or double old-fashioned glass with ice cubes almost to the rim. Pour in the Cognac and fill with Champagne. Garnish with a twist of lemon peel if desired.

—*Warren Picower*

• • •

LE BADINGUET

Guests at Les Prés d'Eugénie, Michel Guérard's renowned spa in the southwest of France, go to take more than the waters. The sparkling house aperitif, fancifully named after Napoleon III's soubriquet, and made with a local Armagnac-based liqueur, Pousse Rapière, seems omnipresent. (A similar sparkling cocktail, called Pousse Rapière, is served at the United Nations Plaza Hotel in New York, which happens to be a Manhattan base of another great French chef from Armagnac country, André Daguin.)

———— 1 Serving ————
½ ounce Pousse Rapière (see Note)
¼ ounce crème de cassis
6 ounces brut Champagne, chilled
Fresh mint leaf, or ½ slice of lemon, or ½ slice of orange, for garnish (optional)

Pour ingredients in above sequence into an 8-ounce Champagne glass. Garnish as desired.

NOTE: Although Pousse Rapière is sold in the United States, it is not widely available. For an optional version of this drink, substitute ¼ ounce of Cointreau and ¼ ounce of Armagnac, or try ½ ounce of Grand Marnier.
—Warren Picower

• • •

KISS ME QUICK

A version of this drink has been in the repertoire of good hotel and restaurant barmen since Prohibition was repealed and Nick and Nora Charles merrily reveled their way from New York to San Francisco in between their *Thin Man* adventures. If you have a liking for anise-flavored preprandials, try this.

———— 1 Serving ————
2 ounces Pernod
½ ounce Curaçao
2 dashes Angostura bitters
Soda water

Shake all the ingredients well with ice and strain into an 8-ounce highball glass or all-purpose wineglass. Add ice cubes. Fill to taste with soda water. Stir gently.
—Warren Picower

• • •

GUBONI

Co-owners and chefs Johanne Killeen and George Germon of Lucky's and Al Forno restaurants in Providence, Rhode Island, were introduced to this drink by a woman in Venice who promised that it would build up the appetite. Marvelously, it does, even though port and Cognac separately are exalted after-dinner drinks.

———— 1 Serving ————
1½ ounces tawny port
1½ ounces Cognac

Mix the port and the Cognac in a snifter and serve.
—Warren Picower

• • •

FOOD & WINE'S HOLIDAY APERITIF

Our holiday offering is refreshingly flavored, a boon to the appetite. If you prefer, by all means stir well rather than shake with ice. This drink is also excellent on the rocks, similarly garnished with a twist of orange rind in a double old-fashioned glass. Or forget about the rocks and top with 2 ounces of chilled brut Champagne in a double old-fashioned glass or a slightly ballooned wineglass.

———— 1 Serving ————
1 ounce sweet vermouth
1 ounce dry vermouth
1 ounce Campari
1 ounce Cointreau
2 dashes Angostura bitters
Twist of orange rind, for garnish

Shake well both vermouths, the Campari, Cointreau and bitters with ice and strain into a stemmed cocktail glass. Garnish with a twist of orange rind.
—Warren Picower

• • •

DUCHESS COCKTAIL

Originally concocted with the now-proscribed liqueur absinthe, this classic may have been the invention of "The King of the Cocktail Shakers," Harry Craddock, who reigned during the Roaring Twenties at The Savoy hotel in London.

———— 1 Serving ————
1 ounce Pernod
1 ounce sweet vermouth
1 ounce dry vermouth
Half-slice of orange, for garnish (optional)

Shake all ingredients well with ice and strain into a cocktail glass. Garnish with a half-slice of orange if desired.
—Warren Picower

• • •

CALVADOS AL GIORNO

One of my favorite restaurants in Chicago, Gordon, serves a lot of these cocktails before dinner during the summer. I find it does wonders for the appetite year-round.

———— 1 Serving ————
1 ounce Calvados
1 ounce orange bitters, such as Aperol
Soda water
Wedge of lemon or lime, for garnish

Pour the Calvados and orange bitters over ice cubes into a highball or double old-fashioned glass. Fill to taste with soda water and stir gently. Garnish with a wedge of lemon or lime.
—Warren Picower

• • •

DECO DELIGHT

The Redwood Room at the Four Seasons Clift Hotel in San Francisco is one of the Bay City's choice watering spots, and this is its choice cocktail.

——————— *1 Serving* ———————
1 ounce Cointreau
1 ounce Dubonnet
1 ounce Cognac
1 ounce fresh lime juice

Stir all ingredients with ice in a mixing glass. Strain into a cocktail glass.
—*Warren Picower*

• • •

WATERMELON AND LIME DAIQUIRI

Pretty and potent, not too sweet and not too tart, a batch of watermelon daiquiris will beat the blahs of summer. For best results, allow enough time to freeze the watermelon chunks in advance.

——————— *4 Servings* ———————
4 cups seeded 1-inch watermelon
  chunks
¼ cup fresh lime juice
¾ cup white rum
1 tablespoon plus 1 teaspoon sugar
Lime slices, for garnish

1. In a roomy plastic bag, place the watermelon chunks in a single layer. Freeze for 6 hours or overnight.
2. In a small bowl, combine the lime juice, rum and sugar. Stir to dissolve the sugar. Pour the mixture into a blender. Add the frozen watermelon chunks, breaking up any clumps. Blend until quite smooth, about 1 minute. Pour into martini glasses and garnish each daiquiri with a slice of lime.
—*Diana Sturgis*

• • •

PERFECTLY GRAND

The "perfect," as it does with all drinks so-named, refers to the equal parts of sweet and dry vermouth in the recipe.

——————— *1 Serving* ———————
1½ ounces Grand Marnier
¾ ounce gin
1 teaspoon dry vermouth
1 teaspoon sweet vermouth
2 dashes Angostura bitters
Twist of orange rind, for garnish
  (optional)

Stir all ingredients with ice in a mixing glass. Strain into a chilled, stemmed cocktail glass. Garnish with a twist of orange rind if desired.
—*Warren Picower*

• • •

THE BIG ORANGE

A friend of mine who was once a confirmed bourbon Manhattan drinker became so fond of bittersweet, orange-flavored Cointreau during a stay in France that he came up with this cocktail to bridge his spiritual divide.

——————— *1 Serving* ———————
1½ ounces bourbon
1 ounce Cointreau
2 dashes Angostura bitters
Twist of orange rind, for garnish
  (optional)

Stir all ingredients with ice in a mixing glass. Strain into a chilled cocktail or balloon wineglass. Garnish with a twist of orange rind if desired.
—*Warren Picower*

• • •

MANSION MARTINI

A bit of cool inspiration from The Mansion on Turtle Creek in Dallas, this is oh so smooth, dry, pleasing and potent.

——————— *1 Serving* ———————
3 ounces premium gin or vodka
Splash of white tequila
Jalapeño-stuffed olive, for garnish

Stir both ingredients well with ice in a mixing glass. Strain into a cocktail glass. Garnish with a jalapeño-stuffed olive (or if not available, use a marinated jalapeño, a slice of pickled green tomato or just a green cocktail olive).
—*Warren Picower*

• • •

CHRISTMAS MELON BALL

This relatively new drink from the Inn on the Park in Houston stirs up pleasant memories of more innocent times. Some of us, when we were kids, would collect freshly fallen snow and drizzle fruit syrup over the top. (We also did it with shaved ice during the summer.) If making crushed ice presents a problem or simply isn't to your liking, this recipe is also excellent on the rocks.

——————— *1 Serving* ———————
1½ ounces Midori
1½ ounces vodka
6 ounces orange juice
Grenadine
Maraschino cherry, for garnish

Mix Midori, vodka and orange juice together and pour over crushed ice (or ice cubes) in a tall Collins glass. Sprinkle with grenadine. Garnish with a cherry.
—*Warren Picower*

• • •

APPETIZERS & FIRST COURSES

SAGE CRISPS

These deep-fried won ton strips can be tossed with another dried herb, such as thyme or oregano, if you prefer.

——————— *Makes About 8 Cups* ———————
1 package (12 ounces) won ton skins
2 teaspoons rubbed sage
1 teaspoon salt
Oil, for deep-frying

1. On a work surface, arrange the won ton skins in stacks of six. Cut them into ¼-inch strips.

2. In a mortar, pound the sage with the salt until the mixture is fine and blended.

3. In a large skillet or a deep-fryer, heat 3 inches of oil to 375°. Meanwhile, toss the won ton skins with your hands to separate the strips. When the oil is hot, add the strips in small batches and fry, stirring with a chopstick to keep them separate, until golden brown, 1 to 2 minutes. Remove with a slotted spoon and drain on paper towels. Let the crisps cool slightly, then sprinkle with the sage salt and toss gently. Repeat with the remaining strips. *(The crisps can be stored in an airtight container for 4 to 5 days.)*
—*Bob Chambers*

• • •

SHREDDED WHEAT SNACK MIX

This is a south-of-the-border version of the snack mix based on breakfast cereal. Here it's made with shredded wheat, peanuts and pretzels—all seasoned with thyme, cumin and chili powder.

——————— *Makes About 10 Cups* ———————
1 box (13½ ounces) bite-size
* shredded wheat*
1 bag (5½ ounces) bite-size pretzels,
* such as Goldfish*
½ pound unsalted, dry roasted
* peanuts*

½ cup olive oil
1 stick (4 ounces) unsalted butter
1 teaspoon thyme
1 teaspoon cumin
1½ teaspoons chili powder
1 teaspoon freshly ground pepper
1½ teaspoons salt

1. Preheat the oven to 350°. In a large bowl, combine the shredded wheat, pretzels and peanuts.

2. In a medium saucepan, combine the olive oil, butter, thyme, cumin, chili powder and pepper. Cook over moderate heat, stirring constantly, until foaming, 3 to 4 minutes.

3. Pour the seasoning mixture evenly over the ingredients in the bowl and toss very well to coat thoroughly. Sprinkle with the salt and toss again.

4. Spread the mixture out on 2 baking sheets in a single layer. Bake, stirring frequently, for 35 to 40 minutes, or until the shredded wheat is golden. Let cool completely. *(The mix can be stored in an airtight container for up to 10 days.)*
—*Bob Chambers*

• • •

GENOA MATCHSTICKS

Blanching and oven drying the meat removes most of the fat, leaving behind a crisp essence of salami. These can be served on their own or combined with Pesto Pita Thins (p. 27) or store-bought sesame sticks.

——————— *Makes About 2½ Cups* ———————
1½ pounds Genoa salami, sliced ⅛
* inch thick*
1½ teaspoons thyme
¾ teaspoon freshly ground pepper

1. Preheat the oven to 325°. Stack 3 or 4 slices of the salami at a time and cut into ⅛-inch-thick matchsticks. When all the salami has been sliced, place it in a medium saucepan and add enough warm water to just cover. Stir once to separate the strips and bring to a boil over high heat. Drain thoroughly and pat dry with paper towels.

2. Toss the salami strips with the thyme and pepper. Spread the strips on a baking sheet in a single layer and bake, stirring frequently, for about 1 hour, until crunchy. Transfer to paper towels to drain and cool. *(The salami sticks can be stored in an airtight container for up to 5 days.)*
—*Bob Chambers*

• • •

SPICY TAMARI NUTS WITH RICE CRACKERS

I've always loved the tamari-roasted nuts sold at health food stores. Here, hot sesame oil is added for a little zip, and the nuts are tossed with rice crackers for another kind of crunch.

——————— *Makes About 8 Cups* ———————
2 pounds mixed unroasted nuts,
* such as walnuts, pecans, almonds*
* and cashews*
¼ cup tamari sauce*
1 tablespoon hot sesame oil*
½ pound Oriental snack mix, such
* as assorted plain and seaweed-*
* wrapped rice crackers and fried*
* green peas**
*Available at Asian markets

1. Preheat the oven to 300°. Place the mixed nuts on a baking sheet in a single layer. Roast in the middle of the oven for 35 minutes, stirring once or twice.

2. Transfer the nuts to a large heat-proof bowl and toss with the tamari sauce and sesame oil. Return the nuts to the baking sheet in a single layer and roast for 5 minutes, stirring occasionally, until glazed and dry.

3. Let the nuts cool completely, then toss them with the rice crackers and peas.

(The mixture can be stored in an airtight container for up to 2 weeks.)
—*Bob Chambers*

• • •

CURRIED PUMPKIN SEEDS AND CORNNUTS

The subtle flavor of pumpkin seeds can be enhanced by any number of spices. Here, curry adds an Indian accent.

—————Makes About 4 Cups —————
2 tablespoons olive oil
1 tablespoon curry powder
1 pound shelled raw pumpkin seeds*
1 teaspoon salt
2 bags (3 ounces each) Cornnuts
*Available at health food stores

1. Preheat the oven to 350°. In a small skillet, combine the oil with the curry powder. Cook over moderately high heat, stirring, until the oil just begins to smoke slightly, 2 to 3 minutes.

2. In a medium bowl, toss the pumpkin seeds with the hot curry oil. Sprinkle on the salt and toss until well distributed.

3. Spread the pumpkin seeds out on a baking sheet and bake in the middle of the oven for 15 minutes, stirring occasionally, until lightly browned.

4. Return the pumpkin seeds to the bowl, add the Cornnuts and toss well to combine. Toss the mixture occasionally as it cools. *(The mixture can be stored in an airtight container for up to 10 days.)*
—*Bob Chambers*

• • •

CARROT CHIPS

Chef Leslie Revsin's bright, chewy chips make convivial partners for poultry dishes. Or serve them to eat out of hand or to scoop into dips.

—————8 to 10 Servings —————
1½ quarts peanut oil
3 to 4 small, firm carrots (about 1 pound total), trimmed and peeled
Salt (optional)

1. In a deep-fat fryer, heat the oil to 350°.

2. Meanwhile, using a small sharp knife, trim off the thin ends to make the carrots fairly uniform in length. Cut off a thin lengthwise strip from each of the carrots. Using a vegetable peeler or a mandoline with the cutting blade set at ¹/₁₆ inch, starting with the cut side, slice the carrots lengthwise into thin strips. Stack the carrot slices into manageable piles and cut into rectangles about 1½ inches long. Alternatively, cut the carrots to fit the feed tube horizontally and slice in a food processor fitted with an extra-thin blade.

3. Divide the carrot slices into 4 batches. Place 1 batch in the fryer basket, lower the basket into the hot oil and fry until the chips are light brown and curled, about 2 minutes. Lift the basket out of the oil; shake gently to remove any excess oil. Transfer the chips to several layers of paper towels to drain. Repeat with the remaining batches, checking the temperature of the oil and adjusting the heat, if necessary, to maintain 350°.

4. Season the chips lightly with salt, if desired, and toss gently. Transfer to a bowl and serve.

—*Doris Tobias*

• • •

RUTABAGA CHIPS

Rutabagas, or meaty yellow turnips, are preferred by chef Anne Rosenzweig for both their deep color and robust flavor.

—————8 to 10 Servings —————
1½ quarts soybean oil
1 very large or 2 medium rutabagas (1½ to 2 pounds total), trimmed and peeled
Salt

1. In a deep-fat fryer, heat the oil to 360°.

2. Meanwhile, using a large heavy knife, cut a thin slice from the end of each rutabaga. Using a mandoline with the cutting blade set at ¹/₁₆ inch, starting with the cut side, slice the rutabagas crosswise. Alternatively, cut the rutabagas to fit into the feed tube and slice in a food processor fitted with an extra-thin blade. Pat the rutabaga slices dry with paper towels.

3. Divide the rutabaga slices into 6 batches. Place 1 batch in the fryer basket, lower the basket into the hot oil and fry until the chips are light golden brown, about 2 minutes. Lift the basket out of the oil; shake gently to remove any excess oil. Transfer the chips to several layers of paper towels to drain. Repeat with the remaining batches, checking the temperature of the oil and adjusting the heat, if necessary, to maintain 360°.

4. Season the chips with salt to taste and toss gently. Pile in a bowl and serve.
—*Doris Tobias*

• • •

CELERY ROOT CHIPS

Chef Gérard Pangaud serves these for nibbles.

——————4 to 6 Servings——————
2 quarts peanut oil
3 tablespoons lemon juice or
    distilled white vinegar
1 firm celery root (¾ to 1 pound
    total), trimmed and peeled
Salt

1. In a deep-fat fryer, heat the oil to 360°.

2. In a medium bowl, combine 4 cups of cold water with the lemon juice.

3. Using a large heavy knife, cut a thin slice from each end of the celery root. Using a mandoline with the cutting blade set at ¹/₁₆ inch, starting with a cut end, slice the celery root crosswise into disks. Alternatively, cut the celery root to fit into the feed tube and slice in a food processor fitted with an extra-thin blade. As you cut them, transfer the slices to the bowl of acidulated water. Let soak for 5 minutes, then drain and pat dry with paper towels.

4. Divide the celery root slices into 3 batches. Place 1 batch in the fryer basket, lower the basket into the hot oil and fry just until the chips are lightly browned, about 2 minutes. Lift the basket out of the oil; shake gently to remove any excess oil. Transfer the chips to several layers of paper towels to drain. Repeat with the remaining batches, checking the temperature of the oil and adjusting the heat, if necessary, to maintain 360°.

5. Season the chips with salt to taste and toss gently.

—*Doris Tobias*

• • •

PARSNIP CHIPS

Serve these chips with broiled meats, roast loin of pork, veal or pork chops, and roast chicken or duckling, recommends chef Seppi Renggli. Or pile them into bowls and serve with drinks. For a sweet version, don't salt but dust liberally with sifted confectioners' sugar and serve with *vin santo*.

——————8 to 10 Servings——————
1½ pounds even-size parsnips,
    trimmed and peeled
About 2 quarts vegetable oil
Coarse (kosher) salt

1. Using a large heavy knife, cut off a little of the thin ends so that the parsnips are fairly uniform in length. Cut off a thin lengthwise strip from each of the parsnips. Using a mandoline with the cutting blade set at ¹/₁₆ inch, starting with the cut side, slice the parsnips lengthwise into thin strips. Alternatively, cut the parsnips to fit into the feed tube horizontally and slice in a food processor fitted with an extra-thin blade. Immediately transfer the parsnip strips to a large bowl, cover with cold water and let soak for 1 hour.

2. Drain well and rinse the parsnip strips under cold running water; pat dry with paper towels.

3. Pour 3 inches of vegetable oil into a deep-fat fryer and heat to 425°. (The amount of oil you use will depend on the size of your fryer.)

4. Divide the parsnip strips into 4 batches. Place 1 batch in the fryer basket, lower the basket into the hot oil and fry just until the chips are golden brown, 2 to 3 minutes. Lift the basket out of the oil; shake gently to remove any excess oil. Transfer the chips to several layers of paper towels to drain. Repeat with the remaining batches, checking the tem-

perature of the oil and adjusting the heat, if necessary, to maintain 425°.

5. Season the chips with coarse salt to taste. Transfer to a bowl and serve.

—*Doris Tobias*

• • •

BEET FRITES

These sweet frizzy chips were created by chef Barry Wine as a garnish for grilled salmon with hot mustard and for lobster with orange. They also make excellent munchies with aperitifs.

——————6 to 8 Servings——————
About 1½ quarts corn oil
1 pound even-size medium beets
    without tops, trimmed and peeled
¼ cup cornstarch
Coarse (kosher) salt (optional)

1. Pour 3 inches of vegetable oil into a deep-fat fryer and heat to 375°. (The amount you use will depend on the size of your fryer.)

2. Using a large heavy knife or a mandoline with the cutting blade set at ⅛ inch, slice the beets crosswise ⅛ inch thick. Alternatively, cut the beets to fit the feed tube and slice in a food processor fitted with an extra-thin blade. Stack the beet slices a few at a time and cut into very thin julienne strips.

3. Place the beet strips in a large bowl. Sprinkle the cornstarch on top and shake the bowl to coat the beets evenly.

4. Divide the beets into 3 batches. Place 1 batch in the fryer basket, lower the basket into the hot oil and fry, stirring constantly at first with tongs or a long-handled metal spoon and then frequently, until the beets darken slightly, 3 to 4 minutes. Lift the basket out of the oil; shake gently to remove any excess oil. Transfer the beet *frites* to several layers of paper towels to drain. Repeat with the remaining batches, checking the temperature of the oil and adjusting the heat, if necessary, to maintain 375°.

5. Season the beet *frites* lightly with coarse salt and toss gently. Pile into a bowl and serve. (If using as a garnish, don't season with salt at all.)

—Doris Tobias

• • •

PARMESAN TREES

A Christmas tree cookie cutter transforms ordinary sliced white bread, topped with a zesty mixture of mayonnaise and grated Parmesan and onion, into holiday treats that are marvelous to munch with drinks. Use other cookie cutters to make these zesty cheese toasts for any occasion.

—————— *Makes 24 Trees* ——————
¾ cup freshly grated Parmesan
  cheese (about 3 ounces)
½ cup good-quality mayonnaise
2 tablespoons grated onion
¼ teaspoon freshly ground white
  pepper
24 slices white sandwich bread

1. Preheat the oven to 400°. In a small bowl, combine the cheese, mayonnaise, onion and white pepper.

2. Lay the bread on a work surface and cut with a tree-shaped cookie cutter. (The scraps can be reserved for another use, such as bread crumbs or stuffing.) Spread about 2 teaspoons of the cheese mixture evenly onto each bread tree. Arrange the trees on a large baking sheet and bake for 5 to 7 minutes, until golden and bubbly. Serve immediately.

—Tracey Seaman

• • •

SPICY CHEDDAR-CHIVE ROUNDS

These crackers get their kick from hot red pepper. Try them with apple wedges or as a crunchy nibble with anything from a cold beer to a Bloody Mary.

—————— *Makes About 100 Crackers* ——————
3 cups grated sharp Cheddar cheese
  (about 8 ounces)
1 cup freshly grated Parmesan
  cheese (about 4 ounces)
3 tablespoons dried chives
¾ to 1 teaspoon hot red pepper flakes
½ teaspoon freshly ground black
  pepper
1½ cups all-purpose flour
6 tablespoons cold unsalted butter,
  cut into pieces
1 teaspoon salt
¾ cup buttermilk

1. In a large bowl, combine the Cheddar, Parmesan, chives, hot pepper flakes and black pepper. Toss well to blend.

2. In a food processor, combine the flour, butter and salt. Pulse until the mixture resembles cornmeal. Add the flour to the cheese mixture and toss until well combined. With a fork, stir in the buttermilk and mix just until the dough can be gathered into a ball.

3. Turn the dough out onto a lightly floured surface and knead it for 10 to 15 seconds. Divide the dough in half and roll each piece into a log 1 inch in diameter. Wrap the logs in waxed paper and refrigerate until firm, 1 to 2 hours. *(At this point, the dough can be frozen for up to 2 months. Thaw before proceeding.)*

4. Preheat the oven to 325°. Slice the logs ⅛ inch thick and arrange the slices about ½ inch apart on 2 large baking

sheets. Bake for 15 minutes, then switch the sheets and bake the crackers for 15 minutes longer, or until golden brown. Transfer to a wire rack to cool completely. *(The crackers can be stored in an airtight container for up to 10 days.)*

—Bob Chambers

• • •

PESTO PITA THINS

The flavor of these pita snacks depends primarily on the quality of the pesto you use. If cut slightly larger before baking, these can be served with assorted cheeses or charcuterie.

—————— *Makes About 7½ Cups* ——————
1 jar (3 ounces) pesto
⅓ cup olive oil
1 package (12 ounces) 7- to 8-inch
  pita bread
⅔ cup freshly grated Parmesan
  cheese (about 3 ounces)
Freshly ground pepper

1. Preheat the oven to 300°. In a food processor, blend the pesto and olive oil, scraping down the sides of the bowl, until smooth. Transfer the pesto to a small bowl.

2. Halve each pita crosswise and generously brush the inside surfaces with the pesto mixture. Trim off the up-curved edges of the pitas to make them flat. Cut each pita in half again, then stack 2 at a time and cut into thin triangles.

3. Separate the triangles and arrange them, pesto-side up, in a single layer on two baking sheets. Sprinkle with the Parmesan cheese and pepper and bake for 10 minutes. Switch the pans and bake for another 8 to 10 minutes, until the pita triangles are evenly browned. Transfer to a rack to cool. *(The triangles can be stored in an airtight container for up to 10 days. Recrisp in a warm oven, if necessary, before serving.)*

—Bob Chambers

• • •

GOLDEN SPICED GOAT CHEESE

Serve this spice-speckled cheese as an hors d'oeuvre or with a salad.

———— *6 Servings* ————
1/2 teaspoon (loosely packed) saffron threads
1 teaspoon cumin seeds
1 teaspoon black peppercorns
1/2 small, dried red chile or 1/4 teaspoon hot red pepper flakes
1/2 cup light olive oil
3 large garlic cloves, crushed through a press
1/4 teaspoon salt
One 11-ounce log of goat cheese, preferably Montrachet, sliced into 1/3-inch rounds
Crackers or French bread, for serving

1. In a small bowl, cover the saffron with 1 tablespoon of hot water. Set aside to infuse for about 5 minutes.

2. In a small skillet, combine the cumin seeds, peppercorns and red chile and toast over high heat, shaking the pan, until fragrant, about 20 seconds. Transfer the spices to a work surface and chop finely or, alternatively, pound to a coarse powder in a mortar.

3. In a small bowl or in the mortar, combine the spice mixture with the olive oil, garlic and salt; stir to combine.

4. Arrange the goat cheese rounds in a wide, shallow dish and spoon about half of the saffron water on top. Flip the cheese over and coat the other side with the remaining saffron water. Pour the garlic-spice oil over the cheese and let marinate at room temperature for at least 5 hours, turning the cheese occasionally to coat both sides. *(The cheese will keep refrigerated for up to 1 week; turn periodically. Return to room temperature before serving.)*

5. To serve, spread some cheese, along with some of the spiced oil, on crackers. Or spread the cheese, oil and spices on slices of bread and toast briefly in a hot oven, just until the cheese is very soft.

—*Marcia Kiesel*

• • •

ROCKY ROQUEFORT DIP

Slightly bitter endive leaves and sweet apple slices are two contrasting accompaniments for this dip rich with Roquefort cheese and walnuts.

———— *Makes About 2 Cups* ————
1/2 cup part-skim ricotta cheese
4 ounces Roquefort cheese, crumbled
1/2 cup sour cream
1/2 cup walnut pieces
3 medium scallions, minced
Juice of 2 large lemons
1/8 to 1/4 teaspoon cayenne pepper, to taste
Salt
3 Belgian endives, leaves separated and rinsed, for serving
3 Red Delicious apples, cored and thinly sliced lengthwise, for serving

In a food processor, combine the ricotta, Roquefort and sour cream; process until smooth. Add the walnuts and process to blend in. Transfer to a medium bowl and stir in the scallions, lemon juice, cayenne and salt to taste. *(The dip can be made up to 1 day ahead; cover and refrigerate.)* Serve with the endive spears and apple slices.

—*Tracey Seaman*

• • •

FRIJOLEMOLE

Similar to guacamole but without the avocado, this dip can (and will) be gobbled up—a real crowd pleaser.

———— *Makes About 5 Cups* ————
1 tablespoon corn oil
1 large Spanish onion, coarsely chopped
4 medium garlic cloves, coarsely chopped
2 cans (15 ounces each) black beans, drained and rinsed
1 tablespoon fresh lemon juice
1 tablespoon fresh lime juice
1 large tomato, finely chopped
2 to 3 medium jalapeño peppers, seeded and minced, or 1 can (4 ounces) chopped mild green chiles
5 medium scallions, minced
1/4 teaspoon salt
1/2 teaspoon freshly ground black pepper
4 to 6 dashes of hot pepper sauce, to taste
1/3 cup (loosely packed) fresh coriander leaves, minced (optional)
1 cup sour cream
Tortilla chips, for serving

1. In a large saucepan, heat the oil over moderate heat. Add the onion and cook until translucent, about 5 minutes. Add the garlic and cook until fragrant, about 2 minutes. Add the black beans and 2/3 cup water. Cook until the beans begin to break apart, about 15 minutes. Transfer the beans to a food processor and puree until smooth. Transfer to a bowl and let cool to room temperature.

2. Meanwhile, in a medium nonreactive bowl, stir together the lemon juice, lime juice, tomato, jalapeños, scallions, salt and black pepper. When the beans are cool, add them to the bowl and stir well to combine. *(The recipe can be prepared to this point up to 8 hours ahead; cover and refrigerate.)*

3. Season the dip to taste with hot pepper sauce and stir in the minced coriander, if using. Pass the sour cream separately and serve with tortilla chips.

—Tracey Seaman

• • •

BRANDIED CHICKEN LIVER MOUSSE

A shortcut pâté, this spread can be made in a jiffy and served chilled within several hours. Besides French bread, serve this with an assortment of crudités, including thinly sliced cucumbers.

——— *Makes About 4 Cups* ———
½ pound sliced bacon
½ cup all-purpose flour
1 pound chicken livers, trimmed
6 medium shallots, halved and thinly sliced
⅓ cup Cognac or other brandy
1 cup heavy cream
½ cup (loosely packed) parsley leaves
2 tablespoons fresh thyme or 2 teaspoons dried
1 teaspoon freshly ground white pepper
½ teaspoon freshly ground black pepper
½ teaspoon salt
Thinly sliced fresh vegetables, such as carrots or cucumber, and/or sprigs of fresh herbs, for garnish
¾ cup canned low-sodium chicken broth
1 teaspoon unflavored gelatin
Toasted French bread slices, for serving

1. In a large heavy skillet, fry the bacon over moderately high heat, turning once, until crisp, about 5 minutes. Transfer the bacon to the bowl of a food processor. Pour all but 2 tablespoons of the bacon fat into a small heatproof bowl and set aside.

2. Place 6 tablespoons of the flour in a shallow bowl. Add the chicken livers and toss lightly to coat. Reheat the bacon fat in the skillet. Add the dredged livers and cook over moderately high heat, stirring occasionally until lightly browned on the outside and barely pink in the center, about 5 minutes. Using a slotted spoon, transfer the livers to the bowl of the food processor.

3. Add 2 tablespoons of the reserved bacon fat to the skillet, reduce the heat to low and add the shallots. Cook until softened, scraping up any browned bits in the pan, about 6 minutes.

4. Pour in the Cognac and increase the heat to moderate. Using a long wooden match, ignite the Cognac and cook until the flames subside, about 1 minute. Whisk in the remaining 2 tablespoons flour until blended. Whisk in ½ cup of the cream and cook until thickened, about 2 minutes. Scrape the sauce into the bowl of the processor.

5. Puree the contents of the food processor until smooth, scraping down the sides once. Add the parsley, thyme, white and black peppers and salt; process until incorporated. With the machine on, pour in the remaining ½ cup cream and process until smooth, creamy and well blended.

6. Scrape the mousse into a 1-quart soufflé dish or rectangular terrine and smooth the top. Decorate the top with the vegetables and/or herbs, pressing them lightly onto the surface. Refrigerate for 1 hour to firm up the mousse.

7. Pour ¼ cup of the chicken broth into a small saucepan. Sprinkle the gelatin on top and let soften for 5 minutes and then warm the mixture over moderate heat until the gelatin dissolves, 1 to 2 minutes. (Or microwave in a heatproof

bowl on High for 25 seconds.) Remove from the heat and stir in the remaining ½ cup chicken broth.

8. Pour the aspic onto the surface of the mousse. Cover and refrigerate for at least 1 hour or overnight. *(The mousse can be made up to 2 days before serving; cover and refrigerate. The texture of the mousse will vary from soft and whipped to firm, depending on how long it sits.)* Serve with toasted French bread.

—Tracey Seaman

• • •

PROVENCALE SPINACH DIP WITH HERB TOASTS

This health-minded dip is chunky with spinach and olives and gutsy with garlic and goat cheese. If you don't have time to make the herb toasts, use slices of a good sourdough bread.

——— *Makes About 3½ Cups* ———
¼ cup olive oil
1 large red onion, finely chopped
1½ tablespoons chopped fresh thyme or 1¼ teaspoons dried
½ cup pine nuts
1 long, thin loaf of French bread, sliced ¼ inch thick
1 teaspoon dried Greek oregano or herbes de Provence
11 ounces goat cheese, such as Bucheron, at room temperature
1½ cups milk
1 package (10 ounces) frozen spinach—thawed, squeezed dry and finely chopped
10 olives, preferably Calamata, chopped
2 garlic cloves, minced
½ teaspoon fresh lemon juice
Salt and freshly ground pepper

1. Preheat the oven to 400°. In a large skillet, warm 2 tablespoons of the olive oil over moderately high heat. Add the onion and thyme; reduce the heat to low. Cook the onion, stirring occasionally, until softened but not browned, about 10 minutes. Set aside to cool.

2. Put the pine nuts on a baking sheet and toast in the oven until golden brown, about 4 minutes. Set aside to cool.

3. Lightly brush 1 side of each slice of bread with the remaining 2 tablespoons olive oil. Arrange the slices, oiled-side up, on a baking sheet and toast in the oven until golden brown, about 5 minutes. Sprinkle the oregano over the toasts.

4. In a medium bowl, mash the goat cheese with a fork until creamy. Gradually blend in the milk. Fold in the spinach, olives, garlic and the cooled onion mixture and toasted pine nuts. Add the lemon juice and season with salt and pepper to taste. Serve with the herb toasts.

—Marcia Kiesel

• • •

CRISPY SHALLOT DIP

It takes very few ingredients—though a whole lot of shallots—to produce this ultimate onion dip.

———— *Makes About 3¹/₂ Cups* ————
²/₃ cup olive oil
2 pounds shallots, thinly sliced
2 sprigs of fresh thyme or ¹/₂ teaspoon dried
1 package (8 ounces) cream cheese, at room temperature
1 pint sour cream, at room temperature
Salt and freshly ground pepper
Potato chips, for serving

1. In a large skillet, warm the olive oil over moderately high heat. Add the shallots and stir in the thyme. Reduce the heat to low and cook, stirring occasionally, until the shallots are browned and crisp, about 30 minutes.

2. Using a slotted spoon, transfer the shallots to paper towels to drain. Discard the thyme sprigs, if used.

3. In a medium bowl, mash together the cream cheese and sour cream with a wooden spoon. Stir in the shallots. Season with salt and pepper to taste. *(The recipe can be made up to 1 day ahead; cover and refrigerate.)* Serve with potato chips.

—Marcia Kiesel

• • •

GOLDEN MADRAS DIP

For the complex flavor of the curry powder to fully develop with the other seasonings and ingredients, this dip should sit at least an hour before serving. It can be made up to one day ahead; keep covered in the refrigerator.

———— *Makes About 3 Cups* ————
2 tablespoons olive oil
1 medium green bell pepper, coarsely chopped
1 large onion, coarsely chopped
1 large tart green apple, such as Granny Smith, peeled and coarsely chopped
2 tablespoons curry powder
1 teaspoon cumin seeds
1 teaspoon finely grated fresh ginger
1 cup sour cream
¹/₂ cup plain yogurt
1 tablespoon chopped fresh dill or 1¹/₂ teaspoons dried
Salt

Papadums,* fried according to package directions, or toasted pita bread, for serving
*Available at Indian markets and specialty food stores

1. In a large skillet, warm the olive oil over moderate heat. Add the green pepper, onion and apple and cook until slightly soft, about 10 minutes.

2. Stir in the curry powder, cumin seeds and ginger. Reduce the heat to low and cook, stirring occasionally, until the vegetables and apple are very soft and the spices are fragrant, about 10 minutes longer. Set aside to cool.

3. Transfer the mixture to a food processor and puree until smooth; stop the machine occasionally to scrape down the sides. Add the sour cream and yogurt and process until thoroughly blended. Pour the dip into a medium bowl and fold in the dill. Season to taste with salt. Let sit at room temperature for at least an hour before serving or refrigerate, covered, for up to 1 day. Serve with fried papadums or toasted pita.

—Marcia Kiesel

• • •

BAKED HORSERADISH CHEDDAR CANAPES

These toasty canapés are an elegant accompaniment to a steaming pot of soup. You can cut them in any variety of shapes and pass them around on a tray so that people can help themselves.

——*Makes 10 Dozen 1-Inch Squares* ——
1 small onion, quartered
¹/₂ pound thinly sliced Canadian bacon or Black Forest ham
¹/₂ pound extra-sharp white Cheddar cheese, cut into small chunks

*1½ tablespoons prepared
    horseradish*
½ teaspoon hot pepper sauce
½ teaspoon salt
*¼ teaspoon freshly ground black
    pepper*
*1 loaf (1 pound) thin-sliced, firm-
    textured white bread (about
    30 slices)*

1. In a food processor, pulse the onion until finely chopped. Transfer the onion to a large mixing bowl. Add the Canadian bacon to the processor and pulse until finely chopped, stopping to scrape down the sides of the bowl as necessary. Add the bacon to the mixing bowl.

2. Working in 2 or 3 batches, add the chunks of cheese to the processor and pulse until finely chopped. Add the cheese to the onions and bacon in the bowl, then add the horseradish, hot sauce, salt and black pepper and mix thoroughly until a chunky spread forms.

3. Preheat the oven to 400°. Spread each slice of bread with a generous ⅛-inch layer of the cheese mixture. Arrange the bread slices side by side, spread-side up, on baking sheets. Place the sheets in the freezer, one at a time if necessary, and freeze until the mixture is just firm enough to slice neatly, about 20 minutes. *(The recipe can be prepared to this point up to 2 weeks ahead. Once firm, stack the bread slices between sheets of waxed paper, wrap well in plastic wrap and freeze.)*

4. Trim off the crusts and cut each slice into 4 squares. Bake the canapés for 12 to 14 minutes, until the cheese is brown and bubbly. Serve hot.

—Paul Grimes

• • •

CROSTINI WITH TOMATO

When we begin to receive ripe, flavorful vine-ripened tomatoes and fresh basil, I know it is time to offer my friends crostini with tomatoes.

———— *Makes 24 Toasts* ————

*1½ pounds ripe plum tomatoes
    (8 to 9 medium), quartered*
1 teaspoon salt
1 garlic clove, minced
1 tablespoon minced basil
*2 tablespoons minced Italian flat-
    leaf parsley*
¼ cup extra-virgin olive oil
Freshly ground pepper
*12 slices country-style round Italian
    bread, halved crosswise, or
    24 slices from a long loaf*

1. Place the tomatoes in a food processor and pulse for 1 second intervals until finely chopped; do not puree. Transfer the tomatoes to a colander or strainer and toss with the salt. Let drain for 1 hour, stirring once or twice.

2. Preheat the oven to 375°. In a medium bowl, combine the drained tomatoes with the garlic, basil and parsley. Gradually whisk in the olive oil until well blended. Season with pepper to taste and more salt if necessary. Set aside.

3. Place the bread on a baking sheet and toast in the oven for about 10 minutes, until crisp and golden.

4. To serve, place the tomato mixture in a small bowl in the center of a platter and surround with toasted bread.

—Lorenza de' Medici

• • •

CROSTINI WITH TARRAGON SPREAD

Tarragon is common in Siena but is practically unknown in the rest of Italy. This spread can be prepared the day before and refrigerated, as the olive oil will prevent the tarragon from discoloring. Serve at room temperature on toast or in a bowl as a dip.

———— *Makes 24 Toasts* ————

*¼ cup finely chopped fresh tarragon
    or Italian flat-leaf parsley*
2 tablespoons capers, finely chopped
2 hard-cooked eggs, finely chopped
¼ cup extra-virgin olive oil
Salt
*12 slices country-style round Italian
    bread, halved crosswise, or
    24 slices from a long loaf*

1. Preheat the oven to 375°. In a medium bowl, combine the tarragon, capers and eggs with a fork. Gradually whisk in the olive oil until well blended. Stir in a pinch of salt.

2. Place the bread slices on a large baking sheet and toast in the oven for 10 minutes, until crisp and golden.

3. Spread each slice with the tarragon mixture and arrange on a platter. Alternatively, spoon the tarragon spread into a small bowl and surround with the toasts.

—Lorenza de' Medici

• • •

CROSTINI WITH BEEF AND BALSAMIC VINEGAR

The best way to begin this dish is to ask your butcher to slice the meat paper thin by machine. However, if you do it at home, freezing the meat for about an hour will help make it easier to shave off thin slices. With all the ingredients ready, you can finish preparing this dish in a few minutes, right before your guests arrive.

Makes 24 Toasts
12 slices country-style round Italian bread, halved crosswise, or 24 slices from a long loaf
¾ pound lean top round, sliced into 24 paper-thin slices
2 tablespoons balsamic vinegar
2 tablespoons extra-virgin olive oil
Salt and freshly ground pepper
4 ounces fresh porcini or button mushrooms, sliced paper thin
4 ounces Parmesan cheese, sliced thin
2 tablespoons finely chopped Italian flat-leaf parsley

1. Preheat the oven to 375°. On a large baking sheet, toast the bread in the oven for 10 minutes, until crisp and golden.

2. Top each piece of toast with a slice of beef, folding in the ends to fit as necessary. Sprinkle lightly with the vinegar and oil; season with salt and pepper to taste.

3. Top each toast with several mushroom slices, a few slices of Parmesan and a sprinkling of parsley. Arrange the toasts on a platter and serve.
—*Lorenza de' Medici*

• • •

ALSATIAN PIZZA

In Alsace this thin, crisp, savory tart is called *flammenküche* or *tarte flambée* because it was originally cooked next to the hot coals in an old-fashioned baker's oven. It's traditionally folded in half and eaten out of hand, like a crêpe, but I like to cut the tart into small squares to serve with drinks.

Makes About 4 Dozen 2-Inch Squares
2 small onions, thinly sliced
¾ cup ricotta cheese
½ cup sour cream
¼ teaspoon salt
⅛ teaspoon cayenne pepper
8 ounces thickly sliced bacon, cut crosswise into ¼-inch strips
Pizza Dough (p. 157), at room temperature
Olive oil, for brushing

1. In a medium bowl, combine the onions, ricotta, sour cream, salt and cayenne. Mix thoroughly. Cover and refrigerate for at least 1 hour.

2. In a large skillet, cook the bacon over moderate heat until slightly crisp but still chewy, about 5 minutes. Drain on paper towels and set aside. *(The recipe can be prepared to this point up to 1 day ahead.)*

3. On a lightly floured surface, roll the Pizza Dough into a small rectangle. Cover with a towel and let rest for ½ hour. Then roll out the dough into a 12-by-17-inch rectangle; it will be very thin. Fold the dough in half and transfer it to a 14-by-17-inch cookie sheet (preferably a black one, for better browning). Unfold the dough to line the sheet.

4. Preheat the oven to 450°. Spread the ricotta and onion mixture evenly over the rolled-out dough. Sprinkle the bacon on top and push it into the topping. Brush the borders of the dough with olive oil.

5. Bake on the lower rack of the oven for 15 minutes, or until the bottom is browned and crisp. Slide the pizza onto a work surface and, using a pizza cutter or large knife, cut it into 2-inch squares.
—*Lydie Pinoy Marshall*

• • •

RADISH AND ARUGULA SANDWICHES

Consider this a contemporary alternative to the classic watercress tea sandwich. Assemble a platter of these and leave a second loaf of bread on a cutting board with a knife. Surround with bowls of grated radishes, arugula, a crock of creamy butter and a pepper mill, and people can make their own.

Makes About 60 Small Sandwiches
2 large bunches of radishes, washed and trimmed
2 baguettes, preferably sourdough
1 stick (4 ounces) unsalted butter, at room temperature
Salt and freshly ground pepper
2 large bunches of arugula, large stems removed

1. Grate the radishes in a food processor or on the large holes of a hand grater.

2. Slice one of the baguettes on the diagonal about ¼ inch thick. Liberally butter one side of each slice; place, buttered-side up, on a work surface. Grind black pepper over each slice and sprinkle with salt. Place a leaf of arugula at one end of each buttered slice and sprinkle with grated radish. *(The sandwiches can be prepared up to 2 hours ahead. Cover and store at room temperature.)*
—*Paul Grimes*

• • •

Tequila-Cured Red Snapper Seviche (p. 39).

Left, New Zealand Mussels with Pommery Mustard Mayonette (p. 225). Above, Fresh Fig Vinaigrette (p. 255), shown here with slices of prosciutto.

THAI FLAVOR PACKAGES

This assemble-your-own hors d'oeuvre, called *mien kham*, is a wonderful introduction to Thai cuisine.

—————— *6 First-Course Servings* ——————
1½ cups freshly grated coconut
½ cup roasted peanuts, coarsely chopped
½ cup dried shrimp* (about ¾ ounce)
3 tablespoons finely chopped fresh ginger
3 tablespoons finely chopped shallots
1 lime, cut into very thin wedges
½ cup fresh coriander leaves
3 tablespoons minced jalapeño pepper
½ cup soy sauce
1 tablespoon palm sugar* or light brown sugar
1 teaspoon nam pla*
3 heads of Bibb lettuce, leaves separated
*Available at Asian markets

1. Preheat the oven to 325°. Spread the coconut on a baking sheet and toast, stirring occasionally, until golden, about 10 minutes. Set aside and let cool.

2. On a medium platter, arrange small piles of the peanuts, shrimp, ginger, shallots, lime wedges, coriander, jalapeño pepper and toasted coconut.

3. In a small saucepan, boil the soy sauce over moderately high heat until it has reduced by half, about 5 minutes. Remove from the heat and stir in the palm sugar and *nam pla*. Pour into a small bowl to be set alongside the platter.

Pork and Olive Finger Pies (p. 37).

4. Arrange the lettuce leaves in a bowl. When all the ingredients are on the table, everyone assembles his own *mien kham*. Begin with a lettuce leaf and use it to hold a small portion of each ingredient. Proportions are a matter of taste, but about 1 teaspoon coconut should first be placed in the middle of the leaf, followed by a bit of the jalapeño pepper, ginger, shallots, peanuts, a few dried shrimp and coriander leaves. Squeeze a small wedge of lime over this. Finally, with a small spoon, pour not more than ¼ teaspoon of sauce on top. Fold the lettuce leaf around what's inside to make a tight package.
—*Jeffrey Alford*

• • •

PORK AND OLIVE FINGER PIES

These Caribbean-inspired finger pies are warm pockets of corn pastry stuffed with a mild mixture of pork, green olives and lemon. They can be assembled weeks ahead and thrown in the oven right from the freezer. Italian green olives, which are easy to find in many delicatessens, add a distinctive flavor to the pastries.

—————— *Makes 12 Finger Pies* ——————
1 pound boneless pork shoulder, cut into 1-inch cubes and chilled
2 tablespoons unsalted butter
1 medium onion, finely chopped
2 garlic cloves, minced
¼ cup dry white wine
1 tablespoon fresh lemon juice
1½ tablespoons all-purpose flour
⅓ cup chicken stock or canned broth
⅓ cup beef stock or canned broth
½ teaspoon freshly ground pepper
8 large green Italian olives, pitted and coarsely chopped
¼ cup minced parsley
Salt
Cornmeal Pastry (recipe follows)
1 egg
1 tablespoon Dijon-style mustard

1. Heat a large heavy skillet over moderately high heat until very hot. Meanwhile, in a food processor, coarsely grind the pork in two batches by pulsing at 2-second intervals, about 10 seconds. Transfer the meat to the hot skillet and cook, stirring to break up the meat, until browned and most of the liquid has evaporated, about 15 minutes.

2. Add the butter to the skillet and reduce the heat to moderate. Add the onion and cook with the meat until the onion is translucent and starting to brown, about 5 minutes.

3. Stir in the garlic and cook for 2 minutes longer. Add the wine and lemon juice and simmer until almost evaporated, about 3 minutes. Sprinkle the flour over the meat and cook, stirring, until the mixture is thick and pasty, about 2 minutes more.

4. Gradually stir in the chicken and beef stocks and ¾ cup of water and bring to a simmer. Season with the pepper. Cover, reduce the heat to low and simmer gently for 30 minutes.

5. Remove from the heat and stir in the olives and parsley. Season to taste with salt and pepper. Let cool completely before filling the pies. *(The pork mixture can be made 1 day ahead and refrigerated overnight.)*

6. On a lightly floured surface, roll out 1 disk of the cornmeal pastry dough into a 6-by-16-inch rectangle. Using a fluted pastry wheel, trim it to 5 by 15 inches, then cut the rectangle into three inch squares.

7. Moisten the edges of each square. Scoop 2 rounded tablespoons of the pork and olive mixture onto the lower half of each square and spread evenly, leaving a ½-inch rim of pastry exposed. Fold the pastry over to enclose the filling, pressing the edges lightly to seal. Trim the edges with the pastry wheel. Continue with the remaining squares, then repeat with the remaining disks of Cornmeal Pastry dough and filling. *(The pies can be made to this point, wrapped well first in plastic and then in foil, and frozen for up to 1 month. If frozen, unwrap the pies and let sit at room temperature for 10 minutes before proceeding and allow 5 extra minutes baking time.)*

8. Preheat the oven to 400°. Place the pies on a large ungreased baking sheet. In a small bowl, beat together the egg and mustard; brush lightly over the top of each pie. With a small sharp knife, cut three small steam vents in the center of each pie. Bake the pies 25 to 30 minutes, until well browned. (Allow an extra 5 minutes if the pies are frozen.) Let cool on a rack about 5 minutes. Serve whole pies in a basket or cut them in half and arrange on a platter.

—Tracey Seaman

• • •

CORNMEAL PASTRY

This dough is firm yet flaky—a good option for any savory or fresh fruit filling. The pastry can easily be prepared in two batches if your processor is not large enough to accommodate the full quantity of ingredients.

Makes Enough for
12 Finger Pies or Two
——— 9-Inch Double-Crust Pies ———
4 cups all-purpose flour
½ cup white cornmeal
1 teaspoon salt
1 stick (4 ounces) plus 2 tablespoons
  cold unsalted butter, cut into
  20 pieces
⅔ cup chilled vegetable shortening
⅔ cup ice water

1. In a food processor, combine the flour, cornmeal and salt; pulse briefly to mix. Add the butter and shortening and process until the mixture resembles coarse meal, about 20 seconds.

2. With the machine on, add the ice water and process just until the dough begins to form a ball. Transfer the dough to a lightly floured surface and knead briefly. Cut the dough in quarters and shape into disks. Wrap each disk in waxed paper and refrigerate until ready to roll out. *(The dough can be prepared to this point and refrigerated overnight if desired. Let the dough sit at room temperature for about 5 minutes before rolling out.)*

—Tracey Seaman

• • •

MANICOTTI CREPES WITH SPINACH AND CHEESE

To appeal to the Italian within us all, I've developed a version of the classic stuffed manicotti. Tomato-cloaked, homemade crêpes envelop a rich filling of spinach, ricotta, mozzarella and Parmesan. You can assemble the crêpes and freeze them right in their baking dish, sauce and all, for up to one month, or you can make the crêpes two days ahead and refrigerate them until ready to bake. Either way, you can bake the finished dish the day before and then reheat it for about a half hour before serving. Sprinkle with plenty of grated cheese.

—Makes About 24 Stuffed Crêpes —
Tomato Sauce (p. 254)
2 pounds fresh spinach, stems
  removed, or 1 box (10 ounces)
  frozen spinach, thawed and
  squeezed dry
2 pounds whole-milk ricotta cheese
½ teaspoon freshly ground pepper
½ teaspoon salt
½ cup freshly grated Parmesan
  cheese (about 4 ounces), plus
  more for serving
24 Crêpes (p. 164)
1 pound mozzarella, coarsely
  shredded

1. Lightly grease an 11-by-15-by-2-inch roasting pan. Pour 2 cups of the Tomato Sauce into the pan and tilt to coat evenly. Set aside.

2. Bring a large pot of lightly salted water to a boil over high heat. Add half of the fresh spinach and stir until wilted. Remove to a colander with a slotted spoon, drain and cool. Repeat with the remaining fresh spinach. When cool, squeeze the spinach to remove as much moisture as possible.

3. Chop the fresh spinach or the frozen spinach leaves and transfer to a medium bowl. Add the ricotta, pepper, salt and ½ cup of the Parmesan cheese; stir to blend well. Set aside.

4. Preheat the oven to 400°. Lay out the Crêpes on a large work surface. Sprinkle 1½ tablespoons of the shredded mozzarella over each crêpe, leaving a 1-inch border around the rim.

5. Mound 2 tablespoons of the spinach and ricotta mixture in the center of each crêpe. Fold the right side of the crêpe over the filling; then fold up the bottom, fold down the top, and fold the left side over to seal. Repeat with the remaining crêpes. Arrange the filled crêpes, seam-side down, in the prepared pan.

6. Spoon 4 cups of tomato sauce over the crêpes. Cover loosely with foil. *The recipe can be made to this point up to 1 month ahead and frozen.)* Bake the assembled dish for about 1 hour, or slightly longer if frozen, until piping hot. Shortly before serving, reheat the remaining 2 cups of tomato sauce. Serve the manicotti crêpes with more of the hot tomato sauce and lots of grated Parmesan cheese on the side.

—Tracey Seaman

• • •

DILLED GRUYERE QUICHE

This quiche can be baked a day ahead and gently rewarmed before serving. However, it is best to serve it freshly baked, so why not bake the crust the day before and simply fill it the next morning?

———— *Makes 40 2-Inch Squares* ————
3 cups unbleached all-purpose flour
2 teaspoons salt
2 sticks (8 ounces) cold unsalted
 butter, cut into ¼-inch pieces
¼ cup ice water
1½ cups grated Gruyère cheese
 (about 5 ounces)
3 cups heavy cream
8 large eggs
½ cup loosely packed fresh dill,
 minced
½ cup freshly grated Parmesan
 cheese (about 4 ounces)
¼ teaspoon freshly ground pepper
⅛ teaspoon freshly grated nutmeg

1. In a food processor, combine the flour and 1 teaspoon of the salt; pulse 5 times to combine. Add the butter and pulse until the mixture resembles coarse meal. With the processor running, add the water and process just until the dough begins to form a ball. Add more water by teaspoons if necessary. Remove the dough from the processor and flatten it into a 6-inch disk. Cover with plastic wrap and refrigerate for 15 minutes.
2. Preheat the oven to 350°. On a lightly floured surface, roll out the dough to a 13½-by-18½-inch rectangle about ¼ inch thick. Roll back onto the rolling pin and transfer the dough to an 11½-by-16½-by-1-inch jelly-roll pan. Push the dough into the corners to line the pan evenly. Even the edges and crimp decoratively. Freeze the shell for 15 minutes.
3. Line the inside of the dough with parchment paper or aluminum foil and fill

with pie weights, rice or dried beans. Bake for 15 minutes. Remove the weights and parchment paper and bake for another 10 minutes to set the pastry. Do not let it brown.
4. Remove the pan from the oven and scatter 1 cup of the grated Gruyère over the hot pastry. It will melt and seal the crust. *(The recipe can be prepared to this point 1 day ahead and kept covered at room temperature.)*
5. In a medium bowl, whisk together the heavy cream, eggs, dill, Parmesan cheese, pepper, nutmeg and the remaining 1 teaspoon salt. Pour the egg mixture into the crust and sprinkle the remaining ½ cup Gruyère on top. Bake for about 30 minutes, or until the custard is set and lightly golden on top.
6. Let cool slightly and cut the quiche into 2-inch squares. Serve warm or at room temperature.

—*Paul Grimes*

• • •

TEQUILA-CURED
RED SNAPPER SEVICHE

This recipe involves very little actual work, but it does call for planning ahead because the fish must marinate for one and a half days in the fridge.

———— *6 First-Course Servings* ————
1½ pounds skinless red snapper
 fillets
¼ teaspoon table salt
½ teaspoon freshly ground black
 pepper
1 large red bell pepper, cut into
 paper-thin rings
1 large green bell pepper, cut into
 paper-thin rings
1 large yellow bell pepper, cut into
 paper-thin rings
1 red onion, sliced paper thin

1 cup fresh lemon juice
½ cup fresh lime juice
3 tablespoons tequila
Unsalted butter and coarse (kosher)
 salt, for the plates
2 tablespoons chopped fresh
 coriander, for garnish

1. In a large glass baking dish, arrange the snapper fillets in a single layer. Season with the table salt and black pepper. Cover with the sliced bell peppers and onion. Pour the lemon juice, lime juice and tequila over the fish and cover with plastic wrap. Marinate in the refrigerator, turning occasionally, until the fish is almost opaque throughout, about 36 hours.
2. Rub a small amount of butter around the rims of 6 glass serving plates. Roll the plate rims in coarse salt as you would a Margarita glass. Place the plates in the refrigerator until the buttered salt rims harden, about 5 minutes.
3. Drain the snapper and cut it into 1-inch cubes. Arrange the bell pepper and onion rings on each plate. Mound the fish in the center and sprinkle the coriander on top.

—*Steve Mellina*

• • •

SHRIMP REMOULADE

The uncooked, fresh-tasting sauce in this dish is a New Orleans trademark.

———— *6 First-Course Servings* ————
1½ pounds medium shrimp, shelled
 and deveined
3 tablespoons Creole mustard*
3 tablespoons distilled white vinegar
½ cup (loosely packed) parsley
 leaves, minced
1 tablespoon paprika
1 garlic clove, minced
2 teaspoons prepared horseradish
⅓ cup olive oil
Dash of hot pepper sauce

Salt
1 small celery rib, minced
3 scallions, minced
1 head of lettuce (such as chicory),
    leaves separated, for serving
*Available at specialty food markets

1. Place the shrimp in a large pot of boiling salted water. When the water returns to a boil, drain the shrimp thoroughly. Set aside.

2. In a medium bowl, whisk together the mustard, vinegar, parsley, paprika, garlic and horseradish. Gradually whisk in the olive oil in a thin stream until thoroughly incorporated. Add the hot pepper sauce and salt to taste. Fold in the celery, scallions and reserved shrimp until well coated. Cover and refrigerate for at least 3 hours and up to 24 hours.

3. Arrange the lettuce on 6 salad plates and top with the marinated shrimp. Serve cold or at room temperature.

—Galatoire's, New Orleans

• • •

GRAVLAX WITH MUSTARD SAUCE

In the days before refrigeration, salmon was cured and buried in the ground to keep through the long winter, hence the name gravlax, which means salmon from the grave.

——— 12 First-Course Servings ———
¼ cup coarse (kosher) salt
¼ cup sugar
1 tablespoon crushed white
    peppercorns
1¾ pounds center-cut salmon fillet
    with skin
2 large bunches of dill
Mustard Sauce (p. 254)
Lemon wedges

1. In a small bowl, combine the salt, sugar and peppercorns. Rub a handful of this seasoning mixture over both sides of the salmon. Set the salmon in a nonreactive dish, skin-side down, and sprinkle

the rest of the seasoning mixture on top.

2. Set aside 12 small dill sprigs for garnish. Cover the salmon with the remaining dill and cover with plastic wrap. Let stand at room temperature for 6 hours, then refrigerate for 24 hours.

3. Scrape the dill and seasoning mixture off the salmon and pat the fish dry. Using a long, sharp knife, thinly slice the salmon on the diagonal about ⅛ inch thick, leaving the skin. Cut out the little gray triangle at the bottom of each slice, if necessary. Arrange the slices on a large platter, overlapping them slightly. Cover tightly with plastic wrap and refrigerate for up to 6 hours.

4. Cut the salmon skin into 12 crosswise strips. Set a large cast-iron skillet on the stove and turn the heat to moderately high. When the pan is hot, add the strips of skin and fry until lightly browned, about 45 seconds per side. Drain on paper towels.

5. To serve, roll up the strips of salmon skin with a dill sprig in the center of each. Garnish the platter of gravlax with the rolls. Serve the Mustard Sauce and lemon wedges on the side.

—Christer Larsson, Aquavit,
New York City

• • •

POACHED MUSSELS
WITH CHENIN BLANC

Try this dish as a dinner appetizer or as a luncheon entrée with an interesting salad and lots of French bread.

❦ Serve the mussels with the crisp and fruity 1986 Chappellet Chenin Blanc.

——— 6 First-Course Servings ———
1 tablespoon unsalted butter
3 large shallots, minced
1 medium garlic clove, minced
1 small jalapeño pepper, minced
2 cups fish stock or bottled clam
    juice

1 medium tomato—peeled, seeded
    and chopped
1 medium onion, chopped
2 large carrots, cut into 2-inch-long
    thin julienne strips
3 medium leeks, trimmed and cut
    into 3-inch-long thin julienne
    strips
Bouquet garni: 2 quartered celery
    ribs, 3 sprigs of parsley, 3 sprigs of
    fresh thyme or ½ teaspoon dried,
    and 1 large bay leaf tied in
    cheesecloth
Salt and freshly ground black
    pepper
1 cup Chappellet Chenin Blanc
4 pounds mussels, scrubbed and
    debearded
6 fresh or preserved kumquats,
    thinly sliced
¼ cup minced parsley

1. In a large nonreactive casserole, melt the butter over moderately high heat. Add the shallots, garlic and jalapeño and cook until softened, about 5 minutes.

2. Add the stock, tomato, onion, carrots, leeks and 2 cups of water. Nestle the bouquet garni among the vegetables and season lightly with salt and black pepper. Bring to a boil over moderately high heat and boil for 5 minutes. Reduce the heat to moderately low and simmer, partially covered, for 20 minutes.

3. Stir in the wine. Increase the heat to moderately high and bring to a boil. Add the mussels, cover and cook until they just begin to open, about 6 minutes. Discard the bouquet garni and any mussels that do not to open.

4. Spoon the mussels and broth into 6 warmed, shallow soup bowls. Garnish with the kumquats and parsley and serve piping hot.

—Molly Chappellet, Chappellet
Vineyard, St. Helena, California

• • •

SOUPS

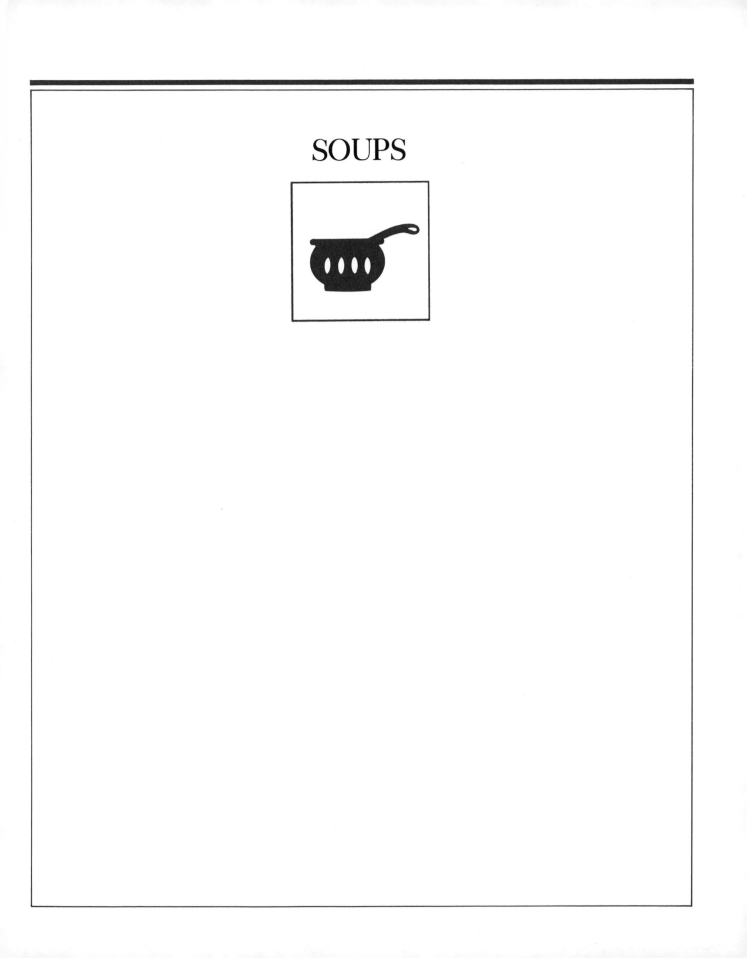

LIGURIAN VEGETABLE SOUP

Don't cut the vegetables too small since the finished soup should have a chunky look. If you're lucky enough to find ripe, fresh tomatoes, use the same volume—peeled, seeded and chopped—as canned.

——————— *8 to 10 Servings* ———————
1 large onion, coarsely chopped
2 celery ribs, coarsely chopped
2 medium carrots, coarsely chopped
¼ cup extra-virgin olive oil
1 pound savoy or green cabbage,
    coarsely shredded or chopped
2 teaspoons salt
½ teaspoon freshly ground pepper
2 cups coarsely shredded romaine
    lettuce or escarole
3 medium potatoes (about 1 pound),
    peeled and cut into ½-inch dice
1¼ cups drained canned plum
    tomatoes, coarsely chopped
4 cups Vegetable Broth (recipe
    follows) or canned low-sodium
    chicken broth
1 cup fresh or frozen peas
⅓ cup minced Italian flat-leaf
    parsley
2 garlic cloves, minced
8 to 10 slices Italian bread, toasted
Freshly grated Parmesan cheese

1. In a large saucepan, cook the onion, celery and carrots in the olive oil over moderate heat until they are softened, about 10 minutes.

2. Add the cabbage, salt and pepper and cook, stirring, until the cabbage is wilted, about 3 minutes. Add the lettuce and cook until wilted, about 1 minute. Stir in the potatoes and tomatoes and cook for another 3 minutes. Increase the heat to moderately high, add the Vegetable Broth and bring to a boil. Reduce the heat to moderately low, cover and simmer for 30 minutes.

3. Add the peas and cook for 5 minutes, covered. Stir the parsley and garlic into the soup; cook for 5 minutes.

4. Place a piece of toasted bread in each soup bowl. Ladle the hot soup on top and serve with a light sprinkling of Parmesan cheese. Serve immediately.

—*Nancy Verde Barr*

• • •

VEGETABLE BROTH

——————— *Makes About 6 Cups* ———————
2 medium carrots, cut into 2-inch
    pieces
2 medium onions, quartered
3 celery ribs, with tops, cut into
    2-inch pieces
2 peeled fresh or drained canned
    plum tomatoes
1 bay leaf
1 small bunch of parsley
½ teaspoon salt

In a large saucepan or stockpot, place the carrots, onions, celery, tomatoes, bay leaf, parsley and salt. Cover with 3 quarts of water and bring to a boil over moderate heat. Reduce the heat to moderately low and simmer for 2 hours. Strain before using. (*The vegetable stock can be cooled and kept covered in the refrigerator for up to 3 days or frozen for up to 3 months.*)

—*Nancy Verde Barr*

• • •

SICILIAN ARTICHOKE AND FRESH PEA SOUP

This delicate soup heralds spring in Italy and can precede the most elegant of meals with finesse.

❢ The subtle flavors of the artichokes and peas would be compatible with a soft, dry white wine, such as 1988 Antinori Orvieto Classico Secco Campogrande.

——————— *4 to 6 Servings* ———————
4 large artichokes
1 lemon, halved
2 garlic cloves, minced
¼ cup olive oil
1 tablespoon minced Italian flat-leaf
    parsley
2 teaspoons salt
6 cups Vegetable Broth (at left) or
    canned low-sodium chicken broth
1 pound fresh peas, shelled, or 1 cup
    frozen peas
Freshly grated Parmesan cheese

1. Trim the artichokes by first snapping off the tough outer leaves near the base. Using a stainless steel knife, cut off the stems. Cut the crowns to within 1½ inches of the base and scoop out the hairy chokes. As you trim the artichokes, rub them with the cut lemon to prevent discoloration. Cut the trimmed bottoms into eight sections.

2. In a large saucepan, cook the garlic in the olive oil over moderately low heat, stirring occasionally, until golden, about 3 minutes.

3. Add the artichokes, parsley and salt and cook until the artichokes are slightly softened, about 5 minutes more. Add the Vegetable Broth, increase the heat to moderately high and bring the soup to a boil. Reduce the heat to moderately low and simmer until the artichokes are tender, about 20 minutes.

4. Add the peas and cook until just tender, about 15 minutes for fresh peas and 20 minutes for frozen.

5. Ladle the soup into serving bowls and serve with a light sprinkling of Parmesan cheese.

—*Nancy Verde Barr*

• • •

CALABRIAN ASPARAGUS SOUP

Thickening soup with bread is typical of rustic Italian cooking, in which nothing goes to waste. The toasts may be made from day-old or slightly stale bread.

♥ Asparagus has a penetrating herbaceousness that has a rapport with Sauvignon Blancs, such as 1988 Buena Vista, which would also happily pair with the accompanying cheese.

———— 6 Servings ————

2 garlic cloves, minced
2 tablespoons extra-virgin olive oil
2 pounds asparagus, cut into 1-inch
*   pieces*
2 teaspoons salt
½ teaspoon freshly ground pepper
4 cups Vegetable Broth (p. 42) or
*   canned low-sodium chicken broth*
4 eggs
½ cup freshly grated Parmesan or
*   Pecorino cheese, plus extra for*
*   serving*
6 slices Italian bread, toasted

1. In a large saucepan, cook the garlic in the olive oil over moderate heat, stirring constantly, until golden, about 3 minutes. Add the asparagus and cook until bright green, about 5 minutes. Add the salt, pepper and Vegetable Broth and bring to a boil. Reduce the heat to moderately low and simmer until the asparagus are tender, about 15 minutes.

2. In a small bowl, beat the eggs with ½ cup of the cheese. Reduce the heat to low so that the soup is no longer simmering, and very slowly ladle about 2 cups of the hot soup into the beaten eggs, whisking constantly. Once incorporated, gradually stir the egg mixture into the soup in the saucepan. Increase the heat to moder-

ately low and cook the soup, whisking constantly, until it just thickens, about 8 minutes. Do not allow the soup to boil or the eggs will curdle. Remove from the heat.

3. Place one slice of toasted bread into each soup bowl. Ladle the hot soup on top and serve with additional grated cheese.

—*Nancy Verde Barr*

• • •

NEAPOLITAN CAULIFLOWER SOUP

As is often the case with Italian food, this soup uses just a few basic ingredients to showcase a star vegetable. A purist would even shudder at the cheese. Make this soup as garlicky and spicy as you like, but be sure to serve it with lots of crusty Italian bread.

———— 6 Servings ————

1 large head of cauliflower (about 2
*   pounds), separated into florets*
2 tablespoons white wine vinegar or
*   cider vinegar*
4 garlic cloves, minced
½ teaspoon crushed hot red pepper
¼ cup olive oil
4 cups hot Vegetable Broth (p. 42) or
*   canned low-sodium chicken broth*
2 teaspoons salt
⅓ cup chopped Italian flat-leaf
*   parsley*
Freshly grated Pecorino cheese

1. Trim the stems from the cauliflower florets and cut the stems into ½-inch pieces, then break the florets into ½-inch pieces. Fill a large bowl with 2 quarts of cold water and stir in the vinegar. Add the cauliflower pieces and stir to clean thoroughly.

2. Bring a large saucepan of salted water to a boil over high heat. Drop the cauliflower into the boiling water, return to a boil and cook over moderately high

heat until just tender, about 4 minutes. Drain the cauliflower thoroughly.

3. In a large saucepan, cook the garlic and hot red pepper in the olive oil over moderately low heat, stirring occasionally, until the garlic is golden, about 3 minutes. Add the cauliflower and cook for 5 minutes, stirring to prevent it from browning. Stir in the hot Vegetable Broth, salt and parsley.

4. Using a slotted spoon, remove 1 cup of the cooked cauliflower from the soup and puree it in a blender or food processor until smooth. Return it to the soup, increase the heat to moderate and heat through. Ladle the soup into bowls and sprinkle on a generous amount of cheese.

—*Nancy Verde Barr*

• • •

TUSCAN RED CABBAGE SOUP

Tuscans pour a little extra-virgin olive oil, often in the shape of the letter *C*, on the surface of each bowl of soup to enrich it. The hot soup releases the fragrance of the fruity oil and, in this case, the rosemary. For this recipe you can soak the beans overnight or use the quicker method of boiling them briefly and allowing them to soak for just one hour.

———— 6 to 8 Servings ————

1 cup dried white beans
⅓ cup plus ¼ cup extra-virgin olive
*   oil*
1 tablespoon chopped fresh
*   rosemary or 1 teaspoon dried*
3 garlic cloves—2 crushed through a
*   press, 1 minced*
1 medium onion, finely chopped
1 large celery rib, finely chopped
1 small carrot, finely chopped
1 head (about 1½ pounds) of red
*   cabbage, shredded or thinly sliced*
2 teaspoons salt
½ teaspoon freshly ground pepper

*⅓ cup drained canned plum
tomatoes, chopped*
*6 cups Vegetable Broth (p. 42) or
canned low-sodium chicken broth*

1. Rinse the beans. Place them in a
large bowl and cover with cold water. Set
aside to soak for 6 to 8 hours or overnight.
Alternatively, rinse the beans and place
them in a large saucepan. Cover with 2
inches of cold water and bring to a boil
over high heat. Boil for 2 minutes, remove from the heat and set aside, covered, to soak for 1 hour.

2. Drain and rinse the soaked beans.
In a medium saucepan, cover the beans
with twice their volume of water and
bring them to a boil, covered, over moderately high heat. Reduce the heat to
moderately low and simmer, covered,
until tender, about 1½ hours. Drain and
reserve.

3. In a small saucepan, combine the ⅓
cup olive oil, rosemary and the 2 crushed
garlic cloves. Cook over moderate heat
until the oil is hot, about 1 minute.
Remove from the heat and set aside.

4. In a large saucepan, cook the onion,
celery, carrot and the minced garlic in the
remaining ¼ cup olive oil over moderate
heat, stirring occasionally, until the vegetables are softened, about 8 minutes.

5. Add the cabbage, salt and pepper
and cook, stirring often, until wilted,
about 4 minutes. Add the tomatoes and
cook 5 more minutes. Add the Vegetable
Broth and bring just to a boil. Reduce the
heat to moderately low, cover and simmer
for 30 minutes.

6. Add the beans and cook, covered,
for 20 minutes.

7. Ladle the soup into bowls and pour
the reserved rosemary oil through a strainer into the soup. Serve immediately.

—*Nancy Verde Barr*

• • •

BUTTERNUT SQUASH SOUP

This dish makes a good first course for a
winter meal. Any hard winter squash,
except spaghetti squash, works well. The
soup is particularly nice topped with a few
croutons, a dollop of sour cream and a
sprinkling of chives.

❦ Serve the soup with the fruity 1988
Iron Horse Fumé Blanc to complement
its round, rich flavors.

———*Makes About 8 Cups* ———
*1 stick (4 ounces) plus 4 tablespoons
unsalted butter*
2 large onions, cut into large dice
1½ tablespoons minced fresh ginger
1 tablespoon curry powder
*2 pounds butternut squash—peeled,
seeded and diced (about 8 cups)*
¾ teaspoon salt
¼ teaspoon allspice
A large pinch of ground cloves

1. In a flameproof casserole, melt 1
stick of the butter over moderately high
heat. Add the onions and ginger and
cook, stirring, until the onions are translucent, about 8 minutes. Stir in the curry
powder and cook for 3 minutes longer.

2. Add the squash and 3 cups of water
and bring to a boil over moderately high
heat. Cover, reduce the heat to moderately low and gently simmer until the squash
is very soft, about 45 minutes.

3. Remove the vegetables with a slotted spoon or strain the contents of the pot
through a sieve, reserving the liquid. In a
food processor, puree the vegetables until
very smooth. Return to the pot with the
reserved liquid and whisk together. Season with the salt, allspice and cloves.
Whisk in the remaining 4 tablespoons
butter and bring to a simmer. Serve hot.
(*The soup can be made up to 2 days
ahead. Cover and refrigerate.*)

—*Martha Buser, Iron Horse Vineyards,
Sebastopol, California*

• • •

ZUCCHINI AND ARBORIO RICE SOUP

This thick, hearty soup is often served at
room temperature in Italy. Its flavors will
blend while it sits.

———*6 to 8 Servings* ———
1 medium onion, minced
1 garlic clove, minced
¼ cup extra-virgin olive oil
*3 medium zucchini (about 1½
pounds), cut into ½-inch dice*
2 teaspoons salt
¼ teaspoon freshly ground pepper
¼ teaspoon freshly grated nutmeg
*1½ cups drained canned plum
tomatoes, chopped*
*6 cups Vegetable Broth (p. 42) or
canned low-sodium chicken broth*
1 cup Arborio rice
*3 tablespoons minced Italian flat-
leaf parsley*
*3 tablespoons chopped fresh basil
(optional)*
Freshly grated Parmesan cheese

1. In a large saucepan, cook the onion
and garlic in the olive oil over moderately
low heat, stirring, until softened but not
browned, about 8 minutes.

2. Add the zucchini and season with
the salt, pepper and nutmeg. Increase the
heat to moderate and cook, stirring, until
the zucchini is barely tender, about 10
minutes.

3. Add the tomatoes, Vegetable
Broth, rice, parsley and basil, if using.
Increase the heat to moderately high and
bring the soup to a boil. Reduce the heat
to moderately low and simmer until the
rice is tender, about 20 minutes.

4. Serve hot or at room temperature
with Parmesan cheese.

—*Nancy Verde Barr*

• • •

PASTA AND BEAN SOUP

I especially like to make this soup in late summer when fresh pink-and-white cranberry beans are in season, although any cooked dried or canned white bean works perfectly well.

──────── *6 Servings* ────────
½ small hot red pepper, such as
*   serrano, or ⅛ teaspoon crushed*
*   hot red pepper*
1 small onion, finely chopped
1 small celery rib, finely chopped
1 medium carrot, finely chopped
2 garlic cloves, minced
¼ cup extra-virgin olive oil
1¼ pounds tomatoes—peeled,
*   seeded and chopped—or 2 cups*
*   drained canned plum tomatoes*
2 teaspoons salt
1½ pounds unshelled cranberry
*   beans or 2½ cups cooked dried or*
*   drained canned white beans*
6 cups hot Vegetable Broth (p. 42) or
*   canned low-sodium chicken broth*
¾ cup short macaroni, such as
*   tubetti*
Freshly grated Pecorino cheese

1. In a large saucepan, cook the hot pepper, onion, celery, carrot and garlic in the olive oil over moderately low heat, stirring occasionally, until the vegetables are softened, about 10 minutes. Add the tomatoes and salt, and cook for 10 more minutes.

2. Add the beans (if using unshelled beans, shell and rinse them first) to the tomato mixture and cook for 3 minutes. If using cooked dried beans or drained canned beans, add the Vegetable Broth and bring just to a gentle boil. If using fresh beans, increase the heat to moderately high, add the broth, and cook until the beans are tender, 45 minutes to 1 hour.

3. Add the macaroni to the soup and continue cooking until the pasta is tender but still firm, about 15 minutes. Remove the soup from the heat and let it rest for 10 minutes before serving. Serve with freshly grated Pecorino cheese.

—Nancy Verde Barr

• • •

FLAGEOLET BEAN SOUP
WITH FRESH THYME

The dried French beans called flageolets have a lovely, subtle flavor that is complemented by fresh thyme. For festive occasions such as this, I garnish the soup with croutons and a cluster of cubed tomatoes. If you can't find flageolets, navy beans can be used instead.

──────── *8 Servings* ────────
1½ cups dried flageolet beans (10
*   ounces)*
1 small onion, quartered
1 garlic clove
1 tablespoon fresh thyme
1 tablespoon coarse (kosher) salt
3 to 3½ cups chicken stock or canned
*   low-sodium broth*
3 plum tomatoes—peeled, seeded
*   and cut into small cubes*
½ baguette, crust trimmed, cut into
*   ½-inch cubes*
2 tablespoons olive oil
½ cup heavy cream
Freshly ground pepper
¼ cup Italian flat-leaf parsley leaves
*   (optional)*

1. In a medium bowl, soak the beans overnight in cold water to cover. Drain the beans and transfer them to a large saucepan. Add the onion, garlic, thyme and 6 cups of fresh water and bring to a boil over high heat. Reduce the heat to low, cover tightly and simmer for 1 hour. Add 2 teaspoons of the salt and continue simmering, covered, until the beans are tender, about 20 minutes longer.

2. Drain the beans and place in a food processor along with the cooked onion and garlic. Puree until smooth. Strain the puree into a saucepan, leaving the bean skins behind. Whisk 3 cups of the chicken stock into the puree. *(The recipe can be prepared to this point up to 2 days ahead. Let cool, then cover and refrigerate.)*

3. Place the tomato cubes in a colander and sprinkle with the remaining 1 teaspoon salt. Set aside to drain for 1 hour.

4. Preheat the oven to 300°. Put the bread cubes on a baking sheet and bake until dry and crisp, about 10 minutes.

5. In a large skillet, heat the olive oil. Add the bread cubes and cook over moderately high heat, tossing frequently, until browned, about 4 minutes. Transfer to paper towels to drain.

6. Shortly before serving, whisk the cream into the soup and reheat over moderate heat. If the soup is very thick, thin it with additional stock or water. Season to taste with salt and pepper. Ladle the soup into 8 soup plates and garnish each serving with some croutons, a cluster of tomato cubes and a few parsley leaves.

—Lydie Pinoy Marshall

• • •

BACON, POTATO, WHITE BEAN AND RED PEPPER SOUP

You'll like this good and satisfying soup.

——— **6 Servings** ———
½ pound slab of hickory-cured
*   bacon, cut into ⅜-inch dice*
1 tablespoon unsalted butter
1 small onion, minced
3 large leeks (white and tender
*   green), cut into ½-inch-thick*
*   slices*
½ large carrot, coarsely chopped
1 small celery rib, coarsely chopped
1 medium red pepper, cut into
*   ¼-inch-thick slices*
4 cups chicken stock or canned low-
*   sodium broth*
¾ teaspoon salt
¼ teaspoon freshly ground white
*   pepper*
2 large all-purpose potatoes (about 1
*   pound), peeled and cut into ½-inch*
*   cubes*
1 can (19 ounces) white kidney
*   beans, drained and rinsed*

1. Place the bacon in a large saucepan and cover with water. Simmer over moderately high heat for 5 minutes. Drain and pat the bacon dry with paper towels. Wipe out the saucepan and return the bacon to the pan. Fry over moderately high heat until golden and crisp, about 4 minutes. Drain the bacon on paper towels, discard all the fat in the pan and wipe out with paper towels.

2. Add the butter to the pan and reduce the heat to moderate. When the butter has melted, add the onion, leeks, carrot, celery and red pepper. Cook until the vegetables are lightly browned and softened, about 5 minutes.

3. Add the bacon, chicken stock, salt and pepper. Simmer, skimming occasionally, for 5 minutes.

4. Add the potatoes and simmer, skimming, until the potatoes are just tender when pierced with a knife, about 15 minutes.

5. Add the white beans and simmer 1 to 2 minutes more. Serve hot. *(This recipe can be made up to 1 day ahead. Cover and refrigerate. Remove any accumulated fat before reheating.)*

—*Lee Bailey*

• • •

HERBED CRAB SOUP IN COCONUT MILK

This is a creamy and slightly sweet soup with undercurrents of tart saltiness.

——— **4 to 6 Servings** ———
3 cups unsweetened coconut milk*
5 shallots, minced
2 stalks of fresh lemon grass,* cut
*   into 1-inch pieces and crushed*
4 live blueclaw or similar medium
*   crabs, quartered*
3 tablespoons fish sauce*
2 tablespoons fresh lime juice
1 teaspoon sugar
1 teaspoon instant tamarind,*
*   dissolved in 2 tablespoons hot*
*   water*
2 tablespoons finely shredded Kaffir
*   lime leaves**
¼ cup chopped fresh coriander
3 small fresh red chiles, seeded and
*   chopped*
*Available at Asian markets

1. In a large saucepan or wok, combine 1 cup of the coconut milk with the shallots and lemon grass and bring to a boil over moderately high heat. Reduce the heat to moderate, add the crabs and bring to a simmer.

2. Stir in the fish sauce, lime juice, sugar, tamarind water and the remaining 2 cups coconut milk. Bring to a simmer and cook until the crabs are bright orange and cooked through, about 5 minutes.

3. Remove from the heat. Sprinkle the soup with the lime leaves, coriander and chopped chiles and serve hot.

—*Thai Cooking School,*
Oriental Hotel, Bangkok, Thailand

• • •

CREAMY MUSSEL CHOWDER

Here's a home-style, roux-thickened chowder with lots of body. Use either light cream or a mix of light cream and milk; any richer than that and I think you mask the mussels' nice briny edge.

——— **6 Servings** ———
1½ cups dry white wine
1 small onion, sliced
2 bay leaves
1 teaspoon thyme
5 pounds mussels, scrubbed and
*   debearded*
2 large all-purpose or waxy potatoes
*   peeled and cut into ¼-inch dice*
Salt
3 tablespoons unsalted butter
1 celery rib, finely chopped
2 shallots, minced
3 tablespoons all-purpose flour
4 cups light cream or 2 cups light
*   cream plus 2 cups milk*
Freshly ground pepper
¼ cup chopped Italian flat-leaf
*   parsley, for garnish*

1. In a large heavy nonreactive pot, combine the wine, onion, bay leaves and thyme and bring to a boil over high heat. Add the mussels and cover tightly. Reduce the heat to moderately high and cook, shaking the pot once or twice, until the mussels steam open, about 5 minutes.

2. With a slotted spoon, transfer the mussels to a large bowl and let cool. Discard any that haven't opened. Set aside 12 mussels in their shells for garnish. Shuck the remaining mussels. Coarsely chop half of the shucked mussels. Combine the whole and the chopped mussels and set aside. Strain the cooking liquid through cheesecloth and set aside.

3. In a medium saucepan, combine the potatoes with enough cold water to barely cover and a pinch of salt. Bring to a boil over high heat and cook the potatoes until just tender, about 10 minutes. Drain and set aside.

4. In a medium nonreactive casserole, melt the butter over moderate heat. Add the celery and the shallots and cook until slightly softened but not browned, about 5 minutes. Sprinkle the flour over the vegetables and cook, stirring constantly, until lightly golden, about 3 minutes.

5. Stir in the reserved mussel liquid and bring to a boil over moderately high heat, stirring. Reduce the heat to moderately low. Stir in the cream and the reserved potatoes and cook, stirring occasionally, until warmed through, about 10 minutes. Add the shucked mussels and simmer—do not boil—stirring occasionally, to combine the flavors, 10 to 15 minutes. Season to taste with salt and pepper. *(The recipe can be made up to 1 day ahead; cover and refrigerate. Reheat before serving.)*

6. Divide the chowder evenly among 6 warm soup bowls; tuck 2 mussels in their shells into each bowl and garnish with a sprinkling of fresh parsley.
—*Ken Haedrich*

• • •

SPICED SOUP WITH SHRIMP

This intensely flavored soup is a skillful blend of hot, tangy and spicy ingredients with just a hint of sweetness.

——————— *6 Servings* ———————
7 small shallots, thinly sliced
5 garlic cloves, thinly sliced
1 tablespoon vegetable oil
3 large dried chiles, such as Anaheim, pasilla or ancho
3 slices fresh or dried galanga,* finely chopped if fresh
1 tablespoon chopped coriander roots or stems
1 teaspoon black peppercorns, crushed
3 stalks of fresh lemon grass,* cut into 1-inch pieces and crushed
3 tablespoons fish sauce*
3 tablespoons fresh lime juice
1 pound medium shrimp, shelled and deveined
1 cup drained canned straw mushrooms*
2 tablespoons very finely shredded Kaffir lime leaves*
¼ cup coriander leaves
2 fresh red chiles, seeded and minced
*Available at Asian markets

1. Preheat the oven to 350°. On a baking sheet, toss the shallots and garlic with the vegetable oil and bake, stirring occasionally, for 30 minutes, or until browned and crisp. Set aside.

2. Meanwhile, soak the dried chiles in hot water until soft, about 20 minutes. Drain well. Discard the stems, seeds and membranes; finely chop the chiles.

3. If using dried *galanga*, soak it in boiling water, changing the water a couple of times, until pliable, about 20 minutes. Drain well and chop fine.

4. In a mortar, pound together the *galanga* (fresh or dried), coriander roots and peppercorns until a dry paste forms.

5. In a large saucepan, bring 5 cups of water to a boil over high heat. Stir in the lemon grass, fish sauce and lime juice. Add the reserved shallots and garlic, the chopped chiles and the *galanga* paste and return to a boil. Add the shrimp and straw mushrooms and return to a boil. Remove from the heat, sprinkle with the shredded lime leaves, coriander leaves and fresh chiles and serve at once.
—*Thai Cooking School, Oriental Hotel, Bangkok, Thailand*

• • •

TURKEY MINESTRONE WITH SAGE-PARMESAN BUTTER

When making the sage-Parmesan butter, you'll discover that whole dried sage leaves will toast just as nicely as fresh—and take less time. Serve this soup with homemade croutons. To make them, simply toss one-inch bread cubes with melted butter and toast them in a 400° oven until browned.

You'll have some turkey breast left over from this recipe for sandwiches. Cover it with plastic wrap and refrigerate.

——————— *Makes 4½ Quarts* ———————
1 whole turkey breast (about 6 pounds)
½ pound sliced smoked bacon, cut crosswise into ½-inch strips
2 medium onions, chopped
2 carrots, thinly sliced into rounds
1 small head of green cabbage— quartered, cored and thinly sliced
2 large celery ribs, thinly sliced
1 fennel bulb, cut into ½-inch dice
1 large red bell pepper, cut into ½-inch dice
5 garlic cloves, minced
1 cup chopped parsley
2 cups drained and rinsed cooked chickpeas
1 pound butternut squash, peeled and cut into ½-inch cubes

1 medium zucchini, halved and
   sliced crosswise ¼ inch thick
⅔ cup elbow macaroni or tubetti
3 tablespoons salted butter
1½ cups (loosely packed) fresh or
   dried whole sage leaves
5 tablespoons unsalted butter,
   softened
¾ cup freshly grated Parmesan
   cheese (about 4 ounces)

1. Place the turkey breast, skin-side down, in a large (10-quart) stockpot. Cover with 16 cups of cold water and bring to a boil over high heat. Reduce the heat to low and simmer very gently, skimming occasionally, until cooked through, about 2 hours. Turn the breast skin-side up for the last 30 minutes of cooking. Remove the turkey to a work surface to cool. With a ladle, skim off any fat from the broth. Set aside.

2. In a very large flameproof casserole or dutch oven, cook the bacon over moderate heat until almost crisp but not browned, about 10 minutes.

3. Drain off all but 2 tablespoons of the bacon fat and add the onions, carrots, cabbage, celery, fennel, red pepper and garlic. Cook the vegetables over low heat, stirring occasionally, until wilted, about 15 minutes.

4. Add the reserved turkey broth and the parsley, increase the heat to high and bring to a boil. Reduce the heat to low and simmer until the vegetables are softened, about 20 minutes.

5. Meanwhile, in a food processor, puree 1 cup of the chick-peas. Remove about two-thirds of the turkey meat from the bone and cut it into 1-inch pieces. Wrap the remaining turkey breast in plastic wrap and reserve for sandwiches.

6. When the vegetables are cooked, add the pureed and whole chick-peas, the turkey pieces, butternut squash, zucchini and macaroni to the casserole and simmer the soup over moderate heat until everything is tender, about 10 minutes. (*The*

recipe can be prepared to this point and refrigerated for up to 5 days or frozen for up to 2 weeks.)

7. In a large skillet, heat the salted butter over moderate heat. When it is very hot, add the sage leaves in an even layer and cook without stirring until they start to brown, about 3 minutes. (If using dried leaves, remove them from the skillet at this point.) Stir the leaves and continue to cook until crisp but not too dark, about 2 minutes longer. Transfer the sage to a food processor and chop fine. Add the unsalted butter and Parmesan cheese and process until just blended.

8. To serve, ladle the soup into bowls and pass the sage butter separately to dollop on top.

—*Marcia Kiesel*

• • •

TURKEY ONION SOUP

Just like freshly baked bread, a pot of soup on the stove is very welcoming. Put a few bowls, mugs or cups—whatever you can find—alongside the soup and let your guests serve themselves.

15 to 20 Servings
About 6½ Quarts
2 tablespoons vegetable oil
2 bunches of scallions (14 to 16),
   coarsely chopped
4 medium leeks (white and tender
   green), coarsely chopped
4 medium onions, finely chopped
6 medium shallots, finely chopped
7 medium-large carrots, sliced into
   ¼-inch rounds
5 celery ribs, coarsely chopped
1 whole turkey breast (about 6
   pounds)
4 large imported bay leaves

1 tablespoon oregano
2 teaspoons fennel seeds
¾ cup chopped Italian flat-leaf
   parsley with stems
1 tablespoon salt
1 teaspoon freshly ground pepper

1. In a 10- to 12-quart stockpot, heat the oil over moderate heat. Add the scallions, leeks, onions, shallots, carrots and celery and stir to combine. Cover and cook, stirring frequently, until the vegetables are softened but not browned, about 20 minutes.

2. Place the turkey breast on top of the vegetables and add water to cover. Increase the heat to moderately high, cover and bring to a boil. Boil for 5 minutes, then remove the lid and skim any foam from the surface.

3. Add the bay leaves, oregano, fennel seeds and ½ cup of the chopped parsley. Reduce the heat to moderately low and simmer gently, partially covered, for 2 hours, until the vegetables are tender. Remove and discard the bay leaves.

4. Remove the turkey and set aside until cool enough to handle, about 20 minutes. Remove the meat from the bones; discard the bones and skin. Cut the meat into bite-size pieces and return them to the soup. Season to taste with salt and pepper. (*The recipe can be prepared to this point 2 to 3 days ahead and kept covered in the refrigerator. When rewarming, make sure to bring the soup to a complete boil for 2 to 3 minutes.*) Add the remaining ¼ cup parsley before serving and serve hot.

—*Paul Grimes*

• • •

FISH & SHELLFISH

FRAGRANT STEAMED FISH

This light, fat-free dish is very simple to prepare and full of taste. The mixture of ginger, black pepper, garlic, pickled plums and salty pancetta seasons the fish inside and out during steaming.

♟ This relatively mild dish could be paired with a simple, lively Italian white, such as 1988 Antinori Galestro or 1988 Principessa Gavi.

————— *2 Servings* —————
6 dried shiitake mushroom caps*
2 garlic cloves
3 tablespoons grated fresh ginger
½ teaspoon black peppercorns, crushed
2 whole Chinese pickled plums,* pitted
2 ounces sliced pancetta or lean unsmoked bacon, cut into thin strips
2 tablespoons light soy sauce
1 tablespoon cornstarch
1 whole red snapper, sea bass or pompano (about 1½ pounds), boned but with the fillets, head and tail intact
3 small fresh red chiles, seeded and minced, for garnish
2 coriander sprigs, cut into 2-inch lengths, for garnish
3 scallions, cut into 2-inch lengths, for garnish
2 tablespoons celery leaves, for garnish
*Available at Asian markets

1. In a small bowl, soak the mushroom caps in hot water to cover until softened, about 20 minutes. Drain and rinse, then slice ¼ inch thick. Set aside.

2. In a mortar, pound together the garlic, ginger, black peppercorns and pickled plums until a paste forms. Blend in the pancetta, soy sauce and cornstarch.

3. Put the fish on a large, round, heat-proof plate and spread 2 tablespoons of

the pounded mixture inside the fish. Close the fish and, with a sharp knife, make 4 crosswise cuts just through the skin on one side. Spread the remaining mixture over and around the fish and scatter the reserved mushrooms on top.

4. Pour 2 cups of water into a wok. Set a round cake rack in the wok over the water. Bring the water to a boil over high heat. Put the plate with the fish on the rack, cover the wok with a lid and steam the fish for 15 minutes. Remove the plate from the steamer. Sprinkle the minced chiles, coriander, scallions and celery leaves over the fish and serve at once.
—*Thai Cooking School, Oriental Hotel, Bangkok, Thailand*

• • •

BAKED COD AND POTATOES

This recipe can be made up to one day ahead. After baking it, let it cool, then cover and refrigerate. Reheat it in a 375° oven.

————— *12 Servings* —————
½ cup salt
½ cup sugar
1 teaspoon cracked white peppercorns plus ¾ teaspoon freshly ground
1 pound cod fillet with skin
2½ pounds medium boiling potatoes
1 medium onion, finely chopped
¼ cup minced dill, plus more for serving
3 eggs
2½ cups half-and-half or light cream
Melted unsalted butter, for serving

1. In a small bowl, combine the salt, sugar and cracked white peppercorns. Rub this seasoning mixture all over the

fish. Place the fish in a glass or ceramic dish, cover and refrigerate overnight.

2. Place the potatoes in a medium pot of salted water and bring to a boil. Reduce the heat to moderate and simmer until tender, about 20 minutes. Drain well and let cool, then peel. Cover and refrigerate overnight.

3. Preheat the oven to 350°. Grease a 12-by-9-by-2-inch oval baking dish. Pat the fish dry. Slice the fish off the skin on the diagonal about ⅛ inch thick, making large slices. Sprinkle each slice with the ground white pepper. Slice the potatoes ¼ inch thick.

4. Arrange some potato slices in the bottom of the prepared baking dish without overlapping them. Cover with a layer of fish slices and sprinkle with some of the chopped onion and dill. Continue layering until all the ingredients are used up, ending with a layer of potato slices.

5. In a small bowl, whisk together the eggs and half-and-half. Pour this mixture evenly over the fish and potatoes. Set the dish on a baking sheet in the oven and bake until the custard is set, about 1 hour. Serve hot or warm, with melted butter and minced dill on the side.
—*Christer Larsson, Aquavit, New York City*

• • •

COLD POACHED BASS WITH MEDITERRANEAN VEGETABLE SALAD

The sale of fished striped bass is restricted in certain areas, but the high-quality farm-raised variety is readily available.

♟ A light savory white, such as 1987 Jean Sauvion Carte d'Or or 1987 Marquis de Goulaine Muscadet, would point up the mild flavors of this dish.

————— *4 Servings* —————
1 European cucumber, cut into ½-inch dice
1 large red bell pepper, cut into ½-inch dice

1 large yellow bell pepper, cut into
    ½-inch dice
2 medium tomatoes, seeded and cut
    into ½-inch dice
1 medium red onion, cut into ½-inch
    dice
¼ cup chopped fresh coriander
6 tablespoons fresh lemon juice
¼ cup plus 1 tablespoon extra-virgin
    olive oil
1 tablespoon coarse (kosher) salt
1 teaspoon sugar
1 teaspoon freshly ground black
    pepper
1 cup (packed) basil leaves
¼ teaspoon Dijon-style mustard
2 tablespoons crushed ice
¼ teaspoon table salt
¼ teaspoon freshly ground white
    pepper
½ cup vegetable oil
2 shallots, minced
4 skinless striped bass fillets (about
    6 ounces each)
½ cup dry white wine

1. In a large bowl, combine the cucumber, red and yellow bell peppers, tomatoes, onion and coriander. Add 3 tablespoons of the lemon juice, ¼ cup of the olive oil, the coarse salt, sugar and black pepper. Mix well and refrigerate, covered, for 2 to 3 hours.

2. In a blender, combine the basil, mustard, ice, ⅛ teaspoon each of the table salt and white pepper and the remaining 3 tablespoons lemon juice. Blend until pureed. With the machine on, pour in the vegetable oil in a thin stream until thoroughly incorporated. Set aside.

3. Spread the remaining 1 tablespoon olive oil evenly over the bottom of a large nonreactive skillet. Sprinkle the shallots on top. Put the bass fillets in the skillet and season with the remaining ⅛ teaspoon each of table salt and white pepper. Pour in the white wine and enough water to just cover the fish. Cover with a damp

kitchen towel or parchment paper and bring to a boil over moderately low heat. Immediately remove the pan from the heat. Let sit for 2 minutes, then remove the towel. Let the fish cool to room temperature in the cooking liquid.

4. Using a slotted spoon, arrange the chilled vegetable salad on 4 large serving plates. Drain the bass fillets on paper towels and place 1 on each salad. Spoon about 2 tablespoons of the basil vinaigrette over each serving.

—Steve Mellina

• • •

COLD POACHED SALMON WITH CUCUMBER SALAD AND FRESH HERB SAUCE

This recipe makes use of a roasting pan to poach the salmon, but if you have a fish poacher, by all means use it instead.

——— **12 Servings** ———
1 cup distilled white vinegar
1 carrot, thinly sliced
1 leek, split and well washed
1 onion, thinly sliced
1 tablespoon black peppercorns
1 tablespoon white peppercorns
1 teaspoon allspice berries
2 bay leaves
3 tablespoons coarse (kosher) salt
1 small bunch of dill
3½- to 4-pound whole salmon,
    cleaned, head removed
Swedish Cucumber Salad (p. 142)
Fresh Herb Sauce (p. 255)

1. Set a large nonreactive roasting pan over 2 burners and add the vinegar, carrot, leek, onion, black and white peppercorns, allspice berries, bay leaves, salt and dill. Add 3 quarts of water and bring to a boil over moderately high heat. Boil for 10 minutes.

2. Add the salmon to the pan and cover loosely with foil. When the water returns to a simmer, reduce the heat to low and simmer for 6 minutes. Using 2 spatulas, turn the salmon over and cook for 6 minutes longer.

3. Remove from the heat and let the fish cool slightly in the liquid. Drain the fish and carefully peel off the skin, leaving the tail attached if you like. Pat the fish dry and place on a plate. Let cool completely, then cover and refrigerate until cold.

4. Set the salmon on a platter. Serve the ice-cold Swedish Cucumber Salad and the Fresh Herb Sauce on the side.

—Christer Larsson, Aquavit,
New York City

• • •

POACHED SALMON PINWHEELS WITH GERMAN CUCUMBER SALAD AND SAUCE VERTE

Because of salmon's high fat content, it tends to firm up when chilled; if you refrigerate the cooked fish, let it return to room temperature before serving. This dish can also be made with salmon steaks.

🍷 The richness of salmon calls for an equally rich, full-bodied white, such as Burgundy or Chardonnay. The 1984 Jadot Corton-Charlemagne would be a splendid accompaniment, as would the 1985 Orlando St. Hugo Chardonnay.

——— **4 Servings** ———
1 European cucumber, very thinly
    sliced
1 teaspoon coarse (kosher) salt
1½ teaspoons sugar
2 teaspoons white wine vinegar
1 teaspoon freshly ground black
    pepper
1 red bell pepper, very finely diced
1 cup (firmly packed) mixed fresh
    herbs, such as parsley, basil,
    tarragon, chives and a small
    amount of watercress, coarsely
    chopped

1 ½ tablespoons fresh lemon juice
½ teaspoon table salt
1 cup mayonnaise
1 whole salmon fillet (about 2
    pounds), skin removed
1 tablespoon olive oil
2 shallots, minced
½ cup dry white wine

1. In a large bowl, toss the cucumber with the coarse salt, sugar, vinegar and ¼ teaspoon of the black pepper. Let marinate for 10 minutes. Drain off the liquid. Add the red bell pepper and set aside.

2. In a food processor or blender, combine the mixed herbs, lemon juice, ¼ teaspoon of the table salt and ½ teaspoon of the black pepper. Process until the herbs are minced. Add the mayonnaise and process to blend thoroughly. Pour the sauce into a bowl.

3. Set the salmon fillet on a work surface. Run your hand over the fillet to locate any stray bones and remove them with tweezers. Starting just off center and using a long sharp knife, slice the salmon fillet lengthwise and slightly on the diagonal, into long strips about 1¼ inches thick. Set aside the 4 longest strips for use in the recipe. Reserve the remaining salmon for another use.

4. Holding the thick end of one of the salmon strips on a work surface, tightly curl the strip around itself to form a neat, tight pinwheel. Repeat with the remaining salmon strips. Insert 2 short bamboo skewers through each salmon pinwheel to hold it together during cooking. Trim the ends of the skewers so the salmon will fit in the pan.

5. Spread the olive oil over the bottom of a large nonreactive skillet and sprinkle with the minced shallots. Set the salmon pinwheels in the skillet and season with the remaining ¼ teaspoon each of table salt and black pepper. Pour in the white wine and add enough water to just cover the salmon. Cover with a damp kitchen towel or parchment paper. Bring to a boil

over moderately low heat. Immediately remove the pan from the heat. Let sit for 2 minutes, then remove the towel. Let the fish cool to room temperature in the poaching liquid.

6. Lift the salmon pinwheels out of the skillet with a spatula and place on paper towels to drain. Carefully remove the skewers. Place the salmon on plates and mound the cucumber salad alongside. Pass the herb sauce separately.

—Steve Mellina

• • •

SALT-COOKED SALMON WITH DILL AND SHALLOT BUTTER

This method of cooking salmon, which may be a little smoky, was passed on to me by my friend Chaz Stevens.

—————— **4 Servings** ——————
2 medium shallots, minced
2 tablespoons unsalted butter,
    softened
¾ cup coarse (kosher) salt
4 salmon fillets (about 6 ounces
    each), cut 1 inch thick, with skin
    on
1 tablespoon fresh lemon juice
2 tablespoons coarsely chopped
    fresh dill

1. In a small bowl, mash the shallots and butter together.

2. Sprinkle the salt in an even layer in a large cast-iron skillet and set over high heat. When the salt is hot, after about 2 minutes, add the salmon to the pan, skin-side down. Spread the shallot butter evenly over the fillets and sprinkle each one with ¾ teaspoon of the lemon juice and 1½ teaspoons of the dill. Cook for 2 minutes, then cover the pan lightly with foil and reduce the heat to moderately low. Cook until the fish is moist and opaque, about 6 minutes. Serve hot.

—Lee Bailey

• • •

SALMON FOR SUPPER

Serves 4

*Salt-Cooked Salmon with Dill and
Shallot Butter (p. 52)*

Warm Cabbage Slaw (p. 143)

*Baked Cornmeal-Coated Green
Tomatoes (p. 131)*

♟ *Rich white wine, such as 1984
Jadot Corton-Charlemagne or 1985
Orlando St. Hugo Chardonnay*

Fresh Fruit Cloud Cake (p. 191)

Coffee

—Lee Bailey

ROAST SALMON WITH ENDIVES AND RIESLING

Gremolata is a fresh Italian seasoning mixture composed of parsley, garlic and lemon zest. It looks pretty and heightens the flavor of whatever it's sprinkled on.

♟ The fattiness of the salmon, underscored with bacon, calls for a rich white with some contrasting acidity, such as 1987 Hanna Chardonnay or 1986 Latour-Giraud Meursault Genevrières.

—————— **6 Servings** ——————
½ pound thick-sliced bacon, cut
    crosswise into ¼-inch strips
2 tablespoons olive oil
1 large onion, chopped
6 carrots, sliced into ¼-inch rounds
16 Belgian endives, sliced crosswise
    1 inch thick

4 sprigs of fresh thyme or ½
  teaspoon dried
1 sprig of fresh rosemary or ¼
  teaspoon dried
⅔ cup dry Riesling
2 teaspoons fresh lemon juice
Salt and freshly ground pepper
1½ teaspoons finely grated lemon
  zest
2 tablespoons minced parsley
2 garlic cloves, minced
1 boneless side of salmon (about 2½
  pounds), skin removed
1 tablespoon unsalted butter, melted

1. In a large flameproof casserole or dutch oven, cook the bacon over moderate heat until crisp but not dark, about 10 minutes. Remove the bacon and drain on paper towels.

2. Pour off all but 1 tablespoon of the bacon fat from the casserole and add the olive oil. Add the onion and carrots, reduce the heat to low and cook, stirring occasionally, until the onion begins to soften, about 10 minutes.

3. Increase the heat to high and add the endives. Cook, stirring occasionally, until the endives are beginning to brown, about 7 minutes.

4. Stir in the reserved bacon, the thyme, rosemary and wine and reduce the heat to low. Cover and cook, stirring occasionally, until all the vegetables are tender, about 10 minutes.

5. Add the lemon juice and season with salt and pepper to taste. Transfer the vegetables to a large, shallow, oval baking dish. *(The recipe can be prepared to this point up to 1 day ahead. Let cool, then cover with plastic wrap and refrigerate.)*

6. To make the *gremolata*, in a small bowl, mix together the lemon zest, parsley and garlic with a fork. Set aside.

7. Preheat the oven to 500°. Set the salmon on a work surface and fold about 3 inches of the tail end under itself to create an even thickness. Place the salmon on top of the vegetables in the baking dish, skinned-side down. Brush the melted butter over the fish and sprinkle lightly with salt and pepper. Roast on the top rack of the oven for about 20 minutes, until the salmon is just cooked through.

8. Remove from the oven and sprinkle the *gremolata* over the fish. Cut the salmon into 6 equal pieces. To serve, place a piece of salmon on each warmed plate and spoon the vegetables with their juices alongside.

—*Marcia Kiesel*

• • •

OVEN-ROASTED SALMON, ASPARAGUS AND NEW POTATOES

❦ Rich salmon, here made with dill and asparagus, would suggest a rich, wood-aged Chardonnay, such as 1988 Belvedere Reserve or 1988 Flora Springs.

——— *4 Servings* ———

1 pound small new potatoes,
  scrubbed and halved
2 tablespoons olive oil
½ pound medium asparagus, sliced
  on the diagonal 1 inch thick
1 tablespoon chopped fresh dill plus
  dill sprigs, for garnish
1 strip of lemon zest (½ by 2 inches)
1 small garlic clove, coarsely
  chopped
½ teaspoon salt
Freshly ground pepper
2 salmon steaks (10 ounces each),
  cut about 1 inch thick
1 lemon, cut into large wedges

1. Preheat the oven to 400°. In a large shallow baking dish (about 10 by 14 inches), toss the potatoes with the olive oil.

Arrange the potatoes, cut-sides down, in the baking dish and roast for 10 to 12 minutes, or until the potatoes begin to brown on the bottom. Turn the potatoes over and roast for 10 minutes longer, or until browned on the top. Remove the baking dish from the oven.

2. In a medium bowl, toss the asparagus with the chopped dill, lemon zest, garlic and salt, and season with pepper to taste. Add the asparagus mixture to the potatoes and stir to combine.

3. Push the vegetables to the sides of the dish and arrange the salmon steaks in the center. Return the baking dish to the oven and roast the salmon and asparagus for 10 to 12 minutes, or until the fish is just cooked through.

4. Spoon the vegetables onto 4 warmed dinner plates. With a small sharp knife, carefully remove the salmon skin and center bone from each steak. Separate the halves. Arrange one half on each plate alongside the vegetables. Squeeze one of the lemon wedges over the 4 salmon steaks. Garnish with dill sprigs and lemon wedges and serve hot.

—*Marie Simmons*

• • •

RED SNAPPER WITH SAFFRON, LEEKS AND CHARDONNAY

This rich dish goes beautifully with sautéed mushrooms and steamed rice.

——— *4 Servings* ———

¼ teaspoon (firmly packed) saffron
  threads
2 tablespoons plus 1 teaspoon
  unsalted butter
2 large leeks (white and tender
  green), halved lengthwise and
  very thinly sliced crosswise
⅔ cup Chardonnay or dry Riesling
1 cup heavy cream
1½ teaspoons tomato paste
½ teaspoon finely grated fresh
  ginger

Salt and freshly ground pepper
4 red snapper fillets (6 to 7 ounces
each), skin on

1. In a small bowl or a measuring cup, cover the saffron with ¼ cup of hot water. Set aside to infuse.

2. Meanwhile, in a medium nonreactive saucepan, melt 2 tablespoons of the butter over moderate heat. Add the leeks and reduce the heat to low. Cover and cook, stirring occasionally, until the leeks are very soft, about 20 minutes. When stirring the leeks, allow any water that collects under the lid to drip onto the leeks for extra moisture.

3. Increase the heat to moderate, add the wine and cook until almost evaporated, about 3 minutes. Stir in the heavy cream, tomato paste and the saffron liquid. Bring to a simmer and cook over moderate heat, stirring occasionally, until the leeks absorb much of the liquid and the mixture is thick and creamy, about 5 minutes. Remove from the heat and stir in the ginger. Season with salt and pepper to taste. Set aside.

4. Preheat the broiler. Season the skin side of the snapper with ¼ teaspoon salt. Let stand at room temperature for at least 5 or up to 20 minutes; the salt will dry the skin to help it crisp.

5. Place a baking sheet in the oven to heat up for about 2 minutes. Remove the sheet, add the remaining teaspoon butter and tilt the hot pan to distribute the butter evenly. Lightly press both sides of each snapper fillet into the butter to coat. Arrange the fillets on the pan, skin-side up. Broil 5 inches from the heat, rotating the pan once, for about 4 minutes, until the skin is crisp and blistery and the flesh is just cooked through.

6. Meanwhile, reheat the leeks if necessary. Spoon the leeks onto 4 warm dinner plates. Place a snapper fillet skin-side up on top of the leeks and serve at once.

—Marcia Kiesel

• • •

SIMPLE SWORDFISH DINNER

Serves 6

Broiled Swordfish Steaks (p. 54)

Fried-Rice Patties (p. 116)

Asparagus with Butter Vinaigrette (p. 120)

🍷 *Crisp California Fumé Blanc, such as 1987 Grgich Hills or 1987 Konocti*

Baked Bananas (p. 212)

Coffee

—Lee Bailey

BROILED SWORDFISH STEAKS

These broiled swordfish steaks are marinated in a garlic and basil vinaigrette.

—————— *6 Servings* ——————
6 swordfish steaks (about 6 ounces
each), 1 inch thick
2 tablespoons Dijon-style mustard
¼ cup fresh lemon juice
½ cup olive oil
½ cup vegetable oil
1 large garlic clove, minced
1 cup (loosely packed) shredded
fresh basil

1. Pat the swordfish steaks with paper towels; place them in a shallow nonreactive dish in a single layer.

2. In a small bowl, whisk together the mustard, lemon juice and the olive and vegetable oils. Whisk in the garlic and basil. Pour the marinade over the swordfish steaks, turning to coat both sides. Marinate for 1 hour, turning once.

3. Preheat the broiler for at least 15 minutes. Place the steaks on a broiler pan and broil about 7 inches from the heat for 5 to 6 minutes per side, turning once, until cooked through. Serve hot.

—Lee Bailey

• • •

FAST-FIRE SWORDFISH

Cooked on a hot grill, this thickly cut swordfish steak is wonderfully crusty outside but moist and juicy inside. This is an easy dish to make, for the fish marinates while you prepare the fire. If you like, tuna or salmon can be used instead.

🍷 To best stand up to the mustard, lemon and garlic accents here—in addition to the smoky flavors from the grilling—we suggest a round, rich and lively Chardonnay, such as 1988 Shafer or 1988 Gundlach-Bundschu.

—————— *6 to 8 Servings* ——————
¼ cup extra-virgin olive oil
2 tablespoons fresh lemon juice
2 tablespoons Spicy Mustard Sauce
(recipe follows)
1 teaspoon salt
1 teaspoon minced garlic
1 large swordfish steak, cut 2 inches
thick (2 to 2½ pounds), rinsed and
patted dry
Peanut oil or corn oil, for brushing
the grill

1. Prepare the fire. In a nonreactive oval dish, combine the olive oil, lemon juice, Spicy Mustard Sauce, salt and garlic. Place the swordfish in the dish and brush to coat with the marinade. Turn the fish occasionally until the fire is ready.

2. Brush the grill with oil. Place the swordfish in the center of the grill and cover, leaving all the vents wide open. Cook the fish for 7 minutes. Uncover, slide a spatula under the fish and rotate it 90° to achieve crisscross grilling marks. Cover and cook for 8 minutes longer. Turn the fish over and repeat the grilling process on the second side.

3. Check to see if the fish is done: Using a spatula, remove the fish from the grill and press it with your fingers; it should feel firm. If not, put it back on the grill, cover and cook for 3 to 5 minutes longer. Remove from the grill and let rest for 5 minutes before slicing against the grain and serving.

—*Karen Lee & Alaxandra Branyon*

• • •

SPICY MUSTARD SAUCE

This sauce is also delicious in salad dressings and on sandwiches.

——— *Makes ⅔ Cup* ———
⅓ cup dry mustard
About ¼ cup medium-dry sherry
¼ cup Dijon-style mustard
¼ cup coarse-grained mustard

Place the dry mustard in a bowl and gradually whisk in the sherry until a smooth, thick paste forms. Whisk in the Dijon and coarse-grained mustards until well blended. The sauce should be thick. Store in a glass jar in the refrigerator for up to 2 months.

—*Karen Lee & Alaxandra Branyon*

• • •

STUFFED TROUT TURKISH STYLE

In Turkey, this dish is usually prepared with rich and pungent mackerel, but I prefer the milder and sweeter trout. Serve with broiled eggplant and zucchini or with sautéed spinach.

——— *6 Servings* ———
¼ cup currants
¼ cup pine nuts
6 tablespoons olive oil, plus more for brushing the fish
2 cups coarse fresh bread crumbs
1 cup finely chopped onions
2 teaspoons ground coriander
1 teaspoon allspice or cinnamon
2 tablespoons chopped parsley
1 tablespoon chopped fresh dill
Salt and freshly ground pepper
6 brook trout or coho salmon trout (about 12 ounces each), bones removed, head and tails intact
Lemon wedges, for garnish

1. Grease a large shallow baking dish. In a small bowl, plump the currants in ¼ cup hot water for 30 minutes. Drain and set aside.

2. Preheat the oven to 375°. Spread the pine nuts on a large baking sheet and bake 5 minutes, or until the nuts are golden brown.

3. In a medium saucepan, heat 3 tablespoons of the olive oil over moderately high heat. Add the bread crumbs and cook, stirring occasionally, until browned, about 5 minutes. Transfer to paper towels to cool.

4. Wipe out the pan and pour in the remaining 3 tablespoons oil. Add the onions and cook, stirring, over moderately low heat until softened but not browned, about 7 minutes. Add the coriander and allspice, stirring, and cook about 2 minutes.

5. In a medium bowl, combine the currants, pine nuts, bread crumbs, on-ions, parsley and dill. Season with salt and pepper to taste. Set aside to cool.

6. Season the insides of the fish with ⅛ teaspoon each salt and pepper. Fill each trout with about ½ cup stuffing. Close and secure tightly with string. Brush each fish lightly with olive oil. *(This recipe can be made to this point up to 6 hours ahead. Cover and refrigerate.)*

7. Transfer the trout to the baking dish, making sure there is room around each trout. Bake about 15 minutes or until the fish is flaky and opaque throughout. Garnish with the lemon wedges and serve.

—*Joyce Goldstein*

• • •

TONNO CON VITELLO

The following recipe is a twist on one of my favorite Italian dishes, *vitello ton-nato*. Here, tuna is dredged in coarsely ground black pepper and seared in an exceedingly hot cast-iron skillet until it is charred on the outside but still cold inside. It's then served cold with a piquant veal sauce. The success of this preparation depends on the tuna remaining raw in the center. So if you're concerned about eating raw fish, or you just don't care for it, this dish may not be for you.

❢ Tuna is a particularly rich fish, and the mayonnaise makes this dish even richer. It needs a white with sufficient acidity to refresh the palate. Try the 1987 Bouchaine Chardonnay or the 1987 Ste. Chapelle Canyon Chardonnay.

——— *6 Servings* ———
½ pound lean veal from the leg, cut into ½-inch cubes
Salt and freshly ground white pepper

FISH & SHELLFISH

¼ cup olive oil
2 tablespoons Cognac or other
brandy
1½ cups mayonnaise
1 anchovy fillet, mashed to a paste
1 teaspoon drained small capers
1 teaspoon caper juice
1½ tablespoons fresh lemon juice
1 teaspoon chopped chives
1 teaspoon chopped parsley
2 tuna steaks (9 ounces each),
preferably bluefin, cut 1 inch thick
2½ teaspoons coarsely ground black
pepper
18 slices (½ inch thick) baguette
1 garlic clove, halved

1. Sprinkle the veal with a pinch of salt and white pepper. In a large skillet, heat 1 tablespoon of the olive oil over moderate heat. Add the veal and cook, stirring occasionally, until cooked through but not browned, about 4 minutes. Add the Cognac and cook until evaporated, about 1 minute. Transfer the veal to a bowl, cover partially and let cool completely.

2. In a food processor, combine the veal with ½ cup of the mayonnaise and the anchovy. Process until smooth. Strain the puree through a coarse sieve into a medium bowl. Fold in the remaining 1 cup mayonnaise, the capers, caper juice, lemon juice, chives, parsley and another pinch of salt and white pepper. Cover and refrigerate for at least 1 hour.

3. Sprinkle the tuna steaks all over with the black pepper, pressing gently to help it adhere. Heat a large cast-iron skillet over high heat until very hot, about 4 minutes. Add 2 tablespoons of the olive oil and immediately add the tuna. Cook, turning frequently, until the tuna is evenly charred on all sides, about 3 minutes total. Transfer the tuna to a plate and let cool slightly. Cover and refrigerate until thoroughly chilled, about 1 hour.

4. Preheat the oven to 350°. Lightly brush one side of each bread slice with the remaining 1 tablespoon olive oil and rub with the garlic clove halves. Put the bread on a baking sheet and bake for 10 minutes or until the edges are golden.

5. Slice each tuna steak into 12 long, thin slices. Arrange 4 slices, slightly overlapping, on 6 chilled plates. Garnish each serving with about 2 tablespoons of the veal sauce and 3 slices of garlic toast.
—*Steve Mellina*

• • •

TERRIFIC TUNA

This quick-seared tuna is excellent hot—straight from the oven—or cold the following day. I like to serve the fish thickly sliced on the bias, like London broil, and accompanied with vegetables, such as baby artichokes and summer squash.

——— *6 Servings* ———
6 tuna steaks (6 ounces each), cut 1
inch thick
¼ cup fresh lemon juice
¼ cup bottled clam juice
¼ cup dry sherry or dry vermouth
1 tablespoon minced fresh ginger
¼ teaspoon sugar
¼ cup plus 2 teaspoons olive oil
¾ teaspoon salt
¼ teaspoon freshly ground pepper
1 medium onion, finely chopped
2 small garlic cloves, minced
1 cup tomato puree
2 medium tomatoes—peeled, seeded
and coarsely chopped
3 tablespoons chopped green olives
plus 6 olives, sliced into thin
strips, for garnish
2 tablespoons Cognac or other
brandy, or bourbon
1 tablespoon basil
1 bay leaf

1. Place the tuna steaks in a glass dish in a single layer. In a bowl, combine the lemon juice, clam juice, sherry, ginger and sugar. Add 3 tablespoons of the olive oil, ¼ teaspoon of the salt and ⅛ teaspoon of the pepper. Mix to blend and pour this marinade over the tuna steaks. Cover and let marinate for at least 2 hours in the refrigerator, turning the steaks once or twice.

2. In a large nonreactive skillet, heat 1 tablespoon of the olive oil. Add the onion and garlic, cover and cook over low heat, stirring occasionally, until the onion is softened, 10 to 15 minutes.

3. Add the tomato puree, fresh tomatoes, chopped green olives, Cognac, basil, bay leaf and the remaining ½ teaspoon salt and ⅛ teaspoon pepper. Cook over very low heat, stirring occasionally, until the sauce thickens, about 20 minutes. Set aside.

4. Preheat the oven to 400°. Remove the tuna steaks from the marinade and pat dry with paper towels. Pour the marinade into a small nonreactive saucepan and cook over high heat until thickened slightly, about 5 minutes.

SUMMER DINNER PARTY

Serves 6

Golden Spiced Goat Cheese (p. 28)

🍷 *Chilled Fino Sherry*

Terrific Tuna (p. 56)

Buttered Zucchini and Summer Squash

Crusty Semolina Bread

🍷 *Crisp California Fumé Blanc, such as 1987 Robert Mondavi or Dry Creek*

Mixed Green Salad with Balsamic Vinaigrette

Gâteau Victoire (p. 202)

Café Filtre

5. In a large heavy skillet, preferably cast iron, heat 1 teaspoon of the olive oil over moderately high heat until almost smoking. Add 3 of the tuna steaks and cook, turning once, until well browned, about 1 minute per side. Using a spatula, transfer the seared tuna to a shallow baking pan. Repeat with the remaining 1 teaspoon olive oil and 3 tuna steaks. Brush the reduced marinade over the tuna steaks and bake until just cooked, 5 to 6 minutes for medium-rare.

6. Reheat the tomato sauce over moderate heat. Spoon the sauce onto 6 serving plates. Thickly slice the tuna steaks on the bias, if you like, or arrange them whole on top of the sauce. Garnish with the sliced olives.

—*W. Peter Prestcott*

• • •

BABY CLAMS, LIVORNO STYLE

Livorno (Leghorn) has been Tuscany's main seaport since the silting up of Pisa's harbor. As with many port towns, its cooking reflects outside influences and employs the widest range of spices and flavorings of any town in the region. Livorno is especially known for its spicy dishes made with an abundance of crushed red pepper, such as the native fish stew called *cacciucco.* The wonderful tiny Mediterranean clams are almost always cooked and served in the shell, even when combined with pasta or, as in this dish, with eggs.

——————— *6 Servings* ———————
2 pounds small clams, such as
*   littlenecks or razor clams*
1 lemon, halved
¼ teaspoon coarse (kosher) salt
½ cup olive oil
1 small red onion, finely chopped
1 large garlic clove, minced
1 pound plum tomatoes, peeled and
*   seeded, or 1 can (28 ounces)*
*   Italian plum tomatoes, drained*
*   and seeded*

Salt and freshly ground black
*   pepper*
About ¼ teaspoon crushed red
*   pepper*
2 eggs
¼ cup coarsely chopped Italian
*   flat-leaf parsley*

1. Wash the clams very well and scrub if necessary. Place the clams in a bowl of cold water to cover. Add the lemon and coarse salt and let soak for 30 minutes.

2. In a large nonreactive skillet, warm the oil over moderate heat. Add the onion and garlic and cook, stirring occasionally, until slightly softened, 2 to 3 minutes.

3. Cut the tomatoes into large pieces and add them to the skillet. Reduce the heat to low and cook for 5 minutes, stirring occasionally. Season with salt, black pepper and crushed red pepper to taste.

4. Drain the clams and rinse well under cold running water. Add them to the skillet, cover and increase the heat to moderately high. Cook, stirring occasionally, until the clams open, 2 to 3 minutes depending on their size. Discard any clams that do not open.

5. Meanwhile, in a medium bowl, lightly beat the eggs with a pinch of salt.

6. Remove the skillet from the heat. Sprinkle the parsley over the clams, pour in the eggs and mix well until thoroughly blended. Return the skillet to moderate heat and cook, stirring frequently, just until piping hot. Serve immediately.

—*Giuliano Bugialli*

• • •

CONFETTI SHRIMP

These stir-fried shrimp are a snowball's throw away from shrimp cocktail. You can serve them hot out of the skillet but the flavors improve when the assembled dish sits at room temperature, making this a great buffet dish.

——————— *Makes About 2 Dozen* ———————
1 medium red bell pepper
¼ cup olive oil
1½ pounds (about 24) large shrimp,
*   shelled and deveined*
3 tablespoons minced fresh ginger
2 garlic cloves, minced
1½ tablespoons fresh lemon juice
1 tablespoon fresh lime juice
¼ teaspoon salt
½ teaspoon Chinese hot (red chili)
*   oil*
¼ cup minced chives or minced
*   scallion greens*

1. Roast the pepper directly over a gas flame or under the broiler as close to the heat as possible, turning, until charred all over, about 5 minutes. Place the pepper in a paper bag, fold to close and let steam for 10 minutes. Scrape off the skin with a knife, rinse briefly under cool water, if necessary, to remove burned bits. Remove the stem and seeds. Mince the pepper and set it aside in a small bowl.

2. In a large heavy skillet, heat 2 tablespoons of the oil over high heat. Add the shrimp and cook, turning, until opaque and firm, about 2 to 3 minutes. Transfer the shrimp to a medium bowl and set aside to cool.

3. Reduce the heat to moderately low and add the ginger and garlic. Cook, stirring, until fragrant and starting to soften, about 3 minutes. Scrape the ginger mixture into a small bowl and whisk in the lemon juice, lime juice and salt. Whisk in the remaining 2 tablespoons olive oil and the hot oil. Pour the mixture over the cooled shrimp, stir to coat and let sit for at least 1 hour to marry the flavors. *(The recipe can be prepared to this point 1 day ahead; cover tightly and refrigerate overnight. Let sit at room temperature for 1 hour before serving.)* Stir in the chives and minced red pepper and transfer to a serving bowl.

—*Tracey Seaman*

• • •

CURRIED PINEAPPLE AND PRAWNS

Tamarind adds a tart, fruity note to this dish. It comes in many forms, the most convenient of which is a strained puree sold as "instant tamarind concentrate."

———— *4 to 6 Servings* ————
3 cups unsweetened coconut milk*
½ cup Chili Jam (p. 258)
¼ cup Panaeng Paste (p. 258)
1½ teaspoons instant tamarind concentrate,* dissolved in 3 tablespoons hot water
3 tablespoons fish sauce*
2 cups chopped fresh pineapple
1 pound large shrimp, shelled and deveined
1 small fresh red chile, seeded and minced
Cooked rice, for serving
*Available at Asian markets

1. In a large saucepan, bring 1 cup of the coconut milk to a boil over high heat. Stir in the Chili Jam and Panaeng Paste and cook, stirring frequently, until fragrant and slightly reduced, about 3 minutes. Reduce the heat to moderate.
2. Add the tamarind water, fish sauce and the remaining 2 cups coconut milk to the pan and bring to a simmer. Stir in the pineapple and return to a simmer.

3. Add the shrimp and cook, stirring occasionally, until opaque throughout, about 2 minutes. Transfer the curry to a serving bowl and garnish with the minced chile. Pass the rice separately.

—*Thai Cooking School, Oriental Hotel, Bangkok, Thailand*

• • •

STEAMED LOBSTER WITH LIME BUTTER

These lobsters are served whole, so be sure to supply four lobster crackers with which to tackle the meal.

———— *4 Servings* ————
4 lobsters (about 1½ pounds each)
1 stick (4 ounces) lightly salted butter
3 tablespoons fresh lime juice
Lime wedges, for garnish

1. In a large pot with a steamer basket, bring 2 inches of salted water to a boil over high heat. Add the lobsters, cover and steam until the lobsters turn bright orange, about 12 minutes.
2. Meanwhile, in a small saucepan, melt the butter over moderate heat. Remove from the heat and stir in the lime juice.
3. Pour the lime butter into 4 small ramekins or bowls. Serve each person 1 lobster with lime wedges and a ramekin of lime butter.

—*Stephanie Lyness*

• • •

SEAFOOD STEW WITH GREEN PEPPERCORNS

This stew is chock-full of lobster, shrimp and squid. Serve it with buttered and toasted baguette slices.
🍷 Crisp California Sauvignon Banc, such as 1987 Matanzas Creek or 1988 Charles Shaw

———— *4 Servings* ————
1 live lobster (1 pound)
1 tablespoon vegetable oil
1 pound large shrimp—shelled, deveined and halved lengthwise, shells reserved
1 medium onion, chopped
2 carrots—1 chopped, 1 halved lengthwise and thinly sliced on the bias
1 sprig of fresh thyme or ½ teaspoon dried
1 tablespoon tomato paste
½ cup brandy or bourbon
⅔ cup fresh orange juice
1 small bulb of fennel, thinly sliced crosswise
1 cup fresh white bread crumbs
2 tablespoons unsalted butter

ZESTY LOBSTER WITH LIME

Serves 4

Steamed Lobster with Lime Butter (p. 58)

Green Salad with Mango and a Citrus Vinaigrette (p. 143)

French Bread

Blueberry Shortcake (p. 180)
—*Stephanie Lyness*

2 shallots, minced
2 garlic cloves, minced
1 small red bell pepper, cut into
    small dice
2½ teaspoons green peppercorns in
    brine, drained and crushed
⅔ cup milk
⅓ cup heavy cream
½ pound cleaned squid—bodies cut
    into thin rings, large tentacles
    split
Salt and freshly ground black
    pepper

1. Fill a large pot with enough water to cover the lobster and bring to a boil over high heat. Add the lobster and cook for 5 minutes. Transfer the lobster to a plate. Reserve 5 cups of the poaching water.

2. When the lobster is cool enough to handle, separate the tail and claws from the body. Crack and discard the shells on the tail and claws; set the lobster meat aside. Using a cleaver, crack the lobster body into 2- to 3-inch pieces.

3. In a large saucepan, heat the oil. Stir in the lobster body pieces and the reserved shrimp shells and cook over high heat, stirring, until the shells turn bright orange and start to brown, about 5 minutes. Add the onion, chopped carrot and thyme and cook, stirring, for 3 minutes. Stir in the tomato paste and cook for 1 minute longer.

4. Reduce the heat to moderate and add the brandy. Using a kitchen match, ignite the brandy and cook, stirring with a metal spoon, until the flames subside. Add the reserved lobster water and the orange juice, increase the heat to high and bring to a boil. Reduce the heat to low and simmer for 40 minutes.

5. Meanwhile, in a small saucepan of boiling salted water, cook the sliced carrot until tender, about 4 minutes. Using a

slotted spoon, transfer the carrot to a plate and set aside. Add the fennel to the boiling water and cook until tender, about 3 minutes. Drain and transfer the fennel to the plate with a slotted spoon.

6. Strain the shellfish stock into a measuring cup. Discard the solids and return the liquid to the saucepan. (If you have more than 4 cups, boil over high heat to reduce the liquid.) Whisk in the bread crumbs and bring just to a boil over high heat. Reduce the heat to moderate and simmer for 1 minute. Strain the stock through a sieve, pushing the bread through with a spatula. Whisk out any lumps that may form.

7. In a large saucepan or medium flameproof casserole, melt the butter over moderate heat. Add the shallots, garlic and red pepper, reduce the heat to low and cook, stirring occasionally, until softened but not brown, about 5 minutes.

8. Whisk in the green peppercorns and cook for 1 minute. Whisk in the milk, cream and the reserved stock. Stir in the reserved carrot and fennel and increase the heat to high. When the liquid comes to a simmer, reduce the heat to moderately high. Add the shrimp and squid and cook, stirring, until the shrimp are pink and loosely curled, about 3 minutes.

9. Remove from the heat and season the stew with salt and black pepper to taste. To serve, divide the lobster meat equally among 4 large soup bowls (1 of the claws or half of the tail per person). Ladle the hot stew over the lobster.

—*Marcia Kiesel*

• • •

FISH STEW WITH FENNEL

This hearty stew is ideal for cold blustery days. I like to serve it in deep soup plates over steamed cubed potatoes or rice or with just some warm crusty bread on the side. Any firm-fleshed fish would work nicely in this dish, and squid, lobster or crab could be added or substituted for the seafood if you like. Don't be put off by the long list of ingredients; this stew is a snap to prepare.

❢ This hearty dish, with its Mediterranean flavors, calls for a crisp white, such as 1988 Caymus Sauvignon Blanc or 1988 Iron Horse Fumé Blanc.

——————— **6 to 8 Servings** ———————

⅓ cup olive oil
2 large garlic cloves, coarsely
    chopped
1 large onion, coarsely chopped
2 large fennel bulbs, cut into ¼-inch
    dice
1 tablespoon fennel seeds, coarsely
    chopped
1 can (35 ounces) Italian plum
    tomatoes, drained
2 bottles (8 ounces each) clam juice
2 cups dry white wine
3 tablespoons tomato paste
1 large bay leaf
½ teaspoon marjoram
1 teaspoon oregano
1 teaspoon salt
½ pound shelled and deveined
    medium shrimp
1½ pounds cod or halibut fillets, cut
    into 3-inch pieces
1 pound red snapper fillets, cut into
    3-inch pieces

2 tablespoons fresh lemon juice
1/2 teaspoon freshly ground pepper
1/2 cup minced parsley
2 tablespoons Pernod (optional)

1. In a large nonreactive saucepan or casserole, heat the oil over moderately low heat. Add the garlic, onion, fennel and fennel seeds. Cover and cook until the onion softens, about 10 minutes.

2. Add the tomatoes, clam juice, wine, tomato paste, bay leaf, marjoram, oregano and salt; bring to a boil over high heat. Reduce the heat to moderately low, cover and cook for 30 minutes.

3. Increase the heat to moderately high. Add the shrimp to the pan and cook, stirring, for 1 minute. Add the cod and snapper and cook until all the seafood is just cooked through, 3 to 4 minutes.

4. Stir in the lemon juice, pepper, parsley and Pernod; simmer for 1 minute longer. Season with additional salt and pepper to taste and serve piping hot.

—*W. Peter Prestcott*

• • •

LAZY-DAY MENU

Serves 6

Jamaican Seafood Stew (p. 60)

Roasted Vegetables with Vinaigrette (p. 132)

Lemon-Blueberry Mousse (p. 201)
—*Melanie Barnard & Brooke Dojny*

JAMAICAN SEAFOOD STEW

🍷 A crisp white, with oak aging that imparts a sweet vanilla nuance, would be a good foil for the flavors in this dish. Try a white Burgundy, such as a 1987 Olivier Leflaive Frères Montagny 1er Cru or a 1988 J.J. Vincent St-Véran.

--- *6 Servings* ---

2 tablespoons unsalted butter
2 tablespoons vegetable oil
1 large onion, chopped
1 large yellow bell pepper, chopped
2 garlic cloves, minced
2 jalapeño peppers—seeded, deribbed and minced
2 teaspoons curry powder
1/3 cup canned unsweetened coconut milk
1 cup fish stock or bottled clam juice
1 pound plum tomatoes, seeded and coarsely chopped
1/4 cup fresh lime juice
1 pound firm white fish fillets—such as red snapper, monkfish or redfish, cut into 2-inch pieces

1/2 pound medium shrimp, shelled and deveined
1/2 pound lump crabmeat, picked over
2 tablespoons minced fresh coriander
1/2 teaspoon salt
1/4 teaspoon freshly ground black pepper
2 cups hot cooked rice, for serving

1. In a large heavy nonreactive saucepan, melt the butter in the oil over moderately low heat. Add the onion and yellow pepper and cook until the pepper is just softened, about 5 minutes.

2. Add the garlic, jalapeño peppers and curry powder and cook for 1 minute. Stir in the coconut milk, fish stock and tomatoes and bring to a boil. Reduce the heat to moderately low and simmer, partially covered, for 10 minutes. *(The recipe can be prepared to this point up to 1 day ahead. Let cool, cover and refrigerate. Reheat before proceeding.)*

3. Stir in the lime juice. Add the fish fillets and shrimp and simmer over low heat until just cooked through, 2 to 3 minutes. Stir in the crabmeat and coriander and simmer for 1 minute. Season with the salt and black pepper.

4. Divide the rice evenly among 6 wide shallow soup bowls. Ladle the hot stew over the rice and serve at once.

—*Melanie Barnard & Brooke Dojny*

• • •

POULTRY

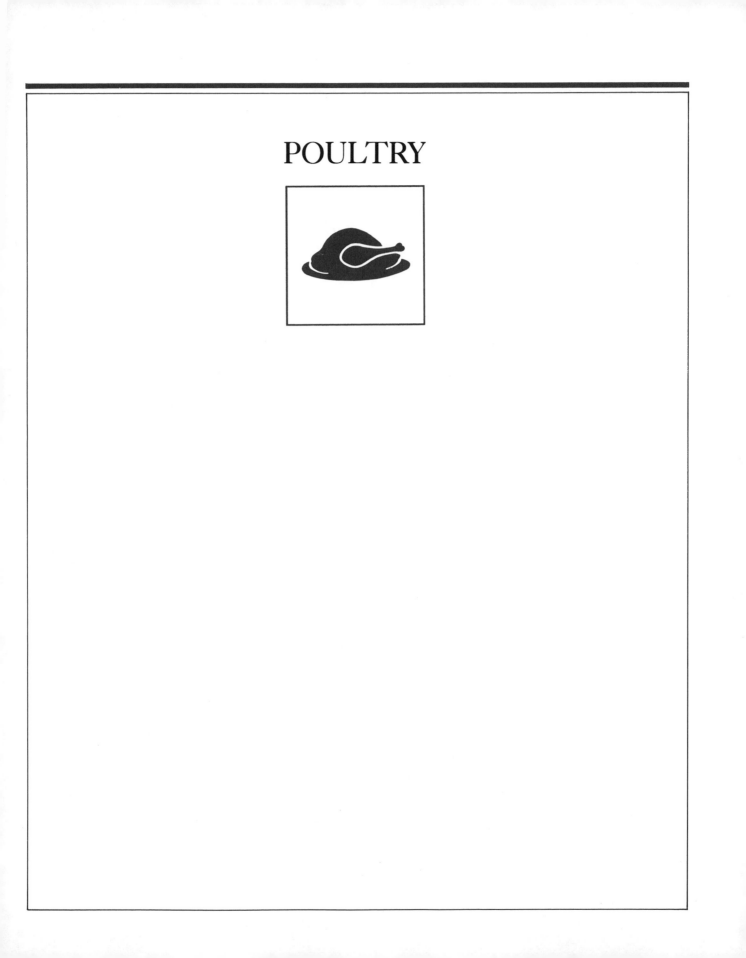

SLOW-FIRE SMOKED CHICKEN

If you won't be eating the chicken immediately, let it cool, then set it on a plate and cover loosely with waxed paper to allow it to breathe. For best flavor and texture, use a free-range or kosher chicken.

❦ To harmonize with but not overwhelm the mild chicken, try a fragrant, light Pinot Noir, such as 1987 Clos du Bois from Sonoma or a Nuits St-Georges 1988 Lupé-Cholet Comte de Lupé.

——— 2 to 3 Servings ———
1 chicken (3½ to 4 pounds)
1 lemon, halved
1 teaspoon salt
1 teaspoon freshly ground black pepper or 2 teaspoons freshly ground Szechuan peppercorns
1 garlic clove, crushed
2 tablespoons unsalted butter
2 shallots
3 sprigs of fresh rosemary or ½ teaspoon dried
1 tablespoon extra-virgin olive oil
Oil, for brushing the grill

1. Start the fire in the grill.
2. Remove the fat from the tail end of the chicken. Squeeze half of the lemon into the cavity and sprinkle in ½ teaspoon each of the salt and black pepper (or 1 teaspoon of the Szechuan pepper). Then place the 2 lemon halves, garlic, butter, shallots and rosemary in the cavity. Rub the chicken with the olive oil and the remaining ½ teaspoon each of the salt and black pepper (or 1 teaspoon Szechuan pepper). Skewer the chicken closed at both ends.
3. Brush the grill with oil. Place the chicken, breast-side up, in the center of the grill and cover, leaving all the vents wide open. Cook the chicken for 1¼ to 1½ hours, turning it with a wide spatula every 15 to 20 minutes. The chicken is done when it is evenly browned and the juices run clear when a thigh is pierced. If the chicken seems to be cooking too fast and getting too dark too soon, move it to the side of the grill where the heat is less intense.
4. Transfer the chicken to a platter and let rest for 15 minutes before carving. If you'll be serving the chicken the next day, let it cool completely, cover and refrigerate.
—Karen Lee & Alaxandra Branyon

• • •

PROVENCAL ROAST CHICKEN

Whether or not this chicken is authentically Provençal, it evokes hill towns and hearty suppers. If the recipe were written in French, it would call for un beau poulet. I start with the beau-est chicken I can find—plump and fresh—flavor it with oranges and basil, give it a massage with melted butter and fragrant olive oil, and fit it into a dutch oven. When cooked through, the chicken is moist and aromatic, with juices that can be served au naturel or used as the base for a gravy. If any chicken remains, the following day I eat it cold, doused with pureed anchovies, garlic and olive oil.

——— 4 Servings ———
1 tablespoon unsalted butter
1 tablespoon olive oil
1½ teaspoons salt
¾ teaspoon freshly ground pepper
6 juice oranges
1 whole chicken (about 3½ pounds)
1 large onion, thinly sliced
6 sprigs of basil, or substitute fresh rosemary or thyme
2 garlic cloves, unpeeled and smashed
1 tablespoon Cognac or other brandy
Orange slices and basil leaves, for garnish

1. Preheat the oven to 375°. In a small saucepan, over moderate heat, melt the butter in the olive oil. Add ½ teaspoon of the salt and ¼ teaspoon of the pepper and set aside.
2. Squeeze the juice from 4 of the oranges and reserve; this should yield about 1 cup. Save the shell from 1 of the juiced oranges. Thinly slice the 2 remaining whole oranges crosswise.
3. Work your fingers between the skin and flesh of the chicken breasts and thighs to separate without tearing the skin. Slip 1 of the orange slices under the skin of each thigh and 2 under each breast. Season the cavity with ½ teaspoon of the salt and ¼ teaspoon of the pepper. Fill the cavity with the reserved orange shell, 4 slices of the onion and 1 sprig of the basil. Truss the bird with string and rub all over with the seasoned melted butter and olive oil.
4. In a lightly buttered ovenproof casserole or dutch oven, combine the remaining orange slices, onion slices, basil sprigs and the garlic cloves. Season with the remaining ½ teaspoon salt and ¼ teaspoon pepper. Toss to mix well.
5. Place the chicken in the pan and pour in ¼ cup of the reserved orange juice. Cover and roast for 15 minutes. Baste with ¼ cup more orange juice. Recover and cook, basting with the accumulated pan juices every 15 minutes, for 1 hour longer.
6. Remove the pan from the oven and increase the oven temperature to 425°. Strain the pan juices into a nonreactive saucepan and set aside. Return the chicken to the oven and roast uncovered, basting once or twice, until nicely browned, about 20 minutes.
7. Meanwhile, add the remaining ½ cup orange juice to the reserved pan juices and boil over moderately high heat

until reduced by half, about 7 minutes. Add the Cognac and boil for 1 minute longer. Carve or quarter the chicken and moisten with a little of the sauce. Garnish with orange slices and basil leaves. Pass the remaining sauce separately.

—*Dorie Greenspan*

• • •

ROAST CHICKEN STUFFED WITH SAUSAGE AND ARMAGNAC PRUNES

The Armagnac-soaked prunes in this chicken recipe from Brittany, France, impart a subtle perfume to the filling.

———— *4 Servings* ————
1 cup pitted prunes (about 6 ounces), cut in half
½ cup Armagnac or other brandy
4 tablespoons unsalted butter
2 medium onions, finely chopped
3 celery ribs, finely chopped
8 garlic cloves, minced
2 tablespoons olive oil
8 ounces lean ground pork
2 teaspoons chopped fresh thyme or ½ teaspoon dried
1 teaspoon freshly grated nutmeg
Salt and freshly ground pepper
1 large chicken (about 4 pounds)

1. In a small bowl, combine the prunes and Armagnac; set aside, covered, for 1 hour or overnight to plump.

2. Preheat the oven to 475°. In a large saucepan, melt 2 tablespoons of the butter over moderate heat. Add the onions and cook, stirring occasionally, until softened but not browned, about 5 minutes.

3. Add the celery and garlic and cook for 5 minutes more. Transfer the vegetables to a medium bowl.

4. Wipe out the saucepan and pour in the olive oil. Add the ground pork and cook, stirring, over high heat until the pork has lost its redness and is cooked through, 3 to 5 minutes.

5. Add the pork to the cooked vegetables. Stir in the thyme, nutmeg, prunes and Armagnac. Season with salt and pepper to taste. Let cool before proceeding.

6. Season the cavity of the chicken with ¼ teaspoon each salt and pepper. Fill the cavity with the pork stuffing. Close the cavity and secure with string, wrapping it tightly around the legs.

7. Rub the chicken with the remaining 2 tablespoons butter and place it, breast-side up, in a roasting pan. Roast for 10 minutes, reduce the heat to 400° and cook for 1¼ hours, or until golden brown and the juices run clear when the thigh is pierced with a knife. Cover loosely with foil and let rest before carving.

—*Joyce Goldstein*

• • •

HEARTY WINTER DINNER

Serves 4

Mixed Bitter Greens with Sautéed Wild Mushrooms

Roast Chicken Stuffed with Sausage and Armagnac Prunes (p. 63)

Crusty Peasant Bread

♟ *Full-bodied red wine, such as Gigondas or California Syrah*

Green Grape Tart (p. 171)

CLAY POT CHICKEN WITH GARLIC AND HERBS

This is a family favorite because all my children love garlic and chicken. They learned from their mother, who likes chicken so much and makes it so often that when they were little, they even thought pork and veal were chicken.

♟ California Chardonnay, such as 1988 Vichon or Kendall-Jackson Vintner's Reserve

———— *4 Servings* ————
1 roasting chicken (4½ to 5 pounds)
Salt and freshly ground pepper
6 sprigs of fresh thyme or ½ teaspoon dried
6 sprigs of parsley
2 imported bay leaves
1 tablespoon unsalted butter, at room temperature
1 medium onion, sliced
1 medium carrot, sliced
1 celery rib, sliced
40 unpeeled garlic cloves (about 2 heads)
4 fresh or dried whole sage leaves
1 sprig of fresh tarragon or ¼ teaspoon dried
Toasted country bread, for serving

1. Cover a 2- to 3-quart clay pot with cold water and let soak for 15 minutes.

2. Meanwhile, sprinkle the inside of the chicken with salt and pepper to taste. Place 2 thyme sprigs (or a pinch of dried), 2 parsley sprigs and 1 bay leaf into the cavity and truss the bird. Rub the butter all over the chicken and sprinkle lightly with salt and pepper.

3. Drain the clay pot and add the onion, carrot and celery. Set the chicken on top of the vegetables and scatter the garlic cloves around the bird. Scatter around the sage leaves, tarragon sprig and the remaining 4 sprigs of thyme (or dried thyme), 4 sprigs of parsley and 1 bay leaf.

4. Cover the clay pot and place it in a cold oven. Turn the oven temperature to 475° and cook the chicken for about 1 hour and 20 minutes or until the juices run clear when a thigh is pierced. Uncover and cook for about 10 minutes longer to brown the breast. Transfer the bird and the garlic cloves to a warmed platter, cover loosely with foil and let rest for about 15 minutes.

5. Strain the braising juices into a sauceboat and keep warm. Carve the chicken and serve with the garlic cloves on the side. Let each person squeeze the garlic from its skin onto the toasted bread.
—*Patrick Clark*

• • •

COUNTRY-STYLE FRIED CHICKEN

When I was growing up, it was considered beneficial for youngsters to have what was called a "change of air." Consequently, although we took vacations as a family as well, each year I was shipped to the country by myself to spend at least 10 days as the guest of a country priest. The house was attached to a beautiful 10th-century church and had a well of crystal-clear, ice-cold water. All the cooking, including frying, was done in an enormous walk-in fireplace, under the supervision of the priest's huge, bossy sister. I'll never forget this simple, succulent dish they made with the chickens they raised. The meat becomes meltingly tender as a result of its marinating in eggs.

❦ The dry, lean nature of a 1986 Chianti, such as Podere Il Palazzino or Cecchi would accent the chicken nicely.

———— 4 Servings ————
1 teaspoon coarse (kosher) salt
1 frying chicken (3½ pounds)
1 teaspoon salt
½ teaspoon freshly ground pepper
1 cup unbleached all-purpose flour
3 eggs

4 cups vegetable oil, for deep-frying
½ cup olive oil, for deep-frying
1 lemon, cut in wedges, for serving

1. Bring a large pot of water with the coarse salt to a boil over high heat. Add the chicken to the pot and parboil for 1 minute. Drain well and let cool.

2. Using a sharp knife, cut the chicken into 8 pieces. Season with the salt and pepper, then dredge in the flour.

3. In a large bowl, beat the eggs lightly with a pinch of salt. Add the chicken pieces and turn to coat evenly. Cover and refrigerate for at least 1 hour and up to 2 hours, turning occasionally.

4. In a large heavy skillet, preferably cast iron, heat the vegetable and olive oils over moderate heat until the temperature reaches 375°. Add half of the chicken pieces and increase the heat to high for 20 seconds. Then reduce the heat to moderate and fry, turning occasionally, until the chicken is golden and crisp and the juices run clear when the meat is pierced with a fork, about 25 minutes.

5. Using tongs, transfer the fried chicken to paper towels to drain. (Keep warm in a low oven.) Fry the remaining chicken pieces. Serve hot, sprinkled with salt and garnished with the lemon wedges.

—*Giuliano Bugialli*

• • •

GREEN CHILE CHICKEN

Fresh green chiles add a lively flavor to this dish, and the dried green chile provides a deep, smoky flavor. Look for corn tortillas labeled "for soft tacos"—they're relatively thick and have an earthy, true corn taste.

———— 6 Servings ————
1 chicken (about 3 pounds), quartered
2 tablespoons olive oil or vegetable oil
1 large onion, chopped
½ pound poblano or other fresh mild green chiles, chopped
8 garlic cloves, minced
1 Idaho potato (about ½ pound), peeled and cut into ½-inch dice
½ ounce dried green chile (optional)
4 fresh tomatillos, chopped
⅓ cup chopped fresh coriander
2 teaspoons salt
Freshly ground black pepper
2 tablespoons unsalted butter
9 corn tortillas (6 inches in diameter)
6 ounces Monterey Jack cheese, grated (about 1½ cups)
6 ounces sharp Cheddar cheese, grated (about 1½ cups)
⅛ teaspoon chili powder or paprika

1. In a large saucepan, pour 4 cups of water over the chicken and bring to a boil over high heat. Reduce the heat to low and simmer for 15 minutes. Turn the chicken pieces over and simmer for 15 minutes longer. Remove the breast pieces and cook the legs for another 10 minutes. Remove the legs.

2. Strain the broth into a bowl and skim off any fat that rises to the surface. Pour the broth into a medium saucepan and boil over high heat until it reduces to 2 cups, about 20 minutes. Pour the reduced broth into a bowl and set aside.

3. Meanwhile, return the large saucepan to high heat and add the oil. When it's hot, add the onion, poblanos and garlic and reduce the heat to low. Cover and cook, stirring occasionally, until the vegetables are softened, about 15 minutes.

4. In a small saucepan, cover the diced potato with water and boil over high heat until tender, about 5 minutes. Drain well.

5. Put the dried green chile, if using, in a small bowl and cover with 1 cup boiling water. Let soak until softened, about 10 minutes. Drain and chop.

6. When the vegetables in the saucepan are soft, add the diced potato, reconstituted dried chile and the reserved chicken broth and simmer over low heat, mashing some of the potatoes, until the mixture thickens slightly and the flavors blend, about 10 minutes. Remove from the heat and stir in the tomatillos, coriander, salt and black pepper to taste.

7. Meanwhile, remove all the meat from the chicken, discarding the skin and bones. Cut the meat into 2-inch pieces. Stir the chicken into the sauce.

8. In a small skillet, heat 1 tablespoon of the butter over moderately high heat. Add 1 corn tortilla and fry until lightly browned, about 1 minute per side. Drain on paper towels. Add the remaining 1 tablespoon butter to the skillet and fry 2 more tortillas, one at a time. Drain well. Cut the fried tortillas in half and set aside.

9. Preheat the oven to 425°. In a bowl, combine the Monterey Jack and Cheddar cheeses. Set aside 1 tablespoon. Spoon one-third of the chicken mixture into a deep 3-quart casserole. Halve the remaining 6 unfried tortillas and arrange 4 halves over the chicken layer. Sprinkle one-third of the mixed cheeses on top. Continue layering in this order until the chicken, unfried tortilla halves and cheese are used up. Decoratively arrange the 6 fried tortilla halves on top and sprinkle with the reserved 1 tablespoon cheese and the chili powder.

10. Bake in the upper third of the oven until bubbly and crisp on top, about 25 minutes. Remove the casserole from the oven and let rest for 15 minutes before serving. Spoon hefty helpings onto 6 warmed plates, making sure to include a crisp tortilla half for each serving.

—*Marcia Kiesel*

• • •

SUMMER PICNIC

Serves 4

Sesame-Fried Lemon Chicken
(p. 65)

Black-Eyed Pea and Corn Salad
(p. 149)

❦ *Red or white jug wine or cold beer*

Giant Anise Sugar Cookies (p. 196)

Watermelon

—*Melanie Barnard*
& Brooke Dojny

SESAME-FRIED LEMON CHICKEN

❦ Because mild and lemony flavors are predominant in this dish, a refreshing, fruity white, such as a Chenin Blanc, would be a good accompaniment. Look for a 1988 Dry Creek or 1988 Hacienda.

———— *4 Servings* ————

1½ cups milk
2½ tablespoons fresh lemon juice
4 skinless, boneless chicken breast halves or thighs (about 6 ounces each)
¼ cup plus 2 tablespoons yellow cornmeal
¼ cup plus 2 tablespoons all-purpose flour
¼ cup plus 1½ teaspoons sesame seeds
2 teaspoons grated lemon zest
1 teaspoon salt
¼ teaspoon freshly ground pepper
3 tablespoons unsalted butter
3 tablespoons vegetable oil
¾ cup chicken stock or canned broth
¾ cup heavy cream
1 tablespoon chopped chives
Thin lemon slices, for garnish

1. In a shallow nonreactive dish, combine the milk and 1½ tablespoons of the lemon juice. Add the chicken and marinate, covered, in the refrigerator for about 1 hour, turning 2 or 3 times.

2. In a shallow dish, combine the cornmeal, flour, sesame seeds, lemon zest, salt and pepper. Remove the chicken from the milk but do not pat dry. Dredge the chicken in the cornmeal mixture to coat completely.

3. In a large skillet, melt the butter in the oil over moderately high heat. Add the chicken and fry, turning once, until deep golden brown on both sides, 8 to 10 minutes for breasts or 10 to 12 minutes for thighs. Drain on paper towels and transfer to a warm platter.

4. Pour off the fat from the skillet. Add the chicken stock and bring to a simmer over moderate heat, scraping up any browned bits in the pan. Add the cream, chives and the remaining tablespoon lemon juice and boil until the gravy thickens slightly, 3 to 5 minutes. Season with additional salt and pepper to taste.

5. Garnish the chicken with lemon slices. Pass the gravy separately.

—*Melanie Barnard & Brooke Dojny*

• • •

ROASTED CHICKEN BREASTS WITH PROSCIUTTO AND LEMON

I serve this flavorful dish with simple buttered mashed potatoes or rice and buttered green beans tossed with pistachios. If you have any chicken left over, thinly slice it and serve cold.

❦ A lively, fruity 1988 California Chenin Blanc, such as Folie à Deux or Pine Ridge, makes a nice contrast to the prosciutto and lemon flavors of this dish.

——— *8 Servings* ———

1½ sticks (6 ounces) unsalted
*   butter, at room temperature*
4 ounces thinly sliced prosciutto,
*   finely chopped*
1 tablespoon grated lemon zest
½ teaspoon salt
½ teaspoon freshly ground black
*   pepper*
½ cup finely chopped parsley
4 large whole chicken breasts on the
*   bone (1 to 1¼ pounds each)*
2 tablespoons olive oil
2 large shallots, minced
2 garlic cloves, crushed
2 medium carrots, minced
1 small green bell pepper, minced
6 cups chicken stock or low-sodium
*   canned broth*
Juice of 1 lemon
½ cup crème fraîche
1½ teaspoons arrowroot, dissolved
*   in 1 tablespoon of water*

1. Preheat the oven to 450°. In a small bowl, combine the butter with the prosciutto, lemon zest, salt, black pepper and ¼ cup of the parsley. Divide the seasoned butter into 8 equal portions.

2. Using your fingers, carefully loosen the skin from the chicken breasts without tearing. Pat one-eighth of the seasoned butter under the skin of each breast half, spreading it evenly.

3. Place the chicken breasts on a rack set over a baking sheet. Roast in the middle of the oven for about 30 minutes, basting frequently with the drippings, until golden brown and firm to the touch but still juicy. Cover with foil and keep warm.

4. Meanwhile, in a large nonreactive skillet, heat the olive oil. Add the shallots and cook over moderate heat until translucent, about 3 minutes. Add the garlic and cook for 1 minute more. Stir in the carrots and green pepper and cook until slightly softened, about 2 minutes.

5. Add the chicken stock, lemon juice and crème fraîche to the pan and bring to a boil over high heat; boil until the sauce reduces to 2 cups, 15 to 20 minutes.

6. Gradually add the arrowroot mixture and simmer, stirring constantly, until the sauce thickens, about 1 minute. Season with salt and pepper to taste.

7. To serve, cut the stuffed chicken breasts off the bones in one piece with a long, thin, sharp knife, using the breastbones as a guide. Place 1 breast half on each of eight warmed plates and spoon the sauce on top.

—*Bob Chambers*

• • •

CHICKEN BREASTS WITH ARTICHOKE HEARTS, OLIVES AND BACON

Frozen artichoke hearts retain their flavor, texture and color when thawed and cooked. This mélange of artichokes, olives and chicken is easily assembled and surprisingly elegant. I like to serve an unexpected grain, such as steamed couscous or bulgur, as an accompaniment.

❦ Since artichokes can make wine taste sweeter, serve a simple, clean-flavored white, such as 1986 Domaines Ott Bandol Blanc, 1987 Parducci French Colombard or 1987 Mirafiore Soave.

——— *6 Servings* ———

6 tablespoons unsalted butter
1 tablespoon olive oil
1½ cups coarsely chopped onions
2 packages (9 ounces each) frozen
*   artichoke hearts, thawed and*
*   halved lengthwise*
¾ cup dry white wine
¾ teaspoon salt
½ teaspoon freshly ground pepper
¼ pound sliced bacon, finely diced
6 skinless, boneless chicken breast
*   halves*
6 Calamata olives, pitted and thinly
*   sliced*
1 tablespoon fresh lemon juice
1 teaspoon grated lemon zest
½ cup minced parsley

1. In a large nonreactive skillet, melt 2 tablespoons of the butter in the oil. Add the onions, cover and cook over moderately low heat until softened, about 10 minutes.

2. Add the artichoke hearts, wine, ½ teaspoon of the salt and the pepper to the skillet. Cover and cook, stirring occasionally, until the artichoke hearts are tender, about 10 minutes.

3. Meanwhile, in another large nonreactive skillet, fry the bacon over moderate heat until browned and crisp, about 5 minutes. Transfer to paper towels to drain. Set aside.

4. Increase the heat under the bacon fat to moderately high. Add the chicken breasts to the skillet and sauté, turning once, until golden brown, 2 to 3 minutes per side. Pour off the bacon fat.

5. Place the chicken breasts on top of the artichoke hearts. Cover and cook over moderate heat until the chicken is just cooked through, 7 to 9 minutes. Transfer the chicken breasts to a warmed platter and sprinkle with the remaining ¼ teaspoon salt. Cover with foil to keep warm.

6. Drain as much liquid as possible from the artichoke hearts into the second skillet. Bring to a boil and cook over high heat until thick and syrupy, about 3 minutes. Remove from the heat. Cut the remaining 4 tablespoons butter into pieces and gradually whisk them into the reduced liquid. Spoon the sauce over the chicken.

7. Add the olives to the artichoke hearts and cook over moderate heat until warmed through, about 1 minute. Add the lemon juice, lemon zest and parsley and toss well. Spoon the artichoke hearts around the chicken and sprinkle with the reserved bacon.

—*W. Peter Prestcott*

• • •

WARMING WINTER FARE

Serves 6 to 8

Pimiento Chicken with Mushrooms (p. 67)

Sour Cream Buttermilk Corn Bread (p. 161)

Warm String Bean Salad (p. 144)

☙ *Fruity red, such as 1986 Castello d'Albola Chianti Classico*

Custard with Apples and Almonds (p. 198)

Coffee

—*Lee Bailey*

PIMIENTO CHICKEN WITH MUSHROOMS

☙ Fruity red, such as 1986 Castello d'Albola Chianti Classico

———— **6 to 8 Servings** ————
6 tablespoons all-purpose flour
¼ teaspoon salt
¼ teaspoon freshly ground pepper
3 large, whole boneless chicken breasts (2½ pounds total)— skinned, trimmed of excess fat, split and halved crosswise
3 tablespoons safflower oil
2 tablespoons unsalted butter
1 large onion, coarsely chopped
2 medium shallots, minced
12 ounces mushrooms, sliced
⅓ cup dry white wine
2 cups chicken stock or canned low-sodium broth
½ cup low-fat sour cream
2 jars (4 ounces each) pimientos, drained and diced
2 tablespoons minced fresh parsley

1. In a small bowl, place 2 tablespoons of the flour. In a medium bowl, combine the remaining ¼ cup flour with the salt and pepper. Add the chicken pieces to the seasoned flour and toss with a slotted spoon to coat, shaking off any excess.

2. In a large heavy flameproof casserole, heat 2 tablespoons of the oil over moderately high heat. Add half of the chicken and cook until well browned and partially cooked, about 3 minutes per side. Transfer the chicken to a bowl or platter and repeat with the remaining 1 tablespoon oil and the chicken pieces.

3. Reduce the heat to moderate and melt the butter in the casserole. Add the onion and cook, stirring to scrape up any browned bits from the bottom of the pan, until the onion is softened and slightly browned, about 5 minutes.

4. Add the shallots and let cook for 1 minute. Add the mushrooms and cook, stirring, until the juices have evaporated, 6 to 8 minutes.

5. Increase the heat to moderately high and add the white wine. Cook until the liquid has reduced by half. Sprinkle in the reserved 2 tablespoons of flour and stir to incorporate; the mushroom mixture will become thick and pasty. Gradually add the chicken stock, stirring. Bring to a simmer and let bubble, until thickened slightly, about 2 minutes. *(The recipe can be made to this point up to 1 day ahead. Wrap and refrigerate the partially cooked chicken breasts with their juices, cover the casserole and refrigerate. To reheat, place the pot over moderate heat, stirring occasionally, until warm.)*

6. Stir in the sour cream and adjust with additional salt and pepper to taste. Stir in the pimientos and parsley. Add the chicken pieces to the sauce and let cook, stirring occasionally, until the chicken is cooked through, about 3 minutes.

—*Lee Bailey*

• • •

GINGERED CHICKEN BREASTS

Boneless chicken breasts lend themselves to being cut into medallions for easy and attractive serving. Chutneys are a wonderful accompaniment.

———— *15 to 20 Servings* ————
16 skinless, boneless chicken breast
*   halves (about 5½ pounds)*
½ cup soy sauce
5 scallions, chopped
¼ cup vegetable oil
3 tablespoons sherry vinegar
3 tablespoons chopped parsley
2 tablespoons ground ginger
1 tablespoon Oriental sesame oil
Assorted chutneys, for serving

1. Place the chicken breasts in a single layer in nonreactive baking pans or large shallow baking dishes.

2. In a small bowl, mix the soy sauce, scallions, vegetable oil, vinegar, parsley, ginger and sesame oil. Pour the mixture over the chicken, turning the breasts to coat evenly. Set aside to marinate for at least 1 hour at room temperature or overnight, covered, in the refrigerator.

3. Preheat the oven to 350°. Bring the chicken to room temperature if refrigerated. Bake, with the marinade, for about 25 minutes, until the chicken is firm with a light spring to the touch. Halfway through cooking, check to make sure the chicken is not dry. If necessary, add a small amount of water to the baking pans or baking dishes. *(The recipe can be prepared to this point up to 1 day ahead. Cover and refrigerate.)*

4. Leave the chicken breasts whole or slice them on the diagonal into medallions. Serve warm or at room temperature. Serve the chutneys alongside.

—*Paul Grimes*

• • •

SAUTEED CHICKEN BREASTS WITH APPLES AND CALVADOS CREAM

Sautéed fresh spinach with a pinch of nutmeg and buttered wild rice or boiled potatoes would be a fine accompaniment to this rich dish.

♟ The richness of this elegant dish would be showcased by an equally rich, full-bodied Chardonnay, such as 1988 William Hill Silver Label, or a grand white Burgundy, such as 1984 Domaine Leflaive Chevalier-Montrachet.

———— *8 Servings* ————
4 ounces sliced bacon, cut into small
*   dice*
8 skinless, boneless chicken breast
*   halves*
Salt and freshly ground black pepper
2 tablespoons unsalted butter
7 medium Granny Smith apples,
*   peeled and cut into eighths*
2 tablespoons dark brown sugar
½ cup Calvados or other apple
*   brandy*
1½ cups crème fraîche
½ teaspoon caraway seeds
Pinch of cayenne pepper

1. Preheat the oven to 250°. In a large nonreactive skillet, cook the bacon over moderate heat until crisp, 8 to 10 minutes. Using a slotted spoon, transfer the bacon to paper towels to drain. Set aside.

2. Pour off all but 1 tablespoon of the bacon fat from the skillet. Lightly sprinkle the chicken breasts with salt and pepper. Set the skillet over high heat and sauté the chicken in batches, turning once, until browned, about 2 minutes per side. Transfer the cooked chicken to a baking dish in a single layer and cover with foil. Place in the low oven for 15 minutes to finish cooking.

3. Meanwhile, in the same skillet, melt the butter over moderately high heat. Add the apples, cover and cook, stirring frequently, until tender, about 5 minutes.

4. Uncover and add the brown sugar and ¼ cup of the Calvados. Increase the heat to high and cook, tossing gently, until the apples begin to brown, about 2 minutes longer.

5. Add the crème fraîche, caraway seeds, cayenne and the remaining ¼ cup Calvados to the apples. Stir in any accumulated juices from the chicken and bring to a boil. Cook until the sauce is thick enough to coat the back of a spoon, about 4 minutes. Season with salt and pepper to taste.

6. To serve, place the chicken on a warmed platter or plates, arrange the apples alongside and pour the cream sauce over all. Garnish with the reserved bacon.

—*Bob Chambers*

• • •

Assorted Meat Satays with
Cucumber Salad (p. 100) and Peanut
Dipping Sauce (p. 255).

**Left, Stuffed Veal Loin (p. 87). Above, Orzo with
Roasted Peppers and Dried Tomatoes (p. 113) and Slow-Fire
Smoked Chicken (p. 62).**

**Above, Ligurian Vegetable Soup (p. 42). Right, Pasta and
Bean Soup (p. 45).**

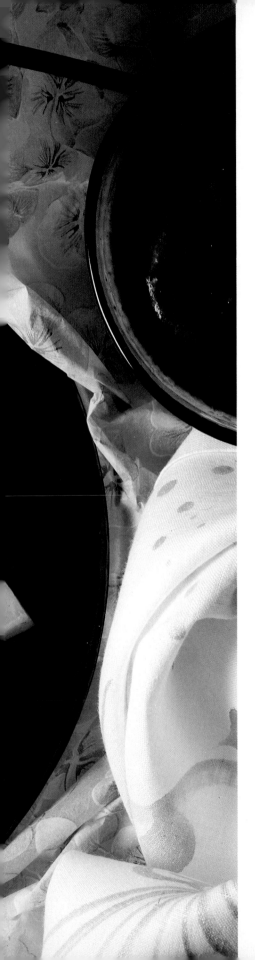

Left, Cold Poached Bass with Mediterranean Vegetable Salad (p. 50). Right, Basil-Orange Vinaigrette (p. 255), shown here with medallions of pork.

CHICKEN BREASTS WITH FENNEL SAUCE

Arrange the slices of chicken in the center of a large platter, slightly overlapping, and surround them with Spinach with Raisins and Pine Nuts (p. 130). I like to put any extra fennel sauce in a separate bowl and let guests serve themselves.

———— 12 Servings ————
1 ounce dried porcini mushrooms
3 eggs
1 tablespoon coarsely chopped fresh sage leaves
¼ cup freshly grated Parmesan cheese
1 teaspoon grated lemon zest
Salt and freshly ground pepper
5 tablespoons unsalted butter
2 large, whole skinless, boneless chicken breasts (12 ounces each), lightly pounded to an even thickness
8 ounces sweet Italian sausage, casings removed
1 cup dry white wine
2 medium fennel bulbs (1 pound total), cut into 1-inch pieces

1. In a medium heatproof bowl, soak the porcini mushrooms in 1 cup hot water for 30 minutes. Drain, squeeze the mushrooms dry and set aside in a small bowl.

2. In a small bowl, using a fork, beat the eggs with the sage, Parmesan cheese, lemon zest and a pinch of salt and pepper.

3. In a 7-inch nonstick skillet, heat 1½ teaspoons of the butter over moderate heat. Pour in half of the egg mixture and cook as you would a pancake, until firm, 1 to 2 minutes per side. Transfer to a large plate and repeat with another 1½ teaspoons butter and the remaining egg mixture. Let the omelets cool slightly.

4. On a work surface, lay the flattened chicken breasts skinned-side down, open like a book in front of you. Spread half of the sausage meat over each breast and sprinkle the reserved porcini mushrooms on top; press the mushrooms into the sausage. Lay the omelets over the mushrooms and roll up the chicken breasts from one side to the other. Secure the rolled chicken with kitchen string.

5. In a heavy, medium flameproof casserole, melt 2 tablespoons of the butter over high heat. Add the chicken rolls and cook, turning, until golden brown on all sides, 6 to 8 minutes.

6. Pour in the wine, add a pinch of salt and ¼ teaspoon pepper. Cover, reduce the heat to low and simmer, turning occasionally until the chicken is cooked through, about 30 minutes.

7. Meanwhile, in a large heavy saucepan, melt the remaining 2 tablespoons butter over low heat. Add the fennel, 1 cup of water and a little salt and pepper. Cover and cook, stirring occasionally, until the fennel is tender, about 20 minutes. Remove from the heat. Transfer the fennel and its cooking liquid to a food processor or blender and puree until smooth.

8. Remove the chicken rolls and clip the strings. Stir the fennel puree into the juices in the casserole and bring to a simmer; if the sauce is too thick to pour, add a little water to thin it. Season with salt and pepper to taste.

9. Slice the chicken rolls into ½-inch rounds and arrange in an overlapping circle on a round platter. Strain the fennel sauce over the chicken and serve any extra sauce on the side.

—*Lorenza de' Medici*

• • •

Roast Duck with Port-Soaked Prunes (p. 83).

CURRIED CAIN CHICKEN

Garnished with toasted sliced almonds, shredded coconut or sesame seeds and served with rice and a vegetable, this curry makes a rewarding lunch or dinner. Ask your butcher to bone the chicken breasts, leaving the skin on.
♇ The soft spicy character of 1986 Cain Cellars Merlot or the 1986 Cain Five goes well with this.

———— 6 Servings ————
4 tablespoons unsalted butter
1 small onion, coarsely chopped
2 large celery ribs, coarsely chopped
1 medium carrot, chopped
1 small green bell pepper, chopped
2 medium garlic cloves, minced
2 tablespoons all-purpose flour
2 tablespoons curry powder
1 medium tart green apple, such as Granny Smith, cored and chopped
2 medium plum tomatoes, chopped
1 large bay leaf
4 cups chicken stock or 1 can (13¾ ounces) chicken broth diluted with 2¼ cups water
2 tablespoons fresh lemon juice
½ teaspoon Worcestershire sauce
3 dashes of hot pepper sauce
6 boneless chicken breast halves with skin (about 2¼ pounds total)

1. In a large saucepan, melt 3 tablespoons of the butter over moderate heat. Add the onion, celery, carrot and green pepper. Cook, stirring occasionally, until they start to turn brown, about 5 minutes.

2. Reduce the heat to low. Stir in the garlic, flour and curry powder and cook until the flavors are blended, about 2 minutes. Add the apple, tomatoes, bay leaf and chicken stock. Bring to a simmer over moderately low heat and cook until the vegetables fall apart when pressed with a spoon, about 45 minutes.

3. Strain the sauce through a sieve into a medium saucepan, pressing through as much vegetable pulp as possible. Stir in the lemon juice, Worcestershire sauce and hot pepper sauce. Cover to keep warm. *(The recipe can be made to this point up to 1 day ahead. Pour into a nonreactive bowl, cover and refrigerate.)*

4. In a large heavy skillet, melt the remaining 1 tablespoon butter over moderately high heat. When the butter begins to foam, add the chicken breasts, skin-side down, and cook until the skin is brown and crisp, about 10 minutes.

5. Turn the breasts and cook until browned on the bottom and firm to the touch, about 10 minutes longer. Reheat the sauce if necessary. Transfer the chicken to warm dinner plates and ladle some of the curry sauce over each portion. Serve hot.

—*Joyce Cain, Cain Cellars,*
St. Helena, California

• • •

CORIANDER CHICKEN WITH TUBETTI

The chicken and pasta cook together in one pot. This dish is best served with simply prepared vegetables such as steamed broccoli or cauliflower or broiled tomatoes.

——— **8 Servings** ———
8 chicken legs
8 chicken thighs
¼ cup olive oil
1 tablespoon Chinese chili sauce
2 teaspoons cumin seeds
1 teaspoon (loosely packed) saffron threads
1 teaspoon salt
Juice of 1 lemon
½ cup coarsely chopped fresh coriander
4 cups chicken stock or canned broth
2 cups tubetti or other small dried pasta

ONE-POT MEAL FOR FAMILY AND FRIENDS

Serves 8

Crispy Shallot Dip (p. 30)

Crudités

———

Coriander Chicken with Tubetti (p. 78)

🍷 *California Chenin Blanc, such as 1988 Pine Ridge or Hacienda*

———

Tossed Salad with Lemon Vinaigrette

———

Blueberry Lime Pie with Coconut Crumble Topping (p. 168)

---

1. Place the chicken legs and thighs in a glass baking dish. In a bowl, combine the oil, chili sauce, cumin seeds, saffron, salt, lemon juice and ¼ cup of the coriander. Pour this mixture over the chicken and turn to coat. Cover and marinate at room temperature for 1 hour or for up to 4 hours in the refrigerator.

2. Heat two deep heavy skillets over moderate heat. Add half of the chicken pieces to each pan and cook, turning frequently, until evenly browned, about 15 minutes. Remove the chicken and set aside.

3. Pour off all the fat from the pans. Add 2 cups of the stock to each pan and bring to a boil over high heat, scraping to dislodge any browned bits from the bottoms. Pour all the stock into one pan, add the pasta and cook for 2 minutes, stirring frequently.

4. Return the chicken to the pan. Reduce the heat to moderately low, cover tightly and simmer until the pasta and chicken are cooked through, about 20 minutes.

5. Transfer the chicken to a warmed platter or plates and sprinkle the remaining ¼ cup chopped coriander on top. Serve the pasta alongside.

—*Bob Chambers*

• • •

CHICKEN THIGHS WITH TARRAGON WINE VINEGAR

This recipe is a variation of a French classic. With its tangy sauce, the best accompaniment is buttered noodles with lots of black pepper.

🍷 The tart notes contributed by the vinegar and tomatoes suggest a medium-bodied, unfussy red, such as Rioja. A 1984 Bodegas Muga or a 1985 Marqués de Cáceres would be a fine choice.

——— **4 Servings** ———
2 tablespoons all-purpose flour
1 teaspoon salt
½ teaspoon freshly ground pepper
½ teaspoon celery seeds
8 chicken thighs
2 tablespoons olive oil
1 head of garlic, cloves peeled
1 cup tarragon wine vinegar
1 can (14 ounces) crushed tomatoes
1 can (10½ ounces) low-sodium chicken broth
1 tablespoon tomato paste
1½ teaspoons tarragon
¼ cup chopped parsley

1. In a shallow bowl, combine the flour, salt, pepper and celery seeds. Dredge the thighs in the flour mixture.

2. In a large nonreactive flameproof casserole, heat the oil over moderately high heat. Add the chicken, skin-side up, and cook, turning once, until well browned all over, 8 to 10 minutes.

3. Reduce the heat to low. Add the garlic, cover and cook until tender, turning the chicken once, about 15 minutes.

4. Tip the pan and drain off all the fat. Add the tarragon vinegar and bring to a boil over high heat; boil until the vinegar reduces by half, 5 to 7 minutes. Add the tomatoes, chicken broth, tomato paste and tarragon to the casserole and return to a boil. Reduce the heat to moderate and simmer the chicken, turning once, until tender, about 15 minutes.

5. Transfer the chicken to a warmed platter and cover with foil to keep warm. Pass the sauce through a food mill or sieve. Alternatively, transfer the sauce to a food processor or blender and puree until smooth. *(The recipe can be prepared to this point up to 2 days ahead. Cover and refrigerate. Reheat before serving.)* Stir the parsley into the sauce and pour it over the chicken. Serve hot.

—*Bob Chambers*

• • •

PESTO CHICKEN CASSOULET

This hearty one-dish meal needs nothing more in the way of accompaniment than a loaf of bread or lightly buttered noodles.
♥ Full-bodied white, such as 1988 Clos du Bois Chardonnay, or fruity red, such as 1986 Louis M. Martini Pinot Noir

——————— 8 Servings ———————

⅔ *cup all-purpose flour*
2 *teaspoons salt*
2½ *teaspoons freshly ground black pepper*
8 *chicken thighs, patted dry*
8 *chicken legs, patted dry*
3 *tablespoons olive oil*
2 *pounds small zucchini*
6 *shallots, thinly sliced*
3 *garlic cloves, crushed*
4 *red bell peppers, cut into ¼-inch strips*

4 *yellow bell peppers, cut into ¼-inch strips*
1 *jar (7 ounces) pesto (¾ cup)*
1½ *cups crème fraîche*
1 *cup freshly grated Parmesan cheese (about 4 ounces)*
1½ *cups fresh bread crumbs*
1½ *teaspoons thyme*
¼ *teaspoon cayenne pepper*

1. In a shallow bowl, combine the flour, salt and 2 teaspoons of the black pepper. Dredge the chicken parts in the flour mixture. Shake off any excess.

2. In a large flameproof casserole, heat 2 tablespoons of the olive oil over moderately high heat. Add the chicken in batches and cook, turning often, until evenly browned, about 15 minutes. Transfer the chicken to paper towels to drain. Wipe out the casserole.

3. Meanwhile, quarter the zucchini lengthwise, then slice crosswise into ½-inch pieces.

4. In a medium casserole, heat the remaining 1 tablespoon olive oil over moderately high heat. Add the shallots and cook until translucent, 2 to 3 minutes. Add the garlic and cook for 1 minute longer, then add the red and yellow bell peppers and the zucchini and cook until softened, 5 to 7 minutes. Remove from the heat.

5. In a small bowl, combine the pesto with the crème fraîche and whisk until blended. In another bowl, toss the Parmesan cheese with the bread crumbs, thyme, cayenne and the remaining ½ teaspoon black pepper.

6. Preheat the oven to 375°. Return the chicken to the large casserole and spread the vegetable mixture evenly on top. Spread the pesto cream over the vegetables. *(The recipe can be prepared to this point up to 2 days ahead and refrigerated. Let return to room temperature before proceeding.)*

7. Sprinkle the Parmesan crumbs evenly over the casserole and bake in the

middle of the oven for 45 minutes. Heat the broiler. Broil the cassoulet for 2 to 3 minutes to brown the topping. Serve hot, directly from the casserole.

—*Bob Chambers*

• • •

PEANUT-FRIED DRUMSTICKS WITH CURRIED CUCUMBERS

Double dipping these drumsticks ensures an even coating, and chopped peanuts give them a special crunch. They're started in a skillet and finished in the oven to avoid deep-frying.

——————— 8 Servings ———————

1⅓ *cups all-purpose flour*
3 *tablespoons plus 1½ teaspoons curry powder*
4½ *teaspoons dried dill weed*
2½ *teaspoons freshly ground black pepper*
2 *teaspoons salt*
16 *chicken drumsticks, skinned and patted dry*
1 *jar (8 ounces) unsalted dry roasted peanuts*
1½ *teaspoons crushed hot pepper*
2 *eggs*
2 *tablespoons milk*
1 *cup olive oil*
2 *European cucumbers*
2 *medium shallots, minced*
1 *teaspoon dill seeds*

1. Preheat the oven to 400°. In a medium bowl, combine the flour with 3 tablespoons of the curry powder, 4 teaspoons of the dill weed, 2 teaspoons of the black pepper and 1½ teaspoons of the salt. Dredge the drumsticks in the flour mixture to coat thoroughly. Shake off the excess flour and set the chicken aside on a rack. Reserve the flour mixture.

2. In a food processor, combine the peanuts, hot pepper and 2 tablespoons of the reserved flour mixture. Pulse until the nuts are finely chopped, then transfer the mixture to a shallow bowl.

3. In another shallow bowl, beat the eggs with the milk. Dredge the drumsticks in the flour mixture once more, then dip them in the egg mixture and then into the ground peanuts, turning to coat completely.

4. Set aside 1½ tablespoons of the olive oil. In a large, high-sided skillet, heat half of the remaining oil over moderately high heat until it just begins to smoke. Add half of the drumsticks and fry, turning, until evenly browned, 10 to 12 minutes. Be careful not to break the delicate crust as you turn the legs. Transfer the chicken to a clean rack set over a baking sheet. Repeat with the remaining oil and drumsticks.

5. Bake the chicken on the rack in the middle of the oven for 35 to 40 minutes, until tender when pierced with a fork.

6. Meanwhile, cut the cucumbers lengthwise into eighths, then slice them crosswise at 1½-inch intervals.

7. In a large skillet, heat the reserved 1½ tablespoons olive oil over moderate heat. Add the shallots and cook until translucent, 2 to 3 minutes. Add the cucumbers and sprinkle with the dill seeds and the remaining 1½ teaspoons curry powder and ½ teaspoon each dill weed, black pepper and salt. Cover and cook, stirring frequently, until the cucumbers are tender, 4 to 6 minutes. Remove from the heat.

8. To serve, reheat the cucumbers if necessary. Mound the cucumbers on a serving platter and arrange the drumsticks alongside.

—Bob Chambers

• • •

SPICED HONEY WINGS WITH POPPY AND SESAME SEEDS

This dish is made with just the meatiest portion of the wing, which is sometimes called the drumette. Save the rest of the wings in the freezer for making stock.

———————— *8 Servings* ————————
24 chicken wings
1 tablespoon dry mustard
1 teaspoon ground ginger
¼ teaspoon allspice
1 teaspoon salt
1 teaspoon freshly ground pepper
⅓ cup poppy seeds
⅓ cup sesame seeds
⅓ cup honey

1. Preheat the oven to 400°. Line a baking sheet with foil and set a rack on top. Remove the tip and mid-section from the wings and reserve for stock. Pat the remaining wing sections (the drumettes) dry with paper towels.

2. In a large bowl, combine the mustard, ginger, allspice, salt, pepper, poppy seeds, sesame seeds and honey; stir well. Toss the drumettes in the honey mixture until thoroughly coated. Transfer them to the rack and bake for 20 minutes.

3. Turn the drumettes and bake for 20 minutes longer. Remove from the oven.

4. Preheat the broiler. Broil the drumettes 4 to 5 inches from the heat, watching them carefully and turning once, for 1 to 2 minutes per side, or until nicely browned. Serve immediately.

—Bob Chambers

• • •

CHICKEN AND SPINACH CAKES WITH SHIITAKE MUSHROOM SAUCE

If the fresh shiitakes called for here are not available, any other wild mushrooms could be used in their place.

❦ The earthy, savory richness of the sauce is best paired with a flavorful but not overbearing red, such as a 1989 Charles Shaw Harvest Wine or 1988 Parducci Pinot Noir.

———————— *8 Servings* ————————
¼ cup plus 2 tablespoons olive oil
¾ pound shallots, thinly sliced
¼ pound bacon, coarsely chopped
1½ pounds skinless, boneless chicken breasts, cut into ½-inch cubes
1 package (10 ounces) frozen chopped spinach, thawed and squeezed dry
¾ cup heavy cream
1½ cups fresh bread crumbs
1½ teaspoons freshly ground black pepper
¾ teaspoon salt
¼ teaspoon cayenne pepper
1 tablespoon unsalted butter
2 pounds fresh shiitake mushrooms, stems discarded, caps thinly sliced
½ teaspoon thyme
1 can (10½ ounces) low-sodium chicken broth

1. In a large heavy saucepan, heat 2 tablespoons of the olive oil. Add the shallots and cook over moderate heat, stirring occasionally, until lightly golden, 8 to 10 minutes. Set aside.

2. Place the bacon in a food processor and pulse until finely chopped. Transfer the bacon to a large bowl. Add half of the chicken to the processor and pulse until minced. Add the minced chicken to the bacon in the bowl. Repeat with the remaining chicken cubes.

3. To the bowl, add the spinach, 6 tablespoons of the heavy cream, ⅓ cup of the bread crumbs, ½ cup of the cooked shallots, 1 teaspoon of the black pepper and the salt and cayenne. Mix well to thoroughly blend the ingredients. Form the mixture into 16 little round cakes.

4. Preheat the oven to 400°. In a shallow bowl, mix the remaining bread crumbs with the remaining ½ teaspoon black pepper. Coat the cakes with the seasoned bread crumbs.

5. In a large skillet, heat 2 tablespoons of the olive oil over moderately high heat. Add 8 of the cakes and fry, turning once, until browned, about 3 minutes per side. Transfer to a baking sheet. Repeat with 1 more tablespoon of the olive oil and the remaining 8 chicken cakes. Bake the cakes for 10 to 12 minutes, until firm.

6. Meanwhile, reheat the shallots over high heat. Stir in the butter, mushrooms, thyme and the remaining 1 tablespoon olive oil. Cover and cook, stirring frequently, until the mushrooms soften and begin to brown, 4 to 5 minutes.

7. Stir in the chicken broth and the remaining 6 tablespoons heavy cream and bring to a boil; cook until the sauce reduces and lightly coats the back of a spoon, 8 to 10 minutes. Season the sauce with salt and pepper to taste.

8. To serve, place 2 chicken cakes on each of 8 warmed plates and spoon a generous amount of mushrooms and sauce on top.

—Bob Chambers

• • •

LIGHT AND EASY DINNER

Serves 8

Scallion and Buttermilk
Pancakes (p. 163)

Smoked Salmon or Golden Caviar
and Crème Fraîche

Roast Cornish Hens with Garlic
Cream (p. 81)

Roasted New Potatoes

♟ California Chardonnay, such as
1988 Vichon or Kendall-Jackson
Vintner's Reserve

Sliced Oranges in Red Wine
Syrup (p. 214)

—Perla Meyers

ROAST CORNISH HENS WITH GARLIC CREAM

——— 8 Servings ———

7 tablespoons unsalted butter
1 tablespoon all-purpose flour
1½ teaspoons Dijon-style mustard
1 teaspoon thyme
1 teaspoon marjoram
1 teaspoon imported sweet paprika
4 Cornish hens (about 1¼ pounds each), patted dry
Coarse (kosher) salt and freshly ground pepper
1 tablespoon peanut oil
2 small onions, halved
1¼ cups chicken stock or canned broth
8 large garlic cloves
1½ cups heavy cream
Watercress, for garnish

1. Preheat the oven to 450°. In a small bowl, rub 1 tablespoon of the butter into the flour until blended to a paste.

2. In another bowl, combine the mustard, thyme, marjoram and paprika. Truss the hens and rub them all over with the mustard-herb mixture. Season lightly with salt and pepper.

3. Spread 2 tablespoons of the butter and the oil in a small roasting pan. Set the hens in the pan on their sides. Arrange the onions around the hens and pour in ¼ cup of the stock. Roast the hens in the middle of the oven for 30 to 40 minutes, turning once and basting every 10 minutes with the pan juices and an additional 2 tablespoons of the chicken stock. The hens are done when the thighs are pierced and the juices run clear. Transfer the hens to a cutting board with tongs, cover loosely with foil and let stand for about 15 minutes before serving.

4. Meanwhile, in a small saucepan of boiling water, blanch the garlic cloves for 1 minute; drain. Add fresh water to the saucepan, bring to a boil and add the blanched garlic cloves. Cook until tender, about 10 minutes; drain well.

5. In a food processor, puree the garlic cloves. Add the cream and process until thick, about 1 minute. Set aside.

6. Discard the onions in the roasting pan and pour the juices into a bowl. Skim off as much fat as possible. Return the juices to the pan and add the remaining chicken stock. Boil over moderately high heat until the liquid reduces to ¾ cup, about 7 minutes.

7. Whisk in the garlic cream and boil to reduce slightly, about 5 minutes. Gradually whisk in the reserved butter-and-flour paste, bit by bit, then remove the pan from the heat and gradually whisk in the remaining 4 tablespoons butter. Season the sauce with salt and pepper to taste.

8. Remove the strings from the hens, cut them in half and place on individual plates. Spoon some of the sauce around the hens and garnish with the watercress. Pass the remaining sauce separately.

—Perla Meyers

• • •

STUFFED CORNISH HENS

Follow the recipe for Roasted Squab with Shiitake Mushroom and Chicken Liver Stuffing (at right), but use eight 1-pound Cornish hens (reserve wing tips and neck trimmings for the Enriched Stock). Loosen the breast and thigh skin of the birds and place ½ cup of the stuffing under the skin of each; press gently to evenly distribute. Truss if you like. Arrange the hens so that they do not touch on two large baking sheets with shallow sides, and spread with the thyme butter. Roast on the top rack of a preheated 500° oven for 15 minutes. Reduce the temperature to 450° and roast, basting occasionally, for 20 to 25 minutes longer, or until an instant-read thermometer inserted in a thigh registers 160°. Halve the hens lengthwise, cover loosely with foil and let rest for 10 minutes while you prepare the sauce. Serve one hen per person.

—*Lydie Pinoy Marshall*

• • •

STUFFED CAPON

Follow the recipe for Roasted Squab with Shiitake Mushroom and Chicken Liver Stuffing (at right), but use a 9- to 10-pound capon (reserve wing tips and neck trimmings for the Enriched Stock). Loosen the breast and thigh skin of the bird with your hands and place the stuffing under the skin; press gently to evenly distribute it. Set the capon in a roasting pan, without trussing, and spread the thyme butter over the breast and thighs. Roast the capon at 425° for 15 minutes, then reduce the temperature to 400° and roast, basting occasionally, for about 1¼ hours, or until an instant-read thermometer inserted in a thigh registers 170°. Remove the capon from the oven and carve off the leg-thigh pieces. Transfer them to a smaller pan and roast for 30 minutes longer, basting occasionally. Set the breast on a large platter and cover

loosely with foil while you prepare the sauce. Carve the legs and thighs and slice the breast carefully so that each slice has some stuffing.

—*Lydie Pinoy Marshall*

• • •

THANKSGIVING DINNER MENU

Serves 8

Alsatian Pizza (p. 32)

🍷 *Alsace Riesling or Champagne*

Flageolet Bean Soup with Fresh Thyme (p. 45)

Roasted Squab with Shiitake Mushroom and Chicken Liver Stuffing (p. 82)

Potato and Celery Root Puree with Glazed Cranberries (p. 129)

Sautéed Broccoli and Cherry Tomatoes (p. 122)

🍷 *1985 Burgundy, such as Joseph Drouhin Pommard-Epenots or Guigal Côte Rôtie*

Chocolate Pecan Tart (p. 169)

—*Lydie Pinoy Marshall*

ROASTED SQUAB WITH SHIITAKE MUSHROOM AND CHICKEN LIVER STUFFING

I suggest that you start preparing this dish two days in advance. First make the stuffing and let it marinate overnight in the refrigerator. The next day cook the stuffing, and when it's cold, stuff the birds. (Since the stuffing will be fully cooked, there is no danger of bacteria developing.) Then, all you'll have to do is roast the birds and make the sauce.

The recipe that follows can be used to roast quail, capon or Cornish hens. Proceed with this recipe, making adjustments for the stuffing and roasting of the various birds as explained in the recipes on pages 82 and 84.

————— *8 Servings* —————
1 pound fresh shiitake mushrooms, stems discarded, caps minced
½ pound chicken livers, trimmed and finely chopped
5 to 6 large shallots, minced (¾ cup)
½ cup minced parsley
2 tablespoons minced garlic
2 tablespoons minced chives
1 tablespoon fresh thyme or 1½ teaspoons dried
1½ teaspoons coarse (kosher) salt
¾ teaspoon freshly ground pepper
1 stick (4 ounces) unsalted butter, at room temperature
2 tablespoons olive oil
1 cup freshly grated Gruyère cheese (about 3 ounces)
8 partially boned squab, necks and wing tips removed and reserved
Enriched Stock (recipe follows)

1. In a medium bowl, combine the mushrooms, chicken livers, shallots, parsley, garlic and chives. Add 1 teaspoon of the fresh thyme (or ½ teaspoon dried) and the salt and pepper; mix well. Cover and refrigerate for 6 hours or overnight to blend the flavors.

2. In a large skillet, melt 2 tablespoons of the butter with the olive oil over moderately high heat. Add the stuffing mixture and reduce the heat to low. Cover tightly and cook, stirring occasionally, until the mushrooms release their liquid and the liver is cooked through, about 10 minutes.

3. Remove from the heat and let cool to room temperature. Stir in the Gruyère cheese and season with salt and pepper to taste. Cover and refrigerate until cold.

4. Meanwhile, in a small bowl, blend 4 tablespoons of the butter with the remaining 2 teaspoons fresh thyme (or 1 teaspoon dried).

5. Stuff the cavity of each squab with ½ cup of the stuffing and fold the neck skin over to enclose it completely. Using your hands, re-form the squab to give them a nice shape; then truss them.

6. Arrange the squab, breast-side up and without touching, on a large jelly-roll pan or other large pan with shallow sides. Spread the thyme butter over the breasts and thighs. *(The recipe can be prepared to this point up to 1 day ahead. Cover the birds with plastic wrap and refrigerate overnight. Let return to room temperature for 1 hour before roasting.)*

7. Preheat the oven to 425°. Roast the squab on the top rack of the oven, basting occasionally with the pan drippings, for about 25 minutes, until golden brown and an instant-read thermometer inserted in a thigh registers 145°. Transfer the birds to a work surface and cut them in half lengthwise with a large, sharp knife. Return to the baking pan and cover loosely with foil. Let rest for 10 minutes while you prepare the sauce.

8. Pour all the juices from the roasting pan into a small saucepan, scraping in all the browned bits from the bottom of the pan. Skim the fat from the surface. Stir in the Enriched Stock and bring to a boil over high heat. Boil, skimming as necessary, until reduced to 1 cup, about 3

minutes. Remove from the heat and whisk in the remaining 2 tablespoons butter. Season with salt and pepper to taste and strain into a sauceboat. Place a halved squab on each of 8 heated dinner plates and pass the sauce separately.

—*Lydie Pinoy Marshall*

• • •

ENRICHED STOCK

──────── *Makes 1 Cup* ────────
2 tablespoons unsalted butter
Reserved wing tips and neck trimmings from the squab
2 shallots, coarsely chopped
1 carrot, coarsely chopped
¼ pound mushrooms, coarsely chopped
5 parsley sprigs
2 cups chicken stock or low-sodium canned broth

1. In a large skillet, melt the butter over high heat. Add the reserved wing tips and necks and cook, stirring occasionally, until well browned all over, about 10 minutes. Add the shallots, carrot, mushrooms and parsley and cook for 5 minutes longer, stirring occasionally.

2. Add 1 cup of the stock to the skillet and bring to a boil. Reduce the heat to moderate and boil until reduced by half, about 5 minutes. Add the remaining 1 cup of stock and boil until 1 cup of liquid remains, about 5 minutes longer. Strain and let cool, then refrigerate. Skim off all the fat that congeals on the surface. *(The stock can be made 1 day ahead.)*

—*Lydie Pinoy Marshall*

• • •

ROAST DUCK WITH PORT-SOAKED PRUNES

The deep black-purple prunes and the golden brown caramelized onions add an autumnal feel to this dish. The duck is delicious with roast potatoes and sautéed Swiss chard.

──────── *4 to 6 Servings* ────────
4 or 5 small garlic cloves, minced
1¼ teaspoons cinnamon
1 tablespoon plus 1 teaspoon fresh lemon juice
2 whole ducks (about 5 pounds each), trimmed of excess fat
¾ teaspoon salt
¾ teaspoon freshly ground pepper
24 pitted prunes (8 ounces)
2¼ cups port
1 pint pearl onions
2 tablespoons unsalted butter
1 teaspoon sugar
1 cup chicken stock or canned low-sodium broth
3 tablespoons orange juice
1 teaspoon grated orange zest

1. Preheat the oven to 500°. In a small bowl, combine the garlic, 1 teaspoon of the cinnamon and the lemon juice. Crush with the back of a spoon into a rough paste.

2. Rub the insides of the ducks with the paste and lightly season the outside with ¼ teaspoon each of the salt and pepper. Place on a rack in a large roasting pan and roast about 1 hour or until browned and the juices run clear when the thigh is pierced with a knife.

3. Meanwhile, in a small nonreactive saucepan, combine the prunes with 1 cup of the port. Bring to a simmer over moderately high heat. Remove from the heat, cover and set aside for at least 30 minutes and up to 2 hours.

4. Make a cross in the root end of each pearl onion. In a medium saucepan of boiling salted water, cook the onions until tender, 5 to 7 minutes; drain and let cool. Peel and trim.

5. In a small skillet, melt the butter over high heat. Add the cooked onions and sprinkle with the sugar. Cook, shaking the pan constantly, until the onions have caramelized to a rich brown, about 3 minutes. Set aside.

6. In a medium nonreactive saucepan, bring the remaining 1¼ cups port and the chicken stock to a boil over high heat and reduce to 1 cup, about 10 minutes.

7. Add the orange juice, orange zest, the remaining ¼ teaspoon cinnamon, the prunes and their liquid and onions to the sauce. Season with the remaining ½ teaspoon each salt and pepper. Cook to warm through, about 3 minutes.

8. Cut the breasts from the ducks and slice each in half. Remove the legs and separate the drumsticks and thighs. Arrange the duck pieces on a large warmed serving platter. Spoon the prunes, onions and sauce on top. Serve hot.

—*Joyce Goldstein*

• • •

DUCK WITH SWEET AND SOUR WILD MUSHROOM CIDER SAUCE

———— *2 Servings* ————
1 whole duck (about 4½ pounds), trimmed of excess fat
Salt and freshly ground white pepper
1 onion, quartered
2 celery ribs, coarsely chopped
1 bay leaf, broken in half
8 ounces sliced bacon, cut into 1-inch pieces
½ pound fresh shiitake mushrooms, stems discarded, caps coarsely chopped

2 cups unfiltered, unpasteurized apple cider
1 tablespoon all-purpose flour
2 tablespoons Cognac or other brandy
2 tablespoons red wine vinegar
½ teaspoon thyme

1. Preheat the oven to 400°. Cut the wing tips off the duck. Sprinkle the duck inside and out with ½ teaspoon each of the salt and white pepper, then truss it with string if desired. Prick the duck all over at 1-inch intervals and place it, breast-side down, in a roasting pan just large enough to hold it. Arrange the onion, celery and bay leaf around it.

2. Roast the duck for 15 minutes. Turn the duck breast-side up and prick again. Continue to roast, turning every 15 minutes, for 45 to 55 minutes more, until the duck is browned and the juices run clear when a thigh is pierced.

3. While the duck roasts, begin making the sauce. In a large skillet, cook the bacon over moderately high heat until lightly browned but not crisp, about 7 minutes. Using a slotted spoon, transfer the bacon to paper towels to drain.

4. Pour off all but 2 tablespoons of the bacon fat from the skillet. Add the mushrooms and cook, stirring, until their juices evaporate, about 10 minutes.

5. Add ½ cup of the cider to the skillet, bring to a boil and cook until the liquid has been reduced by half, about 4 minutes. Whisk in the flour until thoroughly blended. Remove from the heat and set aside.

6. When the duck is cooked, remove it from the roasting pan and cut it in half lengthwise with poultry shears. Cut out and discard the backbone. Cover the duck halves with foil and keep them warm in a low oven. Discard the fat and vegetables in the roasting pan.

7. Pour the remaining 1½ cups cider into the roasting pan and bring to a boil,

scraping the bottom to release any browned bits. Pour the contents of the roasting pan over the mushrooms in the skillet. Add the Cognac, vinegar and thyme and bring to a boil over moderate heat. Cook, stirring frequently, until the sauce thickens slightly, about 10 minutes.

8. Stir in the reserved bacon and season with additional salt and white pepper to taste. Serve the duck on heated plates with the sauce spooned on top.

—*Linda Merinoff*

• • •

STUFFED QUAIL

Follow the recipe for Roast Squab with Shiitake Mushroom and Chicken Liver Stuffing (p. 82), but use 16 partially boned quail (reserve wing tips and neck trimmings for the Enriched Stock). Scoop ¼ cup of the stuffing into the cavities and re-form the birds with your hands. Truss if desired. Arrange the quail so that they do not touch on two large baking sheets with shallow sides, and spread with the thyme butter. Roast the quail on the top rack of a preheated 500° oven for 15 minutes, or until an instant-read thermometer inserted in a thigh registers 145°. (If the quail look pale, you can place them under a preheated broiler, 5 inches from the heat, for 1½ minutes to brown.) Remove from the oven and let rest for 5 minutes while you prepare the sauce. Serve two quail per person.

—*Lydie Pinoy Marshall*

• • •

MEAT

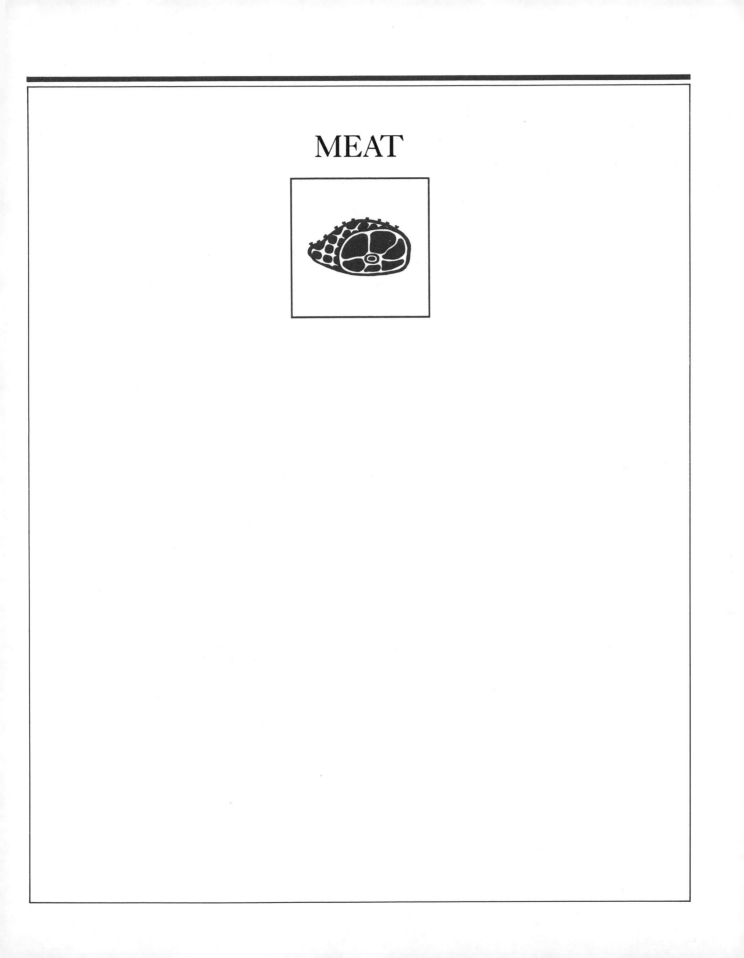

LEMON-HERB VEAL ROAST

Although less expensive than other cuts of veal because it comes from the shoulder, the roast emerges tender and delicious after marinating for 24 hours in a lemony herb mixture. Use the leftovers to make great sandwiches. Serve thin slices of veal on hearty bread slathered with Garlic-Oregano Mayonnaise.

——————— *12 Servings* ———————
*1 boneless veal shoulder roast
  (about 5 pounds), trimmed and
  tied*
2 large garlic cloves, minced
⅔ cup fresh lemon juice
¼ cup white wine vinegar
*2 tablespoons fresh oregano leaves,
  minced, or 1 tablespoon dried*
*1 tablespoon fresh thyme, minced,
  or 1½ teaspoons dried*
½ teaspoon salt
*1½ teaspoons coarsely ground
  pepper*
⅔ cup extra-virgin olive oil
*Garlic-Oregano Mayonnaise
  (p. 254)*

1. Place the veal roast in a large nonreactive bowl. In a medium bowl, whisk together the garlic, lemon juice, vinegar, oregano, thyme, salt and pepper. Add the oil in a slow, steady stream, whisking constantly until incorporated. Pour this marinade over the veal and turn to coat. Cover with plastic wrap and refrigerate overnight, turning once or twice. Remove from the refrigerator and let sit at room temperature for 1 hour before roasting.

2. Preheat the oven to 350°. Remove the veal from the marinade and transfer it to a roasting pan. Roast the veal for 1 hour and 45 minutes, or until the internal temperature reaches 160° on an instant-read thermometer. Remove from the oven and let rest for at least 10 minutes before carving.

3. Thinly slice the veal and arrange on a platter. Before serving, pour any cooking juices over the meat. Serve warm or at room temperature with Garlic-Oregano Mayonnaise.

—*Tracey Seaman*

• • •

TREE-TRIMMING BUFFET

Serves 12

Pork and Olive Finger Pies (p. 37)

Parmesan Trees (p. 27)

Confetti Shrimp (p. 57)

Lemon-Herb Veal Roast (p. 86)

Citrus Green Bean Salad (p. 144)

*Manicotti Crêpes with Spinach and
Cheese (p. 38)*

*Christmas Salad with Red and
Green Vinaigrette (p. 142)*

🍷 *Light, fruity red wine, such as
1988 Mommessin or Georges
Duboeuf Beaujolais-Villages, and a
soft fruity-but-dry white wine, such
as nonvintage Trefethen Eschol
White*

Spiced Angel Cookies (p. 194)

Lazy Linzer Squares (p. 193)

Coffee Cup Truffles (p. 216)

—*Tracey Seaman*

VITELLO TONNATO

This unusual but felicitous pairing of veal and canned tuna is a classic that's enjoyed throughout Italy. The meat can be cooked and refrigerated well ahead. However, since it must be thinly sliced and has a tendency to dry out, the dish should be assembled shortly before serving. Traditionally, the sliced veal is arranged on a large platter, and the sauce is poured over the meat. The classic garnishes for this dish are black olives, anchovies, capers and lemon wedges, plus tomatoes. A crisp mixed salad would be lovely alongside.

🍷 Light red Rioja, such as 1985 Bodegas Olarra Añares or 1985 La Rioja Alta Viña Alberdi

——————— *8 Servings* ———————
*3-pound trimmed veal roast, such as
  leg, top round or shoulder, tied*
*2 medium carrots, halved
  lengthwise*
*1 medium onion, halved, each half
  stuck with 1 clove*
1 celery rib, quartered
1 bay leaf
2 parsley sprigs
1 cup dry white wine
*1 cup chicken stock or canned
  low-sodium broth*
1 can (2 ounces) flat anchovy fillets
1 can (6½ ounces) tuna in olive oil
2 tablespoons fresh lemon juice
1 cup mayonnaise
¼ cup sour cream
*⅛ teaspoon freshly ground white
  pepper*
*Black olives, drained capers and
  lemon and tomato wedges, for
  garnish*

1. In a medium flameproof casserole, combine the veal roast, carrots, onion, celery, bay leaf, parsley, wine and chicken stock. Bring to a boil over high heat. Reduce the heat to low, cover and sim-

mer, turning the veal occasionally, until it is tender and the internal temperature reaches 160° on an instant-read thermometer, about 1 hour and 40 minutes.

2. Remove from the heat, uncover and let cool. Remove and discard the vegetables. Cover the meat and refrigerate overnight or for up to 2 days.

3. Skim the fat from the surface of the jellied cooking liquid. In a food processor, combine 6 tablespoons of the cooking liquid with 3 of the anchovies, the tuna with its oil and the lemon juice. Puree until smooth. Scrape the sauce into a bowl, cover and refrigerate for at least 30 minutes and up to 1 day.

4. Remove the roast from the casserole and place on a cutting board. Using a sharp knife, thinly slice the meat. Arrange the meat on a large platter or on individual plates. (If not serving immediately, cover the platter or the individual plates well with plastic wrap to prevent the meat from drying out.)

5. Add the mayonnaise, sour cream and pepper to the tuna sauce and stir until well blended. Pour the sauce over the plattered veal and pass the remainder separately. Garnish with the remaining anchovies and the olives, capers and lemon and tomato wedges.

—*W. Peter Prestcott*

• • •

STUFFED VEAL LOIN

Ask your butcher to trim off the fat and separate the tenderloin from the loin. Serve this entrée with risotto and broiled tomatoes.

🍷 1986 Robert Mondavi Pinot Noir Reserve goes well with the meaty, yet delicate flavor of the veal.

———— *8 to 10 Servings* ————
1 tablespoon unsalted butter
1 medium leek (white part and 2 inches of green), chopped

4-pound boneless loin of veal with flank attached and tenderloin separated
1 egg
½ cup fresh bread crumbs
¼ cup milk
¼ cup chopped parsley
½ teaspoon salt
¼ teaspoon freshly ground pepper

1. Preheat the oven to 400°. In a small skillet, melt the butter over moderate heat. Add the leek and cook, stirring occasionally, until softened, about 8 minutes. Remove from the heat and set aside.

2. Remove the strip of meat that runs down the length of the tenderloin and chop coarsely. Transfer the chopped meat to a food processor and process until smooth. Add the egg and process again. Using a rubber spatula, scrape the mixture into a medium bowl.

3. In a small bowl, combine the bread crumbs and milk and stir into the veal mixture. Blend in the parsley, salt, pepper and reserved leek.

4. Spread the stuffing over the inner surface of the veal loin where the bones were. Cut the tenderloin in half lengthwise. Lay the tenderloin halves end to end over the stuffing in the crease between the flank and the loin. Starting with the flank side, roll the loin jelly-roll fashion and tie with kitchen string to secure. Season with salt and pepper to taste.

5. Place the meat in a roasting pan and roast, turning every 15 minutes to brown evenly, for about 45 minutes, or until the internal temperature reaches 130°. Let the loin rest for about 15 minutes; then remove the string and carve into ½-inch-thick slices. Drizzle the pan juices on top.

—*Annie Roberts, The Robert Mondavi Winery, Oakville, California*

• • •

SAUTEED VEAL WITH SPINACH AND CREOLE MUSTARD SAUCE

At Brigtsen's, this delicate veal dish typifies new New Orleans cooking.

———— *6 Servings* ————
6 veal scaloppine (about 1½ pounds total)
1½ pounds fresh young spinach, large stems removed, thoroughly rinsed but not dried, or 2 packages (10 ounces each) frozen leaf spinach, thawed and squeezed dry
1 cup heavy cream
3 tablespoons Creole mustard*
2 tablespoons sour cream
6 tablespoons mild olive oil
½ cup all-purpose flour
2 tablespoons Creole Seasoning (p. 258)
2 tablespoons unsalted butter
1 tablespoon sesame seeds
½ cup low-sodium chicken broth
*Available at specialty food markets

1. Using a mallet or the flat side of a cleaver, pound the scaloppine to a ¼-inch thickness. Set aside.

2. In a large covered saucepan, cook the fresh spinach over moderate heat for 1 minute. Squeeze dry and set aside.

3. In a small saucepan, combine the cream, mustard and sour cream. Whisk over low heat and keep warm, whisking occasionally while you prepare the veal.

4. In a large heavy skillet, heat 2 tablespoons of the olive oil over moderately high heat. On a plate, combine the flour and 1 tablespoon plus 1 teaspoon of the Creole Seasoning. Lightly dredge the veal in the seasoned flour and shake off any excess. When the oil is hot, add 2 slices of the veal to the pan and cook until firm but barely cooked through, about 1 minute on each side. Transfer to a platter, cover loosely with aluminum foil and keep warm in a low oven. Repeat with the remaining olive oil and veal.

5. When all the meat has been cooked, drain any excess oil from the skillet. Add the butter and sesame seeds and cook over moderately high heat, stirring, until the seeds are browned and fragrant, about 2 minutes.

6. Add the remaining 2 teaspoons Creole Seasoning and cook for 2 minutes. Add the chicken broth and spinach and cook the mixture until it is nearly dry, about 5 minutes longer.

7. To serve, ladle a scant ¼ cup of the warm mustard sauce onto each of 6 warmed dinner plates. Spoon the spinach onto the sauce and top with the veal.

—*Frank Brigtsen,*
Brigtsen's, New Orleans

• • •

VEAL ROLLS WITH PEAS

When ripe, fresh tomatoes are not in season, I prefer to use canned plum tomatoes rather than fresh ones without any flavor. If you use frozen peas, defrost them by passing them under cold water before adding them to the tomatoes.

——— *12 Servings* ———
24 very thinly sliced veal scaloppine,
(about 1½ pounds total), pounded
to an even thickness
12 thin slices of pancetta, halved
crosswise (about ½ pound)
24 small fresh sage leaves
3 tablespoons extra-virgin olive oil
1 tablespoon finely chopped onion
1 pound plum tomatoes (about 6
medium), peeled and coarsely
chopped, or 1 can (35 ounces)
Italian plum tomatoes, drained
and coarsely chopped
2 tablespoons unsalted butter
1 cup dry white wine
2 pounds fresh peas, shelled, or 1
package (10 ounces) frozen peas,
thawed
Salt and freshly ground pepper
1 tablespoon finely chopped Italian
flat-leaf parsley

1. Trim each scaloppine into a 2-by-3-inch rectangle. Lay 12 of the scaloppine on a work surface. Top each with ½ slice of the pancetta and 1 sage leaf. Roll the scaloppine, starting at the short end. Fasten each roll with a wooden toothpick, threading it into the veal rolls lengthwise, so that they can turn easily in the pan. Alternatively, secure the rolls with thin cotton thread that you can remove before serving. Repeat with the remaining scaloppine, pancetta and sage. Set the rolls aside on a large platter.

2. In a medium nonreactive flameproof casserole, heat 1 tablespoon of the olive oil over low heat. Add the onion; cook until translucent, about 4 minutes. Add the tomatoes with their juices; simmer for 10 minutes.

3. Meanwhile, heat a large, heavy, nonreactive skillet over moderately high heat. Add 1 tablespoon of the olive oil and 1 tablespoon of the butter. Add 12 of the veal rolls and cook, turning until well browned all over, about 7 minutes. Using tongs, transfer the cooked veal to a platter. Repeat with the remaining 1 tablespoon each of oil and butter and the remaining veal rolls.

4. Add the wine to the skillet and bring to a boil, scraping up any browned bits from the bottom of the pan. Boil until the wine is reduced by half, about 1 minute.

5. Add the reduced wine to the tomatoes along with the peas. Place all the veal rolls in the casserole and cook until tender and cooked through but not dry and the sauce is thick, 20 to 25 minutes.

6. Transfer the veal rolls to a deep platter and remove the toothpicks or string. Season the sauce with salt and pepper to taste, stir in the parsley, and ladle over the veal to serve. Serve hot.

—*Lorenza de' Medici*

• • •

SPRINGTIME TUSCAN BUFFET

Serves 12

Crostini with Tarragon Spread
(p. 31)

Crostini with Tomato (p. 31)

Crostini with Beef and Balsamic
Vinegar (p. 32)

🍷 *Chilled Tuscan white, such as*
1987 Badia a Coltibuono or 1988 Il
Cipressino Vernaccia di San
Gimignano

Veal Rolls with Peas (p. 88)

Chicken Breasts with Fennel Sauce
(p. 77)

Risotto Mold with Prosciutto
(p. 115)

Spinach with Raisins and Pine Nuts
(p. 130)

Asparagus with Parmesan Cheese
(p. 120)

Olive Bread (p. 159)

Rosemary Breadsticks (p. 159)

🍷 *Chianti Classico Riserva, such as*
1983 Badia a Coltibuono or 1985
Castello di Querceto

Mascarpone Cream Dessert (p. 198)

Strawberry Sherbet with Cherry
Caramel Sauce (p. 209)

Raisins in Grappa (p. 215)
—*Lorenza de' Medici*

FAST-FIRE VEAL CHOPS

Crusty on the outside and juicy-pink within, these veal loin chops are marinated in a blend of olive oil, sherry, crushed green peppercorns, spicy mustard and Oriental seasonings.

♀ Although highly seasoned, the chops would be attractively matched by a tart, assertive Pinot Noir, served slightly cool for contrast. Try 1987 Knudsen-Erath Vintage Select from Oregon or 1987 De Loach from Sonoma.

——————— 4 Servings ———————
2½ tablespoons olive oil, plus more
   for brushing the grill
1½ tablespoons dark soy sauce
1½ tablespoons Spicy Mustard
   Sauce (p. 55)
1½ tablespoons medium-dry sherry
1 tablespoon light rice miso*
2 large scallions, thinly sliced
2 garlic cloves, minced
1½ tablespoons minced fresh ginger
1 tablespoon brined green
   peppercorns, drained and crushed
½ teaspoon freshly ground black
   pepper
4 veal loin chops, cut 1¼ inches
   thick (about 3 pounds total),
   trimmed
*Available at health food stores

1. In a bowl, whisk together the olive oil, soy sauce, Spicy Mustard Sauce, sherry and miso. Add the scallions, garlic, ginger, green peppercorns and black pepper, and stir to combine.

2. Using a sharp knife, score both sides of the veal chops about ¼ inch deep. Place the chops in a nonreactive dish large enough to accommodate them in a single layer. Rub the marinade into both sides of the chops. Cover and set aside at room temperature for 4 hours, or refrigerate for up to 12 hours. Remove from the refrigerator 30 minutes before cooking.

3. Prepare the fire. Brush the grill with olive oil. Place the marinated veal chops on the grill and cover, leaving all the vents wide open. Cook for 5 minutes, then rotate the chops 90° to achieve crisscross grilling marks. Cover and cook for 5 minutes longer. Turn the chops over and repeat the grilling process on the second side. Remove the chops from the grill and let rest for 5 minutes before serving.

—Karen Lee & Alaxandra Branyon

• • •

VEAL CROQUETTES WITH LEMON

These light croquettes are tender and delicate. Before cooking, the meat mixture is quite soft, so don't be alarmed when you are forming the croquettes. As they bake in the oven, the lemon and butter form a light, piquant sauce.

♀ The delicacy of these light croquettes and the piquancy of the lemon point to a crisp and tart Tuscan white, notably a 1987 Fontodi Meriggio or 1987 Avignonesi Chardonnay "Il Marzocco."

——————— 4 to 6 Servings ———————
12 slices of white sandwich bread,
   crusts removed
2 cups milk
¾ pound ground lean veal shoulder
4 eggs
1 cup freshly grated Italian
   Parmesan cheese (4 ounces)
¼ cup fresh lemon juice
¼ teaspoon salt
½ teaspoon freshly ground pepper
4 cups vegetable oil, for deep-frying
1½ cups unbleached all-purpose
   flour, for dredging
4 tablespoons cold unsalted butter,
   cut into bits

1. In a medium bowl, soak the bread in the milk for 30 minutes.

2. Squeeze the bread as dry as possible and place it in a large bowl; discard the milk. Add the ground veal, eggs, Parmesan, 2 tablespoons of the lemon juice and the salt and pepper. Mix very well with a wooden spoon until blended.

3. Preheat the oven to 300°. In a large, deep skillet or deep-fat fryer, heat the vegetable oil over moderate heat to 375°.

4. Meanwhile, form the veal mixture into egg-shaped croquettes, using ¼ cup of the mixture for each; the mixture will be quite soft. Lightly dredge the croquettes in the flour and fry in batches, turning once, until golden, about 5 minutes per batch. Drain on paper towels.

5. Arrange the croquettes in a single layer in a shallow roasting pan. Dot the tops with the bits of butter and drizzle on the remaining 2 tablespoons lemon juice. Bake for 10 minutes, until heated through. Serve with the pan juices spooned on top.

—Giuliano Bugialli

• • •

BEEF TENDERLOIN
WITH JUNIPER

Juniper berries abound in the woods of the Alps and Apennines. You can also find them in the spice rack at your supermarket. For our *filetto al ginepro*, we recommend using a small tenderloin because it is compact and holds together better than a larger one. Nice accompaniments to this dish are potatoes and green beans or Swiss chard.

♀ Nera Sfursat or 1983 Le Ragose Recioto della Valpolicella Amarone

——————— 6 Servings ———————
1 garlic clove
2½-pound beef tenderloin, trimmed
   and cut into 12 medallions (1 inch
   thick)
½ cup gin
36 juniper berries

1 teaspoon fresh thyme or ¼
    teaspoon dried, plus 6 sprigs of
    fresh thyme, for garnish
1 to 2 tablespoons unsalted butter
¾ cup mascarpone cheese
Salt and freshly ground pepper

1. Make several cuts in the garlic clove and rub the clove over the meat. Then rub the inside of a large heavy skillet, preferably cast iron, with the garlic. Set the skillet aside and discard the garlic.

2. Place the beef in a nonreactive dish. Pour ¼ cup of the gin over the meat. Using the side of a large knife or a mortar and pestle, crush 12 of the juniper berries and sprinkle them over the meat. Sprinkle the 1 teaspoon thyme on top. Cover and refrigerate for 1 hour, turning once.

3. Pat the meat dry, discarding any bits of juniper. Place the prepared skillet on the stove and turn the heat to high. When hot, after about 5 minutes, add 1 tablespoon of the butter. When the foaming subsides, arrange half of the meat slices in the pan and cook, turning once, until browned, about 1½ minutes on each side for medium-rare. Transfer to a platter. Add the remaining 1 tablespoon butter to the skillet if necessary, and repeat with the remaining meat.

4. Reduce the heat to low and add the remaining 24 whole juniper berries and ¼ cup gin to the skillet. Cook for about 45 seconds to burn off the alcohol. Stir in the mascarpone and cook until thoroughly melted, about 2 minutes. Season the sauce with salt and pepper to taste. Return the meat to the skillet and cook, spooning the sauce over the meat, until heated through, about 2 minutes.

5. Arrange the meat on 6 warmed dinner plates and spoon the sauce on top, making sure to include a few juniper berries in each serving. Garnish with the thyme sprigs.

—*Constance and Rosario del Nero*

• • •

STEAK AU POIVRE WITH WILD MUSHROOM CREAM SAUCE

This is a gala version of the classic *steak au poivre*. Black pepper adds a punch to the heavenly combination of cream, wild mushrooms and bourbon that makes up the sauce, but by coarsely grinding the spice instead of cracking it, the result is slightly less hot and spicy. I serve this dish with oven-roasted potatoes and buttered steamed vegetables.

❢ This straightforward peppered steak with its creamy mushroom sauce is a real match for a rich Burgundy, such as 1985 Domaine Dujac Gevrey-Chambertin "Les Combottes," or a fine Rhône, such as 1985 Guigal Côte Rôtie "Blonde et Brune."

——————— *6 Servings* ———————

1½ teaspoons coarsely ground black
    pepper
6 center-cut fillet steaks, 1½ inches
    thick
½ cup bourbon
1½ ounces dried porcini mushrooms
1 cup boiling water
1 tablespoon vegetable oil
2 tablespoons unsalted butter
½ cup minced shallots
1 garlic clove, minced
¾ cup heavy cream
Salt

1. Rub ⅛ teaspoon of the pepper onto each side of the steaks. Place the steaks in

a shallow dish and sprinkle with ¼ cup of the bourbon. Cover with plastic wrap and set aside at room temperature for 1 to 2 hours, turning occasionally.

2. Meanwhile, in a small heatproof bowl, cover the mushrooms with the boiling water. Set aside for 20 minutes.

3. Preheat the oven to 225°. Remove the mushrooms from their soaking liquid, reserving the liquid. Rinse the mushrooms well and drain. Cut off and discard any tough bits and finely chop. Strain the soaking liquid through a fine sieve lined with cheesecloth and reserve ½ cup.

4. In a large heavy skillet, heat the oil and butter over high heat until just beginning to shimmer. Add the steaks and cook until browned, about 2 minutes per side.

5. Remove the pan from the heat and add the remaining ¼ cup bourbon. Stand back and ignite with a long match, then shake the pan until the flames die down. Transfer the steaks to a heatproof platter and cook in the oven until done, about 15 minutes for medium.

6. Meanwhile, add the shallots and garlic to the skillet and cook over moderate heat, covered, until softened, 6 to 8 minutes.

7. Increase the heat to high, add the reserved ½ cup of mushroom soaking liquid and cook, stirring constantly, until syrupy, about 2 minutes. Stir in the cream and cook until slightly reduced, 2 to 3 minutes. Stir in the reserved mushrooms, reduce the heat to low and cook for 2 minutes longer. Season with salt to taste.

8. Transfer the steaks to 6 warmed plates. Stir any juices from the meat into the sauce and spoon over the steaks. Serve at once.

—*W. Peter Prestcott*

• • •

BEEF FILLET STEAKS IN MUSTARD SAUCE

———— *6 Servings* ————
1½ tablespoons grainy mustard
2 tablespoons crème fraîche
5 tablespoons plus 1 teaspoon
  unsalted butter
2 teaspoons all-purpose flour
1 teaspoon peanut oil
6 fillet steaks, ¾ inch thick, patted
  dry
½ teaspoon coarse (kosher) salt
Coarsely ground pepper
½ cup dry white wine
1 cup beef stock or canned broth
Watercress, for garnish

1. In a small bowl, whisk the mustard and crème fraîche until well blended.

2. In another small bowl, blend the 1 teaspoon butter with the flour to form a smooth paste.

3. In a large nonreactive skillet, melt 3 tablespoons of the butter with the peanut oil over high heat. When the foam subsides, add the steaks and sauté until well browned, about 1½ minutes per side. Reduce the heat to moderately high and season the meat with the salt and coarsely ground pepper to taste. Cover and cook for about 2 minutes longer on each side for medium rare. Remove the steaks to a plate.

4. Discard all the fat from the skillet. Add the remaining 2 tablespoons butter and melt over high heat. Add the wine and bring to a boil. Simmer, scraping the bottom of the pan to release any browned bits, until the liquid is reduced to 1 tablespoon, about 5 minutes.

5. Add the stock and the mustard mixture and bring to a boil. Boil until the liquid is reduced by one-fourth, about 4 minutes. Whisk in bits of the butter-and-flour paste until the sauce is just thick enough to coat a spoon. Season the sauce with salt and pepper to taste.

6. Reduce the heat to moderate and return the steaks to the skillet along with any accumulated juices. Spoon the sauce over the meat and simmer just until heated through, about 1 minute. Transfer the steaks to a warm serving platter and top with the sauce. Garnish with the watercress and serve at once.

—*Perla Meyers*

• • •

EARLY SPRING DINNER

Serves 6

Asparagus with Provençale Mayonnaise (p. 120)

Beef Fillet Steaks in Mustard Sauce (p. 91)

Stir-Fry of Snow Peas

Mocha Crème Brûlée (p. 198)

SLOW-FIRE CHINESE STEAK

This is a good example of a thick cut of meat that benefits from marinating and slow cooking.

———— *6 to 8 Servings* ————
2 tablespoons hoisin sauce*
2 tablespoons soy sauce
2 tablespoons medium-dry sherry
1 tablespoon plum sauce*
1 tablespoon miso*
2 scallions, sliced ⅛ inch thick
1 tablespoon minced fresh ginger
1 teaspoon minced garlic
1 boneless sirloin steak, cut 2 inches
  thick (about 2¼ pounds)
Oil, for brushing the grill
*Available at Oriental markets

1. In a medium bowl, whisk together the hoisin sauce, soy sauce, sherry, plum sauce, miso, scallions, ginger and garlic.

2. With a sharp knife, score the sirloin ¼ inch deep on both sides at 1-inch intervals. Place the steak on a large platter and rub the marinade into both sides. Cover and refrigerate for at least 2 hours or overnight. Remove from the refrigerator 30 minutes before cooking.

3. Prepare the fire. Brush the grill with oil. Place the steak in the center of the grill and cover, leaving all the vents wide open. Cook the steak for 5 minutes, then rotate it 90° to achieve crisscross grill marks. Cover and grill for 5 minutes longer or until browned around the edges. (If the steak is cooking too fast and beginning to char, move it to the side of the grill for the remainder of the cooking time.)

4. Turn the steak over and repeat the grilling process on the other side for 13 minutes longer for medium-rare, rotating it once after 5 minutes. Remove the steak from the grill and let rest for at least 10 minutes. Serve hot or at room temperature, thinly sliced against the grain.

—*Karen Lee & Alaxandra Branyon*

• • •

FAST-FIRE FLANK STEAK

The marinade below tenderizes the meat as it seasons it. Because flank steak is such a thin cut, it is cooked as soon as the outside is nicely seared. Any leftover steak, thinly sliced, makes excellent sandwiches the next day.

❦ This spicy, meaty dish calls for a substantial red. It could be a young, vigorous one, such as 1986 Guigal Côtes-du-Rhône, or an older, powerful one, such as 1980 Mastroberardino Taurasi Riserva.

—————— 3 to 4 Servings ——————
1 flank steak, trimmed (about 1¼ pounds)
1½ tablespoons brown sugar
1½ tablespoons soy sauce
1 tablespoon medium-dry sherry
1 tablespoon Oriental sesame oil
2 tablespoons sesame seeds
2 teaspoons minced garlic
1 teaspoon minced fresh ginger
2 scallions, sliced ⅛ inch thick
¼ teaspoon freshly ground pepper
Oil, for brushing the grill

1. With a sharp knife, score the flank steak ⅛ inch deep on both sides at 1-inch intervals. Place the steak in a nonreactive dish.

2. In a small bowl, whisk together the brown sugar, soy sauce, sherry, sesame oil, sesame seeds, garlic, ginger, scallions and pepper. Pour this marinade over the steak and rub it into both sides. Cover and let marinate in the refrigerator for at least 3 hours or overnight. Remove from the refrigerator 30 minutes before cooking.

3. Prepare the fire. Brush the grill with oil. Place the marinated steak in the center of the grill and cover, leaving all the vents wide open. Cook the steak for 3 minutes on each side for rare; 5 minutes per side for medium and 7 minutes per side for well done. Halfway through the cooking on each side, rotate the steak 90° to achieve crisscross grilling marks.

4. Remove the steak from the grill and let rest for 5 minutes. Serve hot, warm or cool, thinly sliced against the grain.

—*Karen Lee & Alaxandra Branyon*

• • •

BROILED FLANK STEAK WITH GARLIC, GINGER AND SOY SAUCE

Marinating this steak overnight will make it even more flavorful. And if you like a smoky barbecued flavor, try this on the outdoor grill whenever weather permits.

❦ Although many red wines are a good match for a steak, the spicy seasonings of the marinade—garlic, ginger and soy—require a gutsy, full-flavored red that won't be overpowered. Try a 1986 Foppiano Petite Sirah or 1988 Vietti Dolcetto d'Alba Sant'Anna.

—————— 4 Servings ——————
1 teaspoon minced fresh ginger
3 garlic cloves, crushed through a press
⅓ cup soy sauce
2 teaspoons vegetable oil
1⅓-pound flank steak

1. In a large shallow baking dish, combine the ginger, garlic, soy sauce and oil. Add the steak to the marinade and let sit for about 10 minutes or longer, turning occasionally. Meanwhile, preheat the broiler.

2. In a large broiler pan, broil the steak 7 inches from the heat about 3 minutes per side for rare, 4 minutes for medium-rare and 5 minutes for medium. Baste the steak with the marinade once or twice as it broils. Transfer the meat to a cutting board.

3. Let the steak sit for about 5 minutes before slicing. Using a very sharp knife, thinly slice the steak on a diagonal against the grain. Serve hot.

—*Pam Parseghian*

• • •

DINNER FOR A BUSY WEEKNIGHT

Serves 4

Broiled Flank Steak with Garlic, Ginger and Soy Sauce (p. 92)

Stir-Fried Sugar Snap Peas and Carrots with Oriental Noodles (p. 126)

❦ *1986 Foppiano Petite Sirah or 1988 Vietti Dolcetto d'Alba Sant'Anna*

Lemon Sorbet with Orange Liqueur (p. 210)

Fortune Cookies

Chinese Tea

—*Pam Parseghian*

GINGER-RUBBED FRESH HAM

Since fresh ginger is thought to have preserving qualities, I decided to use it as an interesting addition to a brine for fresh ham. Ginger, garlic, salt and brown sugar are rubbed into pork to cure it for two days. The brine ensures a very moist roast with a crusty, caramelized exterior. A nice accompaniment is Fried Ginger Rice (p. 116), which is even better if made with the pan juices from the baked ham.

—————— 4 to 6 Servings ——————
1 tablespoon finely grated fresh ginger
8 garlic cloves, minced
2 tablespoons light brown sugar

2 tablespoons coarse (kosher) salt
1 bone-in fresh ham (about 3½ pounds), fat trimmed to a thin layer
1 tablespoon extra-virgin olive oil
1 cup dry white wine

1. In a small bowl, mash the ginger, garlic, brown sugar and salt into a paste with a fork. Rub the paste all over the meat with your fingers. Place the ham in a large nonreactive dish or bowl, cover with plastic wrap and refrigerate for 2 days, turning occasionally.

2. Preheat the oven to 350°. Briefly rinse the ham to remove the bits of ginger and garlic. Pat dry. Place a large oven-proof skillet, preferably cast iron, on the stove and turn the heat to high. Add the olive oil and heat until rippling, about 2 minutes. Add the ham, fat-side down, and cook until browned, about 3 minutes. Turn and cook on the other side until browned, about 3 minutes.

3. Add the wine to the skillet and bake the ham in the upper part of the oven for 45 minutes. Add ½ cup of water and tilt the skillet to coat the pan with the water. Baste the ham. Continue to bake, basting occasionally and adding a few more tablespoons of water when dry, for about 1 hour, or until the internal temperature of the meat reaches 150°.

4. Transfer the ham to a warm platter to rest for about 10 minutes before slicing. Serve with the pan juices passed on the side.

—Marcia Kiesel

• • •

ROASTED LOIN OF PORK

Over the years I've tried all sorts of methods of cooking pork, and I've decided fast and simple is always the best.

—————— *6 Servings* ——————
1 boneless pork loin (about 3 pounds), trimmed of excess fat
½ small garlic clove, crushed
2 teaspoons dried rosemary, crumbled
¼ teaspoon salt
¼ teaspoon freshly ground pepper
¼ cup all-purpose flour

1. Preheat the oven to 500°. Rub the pork with the garlic. Pat on the rosemary and season with the salt and pepper. Lightly sprinkle 2½ tablespoons of the flour over the meat, shaking off any excess. Insert a meat thermometer into the center of the loin and place the meat in a large roasting pan on the bottom oven rack. Roast for 15 minutes, reduce the temperature to 325° and cook until the internal temperature on the thermometer reaches 160°, about 30 minutes. Transfer to a cutting board and cover with foil. Let sit 15 minutes before carving.

2. Meanwhile, skim the fat off the top of the pan juices; reserve 1 tablespoon of fat and put in a medium saucepan. Pour 1 cup of water into the roasting pan, scraping up any browned bits from the bottom of the pan.

3. Whisk the remaining 1½ tablespoons of flour into the fat in the saucepan. Cook over high heat, whisking constantly until the roux begins to brown slightly, about 1 minute. Gradually add the reserved pan juices to the saucepan. Reduce the heat to moderate and cook, whisking until the gravy is thick and smooth, about 3 minutes more. Season with salt and pepper to taste. Slice the pork into ¼-inch-thick pieces and serve with gravy on top.

—Lee Bailey

• • •

BRAISED PORK LOIN WITH APPLES AND CIDER

—————— *8 Servings* ——————
2 tablespoons vegetable oil
1 teaspoon salt
½ teaspoon freshly ground white pepper
¼ teaspoon cinnamon
⅛ teaspoon freshly grated nutmeg
1 boneless pork loin (about 3½ pounds), halved crosswise
1 bay leaf
16 pearl onions, peeled
8 small new potatoes or 4 medium boiling potatoes, halved
3 cups unfiltered, unpasteurized apple cider
4 small tart apples such as Winesap or greening, halved and cored

1. Preheat the oven to 350°. In a dutch oven or other large flameproof casserole, heat the oil. Combine the salt, pepper, cinnamon and nutmeg and rub the mixture into the pork. Add the pork to the casserole and cook over moderately high heat, turning frequently, until browned on all sides, 8 to 10 minutes.

2. Drain the oil from the casserole. Tuck the bay leaf under the meat. Add the onions, potatoes and cider to the pot and bake for 30 minutes.

3. Add the apples to the pot and bake until a thermometer inserted into the meat reaches 160°, about 30 minutes longer.

4. Serve the pork sliced, with some of the pan juices spooned over, and the apples, onions and potatoes on the side.

—Linda Merinoff

• • •

PORK BUNDLES WITH PANCETTA AND SAGE

This dish is known as *uccellini scappati*, or Birds That Got Away, because the little stuffed bundles of pork resemble tiny quail. They don't taste like quail, but no one seems to mind.

🍷 Nino Negri or Rainoldi Grumello or 1983 Ceretto Barbaresco

———— 4 Servings ————

½ cup beef or chicken stock or 1 can (10½ ounces) low-sodium chicken broth
1 pound trimmed, boneless center-cut pork loin, cut into 16 slices (about ¼ inch thick)
¼ cup all-purpose flour
Salt and freshly ground pepper
16 thin slices of pancetta or prosciutto
32 large fresh sage leaves or 3 tablespoons dried sage leaves or 2 tablespoons dried rubbed sage (see Note)
2 tablespoons unsalted butter
1 tablespoon mild olive oil
1 medium shallot, minced
2 tablespoons minced parsley
1 cup Valtellina red wine or other dry red wine
¼ cup tomato puree
Fresh sage leaves, for garnish

1. If using canned chicken broth, reduce it to ½ cup in a small saucepan over high heat.

2. Meanwhile, flatten each pork slice with the palm of your hand to a 4-by-3-inch rectangle. Place the flour on a plate and season it with salt and pepper to taste. Dredge the pork slices in the flour, shaking off any excess.

3. Place 1 slice of pancetta and 2 fresh sage leaves (or a sprinkling of dried) in the middle of each pork slice. Starting at a short end, roll up the pork and secure with a toothpick.

4. In a large nonreactive skillet, heat the butter and oil over high heat. Add half of the meat to the pan and cook, turning once, until browned, 1 to 2 minutes on each side. Transfer to a large plate. Repeat with the remaining meat.

5. Reduce the heat to moderate. Add the shallot and parsley to the skillet and cook, stirring constantly, until softened, about 1 minute. Add the stock (or reduced broth), wine and tomato puree and bring to a boil over high heat, scraping up the browned bits on the bottom of the pan. Cook until the liquid reduces by half, about 5 minutes.

6. Remove the toothpicks from the meat. Add the meat and any accumulated juices to the skillet. Cover and cook over moderate heat, turning once, until heated through, about 5 minutes.

7. Using tongs, transfer 4 of the pork bundles to each of 4 warmed dinner plates. Spoon the sauce over the meat and garnish with fresh sage leaves.

NOTE: If fresh sage is unavailable, be sure to use dried sage leaves or rubbed sage—available in the spice rack of most supermarkets—not powdered sage.

—*Constance and Rosario del Nero*

• • •

STIR-FRIED CURRIED PORK

The hot, salty, sweet and aromatic flavors of this dry Thai curry converge to create what your palate first perceives as one unified taste and then take you on a wild ride through a whole spectrum of flavors and seasonings.

🍷 The sweet-spicy elements in this dish need a tart but mild contrast. Try a crisp, fragrant white, such as 1988 Masson Vineyards Johannisberg Riesling, or a light, fruity (and chillable) red, such as 1988 B&G Beaujolais-Villages.

———— 2 Servings ————

¼ pound thinly sliced pancetta or lean unsmoked bacon, cut into ¼-inch dice
1 tablespoon vegetable oil
½ cup Chili Jam (p. 258)
3 tablespoons Panaeng Paste (p. 258)
½ pound boneless pork loin, trimmed and sliced ⅛ inch thick
6 ounces string beans, sliced on the diagonal into ¼-inch pieces
1 teaspoon palm sugar* or light brown sugar
3 Kaffir lime leaves,* finely shredded
2 tablespoons fresh coriander leaves
1 small fresh red chile, seeded and minced
Lime wedges and cooked white rice, as accompaniment
*Available at Asian markets

1. In a small saucepan of boiling water, blanch the pancetta for 30 seconds; remove with a slotted spoon and drain well.

2. In a wok or large skillet, heat the oil over high heat. When it begins to smoke, add the pancetta and stir-fry until it begins to brown, about 3 minutes.

3. Add the Chili Jam and Panaeng Paste and stir-fry until fragrant, about 1 minute. Add the sliced pork and string beans and stir-fry until the pork is cooked through, about 2 minutes.

4. Add the palm sugar and stir-fry until blended, about 30 seconds. Spoon the curried pork onto a serving platter and sprinkle the lime leaves, coriander leaves and minced chile on top. Serve with lime wedges and white rice.

—*Thai Cooking School, Oriental Hotel, Bangkok, Thailand*

• • •

OLD-FASHIONED SUPPER

Serves 6

Baked Pork Chops (p. 95)

Baked or Roasted Potatoes

Baby Lima Beans, Cherry Tomatoes and Pears (p. 122)

❦ *Cabernet Sauvignon, such as 1985 Columbia Crest or 1987 Rosemount*

Brown Sugar Pie (p. 168)

Coffee

—*Lee Bailey*

BAKED PORK CHOPS

❦ California Cabernet Sauvignon, such as 1983 Beaulieu Vineyard Private Reserve, or red Bordeaux, such as 1986 Château Beau Vallon St-Emilion

6 Servings

1 cup fresh bread crumbs
½ cup all-purpose flour
¼ teaspoon salt
2 egg whites, lightly beaten with 1 tablespoon water
6 pork chops, cut about ¾ inch thick, trimmed of excess fat
1 large garlic clove, lightly crushed
Freshly ground pepper
2 tablespoons unsalted butter
¼ cup olive oil
1 medium onion, finely chopped
⅓ cup dry white wine
½ cup canned low-sodium beef broth
1 bay leaf

1. Place the bread crumbs on a large plate. On another large plate, combine the flour and salt. In a shallow bowl, beat the egg whites until just frothy.

2. Pat the chops dry with paper towels. Rub each chop on both sides with the garlic. Season both sides generously with pepper. One at a time, dredge the chops in the seasoned flour; shake off any excess. Then dip each chop in the beaten egg whites, allowing any excess to drip off. Coat each chop with the bread crumbs, pressing the crumbs onto both sides. Place the breaded chops on a large platter and refrigerate for at least 15 minutes or up to 1 hour.

3. Preheat the oven to 350°. In a large nonreactive skillet, melt 1 tablespoon of the butter in 2 tablespoons of the oil over moderately high heat until bubbling. Add 3 of the chops and cook until browned and crisp, about 3 minutes on each side. Transfer the browned chops to a large roasting pan. Repeat with the remaining 1 tablespoon butter, 2 tablespoons oil and 3 chops.

4. Reduce the heat under the skillet to moderate. Add the onion and cook, stirring constantly, until softened and beginning to brown, about 5 minutes.

5. Add the wine and cook until it has reduced to 2 tablespoons, about 3 minutes. Add the broth and bay leaf, bring to a simmer and cook for 2 minutes longer. Pour this mixture around the chops.

6. Cover the roasting pan tightly with foil and bake the chops for 20 to 25 minutes, or until the meat is white when cut next to the bone, but still juicy. Transfer the chops to a warmed platter. Discard the bay leaf and pour the onion sauce over the meat. Serve hot.

—*Lee Bailey*

• • •

SPICY PLUM PORK

Serve this sweet pork stew with basmati rice and roasted carrots for either lunch or dinner.

❦ The flavors of the dish correspond nicely to the spiciness and fruitiness of the 1987 Sterling Vineyards Winery Lake Pinot Noir.

4 Servings

2 tablespoons vegetable oil
2 garlic cloves, minced
½ cup all-purpose flour
¼ teaspoon salt
¼ teaspoon freshly ground white pepper
2 pounds lean pork shoulder, cut into 1-inch cubes
2 cups dry red wine
1 can (16 ounces) purple plums, pitted and chopped, and their syrup
⅓ cup (packed) dried apricots (2 ounces), chopped
2-inch piece of fresh ginger, peeled and minced
1 bay leaf
½ teaspoon freshly grated nutmeg
¼ teaspoon cinnamon
¼ teaspoon cayenne pepper
Pinch of allspice
Pinch of ground cloves

1. In a medium nonreactive flameproof casserole, heat the oil over moderate heat. Add the garlic and cook until lightly browned and fragrant, 1 to 2 minutes. Transfer the garlic to a small plate and set aside.

2. In a medium bowl, combine the flour, salt and white pepper. Toss the pork in the seasoned flour and shake off any excess.

3. In 2 batches, add the meat to the casserole and cook over moderately high heat until brown and crusty all over, about 8 minutes per batch.

4. Return all the meat to the casserole and add the wine, plums and their syrup,

apricots, ginger, bay leaf, nutmeg, cinnamon, cayenne, allspice, cloves and the reserved garlic. Bring to a simmer over moderately high heat. Cover, reduce the heat to low and simmer gently until the meat is tender and the sauce is thick, about 1½ hours. Remove the bay leaf and serve hot. (*The recipe can be made 2 days ahead. Cover and refrigerate.*)
—*Elaine Bell, Sterling Vineyards, Calistoga, California*

• • •

SLOW-FIRE SPARERIBS

These spareribs need to be watched pretty carefully throughout the cooking.
❦ Hearty red, such as 1987 Nalle Zinfandel or 1988 Torres Coronas

——————— 2 Servings ———————
1 rack of pork spareribs (2½ pounds), trimmed of membranes and excess fat
¼ cup soy sauce
¼ cup mirin (sweet rice wine)*
¼ cup medium-dry sherry
¼ cup Chinese red vinegar* or cider vinegar
1 small Spanish onion, chopped
¼ cup chopped fresh coriander
2 tablespoons minced fresh ginger
1 tablespoon minced garlic
Oil, for brushing the grill
***Available at Asian markets**

1. Using a sharp knife, cut 3-inch-long slits between the largest ribs (leaving them attached) to allow the marinade to penetrate well.
2. In a large nonreactive dish, whisk together the soy sauce, mirin, sherry, vinegar, onion, coriander, ginger and garlic. Add the spareribs and rub the marinade into both sides. Cover and refrigerate for 3 hours or up to 24 hours, turning occasionally. Remove from the refrigerator 30 minutes before cooking.

3. Prepare the fire. Brush the grill with oil. Remove the spareribs from the marinade and place in the center of the grill. Cover, leaving all the vents wide open. Cook the spareribs for 5 minutes, then check; if they seem to be getting too dark too soon, move them to the side of the grill for the next 10 minutes of cooking. Turn the spareribs and cook on the other side for 10 to 15 minutes longer.
4. Continue cooking, turning the ribs over every 15 minutes and watching carefully, until tender and cooked through inside and crisp outside, 1 to 1¼ hours total. Remove the ribs from the grill and let rest for 10 minutes. Using a cleaver or chef's knife, cut the rack into single rib sections and serve hot. (*The recipe can be made up to 1 day ahead. Let cool completely, then cover with plastic wrap and refrigerate. Reheat, uncovered, in a 350° oven until hot.*)
—*Karen Lee & Alaxandra Branyon*

• • •

RISO CON CHORIZO

If you would like to leave the clams in their shells rather than removing them as I do, simply reheat them in a large covered saucepan while the rice bakes (Step 8). You can also make this dish without the clams if you prefer. Just add the saffron to 3½ cups of the sausage poaching liquid instead of to the clam broth.
❦ A tart, herbaceous 1988 California Sauvignon Blanc, such as Quivira or Charles Shaw, would make a crisp, refreshing contrast to this rustic dish.

——————— 6 Servings ———————
1 cup dry white wine
1 dozen littleneck clams, scrubbed
½ teaspoon (lightly packed) saffron threads

½ pound chorizo* or hot Italian sausage
1 tablespoon cumin seeds
2 tablespoons plus 2 teaspoons olive oil
1 pound boneless pork shoulder, cut into ½-inch cubes
1¼ teaspoons salt
1 teaspoon freshly ground black pepper
1 large Spanish onion, chopped
1 large red bell pepper, chopped
3 large garlic cloves, minced
1 can (14 ounces) Italian plum tomatoes, drained and chopped
1 cup drained and rinsed cooked black beans
1⅓ cups basmati rice
1½ teaspoons grated lemon zest
2 tablespoons chopped parsley
1 cup frozen peas, thawed
***Available at specialty shops or Latin American markets**

1. In a large nonreactive saucepan, bring the wine and 2 cups of water to a boil over high heat. Add the clams, cover and cook until they start to open, about 4 minutes. Remove the opened clams, cover and continue to cook, checking frequently, until the rest open, about 2 minutes longer. Discard any that refuse to open.
2. Remove the clams from their shells and set aside. Pour the clam broth into a large measuring cup, leaving behind any grit. Reserve 3½ cups. Sprinkle the saffron threads over the reserved broth and set aside to infuse.
3. In a medium saucepan, cover the sausage with 4 cups of water and bring to a boil over high heat. Reduce the heat to moderate and simmer the sausage until just cooked through, about 10 minutes. Drain and slice ¼ inch thick. Set aside.
4. Preheat the oven to 350°. In a large, dry cast-iron skillet, toast the cumin seeds over high heat, stirring, until fragrant, about 1 minute. Transfer the seeds to a

work surface and chop fine or crush in a mortar. Set aside.

5. In the same skillet, heat 2 teaspoons of the olive oil over high heat. Season the pork cubes with ¼ teaspoon each of the salt and black pepper. When the oil begins to smoke, spread the pork evenly in the pan and cook without stirring until browned, about 2 minutes. Stir once, then cook until well browned all over, about 3 minutes. Remove the pork and set aside.

6. Reduce the heat to low and add the remaining 2 tablespoons olive oil to the skillet. Stir in the onion, red pepper and garlic and cook until the vegetables are softened, about 10 minutes.

7. Add the reserved sausage, pork and cumin as well as the tomatoes, black beans, rice and 3 cups of the saffron-infused broth. Season with the remaining 1 teaspoon salt and ¾ teaspoon black pepper.

8. Cover the pan with foil and bake in the oven for 20 minutes, or until the rice is tender. Remove from the oven and let rest without uncovering for 5 minutes.

9. Meanwhile, in a small saucepan, combine the reserved clams and the remaining ½ cup clam broth with the lemon zest, parsley and peas. Cook over moderately high heat until the clams and peas are warmed through, about 3 minutes. Uncover the rice and stir in the clam mixture. Serve at once.

—*Marcia Kiesel*

• • •

BAKED HAM WITH MUSTARD AND APPLE JELLY GLAZE

The smoked ham called for below is fully cooked, so allow about 10 minutes a pound just to heat it thoroughly and set the glaze.

♟ The salty nature of the ham calls for a fruity, refreshing wine that can also stand up to the tartness of the glaze. A Riesling, such as 1988 Schmitt Söhne Piesporter Michelsberg Spätlese, is one solution; a rich young Burgundy, such as 1985 Joseph Drouhin Pommard-Epenots, is another.

——— *8 to 10 Servings* ———
1 jar (10 ounces) apple jelly
¼ cup Dijon-style mustard
1 skinless, partially boned smoked ham (14 pounds)

1. In a small nonreactive saucepan, combine the apple jelly and mustard and bring to a boil over moderate heat, stirring constantly. Cook until the mixture reduces slightly, about 2 minutes. Set aside half of the glaze to serve with the ham as a condiment. *(The glaze can be made 1 day ahead. Let cool completely, then cover and refrigerate.)*

2. Preheat the oven to 325°. With a sharp knife, trim away any excess fat from the ham, leaving a thin layer. For a decorative effect, score the fat with long shallow cuts at ¼-inch intervals. Set the ham, fat-side up, on a rack in a large roasting pan and bake for 1½ hours. (If you don't have a rack, add 1½ cups of water to the pan.)

3. Remove the ham from the oven and brush all over with the glaze. Continue to bake for about 45 minutes longer, until the ham is heated through to the bone and the glaze is set. Brush the ham again with the glaze 30 minutes before it is done.

4. Transfer the ham to a serving platter. Cover loosely with foil and let rest for 20 to 30 minutes to settle the juices before carving. Slice the ham and pass the reserved glaze separately.

—*Diana Sturgis*

• • •

HEARTY HOLIDAY HAM

Serves 8 to 10

Mixed Salad with Kumquats and Pecans (p. 143)

Baked Ham with Mustard and Apple Jelly Glaze (p. 97)

Blushing Applesauce (p. 213)

Shallots Braised in Red Wine (p. 125)

Sweet Potato and Butternut Squash Puree (p. 130)

Cauliflower and Broccoli with Cream Sauce (p. 123)

♟ *Fruity red, such as 1988 Georges Duboeuf Beaujolais-Villages or 1987 Saintsbury Garnet Pinot Noir*

Chocolate Orange Mousse (p. 202)

—*Diana Sturgis*

MEAT

UMBRIAN PORK SAUSAGE WITH PINE NUTS AND RAISINS

This recipe from the central Italian province of Umbria is delicious with sautéed polenta and a dollop of tomato sauce. The sausage can be crumbled on pizza or put into sausage casings and grilled.

——— *4 to 6 Servings* ———
½ cup raisins
¼ cup pine nuts
2 pounds ground pork
1 tablespoon grated orange zest
4 to 5 small garlic cloves, minced
1½ teaspoons salt
½ teaspoon freshly ground pepper

1. In a small bowl, cover the raisins with ½ cup hot water; set aside for 30 minutes to plump. Drain and reserve the liquid.

2. Meanwhile, preheat the oven to 350°. Spread the pine nuts on a small baking sheet and bake for 5 minutes, or until the nuts are lightly browned. Let cool completely.

3. In a medium mixing bowl, combine the pork, orange zest, garlic, toasted pine nuts, raisins and 2 tablespoons of their soaking liquid. (Discard the remaining liquid.) Season with the salt and pepper. Mix the ingredients well, using your hands, but do not overwork. Form into 16 sausage patties ½ inch thick.

4. Heat a large heavy skillet over high heat. Working in 2 or 3 batches, cook the patties until browned on the outside, about 5 minutes on each side. Transfer to a warm oven, wiping out the skillet between each batch. Serve hot.

—*Joyce Goldstein*

• • •

BAKED HAM AND TURKEY LOAF

This sort of loaf offers a lot of room for flights of fancy. You can leave out the garlic or add more. You can substitute another favorite herb for the thyme. In general, however, keep the seasoning on the bold side. Unless you have a meat grinder, ask your butcher to grind the ham, turkey and pork.

I like this served lukewarm, although served cold the next morning with fried eggs and biscuits, it is almost as good.

♟ California jug wine, such as Gallo Chablis Blanc, or California Chenin Blanc, such as 1988 Simi

——— *8 to 10 Servings* ———
1½ tablespoons unsalted butter
1 medium onion, finely chopped
1 medium green bell pepper, finely chopped
2 garlic cloves, minced
2 teaspoons thyme
1 pound ground boiled ham
½ pound ground turkey
½ pound ground pork
2 large eggs, lightly beaten
½ cup fine dry bread crumbs
¼ cup milk or cream
1 tablespoon Dijon-style mustard
¼ cup minced parsley
¼ teaspoon salt
½ teaspoon freshly ground black pepper

1. Preheat the oven to 375°. Lightly butter a 9-by-5-inch loaf pan.

2. In a medium skillet, melt the butter over moderate heat. Add the onion and green pepper, cover partially, and cook, stirring occasionally, until softened, about 10 minutes. Stir in the garlic and thyme and cook for 2 minutes longer.

3. Transfer the contents of the skillet to a large bowl and stir in the ham, turkey, pork, eggs, bread crumbs, milk, mustard, parsley, salt and black pepper. Using your hands, blend the ingredients thoroughly.

4. Transfer the meat mixture to the prepared loaf pan, pat it down and form a rounded top with your hands. Bake for 1¼ to 1½ hours, until a meat thermometer inserted into the center of the loaf registers 165° to 170°.

5. Remove from the oven and tilt the pan to pour off the fat. Transfer to a rack and let the loaf rest in the pan for at least 10 minutes before serving. *(The loaf can be made up to 2 days ahead; cover and refrigerate. Bring to room temperature, then reheat in a medium oven for 15 minutes.)* Serve directly from the pan or transfer to a platter and slice.

—*Ken Haedrich*

• • •

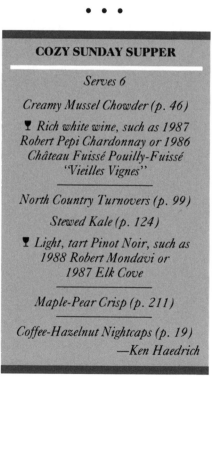

COZY SUNDAY SUPPER

Serves 6

Creamy Mussel Chowder (p. 46)

♟ *Rich white wine, such as 1987 Robert Pepi Chardonnay or 1986 Château Fuissé Pouilly-Fuissé "Vieilles Vignes"*

North Country Turnovers (p. 99)

Stewed Kale (p. 124)

♟ *Light, tart Pinot Noir, such as 1988 Robert Mondavi or 1987 Elk Cove*

Maple-Pear Crisp (p. 211)

Coffee-Hazelnut Nightcaps (p. 19)

—*Ken Haedrich*

NORTH COUNTRY TURNOVERS

These turnovers may convince you that almost anything edible can be improved by wrapping it in pastry. They're a snap to assemble once you've made the pastry and cut out the rounds.

——— *Makes 7 Turnovers* ———
1¼ cups rinsed and drained
  sauerkraut (about 9 ounces)
1 tablespoon German-style mustard
4 ounces thinly sliced Canadian
  bacon or Virginia ham, cut into
  ¼-inch strips
4 ounces sharp Cheddar cheese,
  grated (about 1¼ cups)
1 tart green apple, preferably
  Granny Smith—peeled, cored and
  thinly sliced
Cream Cheese Pastry (recipe
  follows)
1 egg
1 tablespoon milk

1. In a small nonreactive saucepan, combine the sauerkraut and mustard. Cook over moderately high heat, stirring occasionally, until all the liquid evaporates, about 3 minutes. Immediately transfer the sauerkraut onto a plate to cool. Divide into 7 equal piles.

2. Preheat the oven to 400°. Arrange the Canadian bacon, Cheddar cheese and apple in separate bowls nearby.

3. Place the rounds of the Cream Cheese Pastry on a work surface. Working quickly so the dough doesn't get too soft, arrange 3 apple slices on the bottom half of each pastry round, ¼ inch from the outer edge. Place 1 pile of sauerkraut on the apple slices (keep it away from the pastry edge) and top with about 2 tablespoons of the Canadian bacon and about 2½ tablespoons of the cheese. Repeat with the remaining pastry rounds and filling.

4. Lightly moisten the edge of each pastry round with water. Gently stretch and fold the top half of the pastry over the filling; press the edges gently to seal.

Transfer the turnovers to a large baking sheet. Press the edges with the tines of a fork to make a decorative, tightly sealed edge.

5. In a small bowl, lightly beat the egg and milk until blended. Brush the turnovers with the egg wash. Pierce the top of each turnover twice with a fork.

6. Bake the turnovers in the middle of the oven for 10 minutes. Reduce the temperature to 375°, transfer the turnovers to the top rack and bake for 15 to 20 minutes longer, until the bottoms are browned and the tops light golden. Transfer the turnovers to a rack and let cool for 15 minutes before serving.

—*Ken Haedrich*

• • •

CREAM CHEESE PASTRY

—*Makes Enough for 7 Turnovers* —
1¼ cups unbleached or all-purpose
  flour
¼ cup whole wheat flour
¼ teaspoon salt
1 stick plus 2 tablespoons (5 ounces)
  cold unsalted butter, cut into
  small pieces
4 ounces cold cream cheese, cut into
  small pieces
2 to 2½ tablespoons ice water

1. In a large bowl, combine the unbleached and whole wheat flours and the salt; toss to mix. Using a pastry blender or two knives, cut in the butter and cream cheese until broken up into tiny pieces. Just when the mixture starts to clump together, sprinkle in the ice water, 1 tablespoon at a time, tossing and com-

pacting the mixture with a fork just until evenly moistened.

2. Turn the dough out onto a lightly floured work surface and knead once, flattening the dough into a ½-inch-thick disk. Wrap the disk in plastic wrap or place in a plastic bag and refrigerate for 1 hour. (*The dough can be made to this point up to 24 hours ahead. If refrigerated for longer than 1 hour, let the dough sit at room temperature for 10 to 15 minutes before rolling.*)

3. On a lightly floured work surface, roll out the dough into a 14-by-21-inch rectangle approximately ¹⁄₁₆ to ⅛ inch thick; lightly dust the surface of the dough with flour if it sticks to the rolling pin. Using a 6-inch bowl as a guide, cut out 6 circles of dough with a sharp paring knife. Stack the pastry rounds, layered with waxed paper, on a plate. Dust off the excess flour from the dough scraps and pack them into a ball. Roll out the dough and cut out 1 more 6-inch round. Add it to the stack, cover well with plastic wrap and refrigerate for at least 10 minutes and up to 1 day before using.

—*Ken Haedrich*

• • •

HAM 'N' GREENS
BUTTERMILK SPOONBREAD

Serve this as the star of a meal along with a salad of sliced tomatoes and some breadsticks, or add it to the menu as a side dish to accompany grilled chicken.

——————— *4 to 6 Servings* ———————
1 pound young collard, mustard or
  turnip greens or Swiss chard or 1
  package (10 ounces) frozen
  greens, thawed and squeezed dry
4 tablespoons unsalted butter
1 garlic clove, minced
¾ cup diced smoked country ham
  (about 3 ounces)
½ teaspoon salt

¼ teaspoon freshly ground pepper
1 cup white or yellow cornmeal
1 cup buttermilk
3 large eggs, separated
¼ cup freshly grated Parmesan
    cheese (about 1 ounce)

1. Butter a 2-quart soufflé dish. If using fresh greens, wash them well. Discard the tough stems. In a large pot of boiling water, cook the greens until just tender, 5 to 7 minutes. Drain thoroughly, pressing out as much liquid as possible. Coarsely chop the greens.

2. Preheat the oven to 350°. In a large skillet, melt 2 tablespoons of the butter over moderate heat. Add the garlic, ham and greens and cook until the garlic is softened, 3 to 4 minutes. Spread the mixture in the prepared soufflé dish.

3. In a heavy medium saucepan, combine 2 cups of water with the salt and pepper and bring to a boil over moderately high heat. Whisk in the cornmeal in a slow, steady stream. Reduce the heat to moderate and cook, stirring with a wooden spoon, until the mixture is very thick (the consistency of mashed potatoes) and almost comes together in a ball, leaving the bottom of the pan clean, 1 to 2 minutes. Remove from the heat and beat in the remaining 2 tablespoons butter and the buttermilk. Beat in the egg yolks and cheese.

4. In a medium bowl, beat the egg whites until stiff but not dry. Stir one-quarter of the egg whites into the cornmeal batter to lighten it, then fold in the remaining whites.

5. Spoon the batter over the greens and bake in the middle of the oven for 50 to 55 minutes, until puffed and lightly browned on top. The spoonbread will be soft in the center and crusty around the edges. Serve at once and pass a pepper mill at the table.

—*Melanie Barnard & Brooke Dojny*

• • •

ASSORTED MEAT SATAYS WITH CUCUMBER SALAD

The skewered meats—chicken, pork and beef—are marinated before grilling and served with a spicy peanut sauce. Cucumber adds a cool, crisp note to this traditional Thai starter.

—— *6 to 8 First-Course Servings* ——
½ pound skinless, boneless chicken
    breast, cut into 3-by-½-inch strips
½ pound boneless pork loin, cut into
    3-by-½-inch strips
½ teaspoon turmeric
1 teaspoon curry powder
1 teaspoon plus a pinch of salt
½ cup unsweetened coconut milk*
½ teaspoon coriander seeds
½ pound beef top round, cut into
    3-by-½-inch strips
½ cup rice vinegar* or cider vinegar
2 tablespoons sugar
2 tablespoons minced fresh red
    chiles
3 large shallots, thinly sliced
1 European cucumber, thinly sliced
1 tablespoon chopped fresh
    coriander
Peanut Dipping Sauce (p. 255)
*Available at Asian markets

1. Place the chicken and pork in a large shallow dish. Sprinkle evenly with the turmeric, curry powder and the pinch of salt. Pour the coconut milk over the meat and mix to coat thoroughly. Cover and refrigerate for at least 1 hour.

2. Meanwhile, in a small dry skillet, toast the coriander seeds over high heat until fragrant and golden brown, about 30 seconds. In a mortar, finely crush the seeds. In a small bowl, sprinkle the beef with the crushed coriander seeds. Cover and refrigerate for at least 1 hour.

3. In a medium bowl, mix the vinegar, sugar and the remaining 1 teaspoon salt. Stir in the chiles, shallots, cucumber and fresh coriander. Set aside to marinate for up to 1 hour.

4. Soak twenty-four 8-inch bamboo skewers in a bowl of water for at least 20 minutes.

5. Preheat the broiler. Thread the chicken, pork and beef onto separate skewers without crowding. Arrange the skewers on a large baking sheet and broil 5 inches from the heat, turning a few times, for about 4 minutes, or until the meat is browned and cooked through. Serve hot on skewers with the cucumber salad and Peanut Dipping Sauce on the side.

—*Thai Cooking School,*
Oriental Hotel, Bangkok, Thailand

• • •

HERBED-SPICED GRILLED LAMB

The marinade for this grilled lamb dish is cooked and served as a sauce.

❢ The grilled lamb invites a medium-bodied red with a rich, herbaceous flavor, such as a California Merlot, a 1987 Matanzas Creek or a 1987 Clos du Bois.

————— *6 Servings* —————
1 leg of lamb (about 6 pounds)—
    boned, trimmed of fat and
    butterflied (about 3 pounds
    trimmed weight)
⅔ cup dry red wine
⅓ cup olive oil
2 garlic cloves, minced
4 anchovy fillets, chopped
1 tablespoon chopped fresh
    rosemary or 1½ teaspoons dried,
    plus sprigs for garnish
1½ teaspoons ground cumin
½ teaspoon crushed hot red pepper
½ teaspoon freshly ground black
    pepper

OUTDOOR GRILL FOR SIX

Serves 6

*Herbed-Spiced Grilled Lamb
(p. 100)*

Couscous-Stuffed Tomatoes (p. 131)

*Summer Fruit with Orange Liqueur
Custard (p. 212)*
—*Melanie Barnard & Brooke Dojny*

1. Place the lamb in a shallow glass dish. In a small bowl, combine the wine, olive oil, garlic, anchovies, rosemary, cumin, red pepper and black pepper. Pour the marinade over the lamb and set aside at room temperature for about 3 hours, turning the meat once or twice.

2. Light a charcoal fire or preheat the broiler. When the coals are gray, remove the lamb from the marinade and drain on paper towels; leave some bits of herb and garlic on the meat.

3. Grill or broil the lamb about 4 inches from the heat until the outside is nicely charred and the inside is still pink, about 7 minutes on each side. Let rest for about 10 minutes.

4. Meanwhile, pour the marinade into a nonreactive saucepan and boil over moderate heat until reduced to ⅓ cup, about 5 minutes.

5. Carve the lamb on the diagonal into thin slices. Serve on a warm platter, garnished with the rosemary sprigs. Pass the sauce separately.

—*Melanie Barnard & Brooke Dojny*

• • •

LAMB CHOPS WITH CUMIN, CINNAMON AND ORANGE

These chops can be cooked on a charcoal or gas grill. In either case grill them over a moderate fire and not too close to the heat; they should get evenly crusty but not charred. Serve them with Potato-Mushroom Cakes with Cumin (p. 129).

———— *2 Servings* ————
1 tablespoon cumin seeds
¼ teaspoon cinnamon
3 garlic cloves, smashed
3 tablespoons fresh orange juice
2 tablespoons safflower oil
*4 loin lamb chops (about 1 inch
    thick)*

1. In a small dry skillet, toast the cumin seeds, shaking the pan occasionally, over high heat until fragrant, about 30 seconds. Transfer the seeds to a mortar and pound with a pestle to a coarse powder or finely chop with a large knife.

2. In a large shallow nonreactive dish, combine the cumin, cinnamon, garlic, orange juice and oil; mix well. Add the lamb chops and coat thoroughly, pressing the spices and garlic onto both sides of the meat. Let marinate at room temperature for at least 2 hours, turning occasionally, or cover and refrigerate overnight.

3. Preheat the oven to 500°. Remove and discard any bits of garlic from the lamb and set the chops on a baking sheet. Roast on the top shelf of the oven for 8 minutes, without turning.

4. Turn the oven to broil and broil the chops until dark brown, about 3 minutes for medium rare. Let the chops rest for about 3 minutes before serving.

—*Marcia Kiesel*

• • •

URBAN SHEPHERD'S PIE

This version of the country-cooking classic is citified with the addition of shiitake mushrooms and deliciously rich lamb shank meat.

❦ The lamb and mushrooms in this dish suggest an earthy, robust red with some youthful assertiveness. Try 1985 Columbia Crest Cabernet Sauvignon from Washington or 1987 Rosemount Cabernet Sauvignon from Australia.

———— *6 to 8 Servings* ————
3 tablespoons olive oil
*6 large, meaty lamb shanks (about 9
    pounds total)*
Salt and freshly ground pepper
1½ cups dry red wine
*1 large head of garlic, separated into
    unpeeled cloves*
*6 sprigs plus 1 teaspoon chopped
    fresh thyme or 1¼ teaspoons dried*
*2½ pounds Idaho potatoes, peeled
    and quartered*
¼ cup milk
*4 tablespoons unsalted butter plus 1
    tablespoon melted butter*
*½ pound green beans, cut into 1-inch
    pieces*
*1 pound fresh shiitake or oyster
    mushrooms, stems removed, caps
    quartered*
1 medium red onion, chopped
1½ tablespoons all-purpose flour
1 teaspoon fresh lemon juice
¼ cup chopped parsley

1. Preheat the oven to 325°. In a large roasting pan set over 2 burners, heat 1 tablespoon of the olive oil. Season the lamb shanks generously with salt and pepper and add them to the pan. Cook over moderate heat, turning frequently, until well browned all over, about 10 minutes.

2. Pour in 1 cup of the red wine and boil for 3 minutes. Add 1 cup of water and let return to a boil, then add the garlic cloves and thyme sprigs (or 1 teaspoon of the dried thyme). Cover the pan with foil and bake the shanks in the oven for 2 hours, until the meat is very tender. Remove the lamb from the oven and let it cool slightly.

3. Meanwhile, in a large saucepan, cover the potatoes with water and bring to a boil over high heat. Cook until tender, about 15 minutes. Drain well. Return the potatoes to the pan and shake over high heat to dry them completely, about 1 minute.

4. Remove from the heat, add the milk and 4 tablespoons of the butter and mash until smooth. Season with salt and pepper to taste and set aside.

5. In a small saucepan of boiling salted water, cook the green beans until tender, about 4 minutes. Drain and rinse under cold water. Set aside.

6. In a large nonreactive skillet, heat the remaining 2 tablespoons olive oil over high heat. When it begins to smoke, add the mushrooms in an even layer. Do not stir until the mushrooms start to brown, about 2½ minutes. Stir gently and cook until browned all over, about 2 minutes longer.

7. Add the onion and the chopped fresh thyme (or the remaining ¼ teaspoon dried) and reduce the heat to low. Cover and cook, stirring occasionally, until the onion softens, about 10 minutes. Uncover, increase the heat to high and cook without stirring until the onion is browned, about 3 minutes.

8. Add the remaining ½ cup red wine to the skillet and boil, scraping up the brown bits from the bottom of the pan, until the mixture is very dry and beginning to brown again, about 3 minutes. Remove from the heat and set aside.

9. Remove all the lamb from the bones, discarding any gristle and fat; cut the meat into 1-inch pieces. Pour the contents of the roasting pan into a coarse sieve set over a bowl. Using a spoon or

rubber spatula, press the cooked garlic through the sieve. Remove any grease that rises to the surface.

10. Return the mushroom mixture to moderately high heat. Sprinkle on the flour and stir until blended. Whisk in the garlic broth and bring to a boil, stirring constantly. Continue to cook, stirring occasionally until the liquid thickens slightly, about 3 minutes.

11. Stir in the lamb, reserved green beans, lemon juice and parsley. Season with salt and pepper to taste.

12. Spoon the lamb mixture into a large baking dish 2 to 3 inches deep and refrigerate until firm, about 30 minutes. Preheat the oven to 350°.

13. With your hands, take cupfuls of the potato mixture and flatten them into ½-inch-thick patties. Press the patties onto the lamb mixture. Smooth the surface and score decoratively with a fork. Brush with the melted butter. *(The recipe can be prepared to this point up to 2 days ahead. Cover and refrigerate. Let return to room temperature before baking.)*

14. Bake on the top rack of the oven until hot and bubbly, about 45 minutes. Turn on the broiler and brown the top, rotating the pie, about 2 minutes. Let rest for 10 minutes before serving.

—*Marcia Kiesel*

• • •

BRAISED LAMB SHANKS WITH BLACK BEANS

This dish requires a long cooking time, but doesn't need much watching. If your butcher has not already done so, make sure to remove and discard any fat or skin from the shanks.

—————— *6 Servings* ——————
2 tablespoons olive oil
6 small lamb shanks (about 6 pounds total), split across the bone
2 tablespoons unsalted butter
2 cups coarsely chopped onions (about 3 medium)
1 cup coarsely chopped carrots (about 3 medium)
1 cup coarsely chopped celery (about 3 ribs)
3 garlic cloves, minced
1 large sprig of parsley
1½ cups dry red wine
1½ cups beef stock or canned low-sodium beef broth
2 tablespoons tomato paste
1½ teaspoons salt
1½ teaspoons freshly ground pepper
2 teaspoons fresh thyme or 1 teaspoon dried
1 large imported bay leaf
1 tablespoon coarsely grated lemon zest
2 cans (15 ounces each) black beans, rinsed and drained well

1. In a flameproof nonreactive casserole, heat the oil over moderate heat until very hot. Add the lamb shanks and brown on all sides, about 5 minutes. Transfer to a large plate and set aside. Discard the oil.

2. Add the butter to the casserole and melt over moderately high heat. Add the onions, carrots and celery and cook, stirring, until the vegetables start to brown, 3 to 5 minutes. Add the garlic and parsley and cook 1 minute more. Add the wine and beef stock. Stir in the tomato paste, salt, pepper, thyme, bay leaf and lemon zest. Reduce the heat to moderately low and bring to a simmer, about 15 minutes.

3. Return the lamb with its juices to the casserole. Reduce the heat to low, cover and let simmer for 1 hour. Remove the lid and simmer until the liquid is thick enough to coat the back of a spoon, about 30 minutes more. Meanwhile, preheat the oven to 350°.

4. Spread the beans on top of the lamb. Bake for 30 minutes, loosely covered with foil, until the meat is very tender and falls off the bone. *(The recipe can be prepared up to 2 days ahead and reheated.)*

—*Lee Bailey*

• • •

SPICED MIDDLE EASTERN LAMB WITH APRICOTS

This lamb should be marinated overnight. You can make this a day ahead; it reheats beautifully. Serve it with rice or couscous to absorb the delicious juices.

————— 6 to 8 Servings —————
3 pounds boneless trimmed lamb shoulder, cut into 2-inch cubes
1 tablespoon ground coriander
1 tablespoon cumin
2 teaspoons cinnamon
1 teaspoon ground ginger
¼ cup olive oil
1 cup raisins (5 to 6 ounces)
2½ cups dried apricots (¾ pound)
2 tablespoons unsalted butter
2 large onions, finely diced
1 teaspoon saffron threads, crushed
2 cups chicken stock or canned low-sodium broth
Salt and freshly ground pepper
1 tablespoon honey (optional)
Chopped almonds or sesame seeds, for garnish

1. Place the lamb in a large dish. In a small bowl, mix together 1½ teaspoons of the coriander, 1½ teaspoons of the cumin, 1 teaspoon of the cinnamon and ½ teaspoon of the ginger. Rub the seasoning into the lamb. Pour 2 tablespoons of the olive oil over the meat and toss to coat. Cover and marinate in the refrigerator overnight. Return the meat to room temperature before proceeding.

2. In a medium bowl, cover the raisins and apricots with 2 cups of hot water; set aside for 30 minutes to plump. Drain and set aside.

3. Meanwhile, in a large casserole, melt the butter in the remaining 2 tablespoons oil. Working in batches, cook the meat on all sides over high heat until well browned, about 3 minutes per side. Transfer to a platter.

4. Pour off all but 2 tablespoons of the cooking fat. Add the onions and cook, stirring over moderately high heat until translucent, about 5 minutes. Stir in the remaining 1½ teaspoons coriander, 1½ teaspoons cumin, 1 teaspoon cinnamon and ½ teaspoon ginger and cook about 2 minutes.

5. Return the lamb to the casserole along with any accumulated juices. Add the saffron and the chicken stock and bring just to a low boil. Reduce the heat to low, cover and simmer for 1 hour.

6. Add the raisins and apricots to the meat mixture. Continue to cook, uncovered, until the meat is very tender, another 20 to 30 minutes.

7. Season with salt and pepper to taste. Add the honey if a sweeter taste is desired and garnish with chopped almonds or sesame seeds.

—*Joyce Goldstein*

• • •

LAMB CURRY

This spicy curry can be served with any number of condiments. Some favorites include mango chutney, shredded unsweetened coconut, plain yogurt, currants, chopped peanuts, cashews or shelled pistachios, minced scallions, cubed cucumber or banana, and chopped tomato or hard-cooked egg. I sometimes like to toss cooked potato cubes with the lamb before serving.

❧ The heat and spice of the curry dictate a straightforward, not-too-subtle red, such as 1985 Château St-Georges St-Emilion or 1987 Caymus Zinfandel.

————— 4 Servings —————
2½ pounds boneless lamb shoulder, trimmed and cut into 1½-inch cubes
2 tablespoons hot curry powder
½ teaspoon freshly ground pepper
1½ teaspoons ground ginger
1 tablespoon finely grated fresh ginger
3 whole cloves
¼ cup olive oil
2 medium onions, coarsely chopped
1 large garlic clove, crushed
1 cup dry vermouth or dry white wine
2 Granny Smith apples—peeled, cored and cut into large dice
1½ teaspoons salt
2 tablespoons fresh lime juice
Cooked rice and assorted condiments, for serving

1. In a nonreactive bowl, toss the lamb with the curry powder, pepper, ground ginger, fresh ginger and cloves. Set aside.

2. In a large nonreactive flameproof casserole, heat the olive oil. Add the onions and garlic and cook over moderate heat until softened and lightly golden, about 10 minutes. With a slotted spoon, transfer the onions to a large bowl and set aside.

103

3. Increase the heat to high. Working in batches, add the meat to the casserole and cook, turning, until browned on all sides. As each batch is done, transfer it to the bowl with the onions.

4. Reduce the heat to moderately high. Return all the meat and the onions to the casserole and add the vermouth, apples and 1 cup of water. Bring to a boil. Reduce the heat to low and simmer gently, stirring occasionally, until the meat is very tender, about 1½ hours.

5. With a large slotted spoon, transfer the meat to a large platter or plate. Increase the heat to high and boil the sauce, stirring frequently, until thickened, about 10 minutes. Add the salt and lime juice and return the meat to the casserole. *(The recipe can be prepared to this point up to 3 days ahead. Let cool completely, then cover and refrigerate.)* Cook just until heated through, about 2 minutes.

6. Transfer the lamb curry to a serving dish. Pass the rice and assorted condiments separately.

—*W. Peter Prestcott*

• • •

GRILLED LAMB KEBABS WITH HORSERADISH BUTTER

The best cut of lamb to cube for these kebabs is a well-trimmed, boneless leg.

❦ The outdoor setting suggests a casual wine, and the kebabs' hearty flavors point to a rich, but not heavy, red. An Australian Cabernet Sauvignon, such as 1985 Orlando St. Hugo or Rosemount Show Reserve, would be ideal.

———— 6 Servings ————
1 tablespoon prepared horseradish, drained in a fine-mesh sieve
4 tablespoons unsalted butter, softened
1 teaspoon fresh lemon juice
½ teaspoon coarse (kosher) salt
¼ teaspoon freshly ground pepper
½ bay leaf
½ medium onion, thinly sliced

1 garlic clove, crushed
⅓ cup tarragon wine vinegar
½ cup olive oil
2½ pounds well-trimmed lamb, cut into 1½-inch cubes

1. In a small bowl, mash the horseradish into the butter. Mix in the lemon juice. On waxed paper, form into a roll about 1 inch in diameter. Wrap the horseradish butter well and refrigerate until set and ready to use.

2. In a medium nonreactive bowl, combine the salt, pepper, bay leaf, onion, garlic and vinegar. Whisk in the olive oil in a thin stream. Add the lamb and toss to coat. Cover with plastic wrap and refrigerate for at least 4 hours or overnight, turning a couple of times.

3. Preheat a grill or the broiler. Remove the lamb from the marinade and pat dry with paper towels. Thread the cubes onto 6 metal skewers. Grill the kebabs about 6 inches from the heat for 6 minutes on each side (for a total of 12 minutes), or until just pink inside. Alternatively, broil 4 inches from the heat for 6 minutes on each side. Serve hot with slices of horseradish butter.

—*Lee Bailey*

• • •

VENISON STEW WITH DRIED CHERRIES

Serve this stew over a bed of egg noodles as the entrée in a multi-course meal or alone with a green salad and French bread for a more informal lunch or dinner.

❦ The dried cherries in the venison stew bring out the cherry flavor in a 1986 Cakebread Cellars Cabernet Sauvignon.

———— 8 Servings ————
½ cup all-purpose flour
½ teaspoon freshly ground pepper
3 pounds boneless venison stew meat from the leg, cut into 1-inch cubes
3 tablespoons olive oil

1 large onion, coarsely chopped
3 celery ribs, diced
6 carrots, sliced into ½-inch rounds
6 garlic cloves
2 cups dry red wine
¼ cup tomato paste
3 tablespoons fresh orange juice
10 juniper berries, tied in cheesecloth
2 cups beef stock or 1 can (13¾ ounces) beef broth plus ½ cup water
¼ cup dried tart cherries
8 medium red potatoes, quartered
¼ cup brandy

1. In a medium bowl, combine the flour and pepper. Toss the venison in the seasoned flour and shake off any excess.

2. In a large nonreactive flameproof casserole, heat 1½ tablespoons of the oil over moderately high heat. Add half of the venison cubes to the casserole and cook, turning, until browned all over, about 5 minutes. Transfer to a bowl or plate with a slotted spoon. Repeat with the remaining 1½ teaspoons oil and meat and set aside.

3. Add the onion, celery, carrots and garlic cloves to the casserole and cook over moderately high heat until softened and starting to brown, 10 to 12 minutes.

4. Stir in the wine, tomato paste, orange juice and juniper berries until blended. Bring to a boil and cook until the liquid is reduced by half, about 5 minutes. Add the stock and the reserved browned venison and return to a boil. Cover, reduce the heat to low and simmer for 1½ hours.

5. Stir in the dried cherries and potatoes and continue to cook for 30 minutes.

6. Add the brandy and continue to cook until the potatoes are tender, about 30 minutes longer. Discard the juniper berries and serve. *(The stew can be made up to 2 days ahead.)*

—*Dolores Cakebread, Cakebread Cellars, Rutherford, California*

• • •

PASTA, RICE & GRAINS

PASTA, RICE & GRAINS

CAPELLINI WITH BLACK PEPPER AND PROSCIUTTO

What makes this simple dish so special is the great combination of pepper and lemon, here in the form of tart lemon zest strips. The zest is blanched and then lightly browned along with the prosciutto before the capellini is added. This gives the dish such a defined flavor that you may not want to add the Parmesan cheese at the end.

❦ Italian white, such as 1986 La Scolca Gavi or 1987 Fontodi Meriggio

——— **4 to 6 Side-Dish Servings** ———
2 large, firm lemons
4 tablespoons unsalted butter
2 tablespoons olive oil
2 large garlic cloves, minced
2 large shallots, minced
6 ounces thinly sliced prosciutto,
  stacked and cut crosswise into
  ¼-inch strips
¾ pound capellini
1 teaspoon coarsely ground pepper
Freshly grated Parmesan cheese,
  for serving

1. Put on a large pot of water to boil for the pasta. Using a vegetable peeler, remove the zest from the lemons in long strips, avoiding any white pith. Stack the strips and cut them lengthwise into very thin strips with a sharp knife. Measure out ¼ cup of the best strips (discard the remainder).

2. In a small saucepan of boiling water, blanch the zest strips for 1 minute. Drain well and set aside.

3. In a large skillet, melt the butter in the olive oil over low heat. Add the garlic and shallots and cook, stirring occasionally, until softened, about 7 minutes.

4. Increase the heat to moderately high and add the prosciutto and the reserved blanched lemon zest. Cook, stirring to break up the prosciutto, until very lightly browned, about 3 minutes.

5. Meanwhile, salt the boiling pasta water, add the capellini and boil, stirring occasionally with a fork, until al dente, about 3 minutes. Drain well. Add the pasta and black pepper to the skillet and toss to combine thoroughly. Serve at once, with Parmesan cheese on the side.

—*Marcia Kiesel*

• • •

SIMPLE PASTA SUPPER

Serves 4

Pasta with Shrimp, Arugula and Sun-Dried Tomatoes (p. 106)

Romaine Salad with Garlic and Pine Nuts (p. 143)

Semolina Bread

Chilled Orange Salad with Amaretto Cookies (p. 214)

—*Stephanie Lyness*

PASTA WITH SHRIMP, ARUGULA AND SUN-DRIED TOMATOES

To save time, buy the shrimp already shelled and deveined.

——— **4 Servings** ———
¼ cup plus 2 tablespoons olive oil
¼ teaspoon crushed hot red pepper
1 pound medium shrimp, shelled and deveined
¼ teaspoon salt
2 medium shallots, finely chopped
7 sun-dried tomato halves packed in oil, cut crosswise into thin strips
1 teaspoon dried oregano
2 bunches arugula (about 4 cups packed), large stems removed, coarsely chopped
1½ tablespoons fresh lemon juice
12 ounces dried penne or fusilli
Freshly ground pepper

1. In a medium skillet, heat 2 tablespoons of the oil and the hot pepper over moderate heat. Season the shrimp with the salt and add to the skillet. Cook, stirring occasionally, until the shrimp just turn pink, about 2 minutes.

2. Add the shallots, sun-dried tomatoes and oregano and cook, stirring occasionally, until the shallots are soft and the shrimp cooked through, about 2 minutes more. Scrape the contents of the skillet into a large bowl.

3. Add the arugula, the remaining ¼ cup olive oil and the lemon juice to the shrimp mixture; toss to combine. Season with salt to taste.

4. Meanwhile, in a large pot of boiling salted water, cook the pasta until tender, 8 to 9 minutes. Drain well. Add the pasta to the bowl and toss until well coated with the shrimp mixture. Season with salt and pepper to taste and serve hot.

—*Stephanie Lyness*

• • •

TAGLIATELLE WITH CABBAGE AND SAGE

This *pasta alla valtellinese* calls for fresh pasta, but you can use dried. If you do, cook the pasta until almost tender to the bite before adding the greens to the water and proceeding.

❦ Nera Valgella or 1983 or 1985 Dessilani Gattinara

——————— **4 Servings** ———————

Salt
¾ pound fresh tagliatelle or fettuccine
¼ medium head of red cabbage, thinly sliced crosswise (about 2 cups)
¼ medium head of Nappa cabbage, thinly sliced crosswise (about 2 cups)
¼ medium bunch of Swiss chard, sliced crosswise ½ inch thick (about 2 cups)
1 stick (4 ounces) unsalted butter
4 garlic cloves, thinly sliced
8 fresh sage leaves, thinly sliced lengthwise or ¼ teaspoon rubbed sage, plus 4 sprigs of fresh sage, for garnish
Freshly cracked pepper
⅓ cup freshly grated Parmesan cheese

1. In a large pot, bring enough water for the pasta to a rolling boil, add salt and return to a boil again. Stir in the pasta and return to a boil. Stir in the red and Nappa cabbages and the Swiss chard. Cook until the pasta is al dente, about 2 minutes. Do not overcook. Drain the pasta and vegetables thoroughly and place in a large serving bowl.

2. Meanwhile, in a medium skillet, melt the butter over moderate heat. Add the garlic and sage leaves and cook until the garlic is golden, about 4 minutes.

3. Pour the hot butter over the pasta and vegetables, season with salt and pepper to taste and toss to mix well. Sprinkle the Parmesan cheese on top. Garnish with the sage sprigs and serve at once.
—Constance and Rosario del Nero

• • •

ESCAROLE AND RED PEPPER LASAGNA

This light vegetable lasagna offers a plethora of tastes and textures. Sheets of pasta are layered with a sweet red pepper and tomato sauce, slightly bitter steamed escarole leaves and mild, creamy ricotta.

❦ All the elements of this dish point to a simple but flavorful red, such as Zinfandel, as the best partner. Try 1986 Fetzer or 1985 Louis M. Martini.

——————— **6 to 8 Servings** ———————

¼ cup plus 1 tablespoon olive oil
2 large red bell peppers, thinly sliced
2 large Spanish onions—1 thinly sliced, 1 chopped
12 garlic cloves, chopped
1 can (28 ounces) Italian plum tomatoes with their liquid
Salt and freshly ground black pepper
4 heads of escarole (about 4 pounds), leaves separated and rinsed
3 tablespoons unsalted butter plus 2 tablespoons melted butter
1 cup freshly grated Parmesan cheese
3 cups ricotta cheese
½ cup shredded mozzarella cheese
12 lasagna noodles

1. In a large flameproof casserole or dutch oven, heat ¼ cup of the olive oil. Add the red bell peppers, the sliced onion and half of the garlic. Cover and cook over moderate heat, stirring occasionally, until the vegetables are softened, about 10 minutes. Add the tomatoes with their liquid and ½ cup of water and bring to a boil over high heat. Reduce the heat to low and simmer, stirring occasionally, until the vegetables are very tender, about 30 minutes.

2. Transfer the vegetables and their liquid to a food processor and puree in batches until smooth. Strain the sauce through a coarse sieve. Alternatively, just pass the vegetables and their liquid through a food mill. Season the sauce with salt and black pepper to taste and set aside.

3. In a large covered skillet set over high heat, cook the escarole leaves in batches in the water that clings to them, stirring once, until wilted. This should take about 3 minutes per batch. Coarsely chop the wilted escarole and place in a colander. Using your hands, squeeze out all excess moisture.

4. In the same skillet, heat the remaining 1 tablespoon olive oil with 3 tablespoons of the butter over low heat. Add the chopped onion and the remaining garlic and cook, stirring, until softened, about 15 minutes. Increase the heat to moderate, add the escarole and cook, stirring, until blended, about 5 minutes. Season well with salt and black pepper to taste and transfer the escarole to a bowl to cool to room temperature. Stir in ¼ cup of the Parmesan cheese.

5. In a medium bowl, stir together the ricotta, mozzarella and ½ cup of the Parmesan. Season with black pepper to taste.

6. In a large pot of boiling salted water, cook the lasagna noodles until tender, about 10 minutes. Set the pot in the sink and run cold water into it until cool. Lift out the lasagna noodles and drain on paper towels.

7. Preheat the oven to 350°. Pour one-third of the red pepper sauce into a 9-by-13-inch baking dish and spread evenly. Arrange 3 lasagna noodles in the dish and spread one-third of the escarole over the noodles. Spread one-third of the cheese mixture evenly over the escarole. Repeat the layering procedure 2 more times. Top with the remaining 3 lasagna noodles (see Note). Spread the melted butter over the noodles and sprinkle the remaining ¼ cup Parmesan cheese on top. *(The recipe can be prepared to this point up to 1 day ahead. Cover and refrigerate. Let return to room temperature before baking.)*

8. Bake the lasagna on the top rack of the oven for 1 hour or until hot, bubbly and crisp on top. Let cool for 10 minutes. With a sharp knife, cut the lasagna into 6 or 8 equal portions and serve piping hot.

NOTE: For a touch of whimsy, you can cut the last layer of noodles into shapes and place them decoratively on top.

—*Marcia Kiesel*

• • •

CRESCENT CITY SUPPER

Serves 6

Shrimp Rémoulade (p. 39)

Pasta Jambalaya (p. 108)

🍷 *1986 Hugel or Trimbach Gewürztraminer*

French Bread Pudding with Whiskey Sauce (p. 199)

Café Brûlot Diabolique (p. 19)

PASTA JAMBALAYA

At Mr. B's restaurant in New Orleans, a bed of spinach fettuccine brings a modern note to a Creole classic.

——————— **6 Servings** ———————

9 ounces andouille sausage,* cut into ½-inch dice
2 skinless, boneless duck breast halves (about 5 ounces total), pounded ½ inch thick
All-purpose flour, for dredging
6 tablespoons unsalted butter
2 skinless, boneless chicken breast halves (about 7 ounces total), pounded ½ inch thick
1 medium onion, diced
1 small green bell pepper, diced
1 small red bell pepper, diced
1 garlic clove, minced
¾ pound medium shrimp, shelled, shells reserved
2 cans (10½ ounces each) low-sodium chicken broth
2 medium tomatoes, seeded and chopped
1 tablespoon Creole Seasoning (p. 258)
1 pound fresh spinach fettuccine
Pinch of crushed hot red pepper
*Available at specialty food markets

1. Set a large heavy nonreactive skillet over moderately high heat until hot but not smoking. Add the sausage and cook, stirring often, until lightly browned, about 5 minutes. Remove with a slotted spoon and drain on paper towels. Transfer to a medium bowl.

2. Lightly dredge the duck breasts in flour. Return the skillet to moderately high heat and add 1 tablespoon of the butter. When the butter melts, add the duck breasts and cook until firm to the touch and browned, 2 to 3 minutes on each side. Remove from the pan and slice the duck across the grain ½ inch thick. Transfer to the bowl with the sausage.

3. Add 1 tablespoon of the butter to the skillet and repeat the dredging, cooking and slicing procedure with the chicken breasts.

4. Reduce the heat to moderate. Melt 2 more tablespoons of the butter in the skillet. Add the onion, bell peppers and garlic and cook until they begin to soften, about 5 minutes.

5. Add the shrimp and cook until opaque and loosely curled, about 2 minutes longer. Using a slotted spoon, transfer the contents of the skillet to the bowl with the cooked meats.

6. Bring a large pot of salted water to a boil over high heat. Meanwhile, add the reserved shrimp shells and the chicken broth to the skillet and bring to a boil over high heat. Cook until the liquid reduces by half, about 5 minutes. Strain the broth into a measuring cup, then return it to the skillet. If you have more than 1 cup, boil again to reduce the liquid. Add the tomatoes and Creole Seasoning and simmer over moderate heat for 5 minutes. *(The recipe can be prepared to this point up to 1 day ahead. Let cool to room temperature, then cover and refrigerate the sauce and the bowl of meats separately.)*

7. Add the contents of the bowl to the tomato sauce and cook over moderate heat until warmed through, about 5 minutes longer.

8. Cook the fettuccine until tender but still firm to the bite, about 3 minutes. Drain in a colander and place in a large serving bowl or on a platter. Swirl the remaining 2 tablespoons butter into the sauce and season with the hot pepper. Spoon the sauce on top of the fettuccine and serve at once.

—*Gerard Maras, Mr. B's, New Orleans*

• • •

Poached Salmon Pinwheels with German Cucumber Salad and Sauce Verte (p. 51).

Above, Parslied Carrots (p. 123). Right, Tuscan Beans with Tuna, Pancetta and Lemon (p. 121).

ORZO WITH ROASTED PEPPERS AND DRIED TOMATOES

Orzo is a readily available pasta that is shaped like rice. The peppers can be roasted at the edge of a barbecue grill over a fast fire or in the center if the fire is slow.

——————— *6 to 8 Servings* ———————
2 red bell peppers
1 yellow bell pepper
1 tablespoon plus 1 teaspoon salt
1 pound orzo
6 tablespoons extra-virgin olive oil
6 large shallots, minced
3 tablespoons minced garlic
1½ cups air-dried California tomato slices or ¼ cup Italian sun-dried tomatoes with their oil, sliced crosswise
1½ cups chicken stock or low-sodium canned broth
1 teaspoon freshly ground black pepper
1 cup chopped fresh basil
1 cup freshly grated Parmesan or aged domestic asiago cheese (about ¼ pound)

1. Roast the bell peppers directly over a grill or a gas flame, turning frequently, until charred all over. Transfer the peppers to a brown paper bag and set aside for 10 minutes to steam.

2. Using a knife, scrape off the charred skins. Quarter the peppers. Remove the cores and seeds; reserve any juices. Cut the peppers into ½-inch dice.

3. Bring a large pot of water to a boil over high heat. Add 1 tablespoon of the salt and the orzo and cook, stirring once or twice, until al dente, about 6 minutes. Drain well.

4. Meanwhile, heat a large nonreactive skillet over high heat for 1 minute. Add the olive oil and shallots and reduce the heat to low. Cook, stirring occasionally, until slightly softened, about 3 minutes. Increase the heat to moderate. Add the garlic and cook until lightly browned, about 5 minutes. Add the dried tomatoes and cook for a few seconds, then stir in the stock, black pepper and the remaining 1 teaspoon salt.

5. Increase the heat to high and boil until the stock reduces by half, 3 to 5 minutes. Stir in the basil and then the drained orzo. Stir until the stock is absorbed. Add the roasted peppers with their juices and stir well. Remove from the heat. Sprinkle the cheese on top and stir until it is evenly distributed and melted. Serve immediately.

—Karen Lee & Alaxandra Branyon

• • •

RISOTTO WITH PORCINI MUSHROOMS

For *risotto ai porcini*, dried porcini and Arborio rice can be found in Italian food markets and some supermarkets.

♟ Rainoldi Inferno or 1983 or 1985 Ceretto Nebbiolo d'Alba

——————— *4 to 6 Servings* ———————
1¾ ounces dried porcini mushrooms
6 cups beef stock or 2 cans (13¾ ounces each) beef broth plus 2½ cups of water
1 stick (4 ounces) unsalted butter
1 medium white onion, chopped
4 fresh sage leaves, coarsely chopped, or a pinch of rubbed sage
2 cups Arborio rice
¾ cup dry red wine
3 tablespoons minced parsley
¾ cup freshly grated Parmesan cheese

1. In a small bowl, soak the mushrooms in 2 cups of lukewarm water for 30 minutes. Remove the mushrooms with a slotted spoon, rinse and set aside. Strain the mushroom liquid through a triple layer of cheesecloth and set aside.

2. In a saucepan, bring the stock to a boil over high heat; then lower the heat to maintain a simmer until ready to use.

3. Meanwhile, in a large nonreactive saucepan, melt 6 tablespoons of the butter over moderate heat. Add the onion and sage and cook, stirring occasionally, until the onion is translucent, about 5 minutes. Add the rice and cook, stirring constantly, until lightly toasted, about 5 minutes.

4. Add the wine and cook, stirring constantly, until the wine is absorbed, about 3 minutes. Stir in the reserved mushrooms and their liquid. Cook, stirring constantly, until the liquid is absorbed, 3 to 5 minutes. Add 1 cup of the simmering beef stock and stir constantly until it is absorbed. Continue adding the stock, 1 cup at a time when the rice seems dry, stirring constantly, until tender but still firm to the bite and the mixture is creamy but not soupy, about 20 minutes.

5. Remove the saucepan from the heat and stir in the parsley, Parmesan and the remaining 2 tablespoons butter. Mix well and serve at once.

—Constance and Rosario del Nero

• • •

Caramelized Shallot Vinaigrette (p. 256), shown here with mushrooms and potatoes.

PASTA, RICE & GRAINS

MICROWAVED PANCETTA AND MUSTARD-GREEN RISOTTO

Since you already know me for the easy-way-out Philistine that I am, it won't surprise you in the slightest that this risotto is prepared in a microwave oven—the basic technique is from Barbara Kafka, author of *Microwave Gourmet* (William Morrow). Although using this method takes about the same time as the conventional way, it's much easier than standing over a hot stove, constantly stirring. But if you are a purist, the conventional method is also included.

♟ Light crisp white, such as 1988 Torresella Pinot Grigio

——————— *6 Servings* ———————

1/4 pound thinly sliced pancetta, cut into 1/2-inch pieces
1/4 cup olive oil
3 tablespoons unsalted butter
2 cups packed, bite-size pieces of mustard greens (from a 10-ounce bunch)
1 medium onion, chopped
2 cups Arborio rice
6 cups low-sodium chicken broth
Salt and freshly ground pepper
Sprigs of rosemary, for garnish

1. On a microwave-proof plate lined with paper towels, cook the pancetta on High power for 5 minutes, or until crisp and browned. Blot the pancetta with paper towels.

2. Transfer the pancetta to a 9-by-13-inch glass baking dish. Add the oil, butter and mustard greens to the dish and toss to coat. Cook on High for 3 minutes.

3. Stir in the onion and cook on High for 5 minutes. Add the rice and toss to coat; cook on High for 2 minutes. Stir in the chicken broth and cook on High for 10 minutes. Stir the rice again and cook on High for 15 minutes longer. Toss with a fork and season with salt and pepper to taste. Garnish with a sprig of rosemary and serve piping hot.

DINNER ITALIAN-STYLE

Serves 6

Microwaved Pancetta and Mustard-Green Risotto (p. 114)

Belgian Endive and Radicchio Salad (p. 142)

♟ *Light red wine, such as Rioja or Chianti*

—————

Berry Biscuits (p. 210)

Coffee

—Lee Bailey

CONVENTIONAL METHOD:

1. In a large saucepan, bring 8 cups of chicken broth to a simmer over moderately high heat, about 10 minutes. Cover to keep warm and reduce the heat to low.

2. Meanwhile, in a medium flame-proof casserole, cook the pancetta over moderately high heat, stirring frequently, until browned, about 5 minutes. Transfer to paper towels to drain. Drain off all the fat and wipe out the casserole.

3. Add the oil, butter, mustard greens and onion. Reduce the heat to moderately low and cook, stirring, until the onion softens, about 5 minutes. Increase the heat to moderately high. Add the rice and stir to coat the grains. Add 1 cup of the hot broth and cook, stirring constantly, until the liquid is almost completely absorbed, about 2 minutes.

4. Gradually add the remaining hot broth, 1/2 cup at a time, stirring constantly until all the broth is absorbed. The risotto should be creamy with tender yet distinct grains of rice. Season with salt and pepper to taste, garnish with a sprig of rosemary and serve piping hot.

—Lee Bailey

• • •

WILD MUSHROOM RISOTTO

This satisfying risotto makes a good main course, but it can also be a first course or even a side dish.

♟ With the risotto, try the rich and buttery 1986 Simi Chardonnay.

——————— *6 Servings* ———————

5 1/2 cups chicken stock or canned low-sodium broth
6 tablespoons unsalted butter
1/2 pound mixed fresh wild mushrooms, such as shiitake, chanterelles, porcini or oyster mushrooms, trimmed and sliced
1 garlic clove, minced
3 tablespoons olive oil
1 small onion, minced
1 1/2 cups Arborio rice
1/2 cup minced Italian flat-leaf parsley
2 ounces asiago or Parmesan cheese, finely grated
Salt and freshly ground pepper

1. In a medium saucepan, bring the stock to a simmer over moderate heat. Reduce the heat to very low and cover until ready to use.

2. In a large heavy saucepan, melt 3 tablespoons of the butter over moderately high heat. Add the mushrooms and cook until wilted, about 3 minutes. Add the garlic and cook, tossing, for 1 minute. Transfer the mushrooms and garlic to a plate or bowl and set aside.

3. Reduce the heat to moderate. Add the remaining 3 tablespoons butter and the olive oil to the saucepan. When the butter is melted, add the onion and cook until softened, about 5 minutes. Add the rice and stir to coat well.

4. Increase the heat to moderately high. Add about 1/2 cup of the hot stock and stir constantly until the mixture

comes to a simmer. Add 2 more cups of the hot stock, ½ cup at a time, stirring constantly until the stock is absorbed after each addition, about 10 minutes.

5. Toss in the reserved mushrooms and garlic and the parsley. Continue adding the remaining stock, about ½ cup at a time, stirring constantly until the stock is absorbed after each addition and the rice is tender, but still firm, and creamy but not soupy, 8 to 10 minutes longer.

6. Remove the risotto from the heat and stir in the cheese. Season to taste with salt and lots of pepper and serve at once.

—Mary Evely, Simi Winery,
Healdsburg, California

• • •

RISOTTO MOLD
WITH PROSCIUTTO

Instead of a ring mold, a cake pan can be used, but in that case leave it in the oven for a few more minutes to cook through to the center. Test by inserting the tip of a knife into the risotto: when the tip is thoroughly hot, it is ready to be served.

————— **12 Servings** —————
1 stick (4 ounces) unsalted butter,
at room temperature
12 slices prosciutto, preferably from
Parma, thinly sliced
11 cups chicken stock or canned
low-sodium chicken broth
2 tablespoons minced onion
6 cups Arborio rice
1 cup freshly grated Parmesan
cheese
Salt and freshly ground pepper

1. Butter two 6-cup ring molds or two 9-inch cake pans with 1 tablespoon or so of the butter. Evenly line the pans with the slices of prosciutto, patching with small pieces as necessary.

2. In a medium saucepan, heat the stock over moderate heat, covered, until hot. Reduce the heat to very low and keep covered.

3. In a large flameproof casserole or small, heavy stockpot, melt 3 tablespoons of the butter over low heat. Add the onion and cook, stirring frequently, until translucent, about 5 minutes. Increase the heat to moderate, add the rice and stir to coat evenly with the butter.

4. Increase the heat to high and stir in 3 cups of the hot stock. Cook, stirring constantly, until most of the liquid has been absorbed, about 3 minutes. Continue adding stock, 1 cup at a time about every minute, stirring constantly. The rice should always be covered with a thin veil of stock. After 12 minutes, the rice should be quite dry and al dente.

5. Remove from the heat and add the Parmesan cheese and the remaining 4 tablespoons butter. Stir until the butter is incorporated and season with salt and pepper to taste.

6. Pour the warm risotto into a large flat dish or roasting pan to cool completely and to prevent the rice from overcooking. Spoon the cooled rice into the prepared molds. *(The recipe can be prepared to this point several hours ahead; cover and refrigerate.)*

7. Preheat the oven to 400°. Bake the risotto on the lowest rack in the oven, uncovered, for 20 minutes. Cover and bake 10 minutes longer, until heated through. Carefully unmold onto platters.

—Lorenza de' Medici

• • •

PERSIAN RICE

This rice is a adaptation of an ancient dish once made for kings. A blend of spice, rice, fruit and nuts, it has complex flavors, interesting textures and a warm yellow glow.

————— **6 to 8 Servings** —————
1 tablespoon unsalted butter
2 tablespoons light olive oil
1 large onion, chopped

4 garlic cloves, minced
1 dried red chile, seeded and finely
chopped
½ teaspoon cumin seeds, crushed
2 cardamom pods, seeds removed
and crushed
½ teaspoon ground ginger
½ teaspoon (firmly packed) saffron
threads
4½ cups warm chicken stock or
canned low-sodium broth
2 cups long-grain rice, rinsed well
1 cinnamon stick
1 bay leaf
¼ cup dried currants
10 small, whole dried apricots,
quartered
¾ teaspoon salt
½ cup sliced unblanched almonds
2 tablespoons pine nuts
¼ cup shelled unsalted pistachio
nuts
Freshly ground black pepper
3 tablespoons fresh coriander
leaves, torn

1. In a large flameproof casserole, melt the butter in the olive oil over low heat. Add the onion and garlic and cook, stirring, until softened, about 5 minutes.

2. Increase the heat to moderate and add the chile, cumin seeds, cardamom and ginger. Cook, stirring, until fragrant, about 2 minutes. Add the saffron and chicken stock, mix well and remove from the heat. Cover and let the saffron permeate the stock for 5 minutes.

3. Preheat the oven to 400°. Bring the stock to a simmer over moderate heat. Stir in the rice, cinnamon stick, bay leaf, currants, apricots and the salt. Return to a simmer, then reduce the heat to low. Cover and cook for 17 minutes. If the rice is still too wet, cook longer.

4. Meanwhile, place the almonds and pine nuts on a baking sheet and toast in the oven for about 4 minutes, until golden. Add the pistachios and toast for 1 more minute. Transfer to a plate to cool.

5. Uncover the rice and stir once with a fork to fluff up. Season with additional salt and black pepper to taste. Add the nuts and toss. Sprinkle the coriander on top and serve.

—*Marcia Kiesel*

• • •

LOUISIANA DIRTY RICE

Here is Brigtsen's version of a popular Cajun dish. In Louisiana, dirty rice is traditionally served with any poultry dish, such as chicken, duck, turkey or quail. It is also a great side dish with roast pork.

———— *6 Servings* ————
6 ounces chicken gizzards, trimmed
6 ounces chicken livers, trimmed
3 tablespoons unsalted butter,
   chicken fat or duck fat
4 ounces ground lean beef or pork
¾ cup finely chopped onion
½ cup finely chopped green bell
   pepper
½ cup finely chopped celery
¾ cup finely chopped eggplant
½ teaspoon minced garlic
1 large bay leaf
2½ teaspoons salt
½ teaspoon freshly ground black
   pepper
½ teaspoon cayenne pepper
½ teaspoon cumin
½ teaspoon oregano
¼ teaspoon freshly ground white
   pepper
3 cups chicken stock or canned broth
1½ cups converted rice
½ cup thinly sliced scallions

1. In a food processor, place the gizzards and process until finely ground. Set aside. Repeat the procedure with the livers and set aside separately.

2. In a heavy saucepan or cast-iron skillet, heat the butter. Add the chicken gizzards and ground beef and cook over moderate heat, stirring constantly, until thoroughly browned, about 5 minutes.

3. Add the onion, green pepper, celery and eggplant and cook until the vegetables are softened, about 4 minutes.

4. Stir in the garlic, bay leaf, salt, black pepper, cayenne, cumin, oregano and white pepper. Cook for 2 minutes, then add ½ cup of the chicken stock. Cook for 4 minutes, scraping the bottom and sides of the pan with a spoon.

5. Stir in the ground chicken livers and add the remaining 2½ cups chicken stock. Bring to a boil over high heat, reduce the heat to moderate and simmer for 2 minutes. Stir in the rice and cover. Reduce the heat to very low and cook until all the liquid has been absorbed, 17 to 20 minutes. Uncover and stir in the scallions. Serve hot.

—*Frank Brigtsen,*
Brigtsen's, New Orleans

• • •

FRIED GINGER RICE

This is a simple dish of fried ginger, scallions, butter and rice. When sticks of fresh ginger are deep-fried, they turn crunchy with only a hint of spiciness. If you make this as a side dish to go with Ginger-Rubbed Fresh Ham (p. 92), save 2 tablespoons of the pan juices from the ham and stir it into the rice in Step 4 below.

———— *4 to 6 Servings* ————
3 ounces fresh ginger, peeled
½ cup vegetable or corn oil
1½ cups long-grain rice, preferably
   basmati,* rinsed
2 large scallions, thinly sliced
1 tablespoon unsalted butter
Salt and freshly ground pepper
*Available at Indian and specialty
   food markets and at some
   supermarkets

1. Thinly slice the ginger crosswise. Stack the slices and cut crosswise into small sticks.

2. In a medium saucepan, heat the oil over high heat until hot, about 4 minutes. Test by dropping in a piece of ginger: it should sizzle immediately. Add all the ginger and stir briefly to separate. Cook until light brown and starting to crisp, about 5 minutes. Using a slotted spoon, transfer the fried ginger to paper towels.

3. In another medium saucepan, combine the rice with 1¾ cups of water and bring to a boil over high heat. Reduce the heat to low, cover and cook for 16 minutes. Remove from the heat and keep covered for 5 minutes.

4. Fluff the rice and stir in the scallions, butter, salt and pepper to taste, and the reserved fried ginger and serve at once.

—*Marcia Kiesel*

• • •

FRIED-RICE PATTIES

To add some flavor to the rice, cook it in chicken stock or canned low-sodium broth. The rice can be cooked one day ahead. Let come to room temperature before proceeding.

———— *6 Servings* ————
4 tablespoons unsalted butter
1 medium onion, finely chopped
4 cups cooked rice
¼ cup plus 1 tablespoon all-purpose
   flour
2 eggs, lightly beaten
¼ teaspoon salt
¼ teaspoon freshly ground pepper
¼ cup minced parsley
2 tablespoons olive oil

1. In a small saucepan, melt 2 tablespoons of the butter over moderate heat.

Add the onion and cook, stirring, until softened, about 5 minutes.

2. In a medium bowl, combine the cooked rice with the flour, tossing with a fork until all the grains are coated. Add the eggs, salt, pepper, parsley and cooked onion and mix well.

3. Using a 1-cup measure, form 12 patties about 3 inches in diameter. Press lightly to flatten. To set, place finished patties on 2 sheets of waxed paper and microwave at High power for 1 minute. Alternatively, place the patties on a tray or baking sheet lined with waxed paper and refrigerate for 1 hour.

4. In a large heavy skillet, melt the remaining 2 tablespoons butter in the olive oil over moderately high heat. When the fat is foaming, carefully place half of the patties in the pan. Cook until golden, about 2 minutes per side. Drain on paper towels. Fry the remaining patties. Serve hot.

—*Lee Bailey*

• • •

BULGUR PILAF

Bulgur, or cracked wheat, has a nutty flavor and chewy texture when cooked.

──────── *6 Servings* ────────
1 tablespoon vegetable oil
1 medium onion, minced
1 large celery rib, minced, plus
    celery leaves for garnish
3 cups chicken stock or canned
    low-sodium broth
1½ cups bulgur
½ teaspoon salt
1 tablespoon unsalted butter
    (optional)

1. In a large heavy saucepan, heat the oil over moderate heat. When the oil is hot, add the onion and minced celery and cook, stirring occasionally, until softened, about 5 minutes.

2. In a medium saucepan, bring the chicken stock to a boil over high heat. Add the bulgur, cover tightly and reduce the heat to low. Cook until the liquid is absorbed, about 15 minutes.

3. Turn off the heat and add the onion and celery. Let sit, covered, for about 10 minutes.

4. Season with the salt (or to taste) and stir in the butter, if using. Transfer to a serving platter or individual dinner plates and garnish with the celery leaves. Serve the pilaf warm or at room temperature.

—*Lee Bailey*

• • •

GREAT GRANOLA

This recipe dates from the early Sixties, a time when we were all learning our way around the bin-packed aisles of the local health food store. My sister, Sarah, set down the original proportions, and over the years the following recipe evolved. Make a large batch so that there's enough to toss some into cookie doughs and muffin batters or to sprinkle over yogurt or ice cream. When you're having this crunchy medley of grains, nuts and dried fruits for breakfast, you can add yet another texture (and some extra nutrients) by topping it with slices of crisp tart apple or ripe banana, or some berries.

──────── *Makes About 18 Cups* ────────
6 cups old-fashioned rolled oats
    (18 ounces)
2½ cups raw sunflower seeds
    (12 ounces)
1 cup sesame seeds (5 ounces)
2 cups wheat bran (4 ounces)
1 cup oat bran (4 ounces)
1 cup walnut pieces (4 ounces)
2 cups slivered almonds (8 ounces)
½ cup vegetable oil
1½ cups honey
4 cups mixed dried fruit, such as
    dark and golden raisins, currants
    and sliced dried apricots, dates
    and pitted prunes (about 1 pound)

1. Preheat the oven to 350°. In a very large bowl, combine the oats, sunflower seeds, sesame seeds, wheat bran, oat bran, walnuts and almonds. Toss well. Drizzle the vegetable oil over the dry ingredients and toss again to evenly coat.

2. In a small saucepan, warm the honey over low heat until it liquefies, about 5 minutes. Drizzle the honey into the bowl and toss the ingredients very well to coat thoroughly.

3. Divide the granola mixture between two 11-by-17-inch jelly-roll pans, spreading it evenly. Bake for 15 minutes. Remove from the oven and stir the granola with a spatula, mixing it thoroughly by bringing it in from the edges and up from the bottom of the pans.

4. Reduce the oven temperature to 325°. Bake the granola for 30 minutes longer, giving it a good stir every 10 minutes and switching the pans once, until evenly browned.

5. Return the granola to the large bowl and add the dried fruit. Toss well to blend, then let cool completely. Store the granola in plastic bags or airtight tins for up to 2 weeks or freeze for up to 2 months.

—*Bob Chambers*

• • •

VEGETABLES

VEGETABLES

ASPARAGUS WITH PROVENCALE MAYONNAISE

—————— 6 Servings ——————
2 pounds asparagus, trimmed
    and peeled
1/2 cup thawed frozen chopped
    spinach (4 1/2 ounces),
    squeezed dry
2 scallions, minced
1/4 cup minced parsley
2 large garlic cloves, crushed
    through a press
4 to 6 flat anchovy fillets, minced
1/2 cup sour cream
1 cup mayonnaise
Juice of 1 large lemon, or more
    to taste
Salt and freshly ground pepper
1 tablespoon salmon caviar
1 hard-cooked egg yolk, sieved
Sprigs of Italian flat-leaf parsley,
    for garnish

1. In a large pot, steam the asparagus until tender, about 5 minutes. Let cool, then chill, covered, until serving time.

2. In a food processor or blender, combine the spinach, scallions, parsley, garlic, anchovies and sour cream. Process until smooth, about 3 minutes. Add the mayonnaise and lemon juice and process until just combined. Season with salt and pepper to taste. Cover and refrigerate for 4 to 6 hours before serving.

3. Arrange the asparagus on a platter and spoon some of the mayonnaise over them. Garnish with the salmon caviar, egg yolk and sprigs of parsley. Pass the remaining mayonnaise separately.

—Perla Meyers

• • •

ASPARAGUS WITH BUTTER VINAIGRETTE

—————— 6 Servings ——————
2 pounds asparagus
3 tablespoons unsalted butter
1 tablespoon plus 1 teaspoon
    balsamic vinegar
3/4 teaspoon salt
Freshly ground pepper

1. Steam the asparagus until just tender, about 3 minutes. Alternatively, add the asparagus to a large skillet of boiling salted water and let cook about 3 minutes.

2. Meanwhile, in a small nonreactive saucepan, melt the butter over moderate heat. Whisk in the vinegar and salt.

3. Transfer the asparagus to a large warm platter and pour the vinaigrette over it. Season with pepper to taste and serve warm.

—Lee Bailey

• • •

ASPARAGUS WITH PARMESAN CHEESE

I cook fresh asparagus immersed upright in boiling water, but I leave the tender tips standing clear.

—————— 12 Servings ——————
4 pounds medium asparagus
Salt
6 tablespoons lightly salted butter
3/4 cup freshly grated Parmesan
    cheese
Pinch of freshly grated nutmeg

1. Divide the asparagus into 3 bunches and tie each bunch in the center with cotton string. Add enough water to a tall stockpot to almost cover the asparagus when standing vertically (the tips should not be immersed). Lightly salt the water

and bring to a boil over moderately high heat. Stand the asparagus bundles in the pot, cover and simmer until just tender, about 10 minutes. The tips should be barely tender.

2. In a small saucepan, cook the butter over moderate heat until it bubbles and just begins to turn brown, about 5 to 8 minutes. Remove from the heat.

3. Drain the asparagus well. Untie the bundles and heap the asparagus on a deep platter. Pour on 1 tablespoon of the brown butter and turn the asparagus with tongs or 2 spoons to coat.

4. Sprinkle 1/4 cup of the Parmesan cheese and the nutmeg over the asparagus and turn again to distribute the cheese. Pour the remaining browned butter over the asparagus and sprinkle the remaining 1/2 cup Parmesan cheese on top. Serve warm.

—Lorenza de' Medici

• • •

TARRAGON BEETS

The snappy, sharp flavors of tarragon, capers and vinegar balance the natural sweetness of the beets. Tarragon varies in strength, so you may want to add more or less, depending on individual taste. In any case, this sauce should have a pronounced tarragon flavor.

—————— 8 Servings ——————
3 pounds beets without tops
1/3 cup tarragon vinegar
1 tablespoon finely chopped fresh
    tarragon or 1 1/2 teaspoons dried
5 tablespoons unsalted butter, cut
    into pieces
2 tablespoons drained capers
Salt and freshly ground pepper

1. Place the beets in a large saucepan with water to cover and bring to a boil over moderately high heat. Cook until tender

when pierced with a fork, 30 to 40 minutes (depending on the size of the beets). Alternatively, wrap the beets in aluminum foil and bake in a 400° oven for about 1¼ hours, until tender. Peel the beets and cut into 1-inch pieces.

2. In a large nonreactive saucepan, combine ¼ cup of water with the vinegar and tarragon and bring to a boil over high heat. Reduce the heat to moderate and simmer for 3 minutes.

3. Add the butter and stir until melted. Add the beets and cook, stirring, until heated through, about 8 minutes. Remove from the heat, stir in the capers and season to taste with salt and pepper. Toss, transfer to a warmed serving dish and serve hot.

—Marion Cunningham

• • •

BEETS, ARTICHOKES, ASPARAGUS, ONIONS AND RADISHES WITH WHIPPED BUTTER

If white asparagus are unavailable, use another pound of green.

——— *12 Servings* ———
Coarse (kosher) salt
12 young beets without tops
1 large lemon
12 small artichokes
1 pound white asparagus, trimmed
*   and peeled*
1 pound green asparagus, trimmed
*   and peeled*
1 pound young onions with 5 inches
*   of green*
1½ sticks (6 ounces) unsalted
*   butter, softened*
2 bunches of fresh young radishes
*   with leaves*

1. Preheat the oven to 375°. Spread a generous layer of coarse salt in a baking pan and arrange the beets on top, nestling

them down a bit. Bake uncovered until tender, about 2 hours. When cool, peel and trim the beets.

2. Meanwhile, bring a large saucepan of salted water to a boil over high heat. Halve and juice the lemon and add the juice and lemon halves to the water. Trim the stems from the artichokes and trim around the bottoms with a sharp knife to remove the tough, dark outer leaves. Using scissors, cut off the top, thorny parts of the leaves. Add the artichokes to the pan and boil, covered, until tender when pierced, about 10 minutes. Remove from the heat and let cool to room temperature in the liquid.

3. Cook the asparagus in a pot of boiling salted water until just tender, about 4 minutes. Transfer the asparagus to a bowl of ice water to cool them down quickly. Drain well and transfer to a large plate. Cover with plastic wrap and refrigerate.

4. Cook the onions in another pot of boiling salted water until tender, about 5 minutes. Transfer the onions to a bowl of ice water to cool them down quickly. Drain well and transfer to a plate. Cover with plastic wrap and refrigerate. *(The recipe can be prepared to this point up to 6 hours ahead.)*

5. In a medium bowl, beat the butter until very fluffy. Spoon the butter into a pretty crock. Arrange all the cooked vegetables and the radishes on a platter. Serve the butter and a small bowl of coarse salt alongside.

—Christer Larsson, Aquavit,
New York City

• • •

TUSCAN BEANS WITH TUNA, PANCETTA AND LEMON

This is the most Tuscan of all dishes—it combines our love of beans with cooking in terra-cotta in a wood-fired brick oven. The beans can be eaten on their own as a vegetable or as a *zuppa* (soup) served over a slice of Tuscan Bread (p. 158) that has been toasted and rubbed with garlic.

❢ The strong, salty flavors of this hearty dish would be set off by a simple refreshing Italian white, such as 1988 Antinori Galestro from Tuscany or 1988 Mastroberardino Plinius from Campania.

——— *8 Servings* ———
2 cups dried white beans (12
*   ounces), rinsed and picked over*
¼ cup olive oil
12 large sage leaves, fresh or
*   preserved in salt**
4 large garlic cloves
¼ pound thinly sliced pancetta or
*   prosciutto, cut into 1-inch pieces*
½ teaspoon salt
2 tablespoons fresh lemon juice
1 can (6½ ounces) tuna packed in
*   olive oil, drained*
Freshly ground pepper
*Available at Italian markets

1. In a large bowl, soak the beans overnight in cold water to cover. Alternatively, place the beans in a medium saucepan with cold water to cover and bring to a boil over high heat. Cover and set aside for 1 hour.

2. Preheat the oven to 400°. Drain the beans and rinse well. In a medium casserole, combine the beans with 4 cups of water, the oil, sage, garlic, pancetta and salt. Cover tightly and bake for about 1½ hours, stirring occasionally, until the beans are tender. Remove from the oven. *(The recipe can be prepared to this point up to 2 days ahead. Reheat the beans before proceeding.)*

3. Stir the lemon juice and tuna into the beans and bake uncovered for 10 minutes longer. Season with pepper and serve hot.

—*Giuliano Bugialli*

• • •

BABY LIMA BEANS, CHERRY TOMATOES AND PEARS

Lima beans are the one bean I refuse to shell because they are extremely difficult to do, so here I've called for the frozen variety.

——————— *6 Servings* ———————
1½ cups cherry tomatoes
1 package (10 ounces) frozen baby lima beans, thawed
1 lemon
1 firm ripe pear, preferably Anjou or Bosc—peeled, quartered and cored
2 tablespoons unsalted butter
1 teaspoon salt
⅛ teaspoon freshly ground pepper

1. In a small pot of boiling water, blanch the cherry tomatoes for 1 minute; drain. Plunge the tomatoes into a bowl of cold water until the skins split. Peel off and discard the skins. Place the tomatoes in a small bowl.

2. In a small saucepan, steam the lima beans until tender, 12 to 15 minutes.

3. Meanwhile, squeeze the juice from the lemon into a small bowl. Using a grater with large holes, shred the pear into the lemon juice, tossing occasionally.

4. In a medium nonreactive saucepan, melt the butter over moderate heat. Add the pear and any juices, increase the heat to moderately high and cook, stirring

constantly, until the pear is softened and the liquid is slightly reduced, about 1 minute.

5. Drain and discard any tomato juice that may have accumulated in the bowl. Add the tomatoes to the pears and toss over moderate heat for 1 minute. Add the lima beans, salt and pepper and cook, tossing constantly, until heated through, about 1 minute. Serve hot.

—*Lee Bailey*

• • •

SAUTEED BROCCOLI AND CHERRY TOMATOES

When blanched briefly and sautéed quickly in olive oil, broccoli remains bright green. Although the broccoli can be blanched way ahead of time, it has to be sautéed at the last minute.

——————— *8 Servings* ———————
2 large bunches of broccoli, cut into small florets
2 tablespoons olive oil
3 shallots, minced
8 cherry tomatoes, cut in half
¼ cup sour cream
Salt and freshly ground pepper

1. In a large pan of boiling salted water, cook the broccoli until bright green and crisp-tender, about 4 minutes. Drain and refresh under cold running water; drain again thoroughly. *(The broccoli can be prepared up to 2 days ahead to this point. Cover and refrigerate.)*

2. In a large skillet, heat the oil. Add the shallots and cook over moderately high heat, stirring, until softened, about 2 minutes.

3. Add the broccoli and cook for 2 minutes longer. Stir in the cherry tomatoes and cook, stirring gently, until heated through, about 2 minutes longer. Stir in the sour cream and season with salt and pepper to taste. Serve hot.

—*Lydie Pinoy Marshall*

• • •

CABBAGE WITH PINE NUTS

Since it cooks for less than half a minute, the cabbage retains its lovely green color and crisp texture. Toasted pine nuts look pretty on top and add a little crunch and a sweet nutty flavor.

——————— *8 Servings* ———————
½ cup pine nuts
1 large head of green cabbage, coarsely chopped
4 tablespoons unsalted butter, melted
2 tablespoons fresh lemon juice
Salt

1. Preheat the oven to 350°. Spread the pine nuts on a baking sheet and toast for 10 to 12 minutes, until golden and fragrant.

2. Meanwhile, bring a large pot of salted water to a boil. Plunge the cabbage into the water and return to a boil. Cook for 20 seconds. Drain well in a colander and transfer to a warmed bowl.

3. Stir in the butter and lemon juice. Season with salt to taste and toss well to combine. Sprinkle the toasted pine nuts on top. Toss lightly again before serving.

—*Lydie Pinoy Marshall*

• • •

PARSLIED CARROTS

One of the simplest and tastiest side dishes is this combination of cooked carrots with a gloss of butter and a sprinkling of chopped parsley.

———— 8 Servings ————
2½ pounds carrots, cut on the
*   diagonal into ½-inch chunks*
4 tablespoons unsalted butter
Salt
¼ cup finely chopped parsley

1. Bring a large saucepan of salted water to a boil. Add the carrots and cook over moderate heat until just tender, about 10 minutes. Drain off the water.

2. Add the butter to the saucepan and toss to coat the carrots. Season to taste with salt, add the parsley and mix well. Transfer to a bowl and serve hot.
—*Marion Cunningham*

• • •

GLAZED CARROTS, TURNIPS AND PEARL ONIONS

This method is great for other root vegetables, including beets and rutabagas.

———— 6 Servings ————
3 large carrots, cut into ½-inch
*   rounds*
3 medium turnips, peeled, sliced into
*   ¼-inch rounds, then ¼-inch sticks*
1 pint of pearl onions
2 tablespoons unsalted butter
3 tablespoons (packed) light
*   brown sugar*
1 tablespoon fresh lemon juice
2 generous dashes of hot pepper
*   sauce*
Salt and freshly ground pepper

1. Bring a large saucepan of salted water to the boil. Add the carrots and turnips and cook until just tender, about 4 minutes. Drain and place the vegetables in a bowl of cold water.

2. Meanwhile, bring a medium saucepan of salted water to a boil. Add the onions and cook until just tender when pierced with a knife, about 4 minutes. Drain and cool the onions in a separate bowl of cold water. When cool, snip off the stems and roots with shears or a small sharp knife and peel. When all the vegetables are cool, drain and pat dry. *(The recipe can be prepared to this point up to 3 hours ahead. Keep in a cool spot.)*

3. In a large saucepan, melt the butter over moderate heat. Add the vegetables and stir to coat with the butter. Add the brown sugar and stir to coat. Stir in the lemon juice and hot pepper sauce. Simmer for 2 minutes, then increase the heat to moderately high and continue cooking and stirring, until the glaze is thick and the vegetables are coated, about 3 minutes. Season with salt and pepper to taste.
—*Lee Bailey*

• • •

CAULIFLOWER AND BROCCOLI WITH CREAM SAUCE

Use this tasty cream sauce for other vegetables if you prefer. The recipe makes almost 4 cups.

———— 8 to 10 Servings ————
2 medium carrots, chopped
2 celery ribs, chopped
1 medium onion, chopped
2 large imported bay leaves,
*   broken up*
12 white peppercorns
1¼ teaspoons salt
⅛ teaspoon freshly grated nutmeg
4 cups milk
4 tablespoons unsalted butter, cut
*   into pieces*
⅓ cup all-purpose flour
1 large cauliflower (about 2½
*   pounds), cut into 1½-inch florets*
2 heads of broccoli (about 2½
*   pounds total), cut into 1½-inch*
*   florets*

1. In a heavy medium saucepan, combine the carrots, celery, onion, bay leaves, peppercorns, salt, nutmeg and milk. Cover partially and place the pan over moderately low heat, to infuse for 1 hour. Do not boil. Strain the milk and discard the solids.

2. In a heavy medium saucepan, melt the butter over moderate heat. Whisk in the flour and cook, whisking constantly, until foaming, about 3 minutes; do not let the mixture brown. Whisk in 1 cup of the infused milk until completely smooth. Repeat with the remaining milk. Increase the heat to moderately high and bring the sauce to a boil, whisking constantly. Reduce the heat to low and simmer, stirring, until the sauce is satiny and has lost its raw taste, 3 to 5 minutes. *(The recipe can be prepared to this point up to 2 days ahead. Pour the sauce into a medium bowl, place a piece of plastic wrap directly on the surface to prevent a skin from forming and refrigerate.)*

3. In a large casserole or pot, steam the cauliflower over moderately high heat, covered, for 3 minutes. Add the broccoli, cover and steam until the broccoli is bright green and both vegetables are fork-tender, about 8 minutes.

4. Rewarm the sauce over moderate heat, stirring occasionally. (Thin it with a little water if desired.) Transfer the vegetables to a large heated bowl and pour the sauce on top. Serve at once.
—*Diana Sturgis*

• • •

VEGETABLES

BRAISED FENNEL

This braised fennel goes well with roast meats, such as lamb.

6 Servings
3 medium fennel bulbs, tough outer stalks removed (about 2 pounds, trimmed)
2 tablespoons olive oil
2 tablespoons fresh lemon juice
Salt and freshly ground pepper
3/4 cup chicken stock or canned low-sodium broth

1. Preheat the oven to 350°. Cut each fennel bulb in half lengthwise. Cut each half, lengthwise, into three 3/8-inch thick strips.

2. Brush the fennel with the olive oil. Arrange the fennel in a single layer in a large ovenproof pan. Sprinkle with the lemon juice and season with salt and pepper to taste. Pour in the chicken stock, cover with aluminum foil and place in the oven on the top rack. Bake for 30 minutes, or until the fennel is tender when pierced with a knife.

3. Remove the foil and switch the oven to broil. Broil about 7 inches from the heat or until the edges are golden brown, about 4 minutes. Serve hot.

—Lee Bailey

• • •

MIXED GREENS WITH CRACKLINS AND HOT PEPPER VINEGAR

Although I used broccoli raab and escarole here, you can use mustard greens, collard greens or any combination of greens as an alternative. You must make the Hot Pepper Vinegar a week ahead, or you can just serve the greens with your favorite vinaigrette.

6 Servings
1/4 pound double-smoked slab bacon, with rind, cut into 1/4-inch cubes or 6 slices smoked bacon, sliced crosswise 1/8 inch thick
2 teaspoons olive oil
1/2 medium onion, chopped
1/2 cup chicken stock or canned low-sodium broth
1/2 pound broccoli raab—trimmed, tough stems removed and cut into bite-size pieces
1 head of escarole (about 1 pound), torn into bite-size pieces
1/2 teaspoon salt
1/2 teaspoon freshly ground pepper
Hot Pepper Vinegar (see Note)

1. In a large saucepan, cook the bacon over moderately high heat until crisp and browned, about 6 minutes. Transfer to paper towels to drain.

2. Pour off the bacon fat. Add the olive oil and onion to the pan. Reduce the heat to moderate and cook until the onion is softened and lightly browned, about 5 minutes.

3. Add the chicken stock and scrape up any browned bits from the bottom of the pan. Add the broccoli raab, cover and cook, stirring occasionally, until tender, about 10 minutes.

4. Add the escarole and cook, stirring, until wilted, about 5 minutes longer.

5. Season the greens with the salt and pepper and transfer to a large platter. Sprinkle the bits of bacon on top. Serve hot or warm, and pass the Hot Pepper Vinegar at the table.

NOTE: To make Hot Pepper Vinegar, add sliced fresh hot peppers (including seeds to taste for a hotter flavor) to a bottle of red wine vinegar. Let sit at room temperature for 1 week before using.

—Lee Bailey

• • •

MARINATED CUCUMBERS

This simple, unusual and particularly Tuscan dish was traditionally associated with the gathering of the grain at harvesttime. The sweetened cucumbers were probably served as a palate refresher before the dessert course at the big, festive dinner for all the neighbors who helped out. The dish was so well liked that it became a popular snack to have during a small rest break from hard work.

6 Servings
2 European cucumbers, peeled and sliced 1/8 inch thick
2 tablespoons fresh lemon juice
1/2 cup sugar

Place the cucumbers in a medium bowl. Drizzle the lemon juice on top and sprinkle evenly with the sugar. Do not mix. Cover and refrigerate for at least 2 and up to 24 hours. Just before serving, toss well. Spoon the cucumbers and their juices into bowls and serve cold.

—Giuliano Bugialli

• • •

STEWED KALE

This is a gratifyingly full-flavored vegetable dish; I can eat tons of it. It's important to clean the kale thoroughly as outlined here because its curly leaves do a great job of hiding dirt.

6 Servings
1 large bunch of kale (about 2 pounds), stems discarded
1/4 cup olive oil
1 large onion, chopped
2 garlic cloves, minced
1 1/4 cups canned crushed tomatoes with their juices
3/4 teaspoon salt
2 teaspoons red wine vinegar
Freshly ground pepper

1. Place the kale in a large bowl of warm water and rub the leaves with your hands to free any dirt. (Do this in several batches if the leaves are cramped.)

2. Transfer the leaves directly to a large pot. Add ½ cup of water and bring to a boil over high heat. Cover, reduce the heat to moderate, and steam the kale until tender, about 10 minutes. Drain the kale in a colander and set aside.

3. Meanwhile, in a large nonreactive skillet, heat the olive oil. Add the onion and cook over moderate heat until soft, about 10 minutes. Stir in the garlic and cook for 2 minutes. Add the tomatoes and salt and simmer until the sauce reduces slightly, about 5 minutes.

4. Coarsely chop the reserved kale and stir it into the sauce. *(The recipe can be made to this point up to 1 day ahead; cover and refrigerate. Bring to room temperature before proceeding.)* Cover and simmer until heated through, about 5 minutes. Stir in the vinegar and season to taste with pepper. Serve hot.

—*Ken Haedrich*

• • •

ROASTED SHALLOTS

As they roast, these shallots caramelize on the outside and become tender and sweet. They make a fine accompaniment to any grilled meat, fish or fowl.

—————— *6 Servings* ——————
24 large shallots (about 1½ pounds), peeled but with the root ends left on
¾ teaspoon salt
¼ teaspoon freshly ground pepper
2 tablespoons extra-virgin olive oil
2 bay leaves
3 fresh thyme sprigs or ½ teaspoon dried

1. Preheat the oven to 350°. In a medium cast-iron skillet, toss the shallots with the salt, pepper and olive oil. Add the bay leaves and thyme, cover with foil and roast for 30 minutes.

2. Uncover and roast for 30 minutes longer, until the shallots are tender when pierced.

3. Increase the temperature to 450°. Roast the shallots for about 10 minutes, shaking the pan occasionally, until browned. Serve hot.

—*Karen Lee & Alaxandra Branyon*

SHALLOTS BRAISED IN RED WINE

These mild shallots are a nice Thanksgiving alternative to the more traditional onions in cream sauce.

—————— *8 to 10 Servings* ——————
2½ pounds shallots, peeled
5 tablespoons unsalted butter
¾ cup dry red wine
1 tablespoon sugar

1. Combine all the ingredients in a large, heavy nonreactive saucepan. Cover and cook over moderate heat, stirring occasionally, until the shallots are tender, about 40 minutes.

2. Uncover and reduce the heat to low. Cook, stirring occasionally, until the liquid reduces to a syrupy glaze, about 15 minutes. *(The recipe can be prepared up to 3 days ahead. Transfer the shallots to a baking dish, cover with foil and refrigerate. Reheat, covered, in a 325° oven for about 20 minutes.)*

—*Diana Sturgis*

• • •

BAKED ONIONS WITH BALSAMIC VINAIGRETTE

Although you can use any good-quality onion in this recipe, sweet varieties like Vidalia or Walla Walla work best.

—————— *6 Servings* ——————
6 medium Vidalia onions, peeled
¼ cup plus 1 tablespoon olive oil
1½ teaspoons Dijon-style mustard
2 tablespoons balsamic vinegar
½ teaspoon salt
¼ teaspoon freshly ground pepper

1. Preheat the oven to 350°. Cut off the root and stem ends of the onions. Using a sharp knife, make a deep "X" on the top of each onion, cutting halfway down.

2. Place each onion on a 6-by-6-inch square of aluminum foil, with the "X" up. Top each with 1 teaspoon of the oil. Bring up the corners of each square of foil and twist them together tightly to completely enclose the onions. Place the onions, foil twists up, on a large baking sheet and bake for 40 minutes, or until very tender when pierced.

3. Meanwhile, in a small bowl, combine the mustard, vinegar, salt and pepper. Gradually whisk in the remaining 3 tablespoons olive oil until blended.

4. Unwrap the onions and arrange them on a serving platter. Spoon a scant tablespoon of the vinaigrette over each onion. Season with pepper to taste and serve hot, either halved or whole.

—*Lee Bailey*

• • •

VEGETABLES

PEARL ONIONS IN CREAMY ONION SAUCE

Frozen small whole onions are a terrific time saver because they're already peeled.

———— 8 Servings ————

1 stick (4 ounces) unsalted butter
1 cup dry bread crumbs
3 medium onions, finely chopped
1/4 cup all-purpose flour
2 cups milk
2 teaspoons salt
1/2 teaspoon freshly ground pepper
2 packages (16 ounces each) frozen small whole onions

1. Preheat the oven to 350°. Melt the butter in a medium saucepan. Pour half of the butter into a small bowl and stir in the bread crumbs. Set aside.

2. Add the chopped onions to the remaining butter in the saucepan and cook over low heat, stirring occasionally, until the onions are softened but not browned, about 5 minutes.

3. Sprinkle the flour over the onions and whisk to combine, about 1 minute. Increase the heat to moderate, slowly add the milk and cook, whisking constantly, until the sauce is smooth and thickened, about 5 minutes. Stir in the salt and pepper.

4. Place the whole onions in a 2-quart baking dish. Pour the onion sauce over them and mix well, spreading the onions in an even layer. Sprinkle the reserved buttered bread crumbs over the top. Bake for 40 to 50 minutes, or until the topping is crisped and the sauce is bubbling around the edges. Serve hot.

—Marion Cunningham

• • •

CIDER-BRAISED ONIONS

The easiest way to peel small white onions is to score the skin and surface layer from top to root end with a sharp paring knife. This gives you an incision to slip your thumbnail under, so that you can peel off the outer layer. Just try not to cut deeper than the outer layer of the onion.

———— 6 Servings ————

1 pound small (1 inch) white onions
1 tablespoon unsalted butter
3/4 cup fresh apple cider
1/4 teaspoon soy sauce
1 tablespoon chopped parsley (optional)

1. Peel the onions, trimming off the root end as well as about 1/8 inch of the top. With a sharp paring knife, score a shallow cross in the root ends to ensure even cooking.

2. In a medium nonreactive skillet, melt the butter. Add the onions and stir to coat. Add the cider and soy sauce, increase the heat to high and bring to a boil. Reduce the heat to maintain a simmer, cover tightly and braise the onions until tender when pierced with a knife, about 10 minutes.

3. Uncover and increase the heat to high. Boil until the cider reduces to a light amber glaze, about 5 minutes. *(The recipe can be made to this point up to 1 day ahead; cover and refrigerate. Reheat before serving.)* Transfer the onions to a warm dish, scraping the glaze over them. Sprinkle with parsley if desired.

—Ken Haedrich

• • •

STEAMED PEAS WITH MINT

Fresh peas with mint is a classic combination that has been an American favorite since Colonial times.

———— 6 Servings ————

4 pounds of fresh peas, shelled, or 2 packages (10 ounces each) frozen baby peas
1 tablespoon coarsely chopped fresh mint
2 tablespoons unsalted butter
1/2 teaspoon salt
1/4 teaspoon freshly ground white pepper
Pinch of sugar

1. Place the peas in a steamer and sprinkle the mint on top (do not toss). Steam over moderately high heat until the peas are tender, about 10 minutes.

2. Transfer the peas to a bowl. Add the butter, salt, pepper and sugar and toss lightly until the butter melts and coats the peas. Serve hot.

—Lee Bailey

• • •

STIR-FRIED SUGAR SNAP PEAS AND CARROTS WITH ORIENTAL NOODLES

If you have trouble finding sugar snap peas, you can use snow peas instead.

———— 4 Servings ————

1/4 pound Oriental noodles, such as soba*
2 tablespoons vegetable oil
1 tablespoon minced fresh ginger
1 garlic clove, crushed through a press
3 carrots, thinly sliced on the diagonal
1/2 cup canned low-sodium chicken broth

½ pound sugar snap peas
3 scallions, thinly sliced on the diagonal
2½ tablespoons soy sauce
⅔ cup dry-roasted unsalted cashew nuts
*Available at Asian markets and specialty food stores

1. In a large pot of boiling salted water, cook the noodles until almost tender, about 8 minutes. Drain and rinse with cold water.

2. In a large skillet or wok, heat the oil. Add half of the ginger and garlic and stir-fry over high heat for 15 seconds. Reduce the heat to moderately high, stir in the carrots and cook, stirring constantly, for 4 minutes, adding 1 tablespoon of the chicken broth when the vegetables just start to brown.

3. Add the sugar snap peas and the remaining ginger and garlic. Continue to cook, stirring constantly, until the vegetables are tender, about 4 minutes more. Add tablespoons of the chicken broth as needed when the pan gets dry.

4. Stir in the scallions, soy sauce and any remaining chicken broth and cook for 1 minute. Stir in the noodles and cook for 1 minute more, or until the noodles are hot. Stir in the cashews and season to taste with additional soy sauce if desired. Serve hot.

—*Pam Parseghian*

• • •

NANCY SILVERTON'S POTATO PIE

My kids are usually very fussy eaters; they like mild flavors. This recipe contains three of their favorite foods—bacon, potatoes and eggs.

———— *8 Servings* ————
5 medium boiling potatoes
½ pound thinly sliced pancetta or bacon, cut crosswise into thin strips

2 medium onions, thinly sliced
About 1¼ teaspoons salt
Pinch of sugar
¼ teaspoon freshly ground pepper
2 tablespoons olive oil
1½ tablespoons fresh rosemary or 2 teaspoons dried
3 garlic cloves, minced
5 eggs
2 cups heavy cream
Pinch of freshly grated nutmeg
3 cups grated Gruyère cheese (about ½ pound)

1. Bring a large saucepan of water to a boil. Add the potatoes and cook over high heat for 5 minutes. Drain and pat dry; let cool slightly.

2. In a 12-inch ovenproof skillet, cook the pancetta over moderate heat, stirring until almost all the fat has been rendered, about 12 minutes. Using a slotted spoon, transfer the pancetta to paper towels to drain, then finely chop.

3. Set aside 2 tablespoons of the rendered fat. Leave 1 tablespoon of fat in the skillet and add the onions. Season with a pinch each of salt and sugar. Cover and cook over moderate heat, stirring occasionally, until softened and browned, about 25 minutes. Remove the onions from the skillet and set aside.

4. Meanwhile, peel the potatoes and then grate them on the coarse side of a grater or in a food processor fitted with a shredding disk. Season the potatoes with the pepper and 1 teaspoon of the salt.

5. Preheat the oven to 350°. Add the reserved 2 tablespoons of pancetta fat to the skillet and rub it over the bottom and sides generously. Add the grated potatoes and evenly press them into the bottom and sides of the pan to form a crust. Cook over moderately low heat until the potatoes begin to brown on the bottom, about 15 minutes.

6. Meanwhile, in a small skillet, heat the olive oil. Add the rosemary and garlic and cook over moderate heat, stirring, until fragrant, about 3 minutes. Remove from the heat.

7. In a bowl, beat the eggs with the cream until blended. Season with the remaining ¼ teaspoon salt, the nutmeg and two-thirds of the herbed olive oil.

8. When the potato crust has begun to brown, drizzle the remaining herbed oil over the surface. Spread the reserved onions over the potatoes and sprinkle the pancetta and Gruyère on top. Pour the custard mixture into the potato crust and bake the pie for about 50 minutes, rotating the pan once, until the custard is set and golden on top. Remove the pie from the oven and let cool for about 10 minutes before serving in wedges.

—*Nancy Silverton, Campanile, Los Angeles*

• • •

PARMENTIER PIE

Potage Parmentier was the first recipe in the first chapter of Julia Child's first cookbook, *Mastering the Art of French Cooking,* and it was the first soup I ever made. As she promised, it was simplicity itself, just potatoes and leeks, water and cream, but it made me feel like a real country cook from some little French farm town. The fact that the soup wasn't much different from what my Russian grandmother used to serve us was lost on me, for the soup was pure, romantic, peasant French and the start of my love affair with the country and its food. I later learned that the French have a similar affection for this dish. When our au pair arrived from France, the first thing she cooked was Potage Parmentier. And one evening, after my husband and I had eaten a very special meal prepared by Daniel Boulud, chef at Le Cirque, in which each course was a lesson in the cuisine of luxury, I asked what *he* had eaten for dinner: Boulud sighed with contentment when he said, "Potage Parmentier, just as my mother used to make it. I still love it so." I've never stopped cooking this soup and just recently started making a pie based on the same satisfying ingredients, with the addition of mushrooms. I think of it as a solid rendition of the treasured soup.

———— **4 to 6 Servings** ————

1 ounce dried porcini mushrooms
4 Idaho potatoes (about 2¼ pounds), peeled and quartered
¼ cup plus 3 tablespoons olive oil
¼ cup plus 3 tablespoons warm milk
1 teaspoon salt
½ teaspoon freshly ground black pepper
⅛ teaspoon cayenne pepper
3 small leeks (white and tender green), thinly sliced
1 medium onion, chopped
½ pound fresh mushrooms, thinly sliced
2 garlic cloves, minced
2 tablespoons white vermouth
½ teaspoon herbes de Provence, or substitute ⅛ teaspoon each of marjoram, oregano, tarragon and thyme
¼ cup freshly grated Parmesan cheese

1. In a small saucepan, gently simmer the dried mushrooms in 2 cups of water over moderate heat until soft, about 20 minutes. Drain and rinse the mushrooms and reserve the cooking liquid. Cut off and discard any tough bits from the mushrooms. Halve the mushrooms if the pieces are very large. Strain the liquid.

2. Meanwhile, boil the potatoes in a large pot of salted water over moderate heat until very tender, about 30 minutes. Drain well. Return the potatoes to the pot and shake over very low heat for 30 seconds to dry them out.

3. Place the potatoes in a large mixer bowl and beat with a paddle until smooth (or pass them through a food mill or ricer). Mix in ¼ cup of the olive oil, ¼ cup of the warm milk, ½ teaspoon of the salt, ¼ teaspoon of the black pepper and a pinch of the cayenne.

4. Preheat the oven to 425°. In a large skillet, heat the remaining 3 tablespoons olive oil. Add the leeks, onion, fresh mushrooms and garlic. Cook over moderately high heat, stirring occasionally, until the vegetables are softened, about 10 minutes.

5. Mix in the porcini mushrooms and their reserved liquid. Cook, stirring occasionally, until the liquid is almost evaporated, about 8 minutes.

6. Add the vermouth and cook for 1 minute. Season with the remaining salt, black pepper and cayenne and the *herbes de Provence.*

7. Spread half the mashed potatoes over the bottom of a lightly oiled 10-inch pie dish. Spread the mushroom mixture over the potatoes. Spread the rest of the potatoes evenly over the mushrooms. Brush the surface with the remaining 3 tablespoons milk. Run the tines of a fork over the potatoes to form a crisscross pattern and sprinkle the cheese on top. Bake in the upper third of the oven for 20 minutes, or until golden.

—*Dorie Greenspan*

• • •

BOILED NEW POTATOES WITH DILL AND BUTTER

This dish depends entirely on the quality of the potatoes—buy the youngest, freshest ones you can find.

———— **12 Servings** ————

2 pounds very small new potatoes, well scrubbed
2 tablespoons coarse (kosher) salt
1 bunch of fresh dill

4 tablespoons unsalted butter, melted

In a medium pot, cover the potatoes with cold water and add the coarse salt and the dill. Bring to a boil, reduce the heat to moderate and simmer until the potatoes are tender when pierced, about 20 minutes. Drain well and serve hot, drizzled with the melted butter.

—*Christer Larsson, Aquavit, New York City*

• • •

SCALLOPED POTATOES

———— **6 Servings** ————

4 medium all-purpose potatoes
1½ teaspoons salt
¼ teaspoon freshly ground white pepper
1 tablespoon all-purpose flour
2 tablespoons cold unsalted butter, cut into small pieces
1 cup half-and-half or light cream
1 cup grated Gruyère cheese (about ¼ pound)
Freshly ground black pepper

1. Preheat the oven to 325°. Butter a 12-inch shallow oval baking dish. Set aside.

2. Peel the potatoes, cut each in half lengthwise, placing in cold water as you go. Then slice into ¼-inch-thick rounds.

3. Place the potatoes in a large saucepan and cover with water. Add 1 teaspoon of the salt and bring to a boil over moderately high heat. Cook until just tender, about 3 minutes. Drain and let cool.

4. Arrange half of the potatoes in the bottom of the baking dish. Sprinkle with ¼ teaspoon of the salt, the white pepper and flour, and dot with half the butter pieces. Arrange the remaining potatoes in a layer on top and dot with the remaining pieces of butter.

5. In a medium saucepan, scald the half-and-half over moderate heat, 3 to 4 minutes. Pour over the potatoes and sprinkle with the remaining ¼ teaspoon salt, the Gruyère and freshly ground black pepper to taste. *(This recipe can be prepared to this point up to 3 hours ahead. Lightly cover with plastic wrap.)*

6. Bake for 30 minutes, or until the potatoes are tender and the cheese is melted. Switch the oven to broil and broil the potatoes until light golden brown. Let cool for 5 minutes before serving.

—*Lee Bailey*

• • •

POTATO-MUSHROOM CAKES WITH CUMIN

Since I've always had a weakness for potatoes and mushrooms, I've combined them in these crisp fried cakes made of grated potatoes and dried porcini mushrooms. Hot out of the skillet, the cakes are sprinkled with chopped roasted cumin at the last minute.

——— *Makes About 14 Cakes* ———
2½ teaspoons cumin seeds
⅓ cup dried porcini mushrooms (½ ounce)
2 Idaho potatoes (1 pound total)
2 tablespoons unsalted butter, melted
2 tablespoons grated onion
¾ teaspoon salt
½ teaspoon freshly ground pepper
About ¼ cup vegetable oil, for frying

1. In a small dry skillet, toast the cumin seeds, shaking the pan occasionally, over high heat until fragrant, about 30 seconds. Coarsely chop with a large knife.

2. In a small bowl, cover the porcini with ½ cup of hot water. Set aside to soften, about 12 minutes. Rinse the mushrooms, squeeze dry, trim off any tough ends and coarsely chop.

3. Peel the potatoes and grate them on the coarse side of a box grater. Squeeze the potatoes to remove as much liquid as possible. Place the grated potatoes in a medium bowl and add the melted butter; toss well. Stir in the porcini, onion, salt, pepper and 2 teaspoons of the cumin.

4. In a large skillet, heat 2 tablespoons of the oil over moderately high heat until it begins to smoke, about 2 minutes. For each cake, spoon about 3 tablespoons of the potato mixture into the skillet and flatten to about 3 inches in diameter. Cook until the undersides are dark brown, about 2½ minutes, then flip and cook until the second side is brown, 2 minutes longer. Transfer to paper towels to drain, then place on a baking sheet and keep warm in a low oven. Repeat with the remaining oil and potato mixture. *(The cakes can be made up to 5 hours ahead, stored at room temperature and then reheated in a hot oven.)* Sprinkle the remaining cumin over the cakes before serving.

—*Marcia Kiesel*

• • •

POTATO AND CELERY ROOT PUREE WITH GLAZED CRANBERRIES

Late fall and early winter are the best seasons for celery root. Mashed with potatoes, it adds a pleasant tang and sweetness. When the puree is served with cranberries in a light syrup, it becomes a very colorful side dish. The puree should be made on the day it is served, otherwise the vegetables will lose their fresh flavor.

——— *8 Servings* ———
½ cup sugar
1 cup fresh cranberries
2½ pounds celery root (about 3 large), peeled and cut into large dice
2½ pounds Idaho potatoes (about 6), peeled and cut into large dice
1 tablespoon coarse (kosher) salt
1 garlic clove
1 cup milk
4 tablespoons unsalted butter
1½ teaspoons table salt
¼ teaspoon freshly ground pepper

1. In a medium saucepan, combine the sugar with ½ cup water and bring to a boil over high heat. Boil for 5 minutes, then add the cranberries and reduce the heat to moderate. Simmer without stirring until the cranberries pop and the syrup reduces slightly, about 5 minutes. Set aside. *(The cranberries can be cooked up to 2 days ahead. Let cool, then cover and refrigerate.)*

2. In a large pot or dutch oven, combine the celery root, potatoes, coarse salt and garlic. Cover generously with cold water, bring to a boil over high heat and cook until tender, about 20 minutes.

3. Drain well. Transfer the vegetables to a food mill or a ricer and puree, adding the milk, butter, table salt and pepper as you go along. Alternatively, mash with a potato masher.

4. To serve, reheat the cranberries in their syrup. Mound the puree on a platter or individual plates and make a well in the center. Spoon some of the cranberries and their syrup into the well. Serve the remaining cranberries and syrup alongside.

—*Lydie Pinoy Marshall*

• • •

POTATO AND JERUSALEM ARTICHOKE GRATIN

There's really no easy way to peel Jerusalem artichokes, with all those knobby little protrusions. Just do the best you can, using either a sharp paring knife or a swivel-bladed vegetable peeler. Slice each artichoke after it has been peeled, and immediately drop it in the cream. This will prevent the chokes, as well as the finished gratin, from turning a less-than-appetizing shade of tan.

——————— 6 to 8 Servings ———————
1 garlic clove, crushed
1 tablespoon unsalted butter
1½ cups heavy cream
1 cup light cream or half-and-half
1 pound Jerusalem artichokes
5 medium all-purpose potatoes
  (about 1½ pounds), peeled
¾ teaspoon salt
Freshly ground pepper
4 ounces freshly grated Parmesan
  cheese (about 1 cup)

1. Preheat the oven to 350°. Rub the garlic around the inside of a shallow 8-by-12-inch casserole. Discard the garlic. Butter the casserole with the 1 tablespoon butter and set aside.

2. Pour the heavy and light creams into a large nonreactive saucepan. Working with one at a time, peel each Jerusalem artichoke. Slice it about ⅛ inch thick, then immediately drop the slices into the cream, pushing them below the surface.

3. Slice the potatoes ⅛ inch thick and add them to the cream. Stir in the salt.

4. Bring the cream to a boil over moderate heat, stirring occasionally. Pour the mixture into the buttered casserole; spreading the vegetables evenly. Season generously with pepper. *(The recipe can be prepared to this point up to 1 day ahead; cover and refrigerate. Bring to room temperature before baking.)*

5. Bake the gratin for 45 minutes. Push the potatoes and Jerusalem artichokes below the surface of the cream, then sprinkle the Parmesan cheese evenly on top. Bake for 20 to 30 minutes longer, until well browned. Serve hot.

—*Ken Haedrich*

• • •

SPINACH WITH RAISINS AND PINE NUTS

In the springtime, I like to eat fresh tender spinach either uncooked in a salad with just extra-virgin olive oil and a little lemon juice or sautéed with raisins and pine nuts. Don't toast the pine nuts because they will lose their delicate flavor.

——————— 12 Servings ———————
1 cup raisins
Salt
4 pounds fresh spinach leaves with
  stems
¼ cup extra-virgin olive oil
½ cup pine nuts (about 3 ounces)

1. In a small bowl, pour 1 cup of warm water over the raisins and set aside for 30 minutes. Drain thoroughly.

2. In a stockpot, bring 1 cup of salted water to a boil over high heat. Stir in the spinach and cook, stirring, until just wilted, about 2 minutes.

3. Drain the spinach in a colander and refresh under cold running water to keep the bright green color. Once cooled, squeeze out the excess liquid.

4. In a large skillet, heat the oil over moderate heat. Add the drained spinach and the raisins and cook, stirring, until heated through, about 5 minutes. Season to taste with salt and arrange the spinach on a platter. Sprinkle on the nuts.

—*Lorenza de' Medici*

• • •

SWEET POTATO AND BUTTERNUT SQUASH PUREE

The rich flavor of sweet potatoes is enhanced by the juiciness and light texture of butternut squash.

——————— 8 to 10 Servings ———————
4 pounds medium sweet potatoes
1 butternut squash (about 2
  pounds), halved lengthwise, seeds
  scooped out
½ teaspoon salt
¼ teaspoon freshly ground pepper

1. Preheat the oven to 400°. Place the sweet potatoes on a large baking sheet. Place the squash, cut-sides down, on the same sheet. Bake until tender, about 1 hour. Let cool slightly.

2. Scoop the pulp from the squash and sweet potatoes into a food processor; discard the skins. Add the salt and pepper and puree until smooth.

3. Spread the puree in an 8-by-10-inch baking dish and swirl decoratively with a spoon if desired. *(The recipe can be prepared up to 2 days ahead. Let the puree cool, then cover with foil and refrigerate. Reheat, covered, in a 325° oven for about 20 minutes.)*

—*Diana Sturgis*

• • •

TOMATO BREAD CRISP

❦ This lively tomato, olive oil and Parmesan combination would be enhanced by the spicy, full flavors of a young Zinfandel, such as 1987 Buehler or Frog's Leap, both from Napa Valley, California.

────── *6 to 8 Servings* ──────
4 tablespoons unsalted butter, softened
1 long loaf (about ½ pound) Italian bread, sliced ¼ inch thick or 1 Italian peasant bread, sliced into ¼-inch rounds
2½ pounds large beefsteak tomatoes (about 4), thinly sliced crosswise
¼ cup olive oil
½ teaspoon salt
¼ cup minced parsley
¼ teaspoon sugar
1 teaspoon freshly ground pepper
2 English muffins, split and lightly toasted
¼ cup plus 1 tablespoon freshly grated Parmesan cheese

1. Preheat the oven to 350°. Generously butter a 9-by-13-inch glass baking dish with 2 tablespoons of the butter.

2. Arrange the bread slices in a jelly-roll pan and bake until lightly toasted, 10 to 12 minutes.

3. Line the bottom of the baking dish with half the toasted bread slices in a single layer. Patch any empty spaces with small bits of toast. Arrange half the tomato slices on top, overlapping if necessary.

4. Drizzle 2 tablespoons of the olive oil over the layer of tomatoes, then season with ¼ teaspoon of the salt, 2 tablespoons of the parsley, ⅛ teaspoon of the sugar and ½ teaspoon of the pepper.

5. Cover the tomatoes with the remaining toast and layer the remaining tomato slices on top. Drizzle with the remaining 2 tablespoons olive oil and sprinkle the remaining ¼ teaspoon salt, 2 tablespoons parsley, ⅛ teaspoon sugar and ½ teaspoon pepper on top. Dot with the remaining 2 tablespoons butter.

6. Tear the toasted English muffins into large pieces and process in a food processor to form coarse crumbs. In a small bowl, toss the crumbs with the Parmesan cheese. Sprinkle the crumbs evenly over the tomatoes and bake, uncovered, for 45 minutes. Cover with foil and bake for 15 minutes longer, or until the crisp is soft and lightly browned. Serve hot.

—Lee Bailey

• • •

BAKED CORNMEAL-COATED GREEN TOMATOES

Green tomatoes have a distinctive flavor, but you can use red ones instead.

────── *4 Servings* ──────
¼ teaspoon hot pepper sauce
1 egg
1 tablespoon milk
1 tablespoon raspberry vinegar or red wine vinegar
¾ cup yellow cornmeal
1½ teaspoons salt
½ teaspoon freshly ground pepper
2 large green tomatoes (about 1½ pounds total), trimmed and quartered

1. Preheat the oven to 425°. Lightly grease a large baking sheet.

2. In a small bowl, whisk the hot sauce with the egg until blended. Gently whisk in the milk and vinegar.

3. In a pie pan or shallow dish, toss together the cornmeal, salt and pepper.

Dip the tomato wedges in the egg and then lightly dredge in the cornmeal, shaking off any excess. Place on the prepared baking sheet and bake until lightly golden, about 30 minutes. Serve warm.

—Lee Bailey

• • •

COUSCOUS-STUFFED TOMATOES

Quick-cooking, instant or precooked couscous is now widely available.

────── *6 Servings* ──────
1 cup couscous
1½ cups boiling water
1 teaspoon salt
1 small green bell pepper, chopped
1 medium red onion, chopped
⅓ cup dried currants
¼ cup white wine vinegar
2 teaspoons Dijon-style mustard
1 small garlic clove, minced
½ cup olive oil
½ cup chopped parsley
½ cup chopped fresh mint, plus mint sprigs for garnish
¼ teaspoon freshly ground black pepper
6 large tomatoes (about ½ pound each)

1. In a large bowl, stir the couscous into the boiling water with a fork; add ½ teaspoon of the salt and stir briefly. Cover and let stand until the water is absorbed, about 5 minutes.

2. Add the green pepper, onion and currants to the couscous. Stir to mix.

3. In a small bowl, whisk together the vinegar, mustard and garlic. Gradually whisk in the olive oil. Add the parsley and chopped mint and season with the remaining ½ teaspoon salt and the black

131

pepper. Pour the dressing over the couscous and toss well. Cover and refrigerate for at least 1 hour. *(The recipe can be prepared to this point up to 1 day ahead.)*

4. Cut the tomatoes in half horizontally and scoop out the core, seeds and most of the pulp. Place the tomato halves upside down on paper towels to drain for 10 minutes. Lightly season the tomato cavities with additional salt and black pepper.

5. Spoon the couscous filling into each tomato shell. Arrange the tomatoes on a large platter and garnish with mint sprigs.

—Melanie Barnard & Brooke Dojny

• • •

SKILLET RATATOUILLE

This ratatouille is a little unusual both in its composition and in how it is cooked. The vegetables are charred to give them a roasted taste, then they're perked up with soy sauce, sherry, vinegar and crushed hot pepper. Both the texture and the flavor of this side dish improve as it sits.

─── *4 Servings* ───

1 medium red or yellow bell pepper, cut into ½-inch squares
2½ teaspoons salt
1 medium eggplant (about 1 pound), cut into 1-inch cubes
¼ cup tomato sauce, preferably homemade
2 tablespoons medium-dry sherry
1 tablespoon soy sauce
1 tablespoon red wine vinegar
1 teaspoon sugar
¼ teaspoon crushed hot red pepper
3 tablespoons peanut oil
1 small Spanish onion, diced
2 teaspoons minced garlic

1. In a small bowl, toss the bell pepper with ½ teaspoon of the salt. In a medium bowl, toss the eggplant cubes with the remaining 2 teaspoons salt. Set both vegetables aside for about 1 hour.

2. Rinse, drain and dry the bell pepper. Place in a bowl. Repeat the process with the cubed eggplant and place in a separate bowl.

3. In a small bowl, whisk together the tomato sauce, sherry, soy sauce, vinegar, sugar and crushed red pepper.

4. Heat a large cast-iron skillet over high heat just until it begins to smoke, about 1 minute. Add ½ tablespoon of the oil, wait for a few seconds and then add the bell pepper. Cook, stirring and pressing down lightly, until nicely and evenly charred, 2 to 3 minutes. Transfer to a bowl and set aside.

5. Reduce the heat to moderately high and add the remaining 2½ tablespoons oil to the skillet. Add the eggplant and cook, stirring and pressing down lightly, until beginning to char and soften, about 3 minutes.

6. Add the onion and cook, stirring, until softened and beginning to brown, about 4 minutes. Add the garlic and cook, stirring, for 1 minute longer.

7. Stir the tomato sauce mixture and add it to the pan. Cook, stirring, until thickened, 1 to 2 minutes. Stir in the reserved bell pepper. Transfer the ratatouille to a serving bowl and let cool. *(The recipe can be made up to 5 days ahead and refrigerated, covered.)* Serve at room temperature.

—Karen Lee & Alaxandra Branyon

• • •

ROASTED VEGETABLES WITH VINAIGRETTE

Roasting is one of the easiest, quickest and most delicious ways of cooking vegetables. The same method can be applied to asparagus, eggplant, broccoli or tomatoes by varying the roasting time according to the size of the vegetable pieces.

─── *6 Servings* ───

4 medium zucchini (about 1 pound total), cut into 1½-to 2-inch chunks
4 medium, yellow summer squash (about 1 pound total), cut into 1½-to 2-inch chunks
3 large red bell peppers (about 1½ pounds total), cut into 1½- to 2-inch pieces
½ cup olive oil
1½ tablespoons lemon juice
1½ tablespoons white wine vinegar
1 teaspoon Dijon-style mustard
½ teaspoon grated lemon zest
¼ teaspoon salt
¼ teaspoon freshly ground black pepper

1. Preheat the oven to 500°. Place the zucchini, summer squash and red peppers in a large bowl. Drizzle with ¼ cup of the olive oil and toss well. Spread all the vegetables in a single layer on a large rimmed baking sheet or jelly-roll pan. Roast on the upper rack of the oven until crisp-tender and some of the edges begin to char, about 15 minutes.

2. Meanwhile, whisk the remaining ¼ cup olive oil with the lemon juice, vinegar, mustard, lemon zest, salt and black pepper until well blended.

3. Remove the vegetables from the oven and place in a shallow serving dish or on individual plates. Drizzle the vinaigrette over the vegetables while still hot. Serve at room temperature.

—Melanie Barnard & Brooke Dojny

• • •

SALADS

MOLDED SEAFOOD SALAD WITH SHIITAKE MUSHROOMS AND AVOCADO SAUCE

🍷 A crisp, herbaceous white will underscore this salad's rich flavors. A California Fumé Blanc, such as 1987 Grgich Hills or 1987 Konocti, would be ideal.

——————— 4 Servings ———————
6 ounces small shrimp, shelled and deveined
¼ pound bay scallops
½ cup plus 1 tablespoon olive oil
1 pound fresh shiitake mushrooms, stems removed, caps quartered if large
½ teaspoon salt
¼ teaspoon freshly ground white pepper
1 tablespoon plus 1 teaspoon balsamic vinegar
¼ pound cooked lobster meat, cut into small dice (from a 1- to 1½-pound lobster)
½ pound lump crabmeat, picked over to remove any cartilage
1 tablespoon mixed chopped fresh herbs, such as basil, parsley, tarragon and chives
½ medium Hass avocado, finely diced
1 small garlic clove, minced
1 teaspoon chopped fresh coriander
1 teaspoon fresh lemon juice
2 drops hot pepper sauce

1. In a medium saucepan of boiling water, cook the shrimp and scallops together until just opaque throughout, about 1½ minutes. Drain in a colander and refresh under cold running water. Transfer to paper towels to drain. Halve the shrimp crosswise and set aside.

2. In a large skillet, heat ¼ cup of the olive oil over high heat. When the oil is hot, add the mushrooms in an even layer. Season with the salt and white pepper and cook, without turning, until browned on one side, about 2 minutes. Stir and cook the mushrooms until tender, about 1 minute longer. Add 1 tablespoon of the vinegar and cook until evaporated, about 10 seconds. Transfer the mushrooms to a large plate and let cool.

3. In a large bowl, combine the lobster, crabmeat and the reserved shrimp and scallops. Stir in the cooled mushrooms, 1 tablespoon of the olive oil, the remaining 1 teaspoon vinegar and the chopped fresh herbs. Toss well to combine. Tightly pack equal amounts of the seafood salad into four 3½- to 4-inch-wide ramekins or small bowls. Cover with plastic wrap and refrigerate for 1 hour.

4. In a blender, combine the avocado, garlic, coriander, lemon juice and hot sauce. Add ¼ cup of water and blend until smooth. With the machine on, pour in the remaining ¼ cup olive oil in a thin stream and blend until thoroughly incorporated.

5. To serve, unmold the salads by turning each ramekin over onto a plate and giving it a sharp tap. Spoon a heaping tablespoon of the avocado sauce on either side of each salad and serve immediately.
—*Steve Mellina*

• • •

SWEDISH WEST COAST SALAD

This can be served with a fresh herb sauce or with a vinaigrette.

——————— 12 Servings ———————
1½ pounds small or medium shrimp in their shells
2 lobsters (about 1½ pounds each)
1 cup dry white wine
1 large shallot, minced
Freshly ground pepper
1 pound small mussels, scrubbed and debearded
1 pound asparagus, trimmed and peeled
1 cup freshly shelled peas
10 Malpèque or Belon oysters
Lettuce leaves
1 pound fresh lump crabmeat
2 tomatoes—peeled, seeded and cut into thin strips
3 hard-cooked eggs, cut into wedges
1 ounce salmon caviar
2 lemons, cut into wedges
Fresh dill and chervil sprigs, for garnish

1. Bring a large pot of salted water to a boil over high heat. Add the shrimp and cook until just opaque throughout, about 3 minutes. Remove the shrimp from the pot and drain well. Let cool completely, then cover and refrigerate.

2. Bring the water in the pot back to a boil. Add the lobsters and cook for 8 minutes. Drain and let cool completely, then cover and refrigerate until cold.

3. In a medium nonreactive saucepan, combine the wine, shallot and pepper and bring to a boil over high heat. Add the mussels, cover tightly and cook until they open, about 2 minutes. Discard any that do not open. Transfer the mussels to a bowl to cool completely. Cover and refrigerate. *(The recipe can be prepared to this point up to 1 day ahead.)*

4. Cook the asparagus in a pot of boiling salted water until just tender, about 4 minutes. Transfer them to a bowl of ice water to stop the cooking. In the same pot, boil the peas until tender, about 2 minutes. Drain and chill immediately in the ice water. Drain the asparagus and peas. Cover and refrigerate until cold.

5. Shortly before serving, crack the lobster shells. Remove the tail meat and slice ½ inch thick. Crack the claws and knuckles and remove the meat. Peel the shrimp. Remove the mussels from their shells. Shuck the oysters, leaving them on the half shell with their liquor.

6. Line a large platter with lettuce leaves. Arrange the lobster, shrimp, mus-

sels, oysters, crabmeat, peas, asparagus and tomato strips in separate mounds on top. Garnish with the eggs, salmon caviar, lemon wedges and dill and chervil sprigs.

—*Christer Larsson, Aquavit,*
New York City

• • •

SQUID SALAD WITH LEMON AND FRESH MINT

Squid can become firm and elastic if overcooked for even a few seconds. I use an off-the-stove cooking method to keep the squid tender and moist.

————— **6 to 8 Servings** —————
¼ cup Shellfish Boil (p. 258)
2 pounds cleaned small whole squid, with tentacles
1 cup (packed) fresh mint leaves
1 teaspoon dry mustard
¼ cup fresh lemon juice
½ jalapeño pepper, minced
1 teaspoon salt
1½ teaspoons sugar
½ teaspoon freshly ground black pepper
⅔ cup olive oil
Lemon slices and mint sprigs, for garnish

1. Bring a large saucepan of water to a boil. Stir in the Shellfish Boil and the squid. After 1 minute, remove the pan from the heat and set it on a rack. Let the squid cool in the liquid until tepid, about 30 minutes. Drain well.

2. Meanwhile, in a food processor, combine the mint leaves, dry mustard, lemon juice, jalapeño pepper, salt, sugar and black pepper. Process until pureed. With the machine on, pour in the olive oil in a thin stream until blended.

3. Thinly slice the squid bodies crosswise. Leave the tentacles whole. Place the squid in a large bowl and toss with the dressing. Arrange on a serving platter and garnish with lemon slices and mint sprigs.

—*Steve Mellina*

• • •

GREEN PAPAYA SALAD

Som tam is as popular in Thailand as green mangoes and Thai boxing, and that's popular! This salad has its roots in the villages of northeast Thailand, yet it regularly appears on the menus of Bangkok's finest restaurants. If green papaya is unavailable, julienned carrots make a good substitute. To eat the salad, wrap a small amount of it in the cabbage and lettuce leaves.

————— **6 Servings** —————
¼ pound medium shrimp, shelled and deveined
1 garlic clove, chopped
2 serrano chiles, seeded and minced
1 tablespoon chopped roasted peanuts
1 tablespoon palm sugar* or light brown sugar
¼ teaspoon salt
½ pound long beans (asparagus beans) or green beans
1 firm-ripe tomato, sliced
1 green papaya (about 2 pounds)— peeled, seeded and cut into 2-by-⅛-inch strips
¼ cup fresh lime juice
1 teaspoon nam pla*
1 head of leaf lettuce, leaves separated
¼ head of green cabbage, cored and cut into wedges
*Available at Asian markets

1. In a small saucepan, bring 3 cups of water to a boil. Add the shrimp and cook until loosely curled and just opaque throughout, 2 to 3 minutes. Drain and rinse under cold water; drain. Cut the shrimp into ½-inch pieces.

2. In a blender or food processor, combine the garlic, serrano chiles, peanuts, palm sugar and salt. Blend or process to a paste. Set aside.

3. In a saucepan, blanch the long beans in boiling salted water until crisp-tender, about 5 minutes. Drain, rinse under cold water and drain again.

4. In a large mixing bowl, combine the shrimp and tomato. Mash with a wooden spoon until blended. Alternatively, use a mortar and pestle to pound the ingredients. The shrimp will retain their shape for the most part, and the tomato should almost be pureed. Gradually add the papaya strips and mix until incorporated. Add the reserved garlic paste and blend well. Stir in the lime juice and *nam pla*.

5. To serve, arrange some of the lettuce leaves on a platter. Mound the salad on top. Place the long beans, cabbage wedges and remaining lettuce leaves on separate plates and serve alongside.

—*Jeffrey Alford*

• • •

SMOKED SEAFOOD SALAD WITH ROASTED PEPPERS AND CAPERS

❦ The roasted peppers, capers and smoked fish call for wines that offer a contrast to their intense flavors. Straightforward whites such as 1986 Hugel Pinot Blanc Cuvée des Amours or 1987 Torres Viña Sol would work well here.

————— **6 Servings** —————
2 large red bell peppers
2 large green bell peppers
1 large yellow bell pepper
2 teaspoons drained capers
2 tablespoons olive oil
2 tablespoons fresh lemon juice
1 tablespoon chopped fresh basil
½ teaspoon freshly ground black pepper
¼ teaspoon salt

1½ pounds assorted smoked seafood, such as shrimp, scallops, mussels, trout, sturgeon, eel and bluefish, cut into large chunks

1. Roast the red, green and yellow bell peppers directly over a gas flame or under a preheated broiler as close to the heat as possible, turning until charred all over. Immediately place the peppers in a paper bag to steam for 5 minutes. Peel the peppers and remove the cores, seeds and membranes.

2. Cut the peppers into long, thin strips and place in a large bowl. Add the capers, olive oil, lemon juice, basil, black pepper and salt.

3. Add the smoked seafood and toss lightly but thoroughly. Mound the salad on individual serving plates. If desired, remove some of the pepper strips from the salad and use them as a garnish.

—*Steve Mellina*

• • •

SHRIMP, PORK AND WATERCRESS SALAD

Thais, like the Vietnamese, frequently combine shrimp and pork, and the effect is always satisfying.

——————— *6 Servings* ———————
1 pound small fresh shrimp, shelled and deveined
1 tablespoon peanut oil
¼ cup chopped shallots
4 garlic cloves, chopped
½ pound lean ground pork
1 large bunch of watercress, large stems removed
½ cup roasted peanuts, chopped
2 tablespoons nam pla*
3 tablespoons fresh lime juice
1 teaspoon sugar
2 large tomatoes, thinly sliced
2 teaspoons crushed hot red pepper
*Available at Asian markets

1. In a medium saucepan, bring 5 cups of water to a boil. Add the shrimp and cook until loosely curled and opaque throughout, 2 to 3 minutes. Drain and rinse under cold water. Drain well, pat dry and set aside.

2. In a small skillet, heat the peanut oil over moderate heat. Add the shallots and garlic and cook until softened but not browned, about 30 seconds. Add the ground pork and cook, stirring, until no traces of pink remain, 5 to 6 minutes. Remove from the heat. If there is any excess fat in the skillet, drain it off. Let the pork cool slightly.

3. In a large bowl, combine the watercress, reserved shrimp and the peanuts. Add the pork mixture and toss well.

4. In a small bowl, stir together the *nam pla*, lime juice and sugar. Pour the dressing over the salad and toss. Arrange the tomato slices on a serving platter, overlapping them slightly. Spoon the salad on top and garnish with the crushed hot red pepper.

—*Jeffrey Alford*

• • •

CHICKEN SALAD WITH SHRIMP AND FENNEL

Fresh fennel and endive and a light lemony dressing make this a refreshing salad for a hot summer day.

——————— *6 to 8 Servings* ———————
1½ pounds large shrimp, shelled and deveined, shells reserved
2 pounds skinless, boneless chicken breasts, well trimmed
2 large fennel bulbs with tops
⅓ cup fresh lemon juice
½ cup olive oil
1 teaspoon salt
½ teaspoon freshly ground pepper
1½ pounds Belgian endives (4 or 5)

ELEGANT SALAD BAR BUFFET

Serves 12 to 14

🍸 *Cocktails*

Sage Crisps (p. 24)

Genoa Matchsticks (p. 24)

Chicken Salad with Shrimp and Fennel (p. 136)

Shrimp, Pork and Watercress Salad (p. 136)

Swedish Cucumber Salad (p. 142)

Endive and Romaine with Olive Oil and Lemon Juice

Pumpernickel Rolls

Sweet Butter

River Oaks Brownies (p. 193)

Pistachio Ice Cream (p. 206)

---

1. In a medium saucepan, cover the shrimp shells with 3 cups of water and bring to a boil over high heat. Reduce the heat to low and simmer for 5 minutes. Strain the broth and return it to the saucepan; discard the shrimp shells.

2. Add the shrimp to the broth and cook over high heat just until opaque throughout, about 3½ minutes. Drain the shrimp, reserving the broth. Transfer the shrimp to a plate to cool, then refrigerate, covered, until chilled.

3. Pour the broth into a large, straight-sided skillet. Add the chicken and bring to a simmer over moderate heat. Cook until firm and white throughout, about 10 minutes. Transfer the chicken to a plate to cool, then refrigerate, covered, until chilled. *(The recipe can be prepared to this point up to 1 day ahead.)*

4. Trim the fennel, reserving the feathery tops. Halve the bulbs lengthwise and cut out the cores. Thinly slice the fennel crosswise. Mince most of the feathery tops, reserving a few for garnish.

5. In a large bowl, whisk the lemon juice with the oil, salt and pepper. Add the shrimp, fennel and minced fennel tops; toss well.

6. Slice the chicken breasts crosswise ¼ inch thick. Add the chicken to the shrimp and toss well.

7. Separate the endive spears and arrange them around a platter or individual serving plates, yellow tips pointing out. Mound the salad on top, garnish with the reserved fennel tops and serve chilled.

—*Bob Chambers*

• • •

CHICKEN, MUSHROOM AND NAPPA CABBAGE SALAD WITH FRESH CORIANDER

The mushrooms are marinated first to absorb the flavor of the tangy dressing, but the cabbage is tossed in at the very last moment to keep it crisp.

——— 8 to 10 Servings ———
4 scallions, thinly sliced
Juice of 1 lemon
⅓ cup plus 2 tablespoons olive oil
2 tablespoons coarsely chopped fresh coriander (cilantro), plus additional sprigs for garnish
1 teaspoon salt
½ teaspoon freshly ground pepper
½ pound firm white mushrooms, stems removed, caps sliced ⅛ inch thick
6 cups cooked chicken (½-inch cubes)
1 small nappa cabbage (about 1½ pounds), quartered lengthwise, cored and sliced crosswise ⅛ inch thick

1. In a large bowl, combine the scallions, lemon juice, olive oil, chopped coriander, salt and pepper. Add the mushrooms and toss well. Cover and set aside for 1 hour, stirring occasionally.

2. Add the chicken to the mushrooms and toss well. *(The recipe can be prepared to this point up to 4 hours ahead and refrigerated, covered.)* Just before serving, add the cabbage and toss again. Mound the chicken salad on a platter and garnish with the coriander sprigs.

—*Bob Chambers*

• • •

CHICKEN FOR CHICKEN SALAD

In my house, there is never enough chicken left over to make chicken salad the next day. If the same is true for you, the easiest solution is to pick up a freshly roasted chicken at your local deli. Otherwise, you can use one of the recipes that follow for cooking just white meat (sautéed breasts), just dark (roasted legs) or a combination (whole poached chicken); the latter has the added bonus of yielding a tasty stock.

Makes About 3 Cups
———of Cut-up Chicken———

SAUTEED CHICKEN BREASTS:

Season 2 pounds of skinless, boneless chicken breasts with salt and pepper to taste. In a large skillet, heat 2 tablespoons of olive oil over moderately high heat. Add the chicken breasts in a single layer and cook without turning for 5 minutes. Turn the breasts over and cook on the second side until lightly browned and the juices run clear when a skewer is inserted, about 4 minutes longer. Transfer the breasts to a plate and let cool. Cover with plastic wrap and refrigerate for up to 2 days.

ROASTED CHICKEN LEGS:

Preheat the oven to 450°. In a large bowl, toss 3 pounds whole chicken legs (with thighs and skinned) with 3 tablespoons of olive oil. Season with salt and pepper to taste and toss again. Arrange the legs on a baking sheet in a single layer and bake for 20 minutes. Reduce the heat to 375°. Cover the chicken with foil and bake for 30 minutes longer, until cooked through and the juices run clear when a skewer is inserted in a thigh. Transfer to a plate to cool. Remove the meat from the bones. Cover with plastic wrap and refrigerate for up to 2 days.

WHOLE POACHED CHICKEN AND BROTH:

(This recipe also produces 1 quart of broth. If you don't have any use for the broth, skip the last part of the recipe.) Place 1 chicken (3½ pounds), the neck and giblets (without the liver), 1 chopped onion, 2 chopped carrots, 3 chopped celery ribs, 5 peppercorns, 2 bay leaves, 1½ teaspoons salt and 1½ teaspoons *herbes de Provence* (optional) in a small stockpot and add enough water to completely cover the bird. Bring to a boil over high heat. Reduce the heat to low and simmer for 45 minutes, skimming as necessary and turning the chicken in the broth once after 20 minutes. The chicken is done when the meat on the legs and wings begins to pull away from the bones. Transfer the chicken to a platter and let cool slightly. Discard the skin and remove the meat from the bones. Cover the meat with plastic wrap and refrigerate for up to 2 days.

To make the broth, return the bones to the pot and bring to a boil over high heat. Reduce the heat to low and simmer, partially covered, for 1¼ hours. Strain the broth through a fine-mesh sieve. Let the broth cool and refrigerate, covered, for up to 2 days or freeze for up to 2 months.

—*Bob Chambers*

• • •

CURRIED CHICKEN SALAD WITH YOGURT DRESSING

This light salad gets its heat from the curry, its cool from the yogurt and crunch from the carrots, apples and zucchini.

—————— 6 to 8 Servings ——————
1 cup (8 ounces) plain yogurt
3 tablespoons sour cream
2 teaspoons curry powder
1 teaspoon thyme
½ teaspoon ground coriander
1 teaspoon cumin
½ teaspoon celery seeds
1 teaspoon salt
2 tablespoons fresh lemon juice
3 cups cooked chicken (½-inch pieces)
½ cup dried currants
2 medium carrots, grated
2 small zucchini, cut lengthwise into eighths, then sliced 1 inch thick
2 Granny Smith apples, cut into ½-inch cubes
Crisp greens, for garnish
½ cup roasted cashews (about 2½ ounces)

1. In a large bowl, combine the yogurt, sour cream, curry powder, thyme, coriander, cumin, celery seeds, salt and lemon juice. Add the chicken and toss well. Cover and set aside at room temperature for 15 minutes.

2. Meanwhile, in a small bowl, cover the currants with hot water and set aside to plump for 10 minutes. Drain well.

3. Add the carrots, zucchini, apples and plumped currants to the chicken and toss well to combine. Mound the salad on a platter or plates lined with crisp greens and sprinkle the cashews on top. Serve immediately.

—*Bob Chambers*

• • •

TARRAGON CHICKEN SALAD WITH MELON AND CUCUMBER

Crisp cucumbers and juicy melon make this a cooling summer salad that's best served as soon as it's made.

—————— 8 to 10 Servings ——————
2 tablespoons tarragon wine vinegar
2 tablespoons minced fresh tarragon
¾ teaspoon salt
½ teaspoon freshly ground pepper
¼ cup plus 2 tablespoons light olive oil
¼ cup minced red onion
Sautéed Chicken Breasts (p. 137), recipe doubled, meat sliced
1 cantaloupe (about 2½ pounds)
2 cucumbers—peeled, seeded and sliced crosswise ¼ inch thick
Radicchio leaves, for garnish

1. In a large bowl, combine the vinegar, tarragon, salt, pepper and oil. Add

---

LATE-SUMMER LUNCH

Serves 8

Fresh Fig Vinaigrette (p. 255) with Rolled Prosciutto Slices

Mediterranean Chicken-Ratatouille Salad (p. 139)

Garlic and Parmesan Croutons

🍷 *Light, crisp white, such as 1988 Torresella Pinot Grigio*

Upstate Shortcake (p. 189)

Coffee

---

the onion and chicken, toss gently and set aside while you prepare the melon.

2. Halve the cantaloupe and scoop out the seeds. Using a sharp knife, cut each half into quarters. Slice the melon off the peel and cut into ½-inch dice.

3. Add the melon and cucumbers to the bowl and toss well to coat. Serve the salad on a platter or plates on a bed of radicchio leaves.

—*Bob Chambers*

• • •

CHICKEN SALAD WITH BITTER GREENS, PANCETTA AND CHICKEN LIVER CONFIT

In this hearty salad, the richness of the liver confit is balanced by the bitter greens and sweet-tart balsamic dressing.
🍷 The rich confit of chicken livers with the flavorful balsamic dressing would be best matched by a fruity, lively red. A 1988 Rhône, such as a Paul Jaboulet Aîné St-Joseph Le Grand Pompée, or a 1987 Kendall-Jackson Zinfandel from California would be a good match.

—————— 6 to 8 Servings ——————
½ pound pancetta, sliced ⅛ inch thick, cut into 1-inch pieces
1 tablespoon vegetable oil
Chicken Liver Confit (p. 258)
4 scallions, thinly sliced
⅓ cup balsamic vinegar
1 teaspoon salt
½ teaspoon freshly ground pepper
3 cups cooked chicken (1-inch pieces)
¼ cup pine nuts (about 1¼ ounces)
8 cups mixed bitter greens (about 1 pound), such as curly endive, radicchio and dandelion, torn into pieces

1. In a medium skillet, cover the pancetta with water and bring to a boil over high heat. Drain well and wipe the skillet dry. Add the oil to the skillet and fry the

pancetta over high heat, stirring occasionally, until crisp, about 7 minutes. Drain the pancetta on paper towels. Set aside.

2. Remove the chicken livers from their oil, reserving the oil. Cut the livers into ½-inch cubes.

3. In a large bowl, combine the scallions, balsamic vinegar, salt and pepper. Add the chicken, the cubed chicken livers and their oil and toss well. Set aside for 15 minutes to 1 hour to blend the flavors.

4. Meanwhile, in a small dry skillet, toast the pine nuts over moderate heat, shaking the pan frequently, until lightly browned, about 5 minutes. Set aside.

5. Just before serving, add the greens to the chicken and toss well. Mound the salad on plates or a platter and garnish with the reserved pancetta and the toasted pine nuts. Serve immediately.

—*Bob Chambers*

• • •

LEMON-CHICKEN SALAD WITH WILD RICE AND GRAPES

Sweet-tart, juicy grapes are the perfect counterpoint to the tender chicken and chewy, nutty rice.

──────── 6 to 8 Servings ────────
1 cup wild rice (about 6½ ounces)
4 cups Chicken Broth (p. 137) or canned low-sodium broth
1 teaspoon herbes de Provence
1 teaspoon salt
¾ teaspoon freshly ground pepper
⅓ cup fresh lemon juice
1 teaspoon Dijon-style mustard
2 tablespoons olive oil
3 cups cooked chicken (½-inch pieces)
1 celery rib, minced
½ pound seedless red grapes, halved lengthwise
½ pound seedless green grapes, halved lengthwise
Red leaf lettuce, for garnish

1. In a medium bowl, soak the rice in 3 cups of warm water for 1 hour. Drain the rice, rinse well and transfer it to a heavy medium saucepan. Add the chicken broth and bring to a boil over high heat, skimming the surface as necessary.

2. Add the *herbes de Provence*, ½ teaspoon of the salt and ¼ teaspoon of the pepper. Reduce the heat to low and simmer, covered, for 25 minutes. Uncover and continue to cook until the rice is tender and the liquid has been absorbed, about 30 minutes longer. Transfer the rice to a bowl to cool slightly.

3. In another bowl, whisk together the lemon juice, mustard, olive oil and the remaining ½ teaspoon each of salt and pepper. Add this dressing to the rice along with the chicken, celery and red and green grapes. Toss well. Line a platter or plates with the red leaf lettuce and mound the salad on top. Serve warm or at room temperature.

—*Bob Chambers*

• • •

MEDITERRANEAN CHICKEN-RATATOUILLE SALAD

The base of this recipe is a light ratatouille made with roasted eggplant.

──────── 8 to 10 Servings ────────
2 eggplants (1 to 1¼ pounds each)
2 teaspoons salt
½ cup plus 2 tablespoons olive oil
2 medium onions, chopped
2 red bell peppers, cut into 1-by-½-inch strips
2 yellow bell peppers, cut into 1-by-½-inch strips
3 small zucchini, quartered lengthwise and sliced 1 inch thick
3 small yellow summer squash, quartered lengthwise and sliced 1 inch thick
2 garlic cloves, crushed through a press
1 teaspoon fresh thyme or ½ teaspoon dried
½ pound plum tomatoes, halved lengthwise and sliced ½ inch thick
1 teaspoon freshly ground black pepper
6 cups cooked chicken (¾-inch cubes)
1 cup shredded fresh basil, plus whole leaves for garnish
⅓ cup fresh lemon juice

1. Halve the eggplants lengthwise. Set them on a work surface, cut-sides down, and slice lengthwise into eighths. Cut the eggplant slices into 1-inch pieces and place in a colander. Sprinkle 1 teaspoon of the salt on top, toss and set them over a bowl to drain for at least 1 hour at room temperature or overnight, covered.

2. Preheat the oven to 450°. Pat the eggplant dry between paper towels. Transfer the eggplant to a jelly-roll pan and toss with ¼ cup of the olive oil. Spread the eggplant out in a single layer and bake for 40 to 45 minutes, until well browned. Let cool slightly in the pan.

3. Meanwhile, in a large flameproof casserole, heat 2 tablespoons of the olive oil over moderately high heat. Add the onions and cook, stirring frequently, until beginning to brown, about 5 minutes.

4. Add the bell peppers, zucchini and summer squash and cook, stirring frequently, until slightly tender but still crisp, 12 to 15 minutes.

5. Stir in the garlic and cook for 1 minute longer. Stir in the thyme, tomatoes and ½ teaspoon of the black pepper and remove from the heat.

6. Transfer the cooked vegetables to a large bowl and let cool slightly. Fold in the eggplant, chicken, shredded basil, lemon juice and the remaining ¼ cup olive oil, 1 teaspoon salt and ½ teaspoon pepper. Mound the salad on a platter or plates and serve warm or at room temperature, garnished with the basil leaves.

—*Bob Chambers*

• • •

139

CHICKEN SALAD WITH ONIONS AND POTATO CRISPS

Here chicken teams up with crisp potatoes, caramelized onions and garlic. Tangy watercress offsets the sweetness of the onions, and a pungent mustard dressing brings all the elements together.

——————— *8 Servings* ———————
2 pounds small red potatoes, unpeeled
¾ cup plus 2 tablespoons olive oil
2 teaspoons salt
1 teaspoon freshly ground pepper
2 pounds Spanish onions, halved lengthwise and sliced ¼ inch thick
2 garlic cloves, crushed through a press
1 tablespoon grainy mustard
2 tablespoons Dijon-style mustard
⅓ cup fresh lemon juice
⅓ cup chopped Italian flat-leaf parsley
2 teaspoons minced fresh rosemary
6 cups cooked chicken (½-inch pieces)
2 bunches of watercress, large stems removed
2 tomatoes, quartered, for garnish

1. Preheat the oven to 450°. Using a mandoline or a food processor, slice the potatoes ⅛ inch thick. Place in a bowl, add 3 tablespoons of the olive oil and toss until coated. Season with ½ teaspoon each of the salt and pepper.

2. Spray 4 baking sheets with vegetable spray. Arrange the potato slices in a single layer on the baking sheets and roast in the oven, 2 sheets at a time, for 10 minutes. Then switch the sheets and bake for 5 to 7 minutes longer, until the potatoes are nicely browned and crisp. Loosen the potatoes from the sheets as soon as they are done and transfer to paper towels to cool. Repeat with the remaining potatoes.

3. Meanwhile, in a large casserole, heat 3 tablespoons of the olive oil over moderate heat. Add the onions and ½ teaspoon of the salt. Cover tightly and cook, stirring occasionally, until translucent, about 10 minutes. Uncover, increase the heat to moderately high and cook, stirring frequently, until the onions are well browned, about 10 minutes. Add the garlic and cook for 2 minutes longer.

4. In a bowl, combine the grainy and Dijon mustards with the lemon juice, parsley, rosemary and the remaining 1 teaspoon salt and ½ teaspoon pepper. Whisk in the remaining ½ cup olive oil; set aside ¼ cup of this dressing. Add the remainder to the onions and stir well to blend, scraping up any browned bits adhering to the bottom of the casserole. Scrape the onions into a bowl. Add the chicken and potato crisps and toss well.

5. In a bowl, toss the watercress with the reserved ¼ cup dressing. Arrange the watercress on a platter or plates and mound the salad on top. Garnish with the tomato wedges and serve immediately.
—*Bob Chambers*

• • •

BROILED THAI CHICKEN SALAD

The special taste of *yam gai* is in the marinade. Try this same marinade with shark fillets or thin slices of pork for an unusual and delicious barbecue.

❡ Although cold beer is an obvious choice for this salad, a fruity, off-dry white such as 1988 Folie à Deux Dry Chenin Blanc or 1988 Hogue Cellars Chenin Blanc would also work nicely.

——————— *6 Servings* ———————
3½ ounces cellophane noodles* (wun sen)
4 large garlic cloves, chopped
2 teaspoons peppercorns
¼ cup chopped fresh coriander
¼ cup plus 1 tablespoon soy sauce
2 tablespoons plus 1 teaspoon nam pla*
1¼ pounds skinless, boneless chicken breasts, cut into 1-inch cubes
4 cups chicken stock or canned broth
1½ teaspoons sugar
3 tablespoons fresh lime juice
1 head of leaf lettuce, leaves separated
4 medium tomatoes, cut into wedges
3 scallions, chopped
1 European cucumber, cut into 1-inch dice
1 tablespoon chopped roasted peanuts
1 lime, thinly sliced
*Available at Asian markets

1. Place the cellophane noodles in a bowl with hot water to cover. Let soak for 30 minutes to soften.

2. In a blender or food processor, combine the garlic, peppercorns and 2 tablespoons of the coriander. Blend or process to a paste. Scrape down the sides of the bowl and add ¼ cup of the soy sauce and 2 tablespoons of the *nam pla*. Pour the marinade into a shallow pan and add the chicken cubes. Toss well and let marinate for 30 minutes.

3. Preheat the broiler. In a medium saucepan, bring the chicken stock to a boil. Drain the cellophane noodles. Add the noodles to the pan and boil until softened, about 5 minutes. Drain well. Cut the noodles into 4 pieces. Reserve the stock for another use.

4. Remove the chicken from the marinade and place on a baking sheet in a single layer. Broil for 4 to 7 minutes, stirring the pieces from time to time, until browned and cooked through.

5. In a small bowl, stir together the sugar, lime juice and the remaining 1 tablespoon soy sauce and 1 teaspoon *nam pla*, to make the dressing.

6. To assemble the salad, line a large platter with the lettuce leaves. Spread the noodles over the lettuce and top with the tomato wedges, chopped scallions and diced cucumber. Arrange the broiled chicken on the salad and pour on the dressing. Sprinkle the remaining 2 tablespoons coriander and the peanuts on top. Garnish with the lime slices.

—*Jeffrey Alford*

• • •

BOILED BEEF SALAD
WITH TARRAGON SAUCE

Most Italians do not eat leftovers per se; we prefer to convert them into an entirely new dish. So many popular dishes evolved this way that nowadays these *rifatti* (recooked) dishes are started from scratch.

Until the 19th century, it was quite common to have a course of boiled meat or fowl as part of an elaborate dinner. These boiled dishes have retained a strong place in Tuscan cooking.

♟ A full-flavored red would best underscore this dish. Try an earthy 1986 Rosso di Montalcino, such as Poggio Antico or Banfi Centine.

—————— **6 Servings** ——————
2 teaspoons coarse (kosher) salt
1 large carrot
2 red onions—1 medium, halved;
* 1 large, thinly sliced*
1 large celery rib
5 Italian flat-leaf parsley sprigs plus
* ¼ cup coarsely chopped*
3 cherry tomatoes
2½ pounds beef brisket
½ cup olive oil
2 large garlic cloves
3 ounces sweet Italian sausage
* without fennel seeds, casing*
* removed, or 3 ounces ground pork*
½ teaspoon salt
½ teaspoon freshly ground black
* pepper*
Large pinch of crushed hot red
* pepper*

1 can (28 ounces) Italian plum
* tomatoes—well drained, seeded*
* and coarsely chopped*
15 large fresh basil leaves, torn into
* large pieces*
1 tablespoon chopped fresh
* tarragon*

1. In a medium flameproof casserole, combine 8 cups of cold water with the coarse salt and bring to a boil over high heat. Add the carrot, halved onion, celery, parsley sprigs and cherry tomatoes. When the water returns to a boil, add the beef. Reduce the heat to moderately low and simmer gently until tender, about 2½ hours. Using tongs, transfer the meat to a platter and let cool to room temperature. *(The meat can be cooked up to 2 days ahead and refrigerated in its broth.)*

2. In a medium bowl, soak the sliced onion in cold water to cover for 30 minutes. Drain and pat dry.

THAI LUNCHEON

———————————————
Serves 6

Spiced Soup with Shrimp (p. 47)

Thai Beef Salad (p. 141)
♟ *Singha Beer*

Mango Light Ice Cream (p. 209)

---

3. In a medium nonreactive skillet, warm the oil over moderate heat. Add the garlic cloves and cook, stirring, until lightly golden, about 2 minutes. Discard the garlic. Add the onion slices and chopped parsley to the skillet and cook, stirring frequently, until softened, about 5 minutes.

4. Add the sausage meat, salt, black pepper and crushed red pepper. Cook, stirring occasionally to break up the meat, until no trace of pink remains, about 15 minutes. Add the chopped tomatoes and cook until they break down and the sauce is thick and chunky, about 15 minutes longer. Stir in the basil and tarragon and cook for 1 minute more.

5. Thinly slice the boiled beef and arrange on a platter with the slices overlapping. Pour the sauce over the meat and serve.

—*Giuliano Bugialli*

• • •

THAI BEEF SALAD

I first tasted *yam neua* in the dining car of a train rolling through the jungle of south Thailand. It is usually eaten when people get together late in the afternoon to have a glass of Singha beer or Mekong whiskey.

—————— **6 Servings** ——————
1½ pounds beef tenderloin, at room
* temperature*
¼ cup coarsely chopped fresh
* coriander*
2 tablespoons coarsely chopped
* fresh mint*
1 large jalapeño pepper, minced
3 large garlic cloves, crushed
* through a press*
2 tablespoons nam pla*
2 tablespoons palm sugar* or light
* brown sugar*
¼ cup fresh lime juice
1 head of leaf lettuce, leaves
* separated*

2 tomatoes, thinly sliced
1 small cucumber, thinly sliced
1 small red onion, thinly sliced
Freshly ground black pepper
1 lime, cut into thin wedges
*Available at Asian markets

1. Preheat the oven to 500°. Set the beef tenderloin in a small baking dish and roast for 20 minutes, until rare. Let cool for 30 minutes, then refrigerate until cold, about 2 hours. Slice the tenderloin against the grain into ¼-inch-thick slices. Then cut into strips about ¼ inch wide.

2. In a large bowl, combine the meat strips, coriander, mint and jalapeño pepper and toss. In a small bowl, combine the garlic, *nam pla*, palm sugar and lime juice; mix well. Pour this dressing over the meat and toss to coat.

3. Cover a large plate or platter with lettuce leaves. Arrange the tomatoes around the outside, overlapping the slices as necessary. Arrange the cucumber slices inside the tomatoes and then the onion slices inside those.

4. Remove the meat from the dressing and mound it in the center of the vegetables. Pour any dressing that remains in the bowl over the meat. Cover the salad with a damp towel and refrigerate until chilled, at least 1 hour and up to 4 hours. Before serving, sprinkle with black pepper and garnish with the lime wedges.

—*Jeffrey Alford*

• • •

CHRISTMAS SALAD WITH RED AND GREEN VINAIGRETTE

This salad is made with watercress, green leaf lettuce, crunchy Belgian endive and radicchio. The dressing is a blend of balsamic and white wine vinegars and extra-virgin olive oil. Flecks of sun-dried tomatoes, Italian parsley, garlic and (the unpopular but undetected) anchovy delight both eye and tongue.

———— *12 Servings* ————
2 medium anchovies, rinsed well and minced
1 medium garlic clove, minced
¼ teaspoon salt
½ teaspoon freshly ground pepper
¼ cup white wine vinegar
1 tablespoon balsamic vinegar
2 sun-dried tomatoes packed in oil, minced (about 2 tablespoons)
1 tablespoon minced Italian flat-leaf parsley
2 teaspoons grainy mustard
⅔ cup extra-virgin olive oil
1 medium head of green leaf lettuce, torn into bite-size pieces
1 large head of radicchio, torn into bite-size pieces
1 large bunch of watercress, large stems removed
1 medium Belgian endive, sliced crosswise into 1-inch pieces

1. In a medium bowl, mash the anchovies, garlic and salt to form a coarse paste; add the pepper. Whisk in the wine vinegar, balsamic vinegar, sun-dried tomatoes, parsley and mustard until thoroughly combined. Whisk in the oil in a slow, steady stream until well blended. *(The dressing can be made days ahead. Refrigerate in a glass jar and allow to come to room temperature before serving. Shake well before using.)*

2. In a large salad bowl, combine the leaf lettuce, radicchio and watercress. Add the endive and toss to mix the greens. Just before serving, add the dressing and toss again.

—*Tracey Seaman*

• • •

BELGIAN ENDIVE AND RADICCHIO SALAD

Serve this with a wedge of hard cheese.

———— *6 Servings* ————
6 large Belgian endives, sliced crosswise ¾ inch thick
1 large head of radicchio, torn into bite-size pieces
3 tablespoons balsamic vinegar
¼ cup olive oil
Salt and freshly ground pepper

In a large serving bowl, toss the endives and radicchio. In a small bowl, whisk together the vinegar and oil. Pour the vinaigrette over the salad and toss to coat well. Season with salt and pepper to taste and toss once more.

—*Lee Bailey*

• • •

SWEDISH CUCUMBER SALAD

———— *8 to 12 Servings* ————
¾ cup sugar
¾ cup distilled white vinegar
½ teaspoon salt
3 European cucumbers, peeled and very thinly sliced

In a large glass bowl, dissolve the sugar in the vinegar. Stir in the salt. Add the cucumbers and toss well. Cover and refrigerate for at least 3 hours and up to 1 day.

—*Christer Larsson, Aquavit, New York City*

• • •

ROMAINE SALAD WITH GARLIC AND PINE NUTS

————— 4 Servings —————
2 tablespoons pine nuts
½ medium garlic clove, minced
⅛ teaspoon salt
1 tablespoon balsamic vinegar
¼ cup olive oil
1 large head of romaine lettuce,
  torn into bite-size pieces
Freshly ground pepper

1. In a medium skillet, toast the pine nuts over moderately low heat, stirring occasionally, until golden brown, 6 to 8 minutes; transfer to a plate to cool.

2. In a small bowl, combine the garlic, salt and vinegar. Whisk in the oil in a slow, thin stream.

3. In a salad bowl, combine the lettuce with the garlic dressing and toss to coat well. Season to taste with the pepper, sprinkle the toasted pine nuts on top and serve.

—*Stephanie Lyness*

• • •

MIXED SALAD WITH KUMQUATS AND PECANS

Sliced fresh kumquats add a tart, orangey zip to this winter salad. Marinating them in the dressing for half an hour softens their skins nicely. The lettuces can be washed and dried the day before the dinner. Wrap them loosely in paper towels, pack them in a roomy plastic bag and refrigerate until needed.

————— 8 to 10 Servings —————
½ cup olive oil
3 tablespoons white wine vinegar
1 tablespoon Dijon-style mustard
1 small garlic clove, crushed
¼ teaspoon salt
¼ teaspoon freshly ground pepper
10 small fresh kumquats, thinly

sliced into rounds, pits removed
1½ cups pecans (about 5 ounces)
1 head of romaine lettuce, torn into
  pieces
1 head of red oak leaf lettuce, torn
  into pieces
1 small red onion, sliced into thin
  rings
4 Belgian endives—2 thinly sliced
  crosswise, 2 separated into leaves

1. Preheat the oven to 400°. In a large jar, combine the olive oil, vinegar, mustard, garlic, salt and pepper. Cover and shake well. *(The dressing can be made 1 day ahead.)* Add the kumquats to the dressing, shake to coat and set aside to macerate for 30 minutes.

2. Meanwhile, spread the pecans on a cookie sheet and bake for 5 minutes, until fragrant and lightly toasted. Let cool, then break the nuts into large pieces.

3. Just before serving, in a large salad bowl, combine the romaine and red oak leaf lettuces with the onion, sliced endives and pecans. Shake the dressing and pour it over the salad. Toss well to combine. Arrange the endive spears around the salad and serve at once.

—*Diana Sturgis*

• • •

GREEN SALAD WITH MANGO AND A CITRUS VINAIGRETTE

————— 4 Servings —————
3 tablespoons fresh orange juice
1 tablespoon red wine vinegar
2 teaspoons fresh lemon juice
Salt and freshly ground pepper
¼ cup plus 2 tablespoons olive oil
1 ripe medium mango

1 head of Boston lettuce, torn into
  bite-size pieces
1 small head of red leaf lettuce, torn
  into bite-size pieces

1. In a large nonreactive serving bowl, combine the orange juice, vinegar and lemon juice. Season with salt and pepper to taste. Gradually whisk in the olive oil until blended.

2. With a small sharp knife, peel the mango. Place the mango on a flat surface and cut horizontally in half just above the pit. Turn and repeat on the other side. Cut away any remaining flesh and cut into ½-inch dice. Just before serving, add the lettuces and mango to the bowl; toss to coat with the vinaigrette and serve.

—*Stephanie Lyness*

• • •

WARM CABBAGE SLAW

This microwaved dish is just as good cooked on the stove in a tightly covered skillet.

————— 4 Servings —————
5 cups shredded or coarsely chopped
  green cabbage (half of a 2-pound
  head)
½ teaspoon salt
¼ teaspoon freshly ground pepper
1 tablespoon rice wine vinegar
2 tablespoons unsalted butter, cut
  into bits

In a medium glass bowl, toss the cabbage with the salt, pepper and vinegar. Dot with the butter and cover tightly with microwave plastic wrap. Cook on High power until heated through but still crunchy, about 7 minutes. Remove from the microwave and let sit for 2 minutes. Uncover, toss and serve hot. Or, alternatively, in a large nonreactive saucepan, melt the butter over moderately high heat. Add the cabbage, salt and pepper;

toss to coat and cook for 5 minutes. Add vinegar and cook until the cabbage is wilted but still crunchy, about 3 minutes more.

—Lee Bailey

• • •

CARROT AND CABBAGE SLAW WITH CARAWAY SEEDS

——————— 6 Servings ———————
4 cups thinly sliced green cabbage
   (half of a 1½-pound head)
5 medium carrots, shredded
½ small red onion, minced
1½ tablespoons fresh lemon juice
1 tablespoon tarragon wine vinegar
¾ teaspoon salt
½ teaspoon freshly ground pepper
½ teaspoon sugar
1 teaspoon caraway seeds
3 tablespoons olive oil

In a large nonreactive bowl, toss the cabbage with the carrots and onion. In a small bowl, combine the lemon juice, vinegar, salt, pepper, sugar and caraway seeds. Whisk in the oil in a thin stream. Pour over the cabbage mixture and toss well. Serve immediately.

—Lee Bailey

• • •

CAULIFLOWER RAITA

This cool side dish is a great way to use cauliflower in the warmer months.

——————— 4 Servings ———————
1 head of cauliflower (about 2
   pounds), cut into large florets
1½ teaspoons cumin seeds
½ cup plain yogurt
¼ cup chopped fresh mint
½ teaspoon salt
¼ teaspoon freshly ground pepper

1. Place the cauliflower florets in a steamer pot, cover and steam over high heat until barely tender, about 4 minutes. Drain, then refrigerate to chill.

2. Meanwhile, in a small dry skillet, toast the cumin seeds over high heat, shaking the pan, until fragrant, about 30 seconds. Pound in a mortar, grind in a spice mill or chop with a knife to form a coarse powder.

3. In a large bowl, mix the cumin with the yogurt, mint, salt and pepper. Fold in the cauliflower and toss lightly to coat evenly. *(The recipe can be made up to 2 hours ahead; cover and refrigerate.)* Serve slightly chilled.

—Marcia Kiesel

• • •

CITRUS GREEN BEAN SALAD

The light, fresh sweetness of orange is a sunny surprise in this crisp, any-time-of-year salad.

——————— 12 Servings ———————
2 pounds green beans, cut into
   1-inch pieces
½ cup fresh orange juice
1 tablespoon grated orange zest
3 tablespoons balsamic vinegar
1 teaspoon granulated sugar
1 teaspoon grainy mustard
¾ teaspoon salt
¾ cup olive oil
½ cup finely chopped red onion
Freshly ground pepper (optional)

1. In a large pot of boiling salted water, cook the beans until just crisp-tender, about 3 minutes. Drain in a colander and rinse under cold water until cool. Pat dry; transfer the beans to a large nonreactive bowl and set aside.

2. In a medium bowl, whisk together the orange juice, orange zest, balsamic vinegar, sugar, mustard and salt. Gradually whisk in the oil in a slow, steady stream until incorporated. Stir in the red onion.

Pour the dressing over the beans and toss to coat thoroughly. *(The recipe can be made 1 day ahead; cover and refrigerate overnight. Let the beans sit at room temperature about 1 hour before serving.)*

3. Transfer the beans to a serving bowl and season with pepper if desired. Toss once more and serve.

—Tracey Seaman

• • •

WARM STRING BEAN SALAD

——————— 6 Servings ———————
1¼ pounds string beans
2 tablespoons balsamic vinegar
1½ teaspoons fresh lemon juice
¾ teaspoon dry mustard
¾ teaspoon salt
Freshly ground pepper
¼ cup plus 1 tablespoon olive oil
1 garlic clove, minced
¼ cup finely chopped red onion
   (optional)

1. In a large pot of boiling salted water, cook the string beans until just tender but still slightly crunchy, about 3 minutes; drain, refresh and drain again thoroughly.

2. Meanwhile, in a small bowl, combine the vinegar and lemon juice. Whisk in the mustard, salt and the pepper to taste; then whisk in the oil in a thin stream. Add the garlic and season with additional salt and pepper to taste.

3. To serve, place the beans on a serving platter. Pour the vinaigrette over the beans. Sprinkle the onion on the top, if you desire, and season with additional salt and pepper to taste. Serve warm.

—Lee Bailey

• • •

Whole Wheat California Pizza with Fresh Tomatoes and Goat Cheese (p. 220).

Above, Sweet Potato and Butternut Squash Puree (p. 130) baked in acorn squash halves. Right, Ham 'n' Greens Buttermilk Spoonbread (p. 99).

CHICK-PEA AND BAKED BELL PEPPER SALAD WITH CUMIN

Start this recipe a day ahead since the chick-peas need to soak overnight. Baking bell peppers with oil and garlic creates a flavorful liquid to use as a dressing.

—————— *6 Servings* ——————
2 cups dried chick-peas
2 large red bell peppers
6 garlic cloves, unpeeled
¼ cup plus 2 tablespoons extra-virgin olive oil
1 sprig of rosemary (optional)
2½ teaspoons cumin seeds
2 tablespoons fresh lemon juice
1 tablespoon red wine vinegar
1½ teaspoons salt
½ teaspoon freshly ground black pepper
1 small red onion, finely chopped
2 small tomatoes, cut into ½-inch dice

1. In a large saucepan, cover the chick-peas with cold water and let soak overnight at room temperature. The next day, strain off the water. Cover the chick-peas with 6 inches of fresh water and bring to a boil over high heat. Using a ladle, skim the water to remove any impurities that rise to the surface. Reduce the heat to moderately low. Simmer, adding 2 cups of hot tap water to the pan every 30 minutes or so as necessary, until the chick-peas are tender, about 3 hours. Remove from the heat and let cool in the liquid. Drain and transfer to a large bowl. *(The recipe can be made to this point up to 1 day ahead; cover and refrigerate.)*

2. Preheat the oven to 425°. In a small roasting pan, combine the bell peppers, garlic, 2 tablespoons of the olive oil, the rosemary, if desired, and 2 tablespoons of water. Cover with aluminum foil and bake for 20 minutes until the peppers and garlic are soft when pierced with a fork. Remove from the oven and set aside, covered, for 5 minutes. Then transfer the peppers to a large plate and set aside to cool slightly.

3. Meanwhile, peel the garlic cloves and place them in a small bowl. Mash them with a fork. Stir in the juices from the roasting pan; discard the rosemary.

4. In a small skillet, toast the cumin seeds over high heat until fragrant, about 30 seconds. Pound in a mortar, grind in a spice mill or coarsely chop with a knife to form a coarse powder. Stir the cumin into the garlic dressing along with the lemon juice, vinegar, salt, black pepper and the remaining ¼ cup olive oil.

5. Pour the dressing over the chick-peas, add the red onion and mix well. Set aside at room temperature for 30 minutes to blend the flavors.

6. Working over a bowl, peel the peppers; remove and discard the cores, seeds and ribs. Cut into ½-inch dice. Reserve all the juices from the peppers. Shortly before serving, fold the peppers and their liquid into the chick-peas along with the tomatoes. Serve the salad at room temperature or slightly chilled.

—*Marcia Kiesel*

• • •

BLACK-EYED PEA AND CORN SALAD

Use fresh black-eyed peas if you can find them. Otherwise, dried or frozen peas, cooked according to package directions, or canned peas are a fine substitute.

—————— *4 Servings* ——————
1 cup cooked black-eyed peas
1 cup fresh or frozen cooked corn
3 medium celery ribs, thinly sliced
1 medium red bell pepper, cut into ¼-inch dice
3 scallions, thinly sliced
3 tablespoons balsamic vinegar
2 teaspoons honey
1 teaspoon Dijon-style mustard
½ teaspoon salt
⅛ teaspoon freshly ground black pepper
¼ cup plus 3 tablespoons safflower oil
1 bunch of young dandelion leaves, washed and dried (optional)

1. In a large bowl, combine the peas, corn, celery, bell pepper and scallions.

2. In a bowl, whisk together the vinegar, honey, mustard, salt and black pepper. Whisk in the oil until blended. *(The recipe can be prepared to this point up to 4 hours ahead. Refrigerate the vegetables and the dressing separately.)*

3. Pour the dressing over the vegetables and toss well. Divide the dandelion leaves, if using, among 4 chilled plates. Spoon the salad onto the leaves and serve.

—*Melanie Barnard & Brooke Dojny*

• • •

Mixed Salad with Kumquats and Pecans (p. 143).

149

SALADS

THAI RICE NOODLE SALAD

South Chinese influence shows through in *pad thai*, yet the raw vegetables and the bite of the chile-vinegar dressing make this salad distinctively Thai.

—————— 6 to 8 Servings ——————
3 bundles of medium-thin, flat rice noodles* (12 ounces)
2 cups rice wine vinegar*
1 tablespoon sugar
2 Anaheim chiles, thinly sliced
2 tablespoons peanut oil
6 scallions—3 whole, 3 chopped
4 garlic cloves, chopped
1 pound fresh bean sprouts
2 medium tomatoes, cut into small wedges
3 eggs, lightly beaten
1 tablespoon soy sauce
1 tablespoon nam pla*
1 head of leaf lettuce, leaves separated
2 tablespoons chopped roasted peanuts
2 tablespoons fresh coriander leaves
1 lime, thinly sliced
*Available at Asian markets

1. Soak the rice noodles in hot water until softened, 25 to 30 minutes. Drain.

2. For the dressing, combine the rice wine vinegar and sugar and stir until the sugar dissolves. Add the sliced chiles. *(The dressing can be made in advance and refrigerated.)*

3. Heat a wok over moderately high heat. Add the peanut oil and when hot, add the chopped scallions and garlic and stir-fry for 15 seconds. Add half the bean sprouts and stir-fry for 1 minute. Add the tomato wedges and stir-fry for 30 seconds; try not to mash the tomatoes. Push the contents of the wok slightly up the sides and add the eggs to the center. When the eggs begin to set, stir to break into large pieces.

4. Push the contents of the wok as high up the sides as you can and add the drained rice noodles. Stir-fry until heated through, 2 to 3 minutes. Try to use as much of the wok's surface as possible; the noodles have a tendency to bunch up, but keep spreading them out. Add the soy sauce and *nam pla*, then stir well to combine all the ingredients in the wok.

5. To serve, line a large flat platter with the lettuce leaves. Spoon the noodle mixture into the center. Sprinkle the chopped peanuts and the coriander leaves on top. Garnish the platter with the remaining bean sprouts, the lime slices and the whole scallions. Serve the chile-vinegar dressing alongside.

—*Jeffrey Alford*

• • •

WATERMELON AND ORANGE SALAD

Sweet, crisp chunks of watermelon make a pleasing addition to this tangy salad.

—————— 4 to 6 Servings ——————
1 cup walnut or pecan halves, broken
1½ tablespoons red wine vinegar
1 large shallot, minced
½ teaspoon salt
¼ teaspoon freshly ground pepper
¼ cup olive oil
2 navel oranges
1 head of romaine lettuce, torn into bite-size pieces
1 bunch of arugula or watercress, tough stems removed
8 radishes, thinly sliced
½ medium red onion, thinly sliced
4 cups seeded 1-inch watermelon chunks

1. Preheat the oven to 350°. Spread the nuts on a baking sheet and toast for 8 minutes. Set aside to cool.

2. Meanwhile, in a screw-top jar, combine the vinegar, shallot, salt, pepper and olive oil. Cover and shake well.

3. With a small sharp knife, peel the oranges, cutting off all the bitter white pith and the outer membrane. Slice the oranges crosswise, ¼ inch thick. Quarter the slices.

4. In a bowl, toss together the lettuce, arugula, radishes and onion. Add the oranges, watermelon and toasted nuts.

5. Shake the dressing again. Pour it over the salad and toss. Serve at once.

—*Diana Sturgis*

• • •

SANDWICHES & BREADSTUFFS

CRAB ROLL

Although blue crabs are delicious, I prefer the flavor of Dungeness. Either will be just fine in this recipe.

♀ A crisp, flavorful, uncomplicated white, such as Liberty School Lot 17 Chardonnay from Napa or 1988 Preston Estate White from Sonoma, would underscore this rich crab salad.

————— *Makes 4 Sandwiches* —————
½ cup mayonnaise
¼ cup plain yogurt
2 teaspoons fresh lime juice
2 teaspoons fresh lemon juice
1 to 2 celery ribs, finely chopped
1 small shallot, minced
1 teaspoon minced fresh tarragon,
  plus tarragon sprigs, for garnish
Salt and freshly ground white
  pepper
1 pound fresh crabmeat, preferably
  Dungeness, picked over
4 sourdough rolls, split in half
6 large romaine lettuce leaves,
  finely shredded

1. In a medium bowl, whisk the mayonnaise and yogurt. Whisk in the lime and lemon juices, then stir in the celery, shallot and minced tarragon. Season with salt and white pepper to taste; mix well. Fold in the crabmeat and mix gently until thoroughly moistened. Cover and refrigerate for 1 hour.

2. Preheat the broiler. Place the rolls, cut-sides up, on a broiler pan and broil until golden.

3. Stir the crab filling; season with additional salt and pepper if necessary. Spoon the crab onto the bottom half of each roll. Set the roll tops slightly askew over the crab and garnish with tarragon sprigs. Arrange the lettuce alongside and serve immediately.

—*Susan Herrmann Loomis*

• • •

TEA-SMOKED SALMON, SESAME SAUCE AND WATERCRESS SANDWICH

Rich, smoky flavors and crisp, crunchy textures make this sandwich a standout. The smoking technique (an adaptation of the one used by Barbara Tropp at her San Francisco restaurant, China Moon Cafe) is remarkably easy, and the good results are well worth the slight extra effort.

The recipe calls for one large salmon fillet. Smaller fillets can be smoked, but the smoking time should be decreased a little.

————— *Makes 4 Sandwiches* —————
¼ cup light soy sauce
1½ tablespoons dry sherry
1 tablespoon coarse (kosher) salt
4 quarter-size rounds of fresh
  ginger, plus four 2-inch strips of
  ginger peelings
1¼- to 1½-pound center-cut salmon
  fillet in one piece, skin on, rinsed
  and patted dry
1 tablespoon dried sliced lemon
  grass
⅓ cup black tea leaves
⅓ cup raw white rice
⅓ cup (packed) brown sugar
1 cinnamon stick, broken into small
  pieces
½ cup mayonnaise
1 teaspoon Oriental sesame oil
1 teaspoon fresh lemon juice
Eight ¼-inch-thick slices of sour-
  dough bread
1 small European cucumber, peeled
  and very thinly sliced
1 small bunch of watercress, large
  stems removed
2 scallions, very thinly sliced
  lengthwise

1. In a shallow nonreactive baking dish just large enough to hold the salmon, combine the soy sauce, sherry and salt. Using the back of a large knife, crush the ginger rounds to release their flavor, then spread them in the dish. Place the salmon in the dish and turn to coat with the marinade. Refrigerate for 1 hour, turning once after 30 minutes.

2. Remove the salmon from the marinade and set it on a small wire rack to drain until dry and a light film has formed on the surface, about 15 minutes.

3. Meanwhile line a wok and its lid with a double thickness of heavy-duty aluminum foil, leaving a 4-inch overhang on both the wok and lid. In a small bowl, combine the lemon grass, tea leaves, rice, brown sugar, cinnamon stick and ginger peelings. Spread the mixture evenly on the foil in the bottom of the wok. Set the rack with the salmon about 1 inch above the smoking mixture. (Prop up the rack with balls of aluminum foil if necessary.)

4. Set the wok over high heat. When the sugar begins to bubble and smoke in several places, after about 4 minutes, cover the wok and loosely crimp together the foil overhang on the wok and lid, leaving an inch-wide opening for the smoke. Smoke the fish for 10 minutes, then turn off the heat and let sit for 5 minutes.

5. Uncover the wok, remove the rack and let the salmon cool briefly. Using tweezers or pliers, pull out any thin bones you can feel when you run your hand across the top of the salmon fillet. Cut the fish crosswise, up to but not through the skin, into 4 equal pieces. Using a metal spatula, lift each piece of salmon, leaving the skin behind.

6. In a small bowl, mix the mayonnaise, sesame oil and lemon juice. Spread 1 tablespoon of the sesame mayonnaise on each slice of bread. Cover 4 of the slices with a layer of cucumber, several sprigs of watercress, a piece of salmon and a few scallion strips. Top with the remaining 4 slices of bread. Slice the sandwiches in half and serve with any remaining watercress and cucumber as garnish.

—*Susan Herrmann Loomis*

• • •

OPEN-FACED CLAM SANDWICH

This sandwich is filled with sweet, briny clams. For a fine light supper, serve it with steamed artichokes, a fresh green salad and a slightly chilled Chardonnay.

Make sure that each clam you buy is firmly closed. Do not use any that are open. In fact, don't even bring home a clam that won't close immediately when lightly tapped on the shell. Also, be careful to avoid overcooking. Watch the clams so that you can snatch them from the heat as soon as they've opened. And finally, buy top-quality English muffins.

———— *Makes 4 Sandwiches* ————
6 dozen littleneck or Manila clams, scrubbed
2 cups heavy cream
4 English muffins, split in half
1 tablespoon plus 1 teaspoon unsalted butter
Freshly ground pepper
2 teaspoons Cognac or other brandy
¼ cup minced chives

1. In a large heavy pot, add the clams to ½ cup of water and bring to a boil over moderately high heat. Cover and cook, checking the clams frequently and removing them to a plate as soon as they open, 2 to 5 minutes total, depending on the type of clams you use. Discard any clams that do not open.

2. Strain the clam cooking liquid and any liquid on the plate through a fine-mesh sieve lined with dampened cheesecloth and set aside. When the clams are cool enough to handle, remove them from their shells and set aside; discard the shells.

3. In a heavy medium saucepan, bring the cream to a boil over moderately high heat. Boil until the cream reduces by about one-third and is the consistency of a thin gravy, about 12 minutes.

4. Meanwhile, toast the English muffins until crisp and golden brown. Place 2 halves, cut-sides up, on each of 4 plates.

5. In a large heavy skillet, melt the butter over moderate heat until foaming. Add the clams and stir until heated through, about 1 minute. Season lightly with pepper.

6. Stir the Cognac, ¼ cup of the reserved clam cooking liquid and the chives into the reduced cream. Stir constantly over moderately high heat just until hot.

7. Spoon the clams over the English muffins and pour the cream over the clams. Serve immediately.

—*Susan Herrmann Loomis*

• • •

SANDWICH SIT-DOWN

Serves 4

Rocky Roquefort Dip (p. 28) with Endive Spears and Apple Slices

Tea-Smoked Salmon, Sesame Sauce and Watercress Sandwiches (p. 152)

Warm Carrot Slaw Tossed with Chive Vinaigrette

Individual Bittersweet Chocolate Soufflés (p. 203)

Espresso

SALMON CLUB SANDWICH

The key to any club sandwich is using good mayonnaise, freshly ground black pepper, crisp greens and, of course, ripe tomatoes. These satisfying sandwiches, which take just moments to prepare, are even easier to put together if you have your fish market cut the salmon for you.

———— *Makes 4 Sandwiches* ————
8 thin slices of bacon
8 slices of white bread
1 pound skinless salmon fillet, bones removed, cut on the diagonal into 8 very thin slices.
Salt and freshly ground pepper
¼ cup plus 2 tablespoons mayonnaise
2 large tomatoes, sliced crosswise
1 head of butterhead or Boston lettuce

1. In a large skillet, fry the bacon over moderately high heat until crisp, about 5 minutes. Transfer to paper towels to drain.

2. Preheat the broiler. Toast the bread until golden. Place the salmon on a lightly oiled broiler pan in a single layer and broil no more than 3 inches from the heat for 2 to 3 minutes, checking frequently, until pale pink and opaque all the way through. Remove and season lightly with salt and generously with pepper.

3. Spread 1 side of all the toast slices with the mayonnaise. Layer 4 pieces of toast with the sliced tomatoes, 2 pieces of salmon, 2 bacon slices and 3 large lettuce leaves. Season the remaining toast with more pepper and cover each sandwich. Cut in half and serve immediately.

—*Susan Herrmann Loomis*

• • •

GRILLED SHRIMP PITA
WITH PAPAYA SALSA

The lively heat of the salsa can easily be adjusted by removing some or all of the seeds of the jalapeño. The lime juice adds a bright fresh accent. When you buy the avocado, make sure that you get one that gives slightly but is still firm.

──────── *Makes 4 Sandwiches* ────────
1 avocado, preferably Hass, chopped
1 papaya, seeded and chopped
½ cup finely diced jicama
2 scallions, thinly sliced
1 jalapeño pepper, seeded (if
 desired) and minced
1 tablespoon minced fresh coriander
2 tablespoons fresh lime juice
1 pound medium shrimp in their
 shells, patted dry
1 teaspoon safflower oil
½ teaspoon salt
Four 6-inch pita bread pockets
Lime wedges, for garnish

1. Light a charcoal fire. Let the coals burn until they glow red and are covered with gray ash. Alternatively, heat a 10-inch cast-iron skillet over moderately high heat for 5 minutes.

2. In a medium bowl, combine the avocado, papaya, jicama, scallions, jalapeño, coriander and lime juice. Toss and set aside.

3. Toss the shrimp with oil; spread them in a single layer on a piece of heavy-duty aluminum foil and transfer to the grill. Make sure the foil doesn't entirely cover the grill so that the smoke from the fire can reach the shrimp. Grill the shrimp for about 2 minutes, or until just pink around the sides. Turn with tongs and cook for another 2 minutes, until opaque when cut in the thickest part. (Alternatively, spread the shrimp in the hot skillet in a single layer and follow the cooking times for grilling.) Let the shrimp cool, then peel and discard the shells. Slice each shrimp in half lengthwise.

4. Sprinkle the salsa with the salt, stir gently and set aside 1 cup. Stir the sliced shrimp into the remaining salsa.

5. Partially slit open each pita pocket and fill with the shrimp and salsa mixture. Serve immediately, garnished with the remaining salsa and the lime wedges.

—*Susan Herrmann Loomis*

• • •

SNAPPER BURGER WITH
TARTAR SAUCE

Snapper, rockfish, pompano and tilefish all work well with this piquant sandwich. Serve either on homemade hamburger buns made with a touch of whole wheat flour or on the best buns you can buy.

──────── *Makes 6 Sandwiches* ────────
1 cup mayonnaise
2 tablespoons minced dill pickle
1 tablespoon drained capers, minced
1 tablespoon minced red onion, plus
 6 thin slices
1 garlic clove, minced
1 tablespoon fresh lemon juice
½ teaspoon minced parsley
6 hamburger buns, preferably whole
 wheat
1½ pounds skinless red snapper
 fillets, rinsed and patted dry.
Salt
2 cups (lightly packed) arugula
 leaves

1. Preheat the broiler. To make the tartar sauce: in a medium bowl, combine the mayonnaise, pickle, capers, minced onion, garlic, lemon juice and parsley; stir to combine. Set aside.

2. Split the hamburger buns in half. In the broiler, toast the buns, cut-sides up, just until pale golden.

3. Cut the snapper fillets into 6 equal pieces. Place the fish on a baking sheet lined with lightly oiled aluminum foil and season lightly with salt. Broil about 3 inches from the heat for 4 to 6 minutes, turning once and checking frequently to prevent overcooking, just until opaque throughout.

4. Spread the toasted side of each hamburger bun with 1 to 2 tablespoons of the tartar sauce. Place an onion slice on the bottom half of each bun and top with the broiled snapper. Arrange the arugula leaves over the fish and top with the other hamburger bun halves. Serve immediately; pass the remaining tartar sauce separately.

—*Susan Herrmann Loomis*

• • •

MACKEREL FILLET AND
ROSEMARY MAYONNAISE
ON A BAGUETTE

With its lusty flavor and wonderful, meaty mackerel, this sandwich will take you right to the shores of the Mediterranean. Roll up your sleeves before you eat. ❢ This peppery sandwich could be matched by a straightforward Sauvignon Blanc, such as 1988 Quivira from Sonoma or a Bordeaux Blanc, such as 1988 Alfred Schyler Fils Entre-Deux-Mers.

──────── *Makes 4 Sandwiches* ────────
1 medium green bell pepper
1 medium red bell pepper
1 tablespoon olive oil
1 garlic clove, minced
2 teaspoons minced fresh rosemary
 or 1 scant teaspoon dried, plus
 sprigs of rosemary, for garnish
¾ cup mayonnaise
4 fresh mackerel fillets, boned but
 not skinned (5 to 7 ounces each),
 rinsed and patted dry
Salt
Four 6-inch pieces of crisp baguette,
 halved lengthwise

1. Preheat the broiler. Roast the green and red bell peppers directly over a gas flame or under the broiler as close to the heat as possible, turning until charred all over, about 5 minutes. Enclose the peppers in a bag or wrap them in aluminum foil and set aside for about 10 minutes to steam. When cool enough to handle, peel the peppers and remove the cores, ribs and seeds. Rinse the peppers and pat dry, then thinly slice lengthwise.

2. In a small bowl, toss the pepper strips with the olive oil, garlic and 1 teaspoon of the minced rosemary (or ½ teaspoon dried). In another small bowl, stir together the mayonnaise and the remaining 1 teaspoon rosemary (or ½ teaspoon dried). Set both aside.

3. Place a mackerel fillet on a work surface, skin-side down. Using a small sharp knife, cut down to the skin (but not through it) on each side of the dark bony strip that runs down the length of the fillet. Pull out the bony strip and discard. Repeat with the remaining fillets.

4. Arrange the fillets, skin-side down, on a baking sheet lined with lightly oiled aluminum foil. Season with salt and broil about 3 inches from the heat for 5 to 7 minutes, until the meat turns ivory and opaque at the thickest part. Set the fillets aside until cool enough to handle, then remove and discard the skin.

5. Spread each baguette half with a heaping tablespoon of the rosemary mayonnaise. Place a mackerel fillet on each baguette bottom and top with the reserved roasted peppers. Cover with the baguette tops and cut the sandwiches in half. Garnish with a rosemary sprig and serve immediately.

—*Susan Herrmann Loomis*

• • •

TUNA CLUB WITH ROASTED YELLOW PEPPER-BASIL MAYONNAISE

This is inspired by the grilled tuna club at Docks, a seafood restaurant on Manhattan's Upper West Side.

——— *Makes 4 Sandwiches* ———
12 strips of bacon
3 tablespoons bacon fat or olive oil
8 tuna steaks, cut about ½ inch thick (3 ounces each)
12 thin slices white sandwich bread, lightly toasted
Roasted Yellow Pepper-Basil Mayonnaise (p. 254)
Salt and freshly ground pepper
8 thin slices of ripe tomato
8 crisp lettuce leaves

1. In a large skillet, cook the bacon over moderately high heat until crisp, about 10 minutes. Drain on paper towels, cut in half crosswise and set aside.

2. Pour all but 3 tablespoons of bacon fat from the skillet. Heat the bacon fat over moderately high heat. Add the tuna steaks and sauté in batches, turning once, until lightly browned, about 2 minutes per side. Drain on paper towels. *(The tuna can be sautéed up to 2 hours ahead.)*

3. Spread 1 piece of toast with 1 tablespoon of the Roasted Yellow Pepper-Basil Mayonnaise. Lay 1 piece of tuna over the mayonnaise and season lightly with salt and pepper. Top the tuna with three half-strips of bacon. Place a slice of tomato over the bacon and lay a lettuce leaf over the tomato.

4. Spread 1 tablespoon of mayonnaise on both sides of another piece of toast. Set the toast over the lettuce. Top the toast with another tuna steak and season lightly with salt and pepper. Lay 3 more half-strips of bacon over the tuna and top with a tomato slice and a lettuce leaf.

5. Spread a third piece of toast with 1 tablespoon of mayonnaise and set it, mayonnaise-side down, on the lettuce.

6. Repeat with the remaining ingredients to make 3 more sandwiches. Save the remaining mayonnaise for another use. Flatten each sandwich slightly with your palm and secure with toothpicks if desired. With a long sharp knife, trim the crusts and cut each sandwich diagonally in half. Serve immediately.

—*Michael McLaughlin*

• • •

LOBSTER CLUB

Anne Rosenzweig serves a chimney-smoked lobster club at her Manhattan restaurant, Arcadia, on brioche toast, and that, or something equally soft-crusted and eggy (like challah), is just the bread this sandwich calls for. I've never had it at Arcadia, but here is the version I assembled at home.

——— *Makes 4 Sandwiches* ———
2 cups cooked lobster meat (about 10 ounces), from two 1¼-pound lobsters, picked over
About 1 cup mayonnaise
Salt and freshly ground pepper
8 slices of soft egg bread, lightly toasted on one side only
6 slices of crisp cooked bacon, halved crosswise
4 thin slices of ripe tomato
4 crisp lettuce leaves

1. In a medium bowl, combine the lobster and about ¾ cup of the mayonnaise (or more, depending on your conscience). Season with salt and pepper to taste.

2. Set 1 piece of egg bread on a work surface, toasted-side down. Spread one-fourth of the lobster mixture over the untoasted side. Top the lobster with 3 half-strips of bacon, a slice of tomato and a lettuce leaf. Set a second slice of bread, toasted-side up, on the lettuce.

3. Repeat with the remaining ingredients to make 3 more sandwiches. With a serrated knife, trim the crusts. Cut the sandwiches diagonally in half and serve immediately.

—Michael McLaughlin

• • •

THE CLASSIC CLUB

Classic in the title doesn't mean the double-decker version enjoyed years ago, but rather the triple-decker standard by which we now judge all others.

——— *Makes 4 Sandwiches* ———
1 pound cooked chicken breast,
  thinly sliced
12 thin slices white sandwich bread,
  lightly toasted
1 cup mayonnaise
Salt and freshly ground pepper
12 strips of crisp cooked bacon,
  halved crosswise
8 thin slices of ripe tomato
8 crisp lettuce leaves

1. Divide the sliced chicken into 8 portions. Spread 1 piece of toast with 1 tablespoon of mayonnaise. Arrange 1 portion of chicken on the toast. Season lightly with salt and pepper. Lay 3 pieces of bacon over the chicken. Top with 1 slice of tomato and 1 lettuce leaf.

2. Spread 1 tablespoon of mayonnaise on both sides of another piece of toast. Set the toast on the lettuce and top with another portion of chicken. Season lightly with salt and pepper. Lay 3 pieces of bacon over the chicken and top with a slice of tomato and a lettuce leaf.

3. Spread a third piece of toast with 1 tablespoon of mayonnaise and set it, mayonnaise-side down, on the lettuce.

4. Repeat with the remaining ingredients to make 3 more sandwiches. Flatten each sandwich slightly with your palm and secure with toothpicks if desired. With a long sharp knife, trim the crusts and cut each sandwich diagonally in half. Serve immediately.

—Michael McLaughlin

• • •

CALIFORNIA CLUB

The jalapeño in the lime mayonnaise are optional, but they add a pleasant kick to the sandwich. If you do include them, offer your guests a cold beer.

——— *Makes 4 Sandwiches* ———
1 cup mayonnaise
2 pickled jalapeño peppers, seeded
  and minced
1 tablespoon minced lime zest
1 pound thinly sliced smoked turkey
  breast
12 thin slices whole wheat sandwich
  bread, lightly toasted
1 ripe avocado, preferably Hass,
  peeled and cut into 16 thin wedges
12 strips of crisp cooked bacon,
  halved crosswise
8 thin slices of ripe tomato
8 crisp lettuce leaves

1. In a small bowl, whisk together the mayonnaise, jalapeños and lime zest.

2. Divide the turkey into 8 equal portions. Spread 1 piece of toast with 1 tablespoon of mayonnaise. Arrange 1 portion of turkey on the toast and top with 2 avocado wedges and 3 pieces of bacon. Set a tomato slice on the bacon and lay a lettuce leaf on top.

3. Spread 1 tablespoon of mayonnaise on both sides of another piece of toast. Set

the toast on the lettuce. Cover with another portion of turkey and top with 2 more avocado wedges and 3 more bacon pieces. Set a tomato slice and a lettuce leaf on the bacon.

4. Spread a third piece of toast with 1 tablespoon of mayonnaise and set it on the lettuce, mayonnaise-side down.

5. Repeat with the remaining ingredients to make 3 more sandwiches. Flatten each sandwich slightly with your palm and secure with toothpicks if desired. With a long sharp knife, trim the crusts and cut each sandwich diagonally in half. Serve immediately.

—Michael McLaughlin

• • •

**MONDAY NIGHT
FOOTBALL MENU**

Serves 4

Tortilla Chips
Frijolemole (p. 28)

The Classic Club Sandwich (p. 156)
Ligurian Vegetable Soup (p. 42)
🍷 *Amber beer*

Double Crust Apple Pie with
Vanilla (p. 166)

CHEESE AND SAUSAGE CHICAGO DEEP-DISH PIZZA

4 to 6 Servings

1/4 cup extra-virgin olive oil
1 package active dry yeast
2 teaspoons sugar
2/3 cup lukewarm water (105° to 115°)
1 teaspoon coarse (kosher) salt
1 3/4 cups unbleached flour
1/2 cup yellow cornmeal
1/2 cup chopped onion
2 tablespoons minced garlic
2 cups chopped fresh tomatoes, drained, or 3 cans (14 1/2 ounces each) Italian plum tomatoes, drained
2 tablespoons tomato paste
2 tablespoons chopped fresh basil or 2 teaspoons dried
2 tablespoons chopped fresh oregano or 2 teaspoons dried
1/2 teaspoon freshly ground pepper
1 pound sweet Italian sausage links, casings removed
3/4 pound part-skim mozzarella cheese, shredded
1/4 pound provolone cheese, shredded
1/4 cup freshly grated Parmesan cheese (about 3/4 ounce)

1. Oil the bottom of a 14-by-2-inch steel deep-dish pizza pan with 2 tablespoons of olive oil. In a small bowl, dissolve the yeast and sugar in 1/3 cup of the water; set aside until foamy, about 5 minutes.

2. In a food processor combine the salt, flour and cornmeal. With the machine running, add the yeast mixture and the remaining 1/3 cup warm water. Process until a smooth ball forms, about 20 seconds. Transfer the dough to a lightly oiled medium bowl. Turn the dough to coat with oil and cover the bowl with plastic wrap. Set aside to rise in a warm place until doubled in bulk, about 1 hour.

3. In a large skillet, heat the remaining 2 tablespoons olive oil over moderately low heat. Add the onion and garlic and cook, stirring, until the onion is softened but not browned, about 5 minutes.

4. Add the tomatoes and tomato paste. Increase the heat to moderate and simmer, stirring occasionally, until the sauce is very thick and coats the back of a spoon, about 10 minutes. Add the basil, oregano and pepper and set aside.

5. Meanwhile, flatten each sausage link into an oblong patty. In a large skillet, cook the patties over moderately high heat until browned, about 5 minutes per side. Transfer the patties to a platter lined with paper towels and drain.

6. On a lightly floured surface, flatten the dough into a 12-inch round and transfer to the pan. Cover with plastic wrap and set aside for 15 minutes. Using your fingers, spread the dough so that it covers the bottom and comes 1 1/4 inches up the sides of the pan. (The sides should be slightly thicker than the bottom.) Cover with plastic wrap and set aside in a warm place to rise for 30 minutes.

7. Preheat the oven to 475°. Prick the bottom of the dough with a fork at 1/2-inch intervals. Set the pan on the lowest oven rack and bake for 4 minutes, until the crust is set and dry. Remove the crust from the oven.

8. Spread the mozzarella and provolone evenly over the crust. Arrange the sausage patties over the cheese. Spoon the tomato sauce evenly over the cheese and sprinkle with the Parmesan. Bake on the lowest rack for 5 minutes, then reduce the temperature to 400°. Move the pizza to the center oven rack and bake for 20 to 25 minutes, until golden and bubbly. Remove from the oven and let stand 5 minutes before slicing.

—*Sharon Sanders*

• • •

PIZZA DOUGH

You can make this dough three to five days before you need it; once it rises, punch it down and put it in a covered plastic container and refrigerate. Or you can prepare it up to two weeks ahead and freeze it. Either way, let the dough return to room temperature; when it just begins to rise again, it's ready to be rolled out.

Makes One
12-by-17-Inch Crust

1 cup all-purpose flour
3 tablespoons whole wheat flour
3/4 teaspoon coarse (kosher) salt
1/2 cup lukewarm water (105° to 115°)
Large pinch of sugar
1 teaspoon active dry yeast
2 teaspoons olive oil

1. In a small bowl, stir the all-purpose and whole wheat flours with the salt. Set aside.

2. Place the warm water in a medium bowl, add the sugar and stir until dissolved. Sprinkle the yeast over the water; it will sink to the bottom of the bowl at first. When it rises to the surface, stir in the olive oil and add the flour mixture. Mix well with a rubber spatula until a dough forms.

3. Transfer the dough to a floured work surface and knead until smooth and elastic, about 4 minutes. The dough should be just slightly sticky; work in a few teaspoons of flour if it seems too moist. Place the dough in a lightly oiled bowl and turn to coat with oil. Cover tightly with plastic wrap and let rise in a warm place until doubled in bulk, about 45 minutes. Punch down and use immediately or place in a covered plastic container and refrigerate for up to 5 days or freeze for up to 2 weeks.

—*Lydie Pinoy Marshall*

• • •

SANDWICHES & BREADSTUFFS

VALTELLINESE CHRISTMAS BREAD

Called *bisciöla*, this *panettone valtellinese* is a cross between a bread and a cake, chock-full of fruit and nuts.

Fresh chestnuts are not always easy to find, but use them here if you can. Score their flat side with a knife, boil them for 15 minutes and then peel them and proceed. Canned peeled whole chestnuts are easier to use and to find. The best quality are those from France. You can also use dried chestnuts (soak and boil until soft before using) or jarred chestnuts in syrup (drain first).

❦ *Bisciöla's* moderate sweetness invites occasional sips of a nice dessert wine between bites. We suggest two very different wines from opposite ends of the country. I Vignaioli di Santo Stefano (Piedmont) Moscato d'Asti has a whisper of sparkle to highlight its fresh grapey taste. Capo Salina (Hauner/Sicily) Malvasia delle Lipari, of golden honey color, is rich with scents of apricots and citrus. If you've had plenty of wine with dinner, you might opt for the former. On the other hand, just a little of the latter goes a long way.

——*Makes One 8-Inch Cake*——
½ cup raisins
5 dried figs, ends trimmed, coarsely chopped
¼ cup grappa or brandy
¼ cup unsweetened apple juice
¾ cup rye flour
1¾ cups all-purpose flour
1 teaspoon baking soda
2 tablespoons coarsely ground walnuts plus ½ cup walnut pieces
2 tablespoons coarsely ground hazelnuts plus ½ cup whole hazelnuts
¼ cup sugar
¼ tablespoons unsalted butter, cut into pieces, at room temperature
1 egg
¼ cup honey
10 canned chestnuts, drained and coarsely crumbled

1. In a medium bowl, soak the raisins and figs in the grappa and apple juice for at least 2 hours or overnight.

2. Preheat the oven to 350°. In a large bowl, sift together the rye and all-purpose flours with the baking soda. Stir in the ground nuts and sugar. Work in the butter with your fingers until the mixture is the consistency of small peas. Stir in the egg and honey and knead until the texture is uniform, about 2 minutes.

3. Using a slotted spoon, drain the raisins and figs and add them to the dough. Gently work in the dried fruit along with the whole hazelnuts, walnut pieces and chestnuts, until evenly distributed and the dough forms a ball.

4. Dust a pizza stone or cookie sheet with rye flour. Shake off any excess. Place the dough on top and flatten it to form an 8-inch round about 1¼ inches thick. Smooth the edges with moistened fingers. Bake for 45 to 50 minutes, or until lightly golden and a cake tester inserted in the center comes out clean. Remove from the baking sheet and let cool completely on a rack. Serve the bread sliced in thin wedges. (*Wrapped well, the bread will keep refrigerated for up to 1 week and frozen for up to 2 months.*)
—*Constance and Rosario del Nero*

• • •

TUSCAN BREAD

This crusty, large-crumbed bread is traditionally baked in a wood-fired brick oven. If you like, you can replicate the effect by covering an oven shelf with the unglazed Italian or French terra-cotta tiles that are available at gardening shops.

——*Makes One 2-Pound Loaf*——
Two envelopes active dry yeast
About 6 cups unbleached all-purpose flour
¾ teaspoon salt

1. In a small bowl, combine the yeast and ½ cup very warm tap water. Stir well until the yeast dissolves.

2. To make the sponge, put ½ cup of the flour in a large bowl and add the dissolved yeast. Mix with a wooden spoon until a very loose dough forms. Sprinkle 1 tablespoon of the flour over the dough. Cover with a cotton dish towel and let rise in a warm, draft-free place until doubled in bulk, about 1 hour.

3. Mound 5 cups of the flour on a work surface and make a large well in the center. Add the sponge to the well, along with the salt and ½ cup very warm tap water; mix to blend with a wooden spoon. Add another 1¼ cups very warm water and begin mixing the dough with your hands, gradually drawing in the flour from the inside rim of the well.

4. After about 15 minutes, when all but about ½ cup of the flour has been incorporated, knead the dough with your palms, pushing it away from you and folding it over itself, until smooth and elastic, about 20 minutes longer. Incorporate any remaining flour as necessary to keep the dough from sticking to the work surface.

5. Shape the dough into a long or round loaf and wrap it loosely in a floured cotton dish towel. Set aside to rise in a warm, draft-free place until doubled in bulk, about 1 hour.

6. Preheat the oven to 400°. Set the loaf on a large, heavy, lightly floured baking sheet (or directly on heated unglazed oven tiles) and bake for about 55 minutes, until the bread sounds hollow when tapped. (Don't open the oven during the first 30 minutes of baking.)

7. Transfer the bread to a rack. Stand it on its side and let cool for at least 3 hours before slicing.

—Giuliano Bugialli

• • •

ROSEMARY BREADSTICKS

Breadsticks, as well as bread, are usually served with an Italian meal. But they also make delicious appetizers, especially when served with a slice of prosciutto wrapped around one end. If kept in an airtight container, the breadsticks will remain fresh for several days.

——— Makes 36 Breadsticks ———
3 envelopes active dry yeast
1 cup lukewarm water (105° to 115°)
1 cup bread flour
1½ cups whole wheat flour
¾ cup coarse Italian semolina*
1 teaspoon salt
2 tablespoons plus 1 teaspoon
*   extra-virgin olive oil*
2 tablespoons fresh rosemary, finely
*   chopped or 2 teaspoons dried*
*Available at Italian markets

1. In a small bowl, dissolve the yeast in the water for about 10 minutes.

2. On a work surface, combine the bread flour, whole wheat flour, ½ cup of the semolina and the salt. Shape the dry ingredients into a mound, make a well in the center and pour in 2 tablespoons of the olive oil. Pour the dissolved yeast into the well, a little at a time, mixing with a fork in a circular motion and drawing in the flours until all the ingredients are combined and a dough forms.

3. Coat the inside of a large bowl with the remaining 1 teaspoon oil. Add the rosemary to the dough and knead with the heels of your hands until the dough is smooth and elastic, about 10 minutes. Form the dough into a ball and put it in the oiled bowl, turning to coat all sides of the dough with oil. Cover with a cloth and let rise in a warm place until more than doubled in bulk, about 2 hours.

4. Preheat the oven to 350°. On a work surface sprinkled with 2 to 3 tablespoons of the semolina, punch the dough down. Roll the dough out to form a rectangle approximately 8 by 9 inches and ½ inch thick. Cut into ¼-inch strips and roll gently into sticks about 10 inches long.

5. Sprinkle a heavy baking sheet with the remaining semolina and arrange the breadsticks on the baking sheet about 1 inch apart. Cover with a towel and let rise in a warm place for 10 minutes.

6. Bake in the middle of the oven for about 30 minutes, until lightly golden and crisp. Transfer to a rack to cool slightly, arrange in a basket and serve.

—Lorenza de' Medici

• • •

GARLIC TOAST

Although you can make this ahead, it's better if made just before serving.

——————— 4 Servings ———————
1 small loaf of Italian bread, cut into
*   10 slices*
1 garlic clove, halved
2 tablespoons olive oil

Preheat the oven to 400°. Rub one side of each slice of bread with the cut garlic and brush with the olive oil. Arrange on a baking sheet and bake in the top third of the oven for about 15 minutes, or until golden on both sides. Serve hot or at room temperature. *(This recipe can be made up to 2 hours ahead; do not refrigerate.)*

—Marie Simmons

• • •

OLIVE BREAD

This bread is finer in texture than the traditional olive bread because it is made with a lighter dough. I use small brine-cured Tuscan olives, but Sicilian and Greek olives do nicely as well.

——— Makes 1 Large Oval Loaf ———
2 envelopes active dry yeast
1 cup lukewarm milk (105° to 115°)
3 cups bread flour
¼ cup plus 2 teaspoons extra-virgin
*   olive oil*
1 teaspoon salt
½ cup pitted black olives, coarsely
*   chopped*

1. In a small bowl, dissolve the yeast in the milk and set aside until it begins to foam on the surface, about 10 minutes.

2. Sift the flour onto a work surface and make a well in the center. Pour in ¼ cup of the olive oil and add the salt. Pour the milk into the well, a little at a time, mixing with a fork in a circular motion and drawing in the flour until all the ingredients are combined and a dough forms.

3. Coat the inside of a large bowl with 1 teaspoon of the olive oil. Add the olives to the dough and knead with the heels of your hands until it is smooth and elastic, about 10 minutes. Form the dough into a ball and place in the bowl. Turn to coat all sides with oil, cover with a cloth and let it rise in a warm place until it is more than doubled in bulk, about 2 hours.

4. Preheat the oven to 375°. Punch the dough down and roll it out into an oval loaf approximately 10 inches long. Oil the baking sheet with the remaining 1 teaspoon olive oil. Place the loaf on the sheet, cover with a cloth and let rise for another 20 minutes.

5. Bake for about 30 minutes, or until the loaf sounds hollow when tapped. Let cool completely before slicing.

—Lorenza de' Medici

• • •

159

BAKING POWDER BISCUITS

When I took one of my experimental cookery classes at Cornell, I'd made biscuits only once or twice in my growing-up years and will be the first to admit that my lopsided, freckled "rocks" were no match for the ethereal beauties pulled from the oven by my lab partner, a farm girl who had been baking biscuits ever since she was tall enough to reach the dough bowl. So what was her secret? *The* secret? Eight simple steps. Follow them, and with a little practice you, too, will bake perfect biscuits.

——— *Makes About 1 Dozen* ———
⅓ cup chilled lard or vegetable shortening
2 cups sifted all-purpose flour
1 tablespoon baking powder
¾ teaspoon salt
¾ cup cold milk

1. Pack the shortening into a dry measure, level off the top with the broad side of a spatula and chill half an hour or so. Meanwhile, sift the flour (all-purpose works fine), then measure carefully by spooning gently into a dry measure and leveling off with the edge of a spatula.

2. Preheat the oven to 425°. Combine the flour, baking powder and salt, then sift together into a large shallow bowl. If the leavening isn't thoroughly incorporated, your biscuits will be as richly freckled as quail eggs.

3. Using a pastry blender or two knives, cut the shortening into the dry ingredients until the mixture is the texture of small green peas. If you cut the fat in further, the biscuits will be heavy, maybe even soggy, because only largish bits of fat can make biscuits truly flaky. They melt during baking, leaving behind tender wisps or flakes.

4. Make a well in the middle of the fat-flour mixture, dump in the milk and stir briskly with a fork for about 20 seconds.

5. Turn the dough onto a lightly floured board (the dusting of flour should be so gauzy that if you touch your thumb to it, you'll leave a spot of bare board). Knead the dough with the lightest of touches about 8 times (20 seconds) to incorporate all ingredients evenly. Further kneading will develop the gluten (flour protein) and toughen the biscuits.

6. Again using the lightest of touches, roll the dough out ½ inch thick. With a lightly floured biscuit cutter, cut into rounds. Flour the cutter after each cut, tapping off any excess flour.

7. With a spatula, transfer the biscuits to ungreased baking sheets, spacing them so that they almost touch if you want pale-sided biscuits and about an inch apart if you prefer crusty-sided ones.

8. Bake the biscuits, one sheet at a time, on the middle rack of the oven for about 12 minutes, or until pale golden brown. If you bake the biscuits at a lower temperature, they'll dry out before they're done.

—*Jean Anderson*

• • •

BUTTERMILK BISCUITS WITH PARSLEY-CHIVE BUTTER

Light and flaky, these biscuits are a quick and easy complement to almost any meal.

——— *Makes 16 Biscuits* ———
1 stick (4 ounces) unsalted butter, softened, plus 3 tablespoons, chilled
1½ tablespoons chopped parsley
1½ tablespoons snipped chives
2 cups all-purpose flour
2 teaspoons baking powder
1 teaspoon sugar
¾ teaspoon salt
½ teaspoon baking soda
⅓ cup cold vegetable shortening
¾ cup plus 1 tablespoon cold buttermilk

1. Preheat the oven to 450°. Grease a 9-inch square baking pan. In a medium bowl, stir the softened stick of butter with the parsley and chives until blended. Mound in a small dish and set aside.

2. In a large mixing bowl, sift together the flour, baking powder, sugar, salt and baking soda. Cut the 3 tablespoons chilled butter and the shortening into small pieces and, using your fingers, rub into the dry ingredients until the mixture resembles coarse crumbs.

3. Pour in ¾ cup of the buttermilk and stir with a fork until all the ingredients are moistened. Gather the dough into a ball and turn out onto a lightly floured work surface. Knead 5 to 6 times and then pat or roll to a ½-inch thickness. Cut the dough using a 2-inch round biscuit cutter. Pat together or reroll the scraps and repeat the cutting. Arrange the rounds in the prepared baking pan so that they are touching each other. Brush the tops with the remaining 1 tablespoon buttermilk.

4. Bake in the middle of the oven for 15 to 17 minutes, until well risen and golden brown on top. Serve warm with the parsley-chive butter.

—*Melanie Barnard & Brooke Dojny*

• • •

BUTTERMILK SKILLET CORN BREAD

Not too sweet, this corn bread is great for breakfast, spread with jam or clover honey, or for supper with soup or salad.

——— *12 Servings* ———
1 cup yellow cornmeal
1 cup all-purpose flour
2 tablespoons sugar
1½ teaspoons baking powder
1 teaspoon salt
½ teaspoon baking soda
1 cup buttermilk
2 eggs
2 tablespoons unsalted butter, melted

1. Preheat the oven to 425°. Coat a 10-inch cast-iron skillet or 9-inch square baking pan with butter or vegetable spray.

2. In a medium bowl, whisk together the cornmeal, flour, sugar, baking powder, salt and baking soda to evenly distribute the ingredients.

3. In a small bowl, whisk together the buttermilk, eggs and melted butter.

4. Make a well in the center of the dry ingredients and pour in the liquid mixture. Using a wooden spoon, stir just until no dry streaks are visible. Do not overmix.

5. Pour the batter into the prepared pan and bake in the middle of the oven for 20 to 23 minutes, until the top of the corn bread is pale golden brown and a tester inserted in the center comes out clean. Serve warm.

—Melanie Barnard & Brooke Dojny

• • •

BUTTERMILK JALAPENO CORN STICKS

If you don't care for hot peppers, you can make these without them. Either way, they are delicious.

—— Makes About 14 Corn Sticks ——
2 cups white cornmeal
1 tablespoon baking powder
1 teaspoon baking soda
½ teaspoon salt
1½ cups buttermilk
2 tablespoons vegetable oil
1 egg
1 generous tablespoon minced
    pickled jalapeño peppers, drained

1. Preheat the oven to 425°. Spray 2 cast-iron corn-stick pans with vegetable spray and place the pans in the oven while it is preheating, about 20 minutes.

2. Meanwhile, in a large bowl, sift together the cornmeal, baking powder, baking soda and salt. In a separate bowl, combine the buttermilk, oil and egg. Stir in the peppers.

3. Thoroughly combine the dry and liquid ingredients. Work quickly and don't overmix. Spoon the batter into the individual compartments in the pans. Bake for about 18 minutes, or until golden. Serve immediately.

—Lee Bailey

• • •

SOUR CREAM BUTTERMILK CORN BREAD

—— 12 Servings ——
2 cups white cornmeal
3½ teaspoons baking powder
½ teaspoon baking soda
Pinch of salt
1½ cups low-fat sour cream
2 eggs, lightly beaten
2 tablespoons vegetable oil
⅔ cup buttermilk

1. Preheat the oven to 425°. Spray a 9-by-12-inch baking pan with vegetable spray and line the bottom with waxed paper.

2. Sift the cornmeal, baking powder, baking soda and salt into a large bowl.

3. In a medium bowl, lightly beat together the sour cream, eggs, oil and buttermilk. Combine gently with the dry ingredients; do not overmix.

4. Pour the batter into the pan. Bake for 30 to 35 minutes, or until lightly browned.

—Lee Bailey

• • •

LEMON-PECAN BUTTERMILK TEA BREAD

This loaf cake has a moist, firm, sliceable texture. It's wonderful with tea. Or try a dessert version, omitting the nuts and serving it with sweetened berries.

—— Makes One 9-Inch Loaf ——
1 stick (4 ounces) unsalted butter, softened
1¼ cups granulated sugar
3 eggs
1 teaspoon vanilla extract
1 tablespoon (packed) grated lemon zest
1 tablespoon fresh lemon juice
2 cups all-purpose flour
1 teaspoon baking powder
½ teaspoon baking soda
¼ teaspoon salt
⅛ teaspoon mace
¾ cup buttermilk
½ cup coarsely chopped pecans (about 1 ounce)
Confectioners' sugar, for dusting

1. Preheat the oven to 350°. Butter a 9-by-5-inch loaf pan, line the bottom with parchment or waxed paper and butter the paper.

2. In a medium mixer bowl, beat the butter with the granulated sugar until smooth, about 3 minutes. Add the eggs one at a time, beating well after each addition. Beat in the vanilla, lemon zest and lemon juice.

3. In a medium bowl, whisk together the flour, baking powder, baking soda, salt and mace to evenly distribute the ingredients.

4. Using a wooden spoon, stir half the dry ingredients into the batter, then stir in half the buttermilk; repeat with the remaining dry ingredients and buttermilk. Mix just until smooth. Stir in the pecans.

5. Transfer the batter to the prepared pan. Bake in the middle of the oven for 55 minutes to 1 hour, until a cake tester inserted in the center comes out clean. Transfer the loaf to a rack to cool in the pan for 10 minutes, then turn it out and let cool completely. *(The loaf can be well wrapped in plastic and refrigerated for up to 3 days or frozen for up to 1 month. Let return to room temperature before serving.)*

6. To serve, sift confectioners' sugar over the top of the loaf and cut into thin slices.

—Melanie Barnard & Brooke Dojny

• • •

BUTTERMILK BRAN MUFFINS

Serve a crock of orange marmalade alongside these breakfast muffins. They are made with oil, not butter, for a good moist texture. Unprocessed bran is available in health food stores and in the cereal section of supermarkets.

——— *Makes 10 Muffins* ———

1 cup buttermilk
¼ cup vegetable oil, such as safflower
1 egg
1 cup unprocessed bran
⅓ cup dried currants, raisins or chopped dried apricots (optional)
1 cup all-purpose flour
¼ cup (packed) light brown sugar
1 teaspoon baking powder
½ teaspoon baking soda
¼ teaspoon salt

1. In a large bowl, whisk together the buttermilk, oil and egg. Stir in the bran and currants, if using, and let stand for 10 minutes.

2. Preheat the oven to 400°. Grease a 12-cup muffin tin. (Alternatively, coat with vegetable spray or line with paper liners).

3. In a medium bowl, stir together the flour, brown sugar, baking powder, bak-ing soda and salt. Using a wooden spoon, stir the dry ingredients into the butter-milk-bran mixture just until moistened, about 20 strokes; there will be lumps in the batter. Do not overmix.

4. Spoon the batter into 10 of the muffin tins, filling each about three-quar-ters full. Bake in the middle of the oven for 20 to 22 minutes, until the tops are browned and the centers spring back when touched. Turn the muffins out on a rack. Serve warm or at room temperature.

—Melanie Barnard & Brooke Dojny

• • •

BANANA-POPPY SEED MUFFINS

My children like to eat these just-sweet-enough muffins both for dessert and as a snack. They like having a whole muffin of their own, and the recipe is simple enough that I can give them instructions and they can make them themselves.

——— *Makes 16 Muffins* ———

1 stick (4 ounces) unsalted butter
¾ cup coarsely chopped walnuts
2 large overripe bananas, mashed with a fork (1½ cups)
1 cup buttermilk
¾ cup (packed) light brown sugar
2 eggs
1⅔ cups cake flour
1 tablespoon baking powder
2 teaspoons poppy seeds
1 teaspoon baking soda
½ teaspoon salt
1 tablespoon granulated sugar
⅓ teaspoon cinnamon

1. Preheat the oven to 375°. Place paper liners in 16 muffin cups.

2. In a small saucepan, melt the butter over moderate heat and cook until lightly browned, about 5 minutes. Set aside to cool slightly.

3. Spread the walnuts on a baking sheet and place in the oven for about 8 minutes, or until lightly toasted. Set aside.

4. In a large bowl, whisk together the browned butter, mashed bananas, butter-milk, brown sugar and eggs.

5. In a medium bowl, stir together the flour, baking powder, poppy seeds, bak-ing soda and salt. Add the dry ingredients to the banana mixture and stir just until blended. Fold in the walnuts.

6. Spoon the batter into the prepared muffin cups, filling them to the top. Stir together the granulated sugar and cinna-mon and sprinkle a pinch on top of each muffin. Bake the muffins in the upper third of the oven for 18 to 20 minutes, until browned. Remove the muffins from the pan while still hot and transfer to a rack to cool.

—Nancy Silverton, Campanile, Los Angeles

• • •

BACON CRACKLING CRACKERS

Caraway seeds, bits of bacon and corn-meal give these crackers a three-dimen-sional crunch. They're great on their own or spread with softened cream cheese and topped with anything from a cucumber slice to a bit of smoked fish.

——— *Makes About 70 Crackers* ———

½ pound sliced bacon, cut crosswise into thin strips
⅔ cup all-purpose flour
½ cup freshly grated Parmesan cheese (about 2 ounces)
¼ cup whole wheat flour
¼ cup cornmeal
½ teaspoon caraway seeds
¼ teaspoon salt
¾ teaspoon freshly ground pepper
¾ teaspoon baking soda
⅓ cup plain yogurt or sour cream
1½ tablespoons Dijon-style mustard

1. Preheat the oven to 350°. In a medium skillet, cook the bacon over moderately high heat, stirring, until crisp, 5 to 6 minutes. Transfer the bacon to paper towels to drain and cool. Set aside ¼ cup of the bacon fat.

2. Transfer the bacon to a food processor and add the all-purpose flour; pulse until the bacon is finely chopped.

3. Add the Parmesan cheese, whole wheat flour, cornmeal, caraway seeds, salt, pepper and baking soda to the processor; pulse until thoroughly blended.

4. Add the reserved bacon fat and pulse until the mixture resembles coarse meal. Transfer the mixture to a large bowl.

5. In a small bowl, blend the yogurt and mustard. Scrape the yogurt mixture into the dry ingredients and mix with a fork until the dough begins to cohere. Transfer the dough to a lightly floured surface and knead until smooth, about 1 minute.

6. Divide the dough into 2 parts. Roll out each piece ⅛ inch thick. Using a 1½- to 2-inch cookie cutter of any shape, cut out the crackers and place them about ¼ inch apart on lightly greased baking sheets. Bake for 12 to 15 minutes, until lightly browned. Transfer to a rack to cool. *(The crackers can be stored in an airtight container for up to 10 days.)*
—*Bob Chambers*

• • •

BLUEBERRY BUTTERMILK GRIDDLE CAKES

Add the blueberries to the batter after it has been poured on the griddle to avoid having the pancakes turn blue. When fresh blueberries are not in season, frozen berries can be used. This batter, which has a little cornmeal added for texture, also makes great plain griddle cakes. Serve with butter and maple syrup.

——*Makes About 12 Pancakes*——
1 cup all-purpose flour
2 tablespoons cornmeal
1 tablespoon sugar
1 teaspoon baking powder
½ teaspoon baking soda
½ teaspoon salt
⅛ teaspoon cinnamon
1 cup buttermilk
1 egg
2 tablespoons vegetable oil or melted unsalted butter
1½ cups fresh or frozen blueberries

1. Set a griddle or large skillet, preferably cast iron, over low heat. In a large bowl, whisk together the flour, cornmeal, sugar, baking powder, baking soda, salt and cinnamon.

2. In a small bowl, whisk together the buttermilk, egg and oil. Pour over the dry ingredients and stir lightly with a wooden spoon; a few lumps may remain. Do not overmix or the cakes will be tough.

3. Increase the heat under the griddle to moderate. Using an oiled or buttered paper towel, lightly grease the griddle. The griddle is ready when a drop of water skitters on the surface. Ladle about 3 tablespoons of batter onto the griddle for each pancake, allowing room for them to spread to 4 inches. Scatter 2 tablespoons of the blueberries on top of each pancake. Cook until the undersides are golden brown, 2 to 3 minutes, then flip and cook until the centers spring back when lightly

pressed, another 2 to 3 minutes. Repeat with the remaining batter. Serve the cakes hot off the griddle or transfer each batch to a baking sheet lined with a kitchen towel and keep warm in a 200° oven while you cook the remaining cakes.
—*Melanie Barnard & Brooke Dojny*

• • •

SCALLION AND BUTTERMILK PANCAKES

——*Makes 20 to 24 Pancakes*——
5 tablespoons unsalted butter
1 cup sifted cake flour
1 teaspoon baking powder
½ teaspoon baking soda
½ teaspoon salt
¼ teaspoon freshly ground pepper
Pinch of sugar
1 egg, lightly beaten
1 cup buttermilk
3 scallions, minced

1. Melt 2 tablespoons of the butter; let cool. In a bowl, sift together the cake flour, baking powder, baking soda, salt, pepper and sugar. Whisk in the egg, buttermilk and melted butter until blended. Fold in the scallions.

2. In a large skillet, melt 1 tablespoon of the butter over moderately high heat. In batches, add the pancake batter to the skillet by the tablespoonful, without crowding. Cook until bubbles begin to appear on the surfaces and the bottoms are lightly browned, 1½ to 2 minutes. Flip with a spatula and cook until lightly browned on the second side; adjust the heat as necessary. Repeat with the remaining butter and batter, keeping the cooked pancakes warm in a low oven. Serve hot.

—*Perla Meyers*

• • •

CREPES

These crêpes can be filled with just about anything. For dessert crêpes, substitute a pinch of sugar for the salt.

——— *Makes About 24 Crêpes* ———
2 cups all-purpose flour
Pinch of salt
6 eggs
3 cups milk
Soft unsalted butter

1. In a large bowl, whisk together the flour and salt.

2. In a medium bowl, beat the eggs. Gradually whisk in the milk until blended. Add the egg mixture to the flour in 3 batches, whisking until blended after each addition. Transfer the batter to a pitcher or a large measuring cup.

3. Heat a 6-inch crêpe pan or nonstick skillet over moderately high heat. Wipe the pan with buttered paper towels. Pour about ⅓ cup of the batter into the pan to thinly coat the bottom. Tilt and rotate the pan quickly to coat it evenly with batter. Cook until the edges are starting to brown, about 1 minute. Turn the crêpe over and cook until small brown spots appear on the underside, about 30 to 60 seconds more. Transfer the crêpe to a work surface and let cool. Repeat with the remaining batter.

4. On a baking sheet lined with waxed paper, stack the cooled crêpes with more waxed paper in between to prevent sticking. *(The recipe can be refrigerated, well wrapped, overnight.)*

—*Tracey Seaman*

• • •

SUREFIRE STUFFING

This is my husband's method of making stuffing in a skillet. We love the buttery toasted flavor the bread gets when it's cooked this way. This recipe makes enough to loosely fill a 16-pound bird or to serve 16 people if baked separately in a foil packet.

——— *Makes About 8 Cups* ———
1½ loaves of Italian bread (about 1 pound)
1 stick (4 ounces) unsalted butter
1 large onion, chopped
2 celery ribs, minced
4 ounces pecan pieces (about 1 cup)
⅓ cup raisins
½ cup chopped Italian flat-leaf parsley
2 tablespoons chopped fresh thyme or 2 teaspoons dried
1 teaspoon salt
1 teaspoon freshly ground pepper
2 eggs
¾ cup chicken stock or canned broth

1. Cut off 1 inch from the end of the loaves of bread and trim off the bottom crusts. Tear the bread into ½-inch pieces and place in a large bowl.

2. In a large heavy skillet, melt 4 tablespoons of the butter. Add the onion and celery and cook over moderate heat, stirring occasionally, until softened but not browned, about 10 minutes.

3. Add the contents of the skillet to the bread along with the pecans, raisins, parsley, thyme, salt and pepper. Toss well to combine.

4. In a small bowl, lightly beat the eggs with the chicken stock until blended. Pour the egg mixture over the ingredients in the bowl and mix everything together with your hands until thoroughly combined.

5. In the skillet used above, melt 2 tablespoons of the butter. Spread the stuffing in the pan and pat down to flatten. Cook over moderate to moderately low heat, without stirring, until a golden crust forms on the bottom, 10 to 15 minutes. To test, cut the stuffing into 8 wedges and turn one over.

6. Dot the remaining 2 tablespoons butter evenly over the surface of the stuffing and turn over each wedge. Cook until golden and crusty on the bottom, about 10 minutes longer. Remove from the heat and let cool in the pan. *(The recipe can be prepared to this point up to 1 day ahead. Cover and refrigerate. Let return to room temperature before proceeding.)*

7. If you'll be cooking the stuffing in a bird, let it cool completely before breaking it into chunks and placing it in the cavity. Alternatively, wrap the stuffing in heavy-duty aluminum foil, allowing room for it to expand, and form a neat, tightly sealed package. Bake the stuffing in a preheated 325° oven for 1 hour and serve hot.

—*Diana Sturgis*

• • •

PIES, CAKES & COOKIES

APPLE PIE WITH WHIPPED CREAM

Whenever I want a dessert reward, I have apple pie. And I'm very particular—I don't like underdone apples, thickeners or any extra things like nuts or raisins in it. Finally, the crust has to be good and not too thick. So here is my favorite apple pie recipe.

—— *6 Servings* ——
1½ cups all-purpose flour
½ teaspoon salt
1 stick (4 ounces) frozen unsalted butter, cut into tablespoons
2 tablespoons frozen vegetable shortening
3 to 4 tablespoons ice water
⅔ cup sugar
½ teaspoon cinnamon
1 tablespoon finely grated lemon zest
4 medium tart apples (about 1½ pounds total), such as Granny Smith—peeled, cored and cut into ¼-inch slices
1 tablespoon fresh lemon juice
Whipped cream, for garnish

1. In a food processor, combine the flour and ¼ teaspoon of the salt. Process for a few seconds, then add 6 tablespoons of the butter and the shortening and process until the mixture resembles coarse meal. Sprinkle 3 tablespoons of ice water over the mixture and process about 20 seconds. Pinch some of the dough between your fingers. If it is dry and does not hold together add 1 tablespoon water and process briefly until the dough begins to form a ball. Do not overprocess.

2. Divide the dough in half and gather into balls making one slightly larger thin the other. Place each on a large piece of plastic wrap and flatten each disk slightly. *(This recipe can be prepared to this point up to 1 day ahead. Cover with plastic wrap and refrigerate. Let it come to room temperature, about 15 minutes, before rolling it out.)*

3. Preheat the oven to 450°. On a sheet of waxed paper or a lightly floured surface, roll out the larger dough round into an 11-inch circle. Transfer it to an 8-inch metal pie pan, fitting it into the pan without stretching.

4. In a small bowl, toss together the sugar, the remaining ¼ teaspoon salt, the cinnamon and lemon zest. In a large bowl, combine the apple slices and the sugar mixture; toss to coat well.

5. Heap the apples into the pie pan, mounding them in the middle. Sprinkle with the lemon juice and dot with the remaining 2 tablespoons butter.

6. Roll out the other dough round into a 10-inch circle. Place the dough over the apples and seal, crimping the edges together with your fingers. With a paring knife, poke several steam vents in the top crust. (For a golden brown crust, you can paint the top with a little egg wash or light cream or sprinkle the top with a little extra sugar.)

7. Bake for 10 minutes. Reduce the oven to 350° and bake another 35 minutes, until bubbly and the apples are tender. Serve with whipped cream if desired. *(The pie can be prepared up to 1 day ahead. Refrigerate covered or leave out at room temperature.)*

—Lee Bailey

• • •

DOUBLE CRUST APPLE PIE WITH VANILLA

In this apple pie, vanilla intensifies the flavor of the apples and provides a pleasing, fragrant sweetness. This is the apple pie for purists.

—— *8 Servings* ——
Juice of ½ lemon
3 pounds tart-sweet apples, such as Granny Smith—peeled, cored and cut into ⅛-inch slices (about 6 cups)
½ cup plus 1 tablespoon sugar
1 teaspoon vanilla extract
Double Crust Pastry (recipe follows)
2 tablespoons unsalted butter, cut into small pieces
1 egg yolk, lightly beaten with 2 tablespoons heavy cream

1. Pour the lemon juice into a large mixing bowl and add the apples as you slice them, tossing occasionally to coat with the juice. Add ½ cup of the sugar and the vanilla; toss again to mix.

2. On a lightly floured surface, roll out the larger of the two pastry rounds into an 11-inch circle. Line a 9-inch pie pan with the pastry. Sprinkle the remaining 1 tablespoon sugar evenly over the bottom and press lightly into the pastry. Freeze until firm, about 15 minutes.

3. Preheat the oven to 450°. Roll out the remaining pastry into a 10-inch circle.

4. Remove the pie pan from the freezer and distribute the butter pieces over the bottom of the crust. Add the apples with their juices. Moisten the pastry rim with cold water, lay on the top crust and crimp the edges, trimming off any excess dough as necessary.

5. Brush the top of the pie with the beaten egg-cream mixture, cut several steam vents in the top crust and bake for 10 minutes. Reduce the temperature to 350° and bake for 35 to 45 minutes longer, or until nicely browned.

—Robert Farrar Capon

• • •

DOUBLE CRUST PASTRY

— Makes One 9-Inch Double Crust —
2¼ cups all-purpose flour
½ teaspoon salt
1 stick (4 ounces) cold unsalted butter, cut into ½-inch pieces
3 tablespoons cold vegetable shortening or lard
4 to 5 tablespoons ice water

1. In a food processor fitted with the metal blade, combine the flour and salt; pulse a few times just to mix. Add the butter and shortening and pulse just until it is the size of large peas.

2. Add 3 tablespoons of the water, 1 tablespoon at a time, pulsing briefly after each addition. Add another tablespoon and pulse just until the dough begins to hold together. Add 1 more tablespoon of water if necessary.

3. Transfer the dough onto a lightly floured cold surface and gather it into a ball, handling it as little as possible. Divide the dough into two pieces, one slightly larger than the other. Form into rounds and flatten them slightly. Wrap the dough in waxed paper and refrigerate until chilled, at least 20 minutes, before rolling out.

—Robert Farrar Capon

• • •

PEACH AND CURRANT PIE

If you can't find fresh red currants, substitute raspberries and cut back the sugar by one quarter of a cup.

———— 8 Servings ————
All-American Pie Dough (recipe follows)
2 pounds peaches (about 8), peeled and sliced
2 cups fresh red currants
1 cup sugar, plus more for sprinkling
¼ cup quick-cooking tapioca
1 tablespoon fresh lemon juice
¼ to ½ teaspoon cinnamon, to taste
1 tablespoon heavy cream

1. On a lightly floured surface, roll out half of the pie dough into a 12-inch circle, about ⅛ inch thick. Transfer the dough to a 9-inch pie pan, fitting it evenly into the pan without stretching. Leave the edge overhanging. Refrigerate until chilled, at least 20 minutes.

2. On a sheet of waxed paper, roll out the second half of the dough into an 11-inch circle. Leaving the dough on the waxed paper, slide it onto a baking sheet and cover with plastic wrap. Refrigerate until ready to use.

3. Preheat the oven to 425°. In a large bowl, combine the peaches, currants, 1 cup of the sugar, the tapioca, lemon juice and cinnamon; stir together.

4. Scrape the filling into the pastry-lined pie pan. Dip your fingertip in water and moisten the overhang of the pie shell. Place the 11-inch circle of dough on top, pressing at the moistened rim to seal. With a pair of scissors, trim the overhang to ¼ inch. Turn the edge under itself and crimp. With a paring knife, poke several steam vents in the top crust.

5. Brush the top sparingly with the heavy cream. Sprinkle several large pinches of sugar on top. Bake in the middle of the oven for 20 minutes. Lower the heat to 375° and bake for 45 minutes longer, until the top of the pie is a rich golden brown. Transfer to a rack to cool. Serve warm or at room temperature.

—Ken Haedrich

• • •

ALL-AMERICAN PIE DOUGH

This crust incorporates both vegetable shortening for tenderness and butter for flavor. Like most pie doughs, it rolls best when refrigerated long enough to firm up the fat throughout. Also, I find it much easier to roll out pie dough either in the early morning or in the evening rather than at midday. This inhibits a buttery crust from breaking down and your house or apartment from heating up. I recommend rolling it out on a sheet of waxed paper, especially in warm weather. Then if the fat softens and the dough becomes difficult to handle, you can simply lift the waxed paper and dough onto a baking sheet and refrigerate briefly until firm enough to continue.

— Makes One 9-Inch Double Crust —
2½ cups all-purpose flour
1½ tablespoons sugar
¾ teaspoon salt
1 stick (4 ounces) cold unsalted butter, cut into small pieces
½ cup cold vegetable shortening
4 to 5 tablespoons ice water

1. In a large bowl, toss together the flour, sugar and salt to combine. With a pastry cutter or two knives, cut in the butter and shortening until the mixture is rough textured, with particles about the size of split peas.

2. Sprinkle 3 tablespoons of the ice water over the flour mixture. With a fork, toss well to blend. Sprinkle another tablespoon of the ice water on top and toss to combine. With your hands, press the dough against the bowl until it just holds together. If you need more water, add up to 1 more tablespoon. Pack the dough together like a snowball.

3. Divide the dough in half. Place each half on a large piece of plastic wrap and flatten each into a disk about ¾ inch thick. Wrap and refrigerate for at least 1 hour before rolling. *(The dough can be made up to 2 days ahead and refrigerated or frozen for up to 1 month. Let it sit at room temperature for 5 to 10 minutes before rolling.)*

—Ken Haedrich

• • •

BROWN SUGAR PIE

The pie filling will be less than an inch thick and quite wet, but what's there is delicious.

——————— 6 to 8 Servings ———————
1 cup plus 2 tablespoons all-purpose flour
¼ teaspoon baking powder
¼ teaspoon salt
⅓ cup cold vegetable shortening
1 egg yolk
2 tablespoons ice water
3 cups heavy cream
¼ cup granulated sugar
¼ cup (packed) brown sugar
1 tablespoon unsalted butter

1. In a large bowl, combine the flour, baking powder and salt. Cut in the shortening until the mixture resembles coarse meal. Add the egg yolk and ice water and stir with a fork until a dough forms. Pat the dough into a 7-inch disk, wrap in waxed paper and refrigerate until chilled, about 30 minutes.

2. Preheat the oven to 375°. In a large saucepan, combine 2 cups of the cream

with the granulated sugar. Bring to a boil over moderate heat, whisking constantly, and boil for 30 seconds. Reduce the heat to moderately low and simmer gently, whisking occasionally, until the cream reduces by one-third, about 20 minutes.

3. Meanwhile, on a lightly floured surface, roll out the dough into a 12-inch circle. Fit the dough into a 9-inch pie pan and crimp the edges.

4. Stir the brown sugar and butter into the reduced cream until incorporated. Pour the sweet cream filling into the pie crust. Reduce the oven temperature to 350° and bake the pie for 30 minutes, or until the top is browned in patches and the filing jiggles slightly when shaken. Remove from the oven and let cool at room temperature for several hours. *(This pie can be made up to 1 day ahead. Cover and refrigerate.)*

5. Beat the remaining 1 cup heavy cream until stiff. Spread the cream over the pie or serve it on the side. Serve chilled or at room temperature.

—Lee Bailey

• • •

BLUEBERRY LIME PIE WITH COCONUT CRUMBLE TOPPING

For the best blueberry pie ever, use the smaller, tarter wild blueberries when available (check your local market).

——————— 8 Servings ———————
½ cup all-purpose flour
1 cup sugar
3 tablespoons cold unsalted butter, cut into small pieces
⅓ cup shredded coconut, preferably unsweetened
½ recipe All-American Pie Dough (p. 167)
2 pints blueberries
3 tablespoons quick-cooking tapioca
Finely grated zest and juice of 2 limes
Pinch of freshly grated nutmeg

1. In a medium bowl, toss together the flour and ½ cup of the sugar. With a pastry blender, cut in the butter (or rub it in with your fingers) until the mixture is fine textured. Add the coconut and mix in briefly. Cover the coconut crumble topping and refrigerate until needed.

2. On a lightly floured surface or a sheet of waxed paper, roll out the pie dough into a 12-inch circle, about ⅛ inch thick. Transfer to a 9-inch pie pan, fitting it evenly into the pan without stretching. Trim the dough to about 1½ inches all around, then fold the overhanging edge under and crimp. Refrigerate until chilled, at least 20 minutes.

3. Preheat the oven to 425°. In a large bowl, stir together the blueberries, the remaining ½ cup sugar, the tapioca, lime zest, lime juice and nutmeg.

4. Scrape the filling into the pie shell. Lay a piece of aluminum foil on top, leaving the edge of the pie exposed. Bake for 15 minutes. Lower the heat to 375° and bake for 20 minutes longer.

5. Remove the pie from the oven and transfer to a baking sheet. Remove the aluminum foil. Spread the coconut crumble topping evenly over the blueberries. Bake the pie for 25 to 35 minutes, until the topping is golden brown and the juices are bubbling. Transfer to a rack to cool. Serve warm or at room temperature.

—Ken Haedrich

• • •

NEW ORLEANS PECAN PIE

Serve this at room temperature with vanilla ice cream or whipped cream.

——————— Makes One 8-Inch Pie ———————
Basic Pie Dough (recipe follows)
3 eggs
1 cup dark corn syrup
¾ cup sugar
2 tablespoons unsalted butter or margarine, melted and cooled

1 teaspoon vanilla extract
⅛ teaspoon salt
1 cup pecan pieces plus 12 pecan halves

1. Preheat the oven to 350°. On a lightly floured surface, roll out the dough into a 10-inch circle. Fit the dough into an 8-inch pie pan without stretching. Crimp the edge. Refrigerate for 20 minutes.

2. In a medium bowl, with a hand-held electric mixer, lightly beat the eggs. Beat in the corn syrup, sugar, butter, vanilla and salt. Fold in the pecan pieces.

3. Pour the filling into the pie shell and bake for about 15 minutes or until partially set. Remove from the oven and decorate the top with the pecan halves. Return the pie to the oven and bake for 20 to 25 minutes longer, or until a knife or toothpick inserted in the center comes out clean. Set aside on a rack to cool.

—Alex Patout, Alex Patout's Louisiana Restaurant, New Orleans

• • •

BASIC PIE DOUGH

—— *Makes One 9-Inch Crust* ——
1 cup all-purpose flour
¼ teaspoon salt
⅓ cup cold vegetable shortening
About ¼ cup ice water

1. Sift the flour and salt together into a large bowl. Using a pastry blender or two knives, cut in the shortening until the mixture resembles cornmeal. Stir in just enough ice water for the dough to hold together. Gather the dough into a ball.

2. Flatten the dough into a disk and wrap well in plastic wrap. Refrigerate for at least 30 minutes or overnight.

—Alex Patout, Alex Patout's Louisiana Restaurant, New Orleans

• • •

CHOCOLATE PECAN TART

My friend Heidi Trachtenburg, a born baker, helped me develop the recipe for this light, elegant version of the American classic. Unlike most pies, this tart is just as good when baked a day ahead as long as it is not refrigerated.

—————— *8 Servings* ——————
11-inch French Pastry Shell, frozen (recipe follows)
1 stick (4 ounces) unsalted butter
¼ cup honey
¾ cup (lightly packed) dark brown sugar
3 tablespoons granulated sugar
⅓ cup plus ¼ cup heavy cream
2 cups pecans, coarsely chopped (about 8 ounces)
1½ ounces imported bittersweet chocolate, cut into small pieces
Cocoa powder and confectioners' sugar
Fresh mint sprigs, for garnish

1. Preheat the oven to 400°. Line the bottom and sides of the frozen pastry shell with foil and fill with pie weights or dried beans. Bake for 15 minutes. Remove the foil and weights and bake for about 3 minutes longer to dry out the bottom. Transfer the pan to a rack and let the shell cool to room temperature. Reduce the oven temperature to 350°.

2. In a small saucepan, melt the butter and honey together over high heat. Add the brown and granulated sugars and stir until dissolved, then boil for 1 minute without stirring. Add ⅓ cup of the heavy cream and stir constantly until smooth. Remove from the heat and stir in the chopped pecans.

3. Pour the mixture into the baked pastry shell. If necessary, spread the pecans to evenly distribute them over the bottom of the tart. Bake for about 20 minutes, until bubbles appear around the edges and the center is slightly firm. Transfer the tart to a rack to cool.

4. In a small saucepan, bring the remaining ¼ cup heavy cream to a boil over high heat. Remove from the heat, add the chocolate and stir until melted. Spread the chocolate evenly over the cooled tart. *(The recipe can be prepared to this point up to 1 day ahead. Leave the tart out at room temperature, uncovered.)*

5. On the day of serving, decorate the tart. Cut out an 11-inch circle from a piece of parchment or waxed paper. Fold it in eighths, then open it and cut out every other wedge, leaving 4 wedges held together at the center. Place it on top of the tart. Using a fine sieve, dust the cocoa over the exposed tart. Carefully lift the paper and shake off excess cocoa. Set the paper over the cocoa-dusted sections and sift confectioners' sugar over the tart. Carefully remove the paper. Remove the rim of the pan and transfer the tart to a serving platter. Place a cluster of mint sprigs in the center of the tart.

—Lydie Pinoy Marshall

• • •

FRENCH PASTRY SHELL

—*Makes One 11-Inch Tart Shell*—
1 cup all-purpose flour
1 stick (4 ounces) unsalted butter, cut into small pieces
1 tablespoon sugar
Pinch of salt
2 to 3 tablespoons ice water

1. In a food processor, combine the flour, butter, sugar and salt and process for 10 seconds. Add 2 tablespoons of the water and pulse just until the mixture resembles coarse cornmeal. Pinch the dough; it should hold together. If not, add up to 1 more tablespoon of water.

2. Transfer the dough to a work surface and, using the heel of your hand and working a little of the dough at a time, knead lightly and quickly to blend the butter and flour. Gather the dough into a ball and flatten slightly. Wrap in waxed paper and refrigerate just long enough to firm up the butter, about 15 minutes.

3. Roll out the dough to a 13-inch circle. Line a fluted 11-inch tart pan with a removable bottom with the dough, without stretching. Trim the edges and prick the bottom. Wrap well with plastic wrap and freeze until needed.

—*Lydie Pinoy Marshall*

• • •

PECAN BUTTERSCOTCH PIE

Nut crusts, too often overlooked, are easy to make; any type of nut can be used.

———— *8 Servings* ————
2½ cups pecan halves
¼ cup granulated sugar
1 cup (packed) light brown sugar
¼ cup cornstarch
¼ teaspoon salt
2½ cups milk
4 egg yolks plus 1 egg white
6 tablespoons unsalted butter
1½ teaspoons vanilla extract
1 cup heavy cream
1 tablespoon dark rum

1. Preheat the oven to 350°. Lightly coat a 9-inch pie pan with nonstick vegetable cooking spray and set aside.

2. In a food processor, coarsely chop the pecans. Remove ½ cup of the nuts and place them on a baking sheet. Toast for 6 to 8 minutes, or until lightly browned. Set aside to cool. Meanwhile, add the granulated sugar to the remaining 2 cups of pecans in the food processor

bowl, and process until the nuts are finely ground; set the work bowl aside.

3. Sift the brown sugar, cornstarch and salt together into a large saucepan.

4. In a medium bowl, whisk ½ cup of the milk into the egg yolks, then whisk in the remaining 2 cups of milk. Add the milk and egg mixture to the saucepan with the sugar and cornstarch mixture; whisk until incorporated.

5. Place the pan over moderately high heat and cook, whisking constantly, until the mixture becomes very thick and hot, 5 to 7 minutes. Remove from the heat; stir in the butter and vanilla until the butter is melted and the mixture is smooth.

6. Add the reserved toasted pecans and stir to combine. Cover, pressing a sheet of waxed paper directly on the surface of the custard; set aside.

7. With the food processor running, add the egg white to the ground nuts and process until incorporated, about 4 seconds. Transfer the nut mixture to the pie pan and press to spread over the bottom and partially up the sides of the pan. Bake for 10 minutes to set the shell. Transfer the pan to a rack and let cool, about 30 minutes.

8. Pour the custard into the pie shell and let cool to room temperature, about 2 hours. Transfer to the refrigerator and chill at least 3 hours. *(This pie can be made to this point up to 1 day ahead. Cover with plastic wrap and refrigerate.)*

9. Before serving the pie, whip the heavy cream in a medium bowl with an electric mixer until soft peaks form. Add the rum and beat until stiff. Spread the whipped cream over the pie and serve.

—*Lee Bailey*

• • •

BLACKBERRY SILK PIE

One thing to remember about custard pies like this is not to overbake them, lest they turn tough and grainy. You want just a little wobbliness left in the center when it comes out of the oven. As the pie cools, it will firm up. The pie is just as good made a day ahead. It can be served plain, garnished with whole blackberries or even sauced with extra blackberry puree, made just like the puree in the pie.

———— *8 Servings* ————
½ recipe All-American Pie Dough
  (p. 167)
2 cups fresh blackberries or
  1 package (12 ounces) thawed
  frozen
3 eggs, at room temperature
1½ cups heavy cream, at room
  temperature
¾ cup sugar
1 teaspoon vanilla extract
Blackberries, for garnish

1. Preheat the oven to 400°. On a sheet of waxed paper or a lightly floured surface, roll out the pie dough into a 12-inch circle, about ⅛ inch thick. Transfer to a 9-inch pie pan, fitting it evenly into the pan without stretching. Trim the dough to about 1½ inches all around, then fold under and crimp. Refrigerate for 20 minutes or until ready to use.

2. With a fork, prick all over the bottom and sides of the chilled pie shell. Line the shell with aluminum foil and weigh down with pie weights or dried beans, pushing them up the sides. Bake the shell for 15 minutes. Remove the foil and weights. Lower the heat to 375° and bake the shell for 15 to 20 minutes longer, until lightly browned all over. (If the dough has puffed up anywhere, gently press down with the back of a fork.) Transfer to a rack to cool. *(The pie shell can be made to this point up to 3 days* *ahead. Cover the cooled shell with plastic wrap and keep at room temperature.)*

3. Increase the oven temperature to 425°. In a blender or food processor, puree the blackberries. Strain through a fine-mesh sieve to remove the seeds.

4. In a medium bowl, lightly beat the eggs. Stir in the cream, sugar, vanilla and the blackberry puree; mix until thoroughly blended. Pour the filling into the pie shell and bake for 10 minutes. Lower the heat to 325° and bake for 35 minutes longer, until the filling jiggles slightly in the center (but does not ripple in waves). Transfer to a rack and let cool completely. Cover loosely with foil and refrigerate for at least 1 hour before serving. Garnish the top with a few blackberries.

—Ken Haedrich

• • •

TRIPLE STRAWBERRY CREAM PIE WITH CHOCOLATE GRAHAM CRACKER CRUST

This strawberry shortcake rival combines cooked and uncooked berries.

——— *8 Servings* ———
Chocolate Graham Cracker Crust (recipe follows)
3 pints strawberries, halved lengthwise
⅓ cup granulated sugar
Finely grated zest of 1 lemon
1 tablespoon plus 1 teaspoon cornstarch
1½ cups heavy cream, well chilled
¼ cup confectioners' sugar

1. Preheat the oven to 350°. Bake the Chocolate Graham Cracker Crust for 10 minutes, until set. Transfer to a rack to cool completely. Cover snugly with plastic wrap and refrigerate for at least 1 hour. *(The crust can be made to this point up to 2 days ahead.)*

2. Meanwhile, place half of the strawberries in a bowl. Stir in 1 tablespoon of the granulated sugar and the lemon zest and let sit for 10 minutes. With a fork, crush the berries until a coarse puree forms.

3. Transfer the puree to a small nonreactive saucepan. In a small bowl, mix the remaining ¼ cup plus 1 teaspoon granulated sugar with the cornstarch. Stir into the puree and bring to a boil over moderate heat. Cook, stirring frequently, until the mixture thickens and becomes translucent, about 1 minute. Scrape the strawberry filling into a bowl and let cool completely. Cover with plastic wrap and refrigerate until cold, at least 1 hour. *(The filling can be made to this point up to 2 days ahead.)*

4. About ½ hour before assembling the pie, freeze a bowl and a whisk or beaters until cold. In the chilled bowl, whip the cream until it begins to thicken. Add the confectioners' sugar and beat until firm but not grainy. Fold in ½ cup of the strawberry filling.

5. Spread the remaining strawberry filling in the chilled pie crust. Arrange the reserved halved strawberries close together on top of the filling. If you run out of room, coarsely chop any remaining berries and spread over the halves. Spread the strawberry whipped cream on top of the berries. Serve the pie at once.

—Ken Haedrich

• • •

CHOCOLATE GRAHAM CRACKER CRUST

——— *Makes One 9-Inch Pie Shell* ———
1⅓ cups graham cracker crumbs
1½ tablespoons sugar
1½ tablespoons unsweetened Dutch process cocoa powder
5 tablespoons unsalted butter, at room temperature, cut into pieces

1. In a large bowl, combine the graham cracker crumbs, sugar and cocoa powder; mix thoroughly. With your fingers, rub in the butter until the mixture resembles coarse meal.

2. Spoon the crumbs into a 9-inch pie pan. Pat evenly into the bottom and up the sides of the pan; be sure to make the sides and rim as thick as the bottom of the crust. With your fingertips, press firmly all over the crust to pack it down. Cover with foil and freeze for at least 10 minutes before filling or baking.

—Ken Haedrich

• • •

GREEN GRAPE TART

——— *8 Servings* ———
½ recipe All-American Pie Dough (p. 167)
4½ cups seedless green grapes (about 2 pounds)
2 tablespoons plus 1 teaspoon fresh lemon juice
2 tablespoons sugar
1 tablespoon cornstarch

1. Preheat the oven to 400°. On a sheet of waxed paper or a lightly floured surface, roll out the pie dough into a 12-inch circle, about ⅛ inch thick. Place the dough in a 9-inch tart pan with a removable bottom, fitting it evenly into the pan without stretching. Fold the overhanging edge, tucking it in against the side of the pan to make a double-thick rim. Press the dough against the side of the pan and trim it even with the top of the pan. Cover with plastic wrap and refrigerate the shell for at least 20 minutes.

2. With a fork, prick all over the bottom and sides of the chilled tart shell. Line the shell with aluminum foil and weigh down with pie weights or dried beans. Bake for 20 minutes. Remove the foil and weights. Lower the heat to 375° and bake the shell for 15 minutes longer, until lightly browned all over. Transfer to a rack to cool. *(The tart shell can be baked up to 3 days ahead. Cover with plastic wrap and keep at room temperature.)*

3. Meanwhile, make the filling. Set aside 2 cups of the largest, best-looking grapes. In a medium nonreactive saucepan, combine the remaining 2½ cups grapes with 2 tablespoons of the lemon juice and 2 cups of water. Bring to a boil over high heat, reduce the heat to moderately low and simmer until the grapes are soft and plump, about 10 minutes. Drain and let cool slightly. Puree the grapes in a food processor; strain the puree through a fine-mesh sieve (or process in a food mill). Let cool to lukewarm.

4. In the same saucepan used for the grapes, whisk together the sugar and cornstarch. Stir in all but 1 tablespoon of the grape puree. Bring to a boil over moderately high heat, stirring. Cook until the mixture thickens and becomes translucent, about 1 minute. Scrape into a bowl and set aside to cool completely.

5. To assemble the tart, evenly spread the grape puree in the baked shell. Halve the reserved grapes lengthwise. Arrange them in the shell, cut-sides down, in concentric circles.

6. Mix the reserved tablespoon of grape puree with the remaining 1 teaspoon lemon juice. Lightly brush this glaze over the grapes. *(The tart can be assembled up to 3 hours before serving.)* Serve at room temperature or chilled.

—*Ken Haedrich*

• • •

CREAMY STRAWBERRY CHEESECAKE

Cheesecake, like brownies, is one of those desserts that people have very strong feelings about. Some must have it dense and creamy, others like it light and fluffy, and for a few only pumpkin will do. This classic version is rich, creamy and light. The crust can be varied by using different kinds of crushed cookies, or it can be omitted altogether. Sliced kiwis glazed with melted apple jelly are a good alternative to strawberries.

Don't worry if the cheesecake cracks; the flavor and texture won't be affected, and the crack will be concealed by the topping. Plan on baking the cake one day ahead and chilling it overnight. For easy, tidy serving, wipe the knife after each slice is cut.

———— *10 to 12 Servings* ————
1 cup graham cracker crumbs
½ teaspoon ground ginger (optional)
1 cup plus 6 tablespoons sugar
4 tablespoons unsalted butter, melted
2 pounds cream cheese, at room temperature
1½ teaspoons finely grated lemon zest
2 teaspoons vanilla extract
4 eggs, at room temperature
2 cups sour cream, at room temperature
½ cup strawberry jelly
1 teaspoon arrowroot
2 pints strawberries

1. Preheat the oven to 300°. Butter a 10-by-2½-inch springform pan.

2. In a small bowl, mix together the graham cracker crumbs, ginger (if using) and ¼ cup of the sugar. Stir in the melted butter. Transfer the crumbs to the prepared pan and press them into the base in an even layer. Refrigerate the crumb crust for 30 minutes.

3. In a large bowl, combine the cream cheese, lemon zest, vanilla and the remaining 1 cup plus 2 tablespoons sugar. Beat by hand or at low speed in a standing mixer until creamy and smooth. Add the eggs, one at a time, beating just until thoroughly blended. Stir in the sour cream.

4. Pour the cheesecake batter into the prepared pan and place on a cookie sheet. Bake in the middle of the oven for 1¼ hours. Turn the oven off and prop the door open a few inches. Let the cake rest in the oven for 1 hour. Transfer the cake to a rack and let cool to room temperature. Then cover the cake with plastic wrap and refrigerate overnight.

5. In a small saucepan, whisk the strawberry jelly with the arrowroot until blended. Bring to a boil over moderate heat, stirring constantly. Remove from the heat and let cool, stirring occasionally to prevent a skin from forming.

6. Brush the surface of the cheesecake with a thin layer of the glaze. Trim the bases of the strawberries. Set the berries on the cake, points up. Brush with the remaining glaze. Refrigerate for 20 minutes to set the glaze. Serve cold or at room temperature.

—*Diana Sturgis*

• • •

ELIZABETH TERRY'S ROBERT E. LEE CAKE

This is my variation of a traditional southern Huguenot torte made with coconut. For me, white chocolate has a similar quality to coconut, and these days it is very popular.

————— *10 Servings* —————
1 rounded cup pecan halves (4 ounces)
⅓ cup cake flour
1 teaspoon baking powder
⅓ teaspoon freshly grated nutmeg
1 large Granny Smith apple, peeled and finely chopped
2 eggs
½ cup sugar
8 ounces white chocolate, broken into small pieces
2 teaspoons unflavored gelatin
3 cups heavy cream
2 teaspoons Triple Sec or other orange liqueur
½ cup shredded sweetened coconut

1. Preheat the oven to 350°. Butter the bottom and sides of a 9-inch springform pan; flour lightly, tapping out the excess.

2. In a food processor, grind the pecans until fine. In a bowl, combine the ground pecans with the flour, baking powder and nutmeg; mix well. Add the chopped apple and toss.

3. In a medium bowl, beat the eggs at medium speed for 2 minutes. Gradually beat in the sugar until blended, then fold in the apple mixture.

4. Pour the batter into the prepared pan and bake in the middle of the oven for about 30 minutes, until the cake is lightly browned and a cake tester inserted in the center comes out clean. Remove the sides of the pan and let the cake cool completely. Replace the sides of the pan after cooling.

5. While the cake cools, prepare the white chocolate mousse. Place the white chocolate in a large heatproof bowl.

6. In a medium saucepan, sprinkle the gelatin over 1 cup of the cream and bring to a boil over moderate heat, stirring constantly. Pour the hot cream over the white chocolate and stir until completely melted. Set the bowl over a larger bowl of ice and water and stir the mixture until cool and just beginning to set, 2 to 3 minutes.

7. In a large bowl, beat the remaining 2 cups of cream until firm. Beat in the Triple Sec. Lightly fold the whipped cream into the cooled white chocolate mixture. (It's all right if some streaks remain.) Spoon the mousse over the cake base and smooth the surface. Refrigerate until fully set, at least 1 hour.

8. In a dry nonstick skillet, toast the coconut over moderately high heat, stirring constantly, until lightly browned, about 2 minutes. Transfer the coconut to a plate and let cool completely. Garnish the top of the cake with the toasted coconut before unmolding and serving.

—*Elizabeth Terry, Elizabeth on 37th, Savannah, Georgia*

• • •

MOM'S CHOCOLATE CAKE

This is a real old-fashioned American chocolate layer cake. It's very moist, very chocolatey, a snap to make and best baked the day before serving. Test Kitchen Associate Marcia Kiesel acquired the recipe from her friend Joyce Cole, who got it from her mother.

————— *8 to 10 Servings* —————
2 cups all-purpose flour
2 teaspoons baking powder
2 teaspoons baking soda
1 teaspoon salt
2 cups sugar
4 ounces unsweetened chocolate

6 tablespoons unsalted butter
1 teaspoon vanilla extract
2 eggs, lightly beaten
Chocolate Frosting (recipe follows)

1. Preheat the oven to 350°. Butter and flour two 8-by-1½-inch round cake pans. Line the bottoms with waxed paper.

2. In a medium bowl, sift together the flour, baking powder, baking soda and salt; set aside.

3. In a medium saucepan, combine the sugar with 2 cups of water. Bring to a boil over high heat and stir until the sugar dissolves; then pour into a large bowl. Add the chocolate and butter and let sit, stirring occasionally, until melted and slightly cooled. Stir in the vanilla.

4. Beat the eggs into the chocolate mixture at medium speed until combined. Add the dry ingredients all at once and beat at medium speed until smooth.

5. Divide the batter evenly between the prepared pans and bake for about 25 minutes, or until the top springs back when pressed lightly and a cake tester comes out clean. Cool the cakes in their pans for about 25 minutes, then invert onto a rack to cool completely.

6. Set one cake, right-side up, on a serving platter. Using a metal spatula, spread one-third of the Chocolate Frosting evenly over the cake. Top with the second cake and frost the top and sides with the remaining frosting.

—*Marcia Kiesel*

• • •

CHOCOLATE FROSTING

The inspiration for this frosting technique comes from dessert maven Maida Heatter's *Book of Great Chocolate Desserts* (Alfred A. Knopf).

—————— **Makes About 3½ Cups** ——————
1⅓ cups heavy cream
1½ cups sugar
6 ounces unsweetened chocolate
1 stick (4 ounces) plus 2 tablespoons
unsalted butter
1½ teaspoons vanilla extract
Pinch of salt

1. In a medium saucepan, bring the cream and sugar to a boil over moderately high heat. Reduce the heat to low and simmer, stirring occasionally, until the liquid reduces slightly, about 6 minutes.

2. Pour the mixture into a medium bowl and add the chocolate, butter, vanilla and salt. Let stand, stirring occasionally, until the chocolate and butter are melted.

3. Set the bowl in a larger bowl of ice water. Using a hand-held electric mixer, beat the frosting on medium speed, scraping the sides occasionally with a rubber spatula, until thick and glossy, about 5 minutes. Use at once.

—*Marcia Kiesel*

• • •

ALL-AMERICAN CHOCOLATE LAYER CAKE

This is just right for a birthday cake or any celebration: three towering layers, plenty of frosting and enough chocolate flavor to satisfy everyone.

—————— **12 Servings** ——————
3½ ounces unsweetened chocolate,
coarsely chopped
2⅔ cups sifted cake flour
1½ teaspoons baking soda
½ teaspoon salt
1½ sticks (6 ounces) unsalted
butter, softened
1¼ cups granulated sugar
¼ cup (packed) light brown sugar
4 eggs, at room temperature
2 teaspoons vanilla extract

1 teaspoon instant espresso powder
dissolved in 2 tablespoons of hot
water
1½ cups buttermilk, at room
temperature
Chocolate Buttermilk Frosting
(recipe follows)
Milk chocolate shavings (see Note)

1. Preheat the oven to 350°. Butter three 8-inch round cake pans, line the bottoms with waxed or parchment paper and butter the paper.

2. In a double boiler, melt the unsweetened chocolate over hot water until smooth, about 5 minutes. (Alternatively, melt the chocolate in a microwave oven.) Set aside.

3. In a medium bowl, sift together the cake flour, baking soda and salt; set aside.

4. In a large mixer bowl, beat the butter with the granulated and brown sugars on medium speed until light and fluffy. Add the eggs 1 at a time, beating for about 1 minute and stopping to scrape down the sides of the bowl with a rubber spatula after each addition. Beat in the vanilla, the dissolved espresso and the reserved melted chocolate.

5. On low speed, beat in the dry ingredients alternately with the buttermilk in four parts, beginning and ending with the dry ingredients. Transfer the batter to the prepared pans and smooth the tops with a rubber spatula.

6. Bake in the middle of the oven for 25 to 30 minutes, until the layers are firm to the touch and a cake tester inserted in the center comes out clean. Transfer to a rack to cool for 10 minutes, then unmold. Peel off the waxed paper and let cool completely before frosting. *(At this point, the cake layers can be well wrapped in plastic wrap and aluminum foil and frozen for up to 1 month.)*

7. To frost, place 1 cake layer on a serving plate. Spread the surface with a generous ½ cup of the Chocolate Butter-

milk Frosting; top with a second layer and repeat. Add the last layer upside down and spread the remaining frosting on the top and sides of the cake. Decorate the top with the chocolate shavings.

NOTE: To make milk chocolate shavings, use a 3-ounce milk chocolate bar at room temperature. Using a swivel-bladed vegetable peeler and working over a sheet of waxed paper, shave off curls from the longer side of the chocolate bar. Refrigerate on the waxed paper for at least 30 minutes or up to 1 day before sprinkling them over the frosted cake.

—*Melanie Barnard & Brooke Dojny*

• • •

CHOCOLATE BUTTERMILK FROSTING

—————— **Makes About 3 Cups** ——————
6½ ounces unsweetened chocolate,
coarsely chopped
4 cups confectioners' sugar
⅓ to ½ cup buttermilk, at room
temperature
1 tablespoon plus 1 teaspoon vanilla
extract
1 stick (4 ounces) plus 2 tablespoons
unsalted butter, softened

1. In a double boiler, melt the chocolate over hot water until smooth, about 5 minutes. (Alternatively, melt the chocolate in a microwave oven.) Set aside to let cool slightly.

2. In a large mixer bowl, combine the confectioners' sugar with ⅓ cup of the buttermilk and the vanilla. Beat on medium speed until smooth, about 2 minutes. Beat in the melted chocolate. Add the butter and beat until the frosting is light and fluffy, 2 to 3 minutes; if it seems too thick to spread, beat in a little more buttermilk 1 teaspoon at a time.

—*Melanie Barnard & Brooke Dojny*

• • •

CHOCOLATE ANGEL FOOD CAKE

For this cake, the egg whites are beaten to a slightly stiffer consistency in order to support the heavy cocoa powder.

8 to 10 Servings
¾ cup sifted cake flour
⅓ cup unsweetened Dutch process cocoa powder
1½ cups superfine sugar
1¾ cups egg whites (from 14 large eggs), at room temperature
¼ teaspoon salt
1½ teaspoons cream of tartar
6 ounces semisweet chocolate, broken into 1-inch pieces
6 tablespoons unsalted butter
2 tablespoons honey

1. Preheat the oven to 350°. Sift the flour, cocoa and ¾ cup of the sugar onto a sheet of waxed paper. Resift the mixture two more times and set aside.

2. In a large bowl and using an electric mixer, beat the egg whites with the salt on medium speed until thick and foamy. Sift the cream of tartar over the whites. Increase the speed to high and continue to beat, moving the beaters around the bowl, until the whites have almost tripled in volume and form a mass of tiny, even-sized bubbles. When the beaters are lifted, the whites should flop over onto themselves.

3. Sprinkle 6 tablespoons of the remaining sugar over the egg whites and beat on high speed until just incorporated. Repeat with the remaining 6 tablespoons sugar, beating until the whites form stiff, glossy peaks when the beaters are lifted.

4. Sprinkle one-third of the sifted flour mixture over the whites. Using a balloon whisk, fold it in with 4 or 5 light, deep sweeping strokes. (If you don't have a balloon whisk, use a large slotted spoon.) Repeat twice with the remaining flour mixture, whisking until thoroughly incorporated. Do not overmix.

5. Using a spatula, transfer the batter to an ungreased 10-by-4-inch angel food cake pan. Bake in the lower third of the oven for 45 minutes, or until the top of the cake is dry and springs back when lightly pressed.

6. Invert the pan and let the cake cool completely, about 1½ hours. (The pan can be anchored by inserting a narrow-necked bottle into the tube. Support the sides of the pan with boxed dry goods, if necessary.)

7. To unmold, run a thin knife around the sides of the cake to free it from the pan. Pull out the tube. Run the knife around the tube and under the bottom of the cake to free it completely.

8. In a double boiler, combine the chocolate, butter and honey. Set the mixture over barely simmering water and turn off the heat. Stir occasionally until the chocolate is melted and the glaze is smooth, about 5 minutes. Set the pan aside and let the glaze cool to a spreading consistency, about 15 minutes.

9. Invert the cake onto a rack and frost the top with the chocolate honey glaze, letting it run down the sides. Transfer the cake to a large platter and refrigerate for 15 minutes to set the glaze.

—*Diana Sturgis*

• • •

VANILLA ANGEL FOOD CAKE

The tender crumb and light texture of this fatless cake are achieved by gently folding the dry ingredients into beaten egg whites. If you make a lot of light sponge cakes such as angel food, it may be worth investing in a balloon whisk, since it does the job best. If you're wondering what to do with all the leftover egg yolks, make the Vanilla Custard Sauce (p. 259), which calls for 12 egg yolks.

8 to 10 Servings
1¼ cups sifted cake flour
1½ cups superfine sugar
1¾ cups egg whites (from 14 large eggs), at room temperature
¼ teaspoon salt
1½ teaspoons cream of tartar
2 teaspoons vanilla extract
1 teaspoon confectioners' sugar, for dusting
Fresh raspberries (optional)
Sweetened whipped cream or Vanilla Custard Sauce (p. 259), for serving (optional)

1. Preheat the oven to 350°. Sift the flour with ¾ cup of the superfine sugar onto a sheet of waxed paper. Sift again onto waxed paper and set aside.

2. In a large bowl and using an electric mixer, beat the egg whites with the salt on medium speed until thick and foamy. Sift the cream of tartar over the whites. Increase the speed to high and continue to beat, moving the beaters around the bowl, until the whites have almost tripled in volume and form a mass of tiny, even-sized bubbles. When the beaters are lifted, the whites should flop over onto themselves. Quickly whisk in the vanilla.

3. Sprinkle 6 tablespoons of the superfine sugar over the egg whites and beat on high speed until just incorporated. Repeat with the remaining 6 tablespoons superfine sugar, beating until the whites are glossy and form soft peaks when the beaters are lifted.

4. Sprinkle one-third of the sifted flour mixture over the whites and, using a balloon whisk, fold it in with 4 or 5 light but deep sweeping strokes. (If you don't have a balloon whisk, use a large slotted spoon.) Repeat twice with the remaining flour mixture, folding only until evenly incorporated. Do not overmix.

175

5. Using a spatula, transfer the batter to an ungreased 10-by-4-inch angel food cake pan. Run the spatula down deeply through the mixture once to break any large air pockets. Bake in the lower third of the oven for 45 minutes, until the cake is golden and the top springs back when lightly pressed.

6. Invert the pan and let the cake cool completely, about 1½ hours. (The pan can be anchored by inserting a narrow-necked bottle into the tube. Support the sides of the pan with boxed dry goods, if necessary.)

7. To unmold, run a thin knife around the sides of the cake to free it from the pan. Pull out the tube. Run the knife around the tube and under the bottom of the cake to free it completely. Invert the cake onto a serving platter or serve it right-side up. Sift the confectioners' sugar over the top. Serve with raspberries and sweetened whipped cream or Vanilla Custard Sauce if you like.

—Diana Sturgis

• • •

ORANGE ANGEL FOOD CAKE WITH ORANGE GLAZE

Follow the recipe for Vanilla Angel Food Cake (above), but substitute one tablespoon of finely grated zest from a washed navel orange for the vanilla extract. The zest should be sprinkled in with the flour mixture (Step 4). Omit the confectioners' sugar and brush the top and sides of the cake with this simple orange glaze instead.

❦ The citrus notes in this ethereal cake are best complemented by delicate dessert wines with honey-and-lemon nuances, such as 1987 Long Vineyards Late Harvest Johannisberg Riesling or 1983 Beringer Nightingale.

——— 8 to 10 Servings ———
1 cup confectioners' sugar
1½ to 2 tablespoons orange juice
1 tablespoon finely grated orange zest

In a small bowl, combine the confectioners' sugar, 1½ tablespoons of orange juice and the orange zest and stir until smooth. Stir in enough of the remaining orange juice to make a glaze (about the consistency of heavy cream) that is thick enough to brush on the cake without being absorbed.

—Diana Sturgis

• • •

SPICE CAKE WITH LINGONBERRY JAM

If you can find only runny lingonberry jam, scoop it into a strainer to drain until firm, then measure out ½ cup to use here.

——— Makes One 9-by-5-Inch Loaf ———
1 stick (4 ounces) unsalted butter, melted and cooled
2 eggs
1 cup (packed) dark brown sugar
1½ cups all-purpose flour
2 teaspoons finely cracked cardamom seeds or 1½ teaspoons ground
1 teaspoon ground ginger
2 teaspoons baking powder
¼ cup crème fraîche
¼ cup buttermilk
½ cup firm lingonberry jam or 1 jar (10 ounces) loose lingonberry jam, drained

1. Preheat the oven to 350°. Grease a 9-by-5-inch loaf pan. In a medium bowl, combine the melted butter, eggs and brown sugar and beat until a ribbon forms when the beaters are lifted.

2. In a small bowl, stir together the flour, cardamom, ginger and baking powder. Add to the butter-sugar mixture and stir until blended. Fold in the crème

fraîche and the buttermilk, then fold in the lingonberry jam until well blended.

3. Pour the batter into the prepared loaf pan and bake for 50 to 60 minutes, until a cake tester inserted in the center comes out clean. Let cool in the pan before unmolding. *(This loaf can be made up to 2 days ahead. When completely cooled, cover tightly with plastic wrap.)*

—Christer Larsson, Aquavit, New York City

• • •

CHOCOLATE HAZELNUT TORTE

Unsweetened baking chocolate adds a deep chocolate flavor to this nutty torte. You can make this a day ahead (wrap it well to prevent it from drying out), but whip the cream no more than an hour before serving.

——— 8 Servings ———
8 ounces shelled hazelnuts (about 1½ cups)
1 cup granulated sugar
1 stick (4 ounces) unsalted butter
6 ounces unsweetened chocolate, broken into pieces
5 eggs, separated
¼ teaspoon salt
1 teaspoon confectioners' sugar
1 cup heavy cream, chilled
2 tablespoons hazelnut liqueur, such as Frangelico

1. Preheat the oven to 350°. Butter a 9-by-2-inch round cake pan. Line the bottom of the pan with waxed paper, butter the paper and set the pan aside.

2. Spread out the nuts in a baking pan and toast for about 10 minutes, or until the skins are blistered. Let cool, then wrap the nuts in a kitchen towel and rub them together to remove their skins. When the nuts are completely cool, transfer them to a food processor. Add 1 tablespoon of the granulated sugar and pulse until finely ground. Set aside.

3. In a medium heatproof bowl, combine the butter, chocolate and the remaining granulated sugar. Place the bowl in a saucepan filled with 2 inches of simmering water set over low heat until the butter is melted and the chocolate is soft, about 5 minutes. Remove from the heat and stir until the chocolate is melted and the mixture is smooth, 2 to 3 minutes. Set aside to cool to room temperature.

4. With a wooden spoon, beat the egg yolks into the chocolate mixture one at a time until incorporated. Stir in the reserved ground nuts.

5. In a medium bowl, beat the egg whites with the salt on high speed until stiff peaks form. Using a spatula, lightly fold the egg whites into the chocolate mixture, one-third at a time, just until no white streaks remain. Scrape the batter into the prepared cake pan and bake for 35 minutes, or until the cake feels firm in the center when lightly pressed. Let cool on a rack.

6. Run a thin knife around the sides of the pan to loosen the cake. Invert the cake onto a rack and peel off the waxed paper. Set the cake right-side up on a platter and sift the confectioners' sugar evenly over the top.

7. In a medium bowl, beat the heavy cream with the hazelnut liqueur until soft peaks form. Spoon the cream into a bowl and pass separately.

—Diana Sturgis

• • •

CHOCOLATE POLENTA CAKE WITH WHITE CHOCOLATE SAUCE

This chocolate cake, with its deep chocolate flavor, gets its unusual texture from the yellow cornmeal that binds it. It is served, cut in triangles in a shiny pool of white chocolate sauce, at Bice, an elegant Italian restaurant in Chicago.

———— *12 Servings* ————
1 pound bittersweet chocolate,
  preferably Callebaut or Lindt,
  coarsely chopped
2 sticks (8 ounces) unsalted butter
11 eggs, separated, plus 9 egg yolks
1¼ cups granulated sugar
½ cup yellow cornmeal
¼ cup dark rum
2 cups milk
1 cup heavy cream
6 ounces white chocolate, preferably
  Callebaut, finely chopped
1 teaspoon vanilla extract
2 to 3 tablespoons confectioners'
  sugar

1. Preheat the oven to 300°. Lightly butter a 9-by-12-by-2-inch glass baking dish and line the bottom with waxed paper; set aside. In a large metal bowl, melt the bittersweet chocolate and butter over simmering water, stirring occasionally, until smooth. Set aside to cool.

2. In a large bowl, beat 11 egg yolks with ½ cup of the granulated sugar at high speed until light in color and thick enough to hold a ribbon trail when the beaters are lifted. Fold the yolk mixture into the melted chocolate.

3. In a medium bowl, beat the 11 egg whites at high speed until almost stiff. Sprinkle in ¼ cup of the granulated sugar and continue beating on high speed until stiff peaks form. Fold the beaten whites into the chocolate-egg mixture; then fold in the cornmeal and rum. Pour the batter into the prepared pan.

4. Bake the cake for 60 to 65 minutes, until puffed and firm to the touch in the center. Remove from the oven and let cool completely in the pan. The cake will sink at least one-third in height as it cools.

5. Meanwhile, in a small saucepan, scald the milk and cream over moderate heat. In a medium bowl, whisk together the remaining 9 egg yolks and the remaining ½ cup granulated sugar until just blended.

6. Gradually whisk about half of the hot milk into the yolks, then pour the mixture into the saucepan. Return to the heat and cook, stirring constantly with a wooden spoon, over moderately high heat until the mixture is thick, coats the back of the spoon and reaches 165° on a candy thermometer, about 10 minutes. Do not allow to boil or the custard will curdle.

7. Remove from the heat and immediately add the white chocolate, stirring until thoroughly melted. Stir in the vanilla. Strain the white chocolate sauce and chill until ready to use.

8. Turn the cooled cake out onto a sheet of waxed paper. Cut into twelve 3-inch squares, then cut each square diagonally into 2 triangles. Sift confectioners' sugar over the top of each triangle. Place 2 triangles on each plate and surround with a pool of white chocolate sauce.

—Donato DeSantis, Bice, Chicago

• • •

HAZELNUT-ORANGE BUNDT

———— *8 to 10 Servings* ————
1 cup hazelnuts
1¼ cups granulated sugar
8 eggs, separated
1 teaspoon vanilla extract
2 tablespoons finely grated orange
  zest
⅓ cup plus 3 tablespoons fresh
  orange juice
1 cup cake flour
Pinch of salt
3 ounces cream cheese, softened
½ cup confectioners' sugar

1. Preheat the oven to 350°. Butter and flour a 12-cup Bundt or kugelhopf pan.

2. Spread the hazelnuts on a baking sheet and toast until golden brown and the skins begin to crack, about 10 minutes. Let cool. Place the hazelnuts in a towel and rub off the skins. Coarsely chop 12 of the nuts and reserve for garnish. In a food processor or blender, process the remaining nuts and 2 tablespoons of the granulated sugar until finely ground.

3. In a large bowl, beat the egg yolks on medium speed until they turn pale yellow, about 1 minute. Gradually beat in 1 cup of the granulated sugar until thick and light, about 5 minutes.

4. Beat in the vanilla, orange zest and ⅓ cup of the orange juice. In 2 batches, sift the cake flour over the batter and fold in. Fold in the finely ground hazelnuts.

5. In a large bowl, beat the egg whites on medium speed until frothy. Add the salt and continue beating until soft peaks form, about 2 minutes. Beat in the remaining 2 tablespoons granulated sugar; beat until stiff peaks form. Fold one-fourth of the egg whites into the batter, then fold in the remaining egg whites.

6. Scrape the batter into the prepared pan and bake for 40 to 45 minutes, or until a toothpick inserted in the center of the cake comes out clean. Let cool in the pan on a rack for 10 minutes. Invert the cake onto a serving plate.

7. In a small bowl, stir the cream cheese until smooth. Add the confectioners' sugar and beat until blended. Stir in the remaining 3 tablespoons orange juice.

8. Drizzle the orange glaze over the top of the warm cake, allowing it to cascade down the sides. Sprinkle the reserved nuts over the top. Serve at room temperature. *(This cake can be made up to 2 days in advance. Wrap well and refrigerate. Let return to room temperature before serving.)*

—*Mimi Ruth Brodeur*

• • •

PUMPKIN-GINGER CAKE

In this exquisitely tender cake, ginger is blended with another spice—allspice—to produce a deep and complex flavor that is especially pleasing when combined with pumpkin and molasses.

———— *8 Servings* ————
1 stick (4 ounces) unsalted butter, softened
½ cup maple syrup
½ cup (packed) light brown sugar
2 eggs, lightly beaten, at room temperature
2 tablespoons unsulphured molasses
½ teaspoon vanilla extract
1 cup canned unsweetened pumpkin puree
1¾ cups all-purpose flour
2¼ teaspoons ground ginger
1 teaspoon baking soda
½ teaspoon salt
½ teaspoon ground allspice

1. Preheat the oven to 350°. Butter and flour a shallow 4-cup ring mold or a deep, 4-cup kugelhopf pan. In a large bowl, beat together the butter, maple syrup and brown sugar. Stir in the eggs, molasses and vanilla until combined. Stir in the pumpkin puree.

2. In a sifter or sieve set over the bowl, combine the flour, ginger, baking soda, salt and allspice. Gradually sift the dry ingredients into the pumpkin mixture, folding them in with a rubber spatula until just blended.

3. Pour the batter into the prepared pan and smooth the surface with the spatula. Bake the cake for 30 minutes for the shallow pan and up to 45 minutes for the kugelhopf pan, or until a cake tester inserted in the center comes out dry. Let the cake cool for about 10 minutes in the pan before unmolding it onto a rack. Serve warm or at room temperature.

—*Marcia Kiesel*

• • •

CALVADOS APPLE CAKE

———— *10 to 12 Servings* ————
3 cups all-purpose flour
2 teaspoons cinnamon
2 teaspoons baking powder
1 teaspoon baking soda
1 teaspoon ground ginger
½ teaspoon salt
¼ teaspoon freshly grated nutmeg
2 sticks (8 ounces) unsalted butter, at room temperature
2 cups (packed) dark brown sugar
4 eggs
1½ teaspoons vanilla extract
½ cup milk
3 tablespoons Calvados or apple brandy
4 Granny Smith apples—peeled, cored and cut into ½-inch chunks
1 tablespoon confectioners' sugar

1. Preheat the oven to 350°. Grease a 12-cup Bundt or tube pan.

2. In a medium bowl, combine the flour, cinnamon, baking powder, baking soda, ginger, salt and nutmeg.

3. In a large bowl, beat the butter on high speed until light and creamy. Gradually beat in the brown sugar. Add the eggs, 1 at a time, beating until thoroughly blended. Beat in the vanilla.

4. Reduce the speed to low and beat in the flour mixture in 3 batches, alternating with the milk, beginning and ending with the flour, until combined. Using a wooden spoon, stir in the Calvados and the apples thoroughly.

5. Scrape the batter into the prepared pan. Bake for 55 to 60 minutes, or until a toothpick inserted in the center of the cake comes out clean. Let cool on a rack for 10 minutes before inverting onto a wire rack. Sift the confectioners' sugar over the top. Serve slightly warm or at room temperature.

—*Mimi Ruth Brodeur*

• • •

POST-HOLIDAY SHORTCAKE

This heart-shaped shortcake is the answer to my hankering for gingerbread, which begins when the leaves turn red and lasts until those little green shoots begin to poke out of the ground. Pear, the most delicately flavored of the winter fruits, is the perfect foil for ginger's aggressive bite. Pears poached in a lemon and fresh ginger syrup are set on a gingerbread base with a large dollop of crème fraîche. Glistening filaments of candied lemon zest garnish the top.

───────── *5 Servings* ─────────

2 cups all-purpose flour
¼ cup light brown sugar
1 tablespoon baking powder
½ teaspoon salt
2 tablespoons ground ginger
1 teaspoon cinnamon
½ teaspoon freshly grated nutmeg
¼ teaspoon ground cloves
1 stick (4 ounces) cold unsalted
  butter, cut into ¼-inch dice
2 teaspoons instant coffee
2 teaspoons molasses
⅔ cup plus 2 tablespoons milk
2 lemons
2 cups plus 1 tablespoon superfine
  sugar
3 Bosc pears—peeled, halved and
  cored
4-inch piece of fresh ginger, peeled
  and cut into thin slices
1 cup heavy cream
1 cup crème fraîche
1 teaspoon vanilla extract
2 tablespoons finely chopped
  candied ginger

1. Preheat the oven to 375°. In a medium bowl, sift together the flour, brown sugar, baking powder, salt, ground ginger, cinnamon, nutmeg and cloves.
2. Using a pastry blender or two knives, cut in the butter until the mixture is the texture of coarse meal with a few pea-size pieces of butter remaining.

3. In a 1-cup measure, combine the instant coffee, molasses and 1 tablespoon of the milk. Stir to dissolve the coffee; add the ⅔ cup milk and stir to combine.
4. Make a well in the center of the flour mixture and pour in the milk mixture. Using a rubber spatula, quickly combine the ingredients, scraping down the bowl, until the dough comes together, 5 to 6 strokes.
5. Transfer the dough to a lightly floured surface and knead gently 2 or 3 times. Shape the dough into a 12-inch log scraping the work surface as necessary. Flatten the log into a rectangle 3 inches wide and 1 inch thick. Dip a large heart-shaped cookie cutter in flour and cut out 4 hearts. Gently reknead the dough scraps just enough to gather them together; shape into a triangle 1 inch thick and cut out the last heart. Brush the tops of the shortcakes with the remaining 1 tablespoon milk and place on a heavy baking sheet lined with aluminum foil. Refrigerate for 10 minutes.
6. Bake the shortcakes for 30 minutes, until golden brown. Let cool on the baking sheet for 10 minutes. Using a metal spatula, gently transfer to a wire rack to cool further.
7. Meanwhile, using a vegetable peeler, cut the zest from the lemons, being careful to leave behind the bitter white pith. Using a sharp knife, slice the zest lengthwise into very thin julienne strips.
8. In a medium saucepan, combine 2 cups of the superfine sugar with 3 cups of water. Cook over high heat until the sugar dissolves completely, 4 to 5 minutes. Add the pear halves, zest strips and sliced fresh ginger. Reduce the heat to moderately high and simmer, turning the pears occasionally, until tender and easily pierced with a fork, about 10 minutes. Remove the pears with a slotted spoon and set aside.

9. Continue to simmer the syrup, occasionally washing down the sides of the pan with a pastry brush dipped in water, until the zest is transparent and the syrup somewhat thickened, about 30 minutes. Strain the syrup (you should have about 2 cups) and set aside. Discard the ginger but reserve the lemon zest.
10. In a chilled bowl, combine the heavy cream and crème fraîche and beat until the mixture begins to thicken. Add the remaining 1 tablespoon superfine sugar and the vanilla and continue beating until soft peaks form. Set aside.
11. Using a fork, split each shortcake in half. Spoon about 1 tablespoon of the warm lemon-ginger syrup onto each of 5 dessert plates. Place the bottom half of a shortcake on each plate, cover with a ½-inch layer of cream and top with a pear half, the pointy end matching the heart tip. Spoon another tablespoon of syrup over each pear and cover with another layer of cream. Arrange the shortcake tops over the cream, cocked to one side. Garnish with the reserved candied lemon zest and the candied ginger and drizzle with additional syrup.

—*Peggy Cullen*

• • •

MEDITERRANEAN SHORTCAKE

Hazelnuts, figs and mascarpone are the winter flavors of Italy. For this shortcake, plump dried figs are poached in a port syrup, which is then reduced to a glistening sauce the color of Dorothy's ruby slippers. Even if you dislike anise, don't be afraid to use it. It brings out the flavor of the toasted hazelnuts.

───────── *6 Servings* ─────────

1 cup hazelnuts
2 cups all-purpose flour
1 tablespoon baking powder
½ teaspoon salt
1 cup plus 3 tablespoons superfine
  sugar

1 tablespoon anise seeds, finely
    chopped or freshly ground
1 stick (4 ounces) cold unsalted
    butter, cut into ¼-inch dice
⅔ cup plus 1 tablespoon milk
1 vanilla bean
12 moist dried Calimyrna figs
    (about ¾ pound)
2 cups ruby port
½ cup heavy cream
1 cup mascarpone cheese, at room
    temperature

1. Preheat the oven to 350°. Place the hazelnuts on a baking sheet and toast until the skins crack and the centers are golden, about 15 minutes. While still warm, rub the nuts in a terry cloth towel to remove the skins; chop coarsely and set aside.

2. In a medium bowl, sift together the flour, baking powder, salt and 3 tablespoons of the superfine sugar. Stir in the anise seeds. Using a pastry blender or two knives, cut in the butter until the mixture is the texture of coarse meal with a few pea-size pieces of butter remaining. Toss in the cooled hazelnuts.

3. Pour the ⅔ cup of the milk into a measuring cup and scrape the seeds from the vanilla bean into the milk. Make a well in the center of the flour mixture and add the vanilla milk. Using a rubber spatula, quickly combine the ingredients, scraping down the sides of the bowl, until the dough comes together, 5 to 6 strokes.

4. Transfer the dough to a lightly floured surface and knead gently 2 or 3 times. Shape the dough into a 12-inch log. Pat the log into a rectangle 3 inches wide and 1 inch thick. Dip a 3-inch round biscuit cutter in flour and cut out 4 circles. Gently reknead the dough scraps to gather them together. Pat the dough to a 1-inch thickness and cut out another 2 circles. Brush the tops of the shortcakes with the remaining 1 tablespoon milk and place on a heavy baking sheet lined with aluminum foil. Refrigerate for about 10 minutes.

5. Bake the shortcakes for 30 minutes, until golden brown. Let cool on the baking sheet for 10 minutes. Using a metal spatula, gently transfer them to a wire rack to cool further.

6. Meanwhile, cut the stem tips off the figs. In a medium nonreactive saucepan, combine the port and the remaining 1 cup sugar. Cook over high heat to dissolve the sugar, about 3 minutes. Add the figs, bring just to a boil and reduce the heat to moderately high. Continue to simmer the figs until the skins are very soft, about 20 minutes. Remove the pan from the heat and leave the figs to steep in the syrup until cool, 20 to 30 minutes.

7. Meanwhile, in a medium bowl, whisk the heavy cream into the mascarpone. Remove the figs from the syrup and cut each fig into quarters. Reserve the syrup.

8. Using a fork, split each shortcake in half. Spoon about 1 tablespoon of the port syrup onto each of 6 dessert plates. Place the bottom half of a shortcake on each plate and cover with ¼ cup of the mascarpone cream. Arrange 4 fig quarters on the cream with their points facing out. Drizzle about 1 tablespoon of syrup over the figs and top with about 3 tablespoons more cream. Set 4 more fig quarters atop the cream and cover with the other shortcake half. Garnish each shortcake with a dollop of cream and drizzle additional syrup over the top so that it runs down the sides.

—*Peggy Cullen*

• • •

BLUEBERRY SHORTCAKE

——————— *4 Servings* ———————
3 cups blueberries
Juice of ½ lemon
3 tablespoons plus 1 teaspoon sugar
¼ teaspoon cinnamon
½ cup all-purpose flour
½ cup cake flour
1½ teaspoons baking powder

¼ teaspoon salt
4 tablespoons cold lightly salted
    butter, cut into small pieces
1⅓ cups plus 1 tablespoon heavy
    cream

1. Preheat the oven to 450°. In a medium bowl, toss the blueberries with the lemon juice and 2 tablespoons of the sugar; crush some of the berries and set aside. In a small bowl, combine the cinnamon and 1 teaspoon of the sugar.

2. In a food processor, combine the all-purpose and cake flours, the baking powder, salt and the remaining 1 tablespoon sugar; process until blended. Add the butter and process until the mixture resembles coarse meal. Add ⅓ cup plus 1 tablespoon of the cream and process just until a dough forms, 1 to 2 seconds.

3. Turn the dough out on a lightly floured work surface and knead a few times. Form the dough into a ball and place it on an ungreased cookie sheet. Pat the dough out to form a ¾-inch-thick round. Cut the round into quarters and arrange them about 1 inch apart. Sprinkle the tops with the cinnamon sugar. Bake until very lightly browned, about 12 minutes. Let cool for 5 minutes.

4. Meanwhile, in a medium bowl, whip the remaining 1 cup cream until thick peaks form.

5. Split each shortcake biscuit in half and put the bottom halves on 4 plates. Spoon one-fourth of the blueberry mixture over each biscuit, cover with the other biscuit half and spoon the whipped cream on top.

—*Stephanie Lyness*

• • •

Chocolate Pecan Tart (p. 169).

Left, Chocolate Angel Food Cake (p. 175). Above, Banana-Strawberry Sherbet (p. 249).

Above, Chocolate Hazelnut Torte
(p. 176). Near right, New Orleans
Pecan Pie (p. 168). Far right,
Chocolate Cream Napoleon with Hot
Chocolate Sauce (p. 204).

Above, Summer Fruit with Orange Liqueur Custard (p. 212). Right, Vanilla Angel Food Cake (p. 175).

UPSTATE SHORTCAKE

This shortcake was inspired by two of my favorite confections: sticky caramel apples from upstate New York and pecan buttercrunch. The pecan-studded triangular shortcake is split and filled with vanilla ice cream and apples in a buttery caramel sauce. Eat this quickly before the sauce melts the ice cream.

❢ This intensely rich dessert calls for an equally rich dessert wine. Try one whose flavor won't be flattened in comparison, such as Prosper Maufoux Muscat de Beaumes-de-Venise or a cream sherry, such as Harvey's.

───────── *6 Servings* ─────────
2 cups all-purpose flour
3 tablespoons light brown sugar
1 tablespoon baking powder
1 teaspoon cinnamon
½ teaspoon salt
1 stick plus 4 tablespoons cold unsalted butter (6 ounces), the stick cut into ¼-inch dice
1½ cups coarsely chopped pecans (about 5 ounces)
⅔ cup plus 1 tablespoon milk
1 teaspoon vanilla extract
4 medium apples, such as Winesap, Granny Smith or Golden Delicious—peeled, cored and sliced into eighths
¾ cup plus 1 tablespoon superfine sugar
¼ teaspoon lemon juice
¾ cup heavy cream
6 scoops of good-quality vanilla ice cream (about 1 pint)

1. Preheat the oven to 375°. In a medium bowl, sift together the flour, brown sugar, baking powder, cinnamon and salt. Using a pastry blender, cut in the diced butter until the mixture is the texture of coarse meal with a few pea-size pieces of butter remaining. Toss in the pecans.

2. Make a well in the center of the mixture and add ⅔ cup of the milk and the vanilla. Using a rubber spatula, quickly combine the ingredients, scraping down the bowl, until the dough comes together, 5 to 6 strokes.

3. Transfer the dough to a lightly floured surface and gently knead 2 or 3 times. Shape the dough into a 12-inch log, scraping the work surface as necessary. Pat the log into a rectangle, 3½ inches wide and 1 inch thick. Using a sharp knife, cut out 6 triangles.

4. Brush the tops of the shortcakes with the remaining 1 tablespoon milk. Transfer the shortcakes to a heavy baking sheet lined with aluminum foil and refrigerate for 10 minutes.

5. Bake the shortcakes for 30 minutes, until golden brown. Let cool on the baking sheet for 10 minutes. Using a metal spatula, gently transfer the shortcakes to a wire rack to cool further.

6. Meanwhile, in a large skillet, melt the remaining 4 tablespoons butter. Add the apples and cook over high heat, stirring frequently, until lightly browned, about 4 minutes. Sprinkle 1 tablespoon of the superfine sugar over the apples and continue cooking, stirring frequently, until softened and browned, about 4 minutes longer. Remove from the heat and set aside.

7. In a medium saucepan and using your fingers, rub the lemon juice thoroughly into the remaining ¾ cup superfine sugar. Stir in 2 tablespoons of water until blended and bring to a boil over high heat. Using a pastry brush dipped in water, wash down any sugar crystals from the sides of the pan and boil the syrup over high heat until it becomes a light caramel, 4 to 5 minutes.

8. Remove from the heat and slowly whisk in the heavy cream. Return the caramel to the heat and continue whisking until the cream is incorporated. Pour the warm caramel sauce into the skillet and stir gently to coat the apples.

9. Using a fork, split each shortcake in half. Place the bottom half of a shortcake on each of 6 dessert plates and spoon on 2 to 3 slices of apple and about 1 tablespoon of the warm caramel sauce. Set a scoop of ice cream on the apples and coat with another tablespoon of caramel sauce. Top with the other shortcake half. Spoon another 2 or 3 slices of apple and 1 tablespoon of caramel sauce over all and serve immediately.

—*Peggy Cullen*

• • •

MIAMI BEACH SHORTCAKE

When sleigh bells give way to slush puddles and winter begins to get a little tiresome, thoughts turn south to palm trees and a turquoise sea. This tropical shortcake is covered in coconut to resemble a large macaroon. For the filling, sliced ripe bananas are layered with banana-fortified whipped cream and a touch of tangy sour cream. While it won't give you a tan, this dessert is a proven cure for the ubiquitous late-winter malady known as cabin fever.

───────── *6 Servings* ─────────
⅔ cup plus ½ cup sweetened shredded coconut
2 cups all-purpose flour

Winter Fruit Compote (p. 213).

1 tablespoon baking powder
1 teaspoon freshly grated nutmeg
½ teaspoon salt
¼ cup superfine sugar
1 stick (4 ounces) cold unsalted
  butter, cut into ¼-inch dice
⅔ cup plus 1 tablespoon milk
2½ teaspoons vanilla extract
4 large ripe bananas
1 cup heavy cream
2 tablespoons sour cream

1. Preheat the oven to 375°. Toast ⅔ cup of the coconut on a heavy baking sheet for 4 to 5 minutes, stirring once, until lightly browned. Let cool completely. Set aside 3 tablespoons of the toasted coconut for garnish.

2. In a medium bowl, sift together the flour, baking powder, nutmeg, salt and 3 tablespoons of the sugar. Using a pastry blender, cut in the butter until the mixture is the texture of coarse meal with a few pea-size pieces of butter remaining. Toss in the toasted coconut remaining on the baking sheet.

3. Make a well in the center of the mixture and pour in ⅔ cup of the milk and 1 teaspoon of the vanilla. Using a rubber spatula, quickly combine the ingredients, scraping down the bowl, until the dough comes together, 5 to 6 strokes.

4. Using a 2-ounce (¼-cup) ice cream scoop, form a rounded ball of dough. Holding the ball in your hand and using a pastry brush, dab the surface with some of the remaining 1 tablespoon milk. Place the remaining ½ cup untoasted coconut in a medium bowl and roll the ball of dough in it, pressing to help the coconut adhere; let the excess coconut fall back into the bowl. Transfer the shortcake to a heavy baking sheet covered with aluminum foil. Repeat with the remaining 5 shortcakes and the remaining milk and coconut. Refrigerate the shortcakes for 10 minutes.

5. Bake the shortcakes for 30 minutes, or until the coconut is nicely browned and the surfaces are hard to the touch. Let cool on the baking sheet for 10 minutes. Using a metal spatula, gently transfer the shortcakes to a wire rack to cool further.

6. Meanwhile, in a small bowl, mash 1 of the bananas and the remaining 1 tablespoon sugar to a puree. In a medium bowl, combine the heavy cream and sour cream and beat at medium-high speed until soft peaks form, about 2 minutes. Fold in the mashed banana and the remaining 1½ teaspoons vanilla.

7. Using a sharp serrated knife, slice each shortcake in half horizontally. Place the bottom half of a shortcake on each of 6 dessert plates and spread with about ½ cup of the banana cream.

8. Slice the remaining bananas into ¼-inch rounds and arrange the slices on the cream, reserving 6 banana slices for garnish. Top with the other shortcake half. Garnish each shortcake with a dollop of banana cream, a banana slice and about ½ tablespoon of the reserved toasted coconut and serve immediately.

—*Peggy Cullen*

• • •

CREAMSICLE CURRANT SHORTCAKE

As a cold wind blows and the afternoon light is beginning to fade, there's no better place to be than on a divan taking tea with scones and clotted cream. Stateside, you'll happily settle for this shortcake, inspired both by the classic hot cross bun with its felicitous pairing of currants and orange and the flavors of an old-fashioned Creamsicle, with its smooth blend of vanilla ice cream and orange sherbet.

――――――― 6 Servings ―――――――
2 cups all-purpose flour
1 tablespoon baking powder
½ teaspoon salt
¼ teaspoon freshly grated nutmeg
¾ cup superfine sugar
1 stick (4 ounces) cold unsalted
  butter, cut into ¼-inch dice
¾ cup currants
⅔ cup plus 1 tablespoon milk
1½ cups fresh orange juice
¼ cup kirsch
1 cinnamon stick
4 large navel oranges, peeled and
  cut into segments
1 cup heavy cream

1. Preheat the oven to 375°. In a medium bowl, sift together the flour, baking powder, salt, nutmeg and 3 tablespoons of the sugar. Using a pastry blender, cut in the butter until the mixture is the texture of coarse meal with a few pea-size pieces of butter remaining. Toss in the currants.

2. Make a well in the center of the mixture and add ⅔ cup of the milk. Using a rubber spatula, quickly combine the ingredients, scraping down the bowl, until the dough comes together, 5 to 6 strokes.

3. Transfer the dough to a lightly floured surface and knead gently 2 or 3 times. Shape the dough into a 12-inch log, then pat it out into a 12-by-3-inch rectangle 1 inch thick.

4. Dip a 3-inch round biscuit cutter in flour and cut out 4 circles from the dough. Gently reknead the scraps just enough to gather them together. Pat the dough to an even 1-inch thickness and cut out 2 more circles. Lightly brush the tops of the shortcakes with the remaining 1 tablespoon milk. Arrange the shortcakes on a heavy baking sheet lined with aluminum foil and refrigerate for 10 minutes.

5. Bake the shortcakes for 30 minutes, or until lightly browned. Let cool on the baking sheet for 10 minutes. Using a metal spatula, gently transfer the shortcakes to a wire rack to cool further.

6. Meanwhile, in a medium nonreactive saucepan, combine the orange juice, kirsch, ½ cup of the sugar and the cinnamon stick. Bring to a boil over high heat. Reduce the heat to moderate and boil until reduced by about half and thickened slightly, about 30 minutes.

7. Remove from the heat and discard the cinnamon stick. Let cool for about 5 minutes, then fold in the orange segments. (The syrup will thin out when the oranges are added.)

8. In a chilled medium bowl, beat the heavy cream until it just begins to thicken. Add the remaining 1 tablespoon sugar and continue beating until soft peaks form.

9. Using a fork, split each shortcake in half horizontally. Spoon 1 tablespoon of the orange syrup onto each of 6 dessert plates. Place the bottom half of a shortcake on each plate and cover with a ½-inch layer of whipped cream. Spoon 2 tablespoons of the glazed oranges over the cream, then spoon over another layer of cream. Top with the other shortcake half. Garnish the shortcakes with a dollop of whipped cream and 2 to 3 orange segments and serve immediately.

—Peggy Cullen

• • •

FRESH FRUIT CLOUD CAKE

I've seen a number of variations of this cake that my grandmother used to make.

──────── *10 to 12 Servings* ────────
2 cups sifted all-purpose flour
½ teaspoon salt
Pinch of freshly grated nutmeg (optional)
9 eggs, separated
2 cups sugar
1 tablespoon fresh lemon juice
¼ cup fresh orange juice
2 tablespoons orange liqueur
2 tablespoons dark rum

1 pint heavy cream
1 pint strawberries, sliced, 12 left whole
1 pint raspberries

1. Preheat the oven to 350°. Lightly grease three 8-by-1-inch cake pans.

2. In a medium bowl, sift together the flour, salt and nutmeg. In a large mixer bowl, beat the egg yolks with the sugar on high speed until thick and light in color, about 7 minutes. Gradually mix in the dry ingredients on low speed, then increase the speed to high to thoroughly combine.

3. In a large bowl, beat the egg whites until stiff but not dry. Beat one-fourth of the whites into the batter to lighten it and then fold in the remaining whites until barely incorporated. Gently fold in the lemon juice until just blended.

4. Pour the batter into the prepared pans and bake for 15 to 20 minutes, or until the layers are lightly golden and a toothpick inserted into the centers comes out clean. Transfer the cakes to wire racks and let cool for 15 minutes. Loosen the layers from the pans, invert onto the racks and let cool completely. *(This recipe can be prepared to this point up to 1 day ahead. Wrap the cake layers with plastic wrap and store at room temperature.)*

5. In a small bowl, combine the orange juice, orange liqueur and rum. Turn the cake layers top-side up and brush with the orange mixture. In a medium bowl, whip the heavy cream until stiff.

6. To assemble, place one cake layer on a serving plate. Top with one-third of the whipped cream and then the sliced strawberries. Cover with a second cake layer and top with another one-third of the cream. Reserve 15 raspberries and place the remaining raspberries on the whipped cream. Add the last cake layer and cover the top with the remaining whipped cream. Arrange the whole strawberries in the center of the cake and dot with the reserved raspberries. Refrigerate

until ready to serve. Cut with a serrated knife. *(This cake can be kept for 1 day, covered loosely in plastic wrap, in the refrigerator.)*

—Lee Bailey

• • •

BLUEBERRY-ALMOND COFFEE CAKE

Do not thaw the blueberries; use them straight from the freezer.

──────── *16 Servings* ────────
2¾ cups plus 2 teaspoons cake flour
2 cups sugar
¼ teaspoon freshly grated nutmeg
1 tablespoon finely grated lemon zest
2 sticks (8 ounces) unsalted butter— 4 tablespoons chilled and cut into ¼-inch dice, 12 tablespoons at room temperature
½ cup sliced blanched almonds
1 tablespoon baking powder
½ teaspoon salt
3 eggs
1½ teaspoons vanilla extract
1 cup plain yogurt
1½ cups frozen blueberries

1. Preheat the oven to 350°. Grease a 13-by-9-by-2-inch baking pan and set aside. In a small bowl, combine ¼ cup of the cake flour, ½ cup of the sugar, the nutmeg and 1 teaspoon of the lemon zest. Cut in the 4 tablespoons chilled butter bits until the mixture resembles coarse crumbs. Add the almonds and toss to coat. Cover the topping and refrigerate.

2. Meanwhile, in a medium bowl, sift together 2½ cups of the cake flour, the baking powder and salt.

3. In a large bowl, beat the remaining 12 tablespoons butter at medium speed.

Gradually beat in the remaining 1½ cups sugar. Increase the speed to high and whip until fluffy, about 2 minutes. Add the eggs, 1 at a time, beating well after each addition. Beat in the vanilla and the remaining 2 teaspoons lemon zest.

4. Reduce the speed to low and beat in the flour mixture in 3 batches, alternating with the yogurt, beginning and ending with the flour, until combined.

5. In a medium bowl, toss the frozen blueberries with the remaining 2 teaspoons cake flour. Fold into the batter. Scrape the batter into the prepared baking pan. Crumble the topping evenly over the batter.

6. Bake for 45 to 50 minutes, or until a toothpick inserted in the center of the cake comes out clean. Let cool for 10 minutes before cutting into squares. Serve warm.

—Mimi Ruth Brodeur

• • •

WALNUT-DATE CRUMB CAKE

——— *8 to 10 Servings* ———
2½ cups plus 2 tablespoons all-purpose flour
1 cup sugar
1 stick (4 ounces) unsalted butter at room temperature plus 6 tablespoons cold unsalted butter
1 cup walnuts, chopped (about 4 ounces)
2 teaspoons baking powder
¼ teaspoon salt
2 eggs
1 teaspoon vanilla extract
⅓ cup sour cream
1 package (8 ounces) pitted dates, chopped

1. Preheat the oven to 350°. Grease a 10-inch springform pan and set aside.

2. In a medium bowl, combine ½ cup plus 2 tablespoons of the flour and ¼ cup of the sugar. Cut in the 6 tablespoons cold butter until the mixture resembles coarse crumbs. Stir in the chopped walnuts. Cover the topping and refrigerate.

3. In a small bowl, combine the remaining 2 cups flour, the baking powder and salt.

4. In a medium bowl, beat the remaining 1 stick butter on high speed. Gradually add the remaining ¾ cup sugar; beat until fluffy, about 2 minutes. Add the eggs and vanilla and beat until well mixed, about 1 minute. Reduce the speed to low and add half the flour mixture, the sour cream and then the remaining flour mixture. Increase the speed to medium and beat until blended. (The batter will be very thick; do not overmix.) Fold in the chopped dates.

5. Scrape the batter into the prepared pan and smooth the top. Crumble the walnut topping evenly over the batter.

6. Bake the cake for 55 to 60 minutes, or until a toothpick inserted in the center of the cake comes out clean. Let cool in the pan for 15 minutes. Remove the sides. Serve warm or at room temperature. *(This cake can be made up to 1 day in advance. Wrap well and keep at room temperature.)*

—Mimi Ruth Brodeur

• • •

CINNAMON-CREAM CHEESE PULL-APARTS

——— *Makes 8 Rolls* ———
1 envelope (¼ ounce) active dry yeast
¼ cup lukewarm (105° to 115°) water
⅓ cup plus 1 teaspoon granulated sugar
2⅓ cups all-purpose flour
½ teaspoon salt
6 tablespoons unsalted butter, at room temperature
2 eggs—1 separated, 1 whole
1 teaspoon vanilla extract
½ cup scalded milk
⅓ cup plus 2 tablespoons (packed) dark brown sugar
1 teaspoon cinnamon
½ cup coarsely chopped pecans
3 ounces cream cheese, at room temperature
2 tablespoons confectioners' sugar
1 tablespoon boiling water

1. In a small bowl, sprinkle the yeast over the warm water. Stir in 1 teaspoon of the granulated sugar. Set aside until foamy, about 5 minutes. Meanwhile, in a medium bowl, combine the flour and salt.

2. In a large bowl, beat 4 tablespoons of the butter on high speed until creamy. Gradually beat in the remaining ⅓ cup granulated sugar. Add an egg yolk and the whole egg, beating well after each addition. Beat in the vanilla and then the yeast mixture.

3. Reduce the speed to low and beat in the flour mixture in 3 batches, alternating with the scalded milk, beginning and ending with the flour, until combined. (The dough will be very sticky.) Cover with a damp cloth and refrigerate until doubled in bulk, at least 4 hours or up to 24 hours.

4. Butter a 9-inch round cake pan. Turn the dough out onto a well-floured surface and roll the dough into an 8-by-16-inch rectangle about ¼ inch thick. Spread the remaining 2 tablespoons butter over the dough. In a small bowl, mix together ⅓ cup of the brown sugar and the cinnamon. Sprinkle the mixture evenly over the dough and sprinkle ¼ cup of the pecans over the top.

5. Starting at one of the long edges, roll up the dough to form a log. Using a knife dipped in flour, cut 8 slices, each 2 inches thick. Set the dough rounds flat, spiral-side up, in the cake pan.

6. In a small bowl, stir the cream cheese until smooth. Mix in the confectioners' sugar. Beat in the egg white until well blended.

7. Spoon about 1 tablespoon of the cream cheese mixture onto the center of each cinnamon roll and sprinkle the remaining ¼ cup pecans on top. Let the rolls rise until doubled, about 30 minutes. Preheat the oven to 375°.

8. Bake for 35 to 40 minutes, or until a toothpick inserted in the center of a roll comes out clean.

9. In a small bowl, add the boiling water to the remaining 2 tablespoons brown sugar. Stir until the sugar has dissolved. Brush the brown sugar glaze over the warm rolls. Serve warm or at room temperature.

—Mimi Ruth Brodeur

• • •

LOVEY'S BROWNIES

Mother of five (including Tracey Seaman of *Food & Wine's* test kitchen) and grandmother of seven, Mary Seaman has made hundreds of fudgy-brownie lovers happy for years with this recipe.

―――――― *Makes 35* ――――――
2 sticks (8 ounces) unsalted butter
4 ounces unsweetened chocolate, coarsely chopped
2 cups sugar
4 eggs
1 teaspoon vanilla extract
1 cup all-purpose flour
½ teaspoon salt
1 generous cup coarsely chopped walnuts or pecans (about 3 ounces)

1. Preheat the oven to 350°. Lightly grease a 13-by-9-by-2-inch metal or ceramic baking pan.

2. In a large saucepan, heat the butter over moderately low heat until half melted. Add the chocolate and stir until the butter and chocolate are completely melted and combined. Remove from the heat and stir in the sugar with a wooden spoon until incorporated.

3. Using the wooden spoon, beat in the eggs, 1 at a time, stirring after each addition until the eggs are fully incorporated and the chocolate mixture is shiny. Stir in the vanilla. Add the flour and salt all at once and mix until blended. Stir in the chopped nuts.

4. Scrape the batter into the prepared pan. Bake for 30 minutes, or until the brownies are slightly firm to the touch and a cake tester inserted in the center indicates the brownies are moist. Let cool completely in the pan. Cut into 35 bars.

—Mary Seaman

• • •

RIVER OAKS BROWNIES

Marilyn Descours, Houston pastry chef and owner of Descours Desserts, has produced a brownie recipe to satisfy any member of the cakey contingent, anywhere. "This recipe is straightforward, simple and nothing short of heavenly," she says. "I named it after Houston's most exclusive neighborhood, River Oaks, which is rich and luxurious just like these brownies."

―――――― *Makes 20* ――――――
1¼ cups unsweetened Dutch process cocoa powder, preferably Guittard (see Note)
1¼ cups all-purpose flour
½ teaspoon salt
3 sticks (12 ounces) unsalted butter
3 cups sugar
6 eggs
2 teaspoons vanilla extract
1 pound (about 3 cups) pecan pieces

1. Preheat the oven to 350°. Lightly grease a 13-by-9-by-2-inch metal baking pan and line it with parchment paper. In a

medium mixer bowl, sift together the cocoa, flour and salt. Set aside.

2. In a large saucepan, melt the butter over low heat. Remove from the heat and stir in the sugar. Add the eggs, 2 at a time, stirring after each addition. Stir in the vanilla. Add this mixture all at once to the dry ingredients and beat on low speed until combined. Add the nuts and beat on low speed until just evenly distributed.

3. Scrape the batter into the prepared pan and bake for about 50 minutes, or until a cake tester inserted in the center indicates the brownies are slightly moist (it is better to undercook than overcook). Let cool in the pan. Invert the pan to turn out the brownies. Remove and discard the parchment paper and turn the brownies right-side up. Using a serrated knife, cut into 20 bars.

NOTE: You can buy Guittard products at some specialty food markets or can order directly from Guittard Chocolate Company in Burlingame, California.

—Marilyn Descours,
Descours Desserts, Houston

• • •

LAZY LINZER SQUARES

In the classic tradition of the linzer torte, these crisp squares of almond pastry and raspberry jam are a sweet addition to any buffet all year long.

―――――― *Makes 50 Squares* ――――――
1 cup whole blanched almonds (about 4½ ounces)
¼ cup granulated sugar
1⅔ cups all-purpose flour
¼ cup confectioners' sugar
¼ teaspoon salt
⅓ cup cold unsalted butter, cut into small pieces
⅓ cup cold vegetable shortening
1 tablespoon vanilla extract
2 tablespoons ice water

1 jar (12 ounces) seedless raspberry
jam
1 cup sliced blanched almonds
(about 4½ ounces)

1. Preheat the oven to 350°. Place the whole almonds on a 10-by-15-inch jelly-roll pan and toast in the oven as it preheats for 10 minutes. Remove from the oven and let the almonds cool completely.

2. In a food processor, combine the toasted almonds and granulated sugar and process until the nuts are finely ground. Add the flour, confectioners' sugar and salt; process briefly to combine.

3. Add the butter and shortening and process to a coarse meal, about 20 seconds. Add the vanilla and 1 tablespoon plus 1 teaspoon of the ice water and continue to process until the mixture begins to form a ball, about 20 seconds longer. If the dough is not coming together at this point, add another teaspoon of ice water.

4. Transfer the dough to a work surface and form into a ball. Roll the dough between 2 sheets of waxed paper to form an 11-by-16-inch rectangle, about ¼ inch thick. Remove the top sheet of waxed paper and, pulling the bottom sheet, slide the dough onto the jelly-roll pan. Trim off any dough along the sides of the pan with a small sharp knife or a pastry wheel. Bake for 15 minutes.

5. Meanwhile, in a small saucepan melt the jam over moderately low heat.

6. Remove the pan from the oven and drizzle the hot jam over the hot pastry. Working quickly, spread the jam evenly over the surface with a pastry brush. Sprinkle the sliced almonds evenly over the jam and bake for 15 to 20 minutes longer, until the almonds are golden brown and the jam is bubbly.

7. Transfer the pan to a rack and let cool completely. Cut into fifty 2-by-1½-inch cookies. Store in a cookie tin for up to 1 week or wrap well in foil and freeze for up to 2 weeks.

—*Tracey Seaman*

• • •

HAZELNUT CHOCOLATE COOKIES

——— *Makes About 20* ———
½ cup all-purpose flour
½ teaspoon baking powder
7 tablespoons unsalted butter,
softened
¾ cup sugar
1 egg
1 teaspoon vanilla extract
2 tablespoons unsweetened Dutch
process cocoa powder
½ cup coarsely chopped hazelnuts

1. Preheat the oven to 400°. Grease a 9-inch square baking pan and line it with enough parchment paper to reach ½ inch up the sides of the pan.

2. In a small bowl, combine the flour and baking powder.

3. In a medium bowl, cream the butter with the sugar. Stir in the egg and the vanilla until blended. Sift in the cocoa powder and add the flour mixture. Stir until blended.

4. Spread the batter evenly in the prepared pan. Sprinkle the hazelnuts on top and bake for 20 minutes. While still warm, invert the pan and peel off the parchment paper. Turn right-side up and cut the cookies into 1½-inch squares. *(Once cooled, the cookies can be stored for up to 2 days in an airtight container.)*

—*Christer Larsson, Aquavit,
New York City*

• • •

SPICED ANGEL COOKIES

These delicious spice cookies are edible ornaments that can be hung on the tree, given as gifts or washed down with plenty of milk. They will keep for up to two weeks sealed in a cookie tin.

——— *Makes About 3 Dozen* ———
2 cups all-purpose flour
⅛ teaspoon salt
½ teaspoon baking soda
1 teaspoon baking powder
1 teaspoon cinnamon
1 teaspoon allspice
1 teaspoon ground ginger
1 stick (4 ounces) unsalted butter, at
room temperature
½ cup sugar
½ cup unsulphured molasses
1 egg yolk

1. In a medium bowl, whisk together the flour, salt, baking soda, baking powder, cinnamon, allspice and ginger.

2. In another medium bowl, cream the butter and sugar at high speed until fluffy, about 1 minute. Add the molasses and beat on high speed for 1 minute more. Beat in the yolk until incorporated.

3. With the mixer at low speed, beat in the flour mixture in two batches. The dough will be very stiff. Divide the dough in half and place on two large sheets of waxed paper. Flatten the dough into disks, wrap and refrigerate for at least 2 hours or overnight.

4. Preheat the oven to 350°. Remove one package of dough from the refrigerator and split in half. On a generously floured work surface, working quickly, roll one portion of the dough to between ⅛ and ¼ inch thick. (The dough tends to become sticky as it comes to room temperature.) Cut out cookies with a 3-inch angel-shaped cookie cutter.

5. With a metal spatula, transfer the angels to a large ungreased cookie sheet. Bake for about 8 minutes, until firm (but not hard) and golden brown. Be careful not to overbake. With a skewer or toothpick, make a hole in the head of each angel large enough for a string or ribbon to be pulled through. Let the cookies cool on the baking sheet for 2 minutes, then transfer them to a rack to cool completely.

6. Gather up any scraps of dough, wrap in waxed paper and chill. Repeat with the remaining cookie dough. Combine all the dough scraps; reroll, cut out and bake more cookies.

—*Tracey Seaman*

• • •

SPICY SHORTBREAD COOKIES

This spicy shortbread can be either a dessert or an unusual, lightly sweet hors d'oeuvre. Cut neatly into decorative shapes or baked in sheets and broken apart, these rich cookies go well with ice cream and fruit for dessert.

Makes About 70

2½ sticks (10 ounces) unsalted butter, softened
⅔ cup sugar
3 cups all-purpose flour
1½ tablespoons curry powder
1 teaspoon paprika
¼ teaspoon chili powder
1 teaspoon turmeric
⅓ teaspoon cayenne pepper

1. In a mixer bowl, cream the butter on medium speed. Add the sugar and continue beating until light and fluffy.

2. In another bowl, sift together the flour, curry powder, paprika, chili powder, turmeric and cayenne. Stir the dry ingredients into the butter mixture until a dough forms.

3. Preheat the oven to 325°. On a work surface, roll out the dough between two large sheets of plastic wrap to a 12-by-16-inch rectangle about ⅓ inch thick. Slide the dough onto a large cookie sheet. Freeze until firm, about 30 minutes.

4. Remove the top sheet of plastic wrap and invert the dough onto a work surface. Remove the remaining plastic. With a 1½-inch cookie cutter, cut the dough into rounds. Place the cookies back on the cookie sheet and bake for 25 to 30 minutes, until lightly golden.

5. Let the cookies cool slightly on the baking sheet, then transfer to a rack to cool completely. *(The cookies can be baked 4 to 5 days in advance and kept in an airtight container.)*

—*Paul Grimes*

• • •

LITTLE PEPPER-SPICE COOKIES

These are my version of the German pfeffernuss cookie we see around Christmastime. They are easy to make, and the aroma from the spices is heavenly.

Makes About 70

2 sticks (8 ounces) unsalted butter, softened
⅔ cup (packed) light brown sugar
1½ teaspoons finely ground black pepper
1½ teaspoons ground coriander
½ teaspoon anise seeds, finely chopped
½ teaspoon ground ginger
½ teaspoon cinnamon
½ teaspoon allspice
½ teaspoon salt
1 teaspoon vanilla extract
2 teaspoons finely grated lemon zest
2 cups all-purpose flour

1. Preheat the oven to 350°. In a large bowl, cream the butter and brown sugar. Stir in the pepper, coriander, anise, ginger, cinnamon, allspice, salt, vanilla and lemon zest. Then add the flour and mix well. Refrigerate the dough to firm up slightly, about 10 minutes.

2. By the heaping teaspoonful, roll the dough into balls. Place on ungreased cookie sheets about 1 inch apart and flatten them slightly. Freeze for about 10 minutes to set.

3. Bake the cookies for about 18 minutes, until golden brown on the bottom and firm but not hard to the touch. Let cool on the cookie sheets for about 1 minute before transferring to a rack to cool completely. Store the cookies in an airtight tin for up to 2 weeks.

—*Marcia Kiesel*

• • •

FARMERS' COOKIES

Makes About 35

1 cup plus 2 tablespoons all-purpose flour
¼ cup plus 2 tablespoons sugar
6 tablespoons unsalted butter, softened
2 tablespoons coarsely chopped almonds
1½ teaspoons molasses
½ teaspoon baking powder dissolved in 1½ teaspoons water

1. Mound the flour on a work surface and make a well in the center. Add all the remaining ingredients to the well and work them together with your fingers. Beginning at the inside of the well, gradually work in all the flour until a dough forms. Roll the dough into a log about 1½ inches in diameter. Cover and refrigerate until firm, at least 1 hour.

2. Preheat the oven to 400°. Slice the cookies ⅛ inch thick and place on greased

cookie sheets. Bake for about 12 minutes, until lightly golden. Transfer to a rack to cool. *(The cookies can be stored in an airtight container for up to 2 days.)*
—*Christer Larsson, Aquavit, New York City*

• • •

GIANT ANISE SUGAR COOKIES

———— *Makes 16 Cookies* ————
1¾ cups all-purpose flour
½ teaspoon baking soda
½ teaspoon salt
2 teaspoons anise seeds
1 cup sugar
*1 stick (4 ounces) unsalted butter,
    softened*
1 whole egg plus 1 egg yolk
1 teaspoon vanilla extract

1. In a medium bowl, sift together the flour, baking soda and salt; set aside. In a spice grinder or using a mortar and pestle, grind the anise seeds and ¼ cup of the sugar to a powder.

2. In a large bowl, using an electric mixer, beat the butter, anise sugar and ½ cup of the remaining sugar until thick and pale. Beat in the whole egg, egg yolk and vanilla until light and fluffy. Gradually stir in the flour mixture until a dough forms. Wrap in plastic wrap and chill until firm, at least 2 hours.

3. Preheat the oven to 350°. Grease 2 large cookie sheets. Pour the remaining ¼ cup sugar into a shallow dish. Divide the dough into 16 equal pieces and roll into 1½-inch balls. Dredge in the sugar, turning to coat well. Place the cookies on the cookie sheets about 3 inches apart.

4. Bake in the middle of the oven for 18 to 20 minutes, or until the tops of the cookies are very lightly browned and crinkled. Transfer the cookies to a rack to cool. *(The cookies will keep for up to 4 days stored in an airtight container.)*
—*Melanie Barnard & Brooke Dojny*

• • •

ESPRESSO DROPS

These are very sweet, so serve them with something tart like sherbet or berries.

———— *Makes About 7 Dozen* ————
2½ cups sifted all-purpose flour
1 teaspoon baking soda
½ teaspoon cream of tartar
*2 heaping tablespoons instant
    espresso powder*
*2 sticks (8 ounces) unsalted butter,
    softened*
1 cup sugar
3 egg yolks
½ teaspoon vanilla extract

1. Preheat the oven to 350°. Lightly grease 2 cookie sheets. In a medium bowl, sift together the flour, baking soda, cream of tartar and instant espresso.

2. In a large mixer bowl, cream together the butter and sugar on high speed until light and fluffy, about 5 minutes. Beat in the egg yolks and vanilla until incorporated.

3. Add the flour mixture to the butter mixture in batches on low speed, mixing well after each addition.

4. Drop the dough by rounded teaspoons 2 inches apart onto the cookie sheets. Bake, one sheet at a time, for 13 minutes, or until the drops have risen and are lightly golden. Let cool about 1 minute before removing to a rack. *(These can be stored in an airtight tin for up to 1 week.)*
—*Lee Bailey*

• • •

DESSERTS

MASCARPONE CREAM DESSERT

This dessert improves when made one or two days ahead and all the flavors have time to blend in the refrigerator. You can vary the recipe by adding a little melted chocolate instead of coffee and by decorating it with grated chocolate or, in summer, raspberries. Because the filling is very soft and creamy, this may require a spoon for serving.

 A small glass of Tuscany's dessert wine specialty, *vin santo*, such as Badia a Coltibuono or Brolio would add an authentic flourish to the dessert course.

────── *12 Servings* ──────

6 egg yolks
1 cup sugar
1¼ cups dry Marsala
2 tablespoons instant coffee, dissolved in 1 teaspoon of hot water
3 cups mascarpone cheese (about 1½ pounds)
12 ounces ladyfingers (see Note)
¼ cup chocolate-covered coffee beans, for garnish (about 2 ounces)

1. In a large saucepan, bring 3 inches of water to a boil over moderate heat.

2. In a medium stainless steel bowl, whisk the egg yolks with the sugar until light in color, about 2 minutes. Whisk in 1 cup of the Marsala. Set the bowl over, but not touching, the boiling water. Whisk constantly, cook until the egg mixture becomes creamy and foamy and doubles in volume, about 4 minutes. (The mixture should reach a temperature of 160°.)

3. Remove the bowl from the heat. Stir in the dissolved coffee and the mascarpone cheese; mix gently but thoroughly until blended. Set aside.

4. Line the bottom of a 10-inch springform pan with a circle of parchment or waxed paper. Lightly brush both sides of the ladyfingers with the remaining ¼ cup Marsala. Arrange the ladyfingers,

smooth-side up, in a daisy petal pattern on the bottom of the springform pan, being careful not to leave any empty spaces.

5. Cut the remaining ladyfingers in half crosswise and stand them, cut-sides down and smooth-side in, all around the insides of the springform to completely line it. Pour in the cooled mascarpone cream. Cover with plastic wrap and chill until set, at least 8 hours but preferably for one to two days.

6. To serve, trim the tops of the ladyfingers so that they are flush with the mascarpone cream mixture. Invert onto a serving platter; remove the sides and bottom of the springform pan and the parchment paper. Decorate with the coffee beans and serve.

NOTE: Ladyfingers vary in size so be sure to buy enough to completely line the bottom and sides of the pan.

—*Lorenza de' Medici*

• • •

MOCHA CREME BRULEE

────── *6 Servings* ──────

2 cups heavy cream
2 teaspoons instant espresso
6 egg yolks
1 teaspoon vanilla extract
1½ cups sugar

1. Preheat the oven to 350°. In a medium saucepan, combine the cream with the instant espresso. Cook over low heat, stirring occasionally, until the mixture is hot and the coffee is dissolved, 3 to 5 minutes. Remove from the heat.

2. In a medium bowl, whisk together the egg yolks, vanilla and ½ cup of the sugar. Beat until pale and fluffy, about 5 minutes. Whisk in the warm coffee cream

until thoroughly blended. Strain the mixture through a fine sieve and ladle into six 4-ounce ramekins.

3. Place the ramekins in a baking dish and pour in enough boiling water to reach 1 inch up the sides of the ramekins. Cover the custards with a sheet of parchment paper and place the baking dish in the oven. Bake for 25 minutes, or until the custards are just set but still wobbly; do not overcook.

4. Remove the baking dish from the oven and set the ramekins on a rack to cool completely. Refrigerate until cold, about 1 hour.

5. In a small heavy pan, combine the remaining 1 cup sugar with ¼ cup of water. Cook over moderate heat, without stirring, until the caramel is amber colored, about 12 minutes. (This will happen very fast once it begins to darken. Do not let it burn.)

6. Drizzle just enough of the hot caramel over each custard to cover the top. Refrigerate until serving time.

—*Perla Meyers*

• • •

CUSTARD WITH APPLES AND ALMONDS

────── *6 Servings* ──────

5 tablespoons unsalted butter
1 tablespoon sugar
2 cups milk
2 tablespoons honey
4 eggs
¼ cup sliced almonds
¼ cup (firmly packed) light brown sugar
2 Granny Smith or Golden Delicious apples—peeled, quartered and very thinly sliced crosswise
1 tablespoon Calvados or apple brandy

1. Preheat the oven to 300°. Cut 2 tablespoons of the butter into 6 pieces

and place one piece in each of six ½-cup custard cups or ramekins. Sprinkle ½ teaspoon of the sugar into each cup. Place the cups in a 9-by-13-inch roasting pan or baking dish and fill the pan with enough hot water to reach halfway up the sides of the ramekins. Transfer the pan to the preheated oven. Let sit 6 to 7 minutes, or until the butter is melted.

2. Meanwhile, in a small saucepan, scald the milk over moderate heat, about 5 minutes. Remove from the heat and stir in the honey. Crack the eggs into a medium bowl and whisk briefly. Slowly whisk the hot milk into the eggs.

3. Remove the baking dish from the oven and pour the milk mixture into the ramekins. Return to the oven and cook 30 to 35 minutes, or until lightly brown on top and firm but still wobbly. Let cool completely. *(The custards can be prepared to this point up to 1 day ahead. Cover and refrigerate overnight. Let sit at room temperature 1 hour before serving.)*

4. In a medium nonreactive skillet, cook the almonds over moderate heat, stirring occasionally, until lightly toasted, about 3 minutes. Transfer the almonds to a plate to cool.

5. Increase the heat to moderately high and melt the remaining 3 tablespoons butter in the skillet. Add the brown sugar and cook, stirring, until bubbly and caramelized, 4 to 5 minutes.

6. Add the apples and cook, stirring, until the apples are crisp-tender and the sauce is syrupy, about 5 minutes. Add the Calvados and let simmer for 2 minutes. *(The apples can be prepared to this point up to 2 hours ahead. Let cool. Reheat before serving.)*

7. To serve, unmold the custards onto individual plates. Spoon about 2½ tablespoons of the warm apples and sauce over each serving and sprinkle with the toasted almonds. Serve immediately.

—*Lee Bailey*

• • •

FRENCH BREAD PUDDING WITH WHISKEY SAUCE

Here is the Commander's Palace version of a revered New Orleans dessert. Rich and decadent, it will probably yield some leftover portions.

——————*6 to 8 Servings*——————
1 stick (4 ounces) unsalted butter, softened
1 cup sugar
5 eggs, lightly beaten
2 cups heavy cream
1 tablespoon vanilla extract
Dash of cinnamon
¼ cup raisins
12 slices of fresh or stale French bread, cut 1 inch thick
Whiskey Sauce (recipe follows)

1. Preheat the oven to 350°. In a large mixer bowl, beat together the butter and sugar until creamy. Add the eggs, cream, vanilla and cinnamon and beat until thoroughly combined. Stir in the raisins. Pour the mixture into a 9-inch square baking pan.

2. Place the bread slices flat in the pan and let stand for 5 minutes to soak up some of the liquid. Turn the bread over and let stand for 10 minutes longer. Then push the bread down so that most of it is submerged. Don't break up the slices.

3. Set the pan in a larger pan and pour in enough water to reach within ½ inch of the top of the inner pan. Cover with aluminum foil and bake for 35 minutes. Uncover the pudding and bake for 10 minutes longer, until the top is browned and the pudding is still soft.

4. Spoon the pudding onto plates and pass the Whiskey Sauce separately.

—*Commander's Palace, New Orleans*

• • •

WHISKEY SAUCE

At Commander's Palace, this sauce is served slightly warm.

——————*Makes About 1½ Cups*——————
½ teaspoon cornstarch
1 cup heavy cream
1 cup sugar
Pinch of cinnamon
1 tablespoon unsalted butter
1 tablespoon bourbon or other whiskey

1. In a small bowl, dissolve the cornstarch in ¼ cup of water.

2. In a medium saucepan, combine the cream, sugar, cinnamon and butter. Bring to a boil over high heat and cook, stirring frequently to dissolve the sugar, about 3 minutes.

3. Stir in the cornstarch mixture and cook until the sauce thickens slightly, about 3 minutes. Remove from the heat and stir in the bourbon.

—*Commander's Palace, New Orleans*

• • •

APPLE BREAD PUDDING

My Aunt Bert recently unearthed what she calls Grandma's "real" recipe for apple cake. With it came a warning that the dough is tricky, the results only intermittently successful and the whole likely to bring a baker to tears. I followed her recipe, neither crying nor screaming from frustration as predicted, but I produced a cake that didn't live up to my recollection. Opting to keep the memory and forgo exact replication, I devised a dependable, warm, satisfying dessert that fills my house with a smell as sweet as Granny's cake. I sauté apples in butter and sugar until they are caramelized, give them a splash of Calvados and a pinch of cinnamon, then add a small handful of raisins to make a filling for a rich bread pudding. For breakfast, as an after-dinner dessert or a late-night snack, this is the kind of food for which the term comfort was coined.

--------- **6 Servings** ---------
3 tart apples, such as Granny Smith
*   —peeled, quartered and thinly*
*   sliced*
2 teaspoons fresh lemon juice
3 tablespoons unsalted butter
¾ cup plus 2½ tablespoons sugar
1 tablespoon Calvados or apple
*   brandy*
½ cup raisins or dried currants
¾-pound loaf of sweet egg bread,
*   such as challah or brioche, crusts*
*   removed, sliced ¼ inch thick*
3 cups milk
1 cup heavy cream
3 whole eggs, at room temperature
3 egg yolks, at room temperature
1½ teaspoons cinnamon
1½ teaspoons vanilla extract

1. In a medium bowl, toss the apples with the lemon juice. In a heavy skillet, melt 2½ tablespoons of the butter over moderately high heat. Add the apples and sauté, shaking the pan and turning the apples frequently, until beginning to brown, about 5 minutes.

2. Sprinkle 2½ tablespoons of the sugar over the apples and cook, turning the apples until lightly caramelized, about 4 minutes. Add the Calvados and cook for 1 minute longer. Remove from the heat and set aside.

3. Preheat the oven to 400°. Use the remaining ½ tablespoon butter to grease a shallow baking dish (an 8-by-14-inch oval gratin dish is best, but a standard 7-by-11-inch rectangular pan is fine).

4. Sprinkle half the raisins over the bottom of the buttered baking dish. Lay slices of bread around the sides of the pan, overlapping them slightly. If the bread slices are large, cut them in half. Fill in the center of the pan with half the remaining bread slices. Sprinkle with the remaining raisins, spoon on the caramelized apples and lay the remaining bread slices on top.

5. In a medium saucepan, combine the milk, cream and the remaining ¾ cup sugar. Cook over moderate heat, stirring, until the sugar is dissolved and the milk is hot, about 3 minutes.

6. Meanwhile, in a large bowl, whisk together the whole eggs, egg yolks and cinnamon until blended. Gradually whisk in the hot milk mixture. Whisk in the vanilla and pour the hot custard evenly over the bread to moisten it completely.

7. Set the baking dish in a large roasting pan and place in the middle of the oven. Add enough warm water to the pan to reach three-quarters of the way up the sides of the baking dish. Bake for 30 to 35 minutes, until the top of the pudding is puffed and golden and a knife inserted in the center comes out clean. If you prefer a darker top, sprinkle on a bit more sugar and place under a preheated broiler for about 30 seconds; watch carefully so it does not burn. Serve warm, at room temperature or chilled.

—*Dorie Greenspan*

• • •

ODEON'S TRIPLE CHOCOLATE PUDDING

Stephen Lyle, executive chef at New York City's Odeon restaurant, makes this pudding with semisweet chocolate, unsweetened chocolate and cocoa. Be sure to allow plenty of time to let the pudding chill in the refrigerator. You can gild the lily by topping each serving with a little unsweetened whipped cream.

--------- **12 Servings** ---------
6 cups milk
1 vanilla bean, split
6 ounces imported semisweet
*   chocolate, preferably Callebaut*
6 ounces unsweetened chocolate
1 stick (4 ounces) unsalted butter
4 whole eggs
8 egg yolks
2 cups sugar
1 cup unsweetened Dutch process
*   cocoa powder, preferably Droste*
2 cups heavy cream
1 tablespoon cornstarch

1. In a large saucepan, combine the milk and vanilla bean and bring to a boil over moderate heat, about 15 minutes.

2. Meanwhile, in a double boiler, combine the semisweet and unsweetened chocolates with the butter. Melt over simmering water, stirring occasionally, until smooth, about 8 minutes. Remove from the heat and set aside.

3. In a large heatproof bowl, whisk the whole eggs, egg yolks and sugar until well blended. Remove the vanilla bean from the milk and scrape the seeds into the egg mixture; discard the bean. Gradually add the hot milk to the egg mixture and whisk until well blended.

4. Place the bowl over a large saucepan of simmering water and cook over moderate heat, stirring constantly with a wooden spoon, until the custard reaches 175° on a candy thermometer and thinly coats the back of the spoon, 16 to 18 minutes.

5. Remove from the heat and gradually whisk in the reserved melted chocolate. Sift the cocoa powder over the custard and whisk in until fully incorporated.

6. In a medium saucepan, using a small whisk, combine the cream and cornstarch and bring to a boil, stirring, over moderately high heat. Cook until thickened slightly, about 2 minutes. Vigorously whisk the cream into the chocolate custard until blended.

7. Let the pudding cool slightly, stirring occasionally to prevent a skin from forming, about 10 minutes. Pour the mixture into parfait glasses, brandy snifters or ramekins and let cool completely. Refrigerate for at least 6 hours before serving. *(The pudding can be prepared up to 3 days ahead.)*
—*Stephen Lyle, Odeon, New York City*

• • •

RICOTTA PUDDING

This luscious pudding should be made before dinner because it needs some time to chill in the refrigerator.

———— *4 Servings* ————
1 container (15 ounces) whole-milk
  or part-skim ricotta cheese
1/3 cup heavy cream
1/2 cup confectioners' sugar
1 teaspoon grated orange zest
1/4 teaspoon vanilla extract
Grated nutmeg or cinnamon, for
  garnish

In a food processor, combine the ricotta, cream, confectioners' sugar, orange zest and vanilla and process until smooth and creamy. Spoon the mixture into bowls or wineglasses and chill for about 30 minutes or up to 4 hours. Sprinkle a pinch of nutmeg or cinnamon over each pudding and serve cold.
—*Marie Simmons*

• • •

TAPIOCA-APPLE PUDDING

I think tapioca is nostalgic food. People talk about it, but nobody ever makes it. Every time we have it on the menu, though, it sells out. I think people miss it. Tapioca is so easy to work with and so easy to eat—it's the perfect food for kids. They love its soft, gooey texture.

To create different puddings, use this recipe as a master and substitute pear, banana, apricot or any other fruit puree.

———— *Makes About 1 1/2 Cups* ————
2 tablespoons pearl tapioca
1 cup milk
1 egg yolk
1/2 cup Smooth Applesauce (p. 213)

1. In a small heavy saucepan, stir together the tapioca and milk. Cover with plastic wrap and refrigerate for 2 hours to soften the tapioca.

2. Bring the mixture to a boil over moderate heat. Reduce the heat to moderately low and simmer, stirring frequently, until the tapioca is completely translucent but still firm, about 10 minutes.

3. Meanwhile, in a small bowl, mix the egg yolk and Smooth Applesauce until blended. Stir the applesauce mixture into the tapioca and cook over low heat, stirring constantly, until thickened, about 2 minutes. Pour the pudding into small cups or a bowl and refrigerate until cold.
—*Jasper White, Jasper's, Boston*

• • •

LEMON-BLUEBERRY MOUSSE

———— *6 Servings* ————
3 whole eggs
3 egg yolks
1 cup sugar
1 tablespoon grated lemon zest
1/2 cup fresh lemon juice
1/8 teaspoon salt
4 tablespoons unsalted butter,
  melted
1 cup heavy cream
1 1/2 cups fresh blueberries

1. In a medium nonreactive saucepan, whisk together the whole eggs, egg yolks and sugar until thick and lemon colored, about 2 minutes. Whisk in the lemon zest, lemon juice, salt and melted butter.

2. Cook over moderately low heat, stirring constantly, until the custard is thick enough to coat the back of a spoon, 6 to 8 minutes. Do not boil.

3. Strain the custard into a bowl and let cool slightly. Cover and refrigerate until well chilled, about 1 hour. *(The recipe can be prepared up to 1 week ahead.)*

4. In a chilled bowl, beat the cream until soft peaks form. Reserve 1/2 cup of the whipped cream for garnish. Stir a quarter of the remaining whipped cream into the cold lemon custard to lighten it, then fold in the remainder.

5. Reserve 18 blueberries for garnish. Fold the remaining berries into the lemon mousse. Spoon the mousse into 6 dessert glasses or wineglasses. Garnish with a dollop of the reserved 1/2 cup whipped cream and sprinkle 3 blueberries over the top of each serving.
—*Melanie Barnard & Brooke Dojny*

• • •

DESSERTS

CHOCOLATE ORANGE MOUSSE

The orange zest contributes a surprising amount of flavor to this mousse. Of course you can omit it if you prefer a simple chocolate taste. Cooking the egg yolks and egg whites makes this a light but stable mousse that can be made up to two days ahead.

───────── *8 to 10 Servings* ─────────
12 ounces imported extra-
    bittersweet chocolate, such as
    Tobler, broken into pieces
1½ cups milk
4 egg yolks
Finely grated zest of 1 orange
½ cup sugar
6 egg whites
1 cup heavy cream, chilled
Chocolate shavings, for garnish

1. Place the chocolate pieces in a food processor and pulse until finely ground, about 20 seconds. Leave the chocolate in the bowl.

2. In a heavy medium saucepan, combine the milk, egg yolks and orange zest. Cook over moderate heat, whisking constantly, until slightly thickened, about 5 minutes; do not let the custard boil. Strain immediately into a pitcher.

3. With the food processor running, pour the hot custard into the chocolate in the bowl; a smooth mixture will form almost at once. Stop the machine and scrape the chocolate mixture into a large bowl.

4. In a small heavy saucepan, combine the sugar and ¼ cup of water. Bring to a boil over moderate heat, stirring occasionally to dissolve the sugar. With a wet brush, wash down any sugar crystals from the sides of the pan. Cook without stirring until the syrup registers 235° on a candy thermometer, about 10 minutes.

5. Meanwhile, place the egg whites in a large heatproof bowl and beat with an electric mixer until soft peaks form. Carefully add the boiling sugar syrup in a thin, steady stream, beating constantly as you pour. Continue to beat the whites at high speed until stiff, glossy peaks form when the beaters are lifted, about 2 minutes.

6. With a large whisk or a spatula, gently fold one-fourth of the egg whites into the chocolate mixture until no white streaks remain. Repeat with the remaining egg whites. Refrigerate the mixture until cool, about 15 minutes.

7. In a medium bowl, beat the cream until stiff. Fold the whipped cream into the cooled chocolate mixture and pour the mousse into a large serving bowl. Cover with plastic wrap and refrigerate until chilled, about 4 hours, or for up to 2 days. Garnish with chocolate shavings before serving.

—*Diana Sturgis*

• • •

GATEAU VICTOIRE

This airy concoction is a specialty of San Francisco's Zuni Cafe, a restaurant known for flavorful and robust California-Mediterranean cuisine. More chocolate mousse than cake, the Gâteau Victoire is the best of both worlds.

─── *Makes One 9-Inch Round Cake* ───
12 ounces semisweet chocolate,
    preferably Guittard French
    Vanilla
⅓ cup plus 1 tablespoon strong
    brewed coffee
4 whole eggs
2 egg yolks
⅓ cup granulated sugar
¾ cup plus 4 teaspoons heavy cream
Confectioners' sugar, for garnish
Lightly sweetened whipped cream

1. Preheat the oven to 400°. Butter a 9-by-2-inch round cake pan and line the bottom with waxed paper. Set aside.

2. Chop the chocolate into 1½- to 2-inch pieces. In a double boiler, melt the chocolate with the coffee over simmering water, stirring until completely smooth, about 8 minutes. Turn off the heat and leave the melted chocolate over hot water, covered, to keep warm.

3. In a large metal bowl set over a saucepan of simmering water, whisk together the eggs, egg yolks and granulated sugar. Cook, whisking constantly to prevent the eggs from setting on the bottom, until the mixture is quite warm and thickened, about 4 minutes. Remove the bowl from the heat and, using a hand-held electric mixer, beat the mixture at high speed until cool and very fluffy and thick, about 6 minutes.

4. In a medium bowl, whip the cream at high speed until it just holds its shape.

5. In 3 batches, fold the cooked egg mixture into the warm melted chocolate. (It is not necessary to incorporate each addition completely.) In 2 batches, fold the cream into the chocolate-egg mixture. Pour the batter into the prepared pan.

6. Place the cake pan in a large roasting pan and pour in enough boiling water to come halfway up the sides of the cake pan. Bake in the oven for 25 minutes, or until crusty on top and firm to the touch. Remove from the oven and let cool in the pan for 30 minutes. While still slightly warm, invert onto a serving platter. Dust with confectioners' sugar just before serving. Pass the whipped cream separately.

—*Julia Cookenboo,*
Zuni Cafe, San Francisco

• • •

TRIO OF CHOCOLATE DESSERTS: CHOCOLATE SOUFFLE CREPES, CHOCOLATE SORBET AND CHOCOLATE WAFERS

This dazzling dessert from Rick Katz, the pastry chef at Biba restaurant in Boston, is actually a triple threat. An orange-scented crêpe filled with a dense chocolate soufflé is served with a deep, intense chocolate sorbet and crisp, rich chocolate wafers. Each component is wonderful on its own, but together they provide a dynamic contrast of temperature, texture and taste.

——————— *8 Servings* ———————
Chocolate Soufflé Crêpes (recipe follows)
Chocolate Wafers (p. 216)
Chocolate Sorbet (p. 209)
Lightly whipped cream, for serving
Fresh mint sprigs, for garnish

To assemble the dessert, transfer the hot crêpes to 8 large serving plates. Prop 2 chocolate wafers against each crêpe and place a scoop of chocolate sorbet on the plate, using the wafers as a wall between the warm crêpe and the cold sorbet. Place a dollop of the whipped cream next to the sorbet. Garnish with a sprig of mint, if desired, and serve immediately.

—*Rick Katz, Biba, Boston*

• • •

CHOCOLATE SOUFFLE CREPES

——————— *Makes About 8 Crêpes* ———————
6 teaspoons flour
¼ teaspoon salt
½ cup plus 2½ tablespoons sugar, plus more for sprinkling
1 whole egg
1 egg yolk
¼ cup plus 3 tablespoons milk
2 tablespoons unsalted butter, melted
1 tablespoon orange liqueur
8 ounces semisweet chocolate, preferably Valrhona Carraque, coarsely chopped
3 egg whites

1. In a medium bowl, sift together the flour, salt and 1½ teaspoons of the sugar. Make a well in the center and add the whole egg, egg yolk and 1 tablespoon of the milk; whisk until smooth. Gradually whisk in the remaining 6 tablespoons milk, followed by the melted butter and the liqueur. Cover and refrigerate for 30 minutes. *(The recipe can be made to this point 1 day ahead.)* Whisk to blend before cooking.

2. Heat a 6-inch nonstick crêpe pan over moderately high heat. Spoon about 1½ tablespoons of the batter into the pan and rotate at a tilt to evenly coat the bottom of the pan with the batter. Cook until the edges are lightly browned, about 1 minute. Flip the crêpe over with a spatula and cook on the other side, about 30 seconds more. Transfer the crêpe to a sheet of waxed paper. When cooled slightly, sprinkle the crêpes lightly with sugar. Continue making crêpes with the remaining batter, stacking the finished crêpes. *(The crêpes can be made to this point and kept, wrapped, in the refrigerator overnight or frozen for up to 1 week.)*

3. Preheat the oven to 400°. In a medium bowl over simmering water, heat the chocolate until melted, about 3 minutes. Remove from the heat; stir until smooth.

4. In a medium mixer bowl, beat the egg whites at high speed until soft peaks form. Sprinkle in the remaining ½ cup plus 2 tablespoons sugar and continue beating until stiff peaks form.

5. Using a rubber spatula, fold half of the beaten egg whites into the melted chocolate. Fold in the remaining whites.

6. Lightly grease a heavy baking sheet. On a work surface, spoon about 2 tablespoons of the chocolate mixture into the center of each crêpe and fold over to form half-moons. Transfer the filled crêpes carefully to the baking sheet. Bake for 7 minutes, until slightly puffed. Serve hot.

—*Rick Katz, Biba, Boston*

• • •

INDIVIDUAL BITTERSWEET CHOCOLATE SOUFFLES

These chocolate soufflés seem to be indestructible. They always rise, and they can even be prepared a day ahead. If soufflés normally scare you, I urge you to throw caution to the wind and try these.

——————— *8 Servings* ———————
8 ounces semisweet chocolate, preferably Ghirardelli Bittersweet, chopped
1 tablespoon unsalted butter
1 tablespoon all-purpose flour
½ cup milk
3 egg yolks
1 teaspoon vanilla extract
4 egg whites
⅛ teaspoon cream of tartar
¼ cup granulated sugar
Confectioners' sugar, for dusting
Lightly sweetened whipped cream, for serving

1. Preheat the oven to 375°. Lightly butter eight 6-ounce ramekins and dust well with granulated sugar. Place on a baking sheet and set aside.

2. In a double boiler over barely simmering water, melt the chocolate, stirring occasionally, until smooth. (Or melt in a microwave at 50 percent power for about 3 minutes and 30 seconds. Stir until smooth.) Remove from the heat.

3. Meanwhile, in a small saucepan, melt the butter over moderate heat. Stir in the flour and cook until thickened but not browned, 1 to 2 minutes. Add the milk and whisk briskly until smooth and thick, about 3 minutes.

4. Remove from the heat, add the melted chocolate and whisk until smooth. Whisk in the egg yolks and vanilla and set aside.

5. In a medium bowl, beat the egg whites and cream of tartar at medium speed until soft peaks form, about 1 minute. Gradually sprinkle the ¼ cup granulated sugar on top and beat at high speed until the whites are stiff but not dry.

6. Using a rubber spatula, fold one-fourth of the whites into the chocolate mixture to lighten it, then fold in the remaining whites. Spoon the mixture into the prepared ramekins, filling them about three-fourths full. *(The soufflés can be prepared to this point up to 1 day ahead. Cover and refrigerate.)*

7. Bake the soufflés for 15 to 17 minutes, until puffed and slightly cracked and a tester inserted in the center indicates the soufflé is moist but not runny. Dust the soufflés with confectioners' sugar and serve immediately in their ramekins with the whipped cream.

—*Alice Medrich, Cocolat, San Francisco*

• • •

CHOCOLATE CREAM NAPOLEON WITH HOT CHOCOLATE SAUCE

Phyllo dough, rather than the traditional puff pastry, gives this napoleon its crisp, light layers. Filled with a delicate chocolate custard, this is an easy, contemporary dessert with a French accent.

———— *4 Servings* ————

1 cup milk
2½ cups heavy cream
1 cup granulated sugar
2 tablespoons unsweetened Dutch process cocoa powder, preferably Droste
2 vanilla beans, split
9 egg yolks
½ cup ground almonds
8 sheets phyllo dough (see Note)
1 stick (4 ounces) unsalted butter, melted and kept warm
⅓ cup confectioners' sugar
4 ounces semisweet chocolate, preferably Callebaut, coarsely chopped
2 tablespoons orange liqueur

1. Preheat the oven to 325°. In a large saucepan, whisk together the milk, 2 cups of the cream, ¾ cup of the granulated sugar and the cocoa. Add the vanilla beans and bring to a boil over moderately high heat, whisking. Remove from the heat and set aside to steep for 30 minutes.

2. Remove the vanilla beans and scrape the seeds into the cream mixture with a small knife. Add the egg yolks, whisking until thoroughly incorporated.

3. Strain the custard mixture into a 9-by-13-inch glass baking dish. Set in a large roasting pan and pour in enough warm water to come halfway up the sides of the baking dish. Bake for 1 hour, or until set; a knife inserted should come out clean. Remove the custard from the water bath, cool to room temperature and refrigerate, covered, for at least 2 hours or overnight.

4. Preheat the oven to 350°. In a small bowl, combine the remaining ¼ cup granulated sugar with the ground almonds.

5. On a work surface, using a pastry brush, lightly but thoroughly brush 1 sheet of the phyllo with some of the warm melted butter. Sprinkle a generous 2 tablespoons of the sugar and almond mixture on top. Repeat with the next 2 sheets of the dough and cover with a fourth sheet. Lightly press with the palms of your hands to seal. With a sharp knife or a pastry wheel, cut the phyllo into six 3½-inch squares, discarding the trimmings.

6. Using a large metal spatula, carefully transfer the squares to a baking sheet lined with waxed paper or parchment. Repeat with the remaining phyllo, butter and almond mixture to make a total of 12 pastry squares.

7. Bake the pastries for 10 to 12 minutes or until lightly browned. *(The pastries can be made to this point 3 days ahead; store in a tightly sealed tin or container.)* Sift the confectioners' sugar over the top of each pastry. Place under a preheated broiler for a few seconds to glaze until golden brown.

8. In a heavy medium saucepan, melt the chocolate with the remaining ½ cup cream and orange liqueur over low heat, stirring until smooth. Set aside.

9. Place a pastry square in the center of each dessert plate. Using a sharp knife, cut the chilled chocolate custard into 3½-inch squares. With a metal spatula, transfer each custard to the top of each pastry square. Top with another layer of pastry, followed by another layer of custard. Finish with a final layer of pastry. Rewarm the chocolate sauce, if necessary, and pour over the napoleons before serving.

NOTE: When working with phyllo dough, keep the leaves covered with a damp towel or plastic wrap to prevent drying and cracking.

—*Michel Richard, Citrus, Los Angeles*

• • •

WHITE CHOCOLATE LASAGNA WITH PEANUT ICE CREAM AND HOT FUDGE SAUCE

Known for introducing restaurant goers to white chocolate ravioli several years ago, The Rattlesnake Club's chef-owner Jimmy Schmidt has now moved on to lasagna. Detroit diners always have several chocolate masterpieces to choose from on the menu, but none more whimsical than this. White chocolate is surprisingly easy to work with, and the results are dazzling.

———— *4 Servings* ————

3½ cups half-and-half or light cream
8 egg yolks
1¾ cups sugar
Pinch of salt
2 teaspoons vanilla extract
½ cup smooth peanut butter
½ cup heavy cream
1 cup coarsely chopped, unsalted dry-roasted peanuts (about 5 ounces)
Three 3-ounce bars imported white chocolate, preferably Lindt, broken in half widthwise
16 ounces extra-bittersweet chocolate, preferably Tobler
2 sticks (8 ounces) unsalted butter
1 cup evaporated milk
2 to 3 teaspoons strong coffee (optional)
Mint sprigs, for garnish

1. In a medium saucepan, scald the half-and-half over moderate heat; set aside. In a medium bowl whisk together the egg yolks, ¾ cup of the sugar, the salt and 1 teaspoon of the vanilla. Gradually whisk in the half-and-half, then transfer the custard mixture to the saucepan.

2. Cook the custard mixture, stirring constantly with a wooden spoon, over moderate heat until just thick enough to coat the back of the spoon (165° on a candy thermometer), about 12 minutes. Do not allow to boil or the custard will curdle.

3. Remove from the heat and whisk in the peanut butter until combined, then add the heavy cream. Strain the custard into a medium bowl and refrigerate, stirring occasionally, until well chilled. Meanwhile, line a 10-by-15-inch jelly-roll pan with waxed or parchment paper.

4. Transfer the custard to an ice cream mixer and freeze according to the manufacturer's instructions until thickened but still pourable. Add the chopped peanuts. Pour into the prepared jelly-roll pan, cover and freeze overnight.

5. In a small saucepan, whisk together the remaining 1 cup sugar with 1 cup of water. Bring to a boil over moderately high heat to dissolve the sugar, remove from the heat and set the sugar syrup aside.

6. Preheat the oven on the lowest setting for 5 minutes, then turn it off. Place the 6 pieces of white chocolate on a large baking sheet lined with waxed paper or parchment. Place in the warm oven until soft enough to yield when pressed with a finger, about 6 minutes.

7. Using a metal spatula, transfer a piece of softened chocolate to an individual sheet of waxed or parchment paper (at least 12 inches long) and cover with a second sheet of paper. Using a large heavy rolling pin, gently roll the chocolate between the pieces of paper to form a thin sheet of chocolate, about 11 by 4 inches. Set each sheet of chocolate aside to firm up while you roll the remaining pieces of chocolate.

8. Line 3 baking sheets with waxed or parchment paper. When the white chocolate is cooled and firm, remove the top piece of paper from each white chocolate sheet. With a pizza cutter, pastry wheel or long sharp knife, trim the edges of each sheet to make a neat 3-by-10-inch rectangle. Cut the rectangle crosswise to form two 3-by-5-inch rectangles. Transfer 4 rectangles to each of the prepared baking sheets. Keep cool until ready to use.

9. In a double boiler over simmering water, melt the bittersweet chocolate with the butter, stirring until smooth. Transfer to a medium bowl. Whisk in 1 cup of the reserved sugar syrup, discarding any extra. Stir in the evaporated milk and the remaining 1 teaspoon vanilla. Thin the fudge sauce with the strong coffee if desired. Set aside, covered. *(The sauce can be made up to 1 week ahead and kept covered in the refrigerator.)*

10. With a pizza cutter or thin sharp knife, cut the ice cream into ten 3-by-5-inch rectangles. (You will have 2 extras that you can save for another use.) Using a spatula, place a rectangle of ice cream on each of 4 rectangles of white chocolate. Top each with another layer of white chocolate, then another layer of ice cream. Finish with a rectangle of white chocolate on the top. Return to the freezer for up to 3 to 4 hours.

11. To serve, remove the assembled lasagnas from the freezer and allow to soften slightly at room temperature, about 5 minutes.

12. Gently reheat the fudge sauce in the top of a double boiler. Transfer each of the 4 portions of the lasagna to individual serving plates and spoon hot fudge sauce on top. Garnish with fresh mint leaves and serve immediately.

—*Jimmy Schmidt, The Rattlesnake Club*

• • •

GHIRARDELLI'S CHOCOLATE ICE CREAM

This recipe comes direct from the Ghirardelli Chocolate Company of California. It is a silken, creamy chocolate ice cream with a delicate chocolate taste.

——— *Makes About 1½ Quarts* ———
4 ounces bittersweet chocolate, preferably Ghirardelli, chopped
2 cups half-and-half or light cream
¾ cup sugar
2 tablespoons flour
¼ teaspoon salt
3 eggs
1½ cups heavy cream
1½ teaspoons vanilla extract

1. In a heavy medium saucepan, combine the chocolate and half-and-half. Cook over moderate heat, whisking occasionally, until the chocolate is melted and the mixture is smooth, about 5 minutes.

2. In a small bowl, combine the sugar, flour and salt. Gradually whisk the dry ingredients into the melted chocolate and bring to a boil. Reduce the heat to moderately low and cook, whisking occasionally, for 1 minute.

3. In a medium bowl, whisk the eggs briefly. Slowly whisk in about half of the chocolate mixture, then transfer this mixture to the remaining chocolate in the saucepan. Cook the custard until it's thick, smooth and steaming and reaches about 160° on a candy thermometer.

4. Remove from the heat and stir in the heavy cream and vanilla. Let cool to room temperature, then refrigerate or chill in a water bath until cold.

5. Pour the custard into an ice cream maker and freeze according to the manufacturer's instructions. When frozen, transfer the ice cream to a container, cover and freeze for at least 30 minutes before serving. *(The ice cream can be made up to 2 days before serving.)*
—*Ghirardelli Chocolate Company, San Francisco*

• • •

PISTACHIO ICE CREAM

Be sure to add the pistachio mixture to the custard base while it is still warm so that the base has time to absorb the flavors. If desired, you can give the ice cream an old-fashioned pistachio ice cream look by adding 4 drops of green food coloring.

——— *Makes About 3½ Pints* ———
1⅔ cups heavy cream
2⅓ cups milk
1¼ cups sugar
4 egg yolks
Pinch of salt
2 teaspoons vanilla extract
1½ cups shelled unsalted pistachios
1½ teaspoons almond extract

1. In a large saucepan with a heavy bottom, combine the cream, milk and ½ cup of the sugar. Heat gently over low heat almost to the boiling point.

2. Meanwhile, using a whisk or electric beater, beat the egg yolks with the remaining ¾ cup sugar and the salt until light and fluffy.

3. Gradually beat about 1 cup of the hot cream mixture into the eggs. Then, stirring constantly, pour the warmed egg mixture back into the cream mixture in the saucepan.

4. Whisking constantly, cook the custard over moderately low heat until it is thick enough to coat the back of a spoon. Do not let the custard boil. Stir in the vanilla extract and remove from the heat.

5. Stir in the pistachios and almond extract and chill the mixture thoroughly, either over ice or in the refrigerator.

6. Pour the mixture into the canister of an ice cream maker and freeze according to the manufacturer's instructions. Eat while still soft, or place it in the freezer to harden up before serving.
—*F&W*

• • •

TANGERINE LIGHT ICE CREAM

The best way to know whether a tangerine is sweet is to simply ask the greengrocer. (I've yet to meet a produce person who doesn't sample each batch of tangerines that comes into the store.) Otherwise, look for fruit that is heavy in the hand, with a smooth, thin and blemish-free skin.

——— *Makes About 1 Quart* ———
4 large tangerines (about 1½ pounds)
½ cup plus 2 to 4 tablespoons sugar
2 cups half-and-half or light cream
1 to 2 teaspoons fresh lemon juice
1 teaspoon tangerine liqueur (optional)

1. Lightly scrub the tangerines with soapy water; rinse thoroughly. Using a sharp swivel-edged vegetable peeler or a very sharp paring knife, peel the zest from the tangerines directly into a food processor fitted with the metal blade. Be careful not to remove any of the bitter white pith. Add ½ cup of the sugar and process, scraping down the sides of the bowl once or twice, until the zest is finely ground and the sugar is liquefied.

2. Halve and juice the tangerines; strain the juice through a fine-mesh sieve and measure out 1 cup. Add the cup of juice to the processor and blend thoroughly. Transfer the tangerine juice to a nonreactive bowl and stir in the half-and-half. Taste and add up to 4 tablespoons more sugar, if needed, until the mixture is a bit too sweet.

3. Strain the mixture through a fine-mesh sieve into another nonreactive bowl; discard the zest. Add the lemon juice, ½ teaspoon at a time, until the flavor is balanced. Add the tangerine liqueur if using.

4. Pour the mixture into an ice cream maker and freeze according to the manufacturer's instructions. To store, transfer the ice cream to a clean container, press a piece of plastic wrap directly on the surface to retard crystallization and freeze for up to 2 days.

—*Barbara Tropp*

• • •

LEMON-LIME LIGHT ICE CREAM

Look for juicy, fat lemons and limes with thin skin that feel heavy in the hand.

——— *Makes About 1 Quart* ———
2 large or 4 small lemons (about ¾ pound)
4 limes (about ¾ pound)
1 cup plus 1 tablespoon sugar
2 cups half-and-half or light cream
Pinch of salt

1. Lightly scrub the lemons and limes with warm soapy water; rinse thoroughly. Using a sharp swivel-edged vegetable peeler or a very sharp paring knife, peel the zest from the lemons and limes directly into a food processor fitted with the metal blade. Be careful not to remove any

of the bitter white pith. Add 1 cup of the sugar and process, scraping down the sides of the bowl, until the zest is finely ground and the sugar is liquefied.

2. Halve and separately juice the lemons and limes. Strain the juices through a fine-mesh sieve and measure out ⅓ cup each of the lemon and lime juice. Add to the sugar mixture and process until blended.

3. Pour the mixture into a nonreactive bowl and stir in the half-and-half. Taste and add up to 1 more tablespoon sugar, until the mixture is a bit too sweet.

4. Strain through a fine-mesh sieve into another nonreactive bowl and discard the zests. Stir in the salt. Pour the mixture into an ice cream maker and freeze according to the manufacturer's instructions. To store, transfer the ice cream to a clean container, press a piece of plastic wrap directly on the surface to retard crystallization and freeze for up to 2 days.

—*Barbara Tropp*

• • •

RASPBERRY LIGHT ICE CREAM

Summer berries make extraordinary ice creams. Their color and flavor are a joy at meal's end. The sweet taste test is easy: red berries will taste only as sweet as they smell; darker berries should be sampled.

——— *Makes About 1 Quart* ———
½ pound raspberries (about 1 pint)
½ cup plus 2 to 3 tablespoons sugar
2 cups half-and-half or light cream
1 to 1½ tablespoons fresh lemon juice

1. In a food processor fitted with a metal blade, combine the raspberries with ½ cup of the sugar and puree until smooth. For a smooth ice cream, strain

out the seeds by pressing the puree through a fine-mesh sieve into a nonreactive bowl. Alternatively, simply pour the puree into the bowl.

2. Stir in the half-and-half. Taste and add up to 3 more tablespoons sugar, if needed, until the mixture is a bit too sweet. Add the lemon juice by the ½ teaspoon until the flavor is balanced.

3. Pour the mixture into an ice cream maker and freeze according to the manufacturer's instructions. To store, transfer the ice cream to a clean container, press a piece of plastic wrap directly on the surface to retard crystallization and freeze for up to 2 days.

—*Barbara Tropp*

• • •

GINGER-PEACH LIGHT ICE CREAM

My criteria for fresh peaches have not changed since I was six and used to gorge on them in the summer at the Jersey Shore: a peach should smell perfumy from a foot away, be soft to the touch and ripe with juice when you bite into it.

——— *Makes About 5 Cups* ———
1½ pounds large peaches (6 to 8)
¾ cup plus 1 to 2 tablespoons sugar
2 cups half-and-half or light cream
2 teaspoons ginger juice (see Note)
1 teaspoon fresh lemon juice

1. Peel the peaches and slice the peach flesh away from the pit directly into a food processor fitted with the metal blade. Add ¾ cup of the sugar and puree until smooth, scraping down the sides of the bowl once or twice.

2. Transfer the puree to a nonreactive bowl and stir in the half-and-half. Taste and add up to 2 more tablespoons sugar, if needed, until the mixture is very sweet. Stir in the ginger juice, then add the lemon juice by the ½ teaspoon until the flavor is balanced.

3. Pour the mixture into an ice cream maker and freeze according to the manufacturer's instructions. To store, transfer the ice cream to a clean container, press a piece of plastic wrap directly on the surface to retard crystallization and freeze for up to 2 days.

NOTE: To make fresh ginger juice, peel a 2-inch piece of ginger and finely grate it over a small bowl. Strain the grated mixture into another bowl through a fine sieve, pressing to extract all the juice.

—Barbara Tropp

• • •

HONEYDEW LIGHT ICE CREAM

For ice cream making, the melon should be fully ripe and sweet smelling but not so ripe that the flesh is watery, translucent or mushy. To judge a melon for sweetness, smell the round spot opposite the stem end; the melon will taste exactly as sweet as it smells. Press the same spot gently— it should give slightly to pressure.

———— *Makes About 1½ Quarts* ————
1 ripe honeydew melon (about 2½ pounds)
½ cup plus 2 to 3 tablespoons sugar
2 cups half-and-half or light cream
1 tablespoon fresh lemon juice

1. Cut the melon in half and scoop out the seeds. Cut the melon in quarters. Using a long sharp knife, cut the honeydew flesh away from the rind; take care not to cut too close to the rind where the flavor wanes or is sometimes bitter. Cut the flesh into 1-inch chunks; you should have about 4 cups.

2. In a food processor fitted with a metal blade, combine the honeydew with ½ cup of the sugar and puree until smooth. Transfer the puree to a nonreactive bowl and stir in the half-and-half. Taste and add up to 3 tablespoons more sugar, if needed, until the mixture is a bit too sweet. Add the lemon juice by the teaspoon until the flavor is balanced.

3. Pour the mixture into an ice cream maker and freeze according to the manufacturer's instructions. To store, transfer the ice cream to a clean container, press a piece of plastic wrap directly on the surface to retard crystallization and freeze for up to 2 days.

—Barbara Tropp

• • •

PINEAPPLE LIGHT ICE CREAM

Field-ripened pineapples—wearing their status proudly on a little tag around the crown—are the best by far. They will smell sweet if they are sweet, and a golden streaked skin (as opposed to green) will indicate ripeness. You can serve the ice cream in hollowed-out pineapple halves. The ice cream can be molded in the shells when newly frozen and still soft, sealed airtight with plastic wrap and then placed in the freezer.

———— *Makes About 5 Cups* ————
1 ripe pineapple (about 2½ pounds)
½ cup plus 1 to 3 tablespoons sugar
2 cups half-and-half or light cream
1 to 2 teaspoons fresh lime juice

1. With a sharp knife, peel the pineapple by cutting down lengthwise. Make sure to remove all the "eyes." Quarter the pineapple, then cut out the core from each piece and discard. Cut the pineapple into 1-inch chunks; you should have about 3 cups. Reserve any extra for garnish or another use.

2. In a food processor fitted with a metal blade, combine the pineapple with ½ cup of the sugar; puree until well blended. Strain the mixture through a fine-mesh sieve into a nonreactive bowl and stir in the half-and-half. Taste and add up to 3 tablespoons more sugar if

needed until the mixture is a bit too sweet. Add the lime juice by the teaspoon until the flavor is balanced.

3. Pour the mixture into an ice cream maker and freeze according to the manufacturer's instructions. To store, transfer the ice cream to a clean container, press a piece of plastic wrap directly on the surface to retard crystallization and freeze for up to 2 days.

—Barbara Tropp

• • •

GRAPE LIGHT ICE CREAM

Any variety of grape, as long as it is seedless and thin skinned, makes a lovely ice cream.

———— *Makes About 1 Quart* ————
1 pound thin-skinned, seedless grapes
½ cup plus 1 to 2 tablespoons sugar
1 teaspoon finely grated lemon zest
2 cups half-and-half or light cream
1½ to 2 teaspoons fresh lemon juice

1. Wash the grapes in soapy water; rinse thoroughly. Drain well and pat dry with paper towels. Stem the grapes and set aside.

2. In a blender or a food processor, fitted with the metal blade, combine ½ cup of the sugar with the lemon zest. Process, scraping down the sides of the bowl once or twice, until the zest is distributed throughout the sugar. Add the grapes and puree until smooth.

3. Strain the mixture through a fine-mesh sieve into a bowl. Stir in the half-and-half. Taste and add up to 2 more tablespoons sugar until the mixture is quite sweet. Add the lemon juice by the teaspoon until the flavor is balanced.

4. Pour the mixture into an ice cream maker and freeze according to the manufacturer's instructions. To store, transfer the ice cream to a clean container, press a

piece of plastic wrap directly on the surface to retard crystallization and freeze for up to 2 days.

—*Barbara Tropp*

• • •

MANGO LIGHT ICE CREAM

A ripe mango exudes an overwhelming perfume. To ripen mangoes that are not yet fragrant, seal in a plastic bag and leave at room temperature for several days. They will grow soft, sweet and fragrant.

—————*Makes About 1 Quart*—————
1 large, ripe mango (about 1 pound)
6 to 8 tablespoons sugar
2 cups half-and-half or light cream
1 to 2 tablespoons fresh lime juice
1 teaspoon rum (optional)

1. Using a sharp knife, trim the skin off the mango, then cut the soft flesh from around the oblong seed. Cut the flesh into 1-inch chunks; you should have about 1½ cups. In a food processor fitted with the metal blade, combine the mango with 6 tablespoons of the sugar and process until smooth, scraping down the sides of the bowl once or twice.

2. Transfer the puree to a nonreactive bowl and stir in the half-and-half. Taste and add up to 2 more tablespoons sugar, if needed, until the mixture is a bit too sweet. Add the lime juice by the teaspoon until the flavor is balanced, then stir in the rum if using.

3. Pour the mixture into an ice cream maker and freeze according to the manufacturer's instructions. To store, transfer the ice cream to a clean container, press a piece of plastic wrap directly on the surface to retard crystallization and freeze for up to 2 days.

—*Barbara Tropp*

• • •

CHOCOLATE SORBET

—————*Makes About 1 Quart*—————
¼ cup unsweetened Dutch process cocoa powder, preferably Droste
2 tablespoons sugar
2 tablespoons light corn syrup
4 ounces semisweet chocolate, preferably Valrhona Carraque, chopped
2 ounces extra bittersweet chocolate, preferably Valrhona, chopped
2 teaspoons coffee liqueur
¼ teaspoon fresh lemon juice
Pinch of salt

1. In a small saucepan, whisk together the cocoa powder, sugar and corn syrup with 1½ cups of water over moderate heat. Bring to a boil, whisking until the mixture is smooth. Set aside.

2. Add the semisweet and bittersweet chocolates to the cocoa powder mixture and stir until smooth. Stir in the coffee liqueur, lemon juice and salt. Add ¾ cup of water and stir until incorporated.

3. Transfer the mixture to an ice cream maker. (If the mixture is too stiff to transfer, reheat it, stirring, in a double boiler.) Freeze according to the manufacturer's instructions. Transfer the sorbet to a covered container and freeze overnight. The sorbet will be very soft right out of the machine but will firm up overnight.

—*Rick Katz, Biba, Boston*

• • •

STRAWBERRY SHERBET WITH CHERRY CARAMEL SAUCE

It is important to caramelize the sugar in a casserole with sides high enough so that when you add the rest of the ingredients, the foam that is created will not spill over. The caramel syrup is ready when the sugar is completely dissolved and turns a dark golden color.

—————*12 Servings*—————
1 pound black cherries, pitted, or 1 can (17 ounces) pitted black cherries in syrup
2 cups sugar
3 pounds strawberries
2 tablespoons fresh lemon juice
½ cup orange liqueur, such as Grand Marnier

1. In a medium nonreactive casserole, combine the fresh cherries with 2 tablespoons of water and cook over low heat, covered, until softened, about 20 minutes. Puree the cherries in a food processor. (If using canned cherries, puree them in the processor with their syrup without cooking them first.) Set the puree aside.

2. In a medium saucepan, combine 1 cup of the sugar with ⅔ cup water. Bring to a boil over high heat, swirling the pan, until the sugar is dissolved, about 2 to 3 minutes. Set the sugar syrup aside to cool slightly.

3. Reserve a few of the smallest strawberries for garnish. Put the remaining strawberries in a food processor and pour in the cooled sugar syrup. Add the lemon juice and puree until smooth.

4. Transfer the puree to an ice cream maker and freeze according to the manufacturer's instructions. When the sherbet is ready, transfer it to a serving bowl and keep, covered, in the freezer until serving.

5. Meanwhile, pour the remaining 1 cup sugar into a heavy medium saucepan.

Bring to a boil over moderate heat, swirling the pan to dissolve the sugar. Boil without stirring until the sugar becomes dark gold in color and reaches 240° on a candy thermometer, 15 to 16 minutes.

6. Standing back as the mixture may splatter, add the orange liqueur a little at a time, stirring constantly with a long-handled spoon until any lumps of caramel dissolve, about 1 minute. Stir in the reserved cherry puree and remove from the heat. Let cool to room temperature.

7. Pour the cherry caramel sauce over the sherbet and decorate with the reserved strawberries. Serve immediately.

—*Lorenza de' Medici*

• • •

LEMON SORBET WITH ORANGE LIQUEUR

Experiment with different citrus sorbets and liqueurs. A plain wafer or cookie would make a good accompaniment.

——— *4 Servings* ———
1 pint of lemon sorbet
½ cup orange liqueur
Fortune cookies, as accompaniment
(optional)

In 4 glass serving bowls, place 2 scoops of lemon sorbet. Pour 2 tablespoons of liqueur over the sorbet in each bowl. Serve with fortune cookies if desired.

—*Pam Parseghian*

• • •

WATERMELON AND STRAWBERRY ICE

Flavors and colors combine here to make a dazzling poolside refresher. Serve it the same day it's made for the best taste and texture. (This quantity will fit in a quart-size ice cream maker.)

——— *4 Servings* ———
3 cups seeded 1-inch watermelon
chunks
1 pint strawberries, quartered
¼ cup sugar
Fresh mint sprigs, for garnish

1. In a food processor, puree the watermelon, strawberries and sugar. Strain through a fine-mesh sieve to remove the strawberry seeds. Pour into an ice cream maker and freeze according to the manufacturer's instructions.

2. Transfer to a chilled bowl, cover and place in the freezer for the flavors to ripen, 1 to 2 hours. Scoop into chilled glasses and garnish with mint sprigs.

—*Diana Sturgis*

• • •

BERRY BISCUITS

Any combination of berries, like sliced strawberries or whole blueberries, blackberries or raspberries, can be used here.

——— *6 Servings* ———
4 cups fresh berries (about 2 pints)
3 tablespoons sugar
2 cups all-purpose flour
2½ teaspoons baking powder
½ teaspoon salt
6 tablespoons chilled unsalted
*   butter, cut into bits*
¾ cup milk
1 pint heavy cream

1 tablespoon brandy or bourbon or 1
teaspoon vanilla extract
Fresh mint sprigs, for garnish

1. Preheat the oven to 450°. In a medium bowl, toss the berries with 1 tablespoon of the sugar. Cover and refrigerate for at least 1 hour or up to 4 hours.

2. In a large bowl, stir together the flour, baking powder, salt and the remaining 2 tablespoons sugar. Using a pastry blender or two knives, cut in the butter until the mixture resembles very coarse meal. Quickly stir in the milk with a fork just until the dough begins to hold together.

3. Transfer the dough to a floured surface and knead for a few seconds until it forms a ball. Roll or pat the dough ½ inch thick. Using a glass or a biscuit cutter, cut out six 3-inch rounds. Transfer to an ungreased cookie sheet. Bake for 12 to 15 minutes, or until golden; let cool on a rack. *(This recipe can be made up to 4 hours ahead. Cover and keep at room temperature.)*

4. In a medium bowl, beat the heavy cream until it thickens slightly, then beat in the brandy.

5. To serve, place some thickened cream in the center of each dessert plate. Split each biscuit in half and place the bottom half on the cream. Heap the fruit on the biscuit and cap with the biscuit top. Garnish with a mint sprig if desired. Pass any remaining cream at the table.

—*Lee Bailey*

• • •

MAPLE-PEAR CRISP

Pears have a special affinity for maple syrup; I often use the two together. In this case, I've covered them with a cornmeal-enriched topping. For best results, use firm but ripe pears. You can replace the vanilla bean with one teaspoon of vanilla extract—add it to the maple syrup after it comes off the heat.

—————— 6 Servings ——————
½ cup pure maple syrup
1 tablespoon fresh lemon juice
½ vanilla bean
6 large Bartlett or Comice pears—peeled, cored and thinly sliced
6½ tablespoons cold unsalted butter
¾ cup unbleached or all-purpose flour
¼ cup yellow cornmeal, preferably stone-ground
3 tablespoons (packed) light brown sugar
⅛ teaspoon cinnamon
⅛ teaspoon salt

1. Preheat the oven to 375°. Generously butter a shallow, 7-by-12-inch nonreactive baking dish and set aside.

2. In a small nonreactive saucepan, whisk together the maple syrup and lemon juice. Slit the vanilla bean and scrape the seeds into the pan. Warm over low heat until very hot, about 5 minutes.

3. Place the pear slices in a large bowl and pour the warm syrup over them. Let sit for 15 minutes, stirring occasionally.

4. Meanwhile, prepare the topping. Cut 4½ tablespoons of the butter into small pieces. In a large bowl, mix together the flour, cornmeal, brown sugar, cinnamon and salt. Using your fingers or a pastry blender, cut in the butter until the mixture is the texture of coarse meal with a few pea-size pieces of butter remaining.

5. Scrape the pears and their juices into the prepared baking dish. Dot with the remaining 2 tablespoons butter. Sprinkle the topping evenly over the pears. Bake for 45 minutes, until the top is golden and the juices are bubbling. Let cool slightly on a rack. Serve warm.

—*Ken Haedrich*

• • •

CARDAMOM-SCENTED CRANBERRY-APPLE COBBLER

I love the combination of cranberry, apple and orange flavors. This cobbler's slightly sweet, soft topping is somewhere between a biscuit and a cake, fortified with whole wheat flour. The filling has just a touch of applesauce, which gives some body to the juices from the fruit. The raisins can be omitted, if you like, or replaced with chopped, dried apricots—my wife's preference.

—————— 8 Servings ——————
1 package (12 ounces) fresh cranberries
1¾ cups fresh orange juice
¾ cup sugar
2 large Golden Delicious apples—peeled, cored and coarsely chopped
⅓ cup unsweetened applesauce
⅓ cup raisins (optional)
Finely grated zest of 1 orange
⅔ cup whole wheat flour
⅔ cup unbleached or all-purpose flour
⅓ cup (packed) light brown sugar
1½ teaspoons baking powder
¾ teaspoon cardamom
½ teaspoon salt
5 tablespoons cold unsalted butter, cut into ¼-inch dice
1 egg
⅓ cup plus 1 tablespoon milk

1. Preheat the oven to 400°. Butter a shallow 8-by-12-inch nonreactive baking dish and set aside.

2. In a large nonreactive saucepan, combine the cranberries, orange juice and sugar. Bring to a boil over moderate heat, stirring occasionally, and boil gently until the cranberry skins pop and the fruit softens, about 2 minutes. Stir in the apples, applesauce, raisins (if using) and orange zest and cook for 1 minute.

3. In a large bowl, mix together the whole wheat and unbleached flours, brown sugar, baking powder, cardamom and salt. Using a pastry blender or two knives, cut in the butter until the mixture resembles coarse meal with a few pea-size pieces of butter remaining. *(The recipe can be made to this point up to 1 day ahead. Cover the fruit and the flour mixtures separately and refrigerate.)*

4. In a small bowl, beat the egg and stir in the milk. Make a well in the dry ingredients, add the egg mixture and, with a wooden spoon, mix with a few strokes until just blended.

5. Pour the fruit mixture into the prepared baking dish. Distribute the batter over the fruit in 8 large spoonfuls with some fruit peeking out. Bake in the middle of the oven for 25 minutes, until the topping is golden brown (pierce the topping with a fork—it should be dry near the surface but moist where it meets the filling). For best flavor, serve very warm but not piping hot.

—*Ken Haedrich*

• • •

DESSERTS

BUTTERMILK RHUBARB COBBLER

Buttermilk makes an exceptionally light cobbler batter, and rhubarb is the right fruit match.

———— 6 to 8 Servings ————
¾ cup plus 2 tablespoons sugar
1 cup plus 1 tablespoon all-purpose flour
½ teaspoon finely grated orange zest
¼ teaspoon cinnamon
1½ pounds fresh rhubarb, cut into ¾-inch pieces or 1½ pounds frozen rhubarb, thawed (a scant 6 cups)
1 teaspoon baking powder
¼ teaspoon baking soda
¼ teaspoon salt
4 tablespoons cold unsalted butter, cut into small pieces
⅔ cup buttermilk
Softly whipped cream, pouring cream or vanilla ice cream, for serving (optional)

1. Preheat the oven to 400°. Generously butter a 1½- to 2-quart oval or rectangular nonreactive shallow baking dish.

2. In a large bowl, stir together ¾ cup of the sugar, 1 tablespoon of the flour, the orange zest and the cinnamon. Add the rhubarb and toss to combine. Spread the mixture in the prepared baking dish and bake for 10 minutes.

3. Meanwhile, in a large bowl, stir the remaining 2 tablespoons sugar and 1 cup flour with the baking powder, baking soda and salt. Add the butter and, using your fingers, rub it into the flour mixture until the mixture is the size of very small peas. Make a well in the center and pour in the buttermilk. Stir with a fork until all the ingredients are moistened and a soft dough forms.

4. Remove the fruit from the oven. Using a spoon, drop the dough in 6 or 8 evenly spaced mounds atop the hot fruit. Return to the oven and bake for 25 to 30 minutes, until the fruit is bubbling and the topping is a rich golden brown. Serve hot with cream or ice cream.

—Melanie Barnard & Brooke Dojny

• • •

SUMMER FRUIT WITH ORANGE LIQUEUR CUSTARD

———— 6 Servings ————
2 cups half-and-half or light cream
½ cup heavy cream
5 egg yolks
¼ cup sugar
½ vanilla bean
2 tablespoons orange liqueur
6 apricots—peeled, pitted and thinly sliced
1½ cups blueberries

1. In a heavy medium saucepan, combine the half-and-half and heavy cream. Cook over moderate heat until bubbles form around the edge, about 3 minutes.

2. Meanwhile, in a large bowl, whisk the egg yolks and sugar until thick and pale, about 2 minutes. Slowly whisk in the hot cream. Return the mixture to the saucepan, add the vanilla bean and cook over low heat, stirring, until the custard is thick enough to coat the back of a spoon, 10 to 12 minutes; do not boil.

3. Strain the custard into a bowl. Split the vanilla bean in half lengthwise and scrape the seeds into the custard; discard the pod. Stir in the orange liqueur. Lightly whisk the custard for about 2 minutes to cool slightly. Refrigerate uncovered until cold, about 1 hour. *(The recipe can be prepared to this point up to 1 day ahead. Cover the custard with plastic wrap when cold and refrigerate overnight.)*

4. Spoon the custard into 6 shallow bowls. Arrange the apricots and blueberries on top and serve.

—Melanie Barnard & Brooke Dojny

• • •

BAKED BANANAS

You can vary this recipe by combining different types of jams with various fruit liqueurs. Garnish with fresh fruit.

———— 6 Servings ————
6 medium bananas, halved lengthwise
1 tablespoon brown sugar
2 tablespoons unsalted butter, cut into small bits
½ cup seedless red raspberry jam or red currant jelly
1 tablespoon fresh lime juice
1 tablespoon sherry
Crème fraîche (optional)

1. Preheat the oven to 350°. Place the banana halves cut-side down in a 9-by-12-inch glass baking dish. Sprinkle the brown sugar evenly over the bananas and dot with the butter. Bake for 15 minutes.

2. Meanwhile, in a small nonreactive saucepan, combine the jam, lime juice and sherry and melt over low heat, stirring occasionally.

3. Pour the jam mixture over the bananas and bake another 5 minutes. Place two banana halves on each plate and spoon some of the sauce on top. Serve immediately with crème fraîche if desired.

—Lee Bailey

• • •

212

BLUSHING APPLESAUCE

This apple-raspberry sauce is a pleasant accompaniment to ham. The flavor and tartness will be determined by the type of apple you use. Any leftover sauce can be sweetened with a little sugar and served as a dessert.

8 to 10 Servings

3½ pounds apples, such as Cortland or McIntosh—peeled, cored and cut into 1-inch chunks
1 bag (12 ounces) frozen unsweetened raspberries or ¾ pint fresh raspberries

1. Place the apples and 2 tablespoons of water in a large, heavy nonreactive casserole. Cover tightly and cook over moderately low heat, stirring once or twice, until the apples are almost tender, about 30 minutes.

2. Stir in the raspberries, cover and cook until all the fruit is soft, about 10 minutes. Transfer the fruit to a food processor and puree until smooth. Strain the puree through a sieve in batches to remove the raspberry seeds. Serve warm or at room temperature. *(The sauce can be made up to 2 days ahead. Cover and refrigerate.)*

—Diana Sturgis

• • •

JASPER WHITE'S SMOOTH APPLESAUCE

I often make this for our baby, Jasper Paul. It's pure applesauce, with no added sugar or flavorings, and is best made with soft, sweet red apples like McIntosh or Empire. The flavor of the sauce depends entirely on the type of apple used. If you are not satisfied with the flavor, you can add sugar and spices to taste. The sauce will have a pink tinge to it, since I don't pare the apples before cooking.

Makes About 7 Cups

5 pounds sweet red apples, such as McIntosh or Empire, well washed and cut into eighths

1. In a large, heavy nonreactive saucepan, combine the apples with ½ cup water. Cover tightly and cook over moderate heat for 20 minutes.

2. Uncover and stir. Reduce the heat to moderately low, cover and simmer until the apples are uniformly soft, about 30 minutes longer. Remove from the heat, uncover and let cool slightly.

3. Pass the apples through a food mill or coarse strainer into a bowl and let cool completely. Spoon the applesauce into airtight containers and store in the refrigerator for up to 2 weeks. Serve cold (or warmed for the baby).

—Jasper White, Jasper's, Boston

• • •

WINTER FRUIT COMPOTE

This versatile dish makes a lovely winter dessert. It is also a delicious accompaniment to Thanksgiving dinner. Heat with a little Grand Marnier and serve over vanilla ice cream.

8 to 10 Servings

1 cup pitted prunes (about 8 ounces), quartered
1 cup dried apricots (about 8 ounces), quartered
1 cup dried apple slices (about 3 ounces), cut into ½-inch pieces
4 large pears, such as Bartlett or Comice—peeled, cored and cut into ½-inch dice
1½ cups fresh orange juice
2 tablespoons brown sugar
2 teaspoons grated orange zest plus slivered orange zest, for garnish

In a large nonreactive saucepan, combine all the ingredients except the slivered orange zest with ½ cup of water and bring to a boil over high heat. Reduce the heat to low, cover and simmer until all of the fruits are tender, 7 to 8 minutes. Transfer to a bowl, garnish with the slivered orange zest and serve warm.

—Marion Cunningham

• • •

PEACHES ROLLED WITH PECANS AND BROWN SUGAR

You can substitute apricots or nectarines here if you wish.

6 Servings

½ cup pecan halves (about 2 ounces)
2 tablespoons granulated brown sugar
3 large peaches
2 teaspoons fresh lemon juice
Crème fraîche or whipped cream
6 fresh mint sprigs, for garnish

1. Preheat the oven to 350°. In a small baking pan, toast the pecans for 8 to 10 minutes, or until golden brown. Set aside to cool.

2. Transfer the nuts to a food processor; add the sugar and process until finely ground but not pasty. Transfer the pecan-brown sugar mixture to a plate.

3. In a large pot of boiling water, blanch the peaches for 30 seconds. Remove with a slotted spoon and plunge them into cold water. Drain well. Peel, halve and pit the peaches. Place in a medium, nonreactive bowl, add the lemon juice and toss well.

4. Roll each peach half in the pecan-brown sugar mixture until evenly coated. Place each half on a dessert plate, rounded-side up. Garnish each serving with a dollop of crème fraîche or whipped cream and a mint sprig.

—Lee Bailey

• • •

FRUIT SALAD WITH BANANA CREAM

This is a colorful, easy-to-assemble dessert. Sliced fresh fruit is simply layered with a sprinkling of sugar and refrigerated overnight. As the fruit macerates a natural syrup forms. The banana cream is a rich, flavorful sauce to serve with the salad.

———— 8 Servings ————
¾ pound plums
½ cup granulated sugar
2 navel oranges
2 kiwis
2 pears
1¼ cups (about 6 ounces) seedless green grapes
1¼ cups (about 6 ounces) seedless red grapes
1 pint strawberries
1 banana
1 tablespoon honey
1 cup heavy cream, chilled

1. With a sharp paring knife, halve the plums lengthwise and discard the pits. Cut the plums into thin wedges and spread them over the bottom of a deep 1½- to 2-quart glass bowl. Sprinkle 1 tablespoon of the sugar over the plums.

2. Working on a plate to catch the juices and using a sharp knife, peel the oranges. Cut off all the bitter white pith. Slice the oranges crosswise ¼ inch thick, then quarter the slices. Spread the oranges over the plums and add any juices from the plate. Sprinkle a rounded tablespoon of the sugar over the oranges.

3. Peel the kiwis and halve lengthwise, then slice crosswise ¼ inch thick. Spread the kiwis over the oranges and sprinkle with 1 tablespoon of the sugar.

4. Peel, quarter and core the pears. Slice crosswise ¼ inch thick. Spread the pear slices over the kiwis and sprinkle with a rounded tablespoon of the sugar.

5. Halve the green and red grapes lengthwise and spread over the pears. Sprinkle with 1 tablespoon of the sugar.

6. Halve the strawberries lengthwise, or quarter them if large. Arrange them over the fruit in the bowl and sprinkle the remaining sugar evenly on top. Cover with plastic wrap and refrigerate overnight.

7. To make the banana cream, cut the banana into chunks and place in a food processor with the honey. Puree until smooth. With the machine running, pour in the heavy cream and process for 1 minute. *(The banana cream can be prepared up to 4 hours ahead and refrigerated.)* Serve the banana cream on top of the fruit salad or alongside in a pitcher or a bowl.

—*Diana Sturgis*

• • •

CHILLED ORANGE SALAD WITH AMARETTO COOKIES

If you don't have time to slice the oranges using the method below, simply peel and divide four of them into segments. Arrange on salad plates, sprinkle with the juice of the remaining orange and crumble the amaretto cookies on top.

———— 4 Servings ————
5 medium oranges
3 tablespoons fresh lemon juice
2 tablespoons sugar
8 amaretto cookies

1. Squeeze the juice of 1 orange into a medium bowl; discard the orange.

2. Slice off the tops and bottoms of the 4 remaining oranges. Stand the oranges upright on a work surface. With a small sharp knife, cut away the skin and pith to expose the flesh, following the contours of the fruit. Cut the oranges crosswise into ¼-inch- to ⅜-inch-thick slices and add them to the bowl along with any accumulated juice. Add the lemon juice and sugar to the oranges and toss to combine. Chill until very cold, at least 1 hour.

3. To serve, decoratively arrange the orange slices on individual salad plates, spoon on some juice and crumble 2 cookies on top of each portion.

—*Stephanie Lyness*

• • •

SLICED ORANGES IN RED WINE SYRUP

———— 8 Servings ————
2 cups dry red wine
¾ cup sugar
1 cinnamon stick
2 whole cloves
1 large strip of orange zest
6 large navel oranges
3 tablespoons orange liqueur (optional)
Fresh mint sprigs, for garnish

1. In a medium nonreactive saucepan, combine the wine, sugar, cinnamon stick, cloves and orange zest. Bring to a boil, stirring to dissolve the sugar. Reduce the heat and simmer until the liquid is reduced to 1 cup, about 10 minutes. Cool and strain into a bowl.

2. Using a sharp paring knife, peel the oranges; remove all the bitter white pith. Slice the oranges crosswise ¼ to ⅜ inch thick and remove any pits. Place the orange slices, overlapping, in a shallow serving dish.

3. Add the orange liqueur to the syrup and pour over the orange slices. Cover with plastic wrap and refrigerate for at least 4 hours. *(The recipe can be prepared up to 1 day ahead.)* Garnish with mint sprigs before serving.

—*Perla Meyers*

• • •

RICE FRITTERS

These substantial fritters are reminiscent of rice pudding, with a light, citrus fragrance. They are traditionally made for the feast of San Giuseppe on March 19.

— *Makes About 3 Dozen Fritters* —
4 cups milk
1 lemon or orange
1¼ cups Arborio rice (about ½ pound)
2 tablespoons unsalted butter
2 tablespoons sugar, plus more for coating
Pinch of salt
6 eggs, separated
6 tablespoons unbleached all-purpose flour
4 cups vegetable oil, for deep-frying
½ cup olive oil, for deep-frying

1. In a medium saucepan, bring the milk to a boil over moderate heat. Meanwhile, using a vegetable peeler, remove the zest from the lemon or orange. Add the zest strips to the milk and stir in the rice, butter, 2 tablespoons sugar and the salt.

2. Reduce the heat to low. Simmer, stirring occasionally with a wooden spoon, until the rice is completely cooked and the milk almost totally absorbed, about 20 minutes.

3. Scrape the rice into a bowl and let cool completely, about 2 hours. *(The recipe can be prepared to this point up to 1 day ahead. Cover and refrigerate the rice overnight. Let return to room temperature before proceeding.)*

4. Discard the citrus zest. Using a wooden spoon, blend the egg yolks into the rice mixture, one at a time. Stir in the flour until thoroughly incorporated.

5. In a large cast-iron skillet, heat the vegetable and olive oils over moderate heat to 375°.

6. Meanwhile, in a large bowl, beat the egg whites until stiff but not dry. Gently fold the whites into the rice.

7. When the oil is hot, spoon tablespoons of the rice mixture into the oil and fry, turning, until well browned and cooked through, about 5 minutes. Using a slotted spoon, transfer the fritters to paper towels to drain. When all the fritters are cooked, roll them in sugar. Arrange on a platter and serve hot.

—*Giuliano Bugialli*

• • •

RAISINS IN GRAPPA

These raisins last for at least six months, so I usually prepare several jars at a time. The raisins absorb almost all the grappa as they sit until they are barely covered. Dried apricots and prunes can also be conserved in this manner and are delicious served either separately or mixed together. Of course, one should use the best quality grappa.

— *12 Servings* —
¾ cup golden raisins
1 cup good quality grappa
1 whole clove

1. Place the raisins in a glass jar and pour in the grappa. Add the clove and seal with a lid. Store at room temperature for at least 2 weeks before serving.

2. To serve, discard the clove, put the raisins in individual tumblers and serve with a demitasse spoon.

—*Lorenza de'Medici*

• • •

NO-TROUBLE CHOCOLATE TRUFFLES

This recipe—one of the easiest we've tried—is the handiwork of Linda Fabiano, owner of Cakecraft, a candy- and cake-decorating supply store in Red Bank, New Jersey, where she also teaches these crafts. A cup of espresso makes a wonderful accompaniment to these heavenly chocolate morsels.

————*Makes About 2 Dozen*————
8 ounces imported bittersweet chocolate, preferably Callebaut
½ cup heavy cream
½ cup sweetened condensed milk
1 cup plus 2 tablespoons unsweetened Dutch process cocoa powder
2 tablespoons unsalted butter

1. In a double boiler, melt the chocolate over simmering water, stirring occasionally, until smooth. Remove from the heat. (Alternatively, in a small heatproof bowl, heat the chocolate in a microwave oven at 50 percent power, stirring thoroughly every 30 seconds, until melted. Transfer to a medium bowl.)

2. Meanwhile, in a small saucepan, heat the cream and condensed milk over moderate heat for 5 minutes, or until warm to the touch. Add to the melted chocolate and whisk until blended. (Alternatively, warm the cream and condensed milk in the microwave at 100 percent power for 60 seconds and blend into the chocolate.)

3. Stir in 2 tablespoons of the cocoa, then add the butter and stir until melted. Scrape the mixture into a small bowl and let cool to room temperature. Cover and refrigerate until set, at least 4 hours or overnight.

4. Working as quickly as possible, scoop up the cold chocolate mixture by the tablespoonful and roll into 1-inch balls. Set the truffles on a cookie sheet lined with waxed paper and refrigerate for 1 hour.

5. Place the remaining 1 cup cocoa powder in a medium bowl. Add the truffles, about 6 at a time, and roll with your hands to coat them thoroughly with cocoa. Place on a cookie sheet lined with a clean sheet of waxed paper. Cover loosely with plastic wrap and refrigerate until 15 minutes before serving. *(The truffles will keep for up to 2 weeks in the refrigerator. Dust again with cocoa before serving if necessary.)*

—*Linda Fabiano, Cakecraft,
Red Bank, New Jersey*

• • •

COFFEE CUP TRUFFLES

These free-form candies are easier to make than you might think, but be sure to use the best chocolate you can get your hands on. Eat the truffles out of hand or drop into individual cups of hot coffee for a special holiday drink. Reserve any extra candies in the refrigerator or freezer until needed, as they tend to soften quickly.

——— *Makes About 3½ Dozen* ———
**9 ounces bittersweet or semisweet
chocolate, broken into pieces
⅔ cup heavy cream
⅓ vanilla bean
2 tablespoons unsalted butter
Pinch of cinnamon
3 tablespoons unsweetened Dutch
process cocoa powder
Pinch of salt
1 cup confectioners' sugar, sifted**

1. Line the inside of an 8-by-4-inch loaf pan with waxed paper.

2. In a double boiler, melt the chocolate, stirring occasionally, over gently simmering water. Remove from the heat and stir until smooth. Set aside. (Alternatively, in a medium microwave-safe bowl, heat the chocolate at medium power for 60 seconds. Stir to redistribute and cook for 60 seconds more. Stir again; if the chocolate is not completely melted, re-peat the microwave procedure for 30 seconds, just until the chocolate can be stirred smooth. Repeat again as necessary. Take care not to burn the chocolate.)

3. In a small saucepan, warm the cream with the vanilla bean over low heat. (Alternatively, place the cream in a glass measuring cup. Split the piece of vanilla bean, scrape it and add the bean and the scrapings to the cream. Microwave on full power for 60 seconds.) Remove from the heat and remove the vanilla bean.

4. Gradually stir the cream into the melted chocolate until smooth. Add the butter, cinnamon, cocoa and salt; stir until incorporated. Scrape the chocolate mixture into the prepared pan and smooth the top. Cover and refrigerate. *(The recipe can be prepared to this point up to 3 days ahead.)*

5. To unmold, run a thin knife around the edges of the chocolate mixture and invert the pan onto a work surface. Trim the edges of the chocolate loaf, if necessary, with a long thin, very sharp knife. Then cut the chocolate crosswise into ¾-inch strips. Do not draw the knife out by pulling it toward you; pull it straight up after making a cut, holding down the chocolate.

6. Cut each strip crosswise into ¾-inch cubes and place on a baking sheet lined with waxed paper. Cover with plastic wrap and freeze until ready to serve. *(The truffles can be made to this point and kept frozen up to 1 week.)*

7. Place the confectioners' sugar in a bag. Add the frozen chocolate cubes to the bag in batches; shake to coat them with the sugar. Place the truffles on a small decorative plate or in a sugar bowl and serve with freshly brewed coffee and a pitcher of warm milk.

—*Tracey Seaman*

• • •

CHOCOLATE WAFERS

——— *Makes About 2½ Dozen* ———
**3 tablespoons unsalted butter, at
room temperature
2 tablespoons light brown sugar
3 ounces semisweet chocolate,
preferably Valrhona, melted and
cooled
¼ teaspoon vanilla extract
½ cup all-purpose flour
Pinch of salt**

1. In a medium bowl, beat the butter at medium speed until soft. Add the sugar and beat until creamy, about 3 minutes. Add the melted chocolate and vanilla and beat until smooth, about 1 minute. Stir in the flour and salt; mix until smooth.

2. Transfer the chocolate mixture to a sheet of waxed paper and shape into a compact log, about 4 inches long and 3 inches thick. Roll the log up in the waxed paper and refrigerate until chilled and firm, at least 6 hours or overnight. *(The recipe can be prepared to this point and kept frozen, wrapped in foil, for up to 1 month. Defrost in the refrigerator overnight before using.)*

3. Preheat the oven to 350°. Remove the log from the refrigerator and let sit at room temperature for 15 minutes. With a thin sharp knife, cut the log into very thin slices, about ⅛ inch thick. Place the slices on a parchment-lined cookie sheet and bake for 8 to 10 minutes until firm. Cool completely on the cookie sheet. *(The wafers can be baked and stored in a covered tin for up to 1 week.)*

—*Rick Katz, Biba, Boston*

• • •

LOW-CALORIE COOKING

CROUTONS OF CREAMY RED PEPPER

Each serving of this colorful, tasty hors d'oeuvre allows for an ample seven or eight croutons, which amounts to just one ounce of bread if thinly sliced from a very narrow French baguette.

6 Servings
——— *105 Calories per Serving* ———
1 small garlic clove, finely chopped
¼ cup drained canned pimientos or roasted red peppers
1 tablespoon plus 1 teaspoon 1% low-fat cottage cheese
1⅓ ounces Neufchâtel cream cheese (or other reduced-fat soft cream cheese)
¾ teaspoon coarsely chopped fresh dill plus 6 fresh dill sprigs, for garnish
⅛ teaspoon freshly ground black pepper
1½ teaspoons fresh lemon juice
1 long narrow French-type baguette (about 6 ounces), cut into 42 to 48 ¼-inch-thick slices

1. Preheat the oven to 400°. In a food processor, add the garlic, pimientos, cottage cheese, cream cheese, chopped dill, black pepper and lemon juice and process until smooth.
2. Arrange the bread slices on a baking sheet and bake for 10 minutes, or until crisp. Set aside until cool.
3. Spread each crouton with a thin layer of the red pepper spread and garnish with a small sprig of fresh dill.
—*Jacques Pépin*

• • •

LIGHT GUACAMOLE

This luscious guacamole keeps its color and flavor for several hours. Serve with tacos, fajitas and enchiladas or alone surrounded with a mound of carrot and celery sticks.

8 Servings
——— *131 Calories per Serving* ———
1 cup plain low-fat yogurt
2 large firm, ripe California avocados (½ pound each), halved and pitted
¼ cup chopped onion
4 medium jalapeño peppers, seeded and chopped
1 tablespoon plus 1 teaspoon fresh lemon juice
½ teaspoon cumin
½ teaspoon salt
⅛ teaspoon freshly ground black pepper
¼ cup plus 2 tablespoons chopped fresh coriander
1 large tomato, cut into ½-inch dice (1½ cups diced tomatoes)

1. Pour the yogurt into a sieve or cheesecloth and let drain over a bowl for about 10 minutes.
2. With a spoon, scoop the flesh from one avocado into a food processor. Add the onion, jalapeños (and seeds to taste for a hotter flavor), lemon juice, cumin, salt, black pepper, the drained yogurt and ¼ cup of the coriander; process until smooth.
3. Scoop the flesh from the remaining avocado and place in a medium serving bowl; coarsely mash with a fork. Stir in the pureed avocado mixture and gently fold in the tomato. Garnish with the remaining 2 tablespoons coriander. Serve ½ cup per person.

—*Jim Fobel*

• • •

SHRIMP WITH CURRIED ALMOND DRESSING IN LETTUCE CUPS

Since most of the sodium in shrimp is contained in the shells, it is greatly reduced by peeling the shrimp and lowered even further by cooking them in lots of water. Look for salt-free curry powder. Be sure to read the label carefully as many blends contain added salt.

You can also fill the lettuce cups with thin slices of the Oriental Flank Steak Sans Soy (p. 234) or use half shrimp and half steak.

6 First-Course Servings
168 Calories and 103 Mg
——— *Sodium per Serving* ———
¼ cup whole blanched almonds (about 1 ounce)
2 tablespoons pure olive oil
¾ teaspoon salt-free curry powder
1 teaspoon fennel seeds
⅛ teaspoon cayenne pepper
3 garlic cloves, coarsely chopped
1 teaspoon grated fresh ginger
2 teaspoons fresh lemon juice
1 teaspoon salt-free mustard
1 teaspoon honey
1 tablespoon plain low-fat yogurt
1 tablespoon chopped fresh coriander
1 pound medium shrimp, shelled and deveined
4 heads Bibb lettuce, separated into leaf cups
1 tomato, seeded and finely diced

1. Preheat the oven to 400°. Put the almonds on a baking sheet and toast for 8 minutes, until golden brown. Let cool.
2. In a small skillet, combine the olive oil, curry powder, fennel seeds and cayenne. Cook over low heat, stirring, until

fragrant, about 1 minute. Transfer the mixture to a mortar.

3. Add the almonds and garlic and pound to a paste with a pestle. Blend in the ginger, lemon juice, mustard, honey, yogurt and coriander. (Alternatively, combine all the ingredients in a food processor and process until smooth. Add 1 tablespoon of water at the end.) Set the sauce aside at room temperature to develop the flavors.

4. Bring a medium saucepan of water to a boil. Add the shrimp and cook until the water returns just to a boil, about 3 minutes. Drain the shrimp in a colander and rinse under cold running water until cool. Drain well.

5. To serve, arrange the lettuce leaf cups on a platter. Place a shrimp in each cup and then spoon a small dollop of the curried almond dressing on top. Garnish with the diced tomato.

—*Marcia Kiesel*

• • •

DRUNKEN SHRIMP

This traditional dish is prepared along the Chinese coast wherever shrimp are found. It is usually made using live shrimp, which are marinated in rice liquor, then flambéed. I have had them at the Golden Unicorn in Hong Kong, where they are cooked in a pot of boiling chicken broth, and I sampled them in Taipei in a broth pungent with ginseng root. Here is a less daunting variation.

6 First-Course Servings
86 Calories and 193 Mg
——— *Sodium per Serving* ———
24 medium shrimp (about ¾ pound)
3 tablespoons Cognac or other brandy
3 medium scallions, 2 halved crosswise
3 cups chicken stock or 2 cans (13¾ ounces each) low-sodium chicken broth

3 small chile peppers, minced
1½ tablespoons low-sodium soy sauce
2 teaspoons distilled white vinegar
2 teaspoons Oriental sesame oil
½ teaspoon sugar
1 piece of fresh ginger (½ by 1½ inches), peeled and smashed

1. Using kitchen scissors, cut through the shrimp shells along the back from the heads to just before the tails; leave the shells on. Remove the veins. Rinse the shrimp in cold water. Drain and pat dry with paper towels.

2. In a medium bowl, toss the shrimp with the Cognac until thoroughly coated. Cover and marinate in the refrigerator for 2 hours.

3. Meanwhile, make the sauce. Thinly slice the green portion of the whole scallion. In a small bowl, combine 2 tablespoons of the chicken stock with the chile peppers, soy sauce, vinegar, sesame oil, sugar and scallion green. Whisk together and set aside.

4. In a large saucepan, combine the remaining chicken stock with the halved scallions and ginger. Cover and bring to a boil over high heat. Reduce the heat to moderately low and simmer for 2 minutes. Return the heat to high and bring to a rolling boil. Add the shrimp with their marinade and stir to immerse them completely. When the liquid returns to a boil, remove the pan from the heat. Cover and set aside until the shrimp are opaque and loosely curled, about 2 minutes.

5. With a slotted spoon, transfer the shrimp to 6 serving plates, placing 4 on each plate. Pour the reserved sauce into 6 dipping dishes and serve alongside the shrimp.

—*Eileen Yin-Fei Lo*

• • •

STEAMED OYSTERS WITH BLACK BEANS

In the traditional Cantonese kitchen, oysters are usually used in dried form, either in vegetarian preparations or in soup. But recently, at the Mandarin Hotel's Man Wah restaurant in Hong Kong, I chatted with Chef Lai Kam Lun about the possibility of steaming fresh oysters with fermented black beans. "Why not?" he said. Why not indeed.

6 First-Course Servings
69 Calories and 157 Mg
——— *Sodium per Serving* ———
12 large freshly shucked oysters on the half shell
2 teaspoons fermented black beans,* rinsed and drained
1 tablespoon low-sodium soy sauce
1 tablespoon Shao-Hsing wine* or dry sherry
1½ teaspoons sugar
1 tablespoon distilled white vinegar
2 tablespoons chicken stock or canned low-sodium broth
2 teaspoons Oriental sesame oil
1 tablespoon peanut oil
Pinch of freshly ground white pepper
1 tablespoon minced red bell pepper
1 small scallion, green part only, thinly sliced
*Available at Asian markets

1. Place the oysters on a large heatproof dish. Divide the black beans evenly and place atop each oyster.

2. In a small bowl, combine the soy sauce, wine, sugar, vinegar, chicken stock, sesame oil, peanut oil and white pepper. Distribute the mixture over each oyster.

3. In a wok with a steamer rack or in a steamer pot, bring 6 cups of water to a boil over high heat. Place the dish on the steamer rack, cover and steam the oysters until plumped and opaque, 2 to 3 minutes. Do not overcook or the oysters will be tough. Sprinkle the red pepper and scallion on top. Place 2 oysters on each of 6 serving plates. Serve hot.

—*Eileen Yin-Fei Lo*

• • •

WHOLE WHEAT CALIFORNIA PIZZA WITH FRESH TOMATOES AND GOAT CHEESE

This pizza is a reward for the guests at Cal-a-Vie after the weigh-in on Saturday mornings. The recipe yields enough topping for one 12-inch pizza and dough for three crusts. Freeze the remaining dough for later use—it will make excellent rolls.
❦ The tartness of goat cheese is nicely matched by a California Fumé Blanc, such as 1987 Dry Creek or 1987 Chateau St. Jean La Petite Etoile.

8 Servings
——— *394 Calories per Serving* ———
2 tablespoons active dry yeast
1½ cups lukewarm water (105° to 115°)
Pinch of sea salt
1 tablespoon plus 2 teaspoons extra-virgin olive oil
2 cups semolina flour* or all-purpose flour
1½ cups whole wheat pastry flour* or all-purpose flour
1 to 1¼ cups all-purpose flour, plus more for dusting
6 ounces goat cheese, such as Montrachet or Bucheron, chilled and crumbled
20 fresh basil leaves
12 medium plum tomatoes—peeled, seeded and diced
½ medium green bell pepper, cut into thin julienne strips
8 California black olives, coarsely chopped

2 teaspoons minced fresh oregano or 1 teaspoon dried
¼ teaspoon freshly ground black pepper
1 tablespoon freshly grated Parmesan cheese
*Available at specialty and health food stores

1. In a medium bowl, combine the yeast, warm water, salt and 1 tablespoon of the olive oil. Let sit until the yeast is dissolved, 5 to 10 minutes.

2. In a large bowl, toss together the semolina, whole wheat and all-purpose flours. Make a well in the center and pour in the yeast mixture. Using your hands, incorporate the flours until a loose dough forms. Turn the dough out onto a lightly floured surface and knead, dusting with flour as necessary, until smooth, about 5 minutes. Rinse out the bowl and oil it lightly. Return the dough to the bowl, turning to coat with oil, cover with a towel and let sit in a warm place until doubled in bulk, about 40 minutes.

3. Preheat the oven to 350°. Grease a 12-inch pizza pan. Punch down the dough and transfer it to a lightly floured surface. Cut the dough into three equal parts and shape into disks. Wrap 2 of the disks well in plastic wrap and freeze for later use. Roll out the remaining disk into a 14-inch circle. Transfer the dough to the pan. Form a rim with the overhanging edge.

4. Bake the pizza crust on the lower rack of the oven for 10 minutes. Remove from the oven and arrange the goat cheese, basil, tomatoes, green pepper and olives on the crust. Season with the oregano and black pepper. Drizzle the remaining 2 teaspoons olive oil over the pizza and sprinkle the Parmesan cheese on top. Bake for 30 minutes longer.

—*Michel Stroot, Cal-a-Vie, Vista, California*

• • •

CRISPY BALSAMIC CHICKEN WINGS

The rich, sweet balsamic vinegar marinade caramelizes to form a crisp glaze on these wings as they cook. They can be baked or grilled if you prefer.

4 First-Course Servings
254 Calories and 72 Mg
——— *Sodium per Serving* ———
2 pounds chicken wings
⅔ cup balsamic vinegar
3 large scallions, thinly sliced

1. In a large bowl, combine the chicken wings, vinegar and scallions. Toss well to evenly coat the wings. Cover and let marinate at room temperature for 6 hours, stirring occasionally, or refrigerate overnight.

2. Preheat the oven to 450°. Let the chicken wings return to room temperature if refrigerated. Lift them out of the marinade and place on a baking sheet in a single layer. Bake the wings until crisp and deep brown, about 25 minutes. Alternatively, grill the chicken wings over a medium-hot fire, about 5 inches from the heat, for about 8 to 10 minutes per side. Serve hot or at room temperature.

—*Marcia Kiesel*

• • •

Pork Loin in Chile Sauce with Roast Potatoes and Carrots (p. 236).

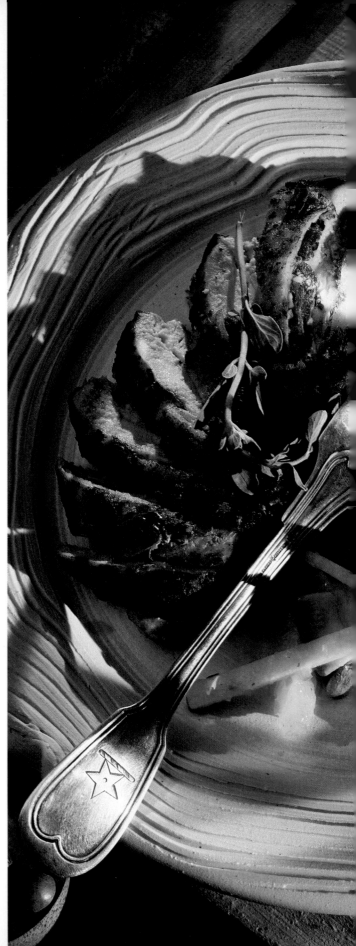

Above, Molded Vanilla Pears (p. 250). Right, Spicy Stuffed Chicken Breasts (p. 228).

NEW ZEALAND MUSSELS WITH POMMERY MUSTARD MAYONETTE

New Zealand, or greenshell, mussels are imported into the United States. They grow to almost twice the size of regular blue mussels. In this dish timing is important. Don't steam the mussels too much in advance, and don't leave them exposed without liquid or they will become dry and rubbery. The mayonette is a lighter version of mayonnaise, made in part with plain yogurt.

6 First-Course Servings
——202 Calories per Serving——
2 dozen large mussels, preferably from New Zealand, scrubbed and debearded
1 large celery rib, cut into 1-inch lengths
¼ cup dry white wine
¼ teaspoon freshly ground pepper
⅓ cup reduced-calorie mayonnaise
⅓ cup plain nonfat or low-fat yogurt
1 medium shallot, minced
2 tablespoons tarragon vinegar
1½ tablespoons grainy mustard
2 teaspoons Dijon-style mustard
1 head of lettuce, leaves shredded, or 4 cups alfalfa sprouts, for the platter
Assorted raw vegetables, such as cherry tomatoes, snow peas and broccoli florets, for garnish

1. Put the mussels in a heavy pot. Add the celery, wine, ⅛ teaspoon of the pepper and 1 cup of water. Cover and steam over high heat until the mussels open, 3 to 4 minutes. Remove from the heat, uncover and let cool, discarding any mussels that have not opened.

2. In a blender, combine the mayonnaise, yogurt, shallot, vinegar, grainy and Dijon mustards and the remaining ⅛ teaspoon pepper. Blend until smooth.

3. Cover a platter with the shredded lettuce or alfalfa sprouts. Remove and discard the top shell from each mussel, leaving the meat on the half shell. Arrange the mussels on the lettuce and spoon a dollop of the mayonette on each one. Garnish the platter with the vegetables. Serve at room temperature.
—*Michel Stroot, Cal-a-Vie, Vista, California*

• • •

BARLEY AND WILD MUSHROOM SOUP

This version is much lighter than the traditional mushroom and barley soup, and the mushroom flavor is developed in a separate broth. If fresh wild mushrooms are available, sauté them separately in butter and add to the finished soup, where they can be seen and enjoyed.

6 Servings
——161 Calories per Serving——
½ cup pearl barley
1 tablespoon unsalted butter
1 small onion or 2 medium leeks, white parts only, finely chopped
4 ounces mushrooms, cut into ¼-inch dice
1 garlic clove, minced
½ teaspoon salt
Mushroom Broth (recipe follows)
1 carrot, cut into ¼-inch dice
1 celery rib, cut into ¼-inch dice
3 tablespoons heavy cream
1 teaspoon red wine vinegar or lemon juice
1 tablespoon chopped parsley
1 tablespoon snipped chives or thinly sliced scallion
½ teaspoon freshly ground pepper

1. In a small bowl, cover the barley with 1 cup of cold water. Set aside to soak for 30 minutes, then drain.

2. Meanwhile, in a large saucepan, melt the butter. Add the onion and cook over moderate heat, stirring frequently, until softened, about 7 minutes. Add the mushrooms, garlic and salt and cook until tender, 2 to 3 minutes.

3. Add the Mushroom Broth and the drained barley to the saucepan. Bring to a boil over high heat. Reduce the heat to low and simmer, covered, for 20 minutes.

4. Add the carrot and celery to the saucepan and cook, partially covered, until tender, about 10 minutes. Stir in the cream and vinegar. Add the parsley, chives and pepper just before serving.
—*Deborah Madison*

• • •

MUSHROOM BROTH

——Makes 7 to 8 Cups——
1 tablespoon light olive oil
1 large onion, chopped
1 ounce dried cèpes (porcini), rinsed briefly in cold water
2 bay leaves
6 fresh sage leaves or 2 pinches dried
8 fresh thyme sprigs or 3 pinches dried
5 parsley sprigs, coarsely chopped
2 celery ribs, coarsely chopped
1 large carrot, coarsely chopped
1 garlic clove, coarsely chopped
1 teaspoon salt

1. In a large heavy saucepan, heat the oil. Add the onion and cook over moderately low heat, stirring occasionally, until beginning to brown, about 15 minutes.

Rhubarb Compote with Cinnamon Corn Bread (p. 251).

2. Add the dried cèpes to the saucepan along with all the remaining ingredients and 2½ quarts of water. Bring to a boil over high heat, then reduce the heat to moderate and simmer, partially covered, for 40 minutes.

3. Strain the broth through a cheese-cloth-lined strainer, pressing on the solids to extract as much liquid is possible. Use immediately or cover and refrigerate for up to 3 days.

—*Deborah Madison*

• • •

ELEGANT LOW-CAL FEAST

Serves 8
740 Calories per Serving

Salad of Bitter Greens with Goat Cheese Phyllo Sticks (p. 239)

Molded Sole and Salmon with Dill (p. 226)

Sorrel Sauce (p. 226)

Braised Leeks with Fusilli (p. 238)

Broiled Tomatoes with Balsamic Vinegar and Mint (p. 239)

Ribboned Peach and Raspberry Mousse (p. 246)

—*Bob Chambers*

MOLDED SOLE AND SALMON WITH DILL

This is nothing more than a very elegant way to serve simple steam-baked fish. The sole encases a chunk of salmon, but thin slices of salmon fillet could be used on the outside instead.

❦ This delicate dish would best be showcased by a polished, mild-mannered 1987 California Chardonnay, such as Saintsbury or Silverado.

8 Servings
——*181 Calories per Serving*——
6 small sole fillets (about 6 ounces each)
Salt and freshly ground white pepper
8 very small dill sprigs
¾ pound skinless salmon fillet (center cut), cut into 1¾-inch chunks
Sorrel Sauce (recipe follows)

1. Preheat the oven to 350°. Using a 12-cup muffin pan, spray 8 cups with vegetable cooking spray. Set aside.

2. Set the sole on a work surface. Using a sharp knife, cut out the central bony strip from each fillet. Arrange the 12 fillets 1 inch apart on a sheet of parchment paper and cover with another sheet. Using a rolling pin or a meat pounder, gently flatten the fillets to an even thickness. Season them lightly with salt and white pepper.

3. Place a dill sprig in the bottom of each prepared muffin cup. Wrap a sole fillet around the sides of each cup with the skinned side facing in, overlapping as necessary.

4. Halve the remaining 4 sole fillets crosswise. Place one piece inside each cup, skinned side in, to line the bottom. Set a salmon chunk in each cup. Fill in

any empty spaces with trimmings from the fish. Press down to make the fish compact. *(The recipe can be prepared to this point up to 1 day ahead. Cover the pan with plastic wrap and refrigerate.)*

5. Spray a piece of foil large enough to cover the muffin pan with vegetable cooking spray. Tightly cover the muffin pan with the foil. Set the prepared pan in a larger baking pan and pour in enough warm water to reach halfway up the sides of the muffin cups.

6. Place the pan in the middle of the oven and bake for 25 minutes, or until the fish feels just firm when gently pressed. Remove the muffin pan from the water bath. Set a baking sheet over the muffin pan, then invert the pan to release the molded fish. Drain well. Using a spatula, transfer the fish to 8 plates and serve warm with the Sorrel Sauce.

—*Bob Chambers*

• • •

SORREL SAUCE

Tart sorrel, which is sometimes called sour grass, complements any fish. Prepared as it is here, it would also be delicious with veal or swirled into a spinach or watercress soup as a tangy garnish.

Makes About 1½ Cups
15 Calories per 3-Tablespoon
——*Serving*——
1 cup fish stock or 1 bottle (8 ounces) clam juice
1¼ pounds fresh sorrel, large stems removed
Salt and freshly ground pepper

1. In a medium nonreactive saucepan, bring the stock to a boil. Add the sorrel, cover and cook over moderately high heat until wilted, about 2 minutes. Uncover, stir and cook for 4 minutes longer.

2. Transfer the sorrel to a food processor or blender and puree, scraping down the sides of the bowl, until smooth. Strain the puree in 3 batches, rinsing the strainer between batches. *(The sauce can be prepared to this point up to 1 day ahead. Cover and refrigerate.)*

3. Return the sauce to a nonreactive pan and season with salt and pepper to taste. Reheat gently before serving. If the sauce is too thick, thin it out with a little stock or water and adjust the seasoning.

—*Bob Chambers*

• • •

LOBSTER STIR-FRIED WITH MELON AND KIWI

In Hong Kong's newer restaurants, particularly the Jade Garden group, stir-frying fruit with shrimp has become commonplace. My own interpretation uses lobster medallions instead of shrimp.

❦ The combination of the perfumed fruit with the delicate lobster requires the subtle fruit and acidity characteristic of Northwest Rieslings, such as 1988 Hogue Cellars Dry Johannisberg Riesling or 1988 Ste. Chapelle Johannisberg Riesling Dry.

6 Servings
155 Calories and 359 Mg
——**Sodium per Serving**——
2 fresh or thawed frozen lobster tails (½ pound each), shelled and cut into ⅓-inch medallions
Ginger Marinade (recipe follows)
⅓ cup chicken stock or canned low-sodium broth
2 teaspoons oyster sauce
1 teaspoon low-sodium soy sauce
1 teaspoon Oriental sesame oil
1⅓ teaspoons cornstarch
½ teaspoon sugar
Pinch of freshly ground white pepper

2 fresh water chestnuts or 3 sliced canned water chestnuts
2½ tablespoons peanut oil
1 tablespoon shredded fresh ginger
2 large scallions, white part only, sliced diagonally into ½-inch pieces
1 medium red bell pepper, cut into ⅓-by-2-inch strips
½ medium cantaloupe, cut into ½-by-1-inch chunks
1¼ teaspoons minced garlic
1 tablespoon dry white wine
2 kiwis—peeled, halved lengthwise and sliced ¼ inch thick

1. In a medium bowl, combine the lobster and the Ginger Marinade. Stir to coat the lobster thoroughly. Set aside to marinate for at least 10 minutes.

2. In a small bowl, combine the chicken stock, oyster sauce, soy sauce, sesame oil, cornstarch, sugar and white pepper. Stir well and set aside.

3. With a small sharp knife, peel the rough, brown outer skin from the water chestnuts. Rinse under cool water. Pat dry with paper towels. Slice ¼ inch thick.

4. Heat a wok over high heat for 30 seconds. Add 1 tablespoon of the peanut oil and stir with a spatula to coat the wok. When the oil is rippling, after about 30 seconds, add ½ tablespoon of the ginger and stir-fry for 10 seconds. Add the scallions and stir-fry for 30 seconds. Add the water chestnuts, red pepper and cantaloupe and stir-fry for 30 seconds. Take the wok off the heat. With a slotted spoon, transfer the contents of the wok to a plate and set aside.

5. Wipe out the wok with paper towels. Return the wok to high heat and add the remaining 1½ tablespoons peanut oil. Stir with a spatula to coat the wok. When the oil is rippling, after about 30 seconds, add the remaining ½ tablespoon ginger and stir-fry for 15 seconds. Add the garlic and stir-fry until golden, about 1 minute.

6. Add the lobster and its marinade; spread the medallions in a single layer over the wok's surface and cook for 1 minute. Turn the medallions over. Drizzle the white wine down the side of the wok and cook until the lobster is white, about 30 seconds. Stir-fry for 30 seconds longer. Take the wok off the stove and reduce the heat to moderate. Transfer the lobster to a plate.

7. Stir the reserved sauce and pour it into the wok. Return to the heat and cook, stirring the sauce constantly in one direction until it begins to bubble, about 2 minutes. Add the lobster and stir to coat. Add the reserved vegetables and melon and mix well. Add the kiwis and stir until heated through, about 1 minute. Spoon the lobster stir-fry onto a warmed serving platter and serve at once.

—*Eileen Yin-Fei Lo*

• • •

GINGER MARINADE

——*Makes About 2 Tablespoons*——
2 teaspoons dry white wine
2 teaspoons oyster sauce
¾ teaspoon ginger juice (see Note)
¾ teaspoon Oriental sesame oil
½ teaspoon low-sodium soy sauce
1 teaspoon cornstarch
¾ teaspoon sugar
Pinch of freshly ground white pepper

In a small bowl, combine all the ingredients. Stir until thoroughly mixed.

NOTE: To make ginger juice, grate fresh ginger on a small grater, then squeeze through a garlic press. Approximately 1 tablespoon grated fresh ginger yields ¾ teaspoon juice.

—*Eileen Yin-Fei Lo*

• • •

SPICY STUFFED
CHICKEN BREASTS

Tomatoes are naturally high in sodium. Drying them concentrates their flavor and intensifies the impact of their acidic sweetness. Some brands of dry, unmarinated sun-dried tomatoes contain small amounts of residual salt from the drying process. Blanching and rinsing the tomatoes well, as I have done in the following recipe, removes most of the added salt.

❢ The sun-dried tomatoes and the other piquant accents here point to a Pinot Noir, such as 1985 Clos du Val or 1986 Louis M. Martini.

4 Servings
520 Calories and 176 Mg
——*Sodium per Serving*——
1 ounce (about 12) dry,
*   unmarinated sun-dried tomato*
*   halves*
1 tablespoon cumin seeds
3 garlic cloves, minced
1 jalapeño pepper, seeded and
*   minced*
2 teaspoons finely grated lemon zest
1 teaspoon freshly ground black
*   pepper*
¼ cup plus 1 tablespoon sour cream
¼ cup chopped fresh coriander
8 large chicken breast halves,
*   boneless, with skin on (about 8*
*   ounces each)*
½ teaspoon pure chile powder
1 tablespoon pure olive oil

1. In a small saucepan, add enough water to just cover the sun-dried tomatoes and bring to a boil over moderately high heat. Reduce the heat to low and simmer until the tomatoes are tender but still slightly chewy, about 3 minutes. Drain the tomatoes, rinse well under cold running water and drain again thoroughly. Cut into ¼-inch dice and set aside.

2. In a small skillet, toast the cumin seeds over moderately high heat, shaking the pan occasionally, until the seeds darken slightly and become very aromatic, about 1 minute. Set aside ½ teaspoon of the seeds. On a work surface or in a mortar with a pestle, finely chop or pound the remaining 2½ teaspoons cumin seeds. If using a mortar, blend in the garlic, jalapeño, lemon zest and black pepper to form a paste. Blend in the sour cream, coriander and tomatoes. Alternatively, combine the chopped seeds with the above ingredients in a bowl. Divide the stuffing into 4 equal portions.

3. Carefully run your fingers under the breast skin to loosen the flesh. Put one-fourth of the stuffing under the skin of each breast and press gently to distribute the filling evenly. Season the chicken breasts on both sides with the reserved cumin and the chile powder. *(The chicken breasts can be stuffed 1 day ahead. Store, covered, in the refrigerator.)*

4. Allow the chicken breasts to come to room temperature if refrigerated. Preheat the oven to 450°. In a large ovenproof skillet, heat the olive oil over high heat. When the oil begins to smoke, add the chicken breasts, skin-side down, and cook until the skin is browned and crisp, about 5 minutes. Turn the chicken over and place the skillet in the oven. Roast until the chicken feels firm to the touch but still juicy, about 8 minutes. Remove the chicken to a warm plate and let rest for 5 minutes before slicing. Cut the breasts on a diagonal into ¼-inch slices or serve whole if desired.

—*Marcia Kiesel*

• • •

WARM CHICKEN SALAD
WITH ORANGES AND SPICY
GINGER DRESSING

Chef Stroot likes to serve this sweet, pungent, gingery salad while the chicken is still slightly warm. He garnishes the dish with shredded fresh vegetables and edible flowers such as nasturtiums.

❢ Citrus and ginger tend to clash with subtle wines; choose more straightforward whites, such as 1987 Masi Masianco or 1987 Trefethen Eschol White.

6 Servings
——*577 Calories per Serving*——
4 skinless, boneless chicken breast
*   halves, trimmed of excess fat*
*   (about 4 ounces each)*
2 tablespoons fresh lime juice
1 teaspoon crushed hot red pepper
2 medium navel oranges
4 ounces fettuccine, dry or fresh
Spicy Ginger Dressing (recipe
*   follows)*
1 tablespoon peanut oil
2 tablespoons chopped fresh
*   coriander*
½ medium red bell pepper, cut into
*   thin julienne strips*
1 head of romaine lettuce, leaves
*   separated*
1 bunch of radishes, sliced, for
*   garnish*

1. In a small nonreactive dish, combine the chicken breasts with the lime juice and hot red pepper; turn to coat. Cover and marinate in the refrigerator for at least 4 hours or overnight.

2. With a small sharp knife, peel the oranges, cutting off all the bitter white pith. Working over a bowl, cut in between the membranes to release the sections. Set aside.

3. In a large saucepan, bring 2 quarts of salted water to a boil over high heat. Add the fettuccine and cook until tender but still firm to the bite, 10 to 12 minutes for dry and about 3 minutes for fresh. Drain and rinse under cool water for several seconds to remove starch and cool slightly. Transfer the pasta to a medium bowl and toss with ½ cup of the Spicy Ginger Dressing. Set aside.

4. In a large heavy skillet, heat the peanut oil over moderately high heat. Add the chicken breasts and cook, turning once, until golden brown and just cooked through, 3 to 4 minutes per side. Transfer the chicken to a cutting board and slice the meat against the grain ½ inch thick. Toss the chicken with the remaining ½ cup dressing and the coriander, red pepper and oranges.

5. Arrange the lettuce leaves on a platter. Mound the fettuccine on the lettuce and top with the warm chicken salad. Garnish the platter with the radish slices and serve at once.

—*Michel Stroot, Cal-a-Vie,*
Vista, California

• • •

SPICY GINGER DRESSING

———— *Makes About 1 Cup* ————
¼ cup coarsely chopped fresh ginger
2 tablespoons red wine vinegar
1 tablespoon rice vinegar
1 tablespoon mirin (sweet sake)*
1 tablespoon honey
1 tablespoon low-sodium soy sauce
1 tablespoon minced fresh basil
½ teaspoon crushed hot red pepper
½ cup peanut oil
*Available at liquor stores and
Oriental markets

In a blender, combine the ginger, red wine vinegar, rice vinegar, mirin, honey, soy sauce, basil, hot red pepper and 1 tablespoon of water. With the machine on, gradually pour in the peanut oil in a thin stream and continue to blend until smooth. *(The dressing can be made up to 1 week ahead and refrigerated in a jar. Remove from the refrigerator at least 20 minutes before using.)*

—*Michel Stroot, Cal-a-Vie,*
Vista, California

• • •

CANTONESE CHICKEN SALAD

Salads featuring meats and poultry are popular in Hong Kong's New Cantonese Cooking. Though we use chicken here, duck is often the preferred ingredient in Hong Kong, perhaps with melon or pistachio nuts. These salads are served at room temperature, a departure from Cantonese tradition in which dishes always come to the table hot.

6 Servings
219 Calories and 325 Mg
———— *Sodium per Serving* ————
1 tablespoon distilled white vinegar
1 tablespoon Oriental sesame oil
1 teaspoon Shao-Hsing wine* or dry
sherry
1½ teaspoons sugar
¾ teaspoon salt
Pinch of freshly ground white
pepper
3 fresh water chestnuts* or 4 sliced
canned water chestnuts
1 tablespoon sesame seeds
5 cups peanut oil
1 ounce rice noodles* or capellini
1½ cups shredded Cantonese Roast
Chicken (recipe follows)
½ small, ripe honeydew melon, cut
into ½-inch pieces
1 celery rib, cut into thin julienne
strips

1 carrot, cut into thin julienne strips
1 small red bell pepper, cut into thin
julienne strips
*Available at Asian markets

1. In a small bowl, combine the vinegar, sesame oil, wine, sugar, salt and white pepper. Whisk together until well blended and set aside.

2. With a small sharp knife, peel the rough brown outer skin from the water chestnuts. Rinse under cool water. Pat dry with paper towels. Cut into matchstick-size pieces and set aside.

3. Heat a wok over high heat for 30 seconds. Add the sesame seeds, reduce the heat to very low and toast, stirring constantly, until the seeds are brown and fragrant, about 1 minute. Transfer to a plate and set aside.

4. Return the wok to high heat. After 20 seconds, add the peanut oil and heat until it is rippling and reaches about 350° on a deep-fat thermometer, about 12 minutes. Add the rice noodles and cook, turning once, until crisp and golden brown, 5 or 6 seconds. With a wire or perforated strainer, remove the noodles and drain well in the strainer over a large bowl. Spread the drained noodles on a serving platter.

5. In a large bowl, combine the chicken, melon, celery, carrot, red pepper, and the reserved water chestnuts and toasted sesame seeds. Pour in the reserved dressing and toss thoroughly to mix. Spoon the salad over the bed of rice noodles and serve at once.

—*Eileen Yin-Fei Lo*

• • •

CANTONESE ROAST CHICKEN

This chicken need not be made exclusively for the Cantonese Chicken Salad (above). It is delicious on its own, straight out of the oven, served with your favorite chicken side dishes.

4 Servings
289 Calories and 535 Mg Sodium
—— per Serving ——

1½ tablespoons distilled white vinegar
3 tablespoons dry white wine
1 tablespoon Oriental sesame oil
1 teaspoon salt
¼ teaspoon freshly ground pepper
1 chicken (about 3½ pounds), excess fat removed
4 large garlic cloves, sliced ¼ inch thick

1. Preheat the oven to 375°. In a bowl, combine the vinegar, wine, sesame oil, salt and pepper. Rub this mixture all over the chicken inside and out. Place half of the garlic in the cavity of the chicken. Set the bird on a rack in a roasting pan, breast-side up. Add the remaining garlic and ¾ cup of cold water to the pan.

2. Roast the chicken for 30 minutes. Lower the heat to 350° and roast for 15 minutes longer. Turn the chicken over and roast for 30 minutes longer. If the pan looks dry, add boiling water, ¼ cup at a time. Turn the chicken breast-side up and roast for another 30 minutes or until the juices run clear when a thigh is pierced. Set aside to cool slightly before serving. *(If using the chicken for the preceding recipe, it can be roasted up to 1 day ahead. To shred the chicken, pull the meat off the bone. With a rolling pin, pound the meat and roll over it to break the fibers. Then shred it with your fingers, setting aside 1½ cups.)*

—*Eileen Yin-Fei Lo*

• • •

CORN CREPES STUFFED WITH CHICKEN AND POBLANOS

6 Servings
—— 350 Calories per Serving ——

2 chicken breast halves (½ pound each), bone in
2 large garlic cloves—1 halved, 1 minced
1 bay leaf
1 pound fresh poblano peppers (about 5 medium)
1 cup milk
⅓ cup all-purpose flour
1 teaspoon crumbled oregano
1 teaspoon cumin
1 teaspoon salt
⅛ teaspoon freshly ground black pepper
1 cup corn kernels, fresh or thawed frozen
Corn Crêpes (recipe follows)
1 cup grated Monterey Jack cheese (about 4 ounces)
¼ cup sour cream
1 large tomato, finely diced

1. In a heavy medium saucepan, combine the chicken with 1½ cups water, the halved garlic clove and the bay leaf. Cover and bring to a boil over moderate heat. Reduce the heat to low and simmer until the chicken is just cooked through, about 15 minutes. Transfer the chicken to a plate and let sit until cool. Discard the bay leaf and strain the broth through a sieve. Reserve 1½ cups of the broth (save the rest for another use) and let it cool.

2. Meanwhile, roast the poblanos directly over a gas flame or under a broiler as close to the heat as possible, turning with tongs until charred all over. Enclose the peppers in a plastic bag and chill until cool enough to handle, 5 to 10 minutes. Working under running water, carefully rub the skins off. Halve the poblanos and remove the stems, seeds and ribs; coarsely chop the poblanos.

3. Preheat the broiler. Lightly coat 6 individual gratin dishes with vegetable cooking spray.

4. In a heavy medium saucepan, combine the reserved chicken broth and the milk. Sift the flour into the saucepan, whisking constantly until all the flour has been added and the mixture is smooth. Add the minced garlic, oregano, cumin, salt and black pepper and bring to a boil over moderately high heat, whisking constantly. Reduce the heat to moderate and simmer. stirring, for 3 minutes.

5. Spoon ⅓ cup of the sauce into a bowl. Add the corn and half of the chopped poblanos to the remaining sauce in the pan and simmer for 2 minutes. Pull the meat from the chicken breast, discarding the skin and bones. Tear the meat into fine shreds and stir it into the sauce in the bowl.

6. To assemble, place one Corn Crêpe on a work surface with the speckled side down. Spoon about 2 tablespoons of the chicken mixture and 1 tablespoon of the chopped poblanos on the crêpe and loosely roll up. Place in the dish seam-side down. Repeat with the remaining Corn Crêpes, chicken and chopped poblanos, arranging 2 in each dish.

7. Spoon a scant ½ cup of the poblano-corn sauce over the crêpes in each dish and top with the cheese and sour cream. *(The recipe can be prepared to this point up to 1 hour ahead and kept, covered, at room temperature.)* Place 3 of the dishes under the broiler for 3 to 5 minutes to melt and lightly brown the cheese and heat the crêpes through. Repeat with the remaining 3 dishes. Garnish with the diced tomato and serve one gratin dish per person.

—*Jim Fobel*

• • •

CORN CREPES

Makes 12 Crêpes
——*About 54 Calories per Crêpe*——
2 large eggs
1 cup skim milk
½ cup masa harina*
¼ cup all-purpose flour
1 tablespoon unsalted butter, melted
¼ teaspoon salt
*Available at specialty food stores and some supermarkets

1. In a large bowl, lightly beat the eggs. Gradually whisk in the milk and masa harina. Whisk in the flour, melted butter and salt. Let stand at room temperature for 30 minutes.

2. Spray a heavy 7-inch crêpe pan (or 8-inch nonstick skillet with a 6½-inch bottom) with vegetable cooking spray and place over moderate heat. When the pan is hot, ladle in 2 tablespoons of the batter, quickly swirling to coat. Cook the crêpe until it's speckled brown on the bottom, 30 seconds to 1 minute. Flip and cook for 15 to 20 seconds longer. Transfer the crêpe to a sheet of waxed paper. Repeat with the remaining batter, spraying the pan between crêpes. Stack the crêpes between sheets of waxed paper and cover to keep warm. *(The crêpes can be frozen. Thaw at room temperature before using.)*

—*Jim Fobel*

• • •

DINNER FOR DIETERS

Serves 6
593 Calories per Serving

Croutons of Creamy Red Pepper
(p. 218)

Turkey Fricassee with Brown Rice
and Cumin (p. 231)

Poached Pears in Lemon-Apricot
Sauce (p. 248)

—*Jacques Pépin*

TURKEY FRICASSEE WITH BROWN RICE AND CUMIN

The combination of rich, spicy turkey and nutty brown rice produces an earthy, satisfying dish. Use the dark meat of the leg, which is moister than white turkey meat when cooked this way.

6 Servings
——*333 Calories per Serving*——
6 garlic cloves
3-inch piece of ginger, peeled and coarsely chopped (about 4 tablespoons)
1 teaspoon salt
1 teaspoon freshly ground black pepper
¼ teaspoon crushed hot red pepper
3 medium onions, cut into 1-inch pieces
1 teaspoon cumin
2 turkey legs (about 2½ pounds total) with skin and any visible fat removed
1 cup uncooked brown rice
½ cup sun-dried tomatoes, cut into 1- to 1½-inch pieces (see Note)
1 cup frozen peas, thawed
Chopped parsley, for garnish

1. With a food processor running, drop the garlic, then the ginger through the feed tube to chop fine.

2. In a medium bowl, combine the chopped garlic and ginger with 2¾ cups water. Add the salt, black pepper and crushed hot pepper and set aside. In a bowl, toss the onions with the cumin.

3. Divide the turkey legs into drumsticks and thighs. Cut the thighs in half lengthwise—one half will have the bone and the other will be all meat. Spray a heavy dutch oven or flameproof casserole with vegetable cooking spray and place over moderate heat. When hot, add the turkey pieces in one layer and cook, turning once, until browned, about 5 minutes per side. Transfer the turkey to a platter.

4. Reduce the heat to low and add the seasoned onions to the casserole. Cook, stirring occasionally, until browned, about 5 minutes. Add the rice and stir to combine with the onions. Return the turkey to the pan and add the reserved garlic and ginger liquid and the dried tomatoes. Increase the heat to high and bring to a boil. Cover, reduce the heat to low and simmer, turning the turkey halfway through, until the meat is tender and the rice is cooked, about 45 minutes. (Depending on the rice, less water and a shorter cooking time or more water and a longer cooking time may be needed.) Stir in the peas.

5. Remove the meat from the leg, slice and arrange with the rice on individual plates. Sprinkle the turkey with the parsley and serve immediately.

NOTE: Those who are very conscientious about sodium intake should look for salt-free or lightly salted sun-dried tomatoes.

—*Jacques Pépin*

• • •

TURKEY TACOS

So simple and fresh-tasting, these low-cal soft tacos can be thrown together in practically no time at all. And if you prefer, chicken breast can be used in place of turkey.

12 Servings
―――*102 Calories per Serving*―――
1 teaspoon vegetable oil
2 large garlic cloves, minced
½ pound boneless uncooked turkey breast, cut into 2-by-¼-inch strips
½ teaspoon cumin
½ teaspoon crumbled oregano
Pinch of salt
¼ teaspoon freshly ground pepper
1 medium onion, finely chopped
⅓ cup chopped fresh coriander
12 corn tortillas
2 medium tomatoes, finely diced
1 cup shredded romaine lettuce

1. In a large, nonstick skillet, heat the oil over moderate heat. Add the garlic and cook for 30 seconds. Add the turkey, cumin, oregano, salt and pepper. Increase the heat to high and sauté until the turkey is almost cooked through, 2 to 3 minutes. Add the onion and cook to warm through, about 1 minute. Remove from the heat; stir in the coriander.

2. Place another medium skillet over moderate heat. Moisten each corn tortilla with drops of water on each side. Add the tortillas to the skillet, one at a time, and flip several times until hot, softened and the water has been absorbed.

3. Spoon 2 tablespoons of the turkey filling across the center of each hot tortilla. Top with the tomatoes and lettuce and fold in half. Serve 1 taco per person.
—*Jim Fobel*

• • •

ZUCCHINI STUFFED WITH TURKEY, BROWN RICE AND SWISS CHARD

According to chef Michel Stroot, this is Cal-a-Vie's most popular dish at lunch and dinner. Serve this entrée with steamed vegetables, radish sprouts or other greens. You can also make a vegetarian variation of this dish: omit the turkey, increase the cooked brown rice to 1½ cups and add ½ cup diced walnuts.

4 Servings
―――*304 Calories per Serving*―――
4 large zucchini, halved lengthwise
2 teaspoons minced fresh thyme or ½ teaspoon dried
1 tablespoon plus 1 teaspoon vegetable seasoning powder (see Note)
1½ teaspoons olive oil
½ medium onion, minced
1 garlic clove, minced
1½ teaspoons minced fresh basil or ½ teaspoon dried
½ pound lean ground turkey
½ cup sliced mushrooms (about 2 ounces)
2 medium tomatoes—peeled, seeded and diced—or 1 can (8 ounces) Italian peeled tomatoes, drained and chopped
½ teaspoon freshly ground pepper
¼ pound Swiss chard, shredded
½ cup cooked brown rice
2 tablespoons chopped parsley
1 tablespoon freshly grated Romano cheese
2 ounces mozzarella cheese, cut into 8 thin slices
1 cup Fresh Tomato Sauce (recipe follows)
Parsley sprigs and basil leaves, for garnish

1. With the tip of a sharp knife, score the cut sides of the zucchini halves in a crisscross pattern. Transfer to a large steamer pot. Season with the thyme and 1 tablespoon of the vegetable seasoning powder. Cover and steam over high heat until crisp-tender, about 10 minutes. Remove from the heat and let cool.

2. Using a teaspoon or a melon baller, scoop out the zucchini flesh without breaking the skin. Set aside the zucchini shells. Coarsely chop the flesh and set aside.

3. In a very large skillet, heat the olive oil over moderately low heat. Add the onion and garlic and cook until softened, 2 to 3 minutes. Increase the heat to moderately high and add the basil and turkey. Cook, stirring with a wooden spoon, until the meat is lightly browned, 8 to 10 minutes.

4. Add the mushrooms, tomatoes, pepper and the remaining 1 teaspoon vegetable seasoning powder. Cook, stirring, until the tomatoes and mushrooms have softened, about 5 minutes.

5. Stir in the Swiss chard, brown rice and the reserved zucchini flesh. Cook until most of the liquid has been absorbed, about 5 minutes. Mix in the parsley and Romano cheese.

6. Preheat the oven to 375°. Spoon the filling into the reserved zucchini shells. Top each shell with 2 mozzarella slices. Place the shells in a large gratin or baking dish with ½ cup of water. Bake for 10 to 15 minutes or until the cheese begins to brown. Transfer 2 zucchini shells to each of 4 plates. Spoon 2 tablespoons of the Fresh Tomato Sauce over each zucchini shell and garnish with a parsley sprig and a basil leaf. Serve at once.

NOTE: Look for chemical-free vegetable seasoning powder, available at some supermarkets and health food stores.
—*Michel Stroot, Cal-a-Vie, Vista, California*

• • •

FRESH TOMATO SAUCE

Serve this sauce with the Zucchini Stuffed with Turkey, Brown Rice and Swiss Chard (above) and save the remainder for another use. It will keep in the refrigerator up to four days and is an easy low-calorie topping for pasta.

Makes About 2 Cups
——— *9 Calories per Tablespoon* ———
1 tablespoon olive oil
2 garlic cloves, minced
2 pounds plum tomatoes—peeled,
*   seeded and coarsely chopped*
¼ cup minced parsley
1 tablespoon minced fresh basil or
*   1 teaspoon dried*
1 large bay leaf
¼ teaspoon freshly ground pepper

In a large skillet, heat the olive oil over moderate heat. Add the garlic and cook, stirring, for 1 minute. Stir in the tomatoes, parsley, basil, bay leaf and pepper and bring to a boil. Reduce the heat to moderately low and simmer, stirring occasionally, until the sauce is reduced by one-third and slightly thickened, 20 to 25 minutes. Remove from the heat and discard the bay leaf.

—*Michel Stroot, Cal-a-Vie,*
Vista, California

• • •

FRICASSEE OF CORNISH HENS WITH CHERRY TOMATOES AND GLAZED SHALLOTS

If you can, have the butcher quarter the birds for you.

❦ This subtle, satisfying fricassee points toward light, flavorful reds such as a California Pinot Noir. Try 1986 Sinskey or Sterling.

8 Servings
——— *397 Calories per Serving* ———
4 Cornish game hens (about 1 pound
*   each)*
1 teaspoon salt
Freshly ground pepper
1½ tablespoons olive oil
1½ pounds shallots, peeled
2 medium onions, finely chopped
4 garlic cloves, crushed
6 cups chicken stock or low-sodium
*   canned broth*
1½ pounds carrots, sliced
*   diagonally ¼ inch thick*
4 celery ribs, sliced diagonally
*   ½ inch thick*
1 teaspoon thyme
½ teaspoon mustard seeds
1 pint cherry tomatoes
½ cup chopped Italian flat-leaf
*   parsley*

1. Cut the wing tips off the birds. Using kitchen shears, cut along both sides of the backbones and remove them. With a large sharp knife, quarter the hens so that you have 2 leg-thigh pieces and 2 breast-wing pieces per bird. Sprinkle the pieces with the salt and pepper to taste.

2. Place 4 of the leg-thigh pieces in a large nonstick skillet, skin-side up. Set the cold pan over low heat and gradually increase the heat to moderately high over a period of 3 minutes. This will melt some of the fat from the hens. Cook, turning occasionally, until all the pieces are nicely browned, about 6 minutes total. Remove from the pan and set aside. Repeat with the remaining hen pieces.

3. Meanwhile, heat ½ tablespoon of the olive oil in a large nonstick skillet. Add the shallots and toss to coat with the oil. Cook over moderately low heat, tossing frequently, until the shallots are browned and glazed, about 25 minutes. Set aside.

4. In a large heavy casserole, heat the remaining 1 tablespoon oil over moderately low heat. Stir in the onions. Cover and cook, stirring occasionally, until translucent, about 5 minutes. Add the garlic and cook for 1 minute longer. Then add 3 cups of the chicken stock.

5. Toss the carrots and celery and add half to the casserole in an even layer. Add the reserved game hen pieces and cover with the remaining carrots and celery. Sprinkle with the thyme and the mustard seeds. Pour in the remaining 3 cups chicken stock. (*The recipe can be prepared to this point up to 1 day ahead. Cover and refrigerate the casserole and the glazed shallots separately.*)

6. Place the covered casserole in the oven. Set the oven at 350° and bake for 1¼ hours or 1½ hours if the casserole was cold. The hens will be very tender but not overcooked.

7. Strain all the cooking liquid into a medium saucepan and bring to a boil over moderately high heat. Boil, skimming frequently, until the liquid reduces to 2 cups, 20 to 25 minutes.

8. Reheat the shallots over moderate heat. When warmed through, add the cherry tomatoes and parsley and toss well. Gently stir the shallots and tomatoes into the casserole and pour in the reduced stock. Reheat the fricassee over moderately high heat until hot, 5 to 7 minutes. Transfer to a large serving dish or arrange on individual plates and serve hot.

—*Bob Chambers*

• • •

ORIENTAL FLANK STEAK SANS SOY

Tart, fruity tamarind gives this dish a rich color and deep flavor. If you can't find the tamarind paste, use a squeeze of fresh lemon juice and an extra teaspoon of molasses instead.

❢ The spicy full-flavored marinade suggests an assertive red, such as 1986 Ferrari-Carano Merlot from California or 1985 Aglianico del Vulture from Italy.

4 Servings
307 Calories and 72 Mg
—— Sodium per Serving ——
4 garlic cloves, coarsely chopped
2½ tablespoons Oriental sesame oil
1 teaspoon instant tamarind paste*
2 teaspoons unsulphured molasses
2 teaspoons grated fresh ginger
1 teaspoon salt-free mustard
1 teaspoon freshly ground pepper
1 flank steak (about 1 pound)
*Available at Indian and Asian markets

1. In a large shallow dish, combine the garlic, sesame oil, tamarind paste, molasses, ginger, mustard and pepper. Add the flank steak and coat it well on both sides with the marinade. Cover and refrigerate overnight.

2. Let the steak return to room temperature. Meanwhile, preheat the broiler. Scrape any bits of garlic off the steak and put the meat on a baking sheet. Broil 5 inches from the heat until medium-rare, about 3 minutes per side. Let the steak rest at least 5 minutes before carving. With a long, thin carving knife, slice the steak against the grain into very thin strips. Serve hot or at room temperature.

—*Marcia Kiesel*

• • •

BEEF AND SCALLION ENCHILADAS

These delicious beef enchiladas have fewer calories than a typical cottage cheese plate.

6 Servings
—— 373 Calories per Serving ——
½ pound extra-lean ground beef
2 large garlic cloves, minced
1½ teaspoons cumin
1 teaspoon crumbled oregano
½ teaspoon salt
⅛ teaspoon freshly ground pepper
½ cup drained and chopped canned Italian-style tomatoes
¼ cup chopped fresh coriander
8 medium scallions, thinly sliced
2 tablespoons vegetable oil, plus more for brushing
2 tablespoons chili powder
3 tablespoons all-purpose flour
⅛ teaspoon cinnamon
2½ cups chicken stock or canned low-sodium broth
⅓ cup canned tomato sauce
12 corn tortillas
¾ cup shredded cheese, such as Cheddar longhorn or Monterey Jack (about 3 ounces)

1. In a large, heavy, nonreactive skillet, fry the beef over moderately high heat, stirring with a wooden spoon to break up any clumps, until browned, about 3 minutes. Drain any fat from the pan. Add half of the garlic, 1 teaspoon of the cumin, the oregano, salt, pepper and tomatoes. Cook until the flavors have blended, 2 to 3 minutes. Remove from the heat and stir in the coriander and three-quarters of the scallions.

2. In a medium nonreactive skillet, heat the oil over moderately high heat. Add the chili powder and the remaining garlic and sauté over moderate heat for 1 minute. Whisk in the remaining ½ teaspoon cumin and the flour, cinnamon, chicken stock and tomato sauce. Cook, stirring constantly, until the sauce is boiling, about 4 minutes. Reduce the heat to low and simmer, stirring occasionally, until slightly thicker, 5 to 8 minutes. Remove ¼ cup of the sauce and stir it into the beef. Reserve the rest of the sauce. *(The recipe can be prepared to this point up to 1 day ahead. Cover both the meat and the sauce and refrigerate. Let come to room temperature before proceeding.)*

3. Preheat the oven to 425°. Lightly coat a 9-by-13-inch baking dish with vegetable cooking spray. On a sheet of waxed paper, very lightly brush both sides of each tortilla with a little vegetable oil and stack, wrinkled side up.

4. Heat a medium skillet over moderate heat. When hot, place two slightly overlapping tortillas in the pan; flip them several times until they're hot and pliable. Either with tongs or by hand, quickly dip them into the reserved enchilada sauce to lightly coat on both sides. Let any excess sauce drip off.

5. Spoon 2 packed tablespoons of the beef in a line across the lower third of each tortilla and roll tightly. Repeat with the remaining tortillas and meat. Arrange the enchiladas in the prepared baking pan seam-side down in two rows of six. Spoon the remaining sauce evenly over the enchiladas and sprinkle the cheese on top. Bake in the upper third of the oven until hot and bubbly, about 12 minutes. Garnish with the remaining sliced scallions. Serve 2 enchiladas per person.

—Jim Fobel

• • •

BEEF AND AVOCADO FAJITAS

The sweet crunchiness of jicama adds a welcome surprise to these fajitas. Marinate the steak for at least 12 hours so that the zesty flavors will penetrate the meat. Serve with Salsa Verde and Salsa Roja (recipes follow).

❢ This piquant dish calls for a light lager beer, such as Corona, Tuborg or Amstel, for a refreshing contrast.

12 Servings
——— *163 Calories per Serving* ———
2 medium jalapeño peppers
1 medium onion, chopped
1 medium tomato, chopped
¼ cup chopped fresh coriander
2 tablespoons fresh lemon juice
1 large garlic clove, thinly sliced
¾ pound lean flank steak, trimmed
12 medium flour tortillas
1 medium-size, firm, ripe California avocado, halved, pitted and cut into 12 wedges
¾ cup finely diced jicama
¾ cup plain low-fat yogurt
Salt and freshly ground black pepper

1. Halve and seed the jalapeños, reserving ¼ to ½ teaspoon of the seeds. Discard the cores and then thinly slice the jalapeños.

2. In a food processor, combine the onion, tomato, coriander, lemon juice, garlic and the jalapeños (with seeds to taste for a hotter flavor). Process to a coarse puree. Pour this marinade into a large bowl.

3. With a fork or sharp small knife, prick the steak all over. Add the meat to the marinade and turn to coat evenly.

Cover the bowl with plastic wrap and marinate in the refrigerator for at least 12 hours or up to 24. Let the steak come to room temperature for 1 hour before broiling or grilling.

4. Preheat the broiler or light a charcoal fire. Wipe off the marinade and pat the steak dry. Broil or grill the meat 4 inches from the heat, 6 to 8 minutes per side for medium-rare. Wrap in aluminum foil and let sit before slicing.

5. Meanwhile, heat a large skillet over moderate heat. One at a time, warm the tortillas in the skillet, about 30 seconds on each side. Cover to keep warm.

6. To serve, slice the beef very thin on the diagonal against the grain. In the center of each tortilla, place lengthwise 4 slices of beef, 1 wedge of avocado, 1 tablespoon jicama and 1 tablespoon yogurt. Season with salt and black pepper to taste. Fold the fajitas burrito style so that one side is open; serve one per person.

—Jim Fobel

• • •

SALSA ROJA

During tomato season use fresh tomatoes instead of the canned variety.

Makes About 1 Cup
——— *8 Calories per Tablespoon* ———
1 can (4 ounces) whole peeled green chiles—drained, rinsed and patted dry
1 can (16 ounces) whole peeled tomatoes—drained, seeded and chopped—or 1 pound ripe tomatoes—peeled, seeded and chopped
1 medium jalapeño pepper, finely chopped
1 scallion, minced
¼ teaspoon salt

Seed the canned chiles, reserving ¼ to ½ teaspoon of the seeds, and then finely chop the chiles. Combine all the ingredients (with seeds to taste for a hotter flavor) in a bowl and stir well.

—Jim Fobel

• • •

SALSA VERDE

For a spicier flavor, add ¼ to ½ teaspoon of jalapeño seeds to the sauce.

Makes About 1 Cup
——— *8 Calories per Tablespoon* ———
½ pound fresh tomatillos (6 medium), husked, or 1 can (13 ounces) tomatillos, drained
1 teaspoon vegetable oil
1 large garlic clove, minced
3 medium jalapeño peppers, seeded and chopped
¼ cup finely chopped onion
¼ cup finely chopped fresh coriander
Salt

1. If using fresh tomatillos, place them in a small nonreactive saucepan with water to cover and bring to a boil over moderate heat. Reduce the heat to moderately low and simmer until soft but not bursting, 6 to 8 minutes; drain and set aside to cool. Remove the stems.

2. In a small skillet, heat the oil over low heat. Add the garlic and cook until softened, 30 seconds to 1 minute. Let cool to room temperature.

3. In a food processor, combine the fresh or canned tomatillos, garlic and oil, jalapeños, onion and coriander. Add 1 tablespoon water and process to a coarse puree. Transfer to a small bowl and season with salt to taste.

—Jim Fobel

• • •

STEWED PORK WITH FRESH LEMON

Stewing pork is a Cantonese tradition, but stewing it with lemon is a very new idea. The tartness of the lemon adds a fine counterpoint to the long-cooked meat. Serve this dish with white rice.

6 Servings
314 Calories and 535 Mg
——— Sodium per Serving ———
1½ pounds lean pork shoulder or butt, cut into 1-inch cubes
2 tablespoons cornstarch
3 tablespoons fresh lemon juice
1½ tablespoons oyster sauce
1½ tablespoons dark soy sauce
1 teaspoon Oriental sesame oil
1½ tablespoons sugar
Pinch of freshly ground white pepper
3½ cups peanut oil
1½ teaspoons minced fresh ginger
1 very large onion, minced
1½ tablespoons dry white wine
1¼ cups chicken stock or canned low-sodium broth
½ of a large lemon, cut in half
Lemon slices, for garnish

1. In a bowl, toss the pieces of pork with the cornstarch to coat thoroughly. Shake off any excess. Place the pork in a flat dish in a single layer.

2. In a small bowl, combine the lemon juice, oyster sauce, soy sauce, sesame oil, sugar and white pepper. Whisk together and set aside.

3. Heat a wok over moderately high heat for 45 seconds. Add the peanut oil and heat until it is rippling and reaches 375° on a deep-fat thermometer, 8 to 10 minutes. With a spatula or slotted spoon, add the pork and fry until light brown and crusty, about 1 minute. With a slotted spoon, transfer the pork to a strainer set over a large bowl to drain.

4. Pour off all but 2 tablespoons of the oil from the wok. Heat the wok over high heat until the oil ripples, about 20 seconds. Add the ginger and stir-fry until light brown, about 30 seconds. Add the onion, reduce the heat to moderate and stir-fry for 2 minutes.

5. Return the heat to high, add the drained pork and stir-fry for 1 minute to combine the ingredients. Drizzle the white wine down the side of the wok and mix well. Add the reserved lemon sauce and cook, stirring, for 3 minutes. Transfer the pork and sauce to a heavy, nonreactive medium pot.

6. Add ½ cup of the chicken stock to the wok and swirl it around, scraping up any browned bits. Stir this liquid into the pot, along with the pieces of lemon. Stir to combine thoroughly.

7. Cover and bring the pork stew to a boil over moderate heat. Stir in the remaining ¾ cup chicken stock. Cover and simmer over low heat, stirring frequently to prevent sticking, until the meat is tender, 45 minutes to 1 hour. (The recipe can be made up to 1 day ahead. Cover and refrigerate in the pot.) Transfer the stewed pork to a serving bowl and garnish with the lemon slices.

—Eileen Yin-Fei Lo

• • •

PORK LOIN IN CHILE SAUCE WITH ROAST POTATOES AND CARROTS

This is a good dish to serve to guests, but be sure to plan ahead because the pork loin needs to marinate for 24 to 48 hours. If you have leftover pork and sauce, wrap both in hot corn tortillas to make tasty fajitas. Included in the calorie count are the roast potatoes and carrots.

♥ Hearty fare such as this needs a red wine with the same characteristics. Two good matches would be 1987 Caymus Zinfandel or 1986 Parducci Petite Sirah.

8 Servings
——— 413 Calories per Serving ———
12 medium garlic cloves, unpeeled
4 large ancho chiles
4 large dried pasilla chiles
2 cups boiling water
2 teaspoons oregano
1 teaspoon cumin
1 teaspoon salt
1 teaspoon freshly ground black pepper
½ teaspoon ground coriander
¼ teaspoon allspice
⅛ teaspoon cinnamon
⅛ teaspoon ground cloves
⅓ cup fresh orange juice
2 tablespoons fresh lime juice
1 tablespoon cider vinegar
2 pounds center-cut boneless pork loin in one piece, trimmed and tied
1 tablespoon plus 1 teaspoon vegetable oil
1 medium onion, coarsely chopped
¾ cup canned tomato sauce
1¾ cups chicken stock or 1 can (13 ounces) low-sodium broth
1 bay leaf
1 teaspoon sugar
8 medium carrots (about 1 pound)
8 medium new potatoes (about 2 pounds), peeled
2 teaspoons sesame seeds
8 parsley sprigs

1. Place the garlic cloves in a small cast-iron skillet and cook over low heat, turning occasionally, until soft and speckled dark brown, about 30 minutes. Remove from the skillet and let cool; then peel them.

2. Meanwhile, place the ancho and pasilla chiles in another skillet and toast over moderate heat until soft and fragrant but not scorched, 1 to 2 minutes on each side. Set the chiles aside to cool slightly, then remove the stems, ribs and seeds. Place the chiles in a large bowl and cover with the boiling water. Let soak until softened, 20 to 30 minutes; drain.

3. In a food processor, combine the chiles, roasted garlic, oregano, cumin, salt, pepper, coriander, allspice, cinnamon, cloves, orange juice, lime juice and

vinegar; process to a paste. Scrape the mixture into a large bowl.

4. Using the tip of a sharp knife, jab small slits, each about ¼ inch deep, all over the pork loin. Add the meat to the bowl and turn to coat with the marinade. Cover with plastic wrap and refrigerate for at least 1 day or up to 2 days. Let the pork come to room temperature for one hour before cooking.

5. Scrape the marinade from the pork; set aside 1 cup and discard the rest. Pat the pork dry with paper towels.

6. In a large, heavy, flameproof casserole, heat 2 teaspoons of the oil over moderate heat. Add the pork loin and brown it well on all sides, about 7 minutes. Transfer the pork to a plate and remove the pan from the heat.

7. In a food processor, combine the reserved 1 cup of marinade with the onion, tomato sauce and 1 cup of the chicken stock; puree. Strain half of the puree into the casserole and bring to a boil, without stirring, over moderate heat. Cook for 2 minutes. Strain in the remaining puree, bay leaf, sugar and the remaining ¾ cup chicken stock and return to a boil. Add the pork loin to the casserole and spoon the sauce over it. Cover tightly and simmer over moderately low heat, turning the meat occasionally, until a meat thermometer inserted in the center registers 160°, about 1½ hours.

8. Transfer the pork to a cutting board and cover with foil. Set aside for 20 minutes before slicing. Remove the bay leaf from the sauce.

9. While the meat cooks, preheat the oven to 425°. In a large pot of lightly salted boiling water, cook the carrots and potatoes together until almost tender, about 8 minutes; drain.

10. Lightly coat a 9-by-13-inch baking pan with vegetable cooking spray. Place the hot potatoes and carrots in the pan and brush with the remaining 2 teaspoons of

oil. Season lightly with salt and pepper to taste. Roast the vegetables in the upper third of the oven for 30 minutes, or until very tender and golden brown.

11. In a small dry skillet, toast the sesame seeds over low heat until golden brown, about 1 minute.

12. To serve, ladle ¼ cup of the sauce onto a large platter. Slice the meat about ¼ inch thick and arrange in overlapping slices on the sauce. Drizzle with a little more sauce. Sprinkle the sesame seeds on top and arrange the carrots and potatoes alongside. Garnish with the parsley.

—Jim Fobel

• • •

PINK AND BLACK BEANS RANCHERO

Although dry beans soaked overnight and cooked would yield a more intense flavor, the canned beans are often more convenient and produce good results.

10 Servings
——— *98 Calories per Serving* ———
2 thick slices lean smoked bacon (about 2 ounces), cut into ¼-inch dice
1 medium onion, chopped
1 medium red bell pepper, cut into ½-inch dice
2 large garlic cloves, minced
½ teaspoon cumin
Pinch of thyme
1 small bay leaf
1 can (16 ounces) pink beans, drained and rinsed
1 can (16 ounces) black beans, drained and rinsed
1 cup chicken stock or canned low-sodium broth
⅛ teaspoon freshly ground black pepper
Salt

1. In a large heavy skillet, cook the bacon over moderate heat until crisp and

browned, about 7 minutes. Spoon off and discard all but 1 teaspoon of the bacon fat.

2. Add the onion, red pepper, garlic, cumin, thyme and bay leaf to the skillet. Cook over moderate heat, stirring frequently, until the onion softens, about 5 minutes. Add the pink and black beans, chicken stock, black pepper and salt to taste; bring to a boil. Reduce the heat to moderately low and simmer for 5 minutes. Remove the bay leaf and serve ½ cup per person.

—Jim Fobel

• • •

CAULIFLOWER WITH HERBED CRUMB TOPPING

In this recipe, cauliflower florets are cooked in boiling water, then covered with flavored crumbs and finished in the oven. If the cauliflower has just been removed from the cooking water and is still hot, 10 minutes in the oven and a few minutes under the broiler are sufficient. If, however, the cauliflower has been cooked ahead and then allowed to cool before the next step, increase the baking time to about 20 minutes before finishing the dish under the broiler.

6 Servings
——— *67 Calories per Serving* ———
1 large head cauliflower (about 2 pounds), separated into florets with large pieces cut in half
1 teaspoon chopped garlic (about 2 small cloves)
3 tablespoons chopped scallions (approximately 1 large scallion)
1 tablespoon chopped Italian flat-leaf parsley
½ teaspoon salt
¼ teaspoon freshly ground pepper
2 teaspoons olive oil
¾ cup fresh bread crumbs (from 1½ slices white bread)

1. Preheat the oven to 425°. In a large saucepan, bring 1½ cups of water to a boil over high heat. Add the cauliflower and cook, covered, until just tender, about 10 minutes. Drain thoroughly and spread the cauliflower in a 9-by-13-inch baking or gratin dish.

2. In a small bowl, mix together the garlic, scallions, parsley, salt, pepper and olive oil. Add the bread crumbs and toss gently. Sprinkle over the cauliflower and bake for 10 minutes. Turn on the broiler. Broil the cauliflower 7 inches from the heat for 3 to 5 minutes, until lightly browned.

—*Jacques Pépin*

• • •

CHAYOTE WITH CORN AND LIME

Chayote has become more available in recent years, but if you can't find it, use zucchini instead. Just cook it for a few minutes less.

4 Servings
—— 87 Calories per Serving ——
1 pound chayote (2 to 3 medium), peeled or 3 medium zucchini
1 tablespoon unsalted butter
1 medium garlic clove, minced
1 cup corn kernels, fresh or thawed frozen
½ teaspoon salt
2 teaspoons fresh lime juice
Freshly ground pepper

1. Cut each chayote in half lengthwise and remove the pits. Cut the chayote crosswise into ¼-inch-thick slices.

2. In a medium skillet, melt the butter over moderate heat. Add the garlic and cook until lightly golden, about 1 minute. Add the corn, increase the heat to moderately high and cook for 3 minutes.

3. Add the chayote, salt and ¼ cup water to the skillet and bring to a boil.

Reduce the heat to low, cover and simmer until tender, 8 to 12 minutes. Add the lime juice, season with pepper to taste and serve hot.

—*Jim Fobel*

• • •

BRAISED LEEKS WITH FUSILLI

This recipe is based on a classic Turkish preparation in which leeks are simmered with rice.

8 Servings
—— 134 Calories per Serving ——
3 pounds leeks (7 to 8 medium)
1½ tablespoons olive oil
1 cup minced onions
2 garlic cloves, crushed through a press
2 teaspoons all-purpose flour
1 teaspoon salt
¼ teaspoon freshly ground pepper
1 cup dry fusilli
¼ cup chopped parsley (optional)

1. Trim the root ends from the leeks and cut off the dark green portions. Slice the leeks in half lengthwise to 1 inch from the root ends, then slice crosswise 1 inch thick. Place in a bowl of cold water and let soak for 10 minutes. Lift the leeks out of the water and drain in a colander. Repeat the soaking process 2 or 3 times using fresh water, until the water is free of sand.

2. In a large heavy casserole, heat the olive oil over moderately low heat. Add the onions and stir to coat with oil. Cover and cook, stirring occasionally, until translucent, 3 to 4 minutes. Stir in the garlic and cook for 1 minute longer.

3. Increase the heat to moderately high and add the flour. Cook, stirring constantly, for 30 seconds. Gradually whisk in 1 cup of warm water. Bring to a boil and add the salt and pepper. Reduce the heat to moderately low, cover and simmer for 5 minutes. Add the leeks. Cover and cook, stirring occasionally, until tender, about 20 minutes. (*The recipe*

can be prepared to this point up to 1 day ahead. Let cool, then cover and refrigerate. Rewarm before proceeding.)

4. Meanwhile, bring a large saucepan of salted water to a boil. Add the fusilli and cook until al dente, tender but still firm to the bite, about 10 minutes. Drain.

5. When the leeks are tender, uncover and stir in the fusilli. Cook just until heated through. Season with additional salt and pepper. If you like, stir in the parsley just before serving.

—*Bob Chambers*

• • •

VEGETABLE-STUFFED BAKED POTATOES

Try sweet corn, red bell pepper or cauliflower in place of any of the vegetables listed below, and serve more steamed, julienned vegetables on the side to create a vegetarian main dish.

4 Servings
—— 333 Calories per Serving ——
4 large baking potatoes
Safflower oil, for rubbing potatoes
1 cup low-fat cottage cheese
½ cup plain low-fat yogurt
1 large celery rib, finely diced
3 medium scallions, chopped
1 tablespoon apple cider vinegar
Dash of cayenne pepper
1 pound broccoli, trimmed of stalk and cut into small florets (about 1 cup)
¼ pound part-skim mozzarella cheese, cut into 8 thin slices
Salt and freshly ground black pepper

1. Preheat the oven to 375°. Rub the potatoes with the oil and bake for 60 to 70 minutes until tender. Let cool slightly.

2. Meanwhile, in a medium bowl, stir together the cottage cheese, yogurt, celery, scallions, vinegar and cayenne.

3. Halve the potatoes lengthwise and scoop out the flesh, leaving a ½-inch potato shell. Stir the scooped-out potato into the cottage cheese mixture. Arrange the potato shells in a medium rectangular baking dish. Stuff with the potato-cheese filling. Top with the broccoli florets and cover with the sliced mozzarella.

4. Bake for about 15 minutes, until the potatoes are heated through and the cheese is golden brown. Season to taste with salt and pepper and serve hot.

—*Michel Stroot, Cal-a-Vie,*
Vista, California

• • •

BROILED TOMATOES WITH BALSAMIC VINEGAR AND MINT

8 Servings
——— *22 Calories per Serving* ———
4 large beefsteak tomatoes, cored
*   and halved*
½ teaspoon salt
Freshly ground pepper
2 tablespoons chopped fresh mint
4 teaspoons balsamic vinegar

1. Score the cut sides of the tomatoes at ¼-inch intervals to form a diamond pattern. Sprinkle evenly with the salt and pepper and then with the mint. Pat gently to help the mint adhere.

2. Set the tomatoes on a nonstick baking sheet and cover with plastic wrap. Set aside at room temperature for 1 hour.

3. Preheat the broiler for 5 minutes. Sprinkle ½ teaspoon of balsamic vinegar over each tomato half. Broil the tomatoes 4 inches from the heat for 4 to 5 minutes, until heated through.

—*Bob Chambers*

• • •

MEDITERRANEAN ROASTED VEGETABLES

I drizzle the extra-virgin olive oil over the vegetables just before serving so that its delicate flavor won't be lost during cooking. Use a good pure olive oil to cook the onions.

4 Servings
146 Calories and 11 Mg
——— *Sodium per Serving* ———
2½ tablespoons pure olive oil
2 medium red onions, thinly sliced
1 tablespoon chopped fresh thyme or
*   1 teaspoon dried*
½ pound small yellow squash, thinly
*   sliced crosswise*
½ pound small zucchini, thinly
*   sliced crosswise*
3 medium tomatoes (about ¾
*   pound), thinly sliced*
½ teaspoon freshly ground pepper
2 teaspoons extra-virgin olive oil
1 tablespoon chopped fresh basil
1 tablespoon chopped fresh mint

1. In a large skillet, warm the olive oil. Add the onions and thyme and cook over low heat, stirring occasionally, until the onions are soft, about 10 minutes. Spread the onion mixture in an even layer over the bottom of a large shallow baking dish.

2. Preheat the oven to 450°. Beginning with the yellow squash, arrange the squash, zucchini and tomato slices in slightly overlapping rows across the dish. Keep them neat and tight by pushing the rows close together as you go.

3. Bake the vegetables on the upper shelf of the oven until tender and golden brown, about 25 minutes. To serve, season the vegetables with the pepper and drizzle the extra-virgin olive oil on top. Sprinkle with the basil and mint and serve hot or at room temperature.

—*Marcia Kiesel*

• • •

SALAD OF BITTER GREENS WITH GOAT CHEESE PHYLLO STICKS

If you can't find Montrachet for the phyllo sticks, choose another fresh goat cheese with a low moisture content.

8 Servings
——— *244 Calories per Serving* ———
1 pound escarole, torn into bite-size
*   pieces*
½ pound dandelion greens, torn into
*   bite-size pieces, or additional*
*   escarole*
¼ pound radicchio, finely shredded
4 ounces soft goat cheese, such as
*   Montrachet, at room temperature*
7 tablespoons freshly grated
*   Parmesan cheese (about 2 ounces)*
1 teaspoon finely chopped fresh
*   thyme or ¼ teaspoon dried*
¼ teaspoon freshly ground pepper
2 sheets of phyllo dough
½ cup olive oil
1½ teaspoons sesame seeds
2 tablespoons sherry vinegar
1 teaspoon dry mustard
¼ teaspoon salt

1. Rinse the escarole, dandelion and radicchio in several changes of cold water. Dry well and set aside.

2. Preheat the oven to 350°. In a small bowl, combine the goat cheese, Parmesan, thyme and ⅛ teaspoon of the pepper. Mash with a fork to combine.

3. Brush 1 sheet of the phyllo dough with 1 tablespoon of the olive oil. Cut the dough into 8 equal squares. Cover all but 1 square with a slightly damp towel.

4. Form ½ tablespoon of the cheese mixture into a 2-inch log. Roll the log in the phyllo square and pinch the ends to seal. Repeat with the remaining 7 squares, then repeat the procedure with the second sheet of phyllo dough. Lightly brush the tops of the sticks with water. Sprinkle the sesame seeds on top and press lightly to help them adhere.

5. Arrange the phyllo sticks on a non-stick baking sheet. Bake on the lower shelf of the oven for 5 minutes. Transfer the baking sheet to the top shelf and bake the phyllo sticks for about 15 minutes longer, until golden. *(The phyllo sticks can be prepared up to 1 day ahead and reheated before serving.)*

6. Meanwhile, in a small bowl, combine the vinegar with the mustard, salt and the remaining ⅛ teaspoon pepper. Gradually whisk in the remaining 6 tablespoons olive oil.

7. In a large bowl, toss the escarole, dandelion and radicchio with the sherry vinaigrette. Arrange the salads on 8 individual plates and garnish each one with 2 warm phyllo sticks.

—*Bob Chambers*

• • •

BEET AND GREEN APPLE SALAD WITH TWO ENDIVES

Sweet, earthy beets and tart apples offset the bitter edge of the endives in this festive fall salad.

8 Servings
—— **135 Calories per Serving** ——
1½ pounds beets without tops, scrubbed
1 tablespoon Dijon-style mustard
Juice of 2 lemons
3 tablespoons olive oil
1 tablespoon safflower oil
Salt and freshly ground pepper
2 tablespoons finely chopped fresh dill plus 8 dill sprigs, for garnish
2 medium Granny Smith apples
1½ pounds Belgian endives, cut crosswise into ½-inch-thick slices
1 medium head of curly endive, torn into bite-size pieces

1. Preheat the oven to 400°. Tightly wrap the beets in aluminum foil and bake for 1 hour and 15 minutes, or until tender when pierced. When the beets are cool enough to handle, peel them under cold running water. Cover and refrigerate until chilled. *(The recipe can be prepared to this point up to 1 day ahead.)*

2. In a bowl, whisk together the mustard and lemon juice. Add the olive and safflower oils in a slow stream, whisking until blended. Season with salt and pepper to taste. Stir in the chopped dill.

3. Cut the beets into ½-inch cubes. In a small bowl, toss the beets with 2 tablespoons of the dressing. Quarter and core the apples; cut into ½-inch cubes. In another small bowl, toss the apples with 1½ tablespoons of the dressing.

4. In a large bowl, toss the Belgian endive with the curly endive and the remaining dressing. Arrange the salad on 8 plates or in a large bowl. Sprinkle the apples on top and mound the beets in the center. Garnish with the dill sprigs.

—*Bob Chambers*

• • •

AVOCADO, ORANGE AND JICAMA SALAD

Green bell peppers have an almost bitter bite, which complements the other elements in the dressing.

4 to 6 Servings
216 Calories and 10 Mg
—— **Sodium per Serving** ——
1 teaspoon finely grated orange zest
½ small green bell pepper, minced
1 shallot, minced
2 teaspoons salt-free mustard
½ teaspoon honey
½ teaspoon marjoram
½ teaspoon freshly ground black pepper

1 tablespoon white wine vinegar
1 tablespoon orange juice
3 tablespoons pure olive oil
2 tablespoons shelled pumpkin seeds
2 large navel oranges
½ of a small jicama (about ¾ pound), peeled and cut into 2-by-½-inch sticks or 1 large Bosc pear—peeled, cored and cut into 8 sections
2 ripe avocados, preferably Hass, cut into ½-inch dice

1. Preheat the oven to 400°. In a small bowl, combine the orange zest, green pepper, shallot, mustard, honey, marjoram, black pepper, vinegar and orange juice. With a fork, blend in the olive oil and set aside.

2. Put the pumpkin seeds on a baking sheet and toast in the oven for about 5 minutes, until golden. Set aside.

3. Using a sharp paring knife, peel the oranges, trimming off all the bitter white pith. Cut in between the membranes to release the sections.

4. In a large bowl, combine the orange sections, jicama and avocados. Add the dressing and toss lightly, just to combine. Place the salad on a serving platter and sprinkle with the pumpkin seeds.

—*Marcia Kiesel*

• • •

QUINOA SALAD

Quinoa, originally from the Andes, is now being grown in the mountains of Colorado and New Mexico. This delicate grain is light and easy to digest and is higher in protein than most other grains. Quinoa should be rinsed well before cooking, or it will have a noticeably bitter edge. This salad is best served warm or at room temperature when first made, but it can also be refrigerated for up to one day. If you're making it ahead, add the pine nuts just before serving.

4 Servings
—————357 Calories per Serving —————
1 cup quinoa
¾ teaspoon salt
¼ cup dried currants
3 tablespoons pine nuts
1 tablespoon fresh lemon juice
1 teaspoon finely grated lemon zest
¼ teaspoon paprika
¼ teaspoon cumin
¼ teaspoon ground coriander
1 tablespoon minced fresh coriander
¼ cup fruity olive oil
6 dried apricots, finely diced
2 tablespoons snipped chives or
    3 small scallions, green part only,
    thinly sliced
3 tablespoons finely diced yellow or
    green bell pepper
Boston or Bibb lettuce leaves

1. Rinse the quinoa very well in a bowl of cool water. Pour into a strainer and rinse briefly.

2. In a medium saucepan, bring 2 cups of water to a boil. Add ½ teaspoon of the salt and stir in the quinoa. Cover and cook over low heat until slightly chewy, about 10 minutes. If all the water has not been absorbed, drain well. Transfer the quinoa to a large bowl and stir in the currants.

3. Meanwhile, toast the pine nuts in a small dry skillet over moderate heat, shaking the pan from time to time, until the nuts are golden brown, about 5 minutes. Set aside.

4. In a medium bowl, combine the lemon juice, lemon zest, paprika, cumin, ground coriander, 2 teaspoons of the fresh coriander and the remaining ¼ teaspoon salt. Whisk in the olive oil.

5. Add the apricots, chives, bell pepper and the toasted pine nuts to the warm quinoa and toss well. To serve, arrange the lettuce leaves on a small platter and mound the salad on top. Sprinkle with the remaining 1 teaspoon fresh coriander before serving.

—Deborah Madison

• • •

ROASTED PEPPER AND SWEET POTATO SALAD

Gremolata is an Italian blend of parsley, garlic and lemon zest, which is often added at the last minute to perk up flavor. I've used the same principle here, embellishing the traditional garlic and lemon zest with sharp caraway, dill and mint.

6 Servings
300 Calories and 27 Mg
—————Sodium per Serving —————
3 pounds (about 3 large or 5 small)
    sweet potatoes
2 large red bell peppers
1 large cucumber—peeled, seeded
    and thinly sliced
1 small onion, chopped
3 garlic cloves, minced
1½ tablespoons chopped fresh dill
2 teaspoons chopped fresh mint
1½ teaspoons caraway seeds,
    crushed
1½ teaspoons finely grated lemon
    zest
½ teaspoon freshly ground black
    pepper
1 tablespoon fresh lemon juice
1 tablespoon red wine vinegar
⅓ cup pure olive oil

1. In a large saucepan, cover the sweet potatoes with cold water and bring to a boil over high heat. Reduce the heat to moderate and simmer until the potatoes are tender, about 15 minutes. Drain and let cool to room temperature. *(The sweet potatoes can be cooked 1 day ahead. Cover and refrigerate once cooked.)* Peel the potatoes and cut into 1-inch chunks. Place in a large bowl.

2. Meanwhile, roast the peppers directly over a gas flame or under a broiler is close to the heat as possible, turning until charred all over, about 5 minutes. Seal the peppers in a paper bag and let steam for about 10 minutes. Peel the peppers and discard the cores, seeds and ribs. Cut the peppers into ¼-inch-thick strips. Add to the sweet potatoes along with the cucumber slices.

3. In a small bowl, combine the onion, two-thirds of the garlic, 1 tablespoon of the dill, 1 teaspoon of the mint, 1 teaspoon of the caraway seeds, 1 teaspoon of the lemon zest and the black pepper, lemon juice and vinegar. With a fork, whisk in the olive oil. Pour this dressing over the potato salad and toss lightly to combine.

4. In another small bowl, mix together the remaining minced garlic with the reserved ½ tablespoon dill, 1 teaspoon mint, ½ teaspoon caraway seeds and ½ teaspoon lemon zest. Arrange the salad on a serving platter and sprinkle the seasoning mixture on top.

—Marcia Kiesel

• • •

HOMINY AND RED CHILE STEW

Hominy is dent corn (so called for its characteristic indentation at the crown of the kernel), which has been treated with slaked lime or ash. Its flavor is nutty and nice, and the chewy texture of the large plump kernels is very satisfying. You can buy it dried and treat it as you would beans, but it's far easier to use the canned variety that's available at supermarkets.

You can easily vary this recipe by adding tomatoes or by using spices like cumin, cinnamon and clove. For the richest flavor possible, use pure ground chile from New Mexico. The amount called for below will make a spicy dish, but the sour cream will soften the heat considerably. So will serving thick tortillas alongside to mop up the sauce. As with most stews, the flavor of this one improves upon sitting. It also freezes well.

❢ The earthy flavors and the heat of the chile call for something equally spicy—a California Zinfandel, preferably 1986 Burgess or 1987 Nalle.

4 Servings
————328 Calories per Serving————
2½ tablespoons light olive,
   safflower or peanut oil
1 medium onion, coarsely chopped
1 large garlic clove, finely chopped
¾ pound butternut or banana
   squash, peeled and cut into ½-inch
   cubes
1 teaspoon Greek or Mexican
   oregano
½ teaspoon salt
2 tablespoons pure chile powder
1 tablespoon all-purpose flour
2 cans (16 ounces each) hominy,
   drained and rinsed
1 green bell pepper, cut into ½-inch
   dice
½ cup sour cream
Chopped fresh coriander (optional)

1. In a large casserole, heat the oil over moderate heat. Add the onion, garlic, squash, oregano and salt and cook, stirring frequently, for 5 minutes. Stir in the chile powder and flour until blended.

2. Add the hominy and enough water to cover generously, about 3 cups. Cook over moderate heat, stirring occasionally, until the squash is barely tender, about 20 minutes.

3. Add the green pepper and cook, stirring occasionally, until the vegetables are tender, about 15 minutes longer. *(The recipe can be prepared ahead to this point and refrigerated, covered, for up to 3 days or frozen for 1 month. Reheat thoroughly before proceeding).*

4. Transfer the stew to a serving bowl and swirl in the sour cream. Sprinkle with coriander if desired.

—*Deborah Madison*

• • •

BUCKWHEAT NOODLES WITH BROWN BUTTER AND CABBAGES

The earthy quality of buckwheat goes extremely well with cabbage and with the nutty flavor of browned butter. Scallions, parsley and toasted black sesame seeds complete the dish.

4 Servings
————470 Calories per Serving————
1 tablespoon black sesame seeds*
1 stick (4 ounces) unsalted butter
1 teaspoon minced garlic
6 brussels sprouts, separated into
   leaves
¾ teaspoon salt
1 pound trimmed Nappa cabbage,
   thinly sliced crosswise
½ pound Japanese buckwheat
   noodles*
3 tablespoons minced parsley
1 bunch of scallions, white portions
   and 3 inches of green, thinly sliced
½ teaspoon freshly ground pepper
*Available at Oriental markets and
   health food stores

1. In a small dry skillet, toast the sesame seeds over moderate heat, shaking the pan frequently, until fragrant, 3 to 4 minutes. Set aside.

2. In a small skillet, cook the butter over low heat just until it becomes pale brown and has a nutty aroma, about 5 minutes. Skim any foam from the surface and pour the butter into a small dish, leaving behind any browned particles.

3. In a large skillet, heat two tablespoons of the browned butter. Add the garlic and brussels sprouts and cook over moderate heat, stirring frequently, until the leaves are shiny, 1 to 2 minutes. Add ¼ cup water and ¼ teaspoon of the salt and continue to cook, stirring, until the leaves are tender and sweet, about 5 minutes longer. Add another tablespoon of water if the garlic begins to stick to the pan.

4. Add the cabbage and the remaining ½ teaspoon salt and cook, stirring occasionally, until just wilted, 3 to 5 minutes.

5. Meanwhile, in a large saucepan, bring 2 quarts of lightly salted water to a boil. Add the noodles and cook until al dente, tender but still firm to the bite, 4 to 5 minutes. Using tongs, transfer the noodles directly to the pan with the cabbages. Add the parsley, scallions, sesame seeds, pepper and the remaining brown butter. Toss well and serve at once.

—*Deborah Madison*

• • •

SAFFRONED MILLET PILAF WITH ROASTED RED PEPPERS

Small, round and yellow, millet is an important grain in Indian and African cooking. It has a pleasant, nutty flavor, but unlike other grains, such as rice, the seeds do not end up completely separate, nor do they cook evenly. Toasting millet in butter, as in this recipe, enhances its flavor and keeps it moist.

4 Servings
————272 Calories per Serving————
2 medium red bell peppers
1 tablespoon olive oil
Pinch of saffron threads
3 tablespoons unsalted butter
1 small onion, finely chopped
½ teaspoon salt
1 small bay leaf
⅛ teaspoon turmeric
1 cup millet
2 tablespoons chopped fresh basil
1 tablespoon chopped parsley
2 teaspoons chopped fresh
   marjoram or ¾ teaspoon dried
Freshly ground black pepper
Finely chopped basil or parsley, for
   garnish

1. Roast the red peppers directly over a gas flame or under the broiler, turning frequently, until the skins are well charred all over. Place the peppers in a bowl, cover with plastic wrap and set aside to steam for 15 minutes.

2. Peel the peppers. Remove and discard the cores, seeds and veins. Cut the peppers into small squares and place in a medium bowl. Strain any pepper juices over the peppers.

3. In a small skillet, warm the oil with the saffron threads over low heat for 1½ minutes. Remove from the heat and let stand for 5 minutes, then stir the saffron oil into the peppers.

4. In a heavy medium saucepan, melt 1½ tablespoons of the butter. Add the onion, salt, bay leaf and turmeric and cook until the onion is softened, about 5 minutes.

5. Meanwhile, in a heavy medium skillet, melt the remaining 1½ tablespoons butter over moderate heat. Add the millet and toast, stirring frequently, until the grains begin to color and pop, 3 to 4 minutes.

6. Stir the millet into the onion mixture with 2 cups of water and bring to a boil. Cover and cook over very low heat, stirring occasionally, until the millet is slightly chewy but not crunchy, about 20 minutes. Stir in the basil, parsley, marjoram and the roasted peppers with their juices.

7. Transfer the millet to a serving bowl and fluff with a fork. Season with black pepper to taste and garnish with additional basil. Serve hot.

—*Deborah Madison*

• • •

BAKED WILD RICE WITH MUSHROOMS

I grew up near the wild rice-producing areas of Minnesota, and my mother was always looking for new ways to use this grain. Here is her overnight method, in which the rice cooks very slowly in a cooling oven.

8 Servings
——— *111 Calories per Serving* ———
1 cup wild rice, well rinsed and drained
2½ cups chicken stock or low-sodium canned broth
1 pound mushrooms, stems removed, caps quartered
2 tablespoons fresh lemon juice
1 tablespoon chopped fresh thyme or 1 teaspoon dried
Salt and freshly ground pepper
3 tablespoons Le Slim Cow (see Note)

1. In a large heavy casserole, combine the wild rice and chicken stock. Cover the casserole, place it in a cold oven and set the temperature at 500°. After 15 minutes, turn the oven off. Leave the door closed overnight or until the oven has cooled completely, at least 6 hours.

2. After 6 hours or the next day, in a medium nonreactive saucepan, combine the mushrooms with the lemon juice and 1 cup of water. Bring to a boil over high heat. Reduce the heat to moderately low and cover partially. Simmer the mushrooms, stirring occasionally, until tender, about 20 minutes. Drain the mushrooms and add to the rice. Season with the thyme and salt and pepper to taste.

3. Shortly before serving, add Le Slim Cow to the rice. Reheat over moderate heat, stirring occasionally, until warmed through, 8 to 10 minutes.

NOTE: Le Slim Cow is a butter substitute with 40 calories per tablespoon. If you use margarine or butter instead, the calorie count for this dish will be about 134.

—*Bob Chambers*

• • •

CARAMEL FLAN

This creamy and satisfying dessert should be prepared a day ahead, as it must chill overnight before unmolding.

6 Servings
——— *209 Calories per Serving* ———
3 tablespoons granulated sugar
3 large eggs
⅓ cup (packed) dark brown sugar
2 teaspoons vanilla extract
¼ teaspoon almond extract
1 can (12 ounces) evaporated whole milk
½ cup whole milk

1. Preheat the oven to 300°. In a small saucepan, combine the granulated sugar with 1 tablespoon water. Stir over moderate heat until the sugar turns a medium caramel color, about 3 minutes. Working quickly, pour the caramel into six (6-ounce) custard cups; don't worry if they are not evenly coated.

2. In a medium bowl, beat the eggs. Whisk in the brown sugar, vanilla and almond extracts. Gradually whisk in the evaporated and whole milk. Strain the mixture through a sieve and then pour it into the custard cups.

3. Place the cups in a baking pan and add enough hot water to reach halfway up the sides. Bake for about 1 hour or until set. Let the flans cool to room temperature in the water bath. Cover and refrigerate overnight.

4. Run a knife tip around the edge of each flan and invert onto dessert plates. Serve cold.

—*Jim Fobel*

• • •

BUTTERNUT SQUASH FLAN

Butternut squash gives this dessert a distinctive flavor and smooth texture.

6 Servings
—— *104 Calories per Serving* ——
1 small butternut squash (about 1½ pounds)
2 tablespoons honey
½ teaspoon vanilla extract
½ teaspoon cinnamon
¼ teaspoon ground cloves
⅛ teaspoon freshly grated nutmeg
1¼ cups low-fat milk (1%)
1 whole egg, at room temperature
1 egg white, at room temperature

1. Preheat the oven to 350°. In a small baking dish, bake the squash for about 1½ hours, turning once, until tender. Quarter the squash and scoop out the flesh, discarding the seeds and skin. Leave the oven on.

2. In a food processor, combine the squash pulp with the honey, vanilla, cinnamon, cloves and nutmeg. Puree until smooth. Transfer to a large bowl.

3. In a small saucepan, scald the milk over moderate heat. In a small heatproof bowl, beat the whole egg with the egg white until blended. Gradually whisk in the hot milk. Strain the milk into the pureed squash. Stir until incorporated. Pour the custard mixture into six (6-ounce) custard cups or ramekins.

4. Place the cups in a shallow baking pan and fill the pan with enough hot water to reach ½ inch up the sides of the custard cups. Bake for 45 minutes, or until a knife inserted in the center comes out clean. Remove the cups from the water bath and transfer to a rack to cool.

—*Michel Stroot, Cal-a-Vie,
Vista, California*

• • •

SWEET SEMOLINA PUDDING SOUFFLES

Semolina is ground hard durum wheat that is pale gold in color. Although usually reserved for pasta, semolina is also used in desserts in some countries. Here, it's cooked in milk infused with orange, cardamom, cinnamon and vanilla. Baked in individual ramekins, the soufflés rise dramatically and then slowly sink as they cool. They can be served warm or at room temperature.

6 Servings
—— *208 Calories per Serving* ——
Unsalted butter and sugar, for coating the ramekins
2 cups milk
1-inch piece of vanilla bean
¼ teaspoon cardamom seeds, lightly crushed
1 cinnamon stick
1 large strip of orange zest
¼ cup plus 1 tablespoon sugar
Salt
½ cup semolina
3 large eggs, at room temperature, separated
1½ cups raspberries
1 medium pomegranate (optional)
1 tablespoon shelled pistachios, chopped

1. Preheat the oven to 350°. Butter six ½-cup ramekins and coat with sugar.

2. In a medium saucepan, combine the milk, vanilla bean, cardamom seeds, cinnamon stick and orange zest. Bring to a boil over low heat. Remove from the heat and set aside for 15 minutes.

3. Strain the milk into a clean, medium saucepan. Scrape the seeds from the vanilla bean into the milk. Add ¼ cup of the sugar and a pinch of salt; bring to a boil over moderate heat. Reduce the heat to low and pour in the semolina, stirring, in a steady stream. Cook, stirring constantly, until the mixture thickens, 2 to 3 minutes. Remove from the heat.

4. In a large bowl, lightly beat the egg yolks. Stir a little of the semolina mixture into the yolks, then gradually stir in the remainder until blended.

5. In another bowl, beat the egg whites with a pinch of salt until stiff peaks form. Stir one-fourth of the beaten whites into the semolina mixture to lighten it, then fold in the remaining whites. Spoon the mixture into the prepared ramekins and arrange them in a small baking pan without touching. Pour enough boiling water into the pan to reach 1 inch up the sides of the ramekins.

6. Bake for 30 minutes, or until the soufflés have risen and are golden brown on top. Remove from the water bath and let them cool on a rack for a few minutes.

7. Meanwhile, in a food processor, puree ¾ cup of the raspberries. Strain the puree into a small bowl and stir in the remaining 1 tablespoon sugar. Break open the pomegranate, if using. Pick out ¼ cup of the seeds and set aside. Squeeze 1 tablespoon of juice from the pomegranate into the raspberry puree to give it a slightly tart edge.

8. Unmold the soufflés by turning them out onto your hand. Place them right-side up on 6 serving plates. Surround each soufflé with raspberry sauce. Garnish with the remaining ¾ cup raspberries, the reserved pomegranate seeds and the pistachios.

—*Deborah Madison*

• • •

PURPLE PLUM CRUMBLE

8 Servings
——— *186 Calories per Serving* ———
*2 pounds Italian prune plums or
other purple plums, cut into
½-inch dice*
*5 tablespoons (packed) dark brown
sugar*
5 teaspoons all-purpose flour
*⅛ teaspoon freshly ground white
pepper*
Pinch of freshly grated nutmeg
Pinch of ground cloves
4 teaspoons unsalted butter
⅔ cup rolled oats
*1½ teaspoons finely grated orange
zest*
1 cup low-fat vanilla yogurt

1. Preheat the oven to 375°. In a medium bowl, toss the plums with 2 tablespoons of the brown sugar and set aside for 15 minutes.

2. On a sheet of waxed paper, toss 2 teaspoons of the flour with the white pepper, nutmeg and cloves. Sprinkle the mixture over the plums; toss to mix.

3. Spoon the plums and any liquid in the bowl into eight ½-cup ramekins. Set the ramekins on a baking sheet and bake in the middle of the oven for 20 minutes.

4. Meanwhile, in a small saucepan, melt the butter with the remaining 3 tablespoons brown sugar over moderate heat.

5. In a food processor, combine the oats with the remaining 1 tablespoon flour and the orange zest. Pulse for 20 seconds. Pour in the butter and pulse again for 20 seconds.

6. Remove the ramekins from the oven. Reduce the oven temperature to 325°. Spoon the oat mixture evenly over the fruit. Return the ramekins to the oven and bake for 20 minutes, or until the tops

are lightly browned and the juices are bubbly. Let cool on a rack. Serve the crumbles warm or at room temperature, with 2 tablespoons of yogurt on each.

—Bob Chambers

• • •

PAPAYA-MELBA PIE

The pie shell in this recipe can be filled with one quart of any frozen yogurt.

8 Servings
201 Calories and 6.6 Gm
——— *Fat per Serving* ———
½ cup wheat germ
½ cup graham cracker crumbs
*3 tablespoons unsalted butter,
melted*
2 cups fresh or frozen raspberries
¼ cup plus 1 tablespoon sugar
*1 tablespoon plus 1 teaspoon vanilla
extract*
*1 papaya—peeled, seeded and cut
into 1-inch chunks*
*1 envelope (¼ ounce) unflavored
gelatin*
*1 pint plain low-fat yogurt, at room
temperature*

1. Preheat the oven to 350°. Lightly spray a 9-inch pie pan with vegetable cooking spray.

2. In a medium bowl, toss together the wheat germ and graham cracker crumbs. Stir in the melted butter with a fork until well incorporated. Transfer the crumbs to the pie pan and gently pat and press them evenly around the bottom and sides of the pan. Freeze until set, about 5 minutes. Bake the shell for 8 minutes. Remove to a rack and let cool completely. Place the pie shell in the freezer until firm, 10 to 15 minutes. *(This pie shell can be stored in the freezer, covered, for up to 1 week.)*

3. In a small, heavy, nonreactive saucepan, toss the raspberries with 1 tablespoon of the sugar and 1 tablespoon of water. Bring to a simmer over low heat

and cook until the fruit reduces to ½ cup, about 30 minutes. Strain the raspberry syrup into a medium bowl, pressing down on the strainer with a spoon; discard the solids. Stir in the vanilla and the remaining ¼ cup sugar.

4. Meanwhile, in a food processor, puree the papaya until completely smooth. Transfer to the bowl with the raspberry syrup.

5. In a small saucepan, sprinkle the gelatin over 3 tablespoons of water and let soften for 5 minutes. Warm over moderately low heat until the gelatin is completely dissolved, about 5 minutes. Alternatively, combine the water and gelatin in a small glass bowl, let soften for 5 minutes and microwave on High power for 30 seconds; stir.

6. Add the gelatin mixture to the fruit puree, stirring until well blended. Stir in the yogurt. Transfer the mixture to an ice cream maker and freeze according to the manufacturer's instructions.

7. When the yogurt is frozen, use a spatula to scoop it into the frozen pie shell. Gently smooth the top. Freeze until set, at least 1 hour or overnight. Remove from the freezer and let sit at room temperature before serving.

—Tracey Seaman

• • •

NUTTY COCONUT YOGURT

This crunchy yogurt gets its texture from shredded coconut. Be sure to use the canned variety, which is moist and chewy.

8 Servings
199 Calories and 12.2 Gm
——— *Fat per Serving* ———
*1 envelope (¼ ounce) unflavored
gelatin*
*1 can (3½ ounces) sweetened, moist
shredded coconut*

¼ cup sugar
1 pint plain low-fat yogurt, at room temperature
2 teaspoons vanilla extract
1 teaspoon coconut extract
⅓ cup almonds (about 1½ ounces), chopped
½ cup pecans (about 2 ounces), chopped

1. In a small saucepan, sprinkle the gelatin over 3 tablespoons of water and let soften for 5 minutes. Warm over moderately low heat until completely dissolved, about 5 minutes. Alternatively, combine the water and gelatin in a small glass bowl, let soften for 5 minutes and microwave on High power for 30 seconds; stir.

2. In a medium bowl, toss together the coconut and sugar. Stir in the yogurt, vanilla and coconut extracts and the gelatin until well blended.

3. Transfer the mixture to an ice cream maker and freeze according to the manufacturer's instructions. When the yogurt is nearly frozen, toss in the almonds and pecans. Freeze until completely frozen, about 5 minutes. *(The frozen yogurt is best when just made, but it can be stored, covered, in the freezer for up to 1 week.)*

—*Tracey Seaman*

• • •

RIBBONED PEACH AND RASPBERRY MOUSSE

This dessert gets its light, airy texture from a base of cooked meringue.

8 Servings
—— *145 Calories per Serving* ——
1½ pounds peaches
1 tablespoon unflavored gelatin (about 1½ envelopes)
½ cup fresh orange juice
1½ pints fresh raspberries
¾ cup sugar
6 egg whites
¼ teaspoon cream of tartar

1. Bring a medium saucepan of water to a boil. Add the peaches in batches and blanch for 30 seconds. Transfer to a colander and rinse under cold running water. Peel and pit the peaches.

2. Place the peaches in a food processor or blender and puree until completely smooth. Strain the puree through a very fine sieve set over a medium bowl.

3. In a small heatproof bowl, sprinkle the gelatin over the orange juice. Set aside to soften for 5 minutes.

4. Reserve 24 perfect raspberries. Puree the remaining raspberries in a food processor or blender. Strain the puree through a very fine sieve to remove the seeds and transfer to a medium bowl.

5. Set the bowl of gelatin over a small pan of gently simmering water until thoroughly melted, about 2 minutes. Divide the gelatin evenly between the peach and the raspberry purees. Set each puree over a larger bowl of ice and water; stir constantly until the mixtures begin to thicken. Remove from the ice and set aside.

6. In a small heavy saucepan, combine the sugar with ¼ cup plus 2 tablespoons of water. Cook over moderate heat until the sugar dissolves. Increase the heat to high and cook the sugar, without stirring, until it reaches 235° on a candy thermometer.

7. Meanwhile, in a heatproof bowl with an electric mixer, beat the egg whites at medium speed with the cream of tartar until frothy. When the sugar syrup reaches 235°, gradually pour it into the whites, beating constantly. Turn the machine to high speed and beat the whites until doubled in volume and satiny smooth, about 4 minutes. Using a large spatula, fold half the beaten whites into each chilled fruit puree.

8. Spoon about 2 tablespoons of the raspberry mixture into the bottom of eight 8-ounce wineglasses. Tap lightly to even the layers. Top with several spoonfuls of the peach mixture. Continue layer-

ing, alternating the raspberry and peach mixtures, until the glasses are full.

9. Insert the blade of a table knife into the bottom of the mousse near the edge of a glass. Draw the knife slowly up the side to form a pattern on the glass. Repeat at ½-inch intervals around the glass. Repeat with the remaining mousses.

10. Garnish each mousse with the reserved raspberries. Cover the glasses with plastic wrap and freeze for 10 minutes, then refrigerate the mousses for at least 2 hours or up to 8 hours before serving. Serve chilled.

—*Bob Chambers*

• • •

FROZEN FRUITY CREAM CHEESE YOGURT

With this recipe you can have your cool, creamy rich cheesecake and eat it, too. Just take your pick of the dried fruits offered below.

8 Servings
163 Calories per Serving for Cherry, 160 for Apricot, 168 for Raisin and 5.4 Gm Fat per Serving
——— *for Each* ———
1 cup dried pitted sour cherries (about 4 ounces) or 1 cup chopped dried apricots (about 4 ounces) or ¾ cup dark and golden raisins (about 4½ ounces)
⅓ cup sugar
1 envelope (¼ ounce) unflavored gelatin
6 ounces Neufchâtel light cream cheese, at room temperature
1 pint plain nonfat yogurt, at room temperature

1. In a small saucepan, combine the cherries, apricots or raisins with 1¼ cups of water and the sugar. Bring to a boil over moderately high heat. Reduce the heat to moderately low and simmer until the syrup is reduced to ¾ cup, about 15 minutes. Let cool slightly.

2. In another small saucepan, sprinkle the gelatin over 3 tablespoons of water and let soften for 5 minutes. Warm over moderately low heat until the gelatin is completely dissolved, about 5 minutes. Alternatively, combine the water and gelatin in a small glass bowl, let soften for 5 minutes and microwave on High power for 30 seconds; stir. Add to the fruit, stirring until blended.

3. In a medium bowl, whisk the cream cheese until smooth. Gradually beat in the fruit mixture. Stir in the yogurt ½ cup at a time until well blended. Transfer the mixture to an ice cream maker and freeze according to the manufacturer's instructions. *(The frozen yogurt is best when just made, but it can be stored, covered, in the freezer for up to 1 week.)*
—Tracey Seaman

• • •

PEANUT BUTTER AND BANANA FROZEN YOGURT

The combination of ingredients in this yogurt is reminiscent of a sandwich my big brother used to make in our younger days. A generous teaspoon of wheat germ will add only 10 calories per serving.

8 Servings
143 Calories and 5.6 Gm
————— *Fat per Serving* —————
1 envelope (¼ ounce) unflavored gelatin
1 very ripe medium banana
⅓ cup creamy peanut butter
¼ cup honey
1 pint plain nonfat yogurt, at room temperature
Wheat germ (optional)

1. In a small saucepan, sprinkle the gelatin over 3 tablespoons of water and let soften for 5 minutes. Warm over moderately low heat until the gelatin is completely dissolved, about 5 minutes. Alter-

natively, combine the water and gelatin in a small glass bowl, let soften for 5 minutes and microwave on High power for 30 seconds; stir.

2. In a medium bowl, mash the banana. Add the peanut butter and honey, stirring with a fork until incorporated. Stir in ½ cup of the yogurt. Add the dissolved gelatin to the peanut butter mixture and stir until well blended. Stir in the remaining 1½ cups yogurt.

3. Transfer the mixture to an ice cream maker and freeze according to the manufacturer's instructions. Serve with a sprinkling of wheat germ if desired. *(The frozen yogurt is best when just made, but it can be stored, covered, in the freezer for up to 1 week.)*
—Tracey Seaman

• • •

STRAWBERRY-RHUBARB FROZEN YOGURT

This familiar pie-filling combo enhances the tartness of the yogurt. If fresh rhubarb is not available, try the frozen variety sold at the supermarket.

8 Servings
106 Calories and 1.1 Gm
————— *Fat per Serving* —————
2 cups sliced fresh or frozen rhubarb (about 8 ounces)
2 cups strawberries, halved
½ cup sugar
1 teaspoon vanilla extract
1 envelope (¼ ounce) unflavored gelatin
1 pint plain low-fat yogurt, at room temperature

1. In a medium nonreactive saucepan, combine the rhubarb, strawberries and sugar. Bring to a simmer over moderately low heat. Cook, stirring occasionally, until the mixture is reduced to 1½ cups,

about 1¼ hours. Remove from the heat and let cool slightly. Stir in the vanilla. Transfer the mixture to a medium bowl.

2. In a small saucepan, sprinkle the gelatin over 3 tablespoons of water and let soften for 5 minutes. Warm over moderately low heat until the gelatin is completely dissolved, about 5 minutes. Alternatively, combine the water and gelatin in a small glass bowl, let soften for 5 minutes and microwave on High power for 30 seconds; stir.

3. Add the gelatin to the fruit. Stir in the yogurt until well blended. Transfer the mixture to an ice cream maker and freeze according to the manufacturer's instructions. *(The frozen yogurt is best when just made, but it can be stored, covered, in the freezer for up to 1 week.)*
—Tracey Seaman

• • •

BLUEBERRY BOMBE

Elegant yet easy to make, this dessert bursts with flavor.

6 Servings
143 Calories and 1.4 Gm
————— *Fat per Serving* —————
2 cups fresh blueberries or 1 package (9 ounces) frozen blueberries, plus a few additional blueberries, for garnish
½ cup sugar
1 envelope (¼ ounce) unflavored gelatin
1 pint plain low-fat yogurt, at room temperature
Pinch of cinnamon

1. In a small, heavy, nonreactive saucepan, combine the blueberries with the sugar and 1 tablespoon water. Bring to a simmer over low heat. Cook, stirring frequently, until thickened and reduced to ¾ cup, about 1 hour.

2. In a food processor, puree the blueberries. Strain the puree and let cool slightly. Transfer to a medium bowl.

3. In another small saucepan, sprinkle the gelatin over 3 tablespoons of water and let soften for 5 minutes. Warm over moderately low heat until the gelatin is completely dissolved, about 5 minutes. Alternatively, combine the water and gelatin in a small glass bowl, let soften for 5 minutes and microwave on High power for 30 seconds; stir.

4. Add the dissolved gelatin to the blueberries, stirring until well blended. Add the yogurt and cinnamon and stir to combine. Transfer the mixture to an ice cream maker and freeze according to the manufacturer's instructions.

5. When frozen, transfer the yogurt to a 1- or 1¼-quart metal mold or stainless steel bowl, cover with plastic wrap and freeze, at least 1 hour or up to 1 week. To unmold, dunk the mold briefly in warm water, wipe dry and invert it onto a serving platter. Let soften at room temperature for 10 minutes before serving. Garnish with fresh berries.

—*Tracey Seaman*

• • •

PEACH AND ORANGE SORBET

When peaches are not in season, substitute ripe mangoes or papayas. Add a squeeze of fresh lime for a tangy accent.

8 Servings
—— *62 Calories per Serving* ——
4 medium peaches or 1 bag (1 pound) frozen unsweetened slices
1½ cups fresh orange juice
1 tablespoon honey
1 tablespoon orange liqueur
Sliced seasonal fruit (optional)

1. Bring a large saucepan of water to a boil over high heat. Drop in the peaches and blanch for 2 to 3 minutes. Remove with a slotted spoon and rinse under cold water. Peel the peaches and cut into wedges, discarding the pits.

2. In a blender, combine the peaches with the orange juice, honey and orange liqueur. Puree until smooth. Transfer the puree to an ice cream maker and freeze according to the manufacturer's instructions. *(Once frozen, the sorbet can be kept in the freezer for up to 4 hours before serving.)* Divide among 8 bowls or goblets and garnish with seasonal fruit.

—*Michel Stroot, Cal-a-Vie, Vista, California*

• • •

SANGRITA SORBET

Sangrita (not to be confused with the wine and fruit concoction sangria) is a traditional, spicy Mexican chaser for tequila, but here it's transformed into an addictive sorbet.

6 Servings
—— *136 Calories per Serving* ——
1 can (6 ounces) frozen orange juice concentrate, slightly thawed
¼ teaspoon grated orange zest
1 cup fresh orange juice
½ cup canned tomato puree
¼ cup fresh lime juice
¼ cup sugar
2 tablespoons tequila
1 tablespoon grenadine syrup
4 drops hot pepper sauce

In a large bowl, combine all the ingredients with ½ cup of water and whisk well. Pour the mixture into an ice cream maker and freeze according to the manufacturer's instructions. Transfer the sorbet to a covered container and freeze until firm. Serve ½ cup per person.

—*Jim Fobel*

• • •

POACHED PEARS IN LEMON-APRICOT SAUCE

This recipe calls for Bosc pears, a very firm variety that requires a long time to cook until tender. If you use Bartlett or Anjou pears, bear in mind that they cook faster. In any case be sure to use only ripe fruit for poaching. Otherwise you will have to double or triple the cooking time, and the dessert will not be as sweet.

6 Servings
—— *155 Calories per Serving* ——
6 small pears, preferably Bosc (about 2½ pounds)
2 large lemons
⅓ cup apricot jam

1. Peel the pears. Using a small melon baller and working from the bottom, scoop out as much of the cores as you can, leaving the pears whole.

2. Using a vegetable peeler, remove 12 strips of zest from the lemons. Squeeze and measure out ⅓ cup of lemon juice.

3. In a nonreactive saucepan large enough to hold the pears on their sides in one layer, combine 8 cups of water with the lemon zest, lemon juice and the jam. Add the pears to the saucepan and weigh them down with a double layer of wet paper towels and an inverted heatproof plate. (The object is to keep the pears submerged; any part of the fruit that rises above the surface is likely to discolor.) Bring to a boil over high heat, then cover the pan and reduce the heat to low. Simmer the pears until tender when pierced, about 10 minutes. Uncover and set the pears aside to cool in the cooking liquid for 30 minutes.

4. Remove the pears and set them upright in an 8-by-10-inch gratin dish. Bring the cooking liquid to a boil over high heat and boil until reduced to ¾ cup, about 1 hour. Strain the sauce over the pears. Allow to cool slightly, then cover with plastic wrap and refrigerate until serving time. *(This dessert can be made several days ahead and stored in the refrigerator.)*

—*Jacques Pépin*

• • •

ROASTED BANANAS WITH POACHED PINK GRAPEFRUIT

If you can find grapefruits from the Indian River region in Florida, use them in this dessert. Choose fruit that is heavy and large with thin, blushed skin.

4 Servings
—— *229 Calories per Serving* ——
2 large pink grapefruits
¼ cup sugar
1 tablespoon lemon juice
4 long strips of lemon zest, very thinly slivered lengthwise
4 large firm-ripe bananas
1½ teaspoons unsalted butter

1. Using a sharp knife, peel the grapefruits, making sure to remove all the bitter white pith. Working over a bowl, cut in between the membranes to release the sections. Squeeze the membranes over the bowl to extract all the juice.

2. Strain the grapefruit juice into a medium nonreactive saucepan. Add the sugar, lemon juice and lemon zest and bring to a boil over high heat. Cook until the liquid is syrupy and reduced to ⅓ cup, about 7 minutes.

3. Remove from the heat and gently stir in the grapefruit sections. Set aside to cool to room temperature. Transfer the grapefruit sections, lemon zest and reduced juice to a glass or ceramic bowl, cover and refrigerate.

4. Preheat the oven to 500°. When the oven is hot, place a large baking sheet in it for 3 minutes. Meanwhile, peel the bananas and halve them lengthwise. When the baking sheet is hot, rub with the butter to coat evenly. Arrange the bananas on the sheet, cut-sides down, and roast until soft and browned on the bottom, about 3 minutes. With a long metal spatula, transfer the bananas to a large warmed plate. Cut each banana half in thirds.

5. To serve, arrange the bananas and grapefruit sections on 4 large plates. Strain some of the grapefruit syrup over the fruit and garnish with the lemon zest. Serve at once.

—*Marcia Kiesel*

• • •

BANANA-STRAWBERRY SHERBET

It is essential that the strawberries and bananas for this dessert be very ripe; if they are not, the dessert will be quite tart. (When the entire banana skin is speckled with black dots, the fruit is ripe and flavorful. The strawberries should be deep purple-red throughout.) Since it's not always possible to buy perfectly ripened fruit, it is a good idea to cut up some ripe bananas and freeze them so that they are available whenever you want to make sherbet.

6 Servings
—— *138 Calories per Serving* ——
1 pound strawberries (about 2 pints), halved, or unsweetened frozen strawberries
1½ pounds very ripe bananas, cut into 1-inch pieces (about 4 medium)
½ cup plain nonfat yogurt
1 tablespoon honey (optional)

1. Arrange the strawberries and bananas in a single layer on a cookie sheet and freeze until hard, about 1 hour. Once frozen, the fruit can be packed in tightly sealed plastic bags and stored in the freezer for up to one month.

2. Chill the bowl of a food processor in the freezer for a few minutes. Put half of the frozen fruit, half of the yogurt and half of the honey in the bowl and process until smooth. Scrape it into a chilled serving bowl. Repeat with the remaining fruit, yogurt and honey. Serve the sherbet immediately or return to the freezer until serving time. *(The sherbet can be prepared ahead and kept frozen, covered, for up to 3 days.)*

—*Jacques Pépin*

• • •

SPICY DRIED SOUR CHERRIES IN PORT

Dried sour cherries have an incredibly deep flavor and well-balanced tartness.

4 Servings
—— *144 Calories per Serving* ——
1 cup ruby port
1 cup dried sour cherries*
2 strips of orange zest
1 cup fresh orange juice
4 very thin slices of fresh ginger
1 cinnamon stick
Vanilla ice cream, frozen yogurt or mascarpone, for serving (optional)
*Available at specialty food shops

In a medium nonreactive saucepan, combine all the ingredients except the ice cream and bring to a boil over high heat. Reduce the heat to low and simmer until the cherries are plump, about 12 minutes. Serve hot or chilled over ice cream.

—*Marcia Kiesel*

• • •

MOLDED VANILLA PEARS

This jewel-like jellied pear dessert could also be molded in a four-cup terrine and served in thick slices.

6 Servings
────*149 Calories per Serving*────
Juice of 2 lemons
3 firm-ripe Bartlett or Bosc pears (about 1½ pounds)
½ cup sugar
½ vanilla bean, split lengthwise
2½ tablespoons pear brandy
1 envelope (¼ ounce) unflavored gelatin

1. Set aside 2 teaspoons of the lemon juice. Fill a medium bowl with water and add the remaining lemon juice. Peel, quarter and core the pears; drop the pears into the acidulated water as you work to prevent them from discoloring.

2. In a large saucepan, combine the sugar, vanilla bean and 4 cups of water. Bring to a simmer over moderate heat and stir occasionally until the sugar dissolves, about 5 minutes. Drain the pears and add them to the syrup. Cook until tender when pierced with a knife, 3 to 8 minutes. With a slotted spoon, transfer the pears to a large plate. Cover and refrigerate until chilled, about 1 hour.

3. Boil the pear poaching liquid over high heat until it reduces to 2 cups, about 12 minutes. Pour the liquid into a stainless steel bowl and let cool to room temperature. Remove the vanilla bean.

4. When the poaching liquid has cooled, add the reserved 2 teaspoons lemon juice and the pear brandy. Sprinkle the gelatin evenly over the surface of the liquid; let stand without stirring until the gelatin softens, about 3 minutes.

5. Set the bowl of poaching liquid directly over low heat. Stir gently with a slotted spoon to melt the gelatin without creating bubbles. The liquid should be warm and clear and the gelatin completely dissolved.

6. Remove the bowl from the heat and set it in a larger bowl of ice water. Stir the pear liquid gently with the slotted spoon, trying not to create any bubbles, until it is cold and slightly thickened, about 2 minutes. Remove the bowl from the ice water and set aside. Stir occasionally to keep the gelatin from setting.

7. Place six ⅔-cup ramekins on a baking sheet and spoon 2 tablespoons of the pear liquid into each. Refrigerate until set, about 10 minutes. Meanwhile, slice the pears crosswise ¼ inch thick.

8. Arrange the pears in the ramekins and pour the remaining liquid on top. Cover the ramekins with plastic wrap and refrigerate until the aspic is completely set, at least 5 hours or up to 2 days.

9. To unmold, dip the bottom of a ramekin into very hot water for about 15 seconds; the aspic should feel barely loose. Dry the ramekin and invert onto a plate to release the molded pears. Repeat with the remaining ramekins. Serve chilled or at room temperature.
—*Marcia Kiesel*

• • •

SPARKLING STRAWBERRIES

The strawberries will release some of their juices as they macerate with the sugar, forming a light syrup.

4 Servings
────*104 Calories per Serving*────
2 pints strawberries, sliced
3 tablespoons sugar
1 tablespoon chopped fresh mint
½ cup high-quality brut Champagne, such as Perrier-Jouet

1. In a large bowl, combine the strawberries, sugar and mint. Toss well and set aside for 5 minutes.

2. Spoon the strawberries and their juices into 4 stemmed glasses or glass bowls. Pour 2 tablespoons of the Champagne into each glass and serve.
—*Marcia Kiesel*

• • •

PINEAPPLE AND PASSION FRUIT GRATIN

Look for a ripe, sweet pineapple, preferably one from Hawaii, with yellow patches on the skin. It should give a little when pressed and smell sweetly fragrant, not fermented. Passion fruits should be deeply wrinkled and feel slightly spongy.

4 Servings
────*178 Calories per Serving*────
5 passion fruits, cut in half
¼ cup sugar
½ of a large, ripe pineapple
⅓ cup heavy cream
2 tablespoons chopped unsalted pistachios (optional)

1. Set a strainer over a medium nonreactive saucepan. Working over the strainer and using a teaspoon, scrape the seeds and pulp from the passion fruits. Press on the seeds to extract as much liquid as possible; you should have about ⅓ cup.

2. Add the sugar and 2 tablespoons of water to the passion fruit juice. Cook over moderate heat, stirring constantly, until the sugar dissolves, about 1 minute. Remove from the heat.

3. With a large sharp knife, peel the pineapple half by cutting down lengthwise. Make sure to remove all the "eyes." Cut the pineapple in half lengthwise, then cut out the core from each piece and discard. Slice the pineapple crosswise ⅓ inch thick.

4. Bring the reserved passion fruit syrup to a simmer over low heat. Add one-fourth of the pineapple slices to the syrup and cook, turning once, until softened, about 4 minutes. As the pineapple is done, transfer it to a large dish with a slotted spoon. Repeat with the remaining pineapple. Remove the syrup from the heat and let cool. Pour any accumulated pineapple juices in the dish into the saucepan.

5. Preheat the broiler. Arrange the pineapple in a large, shallow gratin dish or 4 individual gratin dishes. In a bowl, whip the cream until stiff. Fold in the reserved passion fruit syrup. Pour the cream over the pineapple and spread evenly. Broil 5 inches from the heat for about 2 minutes, rotating the dish frequently, until evenly browned. Sprinkle the pistachios on top, if desired, and serve hot.

—*Marcia Kiesel*

• • •

RHUBARB COMPOTE WITH CINNAMON CORN BREAD

A bit of sugar and vanilla balances the puckery quality of rhubarb, making it smooth and refreshing. Peeling the stalks eliminates stringiness. However, since most of the ruby color is in the peelings, they are simmered in the poaching liquid.

4 Servings
——*326 Calories per Serving*——
¾ pound fresh rhubarb
⅓ cup sugar
1 teaspoon lemon juice
1-inch piece of vanilla bean
⅛ teaspoon cinnamon

CINNAMON CORN BREAD:
1¼ cups yellow cornmeal
¾ cup all-purpose flour
1 tablespoon plus 1 teaspoon baking powder
½ teaspoon salt
1 tablespoon plus 1½ teaspoons sugar
1 cup milk

1 egg
5 tablespoons unsalted butter, melted
1 tablespoon vegetable oil
1 teaspoon cinnamon

1. Peel the rhubarb stalks and reserve the peelings. Slice the rhubarb lengthwise into ¼-inch-wide strips. Stack the strips and cut crosswise into even ¼-inch dice.

2. In a large nonreactive saucepan, combine the rhubarb peelings with the sugar, lemon juice and 3 cups of water. Boil over high heat until the liquid reduces to 1½ cups, about 20 minutes. With a slotted spoon, remove the peelings, pressing to extract any liquid. Add the vanilla bean to the pan, reduce the heat to low and simmer for 3 minutes. Remove the vanilla bean.

3. Return the liquid to a boil over moderately high heat. Add the diced rhubarb and the cinnamon and cook, stirring occasionally, until plumped and tender but still holding its shape, about 4 minutes. Remove from the heat and set aside.

4. *To make the corn bread:* Preheat the oven to 425°. Place a 9- or 10-inch cast-iron skillet in the oven to heat. Meanwhile, in a large bowl, sift together the cornmeal, flour, baking powder, salt and 1 tablespoon of the sugar.

5. In a small bowl, lightly beat the milk with the egg. Add the milk mixture to the dry ingredients and stir with a wooden spoon until almost combined. Add the melted butter and stir just until blended.

6. Remove the hot skillet from the oven and set it over high heat. Add the oil. When it is hot, pour in the corn bread batter and smooth the top with a rubber spatula. Return the skillet to the oven and bake the corn bread for 5 minutes.

7. Meanwhile, mix the remaining 1½ teaspoons sugar with the cinnamon. Remove the corn bread from the oven and sprinkle the cinnamon sugar evenly over the top. Bake the corn bread for 10 minutes longer, or until it feels springy to the touch and a cake tester inserted in the center comes out clean.

8. To serve, rewarm the rhubarb compote. Cut half of the corn bread into 4 wedges. (Wrap the remainder for later.) Place the corn bread on dessert plates and spoon the rhubarb compote around it.

—*Marcia Kiesel*

• • •

HIGH-FIBER SEED BREAD

This bread has an appealing, grainy texture and nutlike flavor and is excellent toasted. It's also high in cholesterol-lowering fiber. The recipe was developed by nutritionist Linny Largent.

Makes 2 Loaves
——*135 Calories per Slice*——
½ cup cracked wheat
2 cups boiling water
1 tablespoon active dry yeast
1½ cups lukewarm water (105° to 115°)
½ cup unsulphured molasses
¼ cup vegetable oil
2 tablespoons honey
3½ cups whole wheat flour
2 cups unprocessed whole bran flakes
½ cup poppy seeds
½ cup sesame seeds
½ cup hulled sunflower seeds
¾ teaspoon salt

1. In a small heatproof bowl, combine the cracked wheat and boiling water and set aside until cool. In a large bowl, stir together the yeast and warm water and let sit until dissolved, about 5 minutes. Stir in the molasses, oil and honey and let sit for 5 minutes longer.

2. Meanwhile, in a medium bowl, toss together the whole wheat flour, bran flakes, poppy seeds, sesame seeds, sunflower seeds and salt. Add to the yeast mixture and stir together. Stir in the cooled cracked wheat and any liquid remaining in the bowl. Mix until combined. Form the dough into a ball, place in a lightly oiled bowl and turn to coat with oil. Cover and let rise in a warm place until doubled in bulk, about 1 hour.

3. Grease two 8-by-5-inch loaf pans. Punch down the dough. Turn it out onto a lightly floured surface and knead until smooth and firm, about 3 minutes. Divide the dough in half and shape into loaves. Place 1 loaf in each pan. Let the loaves rise in a warm place again until doubled in bulk, 1½ to 2 hours.

4. Preheat the oven to 350°. Bake the loaves for 45 to 50 minutes, or until they sound hollow when tapped on the bottom. Transfer them to a rack and let cool completely. Cut each loaf into 16 slices.

—*Michel Stroot, Cal-a-Vie,*
Vista, California

• • •

WILD RICE AND RICOTTA GRIDDLE CAKES

Wild rice provides the foundation for these light, moist breakfast griddle cakes. Any brown rice could also be used. Serve these cakes with honey or syrup, a squeeze of lemon, a dollop of yogurt or sour cream, and some fresh berries.

4 Servings
——*373 Calories per Serving*——
½ cup wild rice, rinsed twice in cold water and drained
½ teaspoon salt
1 cup (8 ounces) ricotta cheese
3 eggs, separated

1 tablespoon sugar
¼ cup plus 1 teaspoon unsalted butter, melted
1 tablespoon finely grated lemon zest (2 to 3 lemons)
¼ cup whole wheat pastry flour or all-purpose flour

1. In a medium saucepan, bring 3 quarts of water to a boil over high heat. Add the wild rice and ¼ teaspoon of the salt. Reduce the heat to moderate and cook until the rice is tender, about 45 minutes. Drain well. Spread the rice on a baking sheet to cool.

2. In a medium bowl, beat the ricotta with the egg yolks, sugar and the remaining ¼ teaspoon salt until smooth. Stir in ¼ cup of the melted butter, the lemon zest and the flour.

3. In a separate bowl, beat the egg whites with a pinch of salt until they hold soft peaks. Gently fold the whites into the batter, then fold in the wild rice.

4. Heat a griddle or large skillet over moderate heat and lightly coat with the remaining 1 teaspoon butter. Using a ⅓-cup measure, scoop the batter onto the griddle and spread into 3- to 4-inch circles with the back of a spoon. Cook until nicely browned on the bottom, 4 to 5 minutes. Carefully turn the griddle cakes and cook until browned on the other side, 4 to 5 minutes. Repeat with the remaining batter. Serve immediately.

—*Deborah Madison*

• • •

BREAKFAST COUSCOUS WITH DRIED FRUIT

As a cereal, couscous has the comforting, familiar flavor of Cream of Wheat, but with much more texture. I like my couscous with diced prunes, but dates and raisins also work well. The couscous can be cooked in milk, water or a mixture of the two, but using all milk produces a richer, creamier texture. This dish calls for instant couscous. You simply stir it into the boiling liquid, turn off the heat and by the time you've showered, it's done. Eat it however you please—with warm milk, a spoonful of cream, a little brown sugar or maple syrup, or perhaps nothing at all. The calorie count below is based on couscous made with whole milk and prunes.

3 Servings
——*313 Calories per Serving*——
2 cups milk, water, or a mixture of the two
¼ teaspoon cinnamon
Pinch of salt
1 cup instant couscous
8 pitted prunes, cut into quarters

In a medium saucepan, combine the milk, cinnamon and salt. Bring to a boil over moderate heat and pour in the couscous. Reduce the heat, add the prunes and return to a simmer; cook for 30 seconds. Remove from the heat, cover and let sit until all the liquid is absorbed, at least 5 minutes. Serve hot.

—*Deborah Madison*

• • •

SAUCES, CONDIMENTS & PRESERVES

SAUCES, CONDIMENTS & PRESERVES

TOMATO SAUCE

This is a zesty sauce for pasta, meats or vegetable dishes. It's slow cooking, but doesn't need much fussing.

Makes About 2 Quarts
3 tablespoons olive oil
1 large onion, chopped
2 large garlic cloves, minced
1 large red bell pepper, chopped
3 cans (35 ounces each) peeled Italian plum tomatoes
1½ tablespoons minced fresh basil or 2 teaspoons dried
1 tablespoon minced fresh oregano or 1 teaspoon dried
½ teaspoon freshly ground black pepper
¼ cup freshly grated Parmesan cheese
¼ teaspoon salt

1. In a large nonreactive saucepan or small dutch oven, heat the oil over moderate heat. Add the onion and cook, stirring, until translucent about 5 minutes. Add the garlic and red bell pepper and cook, stirring, 5 minutes longer.

2. Add the tomatoes with their juice and crush lightly with a fork. Stir in the basil and oregano. Bring just to a boil, reduce the heat to moderately low and simmer, uncovered, for 2 hours, stirring occasionally.

3. Reduce the heat to low and stir in the black pepper and Parmesan and salt. Simmer gently for 1 hour longer. *(The sauce can be made and refrigerated up to 2 days ahead or kept frozen up to one month.)*

—*Tracey Seaman*

• • •

ROASTED YELLOW PEPPER-BASIL MAYONNAISE

This roasted pepper and fresh basil mayonnaise makes a delicious sandwich spread.

Makes About 1¼ Cups
1 small yellow bell pepper
1 cup mayonnaise
3 tablespoons minced fresh basil
½ teaspoon freshly ground black pepper
⅛ teaspoon salt
2 teaspoons fresh lemon juice

1. Roast the pepper directly over a gas burner or under the broiler, turning, until the skin is blackened all over. Transfer the pepper to a bowl, cover with plastic wrap and set aside until cool. Peel the pepper and discard the core, seeds and ribs. Coarsely chop the pepper.

2. In a small food processor, combine the chopped pepper with the mayonnaise and process until smooth. Transfer to a bowl and stir in the basil and black pepper. Season with the salt and lemon juice.

—*Michael McLaughlin*

• • •

GARLIC-OREGANO MAYONNAISE

This is a splendid condiment for any roast and a tasty spread for sandwiches.

Makes About 1 Cup
1 medium head of garlic (about 1½ ounces)
2 teaspoons olive oil
2 tablespoons fresh oregano, minced
1 cup mayonnaise

1. Preheat the oven to 350°. With a sharp knife, cut ½ inch off the top of the head of garlic. Place on a 6-by-6-inch square of aluminum foil and drizzle the olive oil over the top. Seal the garlic in the foil and bake for 60 to 70 minutes, until tender when pierced with a skewer. Remove from the oven, unwrap and let cool.

2. Separate the garlic cloves. Squeeze the stem ends to release the roasted garlic pulp.

3. In a small bowl, combine the oregano, mayonnaise and 2 tablespoons of the roasted garlic (or more if desired). Mix until well blended. Reserve the remaining roasted garlic for another use.

—*Tracey Seaman*

• • •

MUSTARD SAUCE

Makes About 1 Cup
2 tablespoons hot-sweet yellow mustard
1 tablespoon plus 1 teaspoon Dijon-style mustard
3 tablespoons white wine vinegar
½ teaspoon salt
½ teaspoon freshly ground pepper
½ cup vegetable oil
½ cup chopped fresh dill

In a medium bowl, combine the mustards with the vinegar, salt and pepper. Gradually whisk in the oil in a thin, steady stream. Cover and refrigerate. Stir in the dill shortly before serving.

—*Christer Larsson, Aquavit, New York City*

• • •

FRESH HERB SAUCE

———— *Makes About 2 Cups* ————
2 cups crème fraîche or sour cream
1 cup minced mixed fresh herbs,
such as parsley, chives, dill and
chervil
¾ teaspoon salt
½ teaspoon freshly ground pepper
2½ teaspoons fresh lemon juice

Spoon the crème fraîche into a bowl and stir in the herbs. Season with the salt, pepper and lemon juice. Cover and refrigerate for up to 6 hours.
—*Christer Larsson, Aquavit,*
New York City

• • •

PEANUT DIPPING SAUCE

———— *Makes About 1 Cup* ————
3 heaping tablespoons roasted
unsalted peanuts
1 cup unsweetened coconut milk*
1½ tablespoons Panaeng Paste
(p. 258)
1 tablespoon palm sugar* or brown
sugar
2 teaspoons fish sauce*
½ teaspoon instant tamarind,*
dissolved in 2 teaspoons hot water
*Available at Asian markets

1. In a food processor, grind the peanuts to a coarse meal. Set aside.
2. In a medium skillet, bring ½ cup of the coconut milk to a boil over high heat. Stir in the Panaeng Paste and cook, stirring, for 1 minute.
3. Reduce the heat to moderate and stir in the palm sugar, fish sauce, tamarind water, ground peanuts and the remaining ½ cup coconut milk. Bring just to a simmer, stirring constantly. Remove

from the heat and let cool to room temperature. Refrigerate in a covered jar for up to 2 weeks.
—*Thai Cooking School,*
Oriental Hotel, Bangkok, Thailand

• • •

BASIL-ORANGE VINAIGRETTE

A dramatically colored vinaigrette, this emerald and tangerine duet beads like jewels on the plate. Fruity and sweetly herbal, it sets off pork, lamb, veal, chicken, shrimp and scallops.

———— *Makes About ½ Cup* ————
Freshly grated zest of 1 orange
2 cups fresh orange juice
(4 oranges)
¼ cup Basil Oil (recipe follows)
Salt and freshly ground pepper

1. In a medium nonreactive saucepan, combine the zest and orange juice and bring to a boil over moderately high heat; boil until reduced to ¼ cup, about 20 minutes. Strain the juice into a small bowl and let cool slightly.
2. Stir in the Basil Oil and season with salt and pepper to taste. Use immediately or refrigerate the vinaigrette in a covered jar or bottle for up to 2 weeks. Let return to room temperature before serving.
—*Jean-Georges Vongerichten*

• • •

BASIL OIL

You can also use this infused oil on its own tossed with pasta or rice or drizzled over tomatoes and poached fish or fowl.

———— *Makes About 1⅓ Cups* ————
1 cup tightly packed fresh basil
leaves
2 cups olive oil

1. In a large pan of boiling, salted water, blanch the basil leaves for 5 seconds. Drain and rinse with cold water.
2. In a food processor or blender, puree the blanched basil with ¼ cup of the oil. With the machine on, add the remaining 1¾ cups oil and process until well blended and smooth. Transfer to a glass jar, cover and let stand at room temperature for at least 24 hours.
3. Carefully pour off the clear green oil, leaving behind the 6 tablespoons of thick puree. The strained oil can be refrigerated, covered, for up to 1 month.
—*Jean-Georges Vongerichten*

• • •

FRESH FIG VINAIGRETTE

This delicate vinaigrette breaks into a feathery, smoky-rose pattern on the plate. Serve it with prosciutto, thinly sliced ham, smoked duck or goose breast, or foie gras (sautéed fresh or pâté).

———— *Makes About 1¼ Cups* ————
5 ripe red or black fresh figs (about
1 ounce each)
¼ cup dry red wine
¼ cup port
3 tablespoons sherry vinegar
½ cup grape-seed or safflower oil
Salt and freshly ground pepper

1. Trim the tips off the figs and cut the figs lengthwise into sixths. In a small nonreactive saucepan, combine the figs with the red wine, port and 2 tablespoons of the vinegar. Bring to a simmer over moderate heat and cook until the figs soften, 8 to 10 minutes.
2. Puree the figs and their liquid in a food mill fitted with the medium disk. Transfer the puree to a medium bowl and whisk in the grape-seed oil, salt and pepper to taste and the remaining 1 tablespoon vinegar. Use immediately or refrigerate in a covered jar or bottle for up to 1

week. Let return to room temperature and stir lightly before serving.

—*Jean-Georges Vongerichten*

• • •

CARAMELIZED SHALLOT VINAIGRETTE

A fairly dense and hefty vinaigrette, this sauce suits sturdy foods such as potatoes, mushrooms and polenta and meat such as calf's liver, beef and squab.

——— *Makes About 1 Cup* ———
½ cup plus 2 tablespoons hazelnut oil
5 medium shallots (about 4 ounces), very thinly sliced
¼ teaspoon salt
¼ cup sherry vinegar
½ teaspoon minced fresh marjoram or thyme
Freshly ground pepper

1. In a medium skillet, heat 2 tablespoons of the oil over moderate heat. Add the shallots and sprinkle with the salt. Cook, tossing frequently, until deeply browned, 7 to 8 minutes. Add 2 tablespoons of water and stir for a few seconds until the water evaporates. Remove from the heat and let cool slightly.

2. In a medium bowl, whisk the remaining ½ cup oil with the vinegar and marjoram. Stir in the shallot mixture and pepper to taste. Refrigerate in a covered jar or bottle for up to 3 weeks. The vinaigrette is best if allowed to sit for 2 to 3 days. Let return to room temperature and stir or shake lightly before serving.

—*Jean-Georges Vongerichten*

• • •

BEET VINAIGRETTE

This sweet and earthy, carmine-colored sauce breaks into graceful bubbles and splashes on the plate. (If you prefer a lighter, more homogenized effect, emulsify the mixture in the blender before serving.) It suits squab, quail, beef, lamb, chicken, pork or potatoes.

——— *Makes About 2 Cups* ———
1 large beet (about 6 ounces), peeled and cut into 8 pieces
¼ cup sherry vinegar
Ginger Oil (recipe follows)
Salt and fresh ground pepper
Pinch of sugar (optional)

1. In a small nonreactive saucepan, combine the beet with 1½ cups water. Bring to a simmer over moderate heat and cook until soft, about 20 minutes. Drain, reserving ¾ cup of the cooking liquid.

2. In a food processor or blender, combine the beet with the reserved cooking liquid and puree until smooth. Transfer the puree to a medium bowl and whisk in the vinegar, Ginger Oil, salt and pepper to taste. Add a pinch or two of sugar, if necessary, to balance the acid. Use immediately or refrigerate the vinaigrette in a covered jar or bottle for up to 1 week. Let return to room temperature and stir or shake lightly before serving.

—*Jean-Georges Vongerichten*

• • •

GINGER OIL

——— *Makes About ¾ Cup* ———
4 tablespoons ground ginger
1 cup grape-seed or safflower oil

1. In a medium bowl, whisk the ginger with 3 tablespoons water to form a paste. Gradually whisk in the oil. Pour into a jar

and let stand at room temperature, covered, for at least 2 days.

2. Carefully pour the clear oil into a jar and discard the ginger sediment left behind. The oil can be kept covered in the refrigerator indefinitely.

—*Jean-Georges Vongerichten*

• • •

CITRUS VINAIGRETTE

A confetti of coriander and pink peppercorns is suspended in the yellow oil. This brilliant sauce is further embellished with pastel citrus fruits: pink grapefruit, orange, lemon, lime. It is a fine foil for salmon, lobster, shrimp, mahimahi, tuna, swordfish or sturgeon.

——— *Makes About 2 Cups* ———
¼ cup sherry vinegar
2 tablespoons soy sauce
⅔ cup olive oil
1 tablespoon coarsely grated or finely julienned fresh ginger
¼ teaspoon ground ginger
¼ teaspoon celery salt
¼ teaspoon hot pepper sauce
1 teaspoon pink (rose) peppercorns
Salt and freshly ground black pepper
1 large red or pink grapefruit
2 small oranges
2 lemons
2 limes
2 tablespoons minced fresh coriander

1. In a medium bowl, whisk the vinegar and soy sauce. Slowly whisk in the oil, then stir in the grated fresh ginger, ground ginger, celery salt, hot pepper sauce, the pink peppercorns and salt and black pepper to taste. *(The vinaigrette can be prepared to this point up to 3 weeks* *ahead and kept refrigerated in a covered jar or bottle. Let return to room temperature before using.)*

2. To make the citrus garnish: Cut away the peel and the bitter white pith from the grapefruit, oranges, lemons and limes with a very sharp paring knife. Cut in between the membranes of each fruit to release the segments. Cut the large grapefruit segments in half crosswise and combine with the other citrus segments in a bowl.

3. To serve, stir or shake the vinaigrette lightly and stir in the citrus sections and coriander.

—Jean-Georges Vongerichten

• • •

WALNUT VINAIGRETTE

The flavor of this pale beige, nutty sauce is intensified by the bite of the shallots and leek. Earthy foods, such as warm lentils, chicken, squab, mushrooms, cabbage or potatoes, are the best partners.

─────── *Makes About 1 Cup* ───────
3 tablespoons sherry vinegar
¼ cup walnut oil
¼ cup grape-seed or safflower oil
Salt and freshly ground pepper
2 tablespoons coarsely chopped walnuts
1 tablespoon finely minced shallot
1 tablespoon minced tender white of leek

In a small bowl, whisk the vinegar, walnut oil, grape-seed oil and salt and pepper to taste. Whisk in the walnuts, shallot and leek. Use immediately or refrigerate the vinaigrette in a covered jar or bottle for up to 1 week. Let the vinaigrette return to room temperature and stir or shake lightly before serving.

—Jean-Georges Vongerichten

• • •

MUSHROOM, LEMON AND SOY VINAIGRETTE

The mushroom undertones in this deep-colored sauce provide an earthy finish for simply prepared beef, sweetbreads, shrimp, sole or scallops. You could also serve this sauce with sautéed shiitake mushrooms arranged on a bed of curly endive or with warm asparagus.

─────── *Makes About 2 Cups* ───────
1 tablespoon hazelnut oil
1 cup sliced mushrooms (about 3 ounces)
¼ cup soy sauce
¼ cup fresh lemon juice (2 lemons)
1¼ cups olive oil
Salt and freshly ground pepper

1. In a heavy medium skillet, heat the hazelnut oil over moderately high heat. Add the mushrooms and cook, stirring, until well browned, about 6 minutes. Reduce the heat to moderately low and add 2 cups of water. Bring to a simmer and cook for 10 minutes to extract the mushroom flavor.

2. Strain the mixture through a sieve, pressing on the mushrooms to extract all the liquid. Discard the mushrooms and return the mushroom liquid to the skillet and boil over moderately high heat until it is reduced to ¼ cup, about 5 minutes. Set aside to cool slightly.

3. In a medium bowl, whisk together the soy sauce, lemon juice and olive oil. Whisk in the reduced mushroom liquid. Season with salt and pepper to taste. Use immediately or refrigerate in a covered jar or bottle for up to 2 weeks. Let return to room temperature; shake before serving.

—Jean-Georges Vongerichten

• • •

CURRY-LIME VINAIGRETTE

Smooth and emulsified, this green-tinged yellow sauce provides a spicy, tart counterpoint to shrimp, salmon, chicken and rabbit. It is also particularly good with artichokes or mushrooms. Vongerichten always "garnishes" this vinaigrette with finely julienned lime zest and cut segments of fresh lime.

─────── *Makes About ¾ Cup* ───────
Finely grated zest of 1 lime
¼ cup fresh lime juice (3 limes)
½ cup Curry Oil (recipe follows)
Salt and freshly ground white pepper

In a medium bowl, combine the zest and lime juice. Whisk in the Curry Oil and salt and white pepper to taste. Use immediately or refrigerate in a covered jar or bottle for up to 1 week. Let the vinaigrette return to room temperature and shake before serving.

—Jean-Georges Vongerichten

• • •

CURRY OIL

─────── *Makes About ⅔ Cup* ───────
4 tablespoons curry powder
1 cup grape-seed or safflower oil

1. In a medium bowl, whisk the curry with 3 tablespoons of water to form a paste. Gradually whisk in the oil. Cover and let stand at room temperature for at least 2 days.

2. Carefully pour off the oil, leaving behind the curry sediment. The oil can be refrigerated, covered, indefinitely.

—Jean-Georges Vongerichten

• • •

SAUCES, CONDIMENTS & PRESERVES

CHICKEN LIVER CONFIT

This is a great method for putting up delicate chicken livers. They're seasoned first, then cooked slowly in olive oil.

Makes 1 Pound

1 pound chicken livers, lobes separated and trimmed of fat and membrane
1 tablespoon fresh thyme or 1½ teaspoons dried
1 teaspoon coarse (kosher) salt
½ teaspoon coarsely ground pepper
⅔ cup olive oil

1. In a small bowl, toss the livers with the thyme, salt and pepper. Cover and refrigerate for 1 hour.

2. In a medium skillet, spread the livers out in a single layer and pour the olive oil on top. Cook over very low heat, turning once, until the livers feel firm to the touch, about 14 minutes. Transfer the livers to a glass jar and pour the oil on top. Let cool completely, then cover tightly and refrigerate for up to 1 week.

—*Bob Chambers*

• • •

SHELLFISH BOIL

Makes About ⅔ Cup

1 tablespoon fresh thyme or 1 teaspoon dried
3 bay leaves, crumbled
1 teaspoon white peppercorns
1 teaspoon black peppercorns
1 teaspoon celery seeds
½ teaspoon mustard seeds
⅔ cup coarse (kosher) salt

Mix together all the ingredients and store in a covered jar for up to 1 year in a cool, dark place.

—*Steve Mellina*

• • •

CREOLE SEASONING

This pungent, aromatic mixture of herbs and spices is a major component in both Cajun and Creole cooking.

Makes About ⅓ Cup

3 tablespoons salt
2 teaspoons freshly ground black pepper
1 teaspoon freshly ground white pepper
1 teaspoon cayenne pepper
2 teaspoons garlic powder
2 teaspoons thyme
2 teaspoons basil

In a food processor or spice mill, process or grind all the ingredients until fine. Store in an airtight container at room temperature for up to 1 year.

—*Gerard Maras, Mr. B's, New Orleans*

• • •

CHILI JAM

Makes About 1½ Cups

10 garlic cloves, chopped
10 small shallots, chopped
¼ cup vegetable oil
1 cup dried shrimp*
1 teaspoon shrimp paste*
5 fresh chiles, such as serrano or cayenne, seeded and chopped
1 teaspoon instant tamarind,* dissolved in 2 tablespoons hot water
1 tablespoon fish sauce*
2 tablespoons sugar
*****Available at Asian markets**

1. Preheat the oven to 350°. Put the garlic and shallots on a baking sheet and toss with 1 tablespoon of the oil. Bake for 30 minutes, stirring occasionally, until browned and crisp. Set aside to cool.

2. Meanwhile, in a medium bowl, soak the dried shrimp in hot water to soften, about 10 minutes. Drain well and coarsely chop.

3. In a mortar, pound the toasted garlic and shallots with the dried shrimp, shrimp paste and fresh chiles until a coarse paste forms. Alternatively, puree the ingredients in a food processor.

4. In a wok, heat the remaining 3 tablespoons oil. Add the paste and stir-fry over high heat until fragrant, about 1 minute.

5. Add the tamarind water, fish sauce and sugar and stir-fry until most of the moisture has evaporated, about 3 minutes. Set aside to cool. Refrigerate in a covered jar for up to 1 month.

—*Thai Cooking School, Oriental Hotel, Bangkok, Thailand*

• • •

PANAENG PASTE

Makes About 1 Cup

10 large semi-hot dried chiles, such as Anaheim
3 slices of fresh or dried galanga,* chopped if fresh
1 stalk of fresh lemon grass,* thinly sliced
1 teaspoon finely grated lime zest
3 tablespoons chopped fresh coriander roots or stems
7 garlic cloves, chopped
1 large shallot, chopped
10 black peppercorns, crushed
1 teaspoon shrimp paste*
*****Available at Asian markets**

1. In a large bowl, soak the dried chiles in hot water to cover until softened, about 20 minutes. Drain well. Remove and discard the stems, seeds and membranes. Coarsely chop the chiles.

2. If using dried *galanga*, soak the slices in boiling water, changing the water from time to time, until pliable, about 20 minutes. Drain and finely chop.

3. In a mortar, pound together the chiles, *galanga,* lemon grass, lime zest, coriander roots, garlic, shallot, black peppercorns and shrimp paste until a fine paste forms. Alternatively, puree the ingredients in a food processor. Store the paste in a covered jar in the refrigerator for up to 1 month.

—Thai Cooking School, Oriental Hotel, Bangkok, Thailand

• • •

PICKLED WATERMELON RIND

This sweet pickle shows up frequently at southern picnics and buffets.

Makes 2 Pints
6 cups peeled diced (1-inch) watermelon rind
¼ cup coarse (kosher) salt
2 cups sugar
1½ cups distilled white vinegar
1-inch piece of fresh ginger, thinly sliced crosswise
8 whole cloves
2 cinnamon sticks

1. In a bowl, toss the rind with the salt. Cover and set aside at room temperature for 6 hours or overnight.

2. Rinse the rind well. Place in a medium saucepan with enough cold water to cover. Bring to a boil over high heat. Reduce the heat to low and simmer until tender, about 10 minutes. Drain well.

3. In a medium nonreactive saucepan, combine the sugar, vinegar, ginger, cloves, cinnamon and ½ cup of water. Bring to a boil, stirring to dissolve the sugar. Add the watermelon rind and return to a boil. Reduce the heat to low and simmer, stirring occasionally, until the rind is translucent, about 15 minutes.

4. Spoon the rind and the syrup into 2 clean, dry, 1-pint jars. Cover, cool briefly and refrigerate for up to 3 months.

—Diana Sturgis

• • •

CIDER HONEY

Makes About ⅔ Cup
8 cups unfiltered, unpasteurized cider

1. In a large nonreactive saucepan, boil the cider over high heat until reduced by half, about 1 hour. As the cider boils down, use a wet pastry brush to dissolve and release any cider clinging to the sides of the pan.

2. Pour the reduced cider into a smaller saucepan and boil over high heat until it is reduced by half again, about 45 minutes. Pour the cider into yet a smaller saucepan and boil until it is reduced by half again (to about 1 cup), about 45 minutes longer.

3. From this point on you have to watch the cider carefully. Reduce the heat to very low and simmer the cider gently, constantly brushing down any cider that adheres to the sides of the pan. Don't let it get very dark or it will become bitter. When the cider is very thick, after about 30 minutes, pour it into a heatproof measuring cup to see how much is left. If you have more than ⅔ cup, return it to the pan and simmer until you have a scant ⅔ cup. Strain the cider honey through a fine metal sieve into a wide-mouthed glass jar. Stored at room temperature, the cider honey will have the consistency of pancake syrup; if you prefer it thicker, store in the refrigerator.

—Linda Merinoff

• • •

VANILLA CUSTARD SAUCE

Try this delicious custard sauce with cake, or make a rich vanilla ice cream by churning the chilled sauce in an ice cream machine.

Makes About 5 Cups Custard Sauce or 1½ Quarts Ice Cream
1 quart milk
12 egg yolks
½ cup granulated sugar
1 tablespoon vanilla extract

1. Place a 2-quart bowl over a bowl of ice water and set aside.

2. In a heavy medium saucepan, heat the milk over moderate heat until almost boiling, about 5 minutes.

3. Meanwhile, in a large bowl, beat the egg yolks and sugar until foamy, about 2 minutes. Beat in the hot milk until blended. Rinse out the saucepan.

4. Return the mixture to the heavy pan. Cook over moderate heat, stirring constantly with a wooden spoon, until the custard reaches 180° and leaves a creamy film on the back of the spoon, about 10 minutes. (Don't let the custard boil or the eggs will overcook.)

5. Stir in the vanilla. Quickly strain the custard into the bowl set over ice water to stop the cooking. Let cool to room temperature, then cover and refrigerate until chilled, about 2 hours.

—Diana Sturgis

• • •

INDEX

A

All-American Chocolate Layer Cake, 174
Alsatian Pizza, 32
ANGEL FOOD CAKE
  Chocolate Angel Food Cake, 174
  Orange Angel Food Cake with Orange Glaze, 176
  Vanilla Angel Food Cake, 175
APERITIFS. *See Drink, alcoholic*
APPETIZERS
  Baked Horseradish Cheddar Canapés, 30
  Beet Frites, 26
  Brandied Chicken Liver Mousse, 29
  Carrot Chips, 25
  Celery Root Chips, 26
  Confetti Shrimp, 57
  Crispy Shallot Dip, 30
  Crostini with Beef and Balsamic Vinegar, 32
  Crostini with Tarragon Spread, 31
  Crostini with Tomato, 31
  Croutons of Creamy Red Pepper, 218
  Curried Pumpkin Seeds and Cornnuts, 25
  Frijolemole, 28
  Genoa Matchsticks, 24
  Golden Madras Dip, 30
  Golden Spiced Goat Cheese, 28
  Light Guacamole, 218
  Parmesan Trees, 27
  Parsnip Chips, 26
  Pesto Pita Thins, 27
  Provençale Spinach Dip with Herb Toasts, 29
  Radish and Arugula Sandwiches, 32
  Rocky Roquefort Dip, 28
  Rutabaga Chips, 25
  Sage Crisps, 24
  Shredded Wheat Snack Mix, 24
  Spicy Cheddar-Chive Rounds, 27
  Spicy Tamari Nuts with Rice Crackers, 24
APPLES
  Apple Bread Pudding, 199
  Apple Pie with Whipped Cream, 165
  Beet and Green Apple Salad with Two Endives, 240
  Blushing Applesauce, 213
  Calvados Apple Cake, 178
  Cardamom-Scented Cranberry-Apple Cobbler, 211
  Custard with Apples and Almonds, 198
  Double Crust Apple Pie with Vanilla, 166
  Sautéed Chicken Breasts with Apples and Calvados Cream, 68
  Smooth Applesauce (Jasper White's), 213
  Tapioca-Apple Pudding, 201
ARBORIO RICE
  Microwaved Pancetta and Mustard-Green Risotto, 114
  Risotto Mold with Prosciutto, 115
  Risotto with Porcini Mushrooms, 113
  Wild Mushroom Risotto, 114
ARTICHOKES
  Beets, Artichokes, Asparagus, Onions and Radishes with Whipped Butter, 121
  Sicilian Artichoke and Fresh Pea Soup, 42
ASIAN CUISINE. *See Chinese cuisine; Thai cuisine*
ASPARAGUS
  Asparagus with Butter Vinaigrette, 120
  Asparagus with Parmesan Cheese, 120
  Asparagus with Provençale Mayonnaise, 120
  Beets, Artichokes, Asparagus, Onions and Radishes with Whipped Butter, 121
  Calabrian Asparagus Soup, 43
AVOCADO
  Avocado, Orange and Jicama Salad, 240
  Beef and Avocado Fajitas, 235
  Light Guacamole, 218

B

Bacon Crackling Crackers, 162
Baking Powder Biscuits, 160
BANANAS
  Baked Bananas, 212
  Banana-Poppy Seed Muffins, 162
  Banana-Strawberry Sherbet, 249
  Peanut Butter and Banana Frozen Yogurt, 247
  Roasted Bananas with Poached Pink Grapefruit, 249
BARBECUE
  Fast-Fire Flank Steak, 92
  Fast-Fire Swordfish, 54
  Fast-Fire Veal Chops, 89
  Grilled Lamb Kebabs with Horseradish Butter, 104
  Herbed-Spiced Grilled Lamb, 100
  Slow-Fire Chinese Steak, 91
  Slow-Fire Smoked Chicken, 62
  Slow-Fire Spareribs, 96
BARLEY
  Barley and Wild Mushroom Soup, 225
  Barley Tea, 19
Basil Oil, 255
BASS. *See Striped bass*
BEANS, DRIED OR CANNED
  Bacon, Potato, White Bean and Red Pepper Soup, 46
  Black-Eyed Pea and Corn Salad, 149
  Flageolet Bean Soup with Fresh Thyme, 45
  Frijolemole, 28
  Pasta and Bean Soup, 45
  Pink and Black Beans Ranchero, 237
  Tuscan Beans with Tuna, Pancetta and Lemon, 121
BEANS, FRESH. *See also Lima Beans*
  Citrus Green Bean Salad, 144
  Warm String Bean Salad, 144
BEEF
  Beef and Avocado Fajitas, 235
  Beef and Scallion Enchiladas, 234
  Beef Fillet Steaks in Mustard Sauce, 91
  Beef Tenderloin with Juniper, 89
  Boiled Beef Salad with Tarragon Sauce, 141
  Broiled Flank Steak with Garlic, Ginger and Soy Sauce, 92
  Crostini with Beef and Balsamic Vinegar, 32
  Fast-Fire Flank Steak, 92
  Oriental Flank Steak Sans Soy, 234
  Slow-Fire Chinese Steak, 91
  Steak au Poivre with Wild Mushroom Cream Sauce, 90
  Thai Beef Salad, 141
BEETS
  Beet and Green Apple Salad with Two Endives, 240
  Beet Frites, 26
  Beet Vinaigrette, 256
  Beets, Artichokes, Asparagus, Onions and Radishes with Whipped Butter, 121
  Tarragon Beets, 120
Belgian Endive and Radicchio Salad, 142
BELL PEPPERS. *See Peppers, bell*
BERRIES. *See specific types*
BEVERAGES. *See Coffee; Drink, alcoholic; Drink, nonalcoholic*
Big Orange, The, 22
BISCUITS
  Baking Powder Biscuits, 160

Buttermilk Biscuits with Parsley-Chive Butter, 160

BLACK BEANS
Braised Lamb Shanks with Black Beans, 102
Frijolemole, 28
Pink and Black Beans Ranchero, 237
Black-Eyed Pea and Corn Salad, 149
Blackberry Silk Pie, 170
BLUEBERRIES
Blueberry Bombe, 247
Blueberry Buttermilk Griddle Cakes, 163
Blueberry Lime Pie with Coconut Crumble Topping, 168
Blueberry Shortcake, 180
Blueberry-Almond Coffee Cake, 191
Lemon-Blueberry Mousse, 201
Blushing Applesauce, 213
BREAD. *See also Corn bread; Crackers; Croutons; Muffins; Quick breads; Toasts*
High-Fiber Seed Bread, 251
Olive Bread, 159
Tuscan Bread, 158
Valtellinese Christmas Bread, 158
BREAD PUDDING
Apple Bread Pudding, 199
French Bread Pudding with Whiskey Sauce, 199
Breadsticks, Rosemary, 159
BREAKFAST/BRUNCH
Blueberry Buttermilk Griddle Cakes, 163
Blueberry-Almond Coffee Cake, 191
Breakfast Couscous with Dried Fruit, 252
Great Granola, 117
Walnut-Date Crumb Cake, 192
Wild Rice and Ricotta Griddle Cakes, 252
BROCCOLI
Cauliflower and Broccoli with Cream Sauce, 123
Sautéed Broccoli and Cherry Tomatoes, 122
BROCCOLI RAAB
Mixed Greens with Cracklins and Hot Pepper Vinegar, 124
Broth, Vegetable, 42
Brown Sugar Pie, 168
BROWNIES
Lovey's Brownies, 193
River Oaks Brownies, 193
Buckwheat Noodles with Brown Butter and Cabbages, 242
Bulgur Pilaf, 117
BUTTER
Butter Vinaigrette, Asparagus with, 120
Horseradish Butter, Grilled Lamb Kebabs with, 104
Lime Butter, Steamed Lobster with, 58
Parsley-Chive Butter, Buttermilk Biscuits with, 160
Sage-Parmesan Butter, Turkey Minestrone with, 47
Shallot Butter, Salt-Cooked Salmon with Dill and, 52
BUTTERMILK
Blueberry Buttermilk Griddle Cakes, 163
Buttermilk Biscuits with Parsley-Chive Butter, 160
Buttermilk Bran Muffins, 162

Buttermilk Jalapeño Corn Sticks, 161
Buttermilk Rhubarb Cobbler, 212
Buttermilk Skillet Corn Bread, 160
Chocolate Buttermilk Frosting, 174
Lemon-Pecan Buttermilk Tea Bread, 161
Scallion and Buttermilk Pancakes, 163
Sour Cream Buttermilk Corn Bread, 161
BUTTERNUT SQUASH
Butternut Squash Flan, 244
Butternut Squash Soup, 44
Sweet Potato and Butternut Squash Puree, 130

C

CABBAGE
Buckwheat Noodles with Brown Butter and Cabbages, 242
Cabbage with Pine Nuts, 122
Tagliatelle with Cabbage and Sage, 107
Tuscan Red Cabbage Soup, 43
Warm Cabbage Slaw, 143
Café Brûlot Diabolique, 19
CAJUN/CREOLE CUISINE
Café Brûlot Diabolique, 19
Creole Seasoning, 258
French Bread Pudding with Whiskey Sauce, 199
Louisiana Dirty Rice, 116
Milk Punch, 20
New Orleans Pecan Pie, 168
Pasta Jambalaya, 108
Sautéed Veal with Spinach and Creole Mustard Sauce, 87
Shrimp Rémoulade, 39
Whiskey Sauce, 199
CAKES. *See also Cheesecake; Coffee cakes; Cookies and small cakes*
All-American Chocolate Layer Cake, 174
Blueberry Shortcake, 180
Calvados Apple Cake, 178
Chocolate Angel Food Cake, 175
Chocolate Hazelnut Torte, 176
Chocolate Polenta Cake with White Chocolate Sauce, 177
Cinnamon Corn Bread, Rhubarb Compote with, 251
Creamsicle Currant Shortcake, 190
Fresh Fruit Cloud Cake, 191
Hazelnut-Orange Bundt, 177
Mediterranean Shortcake, 179
Miami Beach Shortcake, 189
Mom's Chocolate Cake, 173
Orange Angel Food Cake with Orange Glaze, 176
Post-Holiday Shortcake, 179
Pumpkin-Ginger Cake, 178
Robert E. Lee Cake (Elizabeth Terry's), 173
Upstate Shortcake, 189
Vanilla Angel Food Cake, 175
Calabrian Asparagus Soup, 43
California Club, 156
Calvados al Giorno, 21
Calvados Apple Cake, 178
CANAPES. *See Appetizers*
CANDY

Coffee Cup Truffles, 216
No-Trouble Chocolate Truffles, 215
Cantonese Chicken Salad, 229
Cantonese Roast Chicken, 230
Capellini with Black Pepper and Prosciutto, 106
Capon, Stuffed, 82
Caramel Flan, 243
Caramelized Shallot Vinaigrette, 256
CARROTS
Carrot Chips, 25
Glazed Carrots, Turnips and Pearl Onions, 123
Parslied Carrots, 123
Stir-Fried Sugar Snap Peas and Carrots with Oriental Noodles, 126
Cassoulet, Pesto Chicken, 79
CAULIFLOWER
Cauliflower and Broccoli with Cream Sauce, 123
Cauliflower Raita, 144
Cauliflower with Herbed Crumb Topping, 237
Neapolitan Cauliflower Soup, 43
CELERY ROOT
Celery Root Chips, 26
Potato and Celery Root Puree with Glazed Cranberries, 129
CEREAL
Great Granola, 117
CHAMPAGNE
French 75, 20
Le Badinguet, 20
Poire Royale, 20
Sparkling Strawberries, 250
Chayote with Corn and Lime, 238
CHEESE
Baked Horseradish Cheddar Canapés, 30
Cheese and Sausage Chicago Deep-Dish Pizza, 157
Dilled Gruyère Quiche, 39
Golden Spiced Goat Cheese, 28
Manicotti Crêpes with Spinach and Cheese, 38
Parmesan Trees, 27
Rocky Roquefort Dip, 28
Spicy Cheddar-Chive Rounds, 27
Cheesecake, Creamy Strawberry, 172
CHERRIES
Spicy Dried Sour Cherries in Port, 249
Chicago Deep-Dish Pizza, Cheese and Sausage, 157
Chick-Pea and Baked Bell Pepper Salad with Cumin, 149
CHICKEN. *See also Capon; Chicken livers; Game hens*
Broiled Thai Chicken Salad, 140
Cantonese Chicken Salad, 229
Cantonese Roast Chicken, 230
Chicken Breasts with Artichoke Hearts, Olives and Bacon, 66
Chicken for Chicken Salad, 137
Chicken Salad with Bitter Greens, Pancetta and Chicken Liver Confit, 138
Chicken Salad with Onions and Potato Crisps, 140
Chicken Salad with Shrimp and Fennel, 136
Chicken Thighs with Tarragon Wine Vinegar, 78

Chicken, Mushroom and Nappa Cabbage Salad
with Fresh Coriander, 137
Classic Club, The, 156
Clay Pot Chicken with Garlic and Herbs, 63
Coriander Chicken with Tubetti, 78
Corn Crêpes Stuffed with Chicken and
Poblanos, 230
Country-Style Fried Chicken, 64
Crispy Balsamic Chicken Wings, 220
Curried Cain Chicken, 77
Curried Chicken Salad with Yogurt Dressing,
138
Gingered Chicken Breasts, 68
Green Chile Chicken, 64
Lemon-Chicken Salad with Wild Rice and
Grapes, 139
Mediterranean Chicken-Ratatouille Salad, 139
Peanut-Fried Drumsticks with Curried
Cucumbers, 79
Pesto Chicken Cassoulet, 79
Pimiento Chicken with Mushrooms, 67
Provençal Roast Chicken, 62
Roast Chicken Stuffed with Sausage and
Armagnac Prunes, 63
Roasted Chicken Breasts with Prosciutto and
Lemon, 66
Roasted Chicken Legs, 137
Sautéed Chicken Breasts, 137
Sautéed Chicken Breasts with Apples and
Calvados Cream, 68
Sesame-Fried Lemon Chicken, 65
Slow-Fire Smoked Chicken, 62
Spiced Honey Wings with Poppy and Sesame
Seeds, 80
Spicy Stuffed Chicken Breasts, 228
Tarragon Chicken Salad with Melon and
Cucumber, 138
Warm Chicken Salad with Oranges and Spicy
Ginger Dressing, 228
Whole Poached Chicken and Broth, 137
CHICKEN LIVERS
Brandied Chicken Liver Mousse, 29
Chicken Liver Confit, 258
Louisiana Dirty Rice, 116
Chili Jam, 258
CHINESE CUISINE
Cantonese Chicken Salad, 229
Cantonese Roast Chicken, 230
Drunken Shrimp, 219
Ginger Marinade, 227
Lobster Stir-Fried with Melon and Kiwi, 227
Slow-Fire Chinese Steak, 91
Steamed Oysters with Black Beans, 219
Stewed Pork with Fresh Lemon, 236
CHOCOLATE. *See also White chocolate*
All-American Chocolate Layer Cake, 174
Chocolate Angel Food Cake, 175
Chocolate Buttermilk Frosting, 174
Chocolate Cream Napoleon with Hot
Chocolate Sauce, 204
Chocolate Frosting, 173
Chocolate Graham Cracker Crust, 171
Chocolate Hazelnut Torte, 176
Chocolate Ice Cream (Ghirardelli's), 206
Chocolate Orange Mousse, 202
Chocolate Pecan Tart, 169

Chocolate Polenta Cake with White Chocolate
Sauce, 177
Chocolate Sorbet, 209
Chocolate Soufflé Crêpes, 203
Coffee Cup Truffles, 216
Gâteau Victoire, 202
Hazelnut Chocolate Cookies, 194
Hot Chocolate (La Maison du Chocolat's), 19
Individual Bittersweet Chocolate Soufflés, 203
Lovey's Brownies, 193
Mom's Chocolate Cake, 173
No-Trouble Chocolate Truffles, 215
River Oaks Brownies, 193
Trio of Chocolate Desserts: Chocolate Soufflé
Crêpes, Chocolate Sorbet and Chocolate
Wafers, 203
Triple Chocolate Pudding (Odeon's), 200
Chorizo, Riso con, 96
Chowder, Creamy Mussel, 46
Christmas Melon Ball, 22
**Christmas Salad with Red and Green
Vinaigrette,** 142
CIDER
Cider Honey, 259
Cider-Braised Onions, 126
Mulled Cider, 19
CLAMS
Baby Clams, Livorno Style, 57
Open-Faced Clam Sandwich, 153
Clay Pot Chicken with Garlic and Herbs, 63
COBBLERS
Buttermilk Rhubarb Cobbler, 212
Cardamom-Scented Cranberry-Apple Cobbler,
211
COCKTAILS. *See Drink, alcoholic*
COCONUT
Nutty Coconut Yogurt, 245
Coconut Milk, Herbed Crab Soup in, 46
CODFISH
Baked Cod and Potatoes, 50
COFFEE
Café Brûlot Diabolique, 19
Coffee-Hazelnut Nightcaps, 19
COFFEE CAKES
Blueberry-Almond Coffee Cake, 191
Cinnamon-Cream Cheese Pull-Aparts, 192
Walnut-Date Crumb Cake, 192
Coffee Cup Truffles, 216
COMPOTE
Rhubarb Compote with Cinnamon Corn Bread,
251
Winter Fruit Compote, 213
CONDIMENTS
Chili Jam, 258
Panaeng Paste, 258
Port-Soaked Prunes, Roast Duck with, 83
Confetti Shrimp, 57
Confit, Chicken Liver, 258
COOKIES AND SMALL CAKES
Farmers' Cookies, 195
Giant Anise Sugar Cookies, 196
Hazelnut Chocolate Cookies, 194
Lazy Linzer Squares, 193
Little Pepper-Spice Cookies, 195
Lovey's Brownies, 193
River Oaks Brownies, 193

Spiced Angel Cookies, 194
Spicy Shortbread Cookies, 195
Coriander Chicken with Tubetti, 78
CORN
Black-Eyed Pea and Corn Salad, 149
CORN BREAD
Buttermilk Jalapeño Corn Sticks, 161
Buttermilk Skillet Corn Bread, 160
Cinnamon Corn Bread, Rhubarb Compote
with, 251
Sour Cream Buttermilk Corn Bread, 161
**Corn Crêpes Stuffed with Chicken and
Poblanos,** 230
CORNISH HENS. *See Game hens*
CORNMEAL
Buttermilk Jalapeño Corn Sticks, 161
Buttermilk Skillet Corn Bread, 160
Chocolate Polenta Cake with White Chocolate
Sauce, 177
Cornmeal Pastry, 38
Ham 'n' Greens Buttermilk Spoonbread, 99
Sour Cream Buttermilk Corn Bread, 161
COUSCOUS
Breakfast Couscous with Dried Fruit, 252
Couscous-Stuffed Tomatoes, 131
CRAB
Crab Roll, 152
Herbed Crab Soup in Coconut Milk, 46
CRACKERS
Bacon Crackling Crackers, 162
Parmesan Trees, 27
Pesto Pita Thins, 27
Spicy Cheddar-Chive Rounds, 27
CRANBERRIES
Cardamom-Scented Cranberry-Apple Cobbler,
211
Glazed Cranberries, Potato and Celery Root
Puree with, 129
Cream Cheese Pastry, 99
Crème Brûlée, Mocha, 198
Creole Seasoning, 258
CREPES
Chocolate Soufflé Crêpes, 203
Corn Crêpes, 231
Crêpes, 164
Crisp, Maple-Pear, 211
Croquettes, Veal, with Lemon, 89
CROSTINI
Crostini with Beef and Balsamic Vinegar, 32
Crostini with Tarragon Spread, 31
Crostini with Tomato, 31
Croutons of Creamy Red Pepper, 218
CUCUMBERS
Marinated Cucumbers, 124
Swedish Cucumber Salad, 142
CURRANTS, DRIED
Creamsicle Currant Shortcake, 190
Peach and Currant Pie, 167
CURRY
Curried Cain Chicken, 77
Curried Pineapple and Prawns, 58
Curry Oil, 257
Curry-Lime Vinaigrette, 257
Lamb Curry, 103
Stir-Fried Curried Pork, 94
CUSTARD

Butternut Squash Flan, 244
Caramel Flan, 243
Custard with Apples and Almonds, 198
Mocha Crème Brûlée, 198
Orange Liqueur Custard, Summer Fruit with, 212
Custard Sauce, Vanilla, 259

D

Daiquiri, Watermelon and Lime, 22
DATES
Walnut-Date Crumb Cake, 192
Deco Delight, 22
DESSERTS. *See also Cakes; Cookies and small cakes; Ice cream; Pies and tarts, sweet*
Apple Bread Pudding, 199
Baked Bananas, 212
Berry Biscuits, 210
Blueberry Bombe, 247
Blueberry Shortcake, 180
Blushing Applesauce, 213
Buttermilk Rhubarb Cobbler, 212
Butternut Squash Flan, 244
Caramel Flan, 243
Cardamom-Scented Cranberry-Apple Cobbler, 211
Chilled Orange Salad with Amaretto Cookies, 214
Chocolate Cream Napoleon with Hot Chocolate Sauce, 204
Chocolate Orange Mousse, 202
Chocolate Soufflé Crêpes, 203
Creamsicle Currant Shortcake, 190
Creamy Strawberry Cheesecake, 172
Custard with Apples and Almonds, 198
French Bread Pudding with Whiskey Sauce, 199
Fresh Fruit Cloud Cake, 191
Frozen Fruity Cream Cheese Yogurt, 246
Fruit Salad with Banana Cream, 214
Gâteau Victoire, 202
Individual Bittersweet Chocolate Soufflés, 203
Lemon-Blueberry Mousse, 201
Maple-Pear Crisp, 211
Mascarpone Cream Dessert, 198
Mediterranean Shortcake, 179
Miami Beach Shortcake, 189
Mocha Crème Brûlée, 198
Molded Vanilla Pears, 250
Nutty Coconut Yogurt, 245
Peaches Rolled with Pecans and Brown Sugar, 213
Peanut Butter and Banana Frozen Yogurt, 247
Pineapple and Passion Fruit Gratin, 250
Poached Pears in Lemon-Apricot Sauce, 248
Post-Holiday Shortcake, 179
Purple Plum Crumble, 245
Rhubarb Compote with Cinnamon Corn Bread, 251
Rice Fritters, 215
Ricotta Pudding, 201
Roasted Bananas with Poached Pink Grapefruit, 249

Sliced Oranges in Red Wine Syrup, 214
Smooth Applesauce (Jasper White's), 213
Sparkling Strawberries, 250
Spicy Dried Sour Cherries in Port, 249
Strawberry-Rhubarb Frozen Yogurt, 247
Summer Fruit with Orange Liqueur Custard, 212
Sweet Semolina Pudding Soufflés, 244
Tapioca-Apple Pudding, 201
Trio of Chocolate Desserts: Chocolate Soufflé Crêpes, Chocolate Sorbet and Chocolate Wafers, 203
Triple Chocolate Pudding (Odeon's), 200
Upstate Shortcake, 189
White Chocolate Lasagna with Peanut Ice Cream and Hot Fudge Sauce, 205
Winter Fruit Compote, 213
DIET. *See Low-calorie cooking; Low-sodium cooking*
Dipping Sauce, Peanut, 255
DIPS
Brandied Chicken Liver Mousse, 29
Crispy Shallot Dip, 30
Frijolemole, 28
Golden Madras Dip, 30
Provençale Spinach Dip with Herb Toasts, 29
Rocky Roquefort Dip, 28
Dirty Rice, Louisiana, 116
DRESSING, POULTRY. *See Stuffing*
DRESSING, SALAD. *See Salad dressing*
DRINK, ALCOHOLIC
Big Orange, The, 22
Café Brûlot Diabolique, 19
Calvados al Giorno, 21
Christmas Melon Ball, 22
Coffee-Hazelnut Nightcaps, 19
Deco Delight, 22
Duchess Cocktail, 21
Fragolino, 20
French 75, 20
Guboni, 21
Holiday Aperitif (Food & Wine's), 21
Kiss Me Quick, 21
Le Badinguet, 20
Mansion Martini, 22
Milk Punch, 20
Perfectly Grand, 22
Poire Royale, 20
U.N. Plaza Eggnog, 20
Watermelon and Lime Daiquiri, 22
DRINK, NONALCOHOLIC
Barley Tea, 19
Hot Chocolate (La Maison du Chocolat's), 19
Mango Raspberry Cooler, 18
Mulled Cider, 19
Raspberry or Orange Ice Cubes, 18
Revitalizer, The, 18
Rice-Almond Cooler, 18
Drunken Shrimp, 219
Duchess Cocktail, 21
DUCK
Duck with Sweet and Sour Wild Mushroom Cider Sauce, 84
Roast Duck with Port-Soaked Prunes, 83

E-F

Eggnog, U.N. Plaza, 20
EGGPLANT
Skillet Ratatouille, 132
Elizabeth Terry's Robert E. Lee Cake, 173
Enchiladas, Beef and Scallion, 234
ESCAROLE
Escarole and Red Pepper Lasagna, 107
Mixed Greens with Cracklins and Hot Pepper Vinegar, 124
Fajitas, Beef and Avocado, 235
Farmers' Cookies, 195
Fast-Fire Flank Steak, 92
Fast-Fire Swordfish, 54
Fast-Fire Veal Chops, 89
FENNEL
Braised Fennel, 124
Fish Stew with Fennel, 59
FIGS
Fresh Fig Vinaigrette, 255
FILBERTS. *See Hazelnuts*
FIRST COURSES. *See also Appetizers; Salads; Soups*
Assorted Meat Satays with Cucumber Salad, 100
Crispy Balsamic Chicken Wings, 220
Dilled Gruyère Quiche, 39
Drunken Shrimp, 219
Gravlax with Mustard Sauce, 40
Manicotti Crêpes with Spinach and Cheese, 38
New Zealand Mussels with Pommery Mustard Mayonette, 225
Poached Mussels with Chenin Blanc, 40
Pork and Olive Finger Pies, 37
Shrimp Rémoulade, 39
Shrimp with Curried Almond Dressing in Lettuce Cups, 218
Steamed Oysters with Black Beans, 219
Tequila-Cured Red Snapper Seviche, 39
Thai Flavor Packages, 37
Whole Wheat California Pizza with Fresh Tomatoes and Goat Cheese, 220
FISH/SHELLFISH. *See also specific types*
Baby Clams, Livorno Style, 57
Baked Cod and Potatoes, 50
Broiled Swordfish Steaks, 54
Cold Poached Bass with Mediterranean Vegetable Salad, 50
Cold Poached Salmon with Cucumber Salad and Fresh Herb Sauce, 51
Confetti Shrimp, 57
Crab Roll, 152
Curried Pineapple and Prawns, 58
Drunken Shrimp, 219
Fast-Fire Swordfish, 54
Fish Stew with Fennel, 59
Fragrant Steamed Fish, 50
Gravlax with Mustard Sauce, 40
Grilled Shrimp Pita with Papaya Salsa, 154
Jamaican Seafood Stew, 60
Lobster Club, 155
Lobster Stir-Fried with Melon and Kiwi, 227
Mackerel Fillet and Rosemary Mayonnaise on a Baguette, 154

Molded Seafood Salad with Shiitake
  Mushrooms and Avocado Sauce, 134
Molded Sole and Salmon with Dill, 226
New Zealand Mussels with Pommery Mustard
  Mayonette, 225
Open-Faced Clam Sandwich, 153
Oven-Roasted Salmon, Asparagus and New
  Potatoes, 53
Poached Mussels with Chenin Blanc, 40
Poached Salmon Pinwheels with German
  Cucumber Salad and Sauce Verte, 51
Red Snapper with Saffron, Leeks and
  Chardonnay, 53
Salmon Club Sandwich, 153
Salt-Cooked Salmon with Dill and Shallot
  Butter, 52
Seafood Stew with Green Peppercorns, 59
Shellfish Boil, 258
Shrimp Rémoulade, 39
Shrimp with Curried Almond Dressing in
  Lettuce Cups, 218
Smoked Seafood Salad with Roasted Peppers
  and Capers, 135
Snapper Burger with Tartar Sauce, 154
Squid Salad with Lemon and Fresh Mint, 135
Steamed Lobster with Lime Butter, 58
Steamed Oysters with Black Beans, 219
Stuffed Trout Turkish Style, 55
Swedish West Coast Salad, 134
Tea-Smoked Salmon, Sesame Sauce and
  Watercress Sandwich, 152
Tequila-Cured Red Snapper Seviche, 39
Terrific Tuna, 56
Tonno con Vitello, 55
Tuna Club with Roasted Yellow Pepper-Basil
  Mayonnaise, 155
Flageolet Bean Soup with Fresh Thyme, 45
Flan, Caramel, 243
FLANK STEAK
Broiled Flank Steak with Garlic, Ginger and
  Soy Sauce, 92
Fast-Fire Flank Steak, 92
Oriental Flank Steak Sans Soy, 234
Fragolino, 20
French 75, 20
Fresh Ham, Ginger-Rubbed, 92
FRICASSEE
Fricassee of Cornish Hens with Cherry
  Tomatoes and Glazed Shallots, 233
Turkey Fricassee with Brown Rice and Cumin,
  231
Frijolemole, 28
Fritters, Rice, 215
FROSTING
Chocolate Buttermilk Frosting, 174
Chocolate Frosting, 173
FROZEN YOGURT
Blueberry Bombe, 247
Frozen Fruity Cream Cheese Yogurt, 246
Peanut Butter and Banana Frozen Yogurt, 247
Strawberry-Rhubarb Frozen Yogurt, 247
FRUIT. See also specific types
Baked Bananas, 212
Blushing Applesauce, 213
Chilled Orange Salad with Amaretto Cookies,
  214

Fruit Salad with Banana Cream, 214
Molded Vanilla Pears, 250
Peaches Rolled with Pecans and Brown Sugar,
  213
Pineapple and Passion Fruit Gratin, 250
Poached Pears in Lemon-Apricot Sauce, 248
Rhubarb Compote with Cinnamon Corn Bread,
  251
Roasted Bananas with Poached Pink
  Grapefruit, 249
Sliced Oranges in Red Wine Syrup, 214
Smooth Applesauce (Jasper White's), 213
Sparkling Strawberries, 250
Spicy Dried Sour Cherries in Port, 249
Summer Fruit with Orange Liqueur Custard,
  212
Winter Fruit Compote, 213
FRUIT SALADS
Chilled Orange Salad with Amaretto Cookies,
  214
Fruit Salad with Banana Cream, 214
Fusilli, Braised Leeks with, 238

G

GAME
Stuffed Quail, 84
Venison Stew with Dried Cherries, 104
GAME HENS
Fricassee of Cornish Hens with Cherry
  Tomatoes and Glazed Shallots, 233
Roast Cornish Hens with Garlic Cream, 81
Stuffed Cornish Hens, 82
GARLIC
Garlic Toast, 159
Garlic-Oregano Mayonnaise, 254
Gâteau Victoire, 202
Genoa Matchsticks, 24
Ghirardelli's Chocolate Ice Cream, 206
Giant Anise Sugar Cookies, 196
GINGER
Fried Ginger Rice, 116
Ginger Marinade, 227
Ginger Oil, 256
Ginger-Peach Light Ice Cream, 207
Ginger-Rubbed Fresh Ham, 92
Gingered Chicken Breasts, 68
Pumpkin-Ginger Cake, 178
Spicy Ginger Dressing, 229
Goat Cheese, Golden Spiced, 28
Golden Madras Dip, 30
GRAINS
Barley and Wild Mushroom Soup, 225
Breakfast Couscous with Dried Fruit, 252
Bulgur Pilaf, 117
Great Granola, 117
Quinoa Salad, 240
Saffroned Millet Pilaf with Roasted Red
  Peppers, 242
Granola, Great, 117
GRAPEFRUIT
Roasted Bananas with Poached Pink
  Grapefruit, 249
GRAPES
Grape Light Ice Cream, 208

Green Grape Tart, 171
Grappa, Raisins in, 215
GRATINS
Pineapple and Passion Fruit Gratin, 250
Potato and Jerusalem Artichoke Gratin, 130
Gravlax with Mustard Sauce, 40
Great Granola, 117
GREEN BEANS. See Beans, fresh
Green Chile Chicken, 64
Green Tomatoes, Baked Cornmeal-Coated, 131
GREENS
Ham 'n' Greens Buttermilk Spoonbread, 99
Mixed Greens with Cracklins and Hot Pepper
  Vinegar, 124
Stewed Kale, 124
GRILLED FOODS. See Barbecue
Guacamole, Light, 218
Guboni, 21

H-I

HAM. See also Fresh ham
Baked Ham and Turkey Loaf, 98
Baked Ham with Mustard and Apple Jelly
  Glaze, 97
Ham 'n' Greens Buttermilk Spoonbread, 99
North Country Turnovers, 99
HAZELNUTS
Chocolate Hazelnut Torte, 176
Hazelnut Chocolate Cookies, 194
Hazelnut-Orange Bundt, 177
HERBS
Fresh Herb Sauce, 255
High-Fiber Seed Bread, 251
Holiday Aperitif (Food & Wine's), 21
Hominy and Red Chile Stew, 241
Honeydew Light Ice Cream, 208
HORS D'OEUVRES. See Appetizers
ICE CREAM. See also Frozen yogurt
Chocolate Ice Cream (Ghirardelli's), 206
Ginger-Peach Light Ice Cream, 207
Grape Light Ice Cream, 208
Honeydew Light Ice Cream, 208
Lemon-Lime Light Ice Cream, 207
Mango Light Ice Cream, 209
Peanut Ice Cream and Hot Fudge Sauce, White
  Chocolate Lasagna with, 205
Pineapple Light Ice Cream, 208
Pistachio Ice Cream, 206
Raspberry Light Ice Cream, 207
Tangerine Light Ice Cream, 206
Ice, Watermelon and Strawberry, 210
ICING. See Frosting
ITALIAN CUISINE
Baby Clams, Livorno Style, 57
Beef Tenderloin with Juniper, 89
Boiled Beef Salad with Tarragon Sauce, 141
Calabrian Asparagus Soup, 43
Country-Style Fried Chicken, 64
Crostini with Beef and Balsamic Vinegar, 32
Crostini with Tarragon Spread, 31
Crostini with Tomato, 31
Ligurian Vegetable Soup, 42
Marinated Cucumbers, 124
Neapolitan Cauliflower Soup, 43

Olive Bread, 159
Pasta and Bean Soup, 45
Pork Bundles with Pancetta and Sage, 94
Rice Fritters, 215
Risotto Mold with Prosciutto, 115
Risotto with Porcini Mushrooms, 113
Rosemary Breadsticks, 159
Sicilian Artichoke and Fresh Pea Soup, 42
Spinach with Raisins and Pine Nuts, 130
Tuscan Beans with Tuna, Pancetta and
  Lemon, 121
Tuscan Bread, 158
Tuscan Red Cabbage Soup, 43
Umbrian Pork Sausage with Pine Nuts and
  Raisins, 98
Valtellinese Christmas Bread, 158
Veal Croquettes with Lemon, 89
Veal Rolls with Peas, 88
Wild Mushroom Risotto, 114
Zucchini and Arborio Rice Soup, 44

J-K-L

Jamaican Seafood Stew, 60
JAMBALAYA
  Pasta Jambalaya, 108
Jasper White's Smooth Applesauce, 213
JELLY
  Cider Honey, 259
JERUSALEM ARTICHOKES
  Potato and Jerusalem Artichoke Gratin, 130
JICAMA
  Avocado, Orange and Jicama Salad, 240
Kale, Stewed, 124
KEBABS
  Assorted Meat Satays with Cucumber Salad,
    100
  Grilled Lamb Kebabs with Horseradish Butter,
    104
Kiss Me Quick, 21
KUMQUATS
  Mixed Salad with Kumquats and Pecans, 143
La Maison du Chocolat's Hot Chocolate, 19
LAMB
  Braised Lamb Shanks with Black Beans, 102
  Grilled Lamb Kebabs with Horseradish Butter,
    104
  Herbed-Spiced Grilled Lamb, 100
  Lamb Chops with Cumin, Cinnamon and
    Orange, 101
  Lamb Curry, 103
  Spiced Middle Eastern Lamb with Apricots,
    103
  Urban Shepherd's Pie, 101
Lasagna, Escarole and Red Pepper, 107
Lazy Linzer Squares, 193
Le Badinguet, 20
Leeks, Braised, with Fusilli, 238
LEMONS
  Lemon Sorbet with Orange Liqueur, 210
  Lemon-Blueberry Mousse, 201
  Lemon-Herb Veal Roast, 86
  Lemon-Lime Light Ice Cream, 207
  Lemon-Pecan Buttermilk Tea Bread, 161
Ligurian Vegetable Soup, 42

LIMA BEANS
  Baby Lima Beans, Cherry Tomatoes and Pears,
    122
LIMES
  Blueberry Lime Pie with Coconut Crumble
    Topping, 168
  Lemon-Lime Light Ice Cream, 207
LOBSTER
  Lobster Club, 155
  Lobster Stir-Fried with Melon and Kiwi, 227
  Seafood Stew with Green Peppercorns, 59
  Steamed Lobster with Lime Butter, 58
  Swedish West Coast Salad, 134
Louisiana Dirty Rice, 116
Lovey's Brownies, 193
LOW-CALORIE COOKING
  Avocado, Orange and Jicama Salad, 240
  Baked Wild Rice with Mushrooms, 243
  Banana-Strawberry Sherbet, 249
  Barley and Wild Mushroom Soup, 225
  Beef and Avocado Fajitas, 235
  Beef and Scallion Enchiladas, 234
  Beet and Green Apple Salad with Two
    Endives, 240
  Blueberry Bombe, 247
  Braised Leeks with Fusilli, 238
  Breakfast Couscous with Dried Fruit, 252
  Broiled Tomatoes with Balsamic Vinegar and
    Mint, 239
  Buckwheat Noodles with Brown Butter and
    Cabbages, 242
  Butternut Squash Flan, 244
  Cantonese Chicken Salad, 229
  Cantonese Roast Chicken, 230
  Caramel Flan, 243
  Cauliflower with Herbed Crumb Topping, 237
  Chayote with Corn and Lime, 238
  Corn Crêpes, 231
  Corn Crêpes Stuffed with Chicken and
    Poblanos, 230
  Crispy Balsamic Chicken Wings, 220
  Croutons of Creamy Red Pepper, 218
  Drunken Shrimp, 219
  Fricassee of Cornish Hens with Cherry
    Tomatoes and Glazed Shallots, 233
  Frozen Fruity Cream Cheese Yogurt, 246
  High-Fiber Seed Bread, 251
  Hominy and Red Chile Stew, 241
  Light Guacamole, 218
  Lobster Stir-Fried with Melon and Kiwi, 227
  Mediterranean Roasted Vegetables, 239
  Molded Sole and Salmon with Dill, 226
  Molded Vanilla Pears, 250
  New Zealand Mussels with Pommery Mustard
    Mayonnette, 225
  Nutty Coconut Yogurt, 245
  Oriental Flank Steak Sans Soy, 234
  Papaya-Melba Pie, 245
  Peach and Orange Sorbet, 248
  Peanut Butter and Banana Frozen Yogurt, 247
  Pineapple and Passion Fruit Gratin, 250
  Pink and Black Beans Ranchero, 237
  Poached Pears in Lemon-Apricot Sauce, 248
  Pork Loin in Chile Sauce with Roast Potatoes
    and Carrots, 236
  Purple Plum Crumble, 245

Quinoa Salad, 240
Rhubarb Compote with Cinnamon Corn Bread,
  251
Ribboned Peach and Raspberry Mousse, 246
Roasted Bananas with Poached Pink
  Grapefruit, 249
Roasted Pepper and Sweet Potato Salad, 241
Saffroned Millet Pilaf with Roasted Red
  Peppers, 242
Salad of Bitter Greens with Goat Cheese Phyllo
  Sticks, 239
Salsa Roja, 235
Salsa Verde, 235
Sangrita Sorbet, 248
Shrimp with Curried Almond Dressing in
  Lettuce Cups, 218
Sorrel Sauce, 226
Sparkling Strawberries, 250
Spicy Dried Sour Cherries in Port, 249
Spicy Stuffed Chicken Breasts, 228
Steamed Oysters with Black Beans, 219
Stewed Pork with Fresh Lemon, 236
Strawberry-Rhubarb Frozen Yogurt, 247
Sweet Semolina Pudding Soufflés, 244
Turkey Fricassee with Brown Rice and Cumin,
  231
Turkey Tacos, 232
Vegetable-Stuffed Baked Potatoes, 238
Warm Chicken Salad with Oranges and Spicy
  Ginger Dressing, 228
Whole Wheat California Pizza with Fresh
  Tomatoes and Goat Cheese, 220
Wild Rice and Ricotta Griddle Cakes, 252
Zucchini Stuffed with Turkey, Brown Rice and
  Swiss Chard, 232
LOW-SODIUM COOKING
  Cantonese Chicken Salad, 229
  Cantonese Roast Chicken, 230
  Crispy Balsamic Chicken Wings, 220
  Drunken Shrimp, 219
  Lobster Stir-Fried with Melon and Kiwi, 227
  Oriental Flank Steak Sans Soy, 234
  Shrimp with Curried Almond Dressing in
    Lettuce Cups, 218
  Spicy Stuffed Chicken Breasts, 228
  Steamed Oysters with Black Beans, 219
  Stewed Pork with Fresh Lemon, 236

M

**Mackerel Fillet and Rosemary Mayonnaise on a
  Baguette**, 154
MANGOES
  Green Salad with Mango and a Citrus
    Vinaigrette, 143
  Mango Light Ice Cream, 209
  Mango Raspberry Cooler, 18
Manicotti Crêpes with Spinach and Cheese, 38
Mansion Martini, 22
Marinade, Ginger, 227
Martini, Mansion, 22
Mascarpone Cream Dessert, 198
MAYONNAISE
  Garlic-Oregano Mayonnaise, 254
  Provençale Mayonnaise, Asparagus with, 120

Roasted Yellow Pepper-Basil Mayonnaise, 254
MEAT. *See specific types*
Mediterranean Chicken-Ratatouille Salad, 139
Mediterranean Roasted Vegetables, 239
Mediterranean Shortcake, 179
MEXICAN CUISINE
  Beef and Avocado Fajitas, 235
  Beef and Scallion Enchiladas, 234
  Corn Crêpes Stuffed with Chicken and
    Poblanos, 230
  Chayote with Corn and Lime, 238
  Light Guacamole, 218
  Pink and Black Beans Ranchero, 237
  Pork Loin in Chile Sauce with Roast Potatoes
    and Carrots, 236
  Salsa Roja, 235
  Salsa Verde, 235
  Turkey Tacos, 232
Miami Beach Shortcake, 189
Microwaved Pancetta and Mustard-Green
  Risotto, 114
MIDDLE EASTERN CUISINE
  Persian Rice, 115
  Spiced Middle Eastern Lamb with Apricots,
    103
  Stuffed Trout Turkish Style, 55
Milk Punch, 20
MILLET
  Saffroned Millet Pilaf with Roasted Red
    Peppers, 242
Minestrone, Turkey, with Sage-Parmesan
  Butter, 47
Mom's Chocolate Cake, 173
Mousse, Brandied Chicken Liver, 29
MOUSSE, SWEET
  Chocolate Orange Mousse, 202
  Lemon-Blueberry Mousse, 201
  Ribboned Peach and Raspberry Mousse, 246
MUFFINS
  Banana-Poppy Seed Muffins, 162
  Buttermilk Bran Muffins, 162
MUSHROOMS. *See also Wild mushrooms*
  Baked Wild Rice with Mushrooms, 243
  Chicken, Mushroom and Nappa Cabbage Salad
    with Fresh Coriander, 137
  Mushroom, Lemon and Soy Vinaigrette, 257
  Pimiento Chicken with Mushrooms, 67
MUSSELS
  Creamy Mussel Chowder, 46
  New Zealand Mussels with Pommery Mustard
    Mayonette, 225
  Poached Mussels with Chenin Blanc, 40
  Swedish West Coast Salad, 134
MUSTARD
  Mustard Sauce, 254
  Spicy Mustard Sauce, 55
MUSTARD GREENS
  Microwaved Pancetta and Mustard-Green
    Risotto, 114

N-O

Nancy Silverton's Potato Pie, 127
Napoleon, Chocolate Cream, with Hot
  Chocolate Sauce, 204

Neapolitan Cauliflower Soup, 43
New Orleans Pecan Pie, 168
New Zealand Mussels with Pommery Mustard
  Mayonnette, 225
No-Trouble Chocolate Truffles, 215
NOODLES. *See also Pasta*
  Buckwheat Noodles with Brown Butter and
    Cabbages, 242
  Thai Rice Noodle Salad, 150
North Country Turnovers, 99
NUTS. *See also specific types*
  Spicy Tamari Nuts with Rice Crackers, 24
Odeon's Triple Chocolate Pudding, 200
OILS
  Basil Oil, 255
  Curry Oil, 257
  Ginger Oil, 256
Olive Bread, 159
ONIONS. *See also Pearl onions*
  Baked Onions with Balsamic Vinaigrette, 125
  Cider-Braised Onions, 126
ORANGES
  Avocado, Orange and Jicama Salad, 240
  Chilled Orange Salad with Amaretto Cookies,
    214
  Orange Angel Food Cake with Orange Glaze,
    176
  Peach and Orange Sorbet, 248
  Sliced Oranges in Red Wine Syrup, 214
Oriental Flank Steak Sans Soy, 234
Orzo with Roasted Peppers and Dried
  Tomatoes, 113
Oysters, Steamed, with Black Beans, 219

P

Panaeng Paste, 258
PANCAKES. *See also Crêpes*
  Blueberry Buttermilk Griddle Cakes, 163
  Scallion and Buttermilk Pancakes, 163
  Wild Rice and Ricotta Griddle Cakes, 252
PANCETTA
  Chicken Salad with Bitter Greens, Pancetta
    and Chicken Liver Confit, 138
  Microwaved Pancetta and Mustard-Green
    Risotto, 114
  Pork Bundles with Pancetta and Sage, 94
PAPAYAS
  Green Papaya Salad, 135
  Papaya-Melba Pie, 245
Parmentier Pie, 127
Parmesan Trees, 27
Parsnip Chips, 26
Passion Fruit, Pineapple and, Gratin, 250
PASTA. *See also Noodles*
  Braised Leeks with Fusilli, 238
  Capellini with Black Pepper and Prosciutto,
    106
  Coriander Chicken with Tubetti, 78
  Escarole and Red Pepper Lasagna, 107
  Manicotti Crêpes with Spinach and Cheese, 38
  Orzo with Roasted Peppers and Dried
    Tomatoes, 113
  Pasta and Bean Soup, 45
  Pasta Jambalaya, 108

  Pasta with Shrimp, Arugula and Sun-Dried
    Tomatoes, 106
  Stir-Fried Sugar Snap Peas and Carrots with
    Oriental Noodles, 126
  Tagliatelle with Cabbage and Sage, 107
PASTRIES
  Chocolate Cream Napoleon with Hot
    Chocolate Sauce, 204
  Cinnamon-Cream Cheese Pull-Aparts, 192
PASTRY, PIE
  All-American Pie Dough, 167
  Basic Pie Dough, 169
  Chocolate Graham Cracker Crust, 171
  Cornmeal Pastry, 38
  Cream Cheese Pastry, 99
  Double Crust Pastry, 167
  French Pastry Shell, 169
PATE
  Brandied Chicken Liver Mousse, 29
PEACHES
  Ginger-Peach Light Ice Cream, 207
  Peach and Currant Pie, 167
  Peach and Orange Sorbet, 248
  Peaches Rolled with Pecans and Brown Sugar,
    213
  Ribboned Peach and Raspberry Mousse, 246
Peanut Butter and Banana Frozen Yogurt, 247
PEANUTS
  Peanut Dipping Sauce, 255
  Peanut-Fried Drumsticks with Curried
    Cucumbers, 79
PEARL ONIONS
  Glazed Carrots, Turnips and Pearl Onions, 123
  Pearl Onions in Creamy Onion Sauce, 126
PEARS
  Maple-Pear Crisp, 211
  Molded Vanilla Pears, 250
  Poached Pears in Lemon-Apricot Sauce, 248
PEAS. *See also Sugar snap peas*
  Sicilian Artichoke and Fresh Pea Soup, 42
  Steamed Peas with Mint, 126
  Veal Rolls with Peas, 88
PECANS
  Chocolate Pecan Tart, 169
  Lemon-Pecan Buttermilk Tea Bread, 161
  Mixed Salad with Kumquats and Pecans, 143
  New Orleans Pecan Pie, 168
  Pecan Butterscotch Pie, 170
PEPPERS, BELL
  Chick-Pea and Baked Bell Pepper Salad with
    Cumin, 149
  Orzo with Roasted Peppers and Dried
    Tomatoes, 113
  Roasted Pepper and Sweet Potato Salad, 241
  Roasted Vegetables wiith Vinaigrette, 132
  Roasted Yellow Pepper-Basil Mayonnaise, 254
  Saffroned Millet Pilaf with Roasted Red
    Peppers, 242
  Smoked Seafood Salad with Roasted Peppers
    and Capers, 135
Perfectly Grand, 22
Persian Rice, 115
PESTO
  Pesto Chicken Cassoulet, 79
  Pesto Pita Thins, 27
Pickled Watermelon Rind, 259

PIE CRUST. *See Pastry, pie*
PIES AND TARTS, SAVORY
Dilled Gruyère Quiche, 39
North Country Turnovers, 99
Parmentier Pie, 127
Pork and Olive Finger Pies, 37
Potato Pie (Nancy Silverton's), 127
Urban Shepherd's Pie, 101
PIES AND TARTS, SWEET
Apple Pie with Whipped Cream, 165
Blackberry Silk Pie, 170
Blueberry Lime Pie with Coconut Crumble
Topping, 168
Brown Sugar Pie, 168
Chocolate Pecan Tart, 169
Double Crust Apple Pie with Vanilla, 166
Green Grape Tart, 171
New Orleans Pecan Pie, 168
Papaya-Melba Pie, 245
Peach and Currant Pie, 167
Pecan Butterscotch Pie, 170
Triple Strawberry Cream Pie with Chocolate
Graham Cracker Crust, 171
Pimiento Chicken with Mushrooms, 67
PINEAPPLE
Pineapple and Passion Fruit Gratin, 250
Pineapple Light Ice Cream, 208
Pink and Black Beans Ranchero, 237
Pistachio Ice Cream, 206
PIZZA
Cheese and Sausage Chicago Deep-Dish Pizza,
157
Pizza Dough, 157
Whole Wheat California Pizza with Fresh
Tomatoes and Goat Cheese, 220
PLUMS
Purple Plum Crumble, 245
Poire Royale, 20
POLENTA
Chocolate Polenta Cake with White Chocolate
Sauce, 177
PORCINI
Potato-Mushroom Cakes with Cumin, 129
Risotto with Porcini Mushrooms, 113
PORK
Baked Pork Chops, 95
Braised Pork Loin with Apples and Cider, 93
Ginger-Rubbed Fresh Ham, 92
Pork and Olive Finger Pies, 37
Pork Bundles with Pancetta and Sage, 94
Pork Loin in Chile Sauce with Roast Potatoes
and Carrots, 236
Roasted Loin of Pork, 93
Shrimp, Pork and Watercress Salad, 136
Spicy Plum Pork, 95
Stewed Pork with Fresh Lemon, 236
Stir-Fried Curried Pork, 94
Post-Holiday Shortcake, 179
POTATOES
Bacon, Potato, White Bean and Red Pepper
Soup, 46
Baked Cod and Potatoes, 50
Boiled New Potatoes with Dill and Butter, 128
Parmentier Pie, 127
Potato and Celery Root Puree with Glazed
Cranberries, 129

Potato and Jerusalem Artichoke Gratin, 130
Potato Pie (Nancy Silverton's), 127
Potato-Mushroom Cakes with Cumin, 129
Scalloped Potatoes, 128
Vegetable-Stuffed Baked Potatoes, 238
PROSCIUTTO
Capellini with Black Pepper and Prosciutto,
106
Risotto Mold with Prosciutto, 115
Provençal Roast Chicken, 62
Provençale Spinach Dip with Herb Toasts, 29
PUDDING, SWEET. *See also Custard*
Ricotta Pudding, 201
Tapioca-Apple Pudding, 201
Triple Chocolate Pudding (Odeon's), 200
Pumpkin-Ginger Cake, 178
PUMPKIN SEEDS
Curried Pumpkin Seeds and Cornnuts, 25

Q-R

Quail, Stuffed, 84
Quiche, Dilled Gruyère, 39
QUICK BREADS
Lemon-Pecan Buttermilk Tea Bread, 161
Quinoa Salad, 240
Radicchio, Belgian Endive and, Salad, 142
Radish and Arugula Sandwiches, 32
Raisins in Grappa, 215
Raita, Cauliflower, 144
RASPBERRIES
Mango Raspberry Cooler, 18
Papaya-Melba Pie, 245
Raspberry Light Ice Cream, 207
Ribboned Peach and Raspberry Mousse, 246
RATATOUILLE
Mediterranean Chicken-Ratatouille Salad, 139
Skillet Ratatouille, 132
RED PEPPERS, SWEET
Escarole and Red Pepper Lasagna, 107
Roasted Pepper and Sweet Potato Salad, 241
Saffroned Millet Pilaf with Roasted Red
Peppers, 242
RED SNAPPER
Red Snapper with Saffron, Leeks and
Chardonnay, 53
Snapper Burger with Tartar Sauce, 154
Tequila-Cured Red Snapper Seviche, 39
Revitalizer, The, 18
RHUBARB
Buttermilk Rhubarb Cobbler, 212
Rhubarb Compote with Cinnamon Corn
Bread, 251
Strawberry-Rhubarb Frozen Yogurt, 247
RICE. *See also Wild Rice*
Fried Ginger Rice, 116
Fried-Rice Patties, 116
Louisiana Dirty Rice, 116
Microwaved Pancetta and Mustard-Green
Risotto, 114
Persian Rice, 115
Rice Fritters, 215
Riso con Chorizo, 96
Risotto Mold with Prosciutto, 115
Risotto with Porcini Mushrooms, 113

Wild Mushroom Risotto, 114
Zucchini and Arborio Rice Soup, 44
Rice-Almond Cooler, 18
RICOTTA
Ricotta Pudding, 201
Wild Rice and Ricotta Griddle Cakes, 252
Riso con Chorizo, 96
RISOTTO
Microwaved Pancetta and Mustard-Green
Risotto, 114
Risotto Mold with Prosciutto, 115
Risotto with Porcini Mushrooms, 113
Wild Mushroom Risotto, 114
River Oaks Brownies, 193
Robert E. Lee Cake (Elizabeth Terry's), 173
Rocky Roquefort Dip, 28
ROQUEFORT
Rocky Roquefort Dip, 28
Rosemary Breadsticks, 159
Rutabaga Chips, 25

S

Sage Crisps, 24
SALAD DRESSING. *See also Mayonnaise;
Vinaigrette*
Spicy Ginger Dressing, 229
Yogurt Dressing, Curried Chicken Salad with,
138
SALADS, MAIN-COURSE
Boiled Beef Salad with Tarragon Sauce, 141
Broiled Thai Chicken Salad, 140
Cantonese Chicken Salad, 229
Chicken Salad with Bitter Greens, Pancetta
and Chicken Liver Confit, 138
Chicken Salad with Onions and Potato Crisps,
140
Chicken Salad with Shrimp and Fennel, 136
Chicken, Mushroom and Nappa Cabbage Salad
with Fresh Coriander, 137
Curried Chicken Salad with Yogurt Dressing,
138
Green Papaya Salad, 135
Lemon-Chicken Salad with Wild Rice and
Grapes, 139
Mediterranean Chicken-Ratatouille Salad, 139
Molded Seafood Salad with Shiitake
Mushrooms and Avocado Sauce, 134
Shrimp, Pork and Watercress Salad, 136
Smoked Seafood Salad with Roasted Peppers
and Capers, 135
Squid Salad with Lemon and Fresh Mint, 135
Swedish West Coast Salad, 134
Tarragon Chicken Salad with Melon and
Cucumber, 138
Thai Beef Salad, 141
Warm Chicken Salad with Oranges and Spicy
Ginger Dressing, 228
SALADS, SIDE-DISH. *See also Fruit salads*
Avocado, Orange and Jicama Salad, 240
Beet and Green Apple Salad with Two
Endives, 240
Belgian Endive and Radicchio Salad, 142
Black-Eyed Pea and Corn Salad, 149
Cauliflower Raita, 144

267

Chick-Pea and Baked Bell Pepper Salad with
  Cumin, 149
Christmas Salad with Red and Green
  Vinaigrette, 142
Citrus Green Bean Salad, 144
Cucumber Salad, Assorted Meat Satays with,
  100
German Cucumber Salad, Poached Salmon
  Pinwheels with, and Sauce Verte, 51
Green Salad with Mango and a Citrus
  Vinaigrette, 143
Mediterranean Vegetable Salad, Cold Poached
  Bass with, 50
Mixed Salad with Kumquats and Pecans, 143
Quinoa Salad, 240
Roasted Pepper and Sweet Potato Salad, 241
Romaine Salad with Garlic and Pine Nuts,
  143
Salad of Bitter Greens with Goat Cheese Phyllo
  Sticks, 239
Swedish Cucumber Salad, 142
Thai Rice Noodle Salad, 150
Warm Cabbage Slaw, 143
Warm String Bean Salad, 144

SALAMI
Genoa Matchsticks, 24

SALMON
Cold Poached Salmon with Cucumber Salad
  and Fresh Herb Sauce, 51
Gravlax with Mustard Sauce, 40
Molded Sole and Salmon with Dill, 226
Oven-Roasted Salmon, Asparagus and New
  Potatoes, 53
Poached Salmon Pinwheels with German
  Cucumber Salad and Sauce Verte, 51
Salmon Club Sandwich, 153
Salt-Cooked Salmon with Dill and Shallot
  Butter, 52

SALSA
Papaya Salsa, Grilled Shrimp Pita with, 154
Salsa Roja, 235
Salsa Verde, 235

**Salt-Cooked Salmon with Dill and Shallot
  Butter,** 52

SANDWICHES
California Club, 156
Classic Club, The, 156
Crab Roll, 152
Grilled Shrimp Pita with Papaya Salsa, 154
Lobster Club, 155
Mackerel Fillet and Rosemary Mayonnaise on a
  Baguette, 154
Open-Faced Clam Sandwich, 153
Radish and Arugula Sandwiches, 32
Salmon Club Sandwich, 153
Snapper Burger with Tartar Sauce, 154
Tea-Smoked Salmon, Sesame Sauce and
  Watercress Sandwich, 152
Tuna Club with Roasted Yellow Pepper-Basil
  Mayonnaise, 155

Sangrita Sorbet, 248

SATAYS
Assorted Meat Satays with Cucumber Salad,
  100

SAUCES, SAVORY. *See also Butter; Dipping
  sauce; Mayonnaise; Salad dressing*

Avocado Sauce, Molded Seafood Salad with
  Shiitake Mushrooms and, 134
Creole Mustard Sauce, Sautéed Veal with
  Spinach and, 87
Fennel Sauce, Chicken Breasts with, 77
Fresh Herb Sauce, 255
Fresh Herb Sauce, Cold Poached Salmon with
  Cucumber Salad and, 51
Fresh Tomato Sauce, 233
Garlic Cream, Roast Cornish Hens with, 81
Mustard Sauce, 254
Mustard Sauce, Beef Fillet Steaks in, 91
Papaya Salsa, Grilled Shrimp Pita with, 154
Pommery Mustard Mayonnette, New Zealand
  Mussels with, 225
Provençale Mayonnaise, Asparagus with, 120
Salsa Roja, 235
Salsa Verde, 235
Shiitake Mushroom Sauce, Chicken and
  Spinach Cakes with, 80
Sorrel Sauce, 226
Spicy Mustard Sauce, 55
Sweet and Sour Wild Mushroom Cider Sauce,
  Duck with, 84
Tarragon Sauce, Boiled Beef Salad with, 141
Tartar Sauce, Snapper Burger with, 154
Tomato Sauce, 254
Wild Mushroom Cream Sauce, Steak au Poivre
  with, 90

SAUCES, SWEET
Banana Cream, Fruit Salad with, 214
Cherry Caramel Sauce, Strawberry Sherbet
  with, 209
Hot Chocolate Sauce, Chocolate Cream
  Napoleon with, 204
Hot Fudge Sauce, White Chocolate Lasagna
  with Peanut Ice Cream and, 205
Lemon-Apricot Sauce, Poached Pears in, 248
Red Wine Syrup, Sliced Oranges in, 214
Vanilla Custard Sauce, 259
Whiskey Sauce, 199
White Chocolate Sauce, Chocolate Polenta
  Cake with, 177

SAUSAGES
Cheese and Sausage Chicago Deep-Dish Pizza,
  157
Parmentier Pie, 127
Riso con Chorizo, 96
Roast Chicken Stuffed with Sausage and
  Armagnac Prunes, 63
Umbrian Pork Sausage with Pine Nuts and
  Raisins, 98

Scallion and Buttermilk Pancakes, 163
Scalloped Potatoes, 128
SEAFOOD. *See Fish/shellfish and specific types*
SEMOLINA
Sweet Semolina Pudding Soufflés, 244
Sesame-Fried Lemon Chicken, 65
Seviche, Tequila-Cured Red Snapper, 39
SHALLOTS
Caramelized Shallot Vinaigrette, 256
Crispy Shallot Dip, 30
Fricassee of Cornish Hens with Cherry
  Tomatoes and Glazed Shallots, 233
Roasted Shallots, 125
Shallots Braised in Red Wine, 125

SHELLFISH. *See Fish/shellfish and specific
  types*
Shellfish Boil, 258
Shepherd's Pie, Urban, 101
SHERBET. *See also Sorbet*
Banana-Strawberry Sherbet, 249
Strawberry Sherbet with Cherry Caramel
  Sauce, 209
SHIITAKE
Molded Seafood Salad with Shiitake
  Mushrooms and Avocado Sauce, 134
SHORTBREAD
Spicy Shortbread Cookies, 195
SHORTCAKE
Blueberry Shortcake, 180
Creamsicle Currant Shortcake, 190
Mediterranean Shortcake, 179
Miami Beach Shortcake, 189
Post-Holiday Shortcake, 179
Upstate Shortcake, 189
Shredded Wheat Snack Mix, 24
SHRIMP
Chicken Salad with Shrimp and Fennel, 136
Confetti Shrimp, 57
Curried Pineapple and Prawns, 58
Drunken Shrimp, 219
Grilled Shrimp Pita with Papaya Salsa, 154
Pasta with Shrimp, Arugula and Sun-Dried
  Tomatoes, 106
Seafood Stew with Green Peppercorns, 59
Shrimp Rémoulade, 39
Shrimp with Curried Almond Dressing in
  Lettuce Cups, 218
Shrimp, Pork and Watercress Salad, 136
Spiced Soup with Shrimp, 47
Swedish West Coast Salad, 134
Sicilian Artichoke and Fresh Pea Soup, 42
Skillet Ratatouille, 132
Slow-Fire Chinese Steak, 91
Slow-Fire Smoked Chicken, 62
Slow-Fire Spareribs, 96
SOLE
Molded Sole and Salmon with Dill, 226
SORBET
Chocolate Sorbet, 209
Lemon Sorbet with Orange Liqueur, 210
Peach and Orange Sorbet, 248
Sangrita Sorbet, 248
Sorrel Sauce, 226
SOUFFLES
Chocolate Soufflé Crêpes, 203
Individual Bittersweet Chocolate Soufflés,
  203
Sweet Semolina Pudding Soufflés, 244
SOUPS
Bacon, Potato, White Bean and Red Pepper
  Soup, 46
Barley and Wild Mushroom Soup, 225
Butternut Squash Soup, 44
Calabrian Asparagus Soup, 43
Creamy Mussel Chowder, 46
Flageolet Bean Soup with Fresh Thyme, 45
Herbed Crab Soup in Coconut Milk, 46
Ligurian Vegetable Soup, 42
Mushroom Broth, 225
Neapolitan Cauliflower Soup, 43

Pasta and Bean Soup, 45
Sicilian Artichoke and Fresh Pea Soup, 42
Spiced Soup with Shrimp, 47
Turkey Minestrone with Sage-Parmesan
    Butter, 47
Turkey Onion Soup, 48
Tuscan Red Cabbage Soup, 43
Vegetable Broth, 42
Zucchini and Arborio Rice Soup, 44
Spareribs, Slow-Fire, 96
Spice Cake with Lingonberry Jam, 176
Spiced Angel Cookies, 194
SPINACH
Manicotti Crêpes with Spinach and Cheese, 38
Provençale Spinach Dip with Herb Toasts, 29
Sautéed Veal with Spinach and Creole Mustard
    Sauce, 87
Spinach with Raisins and Pine Nuts, 130
Spoonbread, Ham 'n' Greens Buttermilk, 99
Squab, Roasted, with Shiitake Mushroom and
    Chicken Liver Stuffing, 82
SQUASH. *See also Pumpkin; Zucchini*
Butternut Squash Soup, 44
Roasted Vegetables with Vinaigrette, 132
Sweet Potato and Butternut Squash Puree, 130
SQUID
Seafood Stew with Green Peppercorns, 59
Squid Salad with Lemon and Fresh Mint, 135
STEAK
Beef Fillet Steaks in Mustard Sauce, 91
Broiled Flank Steak with Garlic, Ginger and
    Soy Sauce, 92
Fast-Fire Flank Steak, 92
Slow-Fire Chinese Steak, 91
Steak au Poivre with Wild Mushroom Cream
    Sauce, 90
STEWS
Fish Stew with Fennel, 59
Fricassee of Cornish Hens with Cherry
    Tomatoes and Glazed Shallots, 233
Hominy and Red Chile Stew, 241
Jamaican Seafood Stew, 60
Pasta Jambalaya, 108
Seafood Stew with Green Peppercorns, 59
Turkey Fricassee with Brown Rice and Cumin,
    231
Venison Stew with Dried Cherries, 104
STOCK
Enriched Stock, 83
Whole Poached Chicken and Broth, 137
STRAWBERRIES
Banana-Strawberry Sherbet, 249
Creamy Strawberry Cheesecake, 172
Sparkling Strawberries, 250
Strawberry Sherbet with Cherry Caramel
    Sauce, 209
Strawberry-Rhubarb Frozen Yogurt, 247
Triple Strawberry Cream Pie with Chocolate
    Graham Cracker Crust, 171
Watermelon and Strawberry Ice, 210
STRIPED BASS
Cold Poached Bass with Mediterranean
    Vegetable Salad, 50
STUFFING
Shiitake Mushroom and Chicken Liver
    Stuffing, Roasted Squab with, 82

Surefire Stuffing, 164
Sugar Snap Peas, Stir-Fried, and Carrots with
    Oriental Noodles, 126
Summer Fruit with Orange Liqueur Custard,
    212
SUN-DRIED TOMATOES
Orzo with Roasted Peppers and Dried
    Tomatoes, 113
Pasta with Shrimp, Arugula and Sun-Dried
    Tomatoes, 106
Surefire Stuffing, 164
SWEDISH CUISINE
Baked Cod and Potatoes, 50
Beets, Artichokes, Asparagus, Onions and
    Radishes with Whipped Butter, 121
Farmers' Cookies, 195
Swedish Cucumber Salad, 142
Swedish West Coast Salad, 134
SWEET POTATOES
Roasted Pepper and Sweet Potato Salad, 241
Sweet Potato and Butternut Squash Puree, 130
SWORDFISH
Broiled Swordfish Steaks, 54
Fast-Fire Swordfish, 54

T

Tacos, Turkey, 232
Tagliatelle with Cabbage and Sage, 107
TANGERINES
Tangerine Light Ice Cream, 206
TAPIOCA
Butternut Squash Flan, 244
Tapioca-Apple Pudding, 201
TARTS. *See Pies and tarts*
Tea, Barley, 19
Tea Bread, Lemon-Pecan Buttermilk, 161
Tequila-Cured Red Snapper Seviche, 39
Terrific Tuna, 56
THAI CUISINE
Assorted Meat Satays with Cucumber Salad,
    100
Broiled Thai Chicken Salad, 140
Chili Jam, 258
Curried Pineapple and Prawns, 58
Fragrant Steamed Fish, 50
Green Papaya Salad, 135
Herbed Crab Soup in Coconut Milk, 46
Panaeng Paste, 258
Peanut Dipping Sauce, 255
Shrimp, Pork and Watercress Salad, 136
Spiced Soup with Shrimp, 47
Stir-Fried Curried Pork, 94
Thai Beef Salad, 141
Thai Flavor Packages, 37
Thai Rice Noodle Salad, 150
TOASTS. *See also Croutons*
Baked Horseradish Cheddar Canapés, 30
Crostini with Beef and Balsamic Vinegar, 32
Crostini with Tarragon Spread, 31
Crostini with Tomato, 31
Garlic Toast, 159
TOMATOES. *See also Green tomatoes*
Broiled Tomatoes with Balsamic Vinegar and
    Mint, 239

Couscous-Stuffed Tomatoes, 131
Tomato Bread Crisp, 131
Torte, Chocolate Hazelnut, 176
Trio of Chocolate Desserts: Chocolate Soufflé
    Crêpes, Chocolate Sorbet and Chocolate
    Wafers, 203
Trout, Stuffed, Turkish Style, 55
TRUFFLES, CHOCOLATE
Coffee Cup Truffles, 216
No-Trouble Chocolate Truffles, 215
TUNA
Terrific Tuna, 56
Tonno con Vitello, 55
Tuna Club with Roasted Yellow Pepper-Basil
    Mayonnaise, 155
Tuscan Beans with Tuna, Pancetta and
    Lemon, 121
Vitello Tonnato, 86
TURKEY
Baked Ham and Turkey Loaf, 98
California Club, 156
Turkey Fricassee with Brown Rice and Cumin,
    231
Turkey Minestrone with Sage-Parmesan
    Butter, 47
Turkey Onion Soup, 48
Turkey Tacos, 232
Zucchini Stuffed with Turkey, Brown Rice and
    Swiss Chard, 232
TURNIPS
Glazed Carrots, Turnips and Pearl Onions, 123
Turnovers, North Country, 99
Tuscan Beans with Tuna, Pancetta and Lemon,
    121
Tuscan Bread, 158
Tuscan Red Cabbage Soup, 43

U-V

U.N. Plaza Eggnog, 20
Umbrian Pork Sausage with Pine Nuts and
    Raisins, 98
Upstate Shortcake, 189
Urban Shepherd's Pie, 101
Valtellinese Christmas Bread, 158
VEAL
Fast-Fire Veal Chops, 89
Lemon-Herb Veal Roast, 86
Sautéed Veal with Spinach and Creole Mustard
    Sauce, 87
Stuffed Veal Loin, 87
Tonno con Vitello, 55
Veal Croquettes with Lemon, 89
Veal Rolls with Peas, 88
Vitello Tonnato, 86
VEGETABLES. *See also specific types*
Asparagus with Butter Vinaigrette, 120
Asparagus with Parmesan Cheese, 120
Asparagus with Provençale Mayonnaise, 120
Baby Lima Beans, Cherry Tomatoes and Pears,
    122
Baked Cornmeal-Coated Green Tomatoes, 131
Baked Onions with Balsamic Vinaigrette, 125
Beets, Artichokes, Asparagus, Onions and
    Radishes with Whipped Butter, 121

Boiled New Potatoes with Dill and Butter, 128
Braised Leeks with Fusilli, 238
Broiled Tomatoes with Balsamic Vinegar and
  Mint, 239
Cabbage with Pine Nuts, 122
Cauliflower and Broccoli with Cream Sauce,
  123
Cauliflower with Herbed Crumb Topping, 237
Chayote with Corn and Lime, 238
Cider-Braised Onions, 126
Couscous-Stuffed Tomatoes, 131
Curried Cucumbers, Peanut-Fried Drumsticks
  with, 79
Glazed Carrots, Turnips and Pearl Onions, 123
Marinated Cucumbers, 124
Mediterranean Roasted Vegetables, 239
Mixed Greens with Cracklins and Hot Pepper
  Vinegar, 124
Parmentier Pie, 127
Parslied Carrots, 123
Pearl Onions in Creamy Onion Sauce, 126
Potato and Celery Root Puree with Glazed
  Cranberries, 129
Potato and Jerusalem Artichoke Gratin, 130
Potato Pie (Nancy Silverton's), 127
Potato-Mushroom Cakes with Cumin, 129
Roasted Shallots, 125
Roasted Vegetables with Vinaigrette, 132
Sautéed Broccoli and Cherry Tomatoes, 122
Scalloped Potatoes, 128
Shallots Braised in Red Wine, 125

Skillet Ratatouille, 132
Spinach with Raisins and Pine Nuts, 130
Steamed Peas with Mint, 126
Stewed Kale, 124
Stir-Fried Sugar Snap Peas and Carrots with
  Oriental Noodles, 126
Sweet Potato and Butternut Squash Puree, 130
Tarragon Beets, 120
Tomato Bread Crisp, 131
Vegetable-Stuffed Baked Potatoes, 238
Venison Stew with Dried Cherries, 104
VINAIGRETTE
Balsamic Vinaigrette, Baked Onions with, 125
Beet Vinaigrette, 256
Caramelized Shallot Vinaigrette, 256
Citrus Vinaigrette, 256
Citrus Vinaigrette, Green Salad with Mango
  and, 143
Curry-Lime Vinaigrette, 257
Fresh Fig Vinaigrette, 255
Mushroom, Lemon and Soy Vinaigrette, 257
Walnut Vinaigrette, 257
VINEGAR
Hot Pepper Vinegar, Mixed Greens with
  Cracklins and, 124
Vitello Tonnato, 86

W-Y-Z

WALNUTS
Walnut Vinaigrette, 257
Walnut-Date Crumb Cake, 192
WATERMELON
Pickled Watermelon Rind, 259
Watermelon and Lime Daiquiri, 22
Watermelon and Strawberry Ice, 210
Whiskey Sauce, 199
WHITE BEANS
Bacon, Potato, White Bean and Red Pepper
  Soup, 46
Tuscan Beans with Tuna, Pancetta and
  Lemon, 121
**White Chocolate Lasagna with Peanut Ice
  Cream and Hot Fudge Sauce,** 205
WILD MUSHROOMS
Barley and Wild Mushroom Soup, 225
Mushroom Broth, 225
Potato-Mushroom Cakes with Cumin, 129
Risotto with Porcini Mushrooms, 113
Wild Mushroom Risotto, 114
WILD RICE
Baked Wild Rice with Mushrooms, 243
Lemon-Chicken Salad with Wild Rice and
  Grapes, 139
Wild Rice and Ricotta Griddle Cakes, 252
Yogurt, Nutty Coconut, 245
ZUCCHINI
Roasted Vegetables wiith Vinaigrette, 132
Zucchini and Arborio Rice Soup, 44
Zucchini Stuffed with Turkey, Brown Rice and
  Swiss Chard, 232

CONTRIBUTORS

Jeffrey Alford is a food writer specializing in Asian cuisines and is the author of *Tastes of Travel* (Dharma Enterprises) and the forthcoming *Tastes of Travel 1992* and *Flatbreads: A Baker's Dozen*.

Jean Anderson is a food writer and photographer, newspaper food columnist and the author of, most recently, *The Food of Portugal* (Morrow), *Jean Anderson's New Processor Cooking* (Morrow) and, with Elaine Hanna, *The New Doubleday Cookbook* and *Micro Ways* (both from Doubleday).

Lee Bailey is a designer, the author of the *Entertaining with Lee Bailey* column in *Food & Wine*, and the author of numerous cookbooks, including most recently *Soup Meals* (Clarkson Potter).

Melanie Barnard is a food writer and the co-author, with Brooke Dojny, of *Let's Eat In* and *Sunday Suppers* (both from Prentice Hall).

Nancy Verde Barr is a food writer, cooking teacher and the author of *We Called It Macaroni* (Knopf).

Elaine Bell is the owner of Elaine Bell Catering Company in Sonoma, California.

Alexandra Branyon is co-author, with Karen Lee, of *Nouvelle Chinese Cooking* (MacMillan) and *Soup, Salad and Pasta Innovations* (Doubleday).

Frank Brigtsen is chef/owner of Brigtsen's Restaurant in New Orleans.

Mimi Ruth Brodeur is a food writer and food stylist and the food editor for *Pittsburgh Magazine*.

Giuliano Bugialli is a cooking teacher (New York City and Florence, Italy) and the author, most recently, of *Bugialli on Pasta* (Simon and Schuster).

Martha Buser is chef at Iron Horse Vineyards in Sebastopol, California.

Joyce Cain is the owner/general manager of Cain Cellars Winery in Napa Valley, California.

Dolores Cakebread is Vice President and Culinary and Event Director for Cakebread Cellars in California.

Robert Farrar Capon is an Episcopal priest, cooking teacher, food writer and the author of *The Supper of the Lamb* (Farrar, Strauss & Giroux).

Bob Chambers is executive chef of American Express Publishing Corporation.

Molly Chappellet is the Vice President of Chappellet Vineyard in California and the author of the forthcoming *Inspirations from a Vineyard Garden* (Viking).

Peggy Cullen is a pastry chef, bakery manager and food writer.

Marion Cunningham is a cooking teacher, food writer and the author of *The Breakfast Book*, *The Fannie Farmer Baking Book* and the newly revised (13th edition) *Fannie Farmer Cookbook* (all from Knopf). She is currently working on *The Supper Book*.

Constance and Rosario del Nero are cooking teachers (Cambridge School of Culinary Arts in Cambridge, Massachusetts), restaurant consultants and the authors of *Risotto: A Taste of Milano* (Harper & Row). They are currently working on a book tentatively titled *Our Little Ristorante*.

Lorenza de'Medici is a cooking teacher (The Villa Table in Tuscany) and the author of numerous cookbooks, including most recently *The Renaissance of Italian Cooking* (Ballantine).

Donato DeSantis is the executive chef of Bice restaurant in Chicago. He is currently working on a book called *Spontaneously Italian* to be published in 1992.

Marilyn Descours is the chef/owner of Patisserie Descours in Houston.

Brooke Dojny is a food writer and the co-author, with Melanie Barnard, of *Let's Eat In* and *Sunday Suppers* (both from Prentice Hall).

Mary Evely is chef at Simi Winery in Healdsburg, California. She is currently at work on a book tentatively titled *Simi Cook*.

Jim Fobel is a food journalist, artist and the author of *Jim Fobel's Diet Feasts* (Doubleday), *Jim Fobel's Old-Fashioned Baking Book* (Ballantine) and *Beautiful Food* (Van Nostrand Reinhold). He is currently working on a chicken cookbook to be published in 1991 by Ballantine.

Joyce Goldstein is chef/owner of Square One in San Francisco and the author of *The Mediterranean Kitchen* (Morrow).

Dorie Greenspan is a food writer currently at work on a dessert cookbook called *Sweet Times*, to be published by William Morrow in 1991.

Paul Grimes is a food writer, food stylist and chef instructor (at Peter Kump's New York Cooking School).

Ken Haedrich is a food writer, columnist and the author of *The Maple Syrup Cookbook* (Garden Way Publishing) and *Ken Haedrich's Country Baking* (Bantam).

Rick Katz is the pastry chef at Biba restaurant in Boston.

Marcia Kiesel is Associate Test Kitchen Director of *Food & Wine*.

Christer Larsson is executive chef of Aquavit restaurant in New York City.

Karen Lee is a caterer and cooking teacher and co-author, with Alaxandra Branyon, of *Nouvelle Chinese Cooking* (MacMillan) and *Soup, Salad and Pasta Innovations* (Doubleday).

Eileen Yin-Fei Lo is a cooking teacher (China Institute in America, New York City), food writer and the author of *Eileen Yin-Fei Lo's New Cantonese Cooking* (Viking), *The Dim Sum Book* (Crown) and *The Chinese Banquet Cookbook* (Crown).

Susan Herrmann Loomis is a food writer and the author of *The Great American Seafood Cookbook* and the forthcoming *Foods from the American Farm* (both from Workman).

Stephen Lyle is chef of Odeon restaurant in New York City.

Stephanie Lyness is a food writer and cookbook editor.

Deborah Madison is a food writer, the founder of Greens restaurant in San Francisco and the author of *The Savory Way* and *The Greens Cookbook* (both from Bantam).

Lydie Pinoy Marshall is a cooking teacher (A La Bonne Cocotte, New York City), the author of *Cooking with Lydie Marshall* (Knopf) and the forthcoming *Delicious Potatoes* (Harper & Row).

Elin McCoy and John Frederick Walker are contributing wines and spirits editors for *Food & Wine* and the co-authors of *Thinking About Wine* (Simon and Schuster).

Michael McLaughlin is a food writer and a co-author of *The Silver Palate Cookbook* (Workman), the author of *The New American Kitchen* and the upcoming *The Back of the Box Gourmet* (both from Simon and Schuster).

Alice Medrich is owner of Cocolat in Berkeley, California.

Steven Mellina is executive chef of The Highlawn Pavillion in West Orange, New Jersey.

Linda Merinoff is a cooking teacher, food writer and the author of *Gingerbread* (Fireside Press) and *Pig Out with Peg: Secrets from the Bundy Kitchen*, by Peg Bundy as told to Linda Merinoff (Avon).

Perla Meyers is a cooking teacher (The International Kitchen, New York City), food writer and the author of numerous cookbooks including *Market to Kitchen* (Harper & Row) and the forthcoming *Perla Meyers From Season to Season* (Simon and Schuster).

Pam Parseghian is a New York-based food writer.

Alex Patout is chef/owner of Alex Patout's Louisiana Restaurant in New Orleans and the author of *Patout's Cajun Home Cooking* (Random House).

Jacques Pépin, renowned cooking teacher and cookbook author, has most recently published *The Short-Cut Cook* (Morrow). The low-calorie recipes that appear in this edition of *The Best of Food & Wine* were originally created by Pépin for The Cleveland Clinic and appeared (in slightly different form) in their publication "A Fare That Fits."

Warren Picower is Managing Editor of *Food & Wine*.

W. Peter Prescott is *Food & Wine*'s Entertaining and Special Projects Editor.

Michel Richard is chef of Citrus restaurant in Los Angeles.

Annie Roberts is head chef at The Robert Mondavi Winery in Oakville, California.

Sharon Sanders is a recipe developer, cooking teacher, food reporter for the *Chicago Sun-Times* and the author of *Slim Snacks* (Contemporary Books).

Jimmy Schmidt is chef/owner of The Rattlesnake Club and Tres Vite restaurants in Detroit. His book, *Cooking for All Seasons*, is scheduled for publication in early 1991 by MacMillan.

Tracey Seaman is a recipe tester-developer in *Food & Wine*'s test kitchen.

Nancy Silverton is the pastry chef at Campanile restaurant in Los Angeles.

Marie Simmons is a food writer, cooking teacher and the author of *365 Ways to Cook Pasta* (Harper & Row) and the upcoming book, with co-author Lori Longbotham, *The Best of Microwave* (New American Library).

Michel Stroot is the chef of Cal-a-Vie spa in Vista, California.

Diana Sturgis is the Test Kitchen Director of *Food & Wine*.

Elizabeth Terry is chef/owner of Elizabeth on 37th in Savannah.

Doris Tobias is a food and wine writer and the co-author of *The Golden Lemon* (Atheneum). She is currently working on a book on healthy cooking.

Barbara Tropp is chef/owner of China Moon Cafe in San Francisco and the author of *The Modern Art of Chinese Cooking* (Morrow) and the upcoming *The China Moon Cookbook* (Workman).

Jean-Georges Vongerichten is executive chef of Restaurant Lafayette in New York City and the author of *Simple Cuisine* (Prentice Hall).

Jasper White is chef/owner of Jasper's restaurant in Boston and the author of *Jasper White's Cooking from New England* (Harper & Row).

We would also like to thank the following restaurants and individuals for their contributions to *Food & Wine* and to this cookbook:

Antoine's, New Orleans; **Ella and Dick Brennan,** Commander's Palace, New Orleans; **Patrick Clark; Julia Cookenboo,** Zuni Cafe, San Francisco; **Linda Fabiano,** Cakecraft, Red Bank, New Jersey; **Galatoire's,** New Orleans; **Ghirardelli Chocolate Company,** San Francisco; **Gerard Maras,** Mr. B's, New Orleans; **Gérard Pangaud; Seppi Renggli; Anne Rosenzweig; Thai Cooking School,** Bangkok, Thailand; **Barry Wine.**

If you are not already a subscriber to *Food & Wine* magazine and would be interested in subscribing, please call *Food & Wine*'s toll-free number (800) 247-5470; in Iowa (800) 532-1272.